# Diagnostic Monitoring of Skill and Knowledge Acquisition

# Diagnostic Monitoring of Skill and Knowledge Acquisition

Edited by

Norman Frederiksen
*Educational Testing Service*

Robert Glaser
*University of Pittsburgh*

Alan Lesgold
*University of Pittsburgh*

Michael G. Shafto
*NASA—Ames Research Center*

 LAWRENCE ERLBAUM ASSOCIATES, PUBLISHERS
1990  Hillsdale, New Jersey          Hove and London

This work relates to Department of Navy Grant N00014-85-G-0217
issued by the Office of Naval Research. The United States Government
has a royalty-free license throughout the world in all copyrightable
material contained therein.

Lawrence Erlbaum Associates, Inc., Publishers
365 Broadway
Hillsdale, New Jersey 07642

**Library of Congress Cataloging-in-Publication Data**

Diagnostic monitoring of skill and knowledge acquisition / edited by
   Norman Frederiksen . . . [et al.].
      p.   cm.
   Based on papers presented at a conference held at the Educational
Testing Service in July, 1986.
   Includes bibliographies and index.
   ISBN 0-89859-992-X.—ISBN 0-89859-992-X
   1. Educational tests and measurements—United States—Congresses.
2. Achievement tests—United States—Congresses.   3. Learning—
Evaluation—Congresses.
   [DNLM: 1. Educational Measurement—methods—congresses.
2. Intelligence Tests—standards—congresses.   3. Learning—
physiology—congresses.   4. Transfer (Psychology)—congresses.  LB
3051 D536  1986]
   LB3051.D53  1990
   371.2′6—dc20
   DNLM/DLC                                              89-16858
   for Library of Congress                                 CIP

Printed in the United States of America
10  9  8  7  6  5  4  3  2  1

# Contents

Introduction                                                          ix
*Norman Frederiksen*

1   Intelligent Tutors as Intelligent Testers                          1
    *John R. Frederiksen and Barbara Y. White*

2   Analysis of Student Performance with the
    LISP Tutor                                                        27
    *John R. Anderson*

3   The Role of Cognitive Simulation Models in the
    Development of Advanced Training and Testing
    Systems                                                           51
    *David E. Kieras*

4   Reformulating Testing to
    Measure Learning and Thinking
    *Comments on Chapters 1, 2, and 3*                                75
    *Allan Collins*

5   Evidence from Internal Medicine Teaching
    Rounds of the Multiple Roles of Diagnosis in the
    Transmission and Testing of Medical Expertise                     89
    *Cynthia S. Gadd and Harry E. Pople, Jr.*

v

**6**  Diagnosing Individual Differences in Strategy
Choice Procedures                                          113
*Robert S. Siegler and Jamie Campbell*

**7**  Guided Learning and Transfer: Implications for
Approaches to Assessment                                   141
*Joseph C. Campione and Ann L. Brown*

**8**  The Assisted Learning of Strategic Skills
*Comments on Chapters 5, 6, and 7*                         173
*Sherrie P. Gott*

**9**  Parsimonious Covering Theory in Cognitive
Diagnosis and Adaptive Instruction                         191
*James A. Reggia and C. Lynne D'Autrechy*

**10**  Rules and Principles in Cognitive Diagnosis         217
*Pat Langley, James Wogulis, and Stellan Ohlsson*

**11**  Trace Analysis and Spatial Reasoning:
An Example of Intensive Cognitive Diagnosis
and Its Implications for Testing                            251
*Stellan Ohlsson*

**12**  Assessment Procedures for Predicting and
Optimizing Skill Acquisition After Extensive
Practice                                                   297
*J. Wesley Regian and Walter Schneider*

**13**  Applying Cognitive Task Analysis and Research
Methods to Assessment                                      325
*Alan Lesgold, Susanne Lajoie, Debra Logan, and Gary Eggan*

**14**  Monitoring Cognitive Processing in Semantically
Complex Domains                                            351
*Carl H. Frederiksen and Alain Breuleux*

**15**  Diagnostic Approaches to Learning:
Measuring What, How, and How Much
*Comments on Chapters 12, 13, and 14*                      393
*Judith M. Orasanu*

**16**  Diagnostic Testing by Measuring
Learning Processes: Psychometric
Considerations for Dynamic Testing                    407
*Susan Embretson*

**17**  Generating Good Items for Diagnostic Tests      433
*Sandra P. Marshall*

**18**  Toward an Integration of Item-Response Theory
and Cognitive Error Diagnosis                         453
*Kikumi K. Tatsuoka*

**19**  Diagnostic Testing
*Comments on Chapters 16, 17, and 18*                 489
*Robert L. Linn*

Author Index                                          499

Subject Index                                         507

# Introduction

Norman Frederiksen
*Educational Testing Service*

The chapters in this book are based on papers that were presented at a 3-day conference on "Diagnostic Monitoring of Skill and Knowledge Acquisition." The planning of that conference, at least from my point of view, was motivated by two beliefs. One was that new kinds of tests and assessment methods are needed, not just for the evaluation of school learning, but also to contribute directly to the instructional process. The standardized tests that are commonly used in schools today may actually have harmful effects with regard to what is taught and what is learned in school. The other belief is that the work in cognitive science that has been going on for 30 years or so, largely unnoticed by psychometricians, can provide a theoretical basis for developing new assessment methods that can improve instruction and learning.

## HARMFUL EFFECTS OF CONVENTIONAL TESTS

The harmful effects of conventional tests, I believe, are largely attributable to the almost universal use of the multiple-choice format. The argument is as follows. First, it is difficult (although not impossible) to write multiple-choice items that assess the higher-order skills that are involved in such things as drawing inferences, analyzing text, or demonstrating a deep understanding of a domain; as a result, a large proportion of the items in an achievement test measure only factual knowledge. Choosing the right answer to such an item may in many instances be a matter of simple recognition or a search of the memory store to find a match to one of the options. Sometimes the options provide cues as to what the correct answer is or how to generate it. In any case, it is difficult to be creative while taking a multiple-choice test. Second, there is an increasing tendency for schools to use scores on multiple-choice tests not only in grading students but also in making decisions about promotions and granting high school diplomas. Third, such uses of test scores lead teachers to "teach for the test" and students to learn what the test measures, at the expense of more advanced cognitive skills. And finally, the predicated result is that there will be improved performance on factual items and poorer performance on tasks that require reasoning and understanding of a domain.

Unfortunately, there has been little research aimed directly at the influence of test format on learning and teaching. However, there is some evidence relevant both to the influence of format on the kinds of items written and on what students learn (see Frederiksen, 1984, for more detail).

## Influence of Format on Item Writing

A study by Levine, McGuire, and Natress (1970) involved a multiple-choice test intended to measure competence in orthopedic medicine. Trained raters were instructed to sort the test items into categories. It was found that over half of the items were unanimously believed to require only recall of information, and fewer than 25% were thought by any rater to require even simple interpretation of data, applications of a principle, or synthesis. In revising the test, its authors were explicitly asked to write items that assessed "higher level mental processes," and a systematic review of the items was carried out. Despite these efforts, the majority of the items were again judged to measure only simple recall of information.

A similar investigation involved the GRE Advanced Psychology Test, which is widely used in the selection of students for admission to graduate schools. I was one of five psychologists who were asked to make independent judgments as to which one of four abilities was predominantly involved in answering each of the items in four forms of the test. The four abilities were called *memory, comprehension, analytic thinking,* and *evaluation.* Memory was defined as the "simple reproduction of facts, formulae, or other items of remembered informa- tion" (Bowman & Peng, 1972, p. 1). The consensus was that 70% of the items were in the memory category, and the percentages for the other three categories were 15%, 12%, and 3% respectively. If the item writers had aimed at assessing higher-order cognitive skills, they certainly failed.

## Influence of Format on Student Performance

In contrast with the scene today, tests had little impact on instruction during the 1950s and 1960s (Popham, 1983). However, during the 1970s, when achievement test scores were found to be declining (Womer, 1981) and the media began to report annually on mean test scores, tests began to serve as instruments for use in holding schools accountable for student performance. Many state legislatures passed laws requiring schools to put greater emphasis on teaching the "basic skills," to make testing mandatory, and/or to set standards in terms of test scores for promotion and granting diplomas. All this provided strong incentives for teachers to teach for the test and for students to learn what the tests measured.

The National Assessment of Educational Progress ("The Nation's Report Card") published evidence that may be relevant to the effects of testing on school performance. NAEP was founded in 1969 by congressional mandate to determine and report the trends over time in educational achievement, and since its beginning NAEP has periodically assessed the performance of students at the ages of 9, 13, and 17, using both conventional item types and free-response formats of various kinds.

In 1982, NAEP reported that performance on items measuring "basic skills" was not declining, but there was a decrement in performance on items that require more complex cognitive skills (National Assessment of Educational Progress, 1982). For example, in mathematics 90% of the 17-year-olds could handle simple arithmetic problems (subtraction and addition), but performance on problems that required understanding of mathematical principles dropped from 62% to 58%, and on problem solving from 33% to 29%. Similar drops were noted for reading; 72% could deal with literal comprehension of passages, but for items requiring analysis the percentage dropped from 51% to 41%. Such changes were also noted in writing, where 75% could write sentences with few mechanical errors, but for tasks that required analytic and logical skills the proportion of "competent" writing samples dropped from 21% to 15%. Science performance declined for both kinds of problems, but the decline was twice as large for problems requiring more advanced skills.

Two more recent reports from NAEP give us little reason to believe that the trends have changed. A report on mathematics performance (Dossey, Mullis, Lindquist, & Chambers, 1988) says that "While average performance has improved since 1973, the gains have been confined primarily to lower-order skills . . . Most students, even at age 17, do not possess the breadth and depth of mathematical proficiency needed for advanced study in secondary school mathematics" (p. 10). And the report on science achievement (Mullis & Jenkins, 1988) states that "At age 17, students' science achievement remains well below that of 1969 . . . Only 7% of the nation's 17-year-olds have the requisite knowledge and skills thought to be needed to perform well in college-level science courses" (p. 6). A slight improvement was noted from 1982 to 1986, but "It must be recognized, . . . that improvements in average performance . . . were largely the result of students' increased knowledge *about* science rather than increased skills in scientific reasoning," which "suggests that current reforms tend to be aimed primarily at symptoms rather than the disease" (p. 11).

The NAEP studies were designed to monitor change in the performance of students in schools throughout the country, not to investigate the reasons for changes. There are many possible reasons for the decrements in performance, but the possibility must be considered that the widespread use of minimum competency tests and other tests employing the multiple-choice format has contributed to the decreases in level of performance on tasks that require more advanced problem-solving skills and understanding.

## IF MULTIPLE-CHOICE TESTS ARE BAD, WHY ARE THEY USED?

I can think of five possible reasons for the continued widespread use of multiple-choice tests.

### Economy and Efficiency

The most important reason is no doubt their efficiency and economy. ETS' test-scoring machines can score answer sheets at the rate of 10,000 or more per hour.

### Objectivity

Another reason is that the scores are objectively determined. Once the scoring key is agreed to, no human judgment is required.

### Misleading Research Findings

Several studies have compared performance on multiple-choice tests with performance on other forms of the same tests in which the lists of options were replaced by spaces for writing answers (Traub & Fisher, 1977; Vernon, 1962; Ward, 1982). The findings indicated that there was little or no difference with regard to what the two forms measured. This result can easily be overgeneralized, however, because the multiple-choice items are not likely to assess higher-order cognitive skills.

In another study, a free-response test was used that required students to write hypotheses to account for findings from experiments or field studies. A multiple-choice version was later prepared in which options were representative of the written responses to the same test (Ward, Frederiksen, & Carlson, 1980). Using correlational methods, scores from both free-response and multiple-choice forms were found to require domain knowledge and verbal and reasoning abilities, but only the free-response form was related to measures of ideational fluency—an ability that requires a broad search of long-term memory for relevant ideas and is thought to be related to creative thinking (Guilford, 1967). Format apparently does make a difference if the problems require searching for ideas rather than for a match to each multiple-choice option.

## Test Theory

Conventional testing is supported by a highly sophisticated mathematical test theory that makes it possible to deal with the many important problems having to do with test reliability and validity, item analysis, scaling, norming, equating, test homogeneity, and so forth. However, most of this test theory is based on the conception of a test as a set of items that can be scored in terms of the number of right answers. The theory does not support the development and use of tests that require constructed responses and that may yield qualitative or descriptive information about problem-solving procedures. Some psychometricians, however, are beginning to turn their attention to developing test theory that would be useful in supporting a new generation of tests than better assess procedural skills and understanding of a domain.

## Learning Theory and Achievement Testing

Another possible reason for continuing to use multiple-choice tests is that we lack a strong theory of learning and cognition that could support the development of assessment for use in instruction. This is the topic of the next section.

## A LEARNING THEORY TO SUPPORT INSTRUCTION AND THE ASSESSMENT OF ACHIEVEMENT

In his presentation at the 1985 ETS Invitational Conference, Robert Glaser (1986) stated that "In recent years, the general outline of theoretical grounds for forms of assessment that can assist educators . . . has emerged," and that "the measurement of achievement should rely on our knowledge of learning and of the course of acquisition of competence in the subject matters that we teach" (p. 46). Such knowledge has by now advanced far enough to support achievement testing, if not a full-fledged theory of learning, as is attested by a chapter published in the *Annual Review of Psychology* (Glaser & Bassok, 1989).

According to Glaser and Bassok, there are three essential components of a learning theory: (a) description of the desired state of competence in a domain, (b) analysis of the students' initial state of knowledge and ability, and (c) explication of the process of moving from the initial state to the desired state, usually by means of instruction. They comment that cognitive psychology over the past 25 years has focused primarily on the first of these—the nature of a state of competence—while explication of the process of acquiring expertise has been least investigated.

Glaser's and Bassok's approach to the preparation of the chapter was to choose a set of "seminal programs" of instructional research and to consider their implications for the development of a theory of learning. The set chosen included three contrasting approaches to the study of teaching and learning. One is aimed at acquiring "the compiled, automatized, functional, and proceduralized knowledge characteristic of a well-developed cognitive skill (p. 632), which is exemplified by the work of John Anderson and his colleagues at Carnegie-Mellon. A second approach involves the teaching of "internalized self-regulatory control strategies for fostering comprehension" (p. 632), which is associated with the work of Ann Brown, Scardamalia and Bereiter, Schoenfeld, and many others. And the third approach deals with the structuring of knowledge to facilitate problem solving; this method is exemplified by the work of William Clancey, Barbara White and John Frederiksen, and Allan Collins, to name a few. All three approaches to the study of teaching and learning are illustrated by chapters in this volume.

It was concluded by Glaser and Bassok that as things now stand, we are not ready for a unified theory of learning; some of the reasons, for example, are that the work on automatic proceduralization does not recognize the processes of self-monitoring by a regulatory system, work on control strategies does not deal with automization, and work on knowledge structures does not recognize metacognitive skills. Glaser and Bassok remark that such separation of interests is justified from a methodological point of view—"it is good science to avoid confounded effects" (p. 658)—and that it will be necessary now to embark on research aimed at the integration of different instructional principles in studies of competent performance. Research based on instructional interventions may yield new theories of teaching and learning that can also support the development of greatly improved assessment methods.

It is interesting to note that in all of the studies described by Glaser and Bassok, and in almost all of those described in the following chapters, instruction was embedded in a problem-solving context. Glaser and Bassok commented that all the programs they described advocated learning in the context of specific problems and modeling of the relevant problem-solving structures; and they all agreed that knowledge is strengthened by practice and that failure in solving a problem triggers new learning. All this contrasts sharply with more typical methods of instruction in which the teaching of knowledge and principles is separated from their application in problem solving. The most extreme separation is probably in medical schools, where the knowledge background in anatomy, physiology, biochemistry, and so forth, is taught during the first two years, and not until the third year do the students encounter clinical problems (Schmidt, Dauphine, & Patel, 1987). In school classroom instruction it is common practice to lecture for 40 minutes on knowledge and procedures and then assign the homework problems. The intelligent tutors and other methods of instruction described in the following chapters all teach knowledge and principles in the context of problems, and often the programs provide opportunities for students to discover for themselves the principles in attempting to solve problems. It appears that a learning theory that is concerned with explicating the process of moving from the initial state to the desired state will have to take account of the processes involved in problem-based instruction.

Testing in the future may not be the special province of psychometricians. Rather, assessment may be a useful by-product of problem-based instruction. Through trial and error with feedback, and with the assistance of a tutor (human or otherwise) that provides knowledge, hints, examples, and practice, the students should acquire automatic processing and recognition skills, improved conceptions of problem structures, and metacognitive skills to control problem-solving procedures. Information relevant to the process of learning in the domain can then be recorded and preserved to provide a continuous record of changes in knowledge, skill, and understanding as the student encounters problems of increasing complexity. As our ability to obtain such information during the learning process improves, the need for final examinations may disappear.

## ACKNOWLEDGMENTS

In 1984 I was aware of a large number of books and articles on the implications of cognition for teaching, but I had seen little on its implications for testing. Because of its active role in supporting research on cognition and learning, the Office of Naval Research seemed to be an ideal source for funding in the area of assessment. The idea of a conference on the implications of cognitive psychology for testing was broached to Marshall Farr at the 1984 AERA meeting in New Orleans. Marshall's response was, "Write me a letter." After an exchange of letters and telephone calls, a preliminary proposal was submitted, and after several revisions and a downward adjustment of the budget, the project was approved. By then, Susan Chipman had become Manager of the Training and Personnel Branch of the Office of Naval Research (ONR), and Michael Shafto was designated the Scientific Officer in direct charge of the project. Arrangements were made for Robert Glaser and Alan Lesgold to serve as advisors to the project with regard to arrangements and participants.

Because the proposed conference was to deal with a topic on which relatively little work had been done, we felt that a special effort was desirable in order to orient the participants toward applications of their work in the new area—assessment—and to develop a shared point of view with regard to the kinds of information that would have diagnostic value for both students and teachers. Therefore a preliminary planning meeting was held in November, 1985, at the Learning Research and Development Center (LRDC) in Pittsburgh, at which the theme of the conference was discussed and each participant was given an opportunity to reflect and report on the implications of his or her research on assessment. The 3-day conference was held at the Henry Chauncey Conference Center at the Educational Testing Service (ETS) in July of 1986. I believe that the following chapters will show that the participants did share a common understanding of the purpose of the conference.

There are many acknowledgments due those who helped and sympathized in the course of planning and making arrangements for the conference and editing this book. Marshall Farr gave initial impetus toward approval of the project, and Susan Chipman supported its adoption at higher levels in ONR. Mike Shafto has been very helpful in his role as Scientific Officer, and the advice and help of Bob Glaser and Alan Lesgold has been invaluable in getting the project off to a good start. The encouragement and advice of Ernie Anastasio, at that time Vice President of Research Administration at ETS, is greatly appreciated, as well as the ETS contribution to housing and food for the participants at the conference. Julia Hough of Lawrence Erlbaum Associates has provided much helpful advice about the editing and publishing aspects of preparing for the printing of the book.

## REFERENCES

Bowman, C. M., & Peng, S. S. (1972). *A preliminary investigation of recent advanced psychology tests in the GRE program—an application of a cognitive classification system.* Unpublished report, Educational Testing Service, Princeton, NJ.

Dossey, J. A., Mullis, I. V. S., Lindquist, M. M., & Chambers, D. L. (1988). *The mathematics report card: Are we measuring up? Trends and achievement based on the 1986 national assessment.* Princeton, NJ: Educational Testing Service.

Frederiksen, N. (1984). The real test bias: Influences of testing on teaching and learning. *American Psychologist, 39,* 193–202.

Glaser, R. (1986). The integration of instruction and testing. In E. E. Freeman (Ed.), *The redesign of testing for the 21st century.* Princeton, NJ: Educational Testing Service.

Glaser, R., & Bassok, M. (1989). Learning theory and the study of instruction. *Annual Review of Psychology, 40,* 631–666.

Guilford, J. P. (1967). *The nature of human intelligence.* New York: McGraw-Hill.

Levine, A. G., McGuire, C. H., & Nattress, L. W. (1970). The validity of multiple-choice achievement tests as measures of competence in medicine. *American Educational Research Journal, 7,* 69–82.

Mullis, I. V. S., & Jenkins, L. B. (1988). *The science report card: Elements of risk and recovery. Trends and achievement based on the 1986 national assessment.* Princeton, NJ: Educational Testing Service.

National Assessment of Education Progress. (1982). Graduates may lack tomorrow's "basics." *NAEP Newsletter, 15,* 8.

Popham, W. H. (1983). Measurement as an instructional catalyst. In R. B. Ekstrom (Ed.), *New directions for testing and measurement: Measurement, technology, and individuality in education,* No. 17. San Francisco: Jossey-Bass.

Schmidt, H. G., Dauphine, W. D., & Patel, V. (1987). Comparing the effects of problem-based and conventional curricula in an international sample. *Journal of Medical Education, 62,* 305–315.

Traub, R. E., & Fisher, C. W. (1977). On the equivalence of constructed-response and multiple-choice tests. *Applied Psychological Measurement, 3,* 355–369.

Vernon, P. E. (1962). The determinants of reading comprehension. *Educational and Psychological Measurement, 66,* 736–740.

Ward, W. C. (1982). A comparison of free-response and multiple-choice forms of verbal aptitude tests. *Applied Psychological Measurement, 6,* 1–12.

Ward, W. C., Frederiksen, N., & Carlson, S. (1980). Construct validity of free-response and multiple-choice versions of a test. *Journal of Educational Measurement, 17,* 11–29.

Womer, F. B. (1981). State-level testing: Where we have been may not tell us where we are going. In D. Carlson (Ed.), *New directions for testing and measurement. Testing in the states: Beyond accountability* (No. 10, pp. 1–12). San Francisco: Jossey-Bass.

# Intelligent Tutors as Intelligent Testers

John R. Frederiksen
Barbara Y. White
*BBN Laboratories*

## INTRODUCTION

In the early days of educational testing, tests were developed for the purpose of making quantitative assessments of individuals' general levels of ability and achievement relative to others within a group. The use of such norm-referenced tests was principally for selecting students to enter an educational program or for assessing the outcomes of instruction. The instructional need for precise information about the nature of a student's prior knowledge of a given domain and of its development over the course of learning was not addressed. Criterion-referenced testing was introduced with the goal of promoting individualized, adaptive instruction (Glaser, 1963). These tests were intended to give direct information about what particular knowledge and skills a student has attained, not normative assessments of a student's standing within a skill domain. Viewed from a cognitive perspective, such tests were to provide knowledge of a student's prior mental models, misconceptions, or problem solving skills. This information would have a great bearing on the kinds of problems that the student should be given to promote learning, as well as on the nature of the hints and explanations of problem solving that are likely to be most helpful in learning. By measuring students' knowledge and skills as they are acquired during learning, more effective instructional manipulations could be introduced that would serve the needs of the individual student. This concept of a criterion-referenced test is a precursor to the idea of creating a student model within an intelligent tutoring system.

The great promise of criterion-referenced testing for creating an effective new form of individualized instruction that ensures mastery by all students has not materialized. To a large measure, this may be due to limitations in the technology of testing, that is, in the multiple choice, paper-and-pencil tests that were used to implement the idea. Tests using such a format can be developed relatively easily for purposes of assessing factual knowledge or the performance of a particular skill. However, use of such a testing method makes it very difficult to determine a student's methods and strategies in solving a problem, or his/her mental models and misconceptions within a domain. Thus, developers and users of criterion-referenced tests have tended to focus on individual elements of knowledge and skill rather than on the process of problem solving, and this has led to the fractionation of curricula into collections of knowledge and skill elements. Although each of these individual elements was testable, the higher-order integration of those skill and knowledge elements in mental models for a domain and in strategies for solving problems was not properly addressed using the technology of paper-and-pencil tests (Ward, Frederiksen, & Carlson, 1980). Because these higher level problem solving skills remained unassessed, educational systems were not driven to improve instruction in those skills and strategies (N. Frederiksen, 1984).

The advent of intelligent learning environments in which students are actively engaged in the process of problem solving presents an opportunity for revolutionary changes in the way in which students' competence can be assessed. Within such environments, students interact with a system that simulates real-world problems. Their mode of reasoning is more generative than evaluative. They plan and carry out strategies for solving problems, rather than working backwards from multiple-choice response alternatives. All aspects of their performance are available for measurement purposes, ranging from records of the problems they have solved to inferences about their actual problem-solving processes (based on their solution methods and their past performance). Some developers of intelligent tutoring systems have been so bold as to describe their assessments of the individual as "student models" (Clancey, 1983), or formal representations of the students' declarative and procedural knowledge. These new possibilities for assessment in the course of instruction are being developed by individuals whose primary interest is in learning and instruction, rather than by psychometricians. As in criterion-referenced testing, the goal is the development of effective, individualized instructional systems.

It is important at this early stage of the enterprise to examine the role of assessment within instruction, and to identify (a) those aspects of a student's problem-solving expertise that are capable of measurement (representation) within the framework of a tutoring system, and (b) the set of those measurable aspects that are worthwhile to measure, as viewed from the perspective of current theories of optimal instruction. Since computer-based learning environments can support a variety of learning strategies and types of explanations, it is also important to assess (c) the potential for measurement of a student's preference learning strategies and his or her rate of learning when a particular strategy is employed.

In this chapter we begin with a characterization of a theory of optimal instruction and the constraints it imposes on the design of intelligent learning environments. These are illustrated by describing one such environment, which incorporates many of the features of an optimal instructional environment. We then examine the potential for measurement within such an environment and the instructional purposes to be served by developing such representations of a student's knowledge. We also attempt to map measurement concepts represented within the tutoring system with those of traditional test theory as a way of characterizing the important distinctions we are trying to make. Finally, we consider another form of measurement made possible by tutoring systems, and that is the student's rate of knowledge acquisition within a tutoring system configured to represent a particular learning strategy. Such systems, we argue, may allow an assessment of the particular learning strategies that are most effective or that are preferred by a student. Use of tutoring systems as testers may in this way change fundamentally the kind of knowledge of a student that is the goal of measurement.

## A PLAN FOR AN INTELLIGENT TUTORING SYSTEM

We begin by characterizing some features of an effective instructional system as we (White & Frederiksen, 1986a, 1986b, 1987) and other (e.g., Anderson, Boyle, Farrell, & Reiser, 1984; Collins, Brown, & Newman, 1989) view them. The domain of instruction we have in mind is learning to reason about the behavior of a complex physical system and to solve problems involving that system. In the tutoring system we present, the physical domain is that of electrical circuits, and the problem solving is that involved in predicting the behavior of a circuit, designing and modifying a circuit, and troubleshooting. However, the instructional principles are quite general, applicable to domains as diverse as reading, writing, and mathematics, as well as to physics (see Collins et al., in press, for examples).

*1. Instruction Should be Problem Centered.*    Learning should occur within a problem-solving context. If the student is to acquire knowledge that is not inert but is useful in solving problems, he or she must practice the cognitive processing involved in applying that knowledge in solving problems. This principle is based on one of the oldest maxims of learning theory: You cannot learn a behavior if you do not exercise it (Thorndike, 1898, 1932). In this case, the "behavior" refers to the application of knowledge in the course of solving problems. Learning should therefore be situated in a problem-solving context, in order to engage the desired cognitive processes during learning and to motivate the acquisition of problem-solving strategies and models.

*2. Learning Involves Successive Approximations to the Target Mental Representation.* This principle is also based on a very old idea in learning theory: that complex behaviors can be acquired through the learning of a series of successive approximations to the desired final behavior. In the present context, the "behavior" is again a target mental representation together with strategies and techniques for applying such knowledge in problem solving. The successive approximations constitute an evolutionary progression of mental models, each of which builds on prior models, adding or modifying earlier representations until a target cognitive structure has been achieved. The process of learning is therefore one of *model transformation,* whereby the characteristics of problems and coordinated explanations of a tutor facilitate the modification of a prior model by the student and the synthesis of new concepts with prior mental representations.

*3. Explanations Should be Process Centered.* Explanations should be centered on modelling the reasoning involved in actually solving problems. They should relate the cognitive models that are being taught to (a) prior models for reasoning about the domain developed by the student in the course of learning, and (b) the procedures and strategies needed to use the cognitive models in solving problems within the domain. They thus should facilitate the model transformation to be developed by the student, as well as the application of the model in solving problems.

*4. Instruction Should Employ Cognitively Focused Feedback.* Students should receive feedback concerning not only the correctness of their problem solving, but also concerning the appropriateness of different steps in their solution, from the perspective of the cognitive models and strategies being taught. Such feedback, however, should not necessarily be immediate and intrude into their ongoing problem solving. In "real-time" tasks, for example, Munro, Fehling, and Towne (1987) have found that immediate feedback can be detrimental to learning. Problem solving may be similar. An alternative is to provide a basis for the student to compare his or her problem solving with that of an "expert" (as a coach might do in an post-game analysis). The comparison of problem-solving methods could be left up to the student, or an explicit analysis could be attempted by the tutor. On the other hand, if a student gets stuck and is seen to be "thrashing around" or if the student desires it, immediate feedback may be in order. The student could be coached in such instances by being given some hint as to the strategy that may be appropriate or the principle that is applicable, or the student could be shown some part of the problem solution and then be given an opportunity to complete the problem.

*5. Problem Sequencing Should be Performance Based.*   In a problem-centered learning environment, problem sequences should be based on the mental models and problem-solving strategies required for their solution, and on knowledge of the student's understanding of those models and strategies. The introduction of new problems should support the goals of (a) learning new model transformations, or (b) providing an opportunity to practice applying earlier acquired models in new problem situations. Each of these goals can be best met if the new problems do not require large scale model transformations, but rather incremental changes to an evolving mental model for the domain.

*6. Motivation is Primarily Derived From Success in Solving Problems.*   In a problem-centered learning environment, students are actively engaged in carrying out the intellectual tasks posed by problems, and their motivation for engaging in learning will be intrinsic to their succeeding in the problem-solving enterprise. To capture this motivation, students should have knowledge of the progression of models and problem-solving strategies they are to master and the variety of problem types they will solve. They can then directly interpret their rate of progress within the domain. Expert modeling of problem solving and/or coaching should be employed to ensure success for any student who actively pursues learning within the problem-solving environment.

*7. Multiple Learning Strategies Should be Supported.*   It should not be assumed that all students learn best using the same pedagogical technique (Cronbach & Snow, 1977). Some students may prefer to have solution strategies for a new class of problems modeled for them before they attempt such problems, whereas others may prefer to induce for themselves the new ideas required for solving a new class of problems. Learning environments should therefore provide for the preferences of individual learners.

*8. Reification.*   Learning of cognitive skills such as those involved in problem solving may be enhanced if the cognitive contents of learning are made explicit and represented linguistically and graphically by the tutor in modeling problem solving, in giving explanations, and in providing hints or coaching (Anderson, Boyle, & Reiser, 1985; Brown, 1985; Collins & Brown, 1989). This allows students to develop an understanding of the nature of the cognitive skills that they are learning, and will encourage them to reflect on their own problem-solving processes.

In the next section we describe a tutoring system that incorporates many of these instructional features. With this system as an example, we examine the potential for measurement of cognitive models and problem-solving strategies within such a system, and highlight the instructional uses of such measurement during tutoring.

## Example of a Problem-Based Tutoring System

We have developed a tutoring system called QUEST (Qualitative Understanding of Electrical System Troubleshooting; White & Frederiksen, 1986a, 1986b, 1987) that teaches qualitative models for basic electricity and strategies for solving electrical troubleshooting problems. In this system, we attempted to incorporate many of the features of the optimal problem-based tutoring system just described. QUEST provides an environment in which students can learn basic concepts of electricity along with strategies for solving circuit problems, such as predicting circuit behavior and troubleshooting. The tutoring system combines features of a microworld that provides an interactive simulation of circuit behavior, and a coaching expert that can model how to reason about circuit behavior and can demonstrate troubleshooting strategies. Within this environment, students can construct and modify circuits, and they can attempt to solve problems. The tutoring system is capable of simulating and explaining the behavior of circuits and also of demonstrating how to solve circuit problems, either as an explanation prior to the student's attempting the problem or as feedback following the student's attempted solution of the problem.

*Cognitive Modeling.*   To provide such an explanatory capability, the simulation system built into the tutor incorporates a qualitative, causal model for reasoning about the behavior of electoral circuits, rather than a quantitative model. The qualitative model forms the basis for representing the behavior of circuits within the tutoring system and at the same time provides explanations of how the students should reason about their behavior. This model is a cognitive model derived from studies we have carried out of the problem solving of an expert teacher and troubleshooter (White & Frederiksen, 1986a). As such, it employs the same kind of reasoning that the student is to develop for reasoning about a circuit. Thus, the actual behavior of the simulation, when illustrated using computer graphics and articulated through a speech interface, provides an explanation to the student of how to reason about a circuit. For example, if the student constructs a circuit from a set of elementary objects such as resisters, light bulbs, switches, and batteries, the simulation system can model the behavior of that circuit and explain its functioning in qualitative terms.

Another important feature of the tutoring system is that the cognitive simulation model (as well as the troubleshooting strategy) is not a static, single model for the behavior of circuits, but actually incorporates a set of upwardly compatible models that vary in their complexity. Initially, the models are very simple and only know about simple aspects of electrical theory or simple troubleshooting techniques. These early models are adequate for correctly simulating the behavior of only a limited number of circuits and giving explanations of circuit behavior that are consistent with the model at that level. We motivate transitions to more complex models by choosing problems that (a) cannot be solved correctly by the prior model, and (b) require the new concept or method of reasoning that is incorporated in the more elaborated model. The student's task is to transform his or her current model into a more elaborate model that incorporates the new features needed to solve the new set of circuit problems. Together, the set of models through which the learner may pass forms a *space of models,* and the progression of models mastered by the student forms a trajectory through that space similar to Goldstein's (1982) genetic graph.

Within this framework, the tutoring task can be viewed as one of facilitating the student's model transformations through the choice of problems and the generation of appropriate explanations. The models in the progression are designed to facilitate this evolutionary process of model construction. One can think of the student's task of learning a model of circuit operation as analogous (initially) to developing a piece of computer code, or (later on) to modifying prior code in order to incorporate features of the next model in the progression. Therefore, we have sought to design the progression of models so that at each stage the models are easily modifiable. Computer science has given us some principles to use in specifying such models. One is inheritance: For example, within the tutor all device models inherit a common frame containing slots for features such as device states and fault types, so that when you teach a particular feature such as a type of fault (e.g., open), it will apply to all device models— resisters, bulbs, and so forth. To take another example, a general basis for reasoning about voltage drops within a circuit is developed. This general reasoning is applied whenever any device is reconsidering its state following changes in the states of other devices. Thus, when new fault types are developed or new concepts are introduced for reasoning about voltage drops, their applicability to a large range of circuit components and circuit forms will be facilitated.

*System Architecture.*    The major elements of the tutoring system are shown in Fig. 1.1. These include a circuit simulator and a troubleshooting expert.

*The Circuit Simulator.*    The simulation system consists of a set of component or device models (e.g., for a light bulb) and some general propagation principles. Device models provide representation of (a) *states* of the device (whether the light bulb is in the *on* state or the *off* state), (b) *conditions* under which the device would enter a particular state (e.g., if it has a voltage across it, it enters the *on* state, and if it has no voltage across it, it is in the *off* state), and (c) *variables* describing characteristics of the device that affect the distributions of voltages within the circuit, and thus can have an effect on the states of other devices in the circuit. These include the internal conductivity of the device and its status as a voltage source, each of which is dependent on the state of the device (e.g., a capacitor in the *charged* state is nonconductive and a source of voltage).

In addition to device models, the simulation system includes general propagation principles that enable it to reason about circuit behavior over time, that is,

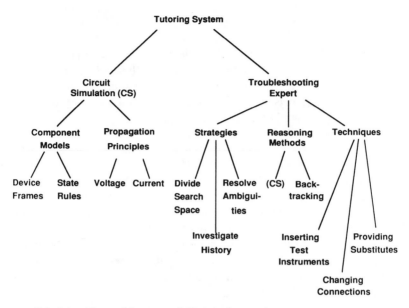

FIG. 1.1.   The architecture of the tutoring system.

to propagate the effects of changes in one device's state on the states of other devices within the circuit. This reasoning is based on a set of qualitative rules used by an expert troubleshooter and teacher whom we have studied, and are ultimately based on constraint equations of circuit theory, such as Kirchhoff's Voltage Law (White & Frederiksen, 1986a). These rules specify how, for example, when a device's conductivity changes (as when a switch is closed), those changes in conductivity alter the voltages applied to other devices in the circuit. These changes in voltages in turn cause other devices to change their states. This ability to reason about the propagations of state changes among devices in a circuit is the purpose of the qualitative simulation. An example of a general rule for propagating state changes is the following simple Voltage Drop Rule: For a device to have a voltage applied to it, it must occur in a circuit containing a voltage source (which is to say, it must have a feed path and a return path to a voltage source). The actual propagation rules used in the qualitative simulation vary in complexity with the particular model that is the focus of instruction at any given point in the model progression. (The aforementioned Voltage Drop Rule, for instance, is the simplest such law, and must be modified in order to hold for circuits containing parallel paths.)

The qualitative simulation is driven by state changes. Changes in the states of devices can be brought about by external interventions (e.g., closing a switch), by changes in the states of other devices (e.g., a transistor becoming saturated), or by increments in time (such as when a capacitor is charging). Whenever a device changes state, its conductivity and status as a voltage source are revised according to the rules of the device model. Changes in these device variables then cause changes in the voltages applied to other components within the circuit, and these changes in voltage can in turn produce changes in the states of those devices. If further changes in device states occur, this propagation cycle continues until the circuit behavior stabilizes

*The Problem-Solving Expert.*    The second major component of the tutoring system is the troubleshooting expert. This is the part of the system that reasons about how faults such as opens and shorts to ground can be located within an electrical circuit. The expert has (a) strategies, such as dividing the search space (dividing a series circuit into two halves, for example) or resolving ambiguities, (b) methods, which include reasoning about the behavior of a circuit in which a fault is presumed (using the same reasoning as that of the circuit simulator), and (c) techniques, such as inserting test instruments and detaching sections of the circuit.

The troubleshooting expert locates faults in, for example, a series circuit, using a "space splitting" strategy in which the circuit is divided by inserting a test light (or voltmeter) at appropriate points in the circuit (i.e., between a point in the middle and the negative, grounded terminal of the battery) and then reasoning about whether the fault can be localized to one or the other part of the circuit based on the condition of the test light.[1] If such an inference cannot be made, the expert adopts the strategy of attempting to reduce the ambiguity of the result. To do this, additional methods (such as detaching part of the circuit) are employed followed by further reasoning about the location of the fault. Once the fault has been localized to one part of the circuit, the troubleshooting strategy is recursively applied within that portion of the circuit, and this continues until the fault has been located. The system can model this strategy for the student, inserting the test light into the circuit, observing its behavior, and articulating its reasoning at all stages in troubleshooting.

*An Example of a Circuit Simulation.*    As an example of how the qualitative simulation works, consider a very simple circuit shown in panel (a) of Fig. 1.2, consisting of a battery, a switch, a wire, and a bulb. When the switch is closed, the switch goes from the nonconductive to the conductive state. The system then evaluates the state of the bulb. To do this, it has to find out if there is a good feed path to the positive side of a voltage source (battery); and as it traces the feed path, the system highlights the path on the screen, as in panel (b) of Fig. 1.2. It

---

[1]This involves reasoning about the expected behavior of the test light in an unfaulted circuit (using the qualitative simulation model), and testing for a discrepancy with its actual behavior. The expert then models the effects on the test light of possible faults within either part of the subdivided circuit to see if the test result can be unambiguously attributed to a single part of the circuit.

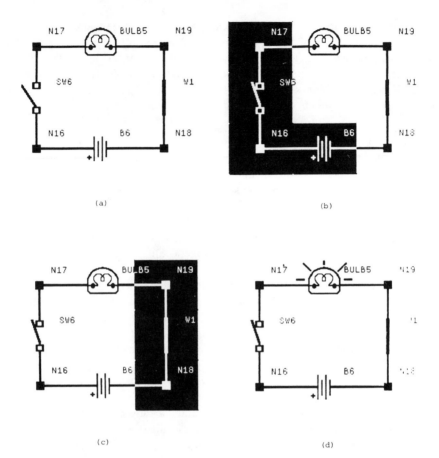

FIG. 1.2.    A visual representation of the model's reasoning for a simple circuit.

also looks to see if it has a good return path to the battery, as in panel (c) of Fig. 1.2. It then announces that, because it has found good feed and return paths, there will be a voltage drop across the light bulb and therefore the bulb's state will change from *off* to *on,* as in panel (d) of Fig. 1.2. This is an example of the simple reasoning used initially for simple series circuits. The initial model that we are trying to develop in the learner uses just this kind of reasoning.

Now, suppose we gave this simple model a circuit such as the one shown at the top of Fig. 1.3. In this circuit, the same sort of reasoning would be applied and the system would find a good feed path from the bulb to the battery through resistor $R_3$ (which is conductive) as well as a good return path, and would conclude (correctly) that the light would be on. However, if the system were then given the circuit in the middle of the figure (in which the switch is closed), it

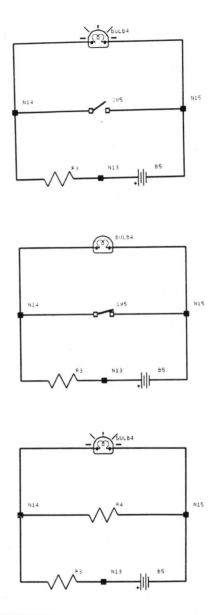

FIG. 1.3. An example of problems used to motivate model transformations.

would (erroneously) conclude that the light is on here as well. In fact, the light will remain off because it has been shorted out by the switch. Problems such as this are used to introduce new ideas; here, the idea is that a purely conductive path (in this case through the switch) has no voltage drop across it. The model—particularly the principle for reasoning about voltage drops—has to be revised to incorporate this new idea. Further, if we were to replace the closed switch with a resistor (or another light bulb) as at the bottom of Fig. 1.3, the light bulb at the top would again be on, requiring yet another model revision. A new concept must again be introduced, namely, that there is an intermediate qualitative possibility: Devices (here, the resistor substituted for the switch) can, in addition to being nonconductive or purely conductive, also be conductive and resistive, and it is only purely conductive devices that allow no voltage drop across them. These examples illustrate how we use a careful choice of problems to motivate students to induce new rules and concepts. The tutor can, of course, articulate these new principles in helping the student to build the new conceptualizations.

*Model Progressions.*    Learning within the tutoring system is based fundamentally on the idea of progressions of models, each of which can be used to simulate and articulate the principles for understanding the behavior of some set of circuits or the strategy for troubleshooting some subset of possible faulted circuits. Each model defines a set of circuit problems that it can solve. Further, any transition between two models in the model space implies a set of problems, such as those given above, that motivate the particular model transformation. These are problems such as those given in Fig. 1.3 for which the transformed model is minimally adequate and the preceding model is no longer adequate. Choosing problems in this way provides a very important pedagogical tool in building subjects' understanding. It allows the student to progressively build a mental model by inductive means through solving problems. The key is to present problem sequences that allow the proper inductions of model transformations to be made, and at the same time provide explanations of key features of the new models to be acquired.

*Multiple Pedagogical Methods.*    An interesting property of the class of tutoring systems we have described is that it is *not* prescriptive with respect to the form of the instructional interaction. For example, by using the system (more particularly, a circuit editor) to create circuits on their own, students can learn in an open-ended exploratory fashion, using the tutoring facilities to provide explanations and feedback whenever they see fit. Alternatively, they can choose to solve problems that have been arranged to represent a progression of models for reasoning about circuit behavior and for troubleshooting. In working through this sequence of problems, they can make decisions as to which set of problems (i.e., which model) they wish to attempt or they can follow the recommendation of the tutor.

When attempting to solve problems, students can, if they wish, try to solve problems on their own, inducing for themselves the characteristics of the model. In this mode of interaction, they can ask for explanations or hints whenever they choose in order to receive assistance from the tutor in developing their models. Alternatively, they can opt for seeing and hearing explanations of how the new model can be applied in solving a new group of problems before they try to solve problems for themselves. This is an example of learning from demonstrations and explanations.

Students may also mix these modes of instructional interaction, for example, by first choosing to learn from demonstrations and explanations, later attempting to learn inductively, and perhaps later using the exploratory tools to construct problems for themselves.

## Need for a Student Model

The instructional strategies employed within the tutoring system depend critically on the evolution of the student's mental model and problem-solving strategies following the model progressions presented to the student. Within the tutor, the emphasis is placed not on the absolute position or "level" of a model within the model space, but rather on the relations among these models. These relations are important because they determine the model transformations that must be developed by the student in order to master the next model in the progression. Models that are adjacent in the model space share most features and involve smaller transformations than nonadjacent models, which have more distinguishing features and involve more complex transformations. For this reason, to facilitate learning, the model progressions generally involve adjacent models. Because the models are runnable, they can be used to analyze the conceptual and cognitive demands of any problem and to partition problems into those that are solvable and those that are not under a particular model.

The instructional strategy is to present problems for which the target model is minimally sufficient and for which the student's current model is insufficient. Exposure to these problems (a) allows students to see the discrepancy between their current model and the demands of the problem, and (b) motivates students to revise their current model along the lines necessary to solve the new problem. Thus, in order to optimally select problems to use in instruction, the tutor must have knowledge not only of the target model, but also of the student's current cognitive model, represented by the preceding model in the progression. Information about the student's current model is thus used both in setting appropriate model transformation goals and in choosing problems.

In addition to its use in selecting model transformation goals and problems, the student model is important in providing a basis for targeting hints and explanations. It is desirable to focus the hints/explanations a student is given so as to highlight the new elements of the target model that the student must master. This again requires information concerning both the student's model and the target model. The measurement problem is therefore one of the inferring the student's current model (the student's competence) on the basis of performance on problems that have been undertaken during the tutoring session.

## INTELLIGENT TUTORS AS MEASUREMENT
## SYSTEMS

### Assessing Student Performance
### Within the Tutoring System

The assessment of a student's current level of expertise is implicit in the operation of the tutor, which uses information about a student's progress within the progression of models as it makes decisions about when to introduce further model transformations. The student model developed by the tutor is *a list of those models within the model space that the student has given evidence of having mastered.* At any stage in learning, mastery of a model transformation is assumed when a student can solve problems that only minimally require the model transformation for their solution. The evaluation of a problem solution can be made not only on the basis of the correctness of the final result, but also on the basis of the reasonableness of the solution steps taken by the student within the context of the expert problem-solving model that is the subject of instruction. To make this evaluation of steps in a problem solution, the intelligent tutoring system we envision can *track* the student's problem-solving actions as he or she works through a problem.

*Tracking Mode.*    The tracking mode serves both an assessment and a pedagogical function. It provides further evidence of successful learning, and it provides a basis for generating helpful hints when a student runs into difficulty. To track a student's problem-solving actions, the expert problem-solving model is run, yoked to the student as the student attempts to solve a problem. With each action taken during problem solving, the expert generates its possible next steps. When the student decides on a next action, that action is evaluated by the expert before it is implemented. The student in essence solves the problem by directing the expert in the actions it is to take. There are two possibilities each time the student selects an action: (a) if the student's action is among the set of possible next steps the expert can take at that point in the problem, the expert follows that action; or (b) if the student's action is not among the possible next steps of the expert, the expert notes a departure from the model's reasoning.

In the first case, an inference is made that the student is following the reasoning/ strategy of the expert. In the second case, an inference is made that there is a departure from the expert's mode of reasoning, particularly in that associated with the possible next steps that the expert could have taken that were not taken by the student. When a discrepant action is attempted by the student, hints can be generated based on the stage in the problem solution reached at the time of the discrepancy and knowledge of the model transformation that the student was attempting. Additional information about the student's source of difficulty could be obtained by asking the student for the reasons for taking the particular discrepant action (Feurzeig & Ritter, 1987). Hints can then increase in their specificity (as in the adaptive testing proposal of Campione & Brown, 1985) until a correct action is selected by the student.

We should note that further inferences of the first type could not be made if the student's reasoning were not brought back into the form of the expert's. As a result of hints and explanations provided when the student departs from the set of "solution paths" generated by the expert, the student's reasoning is kept coherent from the standpoint of the expert.

In coaching the student to follow the problem-solving strategies of the expert, the intent is not to force the student to rigidly take a particular next action at every stage in solving a problem. The flexibility allowed the student within the tracking mode derives from the generative character of the problem-solving expert. The expert must be capable of capturing the range of strategies and approaches that human experts employ in solving problems so that students may follow any of these approaches in their problem solving. This flexibility, however, introduces a complexity into the tutoring system's capability to accurately track the student's problem-solving performance. When the student selects an action, that particular action could have been produced by any one of a number of different strategies. Thus, for any given step, the tutor may be unable to infer which strategy the student is attempting to use. However, by looking at a sequence of actions, and by asking the student to give reasons for actions (as in Feurzeig & Ritter, 1987), this complexity may be manageable.

*Diagnostic Testing.*   It is important to note that, in the above proposal, all information about the student's current mental model is derived from normal instructional interactions between the student and the tutoring system. There is no separate diagnostic testing mode, and no problems are ever presented to the student for purposes other than pedagogical ones. The reason for imposing this condition is that we view the order in which problems are presented as critical to the evolutionary development of models for a domain. The careful sequencing of problems motivates the generation of model transformations by the subject and governs the explanatory strategy of the tutor (which focuses on discrepancies between the actual circuit behavior and that predicted using the prior model; in other words, it focuses on the conceptual changes needed to account for the unexpected behavior). Interpolating problems that are not instructionally appropriate for purely diagnostic purposes would undercut these instructional strategies and cause confusion in the learner. However, information about the particular source of a student's difficulty is nonetheless available, as we have seen, in the tutor's knowledge of the particular model transformation that was being attempted at the time difficulty was encountered and of the requirements of the problem at that stage in its solution.

## Mapping to Conventional Measurement Theory

To further clarify distinctions between measurement concepts developed within the tutoring context and those of conventional psychometric assessment, we attempt to develop some mappings between the psychometric (item–response) theory and tutoring system conceptualizations. In psychometrics, a test is thought to measure a student's underlying ability, which is usually conceived of as a point on an underlying quantitative scale representing "aptitude" or "ability." This point divides the ability scale into a region representing items the student has mastered and a region representing items as yet unmastered. Within the tutoring framework, a student's competence is represented in a way that is fundamentally nonquantitative: Instead of the notion of an ability continuum, the range of ability is represented by a space of possible models. A particular model within this space represents a theory that specifies which problems an individual can solve within a domain, just as in psychometric assessment a point on the ability continuum represents the skill level required to solve problems having particular levels of difficulty. In psychometric assessment, although there may be implicit theories that are used by item writers in preparing items, the only information about an item that is made explicit is that contained in its quantitative characterization (roughly, its position on the ability scale). Successful completion of an item by a student thus provides evidence concerning only the quantitative level of ability of the examinee. In contrast, within the tutoring framework, the models used for generating items (or problems) are made explicit, and a subject's successful solution of a problem—following solution steps prescribed by the model—is taken as evidence that the subject's reasoning is captured by the current model. No quantitative scale is interposed to represent the subject's level of competence within the domain.

In both the psychometric and tutoring frameworks, information about the student's level of competence is derived from the types of problems a student can solve successfully. Within psychometric assessment, a statistical theory is used to relate performance on problems to an individual's ability through the use of a cumulative probability distribution called an item characteristic curve (ICC). The ICC specifies how, as you quantitatively increase ability from a lower to a higher level, performance (the probability of success) on an item will improve. The set of ICC's for a collection of items together provide the statistical basis for relating a person's ability to his or her level of performance on the items requiring that ability. Item–response theory does not provide a formal or cognitive basis for assigning items to locations on the ability axis; rather, the ICC for each item must be determined empirically using an item calibration procedure. Within the tutoring system context, a cognitive model is used to relate performance on a problem to a subject's level of competence. In this framework, model transformations perform the function of ICC's. A model transformation specifies the changes in a student's current model that are necessary to solve problems associated with a new or target model. Model transformations thus describe how, as a student moves from one location in the model space to another during learning, his/her competency in solving problems changes. By running the relevant models, one can determine the additional problems that a student would be able to solve as a result of acquiring the model transformation. Thus, in addition to providing a prediction of performance on problems, model transformations provide an explicit theory of what needs to be learned in order to solve a particular problem based on the student's current model and the requirements of the problem.

Finally, we complete our analogy between measurement within a tutoring system and psychometric measurement by examining the method for selecting items in each form of assessment. In certain kinds of tests called computerized adaptive tests (CATs), some effort is made to use the information about items, and their relationship to ability, in a judicious way in choosing which items are the best to present next in the test. The best items are those that will contribute the most (in the information–theoretic sense) to improving the estimate of the student's ability. Typically, items that are good to present are those that are near (on the ability axis) the current estimate of the student's ability. In other words, it is best to avoid unnecessarily hard or easy items. There is again a parallel to this idea within the tutoring system framework: here, pedagogical principles are used to decide what kind of problems the student should next receive. These pedagogical principles, although different in their motivation from the psychometric item-selection principles, are somewhat similar in their outcome: they generally choose to take small steps rather than large steps in the model space (just as the CAT rules will choose items that are close to the examinee's current estimated ability).

Making these mappings, one could view the entire tutoring session as a computerized adaptive test. Evidence from performance on problems solvable by particular models in the progression provides evidence for mastery of those models. The region of the model space traversed during tutoring constitutes the estimate of a subject's level of competence, which in turn specifies the subset of problems that are solvable. We note that if the models within the model space can be ordered, or even partially ordered, with respect to their underlying structure and place within the model progression, then a scale could be developed representing the level of model that has been mastered by the student. Such a scale would not, however, be a substitute for the detailed representation of cognitive skill contained in the qualitative student model. The student's score on such a hypothetical scale would be analogous to an ability estimate derived from a conventional test.

## Validity of the Student Model

If a student has no difficulty in solving problems associated with the current model employed by the tutor, and has difficulty with new problems that are representative of adjacent models in the model space, there is evidence confirming the current model as a representation of the student's current level of competence. Additional evidence can be derived from (a) the student's performance on problems associated with earlier models in the instructional progression, and (b) the similarity of the student's problem-solving steps to those of the current "expert" model in solving the same problem. Finally, it is possible to query the student during problem solving as to his or her reasons for particular steps taken (Feurzeig & Ritter, 1987), and these reasons should correspond to those of the tutor's current model. Verification of predictions such as these constitutes a validation of the student model.

Furthermore, the assumption that the tutor's model is the same as the student's model is not unreasonable if one considers the instructional context. The student has been solving problems all along that foster the evolution of this model, and the student has been hearing explanations that are generated by the models in the course of learning. Also, it is the case that the models have been designed to be learnable within the sequence used; that is, the progressions have been very carefully constructed so that one can readily induce the model transformations required—the models were designed to be easily modifiable and causally consistent (see White & Frederiksen, 1986a). These arguments for the validity of the tutor's current model as a measure of the student's knowledge thus depend on the tutoring context of the knowledge being assessed. The claim is that, as a result of experience with the tutor, a student model can be developed that represents the student's knowledge as it is developed in interaction with the tutor. No such claim could be made if the problems were to be presented outside the instructional context of the tutor.

Even within the tutoring context, however, there are some circumstances under which one needs to worry about the use of models employed by the tutor as a representation of the student's knowledge of the domain. For instance, students may have other, *prior conceptions* about electricity before they begin tutoring. What we must consider is what might happen to various preconceptions students might have in the course of tutoring. We therefore consider separately preconceptions that are incorrect (misconceptions) and those that simply represent alternative conceptions to those used within the tutor.

*Misconceptions.*   Students may enter tutoring with a misconception about electricity. For example, among the subjects we have studied, we have found a common misconception about the concept of a circuit. Their notion of a circuit is that there need be only one connection between a device such as a light bulb and a voltage source in order for the bulb to light. During tutoring, such misconceptions may either be (a) *eradicated,* (b) *compartmentalized* (that is, students may develop the model presented in the tutoring environment but still think in their old way when placed in a different context, for example, when they repair a toaster), or (c) *coordinated* (that is, students may try to build a bridge between their earlier conception and the new model they have developed). We think it is unlikely that a coordinating theory would be constructed because such a theory would have to predict inconsistent circuit behaviors. It is possible that a student's prior model may be compartmentalized; however, we think it most likely that it would be eradicated because there would be specific instances of problems and feedback presented by the tutoring environment to disconfirm their misconception. We are, therefore, not too concerned about prior misconceptions as invalidating the tutor's model of a student's reasoning.

*Alternative Conceptions.*   On the other hand, alternative conceptualizations are more problematic and could invalidate to some extent the claim that the model employed by the tutor provides a full representation of the student's knowledge. For example, suppose a student's alternate view of electricity is one of current flow viewed as analogous to fluid flow. Cohen, Eylon, and Ganiel (1983) have found that this is a common view, even among teachers of physics, and one that leads to poor performance on qualitative circuit problems. It thus becomes important to build some kind of reductionistic, physical model that enables a student to understand how to limit the inferences one might draw from a "naive" current flow model of electricity. Building such a physical model, however, is not within the domain of the tutoring system as it is currently constituted, and is thus left to the student (if such a theory is developed at all). The more dangerous alternative of allowing students to compartmentalize the alternative model leaves open the possibility that students might inappropriately use this model. In either case, the learner maintains an alternative conceptualization not represented in the current tutoring model, and the existence of such a model partially invalidates the tutor's model as a representation of the student's sole mode for reasoning about circuits. This problem could be remedied if explicit consideration were to be given to alternative conceptions and to their integration within the tutoring context.[2]

A further problem is that we have been discussing a student's knowledge of a domain, such as understanding electrical circuit behavior and troubleshooting, as if it could be represented as a single model. This is a gross oversimplification from several respects. First, as we have argued in prior papers (White & Frederiksen, 1986), "deeply" understanding the behavior of electrical circuits requires that the student acquire a set of linked, alternative models for the domain. These include functional and behavioral models, as well as qualitative and quantitative

---

[2]Recently, we have incorporated a reductionistic, physical model within the tutoring system (White & Frederiksen, 1989).

models. Further, problem solving often requires that the student possess more than causal models of the domain. For instance, in the case of electrical trouble-shooting, the student needs to acquire a set of troubleshooting strategies, as well as decision criteria for selecting an appropriate strategy. However, given a learning environment such as the one we have described, one can tutor the set of linked alternative models and the problem-solving strategies. The above arguments outlining techniques for identifying the student's mental model apply to this expanded set of models and strategies.

## MEASURING THE EFFECTIVENESS
## OF A LEARNING STRATEGY

### Supporting Multiple Learning Strategies

Because the framework of the tutoring system we have described is not prescriptive as to the pedagogical approach or learning strategy followed, such a tutoring system provides an opportunity for studying the effectiveness of alternative learning strategies for the individual undertaking to acquire an understanding of a new domain. It thus allows a reopening of the question as to whether or not measures of rate of learning within particular learning environments are important predictors of a student's success in acquiring knowledge and skills within other training environments, such as in the classroom or in on-the-job training. If measures of gain in knowledge and skill within a tutoring context are strongly predictive of learning in the same or other learning environments (Brown & French, 1979; Campione & Brown, 1984), then such measures could replace conventional aptitude and achievement tests when the purpose is to estimate the learning time required by a particular student and/or his or her eligibility for a particular educational program.

Learning strategies the tutoring environment is designed to support include:

*Exploratory Learning.* In this learning strategy, the student carries out open-ended exploration, using the circuit editor to build or modify circuits. The student can then attempt to predict the circuits' behavior, and invoke the qualitative simulation to obtain hints or explanations of their behavior when needed. In addition, the student can have the system insert faults into circuits and then attempt to troubleshoot them, using the expert as a coach. The expert is capable of demonstrating and explaining the strategies it would use to locate the fault. In each case, the student uses the circuit simulator and troubleshooting expert as learning tools, and invokes them as he or she sees fit in attempting to master the domain.

*Learning From Explanations.*   Alternatively, the student could follow a more directed approach to learning in which new concepts and strategies are always illustrated and explained before the student is given problems to solve on his or her own. Each time a new model within the progression is introduced, the qualitative simulation and/or troubleshooting expert can be used to demonstrate the new model and to apply it in solving problems. The student then tests his or her understanding by attempting to solve similar problems.

*Inductive Learning.*   The student could also follow the model progressions incorporated within the tutoring system, but attempt at each stage to infer the necessary model transformation for himself or herself. The model progressions have been designed to facilitate such inductive learning. Again, the coaching facilities of the tutor can be employed to generate hints and explanations when needed.

*Student-Directed Learning.*   One could also involve the student in a form of self-directed learning. Here, information is provided to the student about the nature and structure of the model space. Students are given a map of the model space, in which the nodes represent models and the arcs stand for transformations between models. Problem sets are associated with each model transformation. The learning environment would provide facilities for moving within the model space, and students could set their own goals as to where they would like to be in the model space, what they would like to learn next, and in general determine their own trajectory through the model space.

These are the kinds of learning strategies (along with mixtures of them) that are supportable within the tutoring system. By providing these options for the student, one could determine the use and mix of learning strategies the student chooses to employ in working with the tutor and in this way determine which among these specific approaches to learning the student prefers. Information concerning the student's preferred mode of learning could be used in optimizing the fit of a learning environment to the student who is entering it.[3]

## Measuring the Rate of Learning

In addition to determining the student's preferred mode of learning, one could impose a particular learning strategy on the student (for example, requiring the student to learn inductively), and then measure how readily the student can gain information within such a learning environment. What we have in mind here is the notion that a good way to predict learning within a learning environment of

---

[3]By way of caveats or limitations, we should point out that there are some learning strategies that the tutoring environment does not support. For example, it does not teach by the use of analogy, and it does not focus on misconceptions.

a particular type is to measure a student's learning in a comparable learning situation. One could have a student use the tutoring system for, say, 5 hours of tutoring, in order to obtain some measures of how the student is gaining information within that period of tutoring. One could then use that information in place of the usual battery of achievement tests in predicting how long it might take for the student to complete some criterion course of training. Measures of information gain one might consider include (a) the highest model mastered within the tutoring period, (b) the rate of information gain, which might be measured in terms of the number of models mastered per constant number of problems, (c) the amount of coaching needed by the student in learning a given model, and (d) the success of tutoring gauged by the quality of model-based reasoning of the student.

It is interesting to speculate about what kinds of instructional variables might turn out to be important when one uses measures of learning such as these to predict information gain in a target "real world" learning environment. It may be, for example, that it is most important to configure the tutoring system to duplicate the kind of *learning strategies* employed in the target training situation that one is trying to predict. For example, if in the target learning environment the student is expected to develop concepts and strategies for himself or herself, then the tutor could be constrained to support the inductive mode of learning. On the other hand, if the target instructional environment relies on learning from examples and explanations, then the tutor could be configured to impose that learning strategy on the student. In addition to using a similar learning strategy, it may also be important that the *subject matter* in the tutoring session be the same as that of the target training environment. The relative importance of having similarity in the subject matter versus similarity in the form of tutoring in predicting learning within the target environment remains an empirical question. Correlations based on similarity of form reflect the importance of subjects' strategies for learning within a particular instructional environment. Correlations due to similarity of content reflect prior knowledge and familiarity with the domain of instruction, information similar to that obtained using more conventional achievement tests.

We propose a research agenda that could reopen some of theses old questions: For example, to what extent do gains in a short period of tutoring, say the first 3 to 5 hours, predict the ultimate levels of learning that are achieved with the very same tutor? If one had a tutor configured for different kinds of learning strategies and different domains, what are the cross-learning strategy and the cross-domain correlations? If in initial experiments using the tutoring system one finds positive correlations, one could then ask whether learning using the tutoring system for a short term (say, 5 hours) is predictive of learning in other kinds of learning environments external to the tutor. And finally, one could determine if such information is an important adjunct to information about the prior knowledge and basic skills people have when they enter a training environment. It is possible that measures of learning within a tutoring system subsume these other measures and provide a more direct basis for assessing a student's potential for learning within a criterion instructional environment, provided that the subject domain and learning strategies used in the tutor correspond with those of the criterion learning situation.

## Modeling Students' Learning Strategies

Imagine that the intelligent learning environment is extended so that it also tutors learning strategies by utilizing the same model progression concept that we employed to teach circuit behavior and troubleshooting. Then, in addition to being able to predict the student's rate of learning and preferred mode of learning, one could use the system to model the student's learning processes. Thus the proposed architecture for an intelligent learning environment potentially enables one to model the student's (a) knowledge of the domain phenomena, (b) problem-solving skills, and (c) learning strategies. The product is a comprehensive representation[4] of the student's domain understanding, problem-solving capabilities, and learning abilities.

## Potential Importance of Learning Strategy Assessments

If learning strategies can form a basis for predicting educational outcomes, then the use of such assessment tools could, we believe, have some desirable effects on education. It could, for example, encourage schools to focus on the process of learning: on the development of learning strategies and learning skills. These include general and metacognitive skills that are applicable across a variety of problem domains, for example, learning how to develop models for domains, qualitative analysis, and general problem-solving strategies (such as dividing a problem space, developing a subproblem, and planning). In addition, schools might be encouraged to focus more on the transfer problem, that is, on how to use what you already know in learning a new domain. Topics here include the use of analogies, mapping theories across domains, and general qualitative, causal reasoning. Developing a new generation of tests based on intelligent tutoring systems could open up the domain of learning skills to measurement. If such tests were in turn adopted widely, they could have an influence on education at least as pervasive as the influence criterion-referenced tests have had over the last 20

---

[4]Of course, if one wants to be able to precisely predict how readily a student can learn within a new domain, one must model not only the student's current knowledge of this domain, but also the student's knowledge of other domains utilized during instruction to help the student understand this new domain. For example, White and Horwitz (1987) taught children about the implications of Newton's laws of motion by building not only on their naive physical theories but also on their knowledge of scalar arithmetic. In cases where one is drawing upon a lot of prior knowledge from a large number of diverse domains, a prediction based on knowledge of the given domain is less reliable.

years. There is an opportunity here for a new approach to testing to improve the educational climate of the future, and to contribute to creating students who are skilled learners as well as experts within their domains of study.

## ACKNOWLEDGMENTS

This paper was prepared with support from the Army Research Institute, Contract MDA-903-87-C-0545, and the Air Force Human Resources Laboratory, Contract No. F33615-84-C-0058.

## REFERENCES

Anderson, J. R., Boyle, C. F., Farrell, R., & Reiser, B. J. (1984). Cognitive principles in the design of computer tutors. In the *Proceedings of the Sixth Annual Conference of the Cognitive Science Society* (pp. 2–9). Boulder, Colorado.

Anderson, J. R., Boyle, C. F., & Reiser, B. J. (1985). Intelligent tutoring systems. *Science, 228,* 456–468.

Brown, A. L., & French, L. A. (1979). The zone of proximal development: Implications for intelligence testing in the year 2000. *Intelligence, 3,* 253–271.

Brown, J. S. (1985). Process versus product: A perspective on tools for communal and informal electronic learning. *Journal of Educational Computing Research, 1,* 179–201.

Campione, J. C., & Brown, A. L. (1984). Learning ability and transfer propensity as sources of individual differences in intelligence. In P. N. Brooks, R. D. Sperber, & C. McCauley (Eds.), *Learning and cognition in the mentally retarded.* Baltimore: University Park Press.

Campione, J., & Brown, A. (1985). Dynamic assessment: One approach and some initial data. Center for the Study of Reading. (Tech. Rep. No. 361). Urbana-Champaign, IL: University of Illinois.

Clancey, W. (1983). Guidon. *Journal of Computer-Based Instruction, 10*(1 & 2), 8–15.

Cohen, R., Eylon, B., & Ganiel, U. (1983). Potential difference and current in simple electric circuits: A study of students' concepts. *American Journal of Physics, 51*(5), 407–412.

Collins, A., & Brown, J. S. (1988). The computer as a tool for learning through reflection. In H. Mandl & A. Lesgold (Eds.), *Theoretical issues in reading comprehension* (pp. 1–18). Hillsdale, NJ: Lawrence Erlbaum Associates.

Collins, A., Brown, J. S., & Newman, S. E. (1989). Cognitive apprenticeship: Teaching the craft of reading, writing, and mathematics. In L. B. Resnick (Ed.), *Knowing, Learning, and Instruction: Essays in honor of Robert Glaser* (pp. 453–494). Hillsdale, NJ: Lawrence Erlbaum Associates.

Cronbach, L. J., & Snow, R. E. (1977). *Aptitudes and instructional methods: A handbook for research on interactions.* New York: Irvington.

Feurzeig, W., & Ritter, F. (1987). Understanding reflective problem solving. In J. Psotka, L. D. Massey, & S. A. Mutter (Eds.), *Intelligent tutoring systems: Lessons learned* (pp. 285–302). Hillsdale, NJ: Lawrence Erlbaum Associates.

Frederiksen, N. (1984). The real test bias. *American Psychologist, 39*(3), 193–202.

Glaser, R. (1963). Instructional technology and the measurement of learning outcomes. *American Psychologist, 18,* 510–522.

Goldstein, I. P. (1982). The genetic graph: A representation for the evolution of procedural knowledge. In D. Sleeman & J. S. Brown (Eds.), *Intelligent tutoring systems* (pp. 51–77). London: Academic Press.

Munro, A., Fehling, M. R., & Towne, D. M. (1987). Instructional intrusiveness in dynamic simulation training. *Journal of Computer-Based Instruction, 12*(2), 50–53.

Thorndike, E. L. (1898). Animal intelligence: An experimental study of the associative processes in animals. *Psychological Monographs #8.*

Thorndike, E. L. (1932). *The fundamentals of learning.* New York: Teachers College, Columbia University.

Ward, W., Frederiksen, N., & Carlson, S. (1980). Construct validity of free-response and multiple-choice versions of a test. *Journal of Educational Measurement, 17,* 11–29.

White, B., & Frederiksen, J. (1986a). Progressions of qualitative models as a foundation for intelligent learning environments. BBN Report No. 6277. Cambridge, MA: BBN Laboratories. (To appear in *Artificial Intelligence.*)

White, B., & Frederiksen, J. (1986b). Intelligent tutoring systems based upon qualitative model evolutions. In *Proceedings of the Fifth National Conference on Artificial Intelligence* (pp. 313–319). Philadelphia, PA.

White, B., & Frederikson, J. (1987). Qualitative Models and Intelligent Learning Environments. In R. Lawler & M. Yazdani (Eds.), *AI and Education* (pp. 281–305). Norwood, NJ: Ablex.

White, B. Y., & Frederikson, J. R. (1989). Causal models as intelligent learning environments for science and engineering education. *Applied Artificial Intelligence: An International Journal.*

White, B. Y., & Horwitz, P. (1987). Thinker Tools: Enabling children to understand physical laws. BBN Report No. 6470. Cambridge, MA: BBN Laboratories.

# 2

# Analysis of Student Performance with the LISP Tutor

John R. Anderson
*Carnegie-Mellon University*

The goal of this chapter is to present our first detailed analysis of student performance with the LISP tutor. First, we describe a little of our general theoretical orientation to the issues of intelligent tutoring. Second, we provide a description of the essential features of the operation of the LISP tutor. Third, we give some general description of characteristics of the data that are obtained with the LISP tutor.

## INTELLIGENT TUTORING AND ITS RELATION TO COGNITIVE THEORY

Research on intelligent tutoring serves two goals. The obvious goal is to develop systems for automating education. Private human tutors are very effective (Bloom, 1984), and it would be nice to be able to deliver this effectiveness without incurring the high cost of human tutors. However, a second and equally important goal is to explore epistemological issues concerning the nature of the knowledge that is being tutored and how that knowledge can be learned. We take it as an axiom that a tutor is effective to the extent that it embodies correct decisions on these epistemological issues.

We chose intelligent tutoring as a domain for testing out the ACT$^*$ theory of cognition (Anderson, 1983). It was a theory that made claims about the organization and acquisition of complex cognitive skills. The only way to adequately test the sufficiency of the theory was to interface it with the acquisition of realistically complex skills by large populations of students. When we read *Intelligent Tutoring,* edited by Sleeman and Brown (1982), it became apparent that the book's authors were explicitly or implicitly performing such tests of theories of cognition and that it was an appropriate methodology for testing the ACT* theory. Fundamentally, the tutoring methodology is predicated on the assumption that one understands a skill and its acquisition. The success of the tutor constitutes a direct test of the sufficiency of the underlying theory.

The ACT* theory has been used to construct performance models of how students actually execute the skills that are to be tutored and learning models of how these skills are acquired. The performance model is used in a paradigm we call *model tracing* in which we try to follow in real time the cognitive states the student goes through in solving a problem. The power of our tutoring approach depends critically on the success of our model-tracing apparatus to correctly interpret the cognitive states of students. When we interrupt students to provide instruction, that instruction is given with respect to an assumed mental state. If this model's assumptions are wrong, the instruction will be off the mark.

The LISP tutor (Anderson & Reiser, 1985) was developed as an instantiation of this model-tracing methodology and serves to test our theory of skill acquisition (Anderson, 1982; Anderson, Farrell, & Sauers, 1984) in two ways. First, it is a sufficiency test of the theory. The fact that a system of this variety does serve to teach LISP programming skills stands as a general confirmation of the theory. Second, it is also a tool to test predictions of the theory.

Although our research is in LISP programming and its tutoring, we are using this as a vehicle to test some fundamental issues about the nature of problem-solving skills and its acquisition. Among these issues are the following:

1. *Skill Representation.* How should a skill be presented? ACT* assumes a representation as a set of production rules.
2. *Procedural Versus Declarative Knowledge.* What is the relationship between the declarative knowledge (which is the original instruction) and the highly proceduralized form that it finally achieves?
3. *Performance Limitations.* How do fundamental performance limitations like working-memory limitations impact on skill performance and skill acquisition?
4. *Organization and Control.* How is the knowledge underlying problem-solving skill organized and controlled to permit coherent problem solving?
5. *Skill Modification.* How is one's knowledge modified to effectively reflect experience? This issue is closely tied up with the issue of feedback.
6. *Mechanisms of Skill Acquisition.* Last but hardly least, what are the fundamental mechanisms of skill acquisition?

LISP programming is an excellent domain for studying these issues because it offers a complex but relatively well-understood domain. The tutor is an excellent tool because it brings control and experimental rigor to what would otherwise be a rather free-form learning experience.

## THE LISP TUTOR

The LISP tutor currently teaches a full-semester, self-paced course at Carnegie-Mellon University. It covers all the basic concepts in LISP. It is the first instance of a practical piece of intelligent tutoring being widely used, and it has been shown to lead to improvement in performance. Roughly, students working on problems with the LISP tutor get one letter grade higher on final exams of general competence than students not working with the LISP tutor (Anderson & Reiser, 1985). It should also be noted that students working with private human tutors have been shown to outperform students with the LISP tutor. So it is by no means a utopian system, but it can claim some pedagogical effectiveness.

Table 2.1 contains a dialogue with a student coding a recursive function to calculate factorial. This does not present the tutor as it really appears. Instead, it shows a "teletype" version of the tutor where the interaction is linearized. In the actual tutor the interaction involves updates to various windows. In the teletype version, the tutor's output is given in normal type whereas the student's input is shown in bold characters. These listings present "snapshots" of the interactions; each time the student produces a response, his input is listed along with the tutor's response (numbered for convenience). The total code as it appears on the screen is shown, although the student has added only what is different from the previous code (shown in boldface type). For instance, in Line 2 he has added "zerop" as an extension of "(defun fact (n) (cond ((. . . . "

In the first line, when the subject typed "(defun", the template (defun <name> <parameters> <body>) appeared. The terms in <—> angle brackets denote pieces of code he will supply. The subject then filled in the <name> slot and the <parameters> slot and had started to fill in the <body> slot. Note that at all points parentheses are balanced and syntax is checked.

Although the student has some difficulty with the syntax of the conditional tests in Lines 1 and 2, he basically codes the terminating case for the factorial function correctly. Typically, we find students have little difficulty with terminating cases but have great difficulty with recursive cases. The dialogue after Line 3 illustrates how the tutor guides the student through a design of the recursive function. Basically, it leads the student to construct a couple of examples of the relationship between fact $(n)$ and fact $(n-1)$ and then gets the student to identify the general relationship. Figure 2.1 shows the screen image at a critical point in the design of this function.

The dialogue after this point shows two errors students make in defining recursive functions. The first, in Line 4, is to call the function directly without

TABLE 2.1

Define the function fact. It takes a number argument, n and computes the factorial of n, which is the result of multiplying n × n−1 × n−2 . . . × 1. For instance, (fact 3) = 3 × 2 × 1 = 6. By definition, the factorial of 0 is 1.

1. **(defun fact (n)**
   **(cond ((equal)** <ACTION>)
   <RECURSIVE-CASE>))

   I assume that you are trying to test if the number argument is equal to the number zero. There is a special function for testing equivalence to zero. Try to use that function instead of EQUAL.

   What code can you write to test if the condition for the terminating case is true? Try writing a predicate.

2. (defun fact (n)
   (cond ((**zero** <ACTION>)
   <RECURSIVE-CASE>))

   Did you mean zerop (y or n)? **y**

3. (defun fact (n)
   (cond ((**zerop n) 1**)
   <RECURSIVE-CASE>))

   Is the value of fact in the recursive cases calculated by:
   PRESS:          IF YOU WANT TO:
   1               Calling fact recursively with n.
   2               Multiplying n by fact of n minus 1.
   3               Getting 1 2 . . . n and then multiplying the results.
   4               have the tutor choose
   Menu choice: **3**

   That is a reasonable way to think of doing factorials but it is not a plan for a recursive function. Since you seem to be having trouble with the recursive cases let us work through some examples and figure out the conditions and actions for each of these cases.

   The recursive relationship is the relationship between fact called with n and fact called with:
   PRESS:          IF YOU WANT TO:
   1               n minus 1
   2               n equal to 0
   3               n plus 1
   4               have the tutor choose
   Menu choice: **1**

   We will consider some concrete examples. We will characterize the recursive relationship between fact called with 1 and fact called with 0
   What is the value of (fact 1)?
   Answer: **1**
   What is the value of (fact 0)?
   Answer: **1**

                        EXAMPLES
                  fact (n)          fact(n − 1)
            A. (fact 1) = 1      (fact 0) = 1

TABLE 2.1 *(continued)*

We will consider some more concrete examples. We will characterize the recursive relationship between fact called with 3 and fact called with 2

What is the value of (fact 3)?

Answer: **6**

What is the value of (fact 2)?

Answer: **2**

EXAMPLES

| fact (n) | fact (n − 1) |
|---|---|
| A. (fact 1) = 1 | (fact 0) = 1 |
| B. (fact 3) = 6 | (fact 2) = 2 |

Since there is only one recursive case characterized by the examples you have just worked out the condition in this case can be just coded at T. We will just focus on characterizing the action in this case.

In examples A and B what do you have to do to get the result of fact called with n?

| PRESS | IF YOU WANT TO: |
|---|---|
| 1 | Multiply n by one less than n. |
| 2 | Multiply n by fact of one less than n |
| 3 | Add n to the result of fact called with one less than n. |
| 4 | have the tutor choose |

Menu choice: **2**

We have now worked through a series of examples that illustrate the recursive relation. We will now return to the goal of trying to produce LISP code that specifies the recursive relation.

4. (defun fact (n)
      (cond ((zerop n) 1)
        **(t (fact)))**

You will have to use fact at some point but right now you want to multiply.

5. (defun fact (n)
      (cond ((zerop n) 1)
        (t (times **n (fact n)**))))

You cannot just code n at this point. What you want to do is subtract one from n.

6. (defun fact (n)
      (cond ((zerop n) 1)
        (t (times n (fact **(difference)**)))))

Difference would work in this case but it is more appropriate to use the function SUB1 when you are subtracting 1 from a number.

7. (defun fact (n)
      (cond ((zerop n) 1)
        (t (times n (fact **(sub1 n)**)))))
                    —YOU ARE DONE. TYPE NEXT TO GO ON AFTER—
                    —TESTING THE FUNCTIONS YOU HAVE DEFINED—

*(continued)*

TABLE 2.1 *(continued)*

THE LISP WINDOW

```
= > (trace fact)
(fact)
= > (fact 3)
1 <Enter> fact (3)
|2 <Enter> fact (2)
|  3 <Enter> fact (1)
|  |4 <Enter> fact (0)
|  |4 <Exit> fact 1
|  3 <Exit> fact 1
|2 <Exit> fact 2
1 <Exit> fact 6
6
```

```
In examples A and B what do you have to do to get the result
of fact called with n?
PRESS:            IF YOU WANT TO:
1.      Multiply n by one less than n.
2.      Multiply n by fact of one less than n.
3.      Add n to the result of fact called with one less than n.
4.      Have the tutor choose.
Menu Choice: 2
```

```
                    CODE FOR fact

(defun fact (n)
     (cond ((zerop n) 1)
               <RECURSIVE-CASE>))




                    EXAMPLES
           fact (n)          fact (n-1)
A.    (fact 1) = 1      (fact 0) = 1
B.    (fact 3) = 6      (fact 2) = 2
```

FIG. 2.1.  A representation of the screen image after line 3 in Table 2.1

combining the recursive call with other elements. The second, in Line 5, is to call the function recursively with the same argument rather than a simpler one.

After the student finishes coding the function he goes to the LISP window and experiments. He is required to trace the function, and the recursive calls embed and then unravel. Figure 2.2 shows the screen image at this point with the code on top and the trace below it.

```
--- YOU ARE DONE.  TYPE NEXT TO GO ON AFTER ---
--- TESTING THE FUNCTIONS YOU HAVE DEFINED  ---

(defun fact (n)
      (cond ((zerop n) 1)
            (t (times n (fact (sub1 n)))))))
```

THE LISP WINDOW

```
= > (trace fact)
(fact)

= > (fact 3)
1 <Enter> fact (3)
|2 <Enter> fact (2)
| 3 <Enter> fact (1)
| |4 <Enter> fact (0)
| |4 <EXIT>  fact  1
| 3 <EXIT>   fact  1
|2 <EXIT>    fact  2
1 <EXIT>     fact  6
6
```

FIG. 2.2.  The final screen image at the end of the dialogue in Table 2.1

## Features of the Model-Tracing Methodology

The example just shown illustrates a number of features of the model-tracing methodology:

1. The tutor constantly monitors the student's problem solving and provides direction whenever the student wanders off a solution path.
2. The tutor tries to provide help with both the overt parts of the problem solution and the planning. However, to address the planning, a mechanism had to be introduced in the interface (in this case menus) to allow the student to communicate the steps of planning.
3. The interface handles details like syntax checking, which are irrelevant to the problem-solving skill being tutored.
4. The interface is highly reactive in that it does make some response to every symbol the student enters.

## The Mechanics of Model Tracing

Sitting within the tutor is a production system consisting of hundreds of ideal and buggy rules. The following are examples of a production rule that codes APPEND and two bugs. Associated with each bug is an example of the feedback we would present to the student should the student display that bug:

*Production Rule in Ideal Model:*

        IF    the goal is to merge LIST1 and LIST2
                into a single list
   THEN   use the function APPEND and set
                subgoals to code LIST1 and LIST2

*Related Bugs:*

        IF    the goal is to merge LIST1 and LIST2
                into a single list
   THEN   use the function LIST and set
                subgoals to code LIST1 and LIST2

*You should combine the first list and the second list, but LIST is not the right function. If you LIST together (a b c) and (x y z), for example, you will get ((a b c) (x y z)) instead of (a b c x y z). LIST just wraps parens around its arguments.*

        IF    the goal is to merge LIST1 and LIST2
                into a single list
                and LIST1 = LIST2
   THEN   use the function TIMES and set
                subgoals to code LIST1
                and the number 2

*You want to put together two copies of the same list, but you can't make two copies of a list by using the function TIMES. TIMES only works on numbers. You should use a function that combines two lists together.*

Altogether we have over 1200 productions (correct and buggy) to model student performance in our lessons, which cover all the basic syntax of LISP, design of iteration and recursive functions, use of data structures, and means–ends planning of code.

## THEORETICAL PREMISES UNDERLYING
## THE LISP TUTOR

The LISP tutor is predicated on a number of assumptions about the cognitive architecture, about the nature of a complex skill like programming, and the nature of its acquisition. The actual student models are implemented in the GRAPES production system, which is a partial simulation of the ACT* theory, and the tutoring interactions are based on assumptions about what the critical factors are underlying skill performance and execution. Without claiming to be exhaustive, the following are among the critical assumptions underlying execution of the LISP tutor:

1. *Production Rule Decomposition*. A skill like programming can be decomposed into an independent set of production rules.

2. *Skill Complexity*. The number of rules underlying such a skill is large— at least in the hundreds and perhaps in the thousands. This is the perspective of the knowledge engineering tradition in AI and implies detailed task analysis is a prerequisite to skill acquisition. It also implies that knowledge is highly specific.

3. *Hierarchical Goal Organization*. All the productions are organized by a hierarchical goal structure, which is traversed in a top–down left-to-right discipline.

4. *Declarative Origins of Knowledge*. All knowledge begins in some declarative representation, typically acquired from instruction or example. Thus, in the LISP tutor we always precede practice with a terse exposition designed to provide the critical declarative knowledge.

5. *Compilation of Procedural Knowledge*. Use of declarative knowledge is inefficient. There is a knowledge compilation process that converts the declarative knowledge into an efficient procedural form specific to a particular use. Knowledge compilation requires the knowledge to be actually used in the content of problem solving. It is by examining the trace of the problem solution that the knowledge-compilation process decides how to cast the production that it produces.

6. *Conscious Correction of Knowledge*. Errors in knowledge do not become automatically corrected with experience. They require that the subject form a declarative representation of the mistake and act to correct the mistake. Thus, the emphasis in the tutor is on explaining the difference between correct and incorrect options.

7. *Centrality of Working Memory Limitations*. A production system operates by matching information in its working memory. In the ACT* theory this working memory is the active portion of long-term memory. This is basically the students' immediate goal, what is attended to in the environment and their strong associates. Activation has a rapid decay; so unattended information quickly drops out of memory. The major performance factor (in contrast to lack of knowledge factor) limiting learning in ACT* is the failure to keep active in working memory all the information for a mental compilation to apply correctly. This view about the major limitation on LISP performance is supported in the research of Anderson and Jeffries (1985). They found that novice errors in LISP were largely slips and not the result of lack of knowledge. Moreover, these slips increased with working-memory load. Working-memory limitations impact on learning as well as performance. Because productions are compiled from declarative representations,

working-memory failures slow down learning and cause incorrect things to be learned.

8. *Minor Relations Between Strength and Learning.* As declarative knowledge or procedural knowledge is practiced it is strengthened. Stronger declarative knowledge is the more active and hence is more likely to be in working memory. Stronger productions are the more rapidly matched to what is in working memory. This means that it is more likely that well-encoded knowledge would overcome the limitations of working memory and would successfully apply. The first-order effect of strength would be on speed of performance, but it would have a second-order effect on working memory (and basically, accuracy). Although these strength factors do affect speed and accuracy performance measures, they should have little direct effect on production learning. Even when strength affects maintenance of information in working memory, these strength effects would occur after productions are learned (at least in the LISP tutor).

In total, these eight assumption constitute some profound claims about the course of skill acquisition. They also paint a rather simple picture of the process. The critical question concerns what the actual data have to say about the theory.

## DATA ANALYSIS

As students interact with the LISP tutor we collect a total record of all of their responses and the time at which they complete these responses. A student's response is defined as something the tutor reacts to. Usually this amounts to a LISP symbol, when typing code, or a menu selection. We do not collect data at the level of inter-keystroke times; that level of data collection would be just too voluminous. We also record the times at which the tutor prints prompts and the identities of these prompts. Finally, in the data files we have records of the correct or buggy productions that the LISP tutor ascribed to students responses.

These data can easily be transformed into a form wherein we organize the data by the sequence of productions that the tutor assumed fired and associate times with the firing of each production. This amounts to ascribing a theoretical interpretation to the data in terms of the simulation program used by the tutor. This is a level of analysis that graduate students used to spend dissertations to achieve for a few subjects solving a few problems. We can achieve it automatically for a class full of students doing a semester's worth of work.

A key feature of the LISP tutor is that it keeps students on a correct path of problem solution. The tutor may be prepared to follow the student on many hundreds of ways of solving a problem, but this is much less than the thousands of ways, mostly incorrect, that students have been observed trying to solve a problem. At any point in time there is a set of possible next correct productions that the tutor is prepared to have the student execute. One of a possible set of things can happen:

1. The student generates an action that matches the action produced by one of the correct productions. The tutor assumes the production that generated this action is the one that fired in the student's head and continues to monitor for the production that follows that.

2. The student makes an error, the tutor responds to that error with feedback, and then the student generates an action that corresponds to a correct production. The tutor assumes that the feedback enabled the student to figure out the correct answer, and the student is back on track.

3. The student asks for the next step either immediately or after an error. The tutor provides the student with an explanation of the correct step and then provides the piece of code that corresponds to that step. The assumption is again that this explanation was sufficient to get the student back on track and the student is in the same mental state as the tutor.

4. The student generates three errors. In this case the tutor offers the same explanation as it would have had the student requested it and provides the next correct action.

The major complication hidden in this description concerns a dichotomy in the types of errors emitted. About 80% of the errors match buggy productions in the LISP tutor, and it is able to generate feedback specific to that error. The other 20% of productions are not matched, and the feedback is a default ("I don't understand that"). The majority of the undiagnosed responses are clearly erroneous on the student's part. Only on rare occasions do we observe a student with a solution that the tutor has not thought of.

The underlying assumption in these interactions is that before doing the next piece of the problem the student and the tutor are in the same mental state. From informal observations we know there are occasions when this is not true, for instance, when the student either misunderstands the problem statement or the feedback given by the tutor. This means that there is a certain noise built into our error attribution. We attribute an error to production applying in state $X$ whereas a different production might be applying in state $Y$. It is difficult to know the magnitude of this "noise" in the data and how it compares with noise in other data. One test is the reliability and interpretability of the data obtained with the LISP tutor. Any experiment has noise in the data, and as in any experiment, we use the ratio of variance between conditions to variance within conditions to decide what effects could not be due to experimental noise.

Given this data base, there are two basic categories of data to collect from the LISP tutor: error measures and time measures. Both of these categories break down into two basic subtypes. For errors, we can calculate the probability of making an error on a production or the total number of errors made on a production. In calculating total number of errors, we score requests for the answer as the maximum, three errors. With respect to time, we can calculate the time for the correct answer to appear irrespective of the number of intermediate errors and whether the answer was provided by the student or the system. This provides a kind of speed through the problem measure. Alternatively, we can restrict our analysis to cases where the first answer is correct.

There are three categories of correct productions. There are productions that do not produce any overt action on the student's part. There are productions whose actions correspond to menu selections. And there are productions whose actions produce code. We restrict our analysis to the third kind and to those situations where the previous production was also a code-producing production. Measuring time from the end of the student's action of the previous production to the end of the action associated with current production gives us a fairly clean measure of time for the production to fire and time for the student to interact with the interface and enter the result. Even in this case we are looking at measures that include a lot of extraneous time such as typing. The actual times we are reporting are much larger than typically associated with production firing.

The data we are analyzing comes from 34 students who were taking LISP in the spring of 1985. The students were in the school of humanities and social science, and this was their first programming course. Although they went through 12 lessons with the LISP tutor, we only analyzed data from the first 6 lessons before their midterm. This midterm was a paper-and-pencil test and so provides us with an external validation of any results we get on performance with the LISP tutor. These lessons involved (a) introduction to some basic LISP functions; (b) introduction to how to define one's own functions; (c) conditionals and logical predicates; (d) helping functions; (e) input-output; and (f) iteration.

The typical history of a production is that it is introduced in a particular lesson and is involved in the coding of a number of problems. After that, it occurs irregularly and less frequently in later lessons. Depending on their centrality, different productions occur with rather different frequencies. This of course creates serious difficulties in trying to perform aggregate measure of performance over lessons.

There are some complications in defining the frequency of occurrence of a production. First, because alternative solutions to problems were possible, it was not guaranteed that the same productions would be used by all subjects. What appears as frequency is a measure of how often the production could have occurred. Some subjects do not contribute to some possible occurrences. This is not as serious a problem as one might think because a lot of the variation concerned changes in order of code or changes in choice of just one or two functions. Thus the variation in production use was much lower than the variation in number of distinct solutions produced.

The other complication is produced by remedial problems. When students are judged weak on certain productions, they are required to do remedial problems, which offers additional practice on these productions. Students need, on average, about 15% extra remedial problems, although there is large individual variation. We ignore remedial problems in the analyses that we report.

Thus our data in its finest grain can be broken down according to the dimensions of lesson, production, and opportunity for that production within the lesson. Crossed with these are the four dependent measures listed earlier—namely, time per production, time for correct production firings, probability of a correct production firing, and mean number of errors for a production firing.

## RESULTS

I would like to present the majority of the data organized by lesson and aggregated over production. However, to explain this aggregation process and to get a better feel for the data, I believe it would be worthwhile to look at one lesson in more detail. Lesson 2 is appropriate for this purpose. Table 2.2 lists the productions we monitored. The first 9 were first introduced in Lesson 2 and the last 9 had been introduced in the previous lesson.

Fig. 2.3 and 2.4 plot the performance on the new productions for this lesson. Fig. 2.3 plots the times for correct use of the production (where the maximum value was set at 200 seconds), and Fig. 2.4 plots the mean number of errors, where this statistic has a maximum of three. We plotted just times for correct productions in order to get a measure that is independent of errors. As noted earlier, we also analyzed time aggregated over corrects and errors. This measure does not seem to reveal any additional insights. We choose to analyze total number of errors per opportunity in Fig. 2.4 rather than probability of error because we believe it is a better measure of student difficulty. Students often make single errors and correct them as slips. Every time an error cannot be corrected, it is further evidence that a student has a fundamental difficulty.

We have plotted these measures as a function of the times a production has been tested in the session. Both scales are logarithmic. Different productions occurred a different number of times, but we calculated a weighted average to provide our best estimate of how the mean changed with practice.[1] As can be seen, this mean shows a marked drop-off from first to second test and a very modest decline after that. The average improvement from first to second trial is almost 50% for time and over 50% for accuracy. We plot this on a log–log scale to make the point that this drop-off is not just part of the power-law improvement normally seen for a skill. Figures 2.5 and 2.6 plot the lesson averages for lessons

---

[1]The average for the first opportunity is the average of the logarithms. The $n$th average, $a_n$, is calculated from $n$-$1$st average $a_{n-1}$ as $a_{n-1} + i_n$ where $i_n$ is the average change in the logarithm values of those productions for which there is both a $n$-$1$st and $n$th observation.

TABLE 2.2
Productions Monitored in Lesson 2

1. specify-function-name: Codes the symbol corresponding to the production name.
2. specify-function-params: Codes the parameters of the function.
3. code-nil: a production for coding the special symbol *nil*.
4. code-append: a production to generate the LISP combining function append.
5. code-reverse: a production to generate the LISP function reverse which codes the reverse of a list.
6. code-cosine: a production to code the LISP function *cosine*.
7. code-sine: a production to code the LISP function *sine*.
8. code-square: a production that codes the square of a number by taking the product of two numbers.
9. check-arg: a production that codes as an argument to a function called a parameter in the function definition.

The following productions were introduced in lesson 1 but reappear in lesson 2

10. code-car: a production to code the LISP function car that gets the first element of a list.
11. code-cdr: a production to code the LISP function *cdr* that gets the rest of a list.
12. code-second: a production that gets the second element of a list. This is coded as a *car-cdr* combination. This is treated separately because students have difficulty with precedence of unary operators.
13. code-cons: a production to code the LISP combiner *cons* that inserts its first argument in front of the list that is its second argument.
14. code-list: a production to code the LISP combiner *list* that wraps parentheses around its arguments.
15. code-divide: a production that codes the LISP function *quotient* that takes the quotient of two numbers.
16. code-difference: a production that codes the LISP function *difference* that subtracts its second argument from its first argument.
17. code-times: a production that codes the LISP function *times* that multiplies its arguments.
18. code-number: a production that codes a number argument to a function.

2, 3, and 5 and the average of these averages (lesson 1 measures are peculiar on the first trials because typically the teacher is coaching, and there are very few new productions introduced on lessons 4 and 6). It makes even clearer the point that the drop-off from the first to second trial is discontinuous.

Note that the rate of improvement after the first trial is basically linear in these two logarithmic measures. This implies a power function relating either time or errors to amount of practice. This is what is typically found in studies of practice. However, the clear discontinuity from trial 1 to trial 2 is something that has not been examined in detail until now. It is consistent with the knowledge compilation mechanism in ACT*, basically a one-trial learning mechanism. One might attribute the drop-off in errors to students just debugging their misconceptions from reading. Thus, it is significant that this discontinuity also shows up in times for errorless trials as well as number of errors.

Another question concerns how performance changes on productions across lessons. Figure 2.7 is an attempt to analyze this. We have plotted performance on

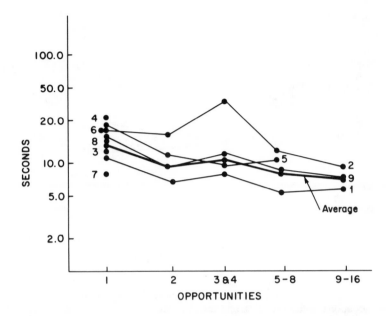

FIG. 2.3.  Mean times for correct coding of the actions corresponding to 9 productions introduced in lesson 2. See text for explanation of the productions.

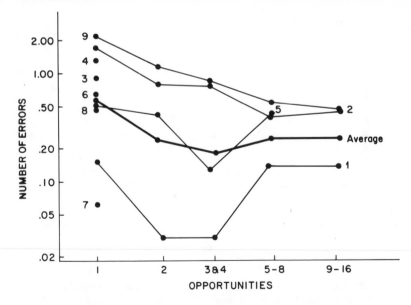

FIG. 2.4.  Mean number of errors in coding the actions corresponding to 9 productions introduced in lesson 2. See text for an explanation of the productions.

41

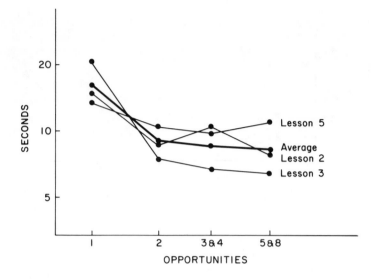

FIG. 2.5.   Average times for coding actions corresponding to new productions in lessons 2, 3, and 5.

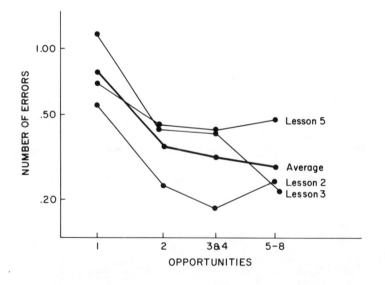

FIG. 2.6.   Average number of errors in coding actions corresponding to new productions on lessons 2, 3, and 5.

last occurrence in lesson *n*-1, first performance in lesson *n*, and last performance in lesson *n*. Figure 2.7 plots these patterns for the lesson pairs 1 and 2, 2 and 3, 3 and 4, and 5 and 6 (there are few shared productions between 4 and 5). The average of these lesson averages makes the pattern even more apparent. There is perhaps a little forgetting between lessons but considerable improvement within lessons. This is more apparent with the accuracy measure than the time measure. Although they are not exactly the same productions plotted in each curve, note that the curves tend to get lower across lessons, also consistent with a gradual improvement with practice.

One might wonder how much support these analyses offer for the existence of the production rules assumed by the LISP tutor. The apparent regularity of the data is consistent with the view that the LISP tutor provides the psychologically correct decomposition of the skill. However, these production rules do tend to correspond to pieces of code in LISP. For instance, *code-car* corresponds to typing *car* and *check-arg* corresponds to typing a variable name. What if we simply monitored how accurately students wrote these pieces of code and ignored the production-rule analysis? Although correlated, it is not the case that a code-based analysis is identical to a production-rule analyses. This is because in some cases there is a many-to-one relationship between production rules and types of LISP code. For instance, although *code-car* usually is responsible for generating *car*, there is a special production, *code-second*, that corresponds to *car* when we

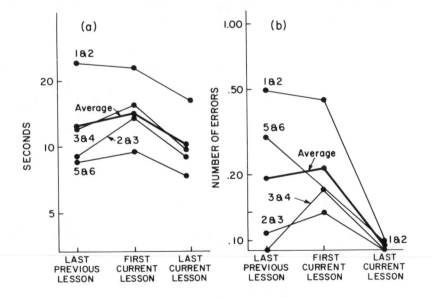

FIG. 2.7.   Average times and errors for old productions in a particular lesson. Plotted is a measure for last opportunity in previous lesson, first opportunity in current lesson, and last opportunity in current lesson.

are composing a *car-cdr* sequence. The first time subjects typed *car* as *code-second* in lesson 1 they made .68 errors. We can go back to their error rate on the preceding *code-car* and find it was just .41. This increase from .41 to .68 deviates from the general improvement within a lesson. All other comparisons we looked at show the same trend. Coding *cond* to terminate an iteration is different than coding *cond* generally. Subject make 1.05 errors in the *cond* in iteration compared to .32 errors for the previous *cond*. Coding a number to initialize a variable is different than passing it as an argument to a function. Subjects make 1.64 errors on their first use of a number to initialize compared to .24 errors in the previous use of a number. Using *setq* to initialize a local variable is controlled by a different production than the one that uses *setq* to initialize a global variable. Subjects make .89 errors on their first local variable *setq* compared to .29 for their previous global variable *setq*. Coding a variable that is a function parameter is governed by a different production than the one that codes a global variable. The difference in error rate is 2.18 versus .38. Coding a parameter is different in turn from coding a local variable in a function. By the time subjects get to local variables, their error rate for parameters has dropped from 2.18 to .03. Their error rate in the first local variable is .84. The upshot of all these comparisons is that subject improvement is better defined in terms of the LISP tutor productions than surface code. The regularity of the data really is evidence for the LISP Tutor's production-rule analysis.

The overall pattern of data displayed in these graphs is consistent with the ACT* learning mechanisms. There is the discontinuous point of learning from first trial to second due to knowledge compilation, a power-law growth in strength (and hence performance measure) with practice, and some forgetting (loss of strength) between lessons. It should also be noted that, with the exception of the first trial discontinuity, we find nothing in LISP learning that would be surprising from the results of verbal learning.

## INTER-PRODUCTION CORRELATIONS

Another question of interest is how well does performance on one production correlate with performance on another production. We looked at the measures of number of errors in calculating these correlations because they prove to yield the largest correlations. In one analysis we looked at patterns of correlation between lessons 1 and 2, 2 and 3, and 3 and 4. We calculated how well a production from one lesson correlated with itself on another lesson. Basically, this involves getting mean number of errors made on a production for each lesson for each subject and looking for a correlation over subjects for each production.

The average correlation of all the productions that repeated across trials was

.26. This might not seem very large, but because most productions only occur a few times in a lesson and the individual measures are inherently quite noisy, correlations will be low. Under one model the expected maximum correlation is only .33.[2]

We gathered two other correlation measures between lessons. First, we broke the productions on individual lessons into those that deal with list operations and those that do not. Thus, we divided the productions into disjoint sets. We looked at correlations within sets (excluding correlations between the same production reported in the preceding paragraph) and between sets. The average correlation was .17 both within and between sets. These numbers are significantly lower than the correlation between the same production on both lessons, and obviously the two correlations were not significantly different. Intuitively, this is surprising because it indicates that there is no tendency for productions of the same type to cluster. Both correlations are quite significantly different than zero, of course, indicating some systematic individual differences among subjects.

We also calculated correlations among productions within the same lesson, excluding correlation of a production with itself, which would be 1. The average within-lesson correlation is .23, which is significantly higher than the between-lesson correlation and does not significantly differ from the between-lesson, same-production correlation. This indicates some tendency for subjects to have good lessons or bad lessons, which is not surprising. Again, if we break up these within-lesson correlations into correlations within list and non-list productions and correlations between list and non-list productions, there is no difference.

The failure to find evidence for a clustering among productions involved with list operations is surprising. We had strongly suspected that some subjects would do well on all list operations and some would not. Although this is in fact the case, it appears that the interproduction correlations are not higher than found between apparently unrelated productions. Thus, there appears to be a general ability factor, but not one associated with list operations.

One possible conclusion is that productions do not break up into thematic clusters, but it is possible that we simply did not intuit properly the factors that would cause productions to cluster. To see if this was the case, we subjected the data from the six lessons to factor analyses. We took the matrix of subject-by-production error means for each lesson and submitted it to a standard factor-analysis program. We then looked at the first two factors extracted for each lesson. We have looked at the other three performance measures, but error totals

---

[2]We have on average about four observations per production per lesson. Assume that each observation is a binomial with a probability $p$ of generating an error. Assume that for half the production $p = .33$ and for the other half $p = .67$. The correlation expected between number of errors for four observations on day 1 and four observations on day 2 is .33.

consistently show largest variance accounted for in the first two factors. The data from the lessons structured as follows.

1. Number of Productions involved in the factor analysis. In all cases there are 34 subjects.
2. Variance accounted for by first factor, second factor, and third factor. The variance accounted for by the second factor indicates what we gain by including it, and the variance accounted for by the third factor indicates what we lose by excluding it.
3. Which productions loaded most heavily on each factor after rotation. If a production loads heavily on both, we report the factor it loads most heavily on. We exclude productions with a factor loading of less than + .6. We report the magnitude of the loadings in parentheses.

## Lesson 1—15 Productions:

| Factor 1 | Factor 2 | Factor 3 |
| --- | --- | --- |
| 41% of the variance | 13% of the variance | 10% of the variance |
| global variables (.81)* | quotient (.74)* | |
| list function (.79)* | formula for square (.61)* | |
| cdr function (.77)* | | |
| coding a number (.76)* | | |
| first arg to setq (.75)* | | |
| cons function (.73)* | | |
| setq function (.72)* | | |
| quoted constant (.63)* | | |
| plan for second element in a list (.61)* | | |

## Lesson 2—19 Productions:

| Factor 1 | Factor 2 | Factor 3 |
| --- | --- | --- |
| 34% of the variance | 12% of the variance | 8% of the variance |
| coding a number (.83) | reverse function (.81)* | |
| cdr function (.81) | coding parameters in function definition (.72)* | |
| coding function name (.78)* | coding NIL (.71)* | |
| difference function (.68) | cons function (.61) | |
| quotient function (.65) | | |
| formula for square (.64) | | |
| defun function (.62)* | | |

## Lesson 3—31 Productions:

| Factor 1 | Factor 2 | Factor 3 |
|---|---|---|
| 28% of the variance | 11% of the variance | 10% of the variance |
| coding a number (.86) | coding an else (*t*) clause (.71)* | |
| cond function (.82)* | coding a parameter (.68) | |
| coding a constant (.78) | member function (.65)* | |
| lessp function (.75)* | reverse function (.64) | |
| cons function (.72) | or function (.63)* | |
| null function (.70)* | not function (.62)* | |
| global variable (.62) | | |

## Lesson 4—18 Productions:

| Factor 1 | Factor 2 | Factor 3 |
|---|---|---|
| 28% of the variance | 12% of the variance | 10% of the variance |
| equal function (.79) | case within a cond (.68) | |
| car function (.74) | coding an else (*t*) clause (.66) | |
| last function (.74) | coding a parameter (.62) | |
| cdr function (.69) | | |

## Lesson 5—28 Productions:

| Factor 1 | Factor 2 | Factor 3 |
|---|---|---|
| 45% of the variance | 10% of the variance | 6% of the variance |
| Prog function (.90)* | code a local variable (.83)* | |
| numberp function (.80)* | print function (.74)* | |
| case within a cond (.77) | coding a parameter (.72) | |
| coding a loop tag (.73) | plus function (.69) | |
| not function (.73) | cond function (.69) | |
| go function (.72) | read function (.69) | |
| resetting a variable (.67)* | coding the variable to be reset | |
| coding a constant (.67) | (.68)* | |
| return function (.64) | list function (.67) | |
| initializing a variable (.62)* | difference function (.61) | |

## Lesson 6—27 Productions:

| Factor 1 | Factor 2 | Factor 3 |
|---|---|---|
| 29% of the variance | 11% of the variance | 7% of the variance |

| Factor 1 | Factor 2 |
|---|---|
| code a local variable (.88) | code an initial value for |
| coding a parameter (.81) | iteration (.83)* |
| coding a loop tag (.76) | initialize a variable for |
| equal function (.76) | iteration (.83)* |
| coding repeat tag (.76) | prog function (.76) |
| coding a variable (.68) | |
| plus function (.68) | |
| coding a number (.63) | |
| difference function (.62) | |
| greaterp function (.61) | |

## WHAT DOES IT MEAN?

We could not make a great deal of sense out of this pattern. Productions were not apparently clustering according to any semantic feature. In an attempt to make sense of this we took each subject's factor scores for the two factors for each lesson and thus got twelve measures for each subject. We subjected these to a factor analysis to determine which lesson factors would cluster together. The first meta-factor extracted accounted for 36% of the variance and the second meta-factor 16% of the variance. The third meta-factor (which we will ignore) accounted for 14% of the variance.

The following factors loaded on the first meta-factor—factor 2, lesson 1; factor 2, lesson 2, factor 2, lesson 3; factors 1 and 2, lesson 5; and factor 2, lesson 6. The following factors loaded on the second meta-factor—factor 1, lesson 3; factors 1 and 2, lesson 4; and factor 1, lesson 6. Factor 1 from lesson 1 and factor 1 from lesson 2 did not load on either meta-factor, suggesting that these may reflect peculiar start-up features in dealing with LISP.

It only became apparent after considerable inspection what unites the factors categorized together under each meta-factor. Twenty-two of the 34 productions organized under meta-factor 1 were introduced in that lesson, whereas only 3 of the 23 productions organized under meta-factor 2. The new productions are starred in the listings just given. Thus the first factor is basically an acquisition factor because it reflects performance in productions being acquired in that lesson, whereas the second is a retention factor because it reflects performance in productions presumably already acquired in previous lessons, and, thus, deficits must be due to forgetting. This helps explain why the actual clustering of productions seemed arbitrary semantically and why the clusters do not stay constant across lessons. The second factor correlates .62 with math SAT; the first factor only correlates .03. Neither factor correlates with verbal SAT or grade-point average at Carnegie Mellon.

It seemed worthwhile to see how these categories did at predicting performance on paper-and-pencil tests. We used the midterm and final exam tests of the 34 students. The midterm was administered right after completing lesson 6, whereas the final was administered after 6 more lessons with the tutor. We have not had the opportunity to analyze the data from these 6 lessons. We took subjects' factor scores on these two meta-factors and classified them into above or below the median. This gave us ten subjects in both the high–high and low–low categories and seven in both the high–low and low–high categories.

Table 2.3 presents the data from the midterm exams in terms of scores out of 24, and Table 2.4 presents the final grades out of 28 similarly classified. There are significant effects of both factors on midterm grades—$F(1,30)=5.1$ for acquisition and $F(1,30)=6.4$ for retention. The interaction is not significant—$F(1,30)=2.8$. Again, only the main effects were significant on final exam—acquisition factor with $F(1,30)=6.3$ and retention factor with $F(1,30)=9.7$

TABLE 2.3
Midterm Grades

|  | Low Acquisition Factor | High Acquisition Factor |
|---|---|---|
| Low Retention Factor | 3.8 ± .9 | 9.7 ± 1.3 |
| High Retention Factor | 10.1 ± 1.9 | 11.0 ± 1.5 |

TABLE 2.4
Final Exam

|  | Low Acquisition Factor | High Acquisition Factor |
|---|---|---|
| Low Retention Factor | 9.8 ± 1.7 | 13.4 ± 1 |
| High Retention Factor | 14.2 ± .9 | 17.8 ± 1.9 |

## CONCLUSIONS

In my opinion this analysis of student behavior is marvelous for the lawfulness and simplicity of the picture it paints. It is particularly consistent with the ACT* production-system analysis of skill acquisition. The behavior is quite regular when analyzed with respect to the production rules used in the LISP tutor. It shows evidence for a one-trial learning episode consistent with knowledge compilation and a more gradual learning consistent with the power-law strengthening process.

Productions are independent and modular, as would be predicted by the ACT* theory. The only production rules with which a particular production correlates especially strongly is with itself. This is consistent with the notion that each production is learned independently. In particular, we found no evidence that productions were being clustered because some subjects were having difficulty with list manipulations. Some productions are clearly more difficult than others and some subjects are clearly more capable than others, but there does not appear to be any interaction between the two factors. Subjects' overall ability impacts on how fact they learn all aspects of LISP, but except through this general ability factor the learning of one production is independent of the learning of others.

When we did an atheoretical factor analysis looking for evidence of an interaction, the only thing we found were two somewhat independent general-ability factors of acquisition and retention on which subjects could be sorted and on which old and new productions could be sorted. This result clearly does not compromise the basic cognitive assumption of independence of productions, although it raises some interesting questions about what the real nature of these two ability factors might be.

## REFERENCES

Anderson, J. R. (1982). Acquisition of cognitive skill. *Psychological Review, 89*, 369–406.
Anderson, J. R. (1983). *The architecture of cognition*. Cambridge, MA: Harvard University Press.
Anderson, J. R., & Jeffries, R. (1985). Novice LISP errors: Undetected losses of information from working memory. *Human-Computer Interaction, 22*, 403–423.
Anderson, J. R., & Reiser, B. J. (1985). The LISP tutor. *Byte, 10*, 159–175.
Anderson, J. R., Farrell, R., & Sauers, R. (1984). Learning to program in LISP. *Cognitive Science, 8*, 87–129.
Bloom, B. S. (1984). The 2 sigma problem: The search for methods of group instruction as effective as one-to-one tutoring. *Educational Researcher, 13*, 3–16.
Sleeman, D., & Brown, J. S. (Eds.). (1982). *Intelligent tutoring systems*. New York: Academic Press.

# The Role of Cognitive Simulation Models in the Development of Advanced Training and Testing Systems

David E. Kieras
*University of Michigan*

The thesis of this chapter is that cognitive simulation modeling is a way to obtain specifications of the knowledge required to do a task, or to evaluate the adequacy of proposed specifications of the body of knowledge. Such specifications should be detailed and precise enough that test questions based on them would allow assessment of the exact knowledge required to perform a skill, and training materials based on them would be made complete, compact, and efficient. Such precision specifications could assist in the development of higher quality, traditional paper-based testing and training systems, and the actual representations of the knowledge contained in a simulation could be the input for intelligent tutoring and other computer-based advanced training and testing systems.

This chapter is organized as follows: First, a brief discussion of cognitive simulation modeling, with a focus on what kind of information is contained in a cognitive simulation. Second is a discussion of how constructing a cognitive simulation can assist in developing training and testing procedures for new tasks. The chapter concludes with an extended discussion of a couple of examples of potential applications of this approach. The first example concerns the acquisition of procedures for operating equipment, and the second example concerns learning and using a mental model for a piece of equipment. A concluding section discusses some of the potential problems with this approach.

## COGNITIVE SIMULATION

A cognitive simulation model is defined here as a computer program that realizes a theoretical idea about mental structures and processes. The computer program contains explicit representations of proposed mental processes and knowledge structures. Changes in the internal state of the model are supposed to represent changes in the internal state of the human mind, at some level of analysis. These programs most commonly involve symbol manipulation, rather than numeric calculation, and use languages such as LISP and programming techniques originally developed in artificial intelligence.

## Goals of Cognitive Simulation

Traditionally, cognitive simulations have been developed in order to turn a vague set of ideas about mental processes into well-defined ideas, whose completeness, adequacy and consistency could be confirmed by determining whether the program produces the correct behavior. Thus, constructing a simulation model is a way to evaluate and make more specific a set of theoretical ideas about cognitive processes.

An important feature of simulation modeling is that it fits in well with the very detailed methodology that is currently available in computer-based psychological experimentation. The deep level of detail in a simulation model corresponds well to the level of detail in data collected with these modern methods. There has been a greater tendency in recent years for simulation models to be tested for empirical accuracy against data at this greater level of detail.

Thus, the simulation itself provides an explicit and detailed theoretical statement that can summarize a large body of data. A fairly new assertion about the simulation approach is that it can provide theory-based predictions and evaluations in practical situations. See Kieras (1985) for more discussion on this topic.

## Cognitive Architecture

The linkage between the psychological theory and the simulation program is best when the theory and the program are both based on definite assumptions about the architecture of cognition, rather than consisting of an arbitrary collection of proposed processes in the psychological theory, and correspondingly arbitrary date structures and code in the simulation program. By working within the structure imposed by an explicit cognitive architecture, the simulation modeler is afforded some degree of protection against accounting for behavior simply by large quantities of *ad hoc* programming. By adhering to a cognitive architecture, the simulation program is forced to have a consistent and principled structure.

A currently popular cognitive architecture assumes that there is both declarative and procedural knowledge in the mind. Declarative knowledge is represented as either a set of propositions, or as a semantic network. Procedural knowledge is represented as a set of production rules, which are elementary If–Then statements. The production rules test for the presence of various conditions in the declarative knowledge representation, and either manipulate the declarative representation or produce behavior. Perhaps the best representative of this cognitive architecture is Anderson's work on cognitive skill (Anderson, 1976, 1983). This architecture has the advantage of supplying a uniform modular notation for both declarative and procedural knowledge; the proposition is the unit of declarative knowledge; the production rule is the unit of procedural knowledge. These units can be counted, to yield quantitative predictors of performance (e.g., Kieras & Bovair, 1986). Although there are alternative cognitive architectures, such as the connectionist framework, the proposition–production rule class of architectures has the virtues that it is theoretically very well developed, and it functions at a level of analysis that applies very well to many important cognitive skills (see Anderson, chap. 2 in this volume). Thus this class of architectures is an ideal theoretical vehicle for applying results and principles from cognitive psychology to practical situations.

## The Information in a Cognitive Simulation

Once a cognitive simulation model has been constructed and appears to behave correctly in the task of interest, a considerable amount of information has been built into the model and in the detailed specifications of the task conditions under which it is supposed to work.

In order to specify a cognitive simulation model, the modeler must provide a detailed task analysis. This analysis is typically far more detailed than what is often meant by the phrase "task analysis." At a global level, before a simulation model can be made to work, the modeler must lay out in specific detail what goals and subgoals the system is supposed to accomplish. In addition to this goal structure, the task analysis provides a detailed and quite explicit description of what the person must do in response to each individual specific aspect of the task situation. The implications of each relevant feature of the stimulus must be specified, along with the impact this is supposed to have on the person's cognitive processes and behavior. This detailed analysis is necessary in order to permit the simulation program to be written. Thus, a successful simulation model is associated with a thorough analysis of the task.

Assuming the cognitive architecture just mentioned, after construction, a working simulation model should contain an explicit description of the declarative knowledge required to do the task. This means that the modeler must lay out in detail exactly what facts about the domain the person must have in order to accomplish the task. In addition, the simulation model should contain an explicit description of the procedural knowledge required to do the task, including all the relevant rules, procedures, and heuristics. In the architecture assumed here, all of this procedural knowledge can be described in terms of production rules.

As an example, consider a hypothetical simulation model that is able to carry out electronics trouble shooting in a psychologically realistic fashion. Such a model contains in it the answers to the following questions: (a) What is the goal structure of the trouble shooting task? (b) What are the critical facts about electronics and the specific electronic system being repaired? (c) What are the rules for inferring the state of a component from various observations? and (d) What are the strategies and heuristics used for isolating the malfunctioning component? If the simulation model is actually able to carry out the electronics trouble shooting task successfully, then we can have some confidence that we have accurately and completely characterized the critical knowledge. Notice that this approach provides essentially a static characterization of the required knowledge. Situations in which the trainee is expected to be flexible or inventive would require making explicit the content of such metacognitive skills before these skills could be taught or assessed under this approach.

## Using the Information in a Simulation

The task analysis and knowledge specifications from the simulation in fact characterize the task itself. This information has several potential uses. First, it can be used to evaluate the design of the system that a trainee must interact with. For example, if a system requires that the user have an extreme amount of knowledge before being able to operate it correctly, there must be something wrong with the design of the system. An improved design would simplify the training process. The approach to cognitive complexity in human–computer interaction taken by Kieras and Polson (1985) is based on this idea.

The second potential use of information in the simulation model is that it could be used to compare tasks in terms of the underlying subtasks. For example, if there were two related tasks, each with a simulation model, the specific knowledge and procedures contained in the simulations could then be compared directly to each other in order to isolate precisely what the tasks have in common. Thus, instead of comparing tasks in terms of intuitions about their relationship, tasks could be compared in terms of their precise knowledge requirements. Such comparisons could be used to "optimize" the set of tasks assigned to individuals in particular jobs. That is, if the ways a set of tasks are related to each other could be precisely characterized, then it should be possible to pick combinations of tasks to assign to an individual that draw on the same body of knowledge. This would make effective training easier, and also would allow the individual to become more expert by being able to concentrate on a specific body of knowledge.

A third potential way to use the information in the declarative and procedural knowledge representations in the simulation model is to provide an explicit specification of the *minimum required knowledge* to accomplish the task. Thus, these representations specify what knowledge is *really* important, as opposed to optional elaboration or detail. Training and testing materials can be inspected to see if they actually contain this information. The examples provided in this chapter show how intuitively prepared material often seriously lacks critical information.

A fourth possibility is to use the knowledge representations directly in computer-based systems such as intelligent tutoring systems. Because the cognitive simulation models are typically constructed using the same AI techniques and concepts used in intelligent tutoring systems, it should be possible to make direct use of the declarative and procedural representations. Thus the effort spent in characterizing the task for purposes of cognitive simulation can be of direct use for the intelligent tutoring or testing system.

## SOME EXAMPLES OF POTENTIAL APPLICATIONS

### The Acquisition of Procedures

If one starts with the assumption that a good way to represent procedural knowledge is in terms of production rules that have a specified syntax and execution properties, then the psychological properties of a body of procedural knowledge should be revealed very directly by examination of the production rule representation for the knowledge. In work reported in Kieras and Bovair (1986), and Polson and Kieras (1985), it seems clear that such a detailed characterization of procedural knowledge in terms of production rules does carry considerable empirical content. In particular, the training time and amount of transfer of training can be accounted for with great precision, at least in some experimental paradigms, by considering the number of production rules that have to be learned, which depends on how many previously learned production rules can be applied in the current procedure being trained. Thus, training time and transfer effects can be predicted with some precision with this explicit representation. The focus of the present discussion, however, is that the same characterization could function as a tool to look at training materials more carefully.

In work done by Kieras and Polson (1985; Polson & Kieras, 1985; Bovair, Kieras & Polson, 1988), production rule simulations of a person using a word processor have been constructed and compared against data. As a result, we have a fairly clear picture of the procedural knowledge required to operate a word processor. A natural step is then to examine the training materials for a word processor to see if they specify a correct and running simulation. A couple of examples appear in the training materials for a commercial word processor, which by current industry standards, are extremely high-quality materials. Table 3.1 presents a portion of a procedure for deleting material on this word processor. Following the instructions is an informal translation of the instructions into production rules. Even though this is an informal translation, it is clear from the Kieras and Polson work how the rules could be made to actually run in a simulation.

If the reader is supposed to be acquiring production rules from this text, then a good training text would be one that conveys a correct and functional set of production rules as directly as possible. Notice in Table 3.1 that the sentence *If*

TABLE 3.1
A Word Processor Deletion Procedure and
Its Informal Production Rule Translation

---

*Instructional Text*

---

Making Deletions

The first step to delete text is to move the cursor under the first character to be deleted. This tells the system where the deletion starts.

The next step is to press the DEL (Delete) key.

When the system prompts, "Delete what?", type the last character of the text to be deleted.

The cursor moves to the last character.

All the text from the first character through the last character is highlighted. You can see exactly what is going to be deleted before it is deleted.

If the wrong characters are highlighted, press CODE + CANCL and try again.

When the text you want to delete is highlighted, press the ENTER key.

The highlighted word is deleted, and the remaining text on the line moves over to take its place.

*Informal Production Rule Translation*

---

IF goal:delete text X THEN do step 1

IF step:1
THEN add goal:move cursor to first of X, do step 2

IF step:2
THEN press DEL, do step 3

IF step:3 and prompt="Delete what?"
THEN type last of X, do step 4

IF step:4 and X not highlighted
THEN press CODE + CANCL, add goal try again

IF step:4 and X highlighted THEN press ENTER

---

*the wrong characters are highlighted, press CODE+CANCL and try again* corresponds very nicely to a production rule in terms of its sentence form. But, in examining the other production rules stated by this portion of the text, one sees that the action of *try again* does not match the condition of any other production rules in the vicinity. This means that after this rule is fired, there are no other rules that match the *try again* situation, and so the procedure grinds to a halt. These training materials in fact did not say what *try again* would consist of. Thus, rather than simply studying the material, the reader must infer the correct procedure, probably by trial and error experimentation with the word processor.

This lack of accuracy and completeness is apparently not an isolated problem. The second example, shown in Table 3.2 shows a more serious situation in the same section of the same manual. The reader is led to believe that this paragraph provides a summary of how to make deletions from the text. Following the text is an attempt to translate it into production rules. As can be seen by examining these rules, the text is in fact quite inaccurate and incomplete in specifying the whole procedure. There are many missing pieces of information. If these rules were put into a simulation, they would either stop in the middle of the task, or generate erroneous behavior such as incomplete deletions.

The point of these examples is that even if the reader is a perfect information processor, the instructional material in fact does not explicitly contain the complete and correct procedures that the learner is supposed to acquire. Instead of simply learning the procedures as stated, the learner must engage in a considerable amount of problem solving and experimentation in order to compose a correct

TABLE 3.2
Summary Description of Deletion Procedure
and Its Production Rule Translation

---

*Instructional Text*

To Make Deletions

    A. Position the cursor under the first character to be deleted.

    B. Press the DEL key.

    C. When the prompt, "Delete what?", appears, type the last character to be deleted. If you are deleting a single character, do not move cursor.

    D. Press ENTER.

*Informal Production Rule Translation (Comments in brackets)*

IF goal:Delete text X THEN do step A

IF step:A THEN add goal:move cursor to first of X, do step B
    [another set of rules satisfies the move cursor subgoal]

IF step:B and cursor at first of X THEN press DEL, do step C
    [this rule waits until the subgoal has been satisfied]

IF step:C and prompt="Delete what?"
THEN type last of X, do step D
    [correct only if last character of X is unique in X]

IF step:C and prompt="Delete what?" and X is single character
THEN delete goal:move cursor
    [the goal deleted here was not added by previous rules; this is not correct—the
    step C rule should be specialized into two rules for the one-character and string
    cases]

IF step:D THEN press ENTER, goal of deleting text X satisfied procedure. Thus, it would be fair to say that the training materials do not assist the person in simply learning the procedures, but in fact require the learner to engage in problem solving to invent the procedures.

Of course, it could be argued that learning by solving problems is more effective than simply absorbing explicitly stated procedures, but this has not yet been demonstrated. It could be that some of the apparent superiority of learning by exploration is simply due to ordinary training materials being badly defective even as rote training materials.

Thus, a first speculation is that better training would result if the complete and correct procedure were explicitly presented in a form that the learner could easily translate into production rules. Attempting to translate the materials into a running production rule set is a way to evaluate the adequacy of the materials. Alternatively, the production rules in a running model could be used as the starting point for the training materials. The deletion procedure on the word processor is probably short and compact enough to present in complete detail, but apparently it is possible for readers to suffer from "overload" effects in attempting to acquire procedures from text (Kieras & Bovair, 1986). Thus, there is apparently a pedagogical problem of how to build a complex procedure without overloading the learner. This question could be addressed with considerable precision by using the production rule characterization of the to-be-learned procedures.

A second speculation is that one could more efficiently test a learner for knowledge of the procedure by using the production rule characterization. Test problems in the form of either paper and pencil questions or tests on the actual equipment could be devised that use paths that traverse all rules within the procedure. If the learner could successfully demonstrate knowledge of each one of the production rules, one could be more confident that all of the components of the procedure were present.

## The Acquisition and Use of a Mental Model

A good example of the use of a cognitive simulation to examine a testing and training situation appears in the work that we have done on the use of a mental model in learning how to operate a simple piece of equipment (Kieras & Bovair, 1984). In this situation, people are acquiring not only a set of procedural skills, but also some declarative knowledge about the organization of a piece of equipment.

*The Task and the Phenomena.*    Subjects learned how to use a simple piece of equipment whose front panel is illustrated in Fig. 3.1. Shown in Fig. 3.2 is the diagram of the fictitious system that subjects were told underlies the control panel. They were told that this system is the control panel for a "phaser bank" on the starship "Enterprise," and they studied the diagram along with a few pages of material that essentially explained the diagram. Subjects studied the material, took a test on it, and were required to study further until they answered all

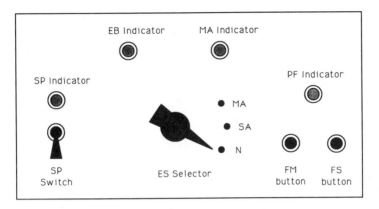

FIG. 3.1.   Sketch of the control panel device.

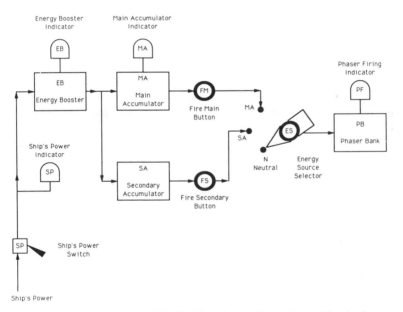

FIG. 3.2.   The diagram of the fictitious internal structure of the device.

questions correctly. The basic manipulation in Kieras and Bovair (1984) was that one group studied the diagram and written material presenting the mental model, while another group learned the device only by rote trial and error.

Two kinds of experimental tasks were used in the different experiments in Kieras and Bovair (1984). In the first, subjects were explicitly trained on the procedures for operating the device in various situations, including those in which some fictitious internal component of the device was malfunctioning and subjects had to determine whether it was possible to compensate for the malfunction and if so, to do so. After training, subjects were tested by being put into the situations repeatedly, without any feedback. The basic measurements are the learning time and trials to criterion and the speed and accuracy of execution. The second type of experimental task consisted of the subject having to *infer* how to operate the device in various situations without any explicit training in the procedures. The subjects were informed what the goal of the operation was, and then were free to attempt to get the device to operate. The performance measures consist of how many actions involving the controls subjects had to perform before they succeeded in getting the device to work, or before they could draw a conclusion that the device could not be made to work.

Briefly, the result was that compared to a group that had no training in the mental model for the device, the group that had the mental model learned the procedures substantially faster, executed them more quickly, and retained them better, even after one week. In the inference task, subjects who knew the mental model were able almost immediately to infer how to operate the device, with little or no trial and error search. In contrast, the subjects without the mental model essentially performed a systematic trial-and-error search that eventually succeeded due to the simplicity of the device, but took substantially more operations on the device. By manipulating the training materials, we concluded that the important content of the mental model material was the information about which components were attached to which controls and indicators and to which other components. In other word, the *topological* information shown in Figure 3.2 was the key information. The fantasy content, or even the supposed explanations of how each of the components worked, was not relevant to this task.

When we devised the training materials, we were guided by intuition; we tried to explain the device, but not to "give away" the procedures for operating it. The test for mastery of the mental model was also prepared intuitively. The comparison of these materials with the simulation makes it very clear what we were *actually* teaching and testing.

*A Simulation of Procedure Inference.*    A simulation model was developed to represent how subjects could infer how to operate this device given knowledge of the system topology and of a set of rules for reasoning with the topological knowledge. Although the model makes inferences on how to solve a problem, it is a model of performance, not learning; the long-term declarative and procedural knowledge is static during the task. Many such models are possible, but this model was built using an intuitive analysis, as are most simulations, based on a characterization of the logical requirements of the task, and observation of the sequence of operations subjects performed. The model can in fact infer the procedures for operating the device. It generates sequences of actions that correspond to the majority of subjects' systematic behavior, and the temporal predictions of the model account reasonably well for the latencies between individual actions. A basic constraint on the model was that it was to be as general as possible so that similar devices with different topological arrangements could also be operated by the model. The model described is an updated version of the one reported in Kieras (1984).

The overall structure of the model is shown in Fig. 3.3. The model consists of two major sections. One is a simulation of the control panel device itself, which simply makes developing the simulation of the human user more convenient, and so need not be discussed further. The simulation of the user's cognitive processes was implemented in terms of production rules that operate on a declarative database consisting of a description of the device topology and ISA facts about each object in the device. This is essentially a propositional paraphrase of the diagram in Fig. 3.2. Table 3.3 shows a few examples of this information.

The goal of the model is to operate the controls so as to get the PF indicator to light (this corresponds to the "phasers" being fired). The model has a top level control structure that divides this task into first starting up the device by switching it on and perhaps setting the selector switch in response to a command as to which "accumulator" should be used. Then the model simulates the internal state of the device, resulting in a set of propositions in working memory that reflect where energy is assumed to be in the system and what the states of some of the internal components are. Then the model constructs a plan for operating the device by starting with the goal of getting energy to the phasers, and working backwards through the diagram until it finds an energy source. Once this plan is constructed, it is then executed by a process that represents stereotypical knowledge of what order controls should be operated in. For example, push buttons are normally operated last. If the goal state is reached (that is, if the PF indicator flashes) the model then signals a successful attempt. If not, the model updates its simulation of the internal state of the device, applies some heuristics to diagnose what the

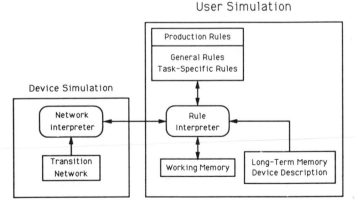

FIG. 3.3.  Overall structure of the simulation model for procedure inference.

TABLE 3.3
Excerpt from Long-Term Memory Description of Device Structure

```
(LTM ISA EB COMPONENT)
(LTM ISA MA COMPENENT)
(LTM ISA SPI INDICATOR)
(LTM ISA EBI INDICATOR)
(LTM ISA EB-OUT TERMINAL)
(LTM ISA MA-FM TERMINAL)
(LTM ISA SP SWITCH)
(LTM ISA FM BUTTON)
(LTM ISA SHIP-POWER POWER-SOURCE)
(LTM ISA SWITCH CONTROL)
(LTM ISA BUTTON CONTROL)
(LTM ISA SELECTOR CONTROL)
(LTM SETTING SP SP ON)
(LTM SETTING ESS-MA ESS MA)
(LTM SETTING FM FM PUSH)
(LTM ASSOCIATED MA FM)
(LTM ASSOCIATED MA ESS-MA)
(LTM CONNECTION SHIP-POWER SP-IN)
(LTM CONNECTION SP-IN SP)
(LTM CONNECTION SP SP-EB)
(LTM CONNECTION SP-EB SPI)
(LTM CONNECTION SP-EB EB)
(LTM CONNECTION EB EB-OUT)
(LTM CONNECTION EB EBI)
(LTM CONNECTION EB-OUT MA)
(LTM CONNECTION MA MA-FM)
(LTM CONNECTION ESS-PB PB)
(LTM CONNECTION ESS-PB PB)
(LTM CONNECTION PB PFI)
```

source of the problem is, which will result in an additional component being labeled as malfunctioning, and then attempts to construct a new plan for operating the device. If this new plan cannot be successfully constructed or fails to succeed and no other plan is available, then the model signals that the device cannot be successfully operated.

***Sample Production Rules.***    It is not necessary to go into any additional detail in this chapter concerning the model's behavior or how it works. What is given is some samples of the production rules to illustrate how this model specifies pieces of knowledge that the user should need to know.

Table 3.4 shows some examples of production rules. The first is an example of a rule that propagates energy forward along a connection. The name of this rule is InferConnectionEnergy, and it specifies that if the goal is to simulate the internal state of the device, and if in working memory we have that energy is at a certain point, indicated by the value of the variable *?T1*, and if we know from

TABLE 3.4
Examples of Production Rules from the Simulation

---

(InferConnectionEnergy
IF      ((GOAL SIMULATE DEVICE)
          (WM AT ENERGY ?T1)
          (LTM CONNECTION ?T1 ?T2)
          (NOT (WM AT ENERGY ?T2))
THEN   ((Add WM AT ENERGY ?T2)
          (Add WM SIMULATION IN PROGRESS)))
(FollowControlBack
IF      ((GOAL FIND PATH)
          (WM GOAL ENERGIZE ?T3)
          (LTM CONNECTION ?T2 ?T3)
          (LTM CONNECTION ?T1 ?T2)
          (NOT (WM GOAL ENERGIZE ?T1))
          (NOT (WM AT ENERGY ?T3))
          (LTM ISA ?T2 ?C2)
          (LTM ISA ?C2 CONTROL)
          (LTM ASSOCIATED ?C3 ?T2)
          (WM COMMAND USE ?C3)
          (NOT (WM STATE ?C3 BAD)))
THEN   ((Add WM GOAL ENERGIZE ?T1)
          (Add WM FINDING IN PROGRESS)
          (Add WM PLAN OPERATE ?T2)
          (Delete WM GOAL ENERGIZE ?T3)))

---

the LTM representation of the device that *?T1* is connected to *?T2*, which is a terminal, and there is not already energy at *?T2*, then we can add to working memory the proposition that there is energy at the point *?T2*, and also a note that we have made some progress in simulating the device. This rule captures the piece of inferential knowledge that necessarily underlies diagrams of the type shown in Fig. 3.2. Namely, the lines shown in the diagram mean that if there is energy at one point in the system, then it can be inferred that this energy is also at the next point "downstream" in the system. This rule, together with several others, is used by the model to update and maintain a representation of where energy must be present in the control panel system.

The second rule in Table 3.4 shows a small piece of planning knowledge. This rule, called FollowControlBack, starts with a goal to find a path through the system, more specifically to get energy to a certain point, *?T3*. It finds two additional points in the system, *?T2*, which is a control of some sort, and *?T1*, which is the point of the system "upstream" from the control. It also identifies a component *?C3* that is associated with this control, and checks to be sure that this component is both supposed to be used, as specified by the command, and is not known to be bad. If so, this rule makes a note that our new goal is to energize the point upstream from the control, *?T1*, and that part of our plan for operating the device is to operate the control *?T2*. Thus, this rule represents a specific piece of the knowledge required for determining how to get energy to a particular point in the system. Namely, if the pathway for the energy involves a switch or control of some sort, then that control must be turned on before the overall operation goal can be accomplished.

The set of rules shown in Table 3.5 illustrate how inferences can be made about the states of the internal components in the system. The first rule,

TABLE 3.5
Some Inference Rules from the Simulation

```
(InferIndicatorEnergy)
IF        ((GOAL SIMULATE DEVICE)
          (DEVICE ?T2 ON)
          (LTM ISA ?T2 INDICATOR)
          (LTM CONNECTION ?T1 ?T2)
          (NOT (WM AT ENERGY /T1)))
THEN      ((Add WM AT ENERGY ?T1)
          (Add WM SIMULATION IN PROGRESS)))
(InferComponentBad
IF        ((GOAL SIMULATE DEVICE)
          (LTM CONNECTION ?T1 ?T2)
          (LTM CONNECTION ?T2 ?T3)
          (LTM ISA ?T1 TERMINAL)
          (LTM ISA ?T2 COMPONENT)
          (LTM ISA ?T3 INDICATOR)
          (WM AT ENERGY ?T1)
          (NOT (DEVICE ?T3 ON))
          (NOT (WM STATE ?T2 BAD)))
THEN      ((Add WM STATE ?T2 BAD)
          (Add WM SIMULATION IN PROGRESS)))
(InferComponentGood
IF        ((GOAL SIMULATE DEVICE)
          (LTM ISA ?T4 COMPONENT)
          (WM AT ENERGY ?T2)
          (NOT (WM STATE ?T2 GOOD)))
THEN      ((Add WM STATE ?T2 GOOD)
          (Add WM SIMULATION IN PROGRESS)))
(InferComponentBad2
IF        ((GOAL DIAGNOSE DEVICE)
          (LTM CONNECTION ?T1 ?T2)
          (LTM CONNECTION ?T2 ?T3)
          (LTM ISA ?T1 TERMINAL)
          (LTM ISA ?T2 COMPONENT)
          (LTM ISA ?T3 TERMINAL)
          (WM AT ENERGY ?T1)
          (WM PLAN OPERTE ?C2)
          (LTM ASSOCIATED ?T2 ?C2)
          (NOT (WM AT ENERGY ?T3))
          (NOT (WM STATE ?T2 BAD)))
THEN      ((Add WM STATE ?T2 BAD)
          (Add WM DIAGNOSIS IN PROGRESS)))
```

InferIndicatorEnergy, states that if an indicator light, *?T2,* on the device is on, then one can infer that the point at which that indicator is connected has energy present. The rule InferComponentGood says that if it is known that energy is at a component, then that component must be good. This rule, working in conjunction with InferIndictorEnergy, results in the system knowing that a component is good if the indicator light attached to it is on. The rule InferComponentBad does the opposite inference. If there is an indicator that is attached to a component that has energy at its input, but the indicator light is not on, then the component must be bad. Thus if it is known that there is energy going into a component, then the failure of the attached indicator light to be on must mean that the component is bad.

The last rule shown in Table 3.5 is InferComponentBad2. This rule is used to diagnose why the device failed to operate after the plan was executed. If there is a component that is known to have energy at its input, and for which part of the plan was to operate a control associated with the component, and there is apparently no energy coming out of the component, then the conclusion is that the component is bad. This rule is actually a heuristic rule, in the sense that even with this simple device it will not always apply correctly. But it does represent the idea of blaming the most "upstream" component in a situation in which it is not possible to determine positively which component is bad. For example, referring to Fig. 3.2, if an attempt was made to use the secondary accumulator (SA), and the phasers did not fire, this could be due either to a defective phaser bank (PB) or to a defective secondary accumulator. Because the secondary accumulator does not have an associated indicator light, the situation is ambiguous. A reasonable heuristic seems to be to assume that the first component upstream must be the defective one, in the absence of any other information. Thus the rule InferComponentBad2 applies and labels the secondary accumulator as bad. When the new plan is formed, it concludes that the main accumulator should be tried.

***Evaluating Training Materials.***    This example shows how the detailed characterization of the task contained in the simulator could be used to examine the instructional materials and testing materials more closely.

At a very general level, one useful result of having developed the simulation is that it shows how much knowledge is actually needed for a usable mental model. The characterization coming from the experiments was simply that a mental model should contain the content necessary to allow the user to infer how to operate the device. It seemed to consist mostly of information about the system topology, along with some inference rules for making use of this topology. However, what we see by looking at the simulation model is that the rules of inference for making use of the topology are many in number, quite specific in their content, and have to be supplemented by additional rules for the overall strategy of performing the task. Beyond this general characterization, we can look in some detail at the instructional materials to see what they actually contain.

For this comparison, I am assuming that the mental model simulation described earlier is in fact an adequate or correct characterization of the reasoning of the typical user. The truth of this statement is another matter; here the model can just be used to illustrate the approach.

Examination of the instructional materials (presented in full in Kieras, 1984) made it clear that they did not state the overall strategies or even the general rules used in the simulation. Instead, the instructional materials contain only limited, highly specific information. For example, the only thing in the material that has any relationship to the rules shown in Table 3.4, such as InferConnectionEnergy, is a single sentence that states *The arrows on the diagram show how power flows through the system*. Elsewhere, the material only states that power can flow from one specific component to another. There is in fact no explicit statement of the general rule that power can flow between connected components in a downstream direction. Apparently the learner is being asked to infer that this is a property of the system.

Likewise, the only general statement about the controls is the sentence, *The switch, selector, and push buttons control the flow of power*. Notice that the material does not state the general rule that when a switch or control is set to the *on* state, then power can flow through the control to the connected points. Instead, what these materials present is each specific case. The bulk of the information about the individual selectors and buttons is always stated only in the specific form and sometimes in a slightly misleading fashion. For example, the instructional material says that *When the selector is set to MA, then power can flow from the main accumulator. When the selector is set to SA, then power can flow from the secondary accumulator*. This material is misleading in that setting the selector is not enough to get the power flowing from the accumulator; rather, the push button must be pressed as well. The material presents this fact a few sentences later, but one wonders whether the subject had at least for a short time an incorrect representation of the relationship of the selector to the accumulators.

The only obvious case in which the materials present a general rule similar to those in the simulation is a sentence describing the indicator lights. This sentence is *The indicator will only light if the component that it is connected to is both receiving power and working properly*. This rule is very similar to the rules in Table 3.5, but it is easy to see that this stated rule does not directly correspond to a single one of the simulation rules for inferring that a component is good (this may actually be a defect in the simulation). Furthermore, the opposite rule, that a component is bad if its indicator is not on when it should be, is being left up to the reader to infer.

The rest of the training material about the indicators presents the inference for each indicator individually, and in an order that is in some sense the reverse of what the subject would actually use. For example, the material states that *The main accumulator indicator will light if the main accumulator is receiving power from the energy booster, and the main accumulator is working properly and putting out power*. This rule states a special case of the general rule discussed earlier, and it does so in a backwards direction. That is, it seems that the subject would start with the perceptual information that the indicator is on and then want to know what conclusion can be drawn. Thus, the readers have to take the information in the training materials sentence and translate it into a form more suitable for their needs.

The training materials contain no apparent information on how to diagnose a malfunction in the system, or how to construct a plan for operating the device. Of course, these materials were deliberately designed not to contain any *procedural* information, but it was not clear to us at the time that we had required the subjects to come up with so many of their own inference rules.

In summary, the training materials lacked explicit specification of: (a) the overall strategy for doing the task; (b) general rules for making inferences about power flow or the state of components; (c) a general procedure for planning how to operate the controls given the inferred state of the device; and (d) rules for diagnosis of failures in the system. On the other hand, the training materials did clearly include specific facts about power flow and the effects of the controls, and some specific inferences that could be made from the indicator lights.

An obvious question is what is the correct characterization of the materials? Notice that the materials definitely lack key facts and procedures, but the simulation is complete (it can perform the task) and is reasonably consistent with subjects' behavior. Thus, if the model is taken as a description of the subjects' knowledge, it is clear that the subjects had to infer a considerable amount of knowledge beyond that presented in the training materials.

*Evaluating Testing Materials.*   In the experiments, we always insisted that subjects demonstrate a knowledge of the material that presented the mental model before proceeding to the rest of the experiment. This was primarily for methodological reasons; we suspected that many of the experiments intended to demonstrate the effects of mental models had not done an adequate job of ensuring that the subjects actually knew the mental model information. However, examining the testing materials for information that was critical in the simulation model produced something of a surprise. Rather than testing for the ability to reason about the system, the test questions focused mostly on the system topology, and most of these could be answered by simply paraphrasing the instructional text.

For example, one question is *Where does the secondary accumulator get its power from?*, with the multiple choice alternatives being *(1) Directly from the ship board circuits (2) From the phaser bank (3) From the energy booster*. This question can be answered almost directly from two sentences appearing in the training materials, *Starting on the lower left of the diagram, you can see that power comes in from the ship board circuits. . . . Power from the energy booster then flows into both accumulators.* Likewise, questions about the indicator lights could also be answered almost directly from the instructional material.

Only 2 of the 12 test questions are more demanding. These are presented in Table 3.6. These 2 questions essentially ask the subject to simulate the operation of the phaser system, based on the diagram (which was present during training and testing) and their knowledge of how to make inferences. In terms of the simulation model, by simulating where the energy is in the system, the subjects should be able to choose the correct alternative answer. The instructional material contains several sentences that are relevant to answering this question, but unlike the other questions, these sentences do not provide the answer by paraphrase. Rather, at least a little bit of inference is required. Thus, these two questions might actually be testing for whether subjects had acquired not only a correct understanding of the system topology, but also the rules for making some inferences from it.

However, these 2 questions are not very strong tests of inferential ability; the tested inference process is only one of several types of inference that the subject must be able to perform in order to operate the device. For example, according to the simulation, some other inferences that have to be made are how to operate the device given the simulated state of the system, and how to determine whether a component is defective, especially if the indicator information is not adequate. But knowledge of how to make these inferences was not addressed by the test at all. Other information missing from the test is an overall strategy for executing the task, and how to operate a device given a plan for operating it. For example, as mentioned, for devices of this general type, push buttons are conventionally operated last in a sequence of operations.

This example shows how exact specifications of the required knowledge for a task from a simulation model can be used to evaluate the content of a test. In this case, it is clear that much of the important required knowledge was not addressed

TABLE 3.6
Test Questions that Require Some Inference

---

Assume that the phaser control system is in full working order, that the SP is on, and that the selector is set to MA.

Now, what will happen if the FM button is pressed?

(1) The Main Accumulator will send power to the Phaser bank.

(2) The Phaser bank will receive power from the Secondary Accumulator.

(3) The Phaser bank will receive power directly from the energy Booster.

---

Assume that the phaser control system is in full working order, that the SP is on, and the selector is set to MA.

Now, what will happen if the FS button is pressed?

(1) Nothing. The selector must be set to SA for power to flow to the Phaser bank when the FS button is pressed.

(2) The Main Accumulator will send power to the Phaser bank.

(3) The Secondary Accumulator will send power to the Phaser bank.

---

by the test at all; a far better test could have been constructed by composing a set of questions that covered the specified knowledge.

***Questions Presented by the Analysis.***    In the experiments, the mental model group still had an advantage over the rote-learning group, even though, as we have seen, the training materials and the test questions were far from adequate in presenting a complete mental model and testing for the acquisition of it. This raises a question about whether a group that knew a mental model would have an even greater advantage if a fully usable model had been explicitly presented and tested before subjects began trying to use it. Furthermore, with the materials that we did use, it appears that subjects would have had to perform a lot of inference and transformation of the materials before they could use them to reason about the device. It should be possible to capture some of these processes at work.

Given that the materials actually presented only specific information about the device, as contrasted to the rather general inference rules in the simulation model, another question is whether subjects who were explicitly taught the more general model could operate the device better, or show superior performance in transferring to a different device.

Another question concerns the formal properties of the relatively specific material that was presented to subjects. Would it be possible to start with the specific rules and descriptions contained in our training materials, and construct a simulation model that could successfully infer how to operate the device? This would be a way to determine just how seriously defective our training materials were. Presenting subjects with these specific rules of inference may have in fact worked fairly well, although we would predict that they would have trouble in transferring such specific knowledge to a different device.

Concerning the test itself, notice that the test questions could have been very different. For example, we could have tested for the acquisition of the general rules for reasoning about the device instead of the specific ones. More specific topology information could have been tested for. The simulation model works on the basis of the individual point-to-point connections in the system; the test could have tested for similar point-to-point connection knowledge. The test questions also could have exercised the specific inference processes that users needed to have. For example, the test questions could have asked people to draw an inference about which components were bad from a specific pattern of the indicator lights.

If subjects could pass a test containing such items, we could be confident that not only did they have the declarative knowledge of how the device was structured, but also the procedural knowledge for how to make the relevant class of inferences from the model. As it was, we were essentially leaving it up to subjects to construct these inferences as they went along, while trying to operate the device. Thus, if we had included items that tested for the specific aspects of the mental model, and if passing the test were the criterion of when the mental model training is complete, we should see superior performance in operating the device. Additionally, given less thorough training, such a test should not only allow us to distinguish good from poor performers, but also determine specifically what declarative and procedural knowledge was lacking.

## CONCLUSIONS

In this chapter I have argued that a working cognitive simulation model contains a specification of the knowledge that a person must have in order to accomplish the task, and this specification can be used as the basis for developing and evaluating training and testing materials. For example, it should be possible to devise very effective tests by composing questions on the same knowledge that is explicitly represented in the simulation.

A possible useful alternate approach would be to start with an existing set of instructional materials that are supposed to be good materials for the domain, and attempt to construct a simulation model using the materials as directly and as naively as possible. If the resulting model cannot perform the task, then it is clear that something is missing from the materials and needs to be added. Once the model can perform the task, then the behavior of the model can be examined in some detail to determine which portions of the material are actually critical and which are not. Thus, rather than using the simulation as a source of specifications for to-be-written training material, the simulation approach could be used as a way to evaluate existing materials. A similar "reverse engineering" approach could be used to evaluate existing tests. If a model has exactly the knowledge required to pass an existing test, could it do the task? If not, what knowledge was not assessed?

Although the example analyses presented here are informal, it does appear that such model-based evaluations of testing and training materials can clarify the actual content and its adequacy relative to the model. The claim was made that training materials that explicitly contain the same knowledge as the model are superior to the normal intuitively prepared materials; but this has to be demonstrated experimentally.

### Puzzles and Obstacles

This discussion of using cognitive simulation to prepare and evaluate training material is obviously speculative, and many problems would have to be solved before such an approach could even be evaluated, much less implemented. However, at this point several obstacles and potential problems can be pointed out.

*Level of Detail.*    The first problem concerns the issue of level of analysis in the model. It should not be necessary for the cognitive simulation modeling to explicitly model all aspects of the cognitive processing involved in a particular task. We should be able to "finesse" some of the more complex processes by assuming their results rather than attempting to represent them in the model.

For example, to model electronics troubleshooting skill, it really should not be necessary to model the perceptual process by which schematic diagrams are perceived. Clearly an electronics troubleshooter must already have this skill, but we could analyze the skill of using schematic diagrams into roughly two components: one is the visual *perception* of the diagram itself, the other is the *interpretation* of the diagram. The interpretation process consists of interpreting the meaning of the symbols in the diagram, determining from the diagram what the relations between these symbols are, and making the appropriate inferences from the diagram about the structure and behavior of the system. Modeling the interpretation processes would, of course, be a major task; modeling the visual perception process involved in examining a schematic diagram would also be a major task, perhaps even more difficult than the interpretation problem.

The argument is that it should not be necessary to model the visual perception process simply because everyone who is likely to be trained in electronics trouble-shooting should be able to perceive lines, squares, circles, and so forth that are printed on paper. For example, every trainee should be able to determine that two circles are connected with a line. What has to be taught as part of electronics training is information such as that two circles with certain additional symbols inside represent two different transistors, and that the line interconnecting specific places on these two circles indicates that the collector of one transistor is electrically connected to the base of the other transistor. This is part of the interpretation process, not a visual perception process. Thus, the modeling effort could bypass the perceptual process by assuming that it produces the appropriate inputs to the interpretation process. Obviously, selectively ignoring the perceptual process is reasonable only if it is true that all trainees have essentially equal and satisfactory perceptual abilities.

Making decisions about what psychological processes can be finessed and which processes have to be explicitly represented would be critical to the success of an attempt to use simulation models to specify the knowledge that has to be learned. The puzzle is whether we can reliably identify, and then focus on, exactly the critical information in the complex tasks that we are interested in training (see Kieras, 1988 for more discussion).

*Nonidentifiability.*    A second problem is that it is impossible to know whether a particular simulation model is *the* correct representation of how a person actually performs a task; basing training on a single model may be misleading. This *nonidentifiability* problem has been discussed at length elsewhere (e.g., see Kieras, 1981; Anderson, 1978). However, it should not discourage us from trying this approach. Notice that although there are many possible simulation models that could account for behavior in a task, only a subset of these appears to the developer of training materials to be relevant, based on expert opinion on how such knowledge and tasks should be organized, presented, and used. For example, troubleshooting strategies for electronics maintenance could be obtained from experts in the domain, and the processes and representations needed to implement these strategies would then be more highly constrained than if a purely AI or intuitive approach were used. Thus, nonidentifiability should not prevent us from arriving at reasonable, intuitively sound, and effective cognitive models.

*Cost-Effectiveness.*    A third obstacle is that, historically, constructing simulation models of complex processes has been a difficult and time-consuming occupation. It would not help an advanced training and testing effort to be more efficient if it required an extremely time-consuming and difficult knowledge analysis to be done beforehand. Thus, the question is whether cognitive simulations can be constructed cost-effectively. Their use should be feasible at least for skills such as electronics troubleshooting, that are in great demand and have a well-understood rational basis that can be used as the foundation for the modeling effort.

The answer to this problem is that we need to have a *technology* of cognitive modeling. The adoption of explicit cognitive architectures is a step in this direction because the cognitive architecture represents a pre-packaged set of decisions and mechanisms; adopting an architecture frees the modeler from having to make these decisions and construct these mechanisms from scratch for each model. But the basic bottleneck in constructing cognitive simulations seems to lie primarily in the task analysis methodology. Apparently, cognitive psychologists know intuitively how to look at a task and break it down in a quick, informal way into its major components; this informal analysis is the first step in constructing a more specific simulation model. We have not codified task analysis methodology, but have always done it intuitively. Thus, we cannot convey task analysis methodology to other people except by long-term apprenticeship in a graduate training program. This limitation clearly makes it very difficult to develop large numbers of simulation models for complex tasks quickly. An effort to make explicit our intuitive analysis methodology would potentially be of great benefit (see Kieras, 1988).

*Portability of Representations.*    A final obstacle is whether the information in a cognitive model can be converted directly into the information needed in intelligent tutoring and advanced testing systems. Based on the examples given in Tables 3.3, 3.4, and 3.5, it seems clear that the information in the simulation model can be expressed in ways that are quite compatible with existing approaches and techniques in artificial intelligence. Thus, once the model was developed, the information in it should be directly exportable as input in intelligent training and testing systems. This is basically a software engineering problem; both the simulation models and the intelligent tutoring and testing systems need to work with compatible knowledge representations, meaning that some kind of common architecture needs to be assumed. In some intelligent tutoring efforts this commonality of representation between the simulation model for the cognitive processes and the intelligent tutoring system is in fact present.

## ACKNOWLEDGMENTS

This work was supported by the Office of Naval Research Personnel and Training Research Programs under Contract Number N00014-85-K-0138, Contract Authority Identification Number NR667-543.

## REFERENCES

Anderson, J. R. (1976). *Language, memory, and thought*. Hillsdale, NJ: Lawrence Erlbaum Associates.

Anderson, J. R. (1978). Arguments concerning representations for mental imagery. *Psychological Review, 85*, 249–277.

Anderson, J. R. (1983). *The architecture of cognition*. Cambridge, MA: Harvard University Press.

Bovair, S., Kieras, D. E., & Polson, P. G. (1988). *The acquisition and performance of text-editing skill: A production-system analysis* (Tech. Rep. No. 28). Ann Arbor, MI: University of Michigan, Technical Communication.

Kieras, D. E. (1981). Knowledge representations in cognitive psychology. In L. Cobb & R. M. Thrall (Eds.), *Mathematical frontiers of the social and policy sciences, AAAS selected symposium 54* (pp. ). Boulder, CO: Westview Press.

Kieras, D. E. (1984). *A simulation model for procedural inference from a mental model for a simple device* (Tech. Rep. No. 15, UARZ/DP/TR-84/ONR-15). University of Arizona, Department of Psychology.

Kieras, D. E. (1985). The why, when, and how of cognitive simulation: A tutorial. *Behavior Research Methods, Instruments, & Computers, 17*(2), 279–285.

Kieras, D. E. (1988). Towards a practical GOMS model methodology user interface design. In M. Helander (Ed.), *Handbook of human-computer interaction*. Amsterdam: North-Holland Elsevier.

Kieras, D. E., & Bovair, S. (1984). The role of a mental model in learning to operate a device. *Cognitive Science, 8*, 255–273.

Kieras, D. E., & Bovair, S. (1986). The acquisition of procedures from text: A production-system analysis of transfer of training. *Journal of Memory and Language, 25*, 507–524.

Kieras, D. E., & Polson, P. G. (1985). An approach to the formal analysis of user complexity. *International Journal of Man–Machine Studies, 22*, 365–394.

Polson, P. G., & Kieras, D. E. (1985). A quantitative model of the learning and performance of text editing knowledge. *CHI'85 Conference Proceedings*, 207–212.

# Reformulating Testing to Measure Learning and Thinking
## Comments on Chapters 1, 2, and 3

Allan Collins
*BBN Laboratories*

## INTRODUCTION

It is well known that testing affects what is taught in the schools. As nationwide tests of math skills or reading comprehension become established, they become the standards by which school systems, teachers, and students are judged. They unconsciously dictate what students should learn, and so education in the schools begins to point toward teaching the skills necessary to do well on these tests. The most flagrant examples of this effect are the courses to prepare students to take the Scholastic Aptitude Test for college entrance, but the effect is far more pervasive in subtle ways throughout the schools.

This phenomenon has potentially beneficial side effects in that the tests form uniform standards by which we can compare different schools, teachers, and students. They establish for all to see, as it were, what is expected of students, and hence point the nation's students and teachers toward specific objectives that can be debated, quantified, and applied equally to all.

But there are insidious side effects that are less well known. First, there is the tendency for testing to drive teaching down to the level of our testing technology— away from learning and reasoning skills toward more easily measurable skills that can be tested by multiple-choice items. Second, testing encourages students to adopt memorization rather than understanding as their goal: Knowledge is learned in a form that can be recalled rather than in a form that can be used in real life tasks. Finally, there is a kind of test-taking mentality that takes over and helps turn many students against school and learning more generally. Each of these issues needs some amplification.

## Education in Service of What Can Be Measured

There is a growing disparity between what we think we should be teaching students and what we actually are teaching. This disparity is reflected in the concern in the education community about teaching critical thinking and metacognitive skills (e.g., Glaser, 1984). I suspect the disparity arises mainly in our escalation of expectations for the schools. Cuban (1984) reports that in historical terms there was more emphasis on rote skills and memorization in former years than now. But machines are taking over the low-level jobs in our society, leaving more and more demand for the kinds of reasoning that only humans are capable of.

However, reasoning and metacognitive skills are the most difficult skills to measure. They include the skills of planning, monitoring your processing during a task, checking what you have done, estimating what a reasonable answer might be, actively considering possible alternative courses of action, separating relevant information from irrelevant information, choosing problems that are useful to work on, asking good questions, and so on. These are skills that current tests for the most part do not measure, nor is it easy to see how such skills could be measured within a single-item, multiple-choice format.

But these are the kinds of skills that have the most payoff in teaching, as evidenced by the success of Reciprocal Teaching and other "cognitive apprenticeship" methods (Collins, Brown, & Newman, 1989; Palincsar & Brown, 1984; Schoenfeld, 1983, 1985). For example, Palincsar and Brown (1984) produced huge gains in students' reading comprehension using their Reciprocal Teaching method that taught students (a) to formulate questions about texts; (b) to summarize texts; (c) to clarify difficulties with texts; and (d) to make predictions about what is coming next in texts. These skills are critical to the ability to monitor one's reading comprehension (Collins, Brown, & Newman, 1989), but they are not the kinds of skills that are easily measured. To the degree that testing technology drives education, it drives teaching away from these high-order thinking skills to the lower-order skills that can be measured easily.

Moreover, to the degree we attempt to develop tests that are truly diagnostic, we may exacerbate the problem even more. There have been some great successes in our ability to identify systematic student errors in arithmetic and algebra (Brown & Burton, 1978; Brown & VanLehn, 1980; Matz, 1982; Sleeman, 1982; Tatsuoka, chap. 18 in this volume). One notion afoot is that because we can diagnose the precise errors students are making, we can then teach directly to counter these errors. Such diagnosis might indeed be useful in a system where diagnosis and remediation are tightly coupled, as for example in the LISP tutor described by Anderson (chap. 2 in this volume). But if diagnosis becomes an objective in *nationwide tests*, then it would drive education to the lower-order skills for which we can do the kind of fine diagnosis possible for arithmetic. Such an outcome would be truly disastrous. It is precisely the kinds of skills for which we can do fine diagnosis, that are becoming obsolete in the computational world of today.

## Conventional Testing Promotes Memorization Rather Than Understanding

Tests are great incentives for students to study. But they lead students into the worst kinds of study strategies. When students learn information for tests, they are developing strategies and memorizing information in forms that are of little or no use for real-world problem solving.

For example, much of students' studying involves memorizing information or procedures that they think they will be asked on a test (Schoenfeld, in press). This leads to the problem of "inert" knowledge (Collins, Brown, & Newman, 1989). Facts and procedures are learned in isolation, apart from the different contexts in which they might be used. As we argued in the earlier paper, learning of information and procedures needs to be "situated" in multiple contexts reflecting its different uses in real-world contexts. Otherwise students are not likely to see how the knowledge they are getting can be applied. The "what" of knowledge is only a third of what needs to be learned; we also need to know the "when" and "how" it applies in different contexts, else we will find that students cannot transfer what they have learned to new, but relevant, contexts.

A related problem was identified by Schoenfeld (1985) for tests covering course material among math students. The students develop strategies for what to do, based on idiosyncrasies of the course and test problems. For example, if an answer doesn't come out to an even integer, they think it is wrong. And the methods they consider using are governed by what material the test covers (e.g., addition of fractions, algebra work problems), rather than all the methods they have learned up to then in their mathematics courses. Thus, they evolve solution methods that are counterproductive for solving real-world problems.

In summary, when testing becomes the raison d'etre for learning, students develop memorization strategies that lead to decontextualized knowledge that cannot be applied later in relevant contexts. Furthermore, they learn problem-solving strategies that are counterproductive for real-world problems.

## Conventional Testing Fosters a Mentality That Turns Some Students Against Learning

Even more subtle and insidious than the previous two side effects is what happens when poorer students see rewards and success going to the students who do well on tests, and disapproval to themselves (c.f. Dweck, 1986). They come to regard learning as synonymous with doing well on tests, and because they do not do well on tests, they do not want to compete in what they perceive to be a losing battle. In consequence, they come to regard education as irrelevant to their interests in life (e.g., becoming an athlete or beautician), and boring as compared with, say, their social life, athletics, and other activities. This is not to say that removing testing from the schools would completely alleviate the problem of students' loss of motivation to learn anything in school, because teachers' expectations undoubtedly contribute to their negative self-image as learners. (Rosenthal & Jacobson, 1968). But tests are a major contributing factor because they are the means by which students are publicly labeled as inferior.

## DESIDERATA FOR A NEW KIND OF TESTING

There are five desiderata that I view as critical for a new more benign learning and testing environment. They may not all be attainable, but they serve as goals to strive toward in redesigning testing:

1. *Tests should emphasize learning and thinking.* A test in any domain should emphasize higher-order thinking skills in that domain: in particular, problem-solving strategies (i.e., heuristics), self-regulatory or monitoring strategies, and learning strategies (Collins, Brown, & Newman, 1989). Dynamic testing (Campione & Brown, chap. 7 in this volume) goes some way toward centering testing on just such issues. These higher-order skills are what we want students to learn, and so tests must focus on them.

2. *Tests should require generation as well as selection.* Most tasks in the real world require planning and executing, but multiple-choice tests only require choosing the best answer. Hence they cannot in fact measure critical aspects of thinking. So it is important that tests require generation of ideas by students (Frederiksen, 1984).

3. *Tests should be integral to learning.* As presently construed, students stop learning when they take a test. Occasionally they may learn something going over a test, but this happens only rarely. The major positive effects of tests on learning, then, are the motivational effects, and these occur mainly with teacher-generated tests. Ideally, tests should not be intrusive to learning, but rather integral to it. This is perhaps the most difficult of the five desiderata to achieve.

4. *Tests should serve multiple purposes.* I have alluded to some of the purposes served by tests, and other researchers (cf. Linn, 1986) have tried to enumerate such purposes. Let me list some of those purposes lest they be overlooked: (a) motivating students to study and directing that study to certain topics or issues; (b) diagnosing what difficulties students are having and selecting what they should study next; (c) placing students in classes, grades, schools, and jobs; (d) reporting to students, teachers, and parents on the progress a student has made; and (e) evaluating how well a teacher, school, or school system is doing

vis-a-vis other teachers, schools, and systems. There may be other purposes for testing but these are the major purposes. And testing must serve all of these purposes in one way or another.

5. *Tests should be valid with respect to all their purposes.* Test makers have worried a great deal about reliability and validity of tests. But for the most part their concerns about validity have only been for content validity and predictive validity of the tests with respect to future schooling. We need to be much more concerned about the validity of tests with respect to the other purposes of testing. For example, do the tests really measure the effectiveness of teaching? Do they motivate students to learn the kinds of knowledge and higher-order skills we want children to learn? As I said in the Introduction, there are reasons to doubt that they do.

Furthermore, as pointed out earlier, when tests become more critical in making decisions, teachers and students direct their teaching and learning to do well on the test. Then tests lose validity. That is, to the degree test validity depends on factors that coincide with, but are not the same as, the skills required in the future school or job, preparing for the test reduces the predictive validity of the test. What starts out as a highly valid test may lose validity as it becomes more visible or decisive in making selections.

Suppose, for example, that aptitude for college is measured with a vocabulary test. Normally a vocabulary test might be a very good predictor of how well someone will do in college, because people who read and study acquire a large vocabulary in the process. But then suppose it becomes known that students are to be selected for college or that teachers are to be evaluated for effectiveness on the basis of such a test. Then it behooves the student or teachers to concentrate on vocabulary, which is a relatively easy thing to learn as compared to, say, an understanding of algebra or literature. When that happens, the vocabulary ceases to be a good predictor of how someone will do in college. In fact, better students are likely to regard learning vocabulary as cheating, whereas lesser students are likely to regard it as necessary for survival; thus, the test might even become negatively predictive if enough attention is focused on it. Furthermore, students would concentrate their energies not on learning what is most valuable for future life, but rather on what is at best a superficial index of learning (i.e., vocabulary). This is what Frederiksen (1984) refers to as the "real test bias."

In this example, it is possible to substitute any number of things for vocabulary. For example, Ravens matrices or analogy problems are probably quite good measures of general problem-solving ability, unless students practice on such items. If they do, they can learn (or be taught) the patterns by which such items are constructed and so they do not then have to figure out nearly as much when they come to take the test. Again, such tests lose their predictive validity if they become the focus of study. The only way to prevent such an occurrence is to have tests that reflect all the knowledge, skills, and strategies necessary for success in college, or whatever outcome the tests are designed to predict.

# TWO SCENARIOS FOR A NEW TESTING
# AND LEARNING ENVIRONMENT

Testing is undoubtedly necessary in a complex society where we need to make decisions about who should go to what schools, who should do what jobs, and what should be taught to different students. The fundamental question about testing, as I see it, is: How can we construct an educational system that embodies testing in a form that sustains its necessary functions and at the same time alleviates the problems that the current system has generated.

The three chapters I have been asked to comment on, by Anderson, Frederiksen and White, and Kieras, point the way to a possible answer. In the rest of the chapter I want to elaborate at some length on how it is possible to use the ideas implicit in intelligent tutoring systems, and in educational computer systems more generally, to construct a new kind of learning and testing environment.

There are two scenarios I can envision for exploiting the potential of computer systems for testing. The first, more conservative, scenario is partly depicted in the papers by Frederiksen and White and by Kieras. It is summarized nicely in Frederiksen and White's title "Intelligent Tutors as Intelligent Testers," and it goes some way toward addressing the desiderata outlined in the previous section. The second, more radical scenario envisions a completely integrated learning and testing environment.

## Intelligent Tutors as Intelligent Testers

In this first scenario, intelligent tutoring systems become the devices for administering tests to students. The tests would be problem-solving tests, where problems differing in difficulty are given to students. The test would start with easier problems, and, depending on how well the student does, the subsequent problems are easier or more difficult, as with adaptive testing.

As they solve problems, students can be given cognitive feedback on how best to solve these kinds of problems. That is, the full capability of the tutoring system to teach the students can be employed as part of the testing procedure. The test then would measure not simply their prior ability to perform the kind of tasks given by the system, but also how well they can learn to perform these tasks given precisely specified cognitive feedback and advice. This gives the intelligent testing system the same kind of capabilities for measurement that Campione and Brown (chap. 7 in this volume) have developed in their work on dynamic assessment.

Intelligent tutoring systems require the student to generate entire sequences of actions that lead to solutions, whether the problems are programming problems, as in Anderson's LISP tutor, or electricity problems as in Frederiksen and White's QUEST tutor, or operational problems as in Kieras's phaser control system. Although the responses allowed by tutoring systems are not open ended (i.e., there is usually a restricted class of inputs that the system can process), they are not single-item, multiple-choice response formats. Thus, the responses required by intelligent tutoring systems are generative in the sense implied in the desiderata listed earlier, but at the same time they are precise enough to be evaluated according to well-defined criteria necessary for constructing tests.

Scoring in such a system can be based on the same kinds of measures now used to evaluate problem solving: percentage correct in solving problems, average time to solve problems, number of incorrect vs. correct steps taken in attempting to solve a problem and so on. But to the degree a system has a characterization of what expert performance requires, as in Anderson's LISP tutor or Frederiksen and White's QUEST, it is possible to evaluate students more directly. In the case of the LISP Tutor, the system has an idealized problem-solving model consisting of some 325 production rules that represent its strategies for solving programming problems. As students work problems, the system can evaluate the degree to which each of these productions is used where appropriate; then we have a measure of how much of the expert model has been acquired. It might also be possible to assess how well the students have learned to suppress those productions in the system representing particular misconceptions. For QUEST, the student's level of performance can be evaluated in terms of how far along the progression of more and more sophisticated models a student has advanced. In either case, it should be possible to measure both the student's current level of understanding of the domain and the rate at which he or she is learning with the tutoring system.

Because the systems can analyze sequences of actions, they have a capability to measure strategic skills as well as domain skills. For example, Anderson, Boyle, and Reiser's (1985) Geometry Tutor allows students to work forward from the givens or backwards from the statement to be proved in constructing geometry proofs. One good strategy to learn is first to work forward from the givens a little way to see their implications and then to work backwards from the statement to be proved in order to close the gap. A good "metacognitive strategy" is that when you are stuck working forward, or backwards (which might be indicated by a long pause), switch to working the other way. In a system such as the Geometry Tutor, it would be possible for the system to analyze sequences of actions (and pauses) by the students, to make suggestions as to what are good strategies, and to evaluate how well students learn to approach problems strategically (Collins & Brown, 1988).

A serious limitation of today's intelligent tutoring systems is that they only exist in the domains of math and science. This is because computational techniques provide the most leverage in these domains. One question, then, is whether computer systems have any role to play as testing systems in domains such as reading, writing, and history. There are in fact less-than-intelligent, computer-based teaching systems in these three domains that might be useful.

For example, in the domain of reading, the IRIS system (developed by WI-CAT—described in Collins, 1986) presents passages to students and then asks questions about the passages, much like a reading comprehension test. But it is an instructional system, so that students receive cognitive feedback on what they do that should help them learn to read better. My reservation about this particular system is that there is not as much instruction on how to make inferences or monitor one's comprehension as there is in the best comprehension instruction (e.g., Palincsar & Brown, 1984). But the structure is potentially there to do so.

The most relevant computer system for testing writing is Writer's Workbench (MacDonald, Frase, Gingrich, & Keenan, 1982), but it is more an advisory system than a teaching system. It can analyze texts in terms of spelling, word usage, and grammar; it can even evaluate overusage of the passive voice, frequency of empty phrases like "there are," and the readability of the text by standard readability measures. But, essentially, it is only evaluating surface features of the text; it cannot evaluate clarity, interest, persuasiveness, or memorability, which are the critical aspects that a good text must possess (Collins & Gentner, 1980). Designing testing around a system that only evaluated surface features would lead the teaching of writing in the wrong direction. But that is all that computer-based systems are capable of evaluating in the foreseeable future.

The most ingenious computer-based teaching system for history is Geography Search developed by Tom Snyder (Kelman et al., 1983). It is a historical simulation of the time after Columbus discovered America and explorers sailed to the New World to bring back its wealth and resources. In the simulation, students have to purchase supplies for their trip to the New World and navigate using sextant and compass. They must plan their voyage as they go, depending on what they find and how many supplies they have left for the voyage home. Historical simulations such as Geography Search or the Civil War Game by Avalon Hill, give students an understanding of the reasons why events take place in a historical context. Although Geography Search does not do so, it would certainly be possible to provide a computer coach to advise students as they engage in these simulations. In such a scenario, it would be possible to evaluate how well students learn to plan and solve problems in historical contexts. This is not what we usually test about students' understanding of history, but it is perhaps an equally valid kind of historical understanding. Moreover, most of the important concerns of history, such as the development of the Constitution or the settling of the American frontier, can be turned into historical simulations.

In summary, the plan to develop intelligent tutors as intelligent testers is feasible in much of the current school curriculum. It has several benefits: (a) testing would be focused on students' problem-solving and planning skills; (b) their ability to learn in a domain as well as their prior knowledge could be tested; and (c) the tests could be adaptive to the students' prior knowledge and would test their generative abilities instead of their recognition abilities. But such a scenario, although feasible, would require a large amount of effort to produce intelligent testing systems that cover a large part of the curriculum. Computer-based teaching systems will in fact be developed to cover much of the school curriculum in the next decade, given the expansion of tools and resources that is taking place in the field. Whether these extend to testing concerns is still an open question, however.

## An Integrated Learning and Testing Environment

The second, more radical scenario for an integrated learning and testing environment is implicit in the way Anderson (chap. 2 in this volume) has analyzed students' learning in the LISP tutor. The tutor was built to teach students LISP, but as a side effect of the teaching, Anderson collected a record of their performance with the tutor that he could analyze to test various hypotheses. Each analysis is a slice through the data to answer certain questions. He can look at students' learning curves, error rates, response times, and even factor out differences between their ability to learn versus their ability to remember. That is, the computational medium enables evaluation to be carried out on the process of learning. Rather than stopping to take a test, the testing comes free in the course of the teaching.

This view of testing first evolved, to my knowledge, in a cognitive-science working group at a conference on testing (Tyler & White, 1979). The analogy we used was to professional sports like baseball or football where extensive records are kept on players (by scorekeeping and videotaping), so that their performance can be evaluated from different perspectives: for instance, in baseball, the batting percentage with men on base, the number of runners left stranded by a player, the batting percentage against left handed vs. right handed pitchers, and so on. Different statistics are used to make different decisions: should you keep the player or send him to the minors; where should he be in the batting order; in what situations should he be used as a pinch hitter; what should he practice. In sports all the variety of questions we try to answer on the basis of tests in school are answered on the basis of analysis of actual performance in the field.

In this scenario, students work with computers either in groups or individually. The teacher's role is that of coach rather than instructor. The teacher suggests tasks and activities for students to engage in, gives them advice or help when they need it, and monitors how they are progressing. This scenario assumes that there is a variety of good educational software, as well as computational tools (e.g., word processors and writing coaches, statistical and graphing programs, and computer-based laboratories). The students would spend their day working with different programs; for example, using the LISP tutor or QUEST, doing science projects with statistical and graphing programs, and debating with students in other schools via electronic networks. The computers and teachers would be assistants to the students' self-learning.

My claim is that in this environment all the functions of testing can be realized without students taking tests per se, and that all the desiderata for testing can be achieved without the bad side effects described. There are three kinds of measures that occur in this scenario that can be used to carry out the multiple functions of testing:

1. *Diagnosis*. Diagnosis is distributed between computer, teacher, and students. Many computer tutors, such as the LISP tutor (Anderson , chap. 2 in this volume), carry out some form of diagnosis. In the case of the LISP tutor the diagnosis is extremely local; it only looks for specific errors students may make at each step and gives advice accordingly. Other computer tutors, such as SOPHIE (Brown, Burton, & deKleer; 1982) and WEST (Burton & Brown, 1982) perform much more global analyses of the students misunderstandings and errors. Frederiksen and White (chap. 1 in this volume) suggest providing aids so that students can do self-diagnosis, which should prove even more effective than computational analysis alone. Finally, the teacher would be available to interact with students on a one-to-one basis as a coach, and hence should be able to build up a better picture of the difficulties particular students are having than in the traditional classroom.

2. *Summary Statistics*. As Anderson (chap. 2 in this volume) has done with the LISP tutor, it is possible to keep records of what students do while they are learning and analyze these records to report to different audiences on students' progress. For example, a report to administrators might summarize how many students went all the way through the LISP tutor and the Geometry Tutor, and how fast they went through each. A report to parents might describe what tutoring systems their child worked with, what kind of progress they made, how hard they tried (in terms of how long they stuck with various programs, particularly when they were having difficulty), and any other measures that parents request, individually or collectively. Reports to teachers might summarize the kinds of difficulties each student is having, and the amount each student learned using the different programs (in terms of the difference between their scores in the beginning and their scores in the final sessions). In fact, teachers could be given the capability of requesting that different kinds of analyses be made on the data, just as Anderson did with the LISP tutor. There are other audiences and other ways of analyzing such data, but these examples suffice to show what might be done.

3. *Portfolios*. Some computer-based teaching systems keep a library of students' best work. As far as I know, the idea was first used in the Plato math curriculum (Dugdale & Kibbey, 1975). An excellent example of a library is the one in Green Globs, a game to teach analytic geometry developed by Sharon Dugdale. The game, which is a part of a larger set of computer-based activities to teach analytic geometry, requires students to write equations for curves to go through fifteen green globs placed randomly on a Cartesian plane. The more green globs any curve goes through (each glob only counts once), the more points students score for that curve (the $n$th glob scores $2^{n-1}$ points). In the library are

stored the highest scoring games played, showing where the globs were placed and the equations written to make the high score. The name of the player who scored each game is also listed, thus garnering fame for a good performance.

The concept of the library can be extended to the personal portfolio that students could keep as a record of their accomplishments. The portfolio could record the students best compositions, game performances, or problem solutions. Art schools and architecture firms require portfolios to help them determine who should be admitted. They know it is impossible to evaluate the creative skills of a person in terms of standard tests. As we move to a society where learning and thinking are critical, the same problems arise with standard tests in other domains. Thus, by basing placement decisions at least in part on student portfolios (they may be based in part on summary statistics described earlier), the decision takes into account creativity as well as selectivity.

Moreover, basing decisions on *accomplishments* rather than simply on measured *aptitudes* reflects more realistically the way decisions are made in the real world. We value employees or students who do good things, not those who merely have the capability to do good things. By stressing accomplishment in our decisions, we change the motivation structure for students in school. The emphasis can change from a concern with doing well on tests to producing good works.

In summary, let me review briefly how this scenario addresses the desiderata and concerns raised in the first two sections. The scenario entails moving away from testing per se to analysis of the ongoing learning and accumulation of the products produced by that learning. There is no lowering of standards to what can be measured, nor any overemphasis on doing well on tests. Moreover, there would be little stigmatizing of students for their poor performance; rather they are rewarded for good products. The emphasis on learning and thinking would be central. Furthermore, the three kinds of measures discussed can validly serve all the purposes of testing in today's school. The scenario describes a truly integrated learning and testing environment.

## CONCLUSION

The introduction of computers into our education system provides an opportunity to rethink the whole relationship between testing and learning. There are serious problems with the way testing currently drives our education system: It fosters emphasis on lower-order rather than higher-order skills and encourages stigmatization of students who do not do well. Further, testing as presently construed has only worried about content and predictive validity rather than about validity with respect to the many other purposes of testing. But by repositioning testing in computer-based learning environments, many of the problems with testing as currently construed can be alleviated.

## ACKNOWLEDGMENTS

This research was supported by the Personnel and Training Research Programs, Psychological Sciences Division, Office of Naval Research under Contract No. N00014-C-85-0026, Contract Authority Identification Number, NR 667-540. I thank Chip Bruce, John Frederiksen, Norman Frederiksen, Robert Glaser, Robert Linn, and Michael Shafto for their comments on a previous draft of the paper.

## REFERENCES

Anderson, J. R., Boyle, C. F., & Reiser, B. J. (1985). Intelligent tutoring systems. *Science, 228,* 456–468.

Brown, J. S., Burton R. R., & deKleer, J. (1982). Pedagogical natural language and knowledge engineering techniques in SOPHIE I, II, and III. In D. Sleeman & J. S. Brown (Eds.), *Intelligent tutoring systems* (pp. 227–282). New York: Academic Press.

Brown, J. S., & Burton, R. (1978). Diagnostic models for procedural bugs in mathematical skills. *Cognitive Science, 2,* 155–192.

Brown, J. S., & VanLehn, K. (1980). Repair theory. A generative theory of bugs in procedural skills. *Cognitive Science, 4,* 379–426.

Burton, R. R. & Brown, J. S. (1982). An investigation of computer coaching for informal learning activities. In D. Sleeman & J. S. Brown (Eds.), *Intelligent tutoring systems* (pp. 79–98). New York: Academic Press.

Collins A. (1986). Teaching reading and writing with personal computers. In J. Orasanu (Ed.), *A decade of reading research: Implications for practice* (pp. 171–187). Hillsdale, NJ: Lawrence Erlbaum Associates.

Collins, A., & Brown, J. S. (1988). The computer as a tool for learning through reflection. In H. Mandl & A. Lesgold (Eds.), *Learning issues for intelligent tutoring systems* (pp. 1–18). New York: Springer.

Collins, A., Brown, J. S., & Newman, S. E. (1989). Cognitive apprenticeship: Teaching the crafts of reading, writing, and mathematics. In L. B. Resnick (Ed.), *Knowing, learning and instruction: Essays in honor of Robert Glaser* (pp. 453–494). Hillsdale, NJ: Lawrence Erlbaum Associates.

Collins, A., & Gentner, D. (1980). A framework for a cognitive theory of writing. In L. W. Gregg & E. Steinberg (Eds.), *Cognitive processes in writing: An interdisciplinary approach* (pp. 51–72). Hillsdale, NJ: Lawrence Erlbaum Associates.

Cuban, L. (1984). *How teachers taught.* New York: Longman.

Dugdale, S., & Kibbee, D. (1975). *The fractions curriculum.* Champaign-Urbana, IL: University of Illinois, Plato Elementary School Mathematics Project.

Dweck, C. S. (1986). Motivational processes affecting learning. *American Psychologist, 41,* 1040–1048.

Frederiksen, N. (1984). The real test bias: Influences of testing on teaching and learning. *American Psychologist, 39,* 193–202.

Glaser, R. (1984). Education and thinking: The role of knowledge. *American Psychologist, 39,* 93–104.

Kelman, P., Bardige, A., Choate, J., Hanify, G., Richards, J., Roberts, N., Walters, J., & Tomrose, M. K. (1983). *Computers in teaching mathematics.* Reading, MA: Addison-Wesley.

Linn, R. L. (1986). Educational testing and assessment: Research needs and policy issues. *American Psychologist, 41,* 1153–1160.

MacDonald, N. H., Frase, L. T., Gingrich, P. S., & Keenan, S. A. (1982). The Writer's Workbench: Computer aids for text analysis. *IEEE Transactions on Communication, 20,* 1–14.

Matz, M. (1982). Toward a process model for high school algebra errors. In D. Sleeman & J. S. Brown (Eds.) *Intelligent tutoring systems* (pp. 25–50). New York: Academic Press.

Palincsar, A. S., & Brown, A. L. (1984). Reciprocal teaching of comprehension-fostering and monitoring activities. *Cognition and Instruction, 1,* 117–175.

Rosenthal, R., & Jacobson, L. (1968). *Pygmalion in the classroom.* New York: Holt, Rinehart & Winston.

Schoenfeld, A. H. (1983). Problem solving in the mathematics curriculum: A report, recommendations and an annotated bibliography. *The Mathematical Association of America.* MAA Notes, No. 1.

Schoenfeld, A. H. (1985). *Mathematical problem solving.* New York: Academic Press.

Schoenfeld, A. H. (in press). On mathematics as sense-making. An informal attack on the unfortunate divorce of formal and informal mathematics. In D. N. Perkins, J. Segal, & J. Voss (Eds.), *Informal reasoning and education.* Hillsdale, NJ: Lawrence Erlbaum Associates.

Sleeman, D. (1982) Assessing aspects of competence in basic algebra. In D. Sleeman & J. S. Brown (Eds.), *Intelligent tutoring systems* (pp. 185–199). New York: Academic Press.

Tyler, R. W., & White, S. H. (1979). *Testing, teaching, and learning.* (Report of a Conference on Research on Testing. August 17–26, 1978). Washington, DC: National Institute of Education.

# Evidence from Internal Medicine Teaching Rounds of the Multiple Roles of Diagnosis in the Transmission and Testing of Medical Expertise

Cynthia S. Gadd
*University of Pittsburgh*

Harry E. Pople, Jr.
*University of Pittsburgh*

Computer-based systems for medical diagnosis have several potential uses, including consultation, tutoring, and evaluation. Each of these uses has profound implications for the design of an underlying expert system's human–machine interaction capability. An awareness of these issues has led us to study the person–person interaction process that takes place in teaching rounds. We believe one of the most significant observations to emerge from our analyses is the presence of multiple levels of diagnostic activity. We propose a representation and process model that defines a general framework for diagnosis, based on the synthesis of a coherent interpretation of multiple (and often inconsistent) phenomena. A discussion of the implications of this model for the development of multiple levels of diagnostic activity within human–machine interaction concludes this chapter.

## COMPUTER-BASED SYSTEMS FOR MEDICAL DIAGNOSIS HAVE SEVERAL POTENTIAL USES

As the development of computer-based systems for medical diagnosis continues to provide us with increasingly sophisticated models of expertise, it is timely, and indeed imperative to future design efforts, that we consider the possible uses to which these systems may be applied. We discuss three of these uses— consultation, tutoring, and evaluation—and, in particular, the current status of these functions in medicine and the implications of introducing computer-based systems into these settings.

We have come to define the role of consultant in the sense of someone who not only provides the answer to a particular diagnostic problem, but also informs the inquiring physician about issues of general relevance to the problem so that the physician is better equipped to handle future cases. Perhaps this distinction can best be explained by using an example from our experiences during the development and tuning of the Internist-I and Caduceus systems for diagnostic problem solving in the domain of internal medicine (see Miller, Pople, & Myers, 1982; Pople, 1982, 1985).

Physicians have often come to our laboratory to request that a particularly difficult clinical case be analyzed by the Internist-I system. The most interesting of these cases, from our point of view, were the ones in which the physician actually ran the case "in real time," with the expert (on whose knowledge the system is modeled) acting as the "interface" between the visiting physician and the system. These interactions provided an opportunity to observe that physicians communicating with one another in a consultation setting engage in a wide variety of activities that frequently diverge from a strict line of reasoning about the specifics of the case. In addition to communicating observations of the patient, the visiting physician often sought confirmation of the opinions and interpretations acquired. The expert, on the other hand, not only sought information to help pin down the patient's problem, but at times the expert's questions and statements were clearly aimed at assessing the competence of the correspondent, advising on how to make measurements and observations, and, in general, trying to educate the correspondent about the problem being discussed.

It is clear that the participants had multiple goals for the interaction goals that were at times oblique to that of a straightforward solution to the clinical problem. The interaction was also effective in facilitating a deeper understanding of the case, enabling the visiting physician to feel that the alternatives considered important were adequately dealt with and that the physician's knowledge of the domain was enhanced. The actual system solution to the case seemed to be relegated to the role of facilitator because it brought these people together and generated a focus for the development of their discussion, but in and of itself, it could not be considered to be a satisfactory response to the visiting physician's inquiry. We came away from these experiences with strong intuitions about the importance of viewing a computer-based consultant for internal medicine as one component of a human–machine partnership—specifically, the need for less restrictive models of human–machine interaction than is possessed by current systems.

The teaching of clinical medicine is seriously limited in its ability to educate students in the *process* of diagnosis. Students are expected to learn diagnostic problem solving by studying medical textbooks and clinicopathological conferences, attending conferences dominated by case presentations, or by observing physicians at work and rediscovering the process of clinical reasoning by trial and error. As Kassirer (1983) pointed out, textbooks do not provide much help in understanding clinical reasoning. They do not explain how to distinguish among a variety of possible diseases in a patient with a constellation of findings, nor how to deal with diagnostic problems that fail to conform to a classical pattern. Even those textbooks devoted solely to problem solving provide only vague advice or theoretical approaches that have little basis in the day-to-day clinical setting. The case presentation format of other teaching methods also has limitations. A well-organized oral case presentation or clinicopathological conference only implicitly incorporates the intermediate reasoning (hypothesis formation and evaluation) that influenced the patient's workup because teaching begins after all the details of the case have been presented (Eddy & Clanton, 1982; Engel, 1971; Lipkin, 1979).

Teaching rounds were meant to overcome some of the deficiencies found in the other methods of medical education; however, as they are typically practiced, this is not likely to be the case. The goal of efficient patient management frequently overshadows any significant elucidation of the *process* of clinical reasoning. This trend is indicated by focusing early in the discussion on laboratory data and radiographic images, rather than using the chief complaint, history, and physical examination to provide a framework in which the workup of a patient can unfold. The opportunity to address process-related issues, such as the appropriateness of requesting an additional piece of data or of entertaining a particular hypothesis, is often lost. We do not imply that all teaching rounds fail to provide an educational experience in which the process of clinical reasoning is featured, but that the quality and character of this experience varies greatly from one clinician–teacher to another.

There are a few seasoned clinician–teachers who are recognized as gifted communicators of their knowledge and reasoning abilities. Their approach is grounded in hypothesis formulation and evaluation, and the interaction often has a distinctively Socratic flavor. (A detailed characterization of the rounds led by one such clinician–teacher is presented later in this discussion.) The strength of this approach is in the expert's ability to help the student "put it all together" by forcing the student to explicitly consider alternative conceptualizations of the problem (which are elicited from the still-fragmented knowledge base has acquired from textbooks and cases) as the student attempts to construct a coherent interpretation of the case data. Findings that are readily available at the beginning of a workup are used to establish expectations that provide a rational guide to subsequent inquiry. As alternatives are hypothesized and pursued, it is the *process* of diagnosis that is featured. We argue that one of the most important contributions expert systems for diagnosis could make to the advancement of medical education would be to make this method of instruction more uniformly available to students, in the form of a computer-based opportunity to explore the process of clinical reasoning.

We also foresee the potential use of computer-based diagnostic systems as a means of evaluating a student's ability to put knowledge to use in a problem-solving setting. This type of evaluation is seen as an alternative or complement to written examinations. A formerly prevalent method of evaluation, oral examination using a case format, has all but died out (with the exception of the internship and residency programs at some teaching hospitals). Performed on the ward, with all of the attendant distractions and subjectivity, the interpretation and normalization of the results from such exercises is often difficult. However, computer-based examinations provide a unique opportunity to gauge the student's declarative knowledge, diagnostic reasoning skills, and reporting/communication skills, in an active problem-solving setting. Expert systems for medical diagnosis could provide a means of reestablishing this method of evaluation, by providing an environment rich in problem-solving opportunities without some of the detracting features noted above. A computer-based system with sophisticated models of human–machine interaction would provide: (a) fewer distractions than the ward setting, (b) interpretative uniformity based on system consistency, and (c) interaction that is more appropriately timed than either written or videotaped cases permit.

## HUMAN PROBLEM-SOLVING DISCOURSE AS A MODEL OF HUMAN–MACHINE INTERACTION

The profound implications of the requirements each of these potential uses would have for the design of an expert system's human–machine interaction capability has led us to begin studies of the person–person interaction process that takes place in teaching rounds. Teaching rounds possess many of the characteristics we have ascribed to the roles proposed above. We have chosen to focus our efforts on consultation dialogues between a recognized expert clinician in the domain of internal medicine and clients with various levels of expertise (medical students, residents, and physicians with expertise in some other specialty). The setting for our initial investigation was teaching rounds in a university-affiliated hospital.

Rounds are commonly used in teaching hospitals as a means of providing clinical diagnosis experience for medical students (and/or residents) under the guidance of an experienced physician. During rounds, one of a group of students (each of whom has primary responsibility for at least one patient) reviews the case data, diagnosis, and treatment with the expert. The ensuing interaction reflects the multiple goals of the expert (assurance of good patient care, evaluation of students' knowledge and ability to apply it within the clinical setting, and instruction) and of the students (provide good care, improve clinical skills, and communicate medical information with clarity). The rounds setting is in some respects more complex than the one-on-one consultation because of more participants and a multiplicity of explicit and implicit goals. However, we believe that the data obtained during bedside rounds discussions are valid evidence of the cognitive processing associated with the communication of expert knowledge. First, the discussions are often explicitly reflective; the discussion leader (expert) requires participants (typically, students) to explain their statements and to reveal the thoughts that have led them to specific conclusions. Second, the interaction is unrehearsed and rapid-fire; students, especially, are working "in the limit."

## TEACHING ROUNDS ARE CHARACTERIZED BY MULTIPLE LAYERS OF DIAGNOSTIC ACTIVITY

Over the past 12 months, we have transcribed and analyzed approximately 8 hours of rounds sessions between Dr. Jack Myers and students at the University of Pittsburgh School of Medicine. The transcripts represent the complete discussion and evaluation of seven cases in internal medicine. They were coded and analyzed using several discourse methods, each of which focused on a different aspect of the complex behavior. We believe one of the most significant observations to emerge from our analyses, and the one on which we focus in this chapter, is the presence of multiple layers of diagnostic activity within the transcripts.

Of course, the most obvious diagnostic activity, performed by both the clinician-teacher and the student, is diagnosing the cause of the patient's illness. The main insights deriving from the Decision Systems Laboratory's study of diagnostic reasoning are detailed by Pople (1982, 1985). In brief, we have found that in a broad domain such as internal medicine, the physician must engage in a heuristic problem-focused strategy so that the set of decision (disease) alternatives actually considered and evaluated is kept to a manageable size. In complicated cases, this strategy becomes even more important because of the frequent necessity of coming to more than one diagnostic decision in a given case. In order to carry out the heuristic problem-focusing aspect of the diagnostic reasoning process, the physician employs a number of pragmatic rules, most notably *Occam's razor*— which argues for choosing the simplest of competing hypotheses. In practical terms, this requires use of what we refer to as *synthesis operators* that combine the partial problem descriptions resulting from diverse sources of patient data into a parsimonious whole. Recognizing, however, that any such framework is based on heuristic constraints, it is important to ensure that new information is used not only to refine the decision problem as formulated, but also that where appropriate it feeds back to the problem-formulation process, causing quite dramatic revision of the problem structure in some cases.

It is this latter feature of diagnostic reasoning, the need to scrupulously question the underlying assumptions of hypotheses and reformulate the diagnostic problem when appropriate, that causes a great deal of trouble for experienced and less experienced physicians, alike. Elstein, Shulman, and Sprafka (1978) noted that physicians were more likely to err on the side of overinterpretation—regarding noncontributory data as confirmation of an existing hypothesis—more frequently than either disregarding the data or regarding it as disconfirming when it was not. Studies of expert–novice differences in diagnostic problem-solving have reported similar results. Feltovich (1981), also reported in Johnson et al. (1981), found that novices in pediatric cardiology responded to early evidence by proposing reasonable hypothesis, but were less likely than experts to recognize the significance of later evidence and change their hypotheses when this was indicated. Lesgold, Feltovich, Glaser, and Wang (1981) reported that the interpretations of novices depended more on finding an explanation for a few features, with a tendency for other details to be assimilated to the initial hypothesis rather than used to generate alternative hypotheses or modifications of existing ones.

As the rounds-participants discuss the diagnostic problem in a specific case, the clinician–teacher frequently demonstrates the synthetic nature of the problem-solving strategy through examination of the "fit" between various interpretations of the data. The clinician–teacher also forces the evaluation of assumptions underlying the favored hypotheses when new data indicate alternatives that have previously been suppressed. By focusing a great deal of the teaching intervention on these troublesome aspects of the diagnostic process, the clinician–teacher is acquainting the student with (and subsequently reinforcing) patterns of reasoning that have the potential to alleviate some of the expert–novice differences noted earlier.

Our analyses of the teaching-rounds transcripts also reveal many statements by the clinician–teacher that are aimed at assessing the latent knowledge and diagnostic competence of the student. There are several reasons for this type of behavior. First, evaluation of competence is an explicit goal of teaching rounds in which the teacher is expected to assign a performance rating to the student at the end of the rotation. Second, the teacher must assess the confidence that can be placed in the student's reports of findings, including how a measurement was taken or an observation was interpreted, so that the findings are evaluated appropriately within the problem-solving framework. Third, another explicit goal of teaching rounds is to provide instruction commensurate with the needs of the student. The teacher has the task of determining the source of a student's error, so that the appropriate remedial intervention can occur (e.g., discuss how to interpret an observation, or "refocus" the student's attention to relevant knowledge that has been overlooked or is missing from the student's disease models).

We view this assessment of latent knowledge and competence as a form of diagnostic activity. From the teacher's previous interactions with a student, in particular, and from experience with other students, in general, opinions (or assumptions) are formed about the current state of the student's knowledge and about errors the student is likely to make. During a specific rounds session, we see the teacher using these assumptions to form expectations about the student's reasoning about this diagnostic case—what knowledge is lacking or is applying incorrectly. The teacher's intervention strategies are frequently aimed at diagnosing the cause of the student's errors, that is, testing and modifying the assumption about the student's knowledge and reasoning ability as applied to this particular case.

The medical problem-solving and instructionally motivated diagnostic activities described here involve both the input and output of complex verbal information, that is, conversation or discourse. We find it useful to think of the other diagnostic activities that occur in the rounds setting as being embedded in another layer of diagnosis—the diagnosis inherent in cooperative discourse. Grice (1975) has described discourse as a cooperative exchange in which each participant attempts to figure out what the other participant "means" (intends) by statements, and formulates responses that are sensitive to the other person's goals (as they are perceived), as well as to the participant's goals. This view of discourse has motivated a great deal of research in computational linguistics, specifically that related to intentionality and speech acts (Allen, 1983). Grice's maxims of cooperative discourse have implications for speakers' statements: quality (give true, rather than false or unsupported, statements), quantity (be as informative as is appropriate to the stage of interaction), relevance, and manner (be brief and orderly, avoid obscurity and ambiguity). The clinician–teacher uses statements to demonstrate the use of these maxims, specifically as they influence the preferred mode of communication for medical consultation. Also, while conducting the rounds session, the teacher (like any participant in a conversation) has the task of determining what speakers mean by their statements, and the constraints of cooperative discourse help to bound the interpretations. We view this feature of medical discourse as yet another form of diagnostic activity—one that facilitates all the others.

## A GENERAL MODEL OF DIAGNOSTIC PROBLEM SOLVING FROM COGNITIVE PSYCHOLOGY

Now that we have identified diagnostic activities in the teaching-rounds discourse, we would like to define diagnosis in such a way that all of these roles may be encompassed. Greeno and Simon (1988) describe diagnostic problem solving as a form of inductive problem solving in which some material is presented and the problem solver tries to find a general principle or structure that is consistent with the material. Induction is characterized as having a dual problem space: a space of stimuli or data and a space of possible structures, such as rules or patterns of relations. The problem-solving task can be viewed as search in the space of structures, and the problem is solved by finding a structure that satisfies the criteria of agreement with the data. Specific to diagnostic problem solving, the space of structures is a set of possible causes of the symptoms, which may include the disease states in medicine or the faulty knowledge of a student. Greeno and Simon (1987) also note that diagnostic problem solving has an *operational thinking* component because it is based on the goal of curing the patient or correcting knowledge deficiencies. Therefore, the processes of providing information and drawing conclusions in diagnosis are directed at decisions about remedial "treatment."

This description of diagnostic problem solving is consonant with the views of cognitive scientists who have studied expertise in medicine (Feltovich, 1981; Lesgold et al., 1981) and in other domains (Larkin, McDermott, Simon, & Simon, 1980; Simon & Gilmartin, 1973), particularly in the importance attached to the expert's ability to represent problems successfully. This ability is attributed to the expert's having a well-integrated structure of knowledge in which patterns of features in the problem are associated with concepts at varying levels of generality, enabling efficient search for hypotheses about the salient features of the problem, as well as methods and operations to be used in solving the problem. We propose here a general framework for diagnostic problem solving that focuses on the evolution of a coherent interpretation of input data (e.g., medical findings, speaker's utterances) through successive attempts to "put together" the partial interpretations and expectations suggested by the data.

## A PROPOSED REPRESENTATION AND PROCESS MODEL FOR DIAGNOSIS: INTERPRETATION SYNTHESIS

A simple way to begin thinking about the process of synthesizing a coherent interpretation of a collection of inputs is to use the metaphor of preparing a presentation of overhead transparencies or overlays. The informative content of the presentation is often built up by selecting component overlays from many that are available, based on the perceived interests or sophistication of the audience. It is possible to arrange components in various ways, beginning with overlays that reveal only partial information and overlaying others that provide clarification or combine concepts to form a more coherent whole. As several overlays are built up, this existing set places certain restrictions and expectations on the subsequent additions. Sometimes the addition of an overlay may require the modification or elimination of previous ones.

In each type of diagnostic activity identified from the teaching-rounds discourse, we see a pattern of reasoning that is, in many ways, suggestive of this overlay metaphor. In the case of the most basic of these activities, discourse-motivated diagnosis, the listener tries out various configurations of knowledge in an attempt to form a coherent interpretation of the speaker's utterances. Initially, this interpretation is incomplete, or even inconsistent. Subsequent dialogue attempts to further specify and clarify earlier interpretations and verify their consistency with information revealed by new utterances. Those contexts and concepts that are relevant to a particular discourse are defined by the process of evolving a coherent interpretation of the utterances that compose that discourse. Medical diagnostic problem solving can be characterized similarly—the physician tries to synthesize a coherent picture of the disease processes present in the patient from the various components of the physician's knowledge that were activated by reported findings. And the instructionally motivated diagnosis, engaged in by the clinician–teacher, can be viewed as the attempt to form a better image of the student's developing knowledge base from the clues provided in their interaction, so that the teaching interventions are appropriate. We now suggest a model of how interpretations are synthesized through a process of context evolution.

We have chosen to represent the expert's knowledge base as a collection of many component structures (corresponding to the overlays just discussed), each of which contains information about some part of his overall medical knowledge. This fragmented or compartmentalized view of expert knowledge is suggested, in part, by the knowledge acquisition process inherent in medical education (and typical of any complex domain), in which organizational techniques, such as categorization (physiology, disease nosologies), have been used to impose some structure on an unwieldy knowledge base. However, such a representation scheme is more strongly indicated by the fragmented and often inconsistent nature of medical knowledge that is due to the variability of phenomena that are to be interpreted as being "the same concept." Take, as an example, the typical textbook description of a disease that consists of many different manifestations and/or pathophysiological states. A patient would rarely present all these manifestations or states, several of which may even contradict one another. Yet the clinician must maintain this inconsistent cluster of descriptors in such a way as to allow for recognizing the disease in what is often a novel setting (i.e., the pattern of presentation for a specific patient). We believe that this characterization of the nature of medical knowledge necessitates the maintenance of a fragmented description of a concept, and that associated with each fragment is a rich set of relations and procedures that determine the appropriateness of its use in a particular setting, as well as expectations about other fragments that should (or should not) coexist with it in a coherent interpretation.

We use an object-oriented, knowledge-representation scheme (see Minsky, 1975) that facilitates decomposition of complex knowledge structures without loss of vital relationships. The information that should be associated with a given knowledge entity, or *object,* can be stored directly in its *slots* or can be identified using *pointers* to other locations in the knowledge base. Objects may also have *demons,* which are procedures that watch for some condition to become true or false and then activate an associated process, at which time the demon is said to have *fired.*

Within this representation scheme, the expert's component-knowledge structures (overlays) are actually complex objects whose slots may be filled with pointers to other objects, reflecting the relationships between overlays. As the expert begins to listen to a speaker, those components of the expert's knowledge that are directly identifiable by concepts introduced in the speaker's utterances are activated. These overlays, through their established associations, indicate other overlays that should be included or rejected for consideration. One of the distinguishing features of the expert's knowledge is that associations are not all equal in their power of indication. Some associations are so strongly indicative of specific, related concepts that *suspicions* regarding these concepts provide expectations for the subsequent interaction. Within our representation framework, these suspicions are embodied in demons that are attached to slots of related concepts and lie in wait for confirmation or denial from subsequent utterances. These suspicions are essentially planting the seeds of multiple contexts—several possible ways of considering the speaker's comments—of which perhaps only a few would ever develop, but all of which have the potential to influence the emergence of a coherent understanding of the diagnostic problem. As the expert continues to get input from the speaker, the existing demons are alertly gathering evidence for or against the pursuit of a particular context. Meanwhile, some newly introduced concepts are positing other overlays for consideration.

Typically, there are many possible configurations suggested by the overlays that were activated by a collection of data. The synthesis process can be viewed as "trying out" these various configurations on the data, using the constraints they impose on the interpretation of the problem (in the form of suspicions and their related contexts) to ensure coherency. It is often the case that the associated knowledge in the early stages of generating an interpretation is very general and/ or tentative in nature; for example, the patient's current gastrointestinal (GI) problem is probably somehow related to a history of liver disease. A possible context for consideration of this patient's symptoms becomes liver disease that has progressed to include significant portal hypertension (a common sequel of which is hyperacidity in the stomach). Other contexts, such as physiological models of the interaction between liver, portal-circulatory, and GI functions, and models of surgical interventions for portal hypertension, may also be seeded at this point. Subsequent input may strengthen some of these contexts, whereas others may find no support. In order to build a coherent interpretation of the data, the configurations (sets of overlays that are associated with these strengthened contexts) that can be developed, both in their own right and in congruence with the others, become the knowledge that is relevant to understanding the problem.

### An Example of Context Evolution and Interpretation Synthesis from the Teaching-Rounds Discourse

To clarify some of these issues, we can follow the representation of the interpreta-tion synthesis process as it applies to an excerpt from one of the teaching-rounds transcripts (see the Appendix for the text of this excerpt). Before beginning with the example, it is useful to define the building blocks of our representation, as used in these figures. In Fig. 5.1, we show the basic components of the expert's evolving interpretation of the patient's disease processes (the descriptive model). The disease process overlays (at the top of the figure) refer to the expert's understanding of the "real time" progression of disease in the patient, based on information that has been revealed in the discourse (sometimes called the disease timeline of the patient). This progression may coincide with the order of introduction of disease processes in the discourse, but more often the most recent problems are mentioned first (i.e., in the history of present illness) and other disease processes get filled in during subsequent dialogue. We indicate real time in increments of $N$, with $N$ corresponding to the time in the patient's timeline at which the first disease process that was mentioned in the discourse occurred. As information about other disease processes that have occurred before or since this initial (arbitrary) starting point is received, the timeline sequence of these disease processes is denoted by $N$-$x$ and $N$+$x$, respectively. The decomposition of these disease processes, represented by the subprocess overlays below them in Fig. 5.1, reveals the expert's interpretation of each specific disease process at a given point in the discourse (or discourse processing time). The interpretation of a disease process is characterized by its subprocesses which, in turn, decompose into manifestations, facets (clusters of manifestations), and links (causal and/or

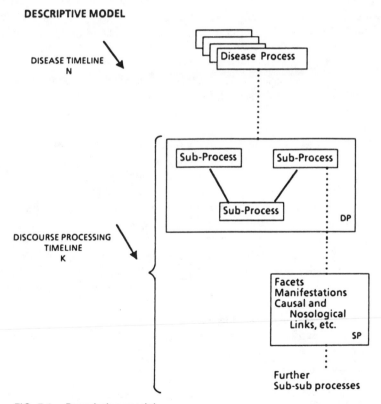

FIG. 5.1.  Descriptive model.

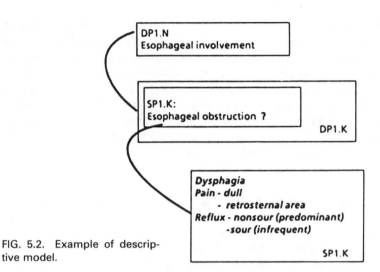

FIG. 5.2. Example of descriptive model.

nosological relationships between manifestations and diseases). As discourse proceeds, the interpretations of a disease process "grow" in complexity and explicitness. Initial findings suggest relationships that percolate upward and allow disease descriptors to be hypothesized, albeit tentatively. With additional findings, more is filled in at the lower levels, relationships between subprocesses are reassessed, and hypotheses at the disease-process level become more concrete. We indicate discourse processing time in increments of $K$, with $K$ corresponding to the first utterance in a discourse and $K+x$ denoting the passage of time as additional utterances are made.

Now, turning to the example from the rounds transcript, we can begin to build a representation of the expert's interpretation of the disease processes in this patient, based on the student's report of positive findings for dysphagia, dull pain in the retrosternal area, and a predominantly nonsour esophageal reflux (see lines 1–4 of excerpt). (These findings are shown together in the bottom box, SP1.$K$. This label denotes subprocess 1 at discourse-processing time $K$ of Fig. 5.2.) This first information that the expert receives about the patient, percolates upward to activate the component of the expert's knowledge (an overlay) that pertains to some, as yet unspecified, form of esophageal obstruction.[1] The initial patient data suggest a tentative interpretation of the disease process, in this patient's disease timeline, of esophageal involvement (shown in box DP1.$N$, which denotes disease process 1 at history-of-illness time $N$).

As we stated earlier, the expert uses the information in the early interpretations of the disease processes as assumption on which to base expectations for additional

---

[1]These findings may also relate to other disease processes not shown in this simple example. Throughout these figures, ellipses are used to denote incompleteness in the medical knowledge represented.

information that helps refine these interpretations. Also recall that within our representation the overlays contain knowledge about associations with other concepts; therefore, the incoming findings and the relationships among disease processes suggested by them are often strongly indicative of other findings and disease processes or subprocesses. These strong indications are the basis for the creation of demons (or suspicions) that reflect the expectations we attribute to the expert. Figure 5.3 shows some of the types of expectations that the expert's

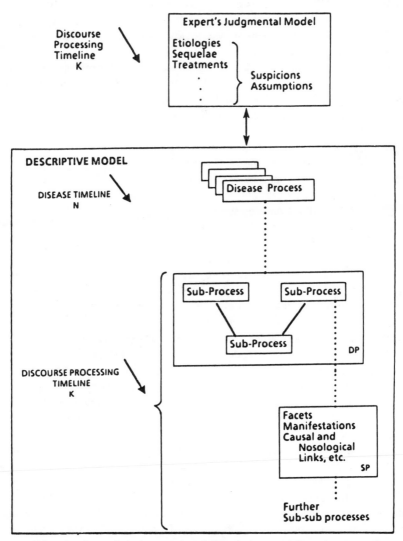

FIG. 5.3.   Expert's judgmental and descriptive models.

judgmental model can accommodate (e.g., etiologies, sequelae, and treatments), suggesting that there are many sources of suspicions. At a specific point in discourse time ($K$), the expert's judgmental model reflects the current set of expectations, based on the corresponding state of the descriptive model being constructed below it. In this example, demons associated with the esophageal obstruction subprocess are activated and create suspicions, in the expert's judgmental model, for reflux esophagitis and aspiration (shown in box EJ.$K$ of Fig. 5.4, which denotes the expert's judgment at discourse-processing time $K$). The first of these, reflux esophagitis, is a suspected etiology of the hypothesized disease process (esophageal obstruction). The second, aspiration, is a suspected secondary complication—a pathophysiological state that often manifests itself in patients who have esophageal obstruction. Each of these suspicions is further expanded into "look-for" structures (LF's), which set the traps for specific findings or other events. In this case, there are LF's for history of ulcers and esophageal stricture associated with reflux esophagitis and LF's for a cough with specific characteristics associated with aspiration. Some suspicions are stronger than others and their resolution may be a prerequisite for the successful conclusion of a discourse. Other suspicions have less strength initially (or are discounted by subsequent input) and may "die on the vine."

In addition to suspicions, the expert's judgment at this point in the discourse has two other attributes: bias and mode. These attributes reflect the fact that the expert is influenced not only by the expert's interpretations of the disease process(es) that could be responsible for the findings in the current case, but also by perceptions of the student: the student's domain knowledge, including perception, reasoning, and reporting skills, and the student's understanding of the current case's disease processes. We propose that these perceptions derive from the expert's assumptions about the diagnostic problem solving in which the student is engaging during the case discussion. These assumptions reside in the expert's model of the student (or *student model*). The expert is actually engaging in two modeling processes: an evolving interpretation of the disease processes in the patient and an evolving understanding of the student. Judgments (e.g., suspicions, constraints) influence and are influenced by both of these modeling processes. The expert is also influenced by the pragmatics of the situation. In this example, the bias represents a judgment made on the basis of assumptions found in the student model (e.g., previous experience has not demonstrated solid reasoning skills) and the mode reflects a pragmatic consideration (e.g., it is very early in the rounds discourse, therefore let the student continue to report case information before interrupting).

Returning to the transcript, the ellipsis indicates that more case-related data are reported by the student. Additional disease processes are now included in the patient's timeline shown in Fig. 5.5, at an earlier point than the esophageal involvement disease process: an old history of ulcers (DP.$N-2$) and a subsequent gastrectomy to relieve their uncontrolled bleeding (DP.$N-1$), the details of which

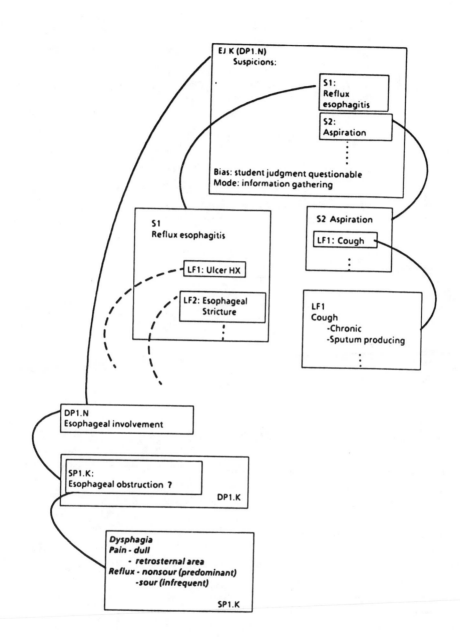

FIG. 5.4. Expert's judgmental and descriptive models after introduction of dysphagia, pain, and reflux findings.

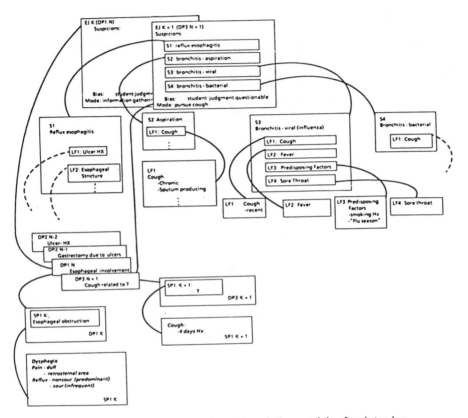

FIG. 5.5. Expert's judgmental and descriptive models after introduction of cough finding.

are not shown here. We pick up the discussion again at the point indicated by line 5 of the excerpt, in which a positive finding for a 4-day history of cough is reported by the student (shown in box SP1.$K+1$, which denotes subprocess 1 at discourse processing time $K+1$). There are many causes of cough; so the disease process descriptor (shown in box DP3.$N+1$, denoting disease process 3 at history-of-illness time $N+1$), is vague with respect to etiology. However, there are several strong relationships that suggest etiological suspicions for the expert's judgment (EJ.$K+1$), including reinforcement of the aspiration context (S2) and the addition of viral and bacterial bronchitis (S3 and S4) with their associated LFs. Taken together, these suspicions create a differential diagnosis of the cause of the patient's cough, within the expert's judgmental model. Particularly because the cough reinforces one of the previous suspicions, the pursuit of this differential diagnosis is pertinent to the immediate discourse.

In line 6 of the excerpt, the expert asks the student if there is a relationship between the cough and the presenting-illness (esophageal obstruction) and, upon receiving what is considered to be disconfirming evidence (the recency and pattern of the cough described in line 9), the expert attempts to elicit from the student an indication that the aspiration alternative was at least considered (line 10). When this attempt fails, the expert explains the connection (lines 14–19), and then proceeds to consider other alternatives by pursuing the LFs of the remaining cough-related suspicions (lines 20–32). Within this episode, the student reports other positive findings (fever in line 25 and a history of smoking in line 30) and the expert notes others (sore throat and the relative mildness of the disease this year, in lines 28–29) that support the viral (influenza) alternative. Figure 5.6

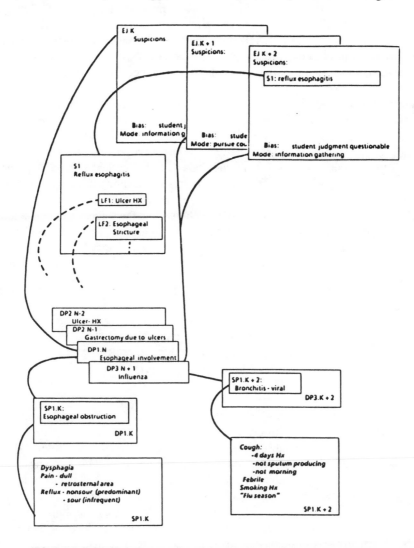

FIG. 5.6.   Expert's judgmental and descriptive models after resolution of cough finding.

shows these additional findings as a more complete description of the cough subprocess (see box SP1.$K+2$, which denotes the understanding of subprocess 1 at discourse processing time $K+2$). The expert's judgment at discourse-processing time $K+2$ (see box EJ.$K+2$) reflects the downgrading or elimination of the cough-related suspicions and the unresolved status of the reflux esophagitis suspicion. The process of synthesizing a coherent interpretation of the diagnostic problem embedded in this discourse would continue in a similar manner.

Before leaving this example, we briefly describe the salient features of the expert's model of the student, alluded to in the previous discussion. The student model resembles the expert's discourse-processing model already described (judgment and disease processes), reflecting the expert's assumption that the student makes hypotheses about disease processes, establishes expectations for subsequent discourse, and uses these hypotheses and expectations in much the same manner as the expert (although the student's proficiency does not yet approach the expert's). However, the expert has the additional tasks of recognizing divergences between the expert's own reasoning and that of the student and redirecting the student's inference process to a more appropriate focus. Therefore, the expert's model of the student includes assumptions (based on previous interactions with this student and/or others) about the status of the student's general domain knowledge and possible alternatives to preferred reasoning models. The suspicions formed in the expert's judgment can be triggered by any of three sources (understanding of the case-specific data, beliefs about the student's understanding of that data, and beliefs about the status of the student's general domain knowledge), whereas the student's suspicions are formed primarily by attempts to reconcile the case data with the student's own declarative domain knowledge.

## IMPLICATIONS OF THIS FRAMEWORK FOR THE MULTIPLE ROLES OF DIAGNOSIS OBSERVED IN TEACHING ROUNDS

Earlier we described the synthetic nature of medical diagnostic problem solving: that partial problem descriptions result from the diverse sources of patient data; that partial descriptions must be combined into a parsimonious whole; and that physicians need to question the underlying assumptions of their hypotheses and reformulate the problem when indicated, or risk overinterpretation errors such as those reported by Elstein et al. (1978). Within our framework, we use the knowledge-organizing strategies in the medical domain as the stimuli for our component view (via overlays) of the expert's knowledge. These strategies include the many ways that physicians have learned to organize their knowledge, such as disease etiologies and nosologies, physiological and anatomical models, and standard operating procedures (SOP)[2] for rounding. Represented as strong indicators of related concepts, which translate into bases for suspicions, physicians' organizing strategies ensure that the evolving interpretations of disease processes are evaluated from many possible points of view.

The instructionally motivated diagnostic activities in the teaching-rounds discourse are facilitated by the two modeling processes we have attributed to the expert: an evolving interpretation of the disease processes in the patient and an evolving understanding of the student. The expert's ability to gain an understanding about the case and about the other participants' knowledge from incomplete, poorly stated, or even wrong information is a particularly striking feature of the rounds discourse. Our framework provides some insight into this issue. Just as the expert is being guided by the suspicions and contexts generated by the input received, so are the other participants in the discourse. When the expert is confronted with statements that conflict with concepts within the contexts of consideration, the expert may hypothesize that there are discrepancies between the expert's interpretations and those of the speaker that are responsible for the incomplete or wrong information in the utterances. Subsequent statements are aimed at confirming this hypothesis through better illumination of the model of the student, and at guiding the discourse toward more appropriate interpretations.

The expert often appears to discover missed or confused inferences in the rounds discourse through responses to non-statements—those expected utterances that were left unsaid. The expert's sensitivity to failed expectations of what could or should be said in a conversation acts as a triggering mechanism for an interaction with the student that reveals the basis for the omissions or discrepancies (usually knowledge deficits) and provides the information required to correct them. It would seem a difficult task to enable a program of significant complexity to be sensitive to what is left unsaid (missing from input), as well as what is said. However, the use of demons to embody a suspicion, by setting "traps" that watch for specific conditions, appears to be a tailor-made method of recognizing non-statements. Some of the demons associated with a suspicion may be encoded with procedures that fire when input has *failed* to activate them instead of (or in addition to) the more usual procedures that fire when activation is successful. This process entails the notion of impatience. The discourse processor must set some limits on the extent to which it allows an issue to go unresolved. This could be accomplished either through a rather rigid establishment of temporal cut-offs or through a more rational agenda-type mechanism, in which a suspicion is "shelved" until some event indicates that it can no longer be ignored. If, as in the excerpt in the Appendix, an expert suspects esophageal obstruction and the related problem of aspiration, a student's report of cough in the history of present illness triggers a suspicion of chronic cough related to the aspiration. This

---

[2]SOP refers to the default script for the rounds interaction, which suggests that the case will be discussed in the following order: presenting condition, previous diagnoses, history, review of systems, physical examination, and laboratory and radiographic data.

suspicion could be pursued immediately with the student or it could be placed on an agenda, to be resolved before the topic is changed (i.e., another aspect of the patient's history of present illness is introduced) or before the next phase of the SOP is initiated.

The types of diagnostic activity discussed above have implications for discourse as well as for instruction, in that they are actually motivated by the more basic task of determining what speakers mean by their statements. As Grice pointed out, the task of "diagnosing" the meaning of a speaker's utterances is facilitated by the cooperative nature of discourse (Grice, 1975). The context evolution aspects of our framework provide a means of using this sense of cooperation to constrain the diagnostic tasks associated with man–machine interaction. Grice's imperatives to "be relevant," to "avoid obscurity," and to "be unambiguous," are facilitated in medical communication by the impressive vocabulary of specialized terminology in the domain. However, there are many subtleties of meaning that are not captured. The use of contexts in our model of discourse provides a means of sensitizing this vocabulary to changes in meaning associated with a particular way of viewing the data. It is possible to activate context-sensitive terminology with the same demon mechanism that generates the contexts. Therefore, when concepts and their relationships are being considered in several contexts, the appropriate terms and referents are used. Another of Grice's maxims, that of quantity ("be as informative as is appropriate to the state of interaction"), is demonstrated in the rounds discourse by the variability of descriptive precision (or abstraction) in which concepts are used. For example, in a dialogue, more abstract pathophysiological terms (such as *impaired function, shunt formation, elevated pressure, blockage, loss of fluid volume*), are generally integrated with more precise terms in such a way as to respond to the demands of the communication (i.e., are we talking about the formation of shunts, in general, or about a specific kind of shunt). Within our proposed framework, we can accommodate much of this descriptive flexibility through the decomposition feature of objects. Abstract or complex concepts are simply objects that have been built up from component objects; therefore we can build mechanisms for decomposing them to achieve a richer level of description and for generalizing across them to integrate, contrast, analogize, and so on.

Although we appear to be able to model significant features of ward-rounds discourse within the interpretation synthesis framework, there are some important features that require further consideration. Although our focus has been on understanding the identification and use of relevant domain knowledge in the generation of coherent discourse, we recognize the critical role of the specific goals (and plans for achieving them) of the participants, which may not be directly related to problem solving in the domain (e.g., reinforcing a critical concept, engaging quiet participants, and others). These goals provide a great deal of the global control in the discourse. A complete model also includes the discourse-level rhetorical "acts" required to bring linguistic expression to our evolving contexts—producing a question, restatement, explanation, or summary when appropriate. If we are to achieve our objective of understanding the complex behavior we have observed in rounds discourse, it is necessary that we integrate goal structures and rhetorical structures with our framework of interpretation synthesis. We are encouraged by the power of the *active* component of objects— that demons can communicate much of the goal and rhetorical knowledge needed to shape the development of contexts.

## CONCLUSION

Although not yet addressing the full range of capabilities observed in the teaching-rounds discourse, our proposed model of diagnostic problem solving has provided a framework within which to approach our current goals regarding the Caduceus expert system (Pople, 1982, 1985): to restructure the knowledge base and reasoning algorithms for more effective diagnosis, and to implement a less restrictive model of human–machine interaction, thereby facilitating a more natural consultation dialogue. We intend to use the computer implementation of our framework as a means of testing its validity and appropriateness to the tasks associated with these goals.

Currently, interaction with the Caduceus system is characterized by an initial entry of positive and negative findings using a highly restricted vocabulary, and by the system's subsequent reports of its reasoning status and queries for additional information. Our strategy is to use the interpretation synthesis framework as the basis for creating, for the Caduceus system, a discourse manager that emulates some of the important features of human medical discourse. Thus, the new Caduceus system, in addition to assuming the initiative and conducting a diagnostic work-up on its own, can engage in a more collegial joint man–machine problem-solving experience.

We view this research as laying a foundation for (a) improving the models of expertise and human–machine interaction in the Caduceus consultation system, (b) incorporating its knowledge and problem-solving strategies in a tutorial setting, and (c) providing an alternative method of evaluating medical competence. The development of this family of systems is necessarily an evolutionary process. Our initial focus is on the consultation system, for which we have undertaken to support the collegial kind of interaction attributed to the consultant in the first section of this chapter. A tutoring system would require a more sophisticated student/client modeling capability than the consultation system, one that allows it to recognize cues from the discourse that indicate deficiencies in the student's knowledge, and to respond by revealing more appropriate concepts. Finally, a system that assumes an evaluative role in medical education may have less expected of its intervention capabilities than its tutoring counterpart; however, the modeling capabilities need to be even more sensitive to the student's knowledge deficiencies.

## ACKNOWLEDGMENTS

The research reported here has been supported by a grant from the Josiah Macy, Jr. Foundation, the National Institutes of Health–Division of Research Resources (2R01 LM03710-06), and the National Library of Medicine (2R24 RR91191-09). The authors wish to thank David Evans and Dr. Jack Myers for useful discussions and valuable comments.

## APPENDIX:
## EXCERPT FROM TEACHING-ROUNDS CASES

{*Note: Dr. Myers' comments are denoted by* m: *and the student's comments by* s1:. *Some paraphrasing was used to condense this excerpt from the transcribed text of Case 4 (lines 30–65, 196–206, 263–301, and 646–743).*}

| | | |
|---|---|---|
| 1 | s1: | His complaints are those of dysphagia, which is marked by sticking in the low |
| 2 | | retrosternal area, and a dull pain in that area. He also gives a history of drinking |
| 3 | | fluids and then when he lies down, if he turns on his side, sometimes the fluid |
| 4 | | will come up to his mouth and then he swallows it again. |

.
.
.

| | | |
|---|---|---|
| 5 | s1: | Incidentally he's had a cough. |
| 6 | m: | Is it incidental? |
| 7 | s1: | I think so. It's incidental to the complaint for which he's here. |
| 8 | m: | I ask that question very seriously. Well let's hear about it. |
| 9 | s1: | He's had a four-day-old cough. He denies morning cough or sputum production. |
| 10 | m: | So, I suppose it is incidental then. I was concerned. Why? |
| 11 | s1: | Well, maybe some irritation, a nerve irritation. |
| 12 | m: | No. |
| 13 | s1: | Well, I would certainly wonder, if he had a chronic cough, from what reason. |
| 14 | m: | Well if he has a chronic cough, I can predict what he has it from. You told us |
| 15 | | this man has retention of fluid, at least in his esophagus. When he lies down, it |
| 16 | | comes up. And it's very frequent that those people will aspirate some of it. So, |
| 17 | | aspiration disease, if you want to call it that. Bronchitis, even bouts of aspiration |
| 18 | | pneumonia, sometimes even bronchiectasis, are associated with esophageal |
| 19 | | obstruction. That's the reason my ears pricked up when you said cough. Well, |
| 20 | | the best explanation for his cough is what? |
| 21 | s1: | Bronchitis. |
| 22 | m: | But there are many kinds of bronchitis. That's the problem. |

23  s1:  Your choices would be viral or bacterial.
24  m:   What's your choice?
25  s1:  Well he's got a very low grade fever this morning 38.2 I would go with the
         viral.
26  m:   Well, unfortunately there are hundreds of viruses. What's your explanation for
         it?
27  s1:  Influenza.
28  m:   Sure. He's got influenza. He's febrile. It's a fresh cough. He had a sore throat.
29       And it's been a comparatively mild illness this year.
30  s1:  And he's a heavy cigarette smoker.
31  m:   That predisposes him to it. I think that I agree with you that it's incidental. As
32       long as he doesn't get sicker than this, we're not gonna' worry much about it.

# REFERENCES

Allen, J. (1983). Recognizing intentions from natural language utterances. In M. Brady & R. C. Berwick (Eds.), *Computational models of discourse* (pp. 107–166). Cambridge, MA: MIT Press.

Eddy, D. M., & Clanton, C. H. (1982). The art of diagnosis: Solving the clinicopathological exercise. *New England Journal of Medicine, 306,* 1263–1268.

Elstein, A. S., Shulman, L. S., & Sprafka, S. A. (1978). *Medical problem solving: An analysis of clinical reasoning.* Cambridge, MA: Harvard University Press.

Engel, G. L. (1971). The deficiencies of the case presentation as a method of clinical teaching: Another approach. *New England Journal of Medicine, 284,* 20–24.

Feltovich, P. J. (1981). *Knowledge-based components of expertise in medical diagnosis* (Report PDS-2). Pittsburgh, PA: University of Pittsburgh, Learning Rearch and Development Center.

Greeno, J. G., & Simon, H. A. (1988). Problem solving and reasoning. In R. C. Atkinson, R. J. Herrnstein, G. Lindzey, & R. D. Luce (Eds.), *Stevens' handbook of experimental psychology* (Vol. 2, pp. 589–672). New York: Wiley.

Grice, H. P. (1975). Logic and conversation. In Cole & Morgan (Eds.), *Syntax and sematics: Vol. 3, Speech acts* (pp. 41–58). New York: Academic Press.

Johnson, P. E., Duran, A. S., Hassebrock, F., Moller, J., Prietula, M., Feltovich, P. J., & Swanson, D. B. (1981). Expertise and error in diagnostic reasoning. *Cognitive Science, 5,* 235–283.

Kassirer, J. P. (1983). Teaching clinical medicine by iterative hypothesis testing: Let's practice what we preach. *New England Journal of Medicine, 309,* 921–923.

Larkin, J., McDermott, J., Simon, D. P., & Simon, H. A. (1980). Expert and novice performance in solving physics problems. *Science, 208,* 1335–1342.

Lesgold, A. M., Feltovich, P. J., Glaser, R., & Wang, Y. (1981). *The acquisition of perceptual diagnostic skill in radiology* (Report PDS-1). Pittsburgh, PA: University of Pittsburgh, Learning Research and Development Center.

Lipkin, M. (1979). The CPC as an anachronism. *New England Journal of Medicine, 301,* 1113–1114.

Miller, R. A., Pople, H. E., & Myers, J. D. (1982). Internist: An experimental computer-based diagnostic consultant for general internal medicine. *New England Journal of Medicine, 307,* 468–476.

Minsky, M. (1975). A framework for representing knowledge. In Winston (Ed.), *The psychology of computer vision.* New York: McGraw-Hill.

Pople, H. E. (1982). Heuristic methods for imposing structure on ill-structured problems: The structure of medical diagnostics. In P. Szolovits (Ed), *Artificial intelligence in medicine* (pp. 119–190). Boulder, CO: Westview Press.

Pople, H. E. (1985). Evolution of an expert system: From internist to Caduceus. In I. De Lotto & M. Stefanelli (Eds.), *Artificial intelligence in medicine* (pp. 179–208). Amsterdam, The Netherlands: Elsevier.

Simon, H. A., & Gilmartin, K. (1973). A simulation of memory for chess positions. *Cognitive Psychology, 2,* 29–46.

# 6

# Diagnosing Individual Differences in Strategy Choice Procedures

Robert S. Siegler
Jamie Campbell
*Carnegie-Mellon University*

In the past 25 years, researchers have described in considerable detail children's problem-solving, mnemonic, and linguistic strategies. In the large majority of cases, the descriptions suggest either that children in general use a particular strategy or that children of one age use one strategy and children of another age use another. Such depictions may be too simple, however. Whether the task is attributing causation, reasoning about spatial location, or solving referential communications problems, children and adults know and use a variety of strategies (Kahan & Richards, 1986; Ohlsson, 1984; Shultz, Fisher, Pratt, & Rulf, 1986). This is true at the level of individuals as well as groups. Individual children often use one strategy on one occasion and a different strategy on the next occasion, even when the two occasions occur within a few minutes of each other (Siegler, 1987a).

The main purposes of the present article are to demonstrate the importance of recognizing that children use multiple strategies; to consider the adaptive value to the children of using these diverse strategies; to present a model of how children choose which strategy to use on a given occasion; to present new data concerning the model's usefulness for diagnosing the sources of individual differences in strategy choices; and to use the individual diagnoses in conjunction with the general model to make different instructional recommendations for children who show different patterns of performance.

## THE DIVERSITY OF CHILDREN'S STRATEGY USE

A literal reading of many contemporary models of children's thinking would suggest that all children of a given age, ability, and knowledge level perform a given task by using a particular strategy. To cite one well-known example, 5-

year-olds are said to solve liquid quantity conservation problems by judging which glass has the taller liquid column, whereas 8-year-olds are said to base judgments on the type of transformation that was performed (Piaget, 1952; Siegler, 1981). To cite another, 6-year-olds are said to solve simple addition problems by counting up from the larger number, whereas adults are said to solve the problems by retrieving answers from memory (Ashcraft, 1982; Groen & Parkman, 1972).

More detailed analysis, however, has indicated that children of a given age use a variety of strategies to solve particular problems. This is not just a slightly inconvenient detail. Ignoring the diversity of children's strategy use has resulted in some fundamentally incorrect depictions of cognitive development.

This point was illustrated in a recent study of 5- to 7-year-olds' addition strategies (Siegler, 1987b). In previous studies of young children's addition, chronometric analyses of data aggregated across trials led to the conclusion that children of these ages consistently used the strategy of counting up from the larger addend the number of times indicated by the smaller addend (Ashcraft, 1982, 1987; Groen & Parkman, 1972; Kaye, 1986; Resnick & Ford, 1981). Thus, on 3+5, the child would think, "5, 6, 7, 8." Groen and Parkman (1982) labeled this approach the "min strategy," because within it, solution times would be proportional to the amount of counting that needed to be done, that is, to the size of the minimum addend. The main source of evidence that children consistently used this min strategy was that the lengths of young children's solution times on each problem increased linearly with the size of the smaller addend on that problem.

To examine the validity of the conclusion that young children consistently use the min strategy, Siegler (1987b) presented 5- to 7-year-olds a set of addition problems and obtained solution times, as well as self-reports of strategy use, on each one. The data were analyzed in two ways: in the usual manner, in which performance on each problem is averaged across all trials (and therefore across all strategies), and by examining data produced by each strategy separately.

When the usual procedure of averaging performance across trials and strategies was followed, the results were like those found previously. The size of the smaller number was the best predictor of both solution times and errors. It accounted for between 70% and 80% of the variance on both variables.

Analyzing separately the data generated by each strategy led to a very different picture. Children reported using the min strategy on only 36% of problems. Their descriptions indicated that they used a number of other strategies, such as retrieval and counting from 1, on the other 64% of trials. The majority of children reported using at least three strategies, and a substantial minority reported using at least four.

Considerable converging evidence supported the validity of the children's verbal reports. On the 36% of trials on which they said they used the min strategy, the size of the smaller addend was by far the best predictor of both percentage of errors and lengths of solution times on each problem. It was also an excellent predictor in absolute terms. On trials where children said they used the min strategy, the size of the smaller addend accounted for 86% of the variance in solution times on each problem and 74% of the variance in errors. In contrast, on parallel analyses of performance on those trials where children reported using one of the other strategies, the size of the smaller addend was never either the best or the second best predictor of either errors or solution times on each problem and never accounted for more than 40% of the variance on either measure.

Analyses of both the actual data and of hypothetical data created for purposes of illustration indicated that there were two main reasons why the size of the smaller addend was such a good predictor of the averaged data, despite the min strategy being used on only a minority of trials. These were frequency of use and variability of performance on different problems. Two strategies, the min strategy and retrieval, were used much more often (36% and 35% of trials) than the other three strategies (14%, 8%, and 7% respectively). Variance of median solution times on the 45 problems was almost four times as great on min strategy trials as on retrieval trials. The combination of relatively frequent use and high variance of errors and solution times led to the min model fitting children's performance on all trials quite well, despite the strategy being used on fewer than 40% of trials. The general point is clear: Cognitive diagnoses can go seriously awry if they ignore the diversity of people's strategies.

## THE ADAPTIVE VALUE OF USING DIVERSE STRATEGIES

That people use diverse strategies to solve given problems is not a mere idiosyncracy of human cognition. Good reasons exist for us to know and to use multiple strategies. Strategies differ in their accuracy, in the amounts of time needed for execution, in their memory demands, and in the range of problems to which they apply. Strategy choices involve tradeoffs among these properties; people try to choose strategies that enable them to cope with cognitive and situational constraints. The broader the range of strategies that we know, the more we can shape our approaches to the demands of particular circumstances.

Even young children are adept at using strategies adaptively. To illustrate, 4-year-olds use at least four strategies to add and subtract: retrieval, counting fingers, putting up fingers but answering without counting them, and counting without any obvious external referent (Siegler & Robinson, 1982). Retrieval is the fastest strategy, but not the most accurate. Its accuracy declines sharply with increases in problem size. In contrast, the putting-up-fingers and counting-fingers strategies are considerably slower, but their accuracy decreases only slowly with increasing problem size. Siegler and Robinson found that children vary their use of strategies in a way that takes advantage of the speed and accuracy characteristics of each type of strategy. On problems where retrieval was almost as accurate as (and considerably faster than) counting fingers or just putting up fingers, children usually used retrieval. On problems where retrieval was much less accurate than the other strategies, children usually used one of the other strategies.

This adaptive pattern of strategy use can be seen in the relation among children's strategy use, errors, and solution times on each problem. On all of the tasks where my colleagues and I have examined strategy choices, strong correlations have emerged among these three variables. Children consistently use overt strategies (strategies involving audible or visible behavior between presentation of the problem and statement of the answer) most often on the most difficult problems, with problem difficulty measured either in terms of percentage of errors or length of solution times. Thus, they use such strategies as counting fingers in addition and subtraction, repeated addition in multiplication, sounding out in reading, and counting from the hour in time telling most often on the problems that cause the most errors and require the most time to solve. As shown in Fig. 6.1, the correlations among the variables are consistently high.

These strong correlations are not attributable to use of the overt strategies causing the high error rates and long solution times. When comparisons are made within a given problem, performance is usually more accurate when children use the overt strategies, and the amount of advantage gained by using overt strategies is greatest on the most difficult problems. Rather, children use overt strategies most often on those problems where they benefit most from them, that is, on problems where they otherwise could not perform accurately. This allows children to proceed quickly and accurately when that is possible, and to proceed slowly but still accurately when fast, accurate performance is impossible.

## A MODEL OF STRATEGY CHOICE

Siegler and Shrager (1984) developed the distribution-of-associations model to account for 4- and 5-year-olds' strategy choices on simple addition problems. The model has proved applicable to 5- and 6-year-olds' subtraction, to 6-year-olds' reading, to 8- and 9-year-olds' multiplication and time telling, and to 10- to 14-year-olds' balance scale performance (Siegler, 1986, 1987a; Siegler & McGilly, 1989; Siegler & Taraban, 1986). Here, we illustrate it in the context of 5- and 6-year-olds' subtraction.

The model of subtraction is organized into a representation and a process. The representation consists of associations of varying strength between each problem and possible answers to the problem. The numerical values in Table 6.1 are the estimated strengths of these associations. The estimates were derived from a separate overt-strategies-prohibited experiment in which children were asked to advance the first answer to the problem that they recalled. The associative strengths are the proportion of children who advanced a given answer. Thus, the

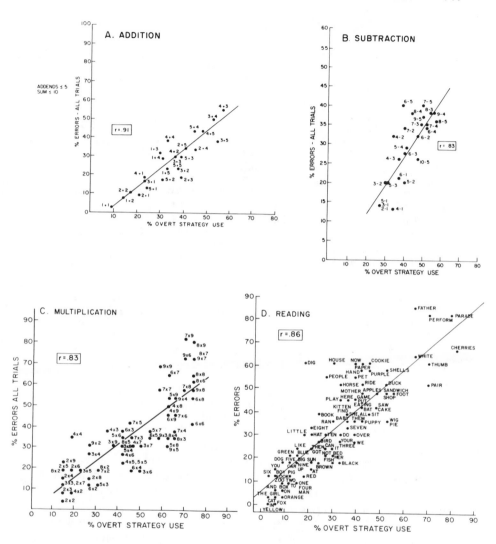

FIG. 6.1.   Relations between percent errors and percent overt strategy use on each problem.

associative strength of .02 linking the problem 2-1 and the answer 0 indicates that children advanced this answer on 2% of trials, and the associative strength .87 linking 2-1 and 1 means that children advanced this answer on 87% of trials.

The process that operates on this representation can be divided into three phases: retrieval, elaboration of the representation, and counting. As shown in Fig. 6.2, the child (who we here imagine as a girl) first retrieves an answer. If she is sufficiently confident of it, or is unwilling to search further, she states it.

TABLE 6.1
Distribution of Associations for Subtraction

| | Response | | | | | | | | | | | |
| | 0 | 1 | 2 | 3 | 4 | 5 | 6 | 7 | 8 | 9 | 10 | other |
|---|---|---|---|---|---|---|---|---|---|---|---|---|
| 2-1 | 0.02 | 0.87 | 0.05 | 0.03 | | | 0.01 | 0.01 | | | | |
| 3-1 | 0.01 | 0.02 | 0.85 | 0.01 | 0.05 | 0.02 | | 0.02 | 0.01 | | | |
| 4-1 | | 0.02 | 0.03 | 0.86 | 0.03 | 0.03 | | 0.01 | | | 0.01 | |
| 5-1 | 0.01 | | 0.02 | 0.04 | 0.84 | 0.03 | 0.03 | 0.01 | 0.01 | | | |
| 6-1 | | | 0.01 | | 0.05 | 0.87 | | 0.05 | 0.01 | | | |
| 3-2 | 0.03 | 0.87 | 0.01 | 0.01 | | 0.02 | 0.01 | 0.03 | | 0.01 | | |
| 4-2 | 0.01 | 0.10 | 0.71 | 0.14 | | 0.01 | | 0.03 | | | | |
| 5-2 | 0.01 | 0.03 | 0.07 | 0.74 | 0.05 | | 0.01 | 0.03 | 0.02 | 0.01 | 0.01 | |
| 6-2 | 0.01 | 0.02 | 0.02 | 0.11 | 0.68 | 0.09 | 0.02 | 0.04 | | | 0.01 | |
| 7-2 | 0.01 | 0.06 | 0.01 | 0.04 | 0.05 | 0.69 | 0.06 | 0.01 | 0.04 | | | 0.01 |
| 4-3 | 0.05 | 0.60 | 0.20 | 0.02 | 0.02 | 0.05 | 0.01 | 0.01 | 0.02 | | 0.01 | |
| 5-3 | | 0.14 | 0.62 | 0.06 | 0.07 | 0.01 | 0.02 | 0.04 | 0.01 | 0.02 | | |
| 6-3 | 0.01 | 0.03 | 0.14 | 0.55 | 0.17 | 0.02 | | 0.03 | 0.03 | 0.10 | | |
| 7-3 | 0.01 | 0.01 | 0.10 | 0.05 | 0.55 | 0.18 | 0.04 | | 0.03 | 0.02 | | |
| 8-3 | 0.02 | 0.03 | 0.03 | 0.01 | 0.15 | 0.53 | 0.06 | 0.13 | | 0.02 | | 0.01 |
| 5-4 | 0.09 | 0.65 | 0.06 | 0.03 | | 0.03 | 0.04 | 0.03 | 0.01 | 0.03 | 0.02 | |
| 6-4 | 0.02 | 0.14 | 0.43 | 0.18 | 0.02 | 0.12 | 0.02 | 0.03 | 0.02 | 0.01 | | 0.01 |
| 7-4 | 0.01 | 0.02 | 0.17 | 0.43 | 0.12 | 0.11 | 0.04 | 0.02 | 0.05 | 0.01 | 0.01 | 0.01 |
| 8-4 | 0.02 | 0.01 | 0.09 | 0.15 | 0.40 | 0.12 | 0.11 | 0.02 | 0.04 | 0.03 | 0.01 | |
| 9-4 | 0.01 | | 0.01 | 0.07 | 0.05 | 0.54 | 0.19 | 0.04 | 0.06 | | 0.01 | |
| 6-5 | 0.05 | 0.69 | 0.06 | 0.06 | 0.07 | | 0.02 | | 0.02 | 0.01 | | |
| 7-5 | 0.01 | 0.10 | 0.44 | 0.18 | 0.13 | 0.01 | 0.03 | | 0.07 | 0.01 | | 0.02 |
| 8-5 | 0.01 | 0.07 | 0.07 | 0.49 | 0.12 | 0.05 | 0.10 | 0.03 | 0.01 | 0.02 | 0.01 | 0.01 |
| 9-5 | 0.02 | 0.03 | 0.09 | 0.06 | 0.53 | 0.06 | 0.07 | 0.05 | 0.05 | 0.01 | 0.01 | |
| 10-5 | 0.01 | | | 0.02 | 0.04 | 0.73 | 0.10 | 0.03 | 0.01 | 0.03 | | 0.02 |

Otherwise, she generates a more elaborate representation of the problem, perhaps by putting fingers up and then down. If she is sufficiently confident of the answer at this point, she states it. Otherwise, she counts the objects in the representation and states the last number as the answer.

Now we can examine the process in greater detail. The first phase (Steps 1–10) is retrieval. Each time a problem is presented, the child randomly selects values for two parameters: a confidence criterion and a search length. The confidence criterion defines a value that must be exceeded by the associative strength of a retrieved answer for the child to state that answer. The search length indicates the maximum number of retrieval efforts the child will make before moving to the second phase of the process.

Next, the child retrieves an answer. The probability of any given answer being retrieved on a particular retrieval effort is proportional to the associative strength of that answer for that problem relative to the associative strengths of all answers to the problem. Thus, the probability of retrieving *1* as the answer to *2-1* would be .87. If the associative strength of the retrieved answer exceeds the confidence

B.  Process

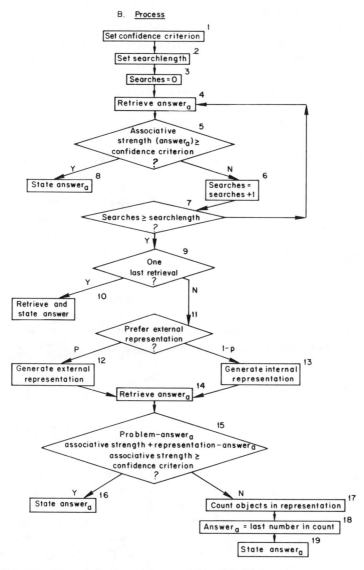

FIG. 6.2.  Process for 5- and 6-year-olds' subtraction.

criterion, the child states that answer. Otherwise, the child examines whether the number of searches that has been conducted is within the permissible search length. If so, the child again retrieves an answer, compares its associative strength to the confidence criterion, and advances it as the solution if its associative strength exceeds the criterion.

If the point is reached at which the number of searches equals the search length, the child may optionally use an alternate form of retrieval. This form could be labeled the "sophisticated guessing approach." It involves lowering the confidence criterion to 0, retrieving one last answer, and stating that answer. The probability of retrieving any given answer is again proportional to the answer's associative strength. Intuitively, this process can be likened to trying to spell a difficult word such as *fusillade,* not having great confidence that any retrieved spelling is correct, and writing out one of the spellings anyway rather than looking up the word in a dictionary or spelling it phonetically.

If the child does not use this sophisticated guessing approach, the next step is to elaborate the representation of the problem. The child can generate either an elaborated external representation or an elaborated internal representation. An elaborated external representation involves putting up the number of fingers indicated by the larger number and putting down the number indicated by the smaller number. An elaborated internal representation involves forming a mental image of the number of objects indicated by the larger number and deleting the number indicated by the smaller number.

Putting up fingers or forming an image adds visual associations between the elaborated representation and various answers to the already-existing problem–to–answer associations. An elaborated external representation involving the child's fingers would add kinesthetic associations as well. We refer to these visual and kinesthetic associations as "elaborated representation–answer associations" as opposed to the "problem–answer associations" discussed previously. Having formed the elaborated representation, the child again retrieves an answer. If that answer's associative strength exceeds the confidence criterion, the child states it as the answer. If it does not, the child proceeds to the third phase, in which she counts the remaining objects in the elaborated representation and advances the number assigned to the last object as the difference.

An example may help illustrate how the model works. Suppose a girl was presented *7–4*. Initially she randomly selects a confidence criterion and a search length. For purpose of illustration, we assume that she selects the confidence criterion .50 and the search length 2. Next she retrieves an answer. As shown in Table 6.1, the probability of retrieving 2 is .17, the probability of retrieving 3 is .43, and so on. Suppose she retrieves 2. The answer's associative strength, .17, does not exceed the current confidence criterion, .50. Therefore, she does not state it as the answer. And because the girl has not yet exceeded the number of searches in her search length, she again retrieves an answer. This time she might retrieve 3. The associative strength of 3, .43, again does not exceed the confidence criterion, .50.

Because the number of searches, 2, has reached the allowed search length, the girl may next use the sophisticated guessing approach in which she would retrieve one final answer from the distribution of associations and state it. If she does not, she next elaborates the problem representation. Suppose that she puts up 7 fingers and then puts down 4, leaving 3 fingers up. She could then count the fingers she has up and state the last number as the answer to the problem. If she counts correctly, she will say "3."

This model accounts for the strategies that children use to subtract, the relative durations of the strategies, and the close relations among the percentage of overt strategy use, the percentage of errors, and the mean solution times on each problem. First, consider how it accounts for the existence of the four strategies. The retrieval strategy appears if children retrieve an answer whose problem–answer associative strength exceeds their confidence criterion (Steps 1–5, sometimes Steps 6 and 7, Step 8). It also appears when they use the sophisticated guessing approach (Steps 1–7, 9–10). The fingers strategy emerges when children fail to retrieve an answer whose problem–answer associative strength exceeds their confidence criterion, put up their fingers, and then retrieve an answer where the sum of the problem–answer and the elaborated representation–answer associative strengths exceeds their confidence criterion (Steps 1–7, 9, 11–12, 14–16). The counting-fingers strategy appears if children fail to retrieve an answer whose problem–answer associative strength exceeds their confidence criterion, put up their fingers, fail to retrieve an answer where the sum of the elaborated representation–answer and problem–answer associative strengths exceeds the confidence criterion, and finally count their fingers (Steps 1–7, 9, 11–12, 14–15, 17–19). The counting strategy is observed if children fail to retrieve an answer whose problem–answer associative strength exceeds their confidence criterion, form an elaborated internal representation, fail to retrieve an answer where the sum of the elaborated representation–answer and problem–answer associative strengths exceeds the confidence criterion, and finally count the objects in the internal representation (Steps 1–7, 9, 11, 13–15, 17–19).

Perhaps the most important feature of the model is that it accounts for the high correlations among percentage of overt strategy use on a problem, percentage of errors on the problem, and mean solution time on the problem. The correlations arise because all three dependent variables are functions of the same independent variable: the distribution of associations linking problems and answers. The more that the associative strength is concentrated in a single answer, the more often retrieval, rather than an overt strategy, is used (because the greater the concentration of associative strength in one answer, the more often the answer that is retrieved would have sufficient associative strength to exceed the confidence criterion and be stated). Because the answer with the greatest associative strength ordinarily is the correct answer, the greater the concentration of associative strength in that answer, the more often the answer is likely to be correct. Finally, the greater the concentration of associative strength in one answer, the greater the likelihood of short solution times because children would retrieve statable answers early in the retrieval process. Thus, the same problems, the ones with associative strengths concentrated in a single answer, would produce frequent use of retrieval, low percentages of errors, and short mean solution times.

The model made a further prediction: that the correlations among overt strategy use, errors, and solution times are due to the patterns of errors and solution times on a subset of trials. Percentage of errors and mean solution times *on retrieval trials,* like percentage of overt strategy use, should depend entirely on the distribution of associations. On these trials a peaked distribution of associations (one where most associative strength is concentrated in a single answer) would lead to fewer errors, shorter solution times, and more use of retrieval. However, errors and solution times on counting-fingers and counting trials should be unaffected by the peakedness of the distribution. Here, children have given up on retrieving a statable answer, so the distribution of associations cannot directly affect errors and solution times. Instead, the number of counts that children would need to make to execute the strategy on that problem should at least partially determine how long it takes to execute and how many errors it elicits. Thus, percentage of overt strategy use on each problem should be more highly correlated with percentage of errors and mean solution times on retrieval trials on the problem than with errors and solution times on counting-fingers and counting trials on it.

These predictions have been confirmed experimentally (Siegler, 1986). Percentage of errors on retrieval trials on each subtraction problem correlated significantly higher with percentage of overt strategy use on the problem, $r=.83$, than did percentage of errors on counting and counting-fingers trials, $r=.25$. When the number of counts required to solve the problem was partialed out from both correlations, the difference remained highly significant, $r=.72$ versus $r=.00$. The correlations involving solution times showed a similar pattern. Solution on retrieval trials on each problem correlated $r=.83$ with percentage of overt strategy use on the problem; solution times on counting and counting-fingers trials correlated $r=.73$ with it. This difference was in the expected direction, though it was not significant. The difference between the correlations became significant, however, when the number of counts was partialed out, $r=.62$ versus $r=.25$. As shown in Table 6.2, similar patterns of correlations have emerged on a number of other tasks.

## How Strategy Choices Develop

The model's basic assumption about acquisition is that people associate whatever answer they state, correct or incorrect, with the problem on which they state it. This assumption reduces the issue of what factors lead people to develop a particular distribution of associations on each problem to the issue of what factors lead them to state particular answers on each problem.

The same three factors are hypothesized to influence acquisition in all of the domains that have been studied. One factor concerns the relative likelihood of errors in executing backup strategies (strategies other than retrieval) on each problem. The more operations, and the more difficult the operations, needed to use a backup strategy, the more likely that errors will be made when using it. For example, solving the problem $6 \times 9$ through repeated addition is more likely

TABLE 6.2
Source of Correlations of Overt Strategy Use with Errors
and Solution Times[a]

A. Zero-Order Correlations

| | Errors | | Solution Times | |
|---|---|---|---|---|
| | Retrieval Trials | Overt Strategy Trials | Retrieval Trials | Overt Strategy Trials |
| Addition | .83 | .51 | .79 | .42 |
| Subtraction | .83 | .25 | .83 | .73 |
| Multiplication | .82 | .58 | .72 | .78 |
| Reading | .69 | .32 | .50 | .12 |

B. Partial Correlations[b]

| | Errors | | Solution Times | |
|---|---|---|---|---|
| | Retrieval Trials | Overt Strategy Trials | Retrieval Trials | Overt Strategy Trials |
| Addition | .67 | .42 | .75 | .10 |
| Subtraction | .72 | .00 | .62 | .25 |
| Multiplication | .43 | .11 | .58 | .02 |
| Reading | .59 | .27 | .34 | .10 |

[a] Numbers in the Table indicate correlations of percentage of overt strategy use on each problem with the variable specified in the Table. For example, the top left value of .83 indicates a raw correlation of $r = .83$ between percentage of errors on retrieval trials on each problem and percentage of overt strategy use on that problem for addition.

[b] The variables partialed out were: in addition, the sum; in subtraction, the size of the larger number; in multiplication, the product; in reading, the number of letters in the word.

to produce erroneous answers than solving $5 \times 3$ in the same way. The former problem requires more additions of bigger numbers. Because people are assumed to associate the answer they produce with the problem on which they state it, learning $6 \times 9$ through use of repeated addition will be harder than learning $5 \times 3$.

The second factor believed to affect the acquisition process is associations with related but separate operations. For example, associations from knowledge of the counting string appeared to influence preschoolers' learning of addition, and associations from knowledge of addition appeared to influence their learning of subtraction and multiplication. The influences include both helpful and harmful effects. As an example of a helpful effect, Siegler (1987a) found that the better known an addition problem (e.g., $2 + 4 = 6$), the easier it is to learn the exact inverse subtraction problem (e.g., $6 - 4 = 2$). As an example of a harmful effect, Siegler and Shrager (1984) found that preschoolers' most frequent error on addition problems where the second addend was greater than the first (e.g.,

3 + 4; 2 + 5) was consistently the number one greater than the second addend (e.g., 3+4 = 5; 2+5 = 6). Similarly, Siegler (1988a) found that a high proportion of errors in multiplication involved stating the answer that would have been correct for addition (e.g., 3 × 4 = 7). Winkelman and Schmidt (1974) and Miller, Perlmutter and Keating (1984) have reported similar interference with adults. Such mistakes seem to come about through confusing less well known with better-known arithmetic operations.

The third factor hypothesized to influence acquisition is frequency of presentation. Parents, teachers, textbooks, and everyday situations present some problems more often than others; this may contribute to superior learning of these problems. Consistent with this view, Ashcraft (1987), Siegler and Shrager (1984), and Siegler (1988a) found that considering frequency of presentation of problems by parents and textbooks contributed significantly to the amount of variance that could be explained in the relative difficulty of addition and multiplication problems. In particular, it helped to explain why tie problems such as 4 + 4 and 4 × 4 were easier than otherwise might have been expected.

Two main types of evidence indicate that these hypotheses about performance and development can account for children's strategy choices in addition, subtraction, and multiplication, the three domains where formal models have been constructed. The two types of evidence are the results of regression analyses and of computer simulations. First consider the results of the regression analyses. These examined the variance in the difficulty of problems that could be accounted for by the three hypothesized developmental factors. The analyses showed that in all three domains, the three developmental factors together accounted for more than 80% of the variance in problem difficulty across the problems examined. Further, within each analysis, each factor individually contributed significant independent variance to that which could be accounted for by the other two.

The second type of evidence involves the results of computer simulations of performance and development in addition, subtraction, and multiplication. Computer models of the acquisition of strategy choices have been developed in each of these areas. These simulations can be characterized in terms of their representation and process at the outset, and in terms of seven features of their operation that result in learning beyond this initial state. Initially, the representation includes only a set of undifferentiated, minimal associations (associative strengths = .01) between each problem under consideration and each whole number within a reasonable range for that problem set (all whole numbers between 0 and 12 for the addition and subtraction problems; all whole numbers between 0 and 100 for the multiplication problems).

The process that operates on the representation to produce performance, and that also embodies the system's capability for learning, is considerably more powerful. It includes both a retrieval mechanism and various backup strategies such as counting fingers in addition and subtraction and repeated addition in multiplication. Retrieval is presumably innate to humans; the backup strategies often are explicitly taught by parents, teachers, and textbooks early in the learning process. Thus, the initial state of each simulation was intended to model children's knowledge early in the learning of each skill—at a point where they generate immature performance but have the capacity to learn.

The way in which the simulations progress beyond this initial state can be summarized in terms of seven features of their operation:

1. The simulation is presented each problem in proportion to that problem's relative frequency either in the textbook used by the children or in parents' presentation of the problems to their children in a laboratory (depending on whether the simulation involves school age children or preschoolers).

2. Before each item, the simulation generates a confidence criterion and a search length. Both are selected by a random process, with the confidence criterion varying from .05 to .95, and the search length from 1 to 3.

3. The simulation next retrieves an answer. The probability of retrieving any given answer is proportional to its associative strength compared to the associative strength of all answers to the problem.

4. A retrieved answer is stated if its associative strength exceeds the current confidence criterion. Retrieval attempts continue until either the associative strength of a retrieved answer exceeds the confidence criterion or the number of searches matches the allowed search length.

5. On 20% of trials on which no answer has yet been advanced, one last answer is retrieved and stated (the sophisticated guessing approach). The probability that a given answer would be retrieved and stated is proportional to its associative strength relative to the associative strengths of all answers connected to that problem.

6. If no answer has been stated, the child executes a backup strategy. In each arithmetic operation, the child first elaborates the representation of the problem, for example by putting up fingers. The visual and/or kinesthetic cues associated with the elaboration may allow the child to state an answer at this point. If not, the child executes an algorithm that is sure to lead to a correct answer if executed correctly. This might involve counting the fingers in addition and subtraction or repeatedly adding the one addend the number of times indicated by the other in multiplication.

7. Every time the system advances an answer, the association between that answer and the problem increases. The increment is twice as great for correct answers, that presumably are often reinforced, as for incorrect answers, that presumably are rarely reinforced.

*Results of the Simulation.*   The simulations have produced performance that resembles that of children in many ways. They generate most of the strategies that the children do. The relative solution times of the strategies are the same.

As with children's performance, use of strategies changes with experience, from a greater use of backup strategies to a greater use of retrieval. The particular errors made also are similar. For example, in multiplication, the two predominant types of errors made by both the children and the simulation are close-misses (errors that are within 10% of the correct answer, such as $6 \times 9 = 52$), and multiplicand-based errors (errors where the answer is a multiple of one of the multiplicands, such as $6 \times 9 = 45$).

Perhaps most important, the simulation, like the children, produces close parallels among percentage of use of backup strategies, percentage of errors, and lengths of solution times on each problem. These relations are evident both in examining the simulation's performance on the three variables, and in examining the correspondence between the children's and the simulation's performance on each variable. The within-simulation correlations (e.g., the correlation between the simulation's percentage of overt strategy use and its percentage of errors) exceeded $r = .90$ for all 3 correlations on all 3 simulations. The simulation–child correlations (e.g., the correlation between the simulation's percentage of errors on each problem and the child's percentage of errors on each problem) equalled or exceeded $r = .80$ on all 3 correlations for all 3 simulations. These parallels indicate that the processes hypothesized by the simulation are sufficient to produce patterns of strategy use, errors, and solution times much like those of children.

## INDIVIDUAL DIFFERENCES IN STRATEGY CHOICES

What are the implications of the strategy choice model for understanding individual differences? The model implies that all children use the same basic strategy choice procedure, involving a process operating on a distribution of associations to produce the various aspects of performance. It also implies that the same learning mechanism produces changes in the distribution of associations, and therefore in performance, over time. However, differences in parameter values within the model could produce substantial individual differences in absolute percentage of errors, length of solution times, and percentage of use of each strategy, even if all children used the hypothesized strategy choice procedure.

To illustrate, consider what would happen if two children used the hypothesized strategy choice procedure, but one child habitually set lower confidence criteria than the other. The first child would use the retrieval strategy more often, and backup strategies less often, even if their distributions of associations were identical. The reason is that for any given distribution of associations, more answers would exceed the lower confidence criteria, and therefore would be stated. Similarly, the first child would have a higher percentage of errors on retrieval trials, because incorrect answers would at times have sufficient associative strengths to exceed the lower confidence criteria.

## An Experiment on Individual Differences in Strategy Choices

We recently conducted an experiment examining individual differences in first graders' strategy choices across three tasks: addition, subtraction, and word identification (reading). In all cases, children were told that they should solve the problem or read the word in whatever way they wanted. The goals were to examine relations across tasks in children's strategy choices, as well as in their errors and solution times.

These particular three tasks were chosen because they allowed a number of potentially interesting comparisons. Several considerations suggested that strategy choices in addition and subtraction would be more closely related to each other than strategy choices in either of them would be to those in reading. Addition and subtraction are both numerical tasks. Children use very similar strategies on them: for example, counting fingers and putting up fingers and answering without counting. Addition and subtraction also appear to be directly related, in the sense that the associative strengths linking addition problems and their answers are highly correlated with performance on the exact inverse subtraction problems (Siegler, 1987a). Finally, addition and subtraction are usually taught by the same teacher using the same textbook; this may contribute motivational similarities (e.g., a child wants very much to do well in math because he like the subject and the teacher, and therefore sets high confidence criteria in both addition and subtraction).

Reading does not share any of these qualities with addition and subtraction. However, other recently completed research suggests that it does share with them the same basic strategy choice procedure. Children seem to first retrieve a pronunciation and state it if they are sufficiently confident; if they cannot do this, they use the backup strategy of overtly sounding out the word. Although the backup strategies differ substantially between the arithmetic and reading tasks, and although some specific motivational factors may vary, the basic strategy choice procedure, along with general motivational factors, may lead to similar performance across domains.

These considerations suggested four types of relations that might emerge among the three tasks.

1. Strategy choices might be similar on all three tasks.
2. Strategy choices in addition and subtraction might be similar, with strategy choices in word identification somewhat related to each of them.

3. Strategy choices in addition and subtraction might be similar, with strategy choices in word identification being unrelated.
4. Strategy choices might be unrelated on the three tasks.

One purpose of the experiment was to determine which of these possible scenarios best described the pattern of individual differences on the three tasks.

A second purpose was to determine whether individual differences across these tasks could be analyzed in terms of children falling into one of several subgroups within the sample. The performance of children within a subgroup would show more similarity to that of others within the same subgroup than to that of children in different subgroups. Thus, the subgroups would provide a characterization of performance at a level higher than the individual child but lower than the total sample. Children within a particular subgroup would be united not only by a common strategy choice procedure but also by similar parameter values within the model, whereas children in different subgroups would share only the common strategy choice procedure. In the present experiment, we examined whether children could be divided into such groups, tested the external validity of a proposed grouping by contrasting the standardized aptitude and achievement test scores of children in different groups, and interpreted the group differences in terms of the strategy choice model's parameters.

## Method

The children were 36 first graders, attending a middle-class suburban public school in the Pittsburgh, PA, area. Their mean age at the time of testing was 81 months. The addition problems were 14 items with sums ranging from 3 to 18 and smaller addends ranging from 1 to 6. The subtraction problems were the 14 exact inverse problems from those presented in addition. That is, for every addition problem such as $8 + 4 = 12$, there would be a subtraction problem such as $12 - 4 = 8$. The reading items were 50 words ranging in difficulty from 2- and 3-letter-words (*in, bed*) to 7- and 8-letter-words (*sandwich, perform*). Each word was printed in lower case letters on a $4 \times 6$ inch index card. The words and arithmetic problems were sampled from those in the children's textbooks— the Addison-Wesley Series in arithmetic (Eicholz, O'Daffer, & Fleenor, 1985) and the Scott Foresman Series (Aaron et al., 1974) in reading. Approximately 70% of the words and problems appeared in lessons that the children had already completed before the time of testing; the remaining items were in lessons that they had not yet encountered.

Each child was brought individually from the classroom to a vacant room in the school and seated at a table directly across from the experimenter. Before each session, the child was told that on that day, he or she would be adding, subtracting, or reading. (A child did only one task on a given day.) Equal numbers of children were presented each of the three tasks in each of the six possible orders. The three tasks were presented on three consecutive school days whenever possible; these usually were literally consecutive days, though at times they were separated by a weekend.

The task instructions emphasized that the child could use any approach to get the right answer: remember it, count on fingers, sound out words, and so on. All that was important was that the child try as hard as possible to be correct.

Each child's behavior was recorded on a videocassette recorder, with digital solution times printed across the bottom of the taped scene. To supplement the videocassettes, the experimenter made notes about the child's observable behavior on each problem where such behavior was detected.

## Results

For purposes of comparability across tasks, the different strategies that children used on each task were reduced to two groups: retrieval and overt strategies. Overt strategies included all trials on which children produced audible or visible behavior relevant to the task between presentation of the problem and statement of the answer; retrieval included all trials on which children did not produce such overt behavior. Thus, in this experiment, backup strategy trials were equated with trials on which *overt* backup strategies were used. A subsequent experiment in which strategy use was assessed by asking children immediately after each trial how they had solved the problem (Siegler, 1988b) indicated that this strategy-assessment procedure may have underestimated the absolute frequency of use of backup strategies, because children sometimes reported using backup strategies on trials where no overt behavior was evident. However, the study also indicated that basing strategy classifications on presence or absence of overt behavior had little effect on the relative number of uses of backup strategies on different problems or on the pattern of individual differences in strategy use, which were the primary issues in the experiment.

Seven measures of each child's performance on each of the three tasks were examined: percentage use of overt strategies, percent correct, median solution time, percentage correct on retrieval trials, percentage correct on overt strategy trials, median solution time on retrieval trials, and median solution time on overt strategy trials. Correlations of each child's performance on the three pairs of tasks were computed for each of the seven measures. The results can be summarized quite simply. On all seven measures, addition and subtraction performance was significantly correlated. The correlations ranged from $r = .48$ to $r = .98$ on the seven measures; on 6 of the 7, the correlation was at least $r = .60$. Performance in reading showed some similarity to that in addition and subtraction, but the relations were weaker and more variable. Of the 14 correlations, 4 were significant: percentage correct on addition and reading, percentage correct in subtraction and reading, percentage correct on retrieval trials in addition and reading, and percentage correct on retrieval trials in subtraction and reading. These significant correlations ranged from $r = .36$ to $r = .61$.

## Good Students, Not-So-Good Students, And Perfectionists

Perhaps the most revealing of the data analyses was a cluster analysis, performed to indicate whether different children's performance fell into characteristic patterns. The input to the cluster analysis was 9 data points for each child: 3 measures (percentage of use of retrieval, percentage correct on retrieval trials, and percentage correct on overt strategy trials) on each of the 3 tasks (addition, subtraction, and reading). The clustering algorithm (PKM) is a nonhierarchical method that establishes a fixed number of homogeneous groups of cases using Euclidean distances (BMDP, 1985). We examined the results when children were divided into two and three groups. The three-groups analysis provided considerably better discrimination among the 9 variables (3 measures on 3 tasks), and therefore is focused on here.

The three groups identified by the clustering algorithm included 12, 9, and 15 children respectively. Performance of the three groups differed significantly on 7 of the 9 task/measure comparison ($Fs < .05$). The only two that did not differ significantly were percentage use of retrieval on the reading task and percentage correct on retrieval trials on the reading task.

To provide convergent validation for the results of the cluster analysis, the groups yielded by it were also contrasted for 6 task/measure combinations that were not used as input to the cluster analysis. These were made up of 2 additional measures on the 3 tasks. The two additional measures were solution times on retrieval trials and solution times on overt strategy trials. Here, the performance of the 3 groups differed significantly ($Fs < .05$) on all 4 of the task/measure comparisons on the arithmetic tasks. The comparisons involving the 2 measures of reading performance did not reach significance, though the pattern of means was similar, and the results for solution times on retrieval trials were very close to significance ($p = .06$).

Perhaps most important, each group's performance was readily interpretable in straightforward terms. For reasons that become evident, we refer to the three groups as the "good students", the "not-so-good students," and the "perfectionists."

The difference between the good and not-so-good students was present along all of the dimensions that might be expected from the names. As shown in Fig. 6.3A, the good students used retrieval more often in both addition and subtraction, though they and the not-so-good students were virtually identical in their frequency of retrieval in reading. As shown in Fig. 6.3B and 6.3C, the good students also were correct more often on both retrieval and overt strategy trials on all three tasks. As shown in Fig. 6.3D and 6.3E, they also were faster in executing the

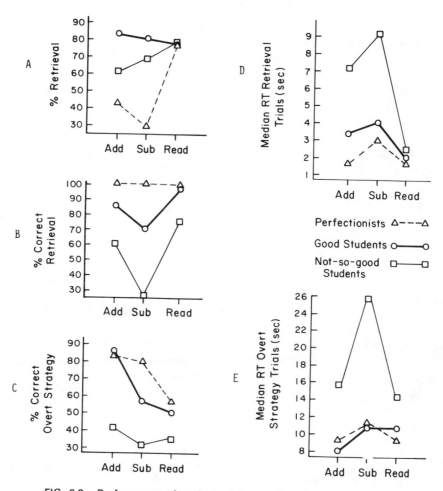

FIG. 6.3.   Performance of perfectionists, good students, and not-so-good students on five measures.

over strategies on all three tasks, and were also faster in retrieving answers on addition and subtraction problems.

The relation of the performance of the "perfectionists" to that of children in the other two groups was more complex. They broke the usual relation among strategy use, errors, and solution times. As shown in Fig. 6.3B and 6.3C, they were the most accurate of the three groups on both retrieval and overt strategy trials. As shown in Fig. 6.3A, however, they used retrieval the least often of the three. This was not due to their having any special difficulty in retrieving. When they did state a retrieved answer, they were the fastest as well as the most accurate of the three groups in doing so (Fig. 6.3D and 6.3E). They just did so less often.

The contrast between the perfectionists' relatively rare use of retrieval, yet excellent performance when they did state retrieved answers, can be seen especially vividly in their absolute levels of performance. On the addition and subtraction tasks (the tasks on which the three groups performed most differently), the perfectionists were correct on 98% of retrieval trials, the good students on 76%, and the not-so-good students on 42%. Despite their facility with retrieval, the perfectionists used retrieval on only 42% of trials, versus 80% for the good students and 74% for the not-so-good ones.

One possible explanation for this pattern is that the perfectionists' superior speed and accuracy on retrieval trials was due to their using retrieval on easier problems. Both the strategy choice model and common sense indicate that children use retrieval primarily on the earliest problems. If this is the case, the fact that the perfectionists used retrieval on only the easiest problems, rather than on both very and fairly easy problems, might account for their greater accuracy and speed relative to the other two groups.

To estimate the contribution of the difficulty of problems on which retrieval was used to the differences in the three groups' accuracy on retrieval trials, an average problem–difficulty score for retrieval trials was calculated separately for each group. The calculation involved multiplying the percent use of retrieval on each problem of children in a particular group by the total sample's percent correct on that problem, and then summing across all problems for that group. Dividing this product for $Group_j$ by $Group_j$'s percentage use of retrieval yields an expected percentage correct retrieval (expected on the basis of the difficulty of the items on which children in the group used retrieval). Thus, the formula for computing the expected percent correct retrieval for the trials on which children in $Group_j$ used retrieval was:

$$\text{EXPECTED \% CORRECT RETRIEVAL FOR GROUP}_j = \frac{\sum_{i=1}^{I} R_{ij} D_i}{\sum R_{ij}}$$

where $I$ = number of problems
$R_{ij}$ = percentage retrieval on problem $i$ by children in group $j$
$D_i$ = percentage correct on problem $i$ across all groups

The results of this analysis indicated that the ease of problems on which retrieval was used by children in each group was part of the explanation of the perfectionists' superior speed and accuracy on retrieval trials, but not the whole story. The problems on which the perfectionists used retrieval were on average easier than the problems on which children in the other two groups used retrieval. Averaging across the addition and subtraction tasks, the expected percentage correct retrieval for the problems on which the perfectionists used retrieval was 80%; it was 68% for the problems on which both the good students and the not-so-good students used it. However, the three groups' actual percentage correct retrieval, 98%, 76%, and 42%, showed greater differences than the differences in expected percentage correct would have suggested. Because the difference between the perfectionists and the good students expected on the basis of problem difficulty was 12%, and because the observed difference was 22%, approximately half of the difference between the two groups in percentage correct on retrieval trials could be attributed to the perfectionists using retrieval on easier problems. Less than one fourth (12%/56%) of the difference between the perfectionists and the not-so-good students could be explained in this way. In sum, when the difficulty of problems on which retrieval was used was taken into account, the perfectionists remained somewhat more accurate than the good students and a great deal more accurate than the not-so-good ones.

*External validation of the groupings.*   Four months after the experiment was run, all of the children in the school were given the Otis-Lennon School Aptitude Inventory (1979 Revision, Form L) and the Metropolitan Achievement Test (1985 Revision, Form R). The Otis-Lennon test yields a measure comparable to an IQ score. The Metropolitan Test included six achievement test scores that seemed relevant to the present experiment: total mathematics, mathematics computation, mathematics problem solving, total reading, word recognition, and reading comprehension. Of these, the mathematics computation and word recognition tests seemed the closest to the skills that were measured in the experiment, the mathematics problem solving and the reading comprehension seemed the farthest measure of the generality of the skills; and the overall mathematics and reading scores seemed the most encompassing measure of the skills tapped.

As shown in Table 6.3, the differences on the experimental tasks between

TABLE 6.3
Aptitude and Achievement Test Scores of Perfectionists,
Good Students, and Not-so-good Students

| Measure | Perfectionists | Good Students | Not-so-good Students |
|---|---|---|---|
| Otis-Lennon | | | |
| School Aptitude | 119 | 120 | 98 |
| Total Math | 86 | 81 | 37 |
| Math Computation | 84 | 68 | 22 |
| Math Problem Solving | 80 | 80 | 38 |
| Total Reading | 81 | 83 | 52 |
| Word Recognition | 79 | 84 | 54 |
| Reading Comprehension | 76 | 83 | 57 |

Note: Otis-Lennon Aptitude Test measure is an absolute score, comparable to an IQ score. Six Metropolitan Achievement Test scores indicate percentiles according to national norms.

perfectionists and good students on the one hand and not-so-good students on the other were echoed in the standardized test scores. The perfectionists and the good students both scored 20 points higher than the not-so-good students on the aptitude test (means of 119 and 120 versus 98). Similar differences showed up on all of the mathematics and reading achievement scores that were examined. Across the 6 tests, the perfectionists' average scores were at the 81st percentile, the good students' average scores were at the 80th percentile, and the not-so-good students' average scores were at the 43rd percentile.

The three groups' achievement test scores also paralleled their performance in the experiment in several more specific ways. In the experimental data, the difference between the perfectionists and the good students was greater on the addition and subtraction tasks than on the reading task, as was the difference between each of these groups and the not-so-good students. This pattern was mirrored in performance on the achievement tests. The perfectionists averaged 16 percentile points higher than the good students on the mathematics computation test, exactly as high on the mathematics problem-solving task, and 5 points higher on the overall mathematics test. In contrast, they scored 5 percentile points lower on the word recognition reading test, 7 percentile points lower on the reading comprehension test and 2 points lower on the overall reading test (there were other subtests on both the math and reading sections of the test that were not analyzed).

With regard to the difference between the not-so-good students and the other two groups, the difference between the average of the other two groups and the not-so-good students was 56 percentiles in the total math achievement score, 55 percentiles on the math computation score, and 42 percentiles on the math problem-solving score. These were all considerably more than the differences of 30 percentiles in the total reading achievement score, 28 percentiles in the word recognition test score, and 22 percentiles on the reading comprehension test. Thus, the aptitude and achievement test performance of the perfectionists, good students, and not-so-good students differed in several specific ways suggested by their performance in the experiment.

*Interpreting the Pattern of Individual Differences.*    How can these differences among the perfectionists, good students, and not-so-good students be explained? Differences in two variables that influence performance within the strategy choice model, the confidence criteria and the peakedness of the distributions of associations, provide a straightforward explanation. Specifically, the pattern of results suggests that perfectionists are children who set very high confidence criteria and have highly peaked distributions; that the good students are children who set somewhat less high confidence criteria and also have somewhat less peaked distributions; and that the not-so-good students set lower confidence criteria and have less peaked distributions than children in the other two groups.

First consider the hypothesis that the perfectionists set higher confidence criteria than children in the other two groups. Within the model, a high percentage of retrieval ordinarily accompanies high accuracy and short solution times on retrieval trials. The performance of the perfectionists defies this pattern, however. Of the three groups, they were the fastest and most accurate on retrieval trials on all three tasks, but also the *least* likely to use retrieval. Within the model, the only way such a pattern would be produced would be if the perfectionists set higher confidence criteria than children in the other two groups. This would lead to relatively infrequent use of retrieval, because the only retrieved answers that would be stated would be ones with very high associative strength. However, such answers, when they exist, would be likely both to be correct and to be retrieved on the first retrieval effort.

In addition to setting high confidence criteria, the perfectionists also appear to have highly peaked distributions of associations. Although they used retrieval on somewhat easier problems than children in the other two groups, the difference in the degree of difficulty was less than the difference in the percentage correct on retrieval trials. One means by which such differences could arise is through differences in relative accuracy in executing the backup strategies. Recall that within the strategy choice model, the more accurately the backup strategies are executed, the more peaked the distributions of associations become. Consistent with this assumption, on all three tasks in the present experiment, a child's accuracy in executing backup strategies was significantly correlated with the child's accuracy in using retrieval. The perfectionists were the most accurate of the three groups in executing the backup strategies. This provided a means through which their distributions of associations could become more peaked than those of other children.

The not-so-good students appeared to have less peaked distributions than either of the other two groups, and also to set lower confidence criteria. First consider evidence that their distributions are less peaked. On all three tasks, the not-so-good students' performance on retrieval trials was both slower and less accurate than that of children in the other two groups. A means by which these less peaked distribution could have evolved was these children's less accurate use of backup strategies. On all three tasks, their execution of backup strategies was much less accurate than that of children in the other two groups. In spite of this lower accuracy, the not-so-good students actually used retrieval more often than the perfectionists on two of the three tasks and as often on the third. Given their less peaked distributions, the not-so-good students must have been setting much lower confidence criteria than the perfectionists.

At first glance, all of the differences between the not-so-good students and the good student might seem attributable to differences in the peakedness of their distributions. As would be expected from the distributions of the not-so-good students being less peaked, they used retrieval on a lower percentage of trials and used it more slowly and less accurately. However, the magnitudes of the differences suggested that they also probably set lower confidence criteria. As shown in Fig. 6.3A, the good students used retrieval on 10% more trials than the not-so-good students. However, they were correct on 28% more of retrieval trials (Fig. 6.3B), and their solution items on retrieval trials were less than half as long (Fig. 6.3D). The combination of less peaked distributions and lower confidence criteria would produce these relations.

This analysis allows an ordering of the three groups along the dimensions of peakedness of distributions and stringency of confidence criteria. With respect to the peakedness of distributions of associations, the perfectionists may have possessed distribution somewhat more peaked than those of the good students. Both the perfectionists and the good students possessed much more peaked distributions than the not-so-good students. With respect to the confidence criteria, the perfectionists set criteria considerably higher than those of children in either of the other groups. The criteria of the good students also were probably higher than those of the not-so-good students. The more aggregate-level differences in mathematics and reading achievement scores that characterized the three groups may stem at least in part from these fine-level differences in distributions of associations and confidence criteria.

## EDUCATIONAL IMPLICATIONS
## OF THE COGNITIVE DIAGNOSES

These analyses of individual differences in strategy choices suggest different recommendations for teaching perfectionists, good students, and not-so-good students. The implications are clearest for the not-so-good students. The poor performance of children in this group seems attributable to two factors: a lack of peaked distributions of associations, and the setting of low confidence criteria. The model suggests remediation strategies for each of these problems.

A strategy that might prove effective in building more peaked distributions of associations would be to teach the not-so-good students to execute their backup strategies more accurately. A basic assumption of the strategy choice model is that the less accurate the execution of backup strategies, the slower the building of peaked distributions of associations. The results of the experiment provided evidence consistent with this assumption at the level of individual children. On all three tasks, a child's accuracy in executing overt strategies correlated significantly with that child's accuracy in retrieval. Teaching children how to execute backup strategies more accurately would be expected to afford them better opportunities to learn the correct answer (i.e., to build distributions with strong peaks at the correct answer). In the case of the reading task, the view implies a strong phonics emphasis for the not-so-good students. This remedy dovetails with the frequent finding that low-ability students benefit especially from phonetically oriented curricula (Chall, 1967, 1979). In the cases of addition and subtraction, it suggests that explicit instruction in how to execute counting-fingers, the min strategy, and other backup approaches would pay dividends for these children.

The other apparent source of the not-so-good students' difficulty was that they set such low confidence criteria that they would state many incorrect answers on retrieval trials. Little is known about why children set the standards they do for stating a retrieved answer rather than resorting to an overt strategy. One possibility is that they adjust confidence criteria in response to their experience with backup strategies. If such backup strategies result in consistently successful performance, children may set higher confidence criteria that would lead to their using backup strategies more often. If the backup strategies do not result in consistently successful performance, children may see little point in investing the considerably greater time needed to use them. From this perspective, helping children execute backup strategies more effectively may by itself lead them to set higher confidence criteria.

Another, not necessarily exclusive, possibility is that children would set higher confidence criteria in response to simple verbal encouragement to do so. Just telling them "It might be a good idea to sound out the word (count out the answer to the problem) unless you are quite sure that your answer is correct" might raise their standards for using retrieval. The two instructional strategies—helping children to more accurately execute backup strategies and verbally encouraging them to set higher confidence criteria—seem worth trying with the not-so-good students.

A quite different instructional approach might help the perfectionists. In some ways, it seems odd to suggest changes at all for children whose overall performance is the most accurate of those in any group, who execute both overt strategies and retrieval the most accurately, and whose mathematics achievement scores are the highest. Even here, however, improvement may be possible, particularly along the dimension of speed. The perfectionists, on average, required 1½ seconds longer to solve each addition problem and 3½ seconds longer to solve each subtraction problem than did the good students. This could not be attributed to slowness in executing either the overt strategies or retrieval. Their average time to use the overt strategies equalled that of the good students and their average time to use retrieval was faster. Rather, their slower times were due to their using the more-time-consuming overt strategies much more often.

Given the exceptionally high accuracy with which these children used retrieval, an average of 97% correct, it might be possible for them to achieve greater speed with little cost in accuracy. Suggesting to them that they experiment with stating retrieved answers when they are pretty sure but not very sure, might lead them to reduce their confidence criteria. If their distributions of associations are already highly peaked, as seems likely given their speed and accuracy on retrieval trials, they might still produce accurate performance while using retrieval on a higher percentage of trials. From the perspective of the strategy choice model, there is no reason to use backup strategies if retrieval produces equally accurate performance. The results of such instructional experiments would have to be carefully monitored, though. Given how well the perfectionists are already doing, it would be essential to tell them to return to their usual way of solving the problems if their accuracy fell off sharply after the new suggestion.

The optimal instructional direction for the good students might be exactly the opposite: persuade them to set higher confidence criteria. Although they used retrieval on almost 80% of trials, the most of any group, their accuracy on retrieval trials was good but not very good (82% correct). Setting somewhat higher confidence criteria might reduce their use of retrieval on difficult problems where their probability of answering correctly is relatively low. Again, though, careful monitoring would be necessary. The good students' combination of speed and accuracy seems sufficiently advantageous that an instructional intervention would best be viewed as fine tuning rather than major overhaul.

These instructional suggestions illustrate the types of benefits that may emerge from fine-grain analyses of cognitive processes and diagnoses of individual differences in execution of those processes. This coming year, we hope to test the usefulness of the recommendations in the classrooms of the perfectionists, good students, and not-so-good students.

## ACKNOWLEDGMENTS

This research was supported in part by Grant #HD-19011 from the National Institutes of Health and in part by Grant #83-0050 from the National Institute of Education. Thanks are due to Miss Hawkins, Miss Perry, and the teachers and students of University Park Elementary of Monroeville, PA, who made the research possible. Thanks also are due to Denise Wilk, who conducted the experiment on individual differences.

## REFERENCES

Aaron, I. E., Artley, A. S., Jenkins, W. A., Manning, J. C., Monroe, M., Pyle, W. J., Robinson, H. M., Schiller, A., Smith, M. B., Sullivan, L. M., Weintraub, S., and Wepman, J. M. (1976). *Studybook: Levels 1-4.* Glenview, IL: Scott Foresman.

Ashcraft, M. H. (1982). The development of mental arithmetic: A chronometric approach. *Developmental Review, 2,* 213–236.

Ashcraft, M. H. (1987). Children's knowledge of simple arithmetic: A developmental model and simulation. In C. J. Brainerd, R. Kail, & J. Bisanz (Eds.), *Formal methods in developmental psychololgy.* New York: Springer-Verlag.

BMDP Stastical Software Manual (1985). Berkeley CA: University of California Press.

Chall, J. S. (1967). *Learning to read: The great debate.* New York: McGraw-Hill.

Chall, J. S. (1979). The great debate: Ten years later, with a modest proposal for reading stages. In L. B. Resnick & P. A. Weaver (Eds.), *Theory and practice of early reading* (pp. 29–55). Hillsdale, NJ: Lawrence Erlbaum Associates.

Eicholz, R. E., O'Daffer, P. G., & Fleenor, C. R. (1985). *Addison-Wesley mathematics*. Menlo Park, CA: Addison-Wesley.

Groen, G. J., & Parkman, J. M. (1972). A chronometric analysis of simple addition. *Psychological Review, 79*, 329–343.

Kahan, L. D., & Richards, D. D. (1986). The effects of context on children's referential communication strategies. *Child Development, 57*, 1130–1141.

Kaye, D. B. (1986). The development of mathematical cognition. *Cognitive Development, 1*, 157–170.

Miller, D., Perlmutter, M., & Keating, D. (1984). Cognitive arithmetic: Comparison of operations. *Journal of Experimental Psychology: Learning, memory, and cognition, 10*, 46–60.

Ohlsson, S. (1984). Induced strategy shifts in spatial reasoning. *Acta Psychologica, 57*, 47–67.

Piaget, J. (1952). *The child's concept of number*. New York: Norton.

Resnick, L. B., & Ford, W. W. (1981). *The psychology of mathematics for instruction*. Hillsdale, NJ: Lawrence Erlbaum Associates.

Shultz, T. R., Fisher, G. W., Pratt, C. C., & Rulf, S. (1986). Selection of causal rules. *Child Development, 57*, 143–152.

Siegler, R. S. (1981). Developmental sequences within the between concepts. *Monographs of the Society for Research in Child Development, 46*(189), 1–74.

Siegler, R. S. (1986). Unities across domains in children's strategy choices. In M. Perlmutter (Ed.), *Perspectives on intellectual development: Minnesota symposium on child development, Vol. 19*, (pp. 1–48). Hillsdale, NJ: Lawrence Erlbaum Associates.

Siegler, R. S. (1987a). Strategy choices in subtraction. In J. Sloboda & D. Rogers (Eds.), *Cognitive process in mathematics*, (pp. 81–106). New York: Oxford University Press.

Siegler, R. S. (1987b). The perils of averaging data over strategies: An example from children's addition. *Journal of Experimental Psychology: General, 116*, 250–264.

Siegler, R. S. (1988a). Strategy choice procedures and the development of multiplication skill. *Journal of Experimental Psychology: General, 117*, 258–275.

Siegler, R. S. (1988b). Individual differences in strategy choices: Good students, not-so-good students, and perfectionists. *Child Development, 59*, 833–851.

Siegler, R. S., & McGilly, K. (1989). Strategy choices in time telling. In I. Levin & D. Zakay (Eds.), *Time and Human Cognition: A life span perspective*. The Netherlands: Elsevier.

Siegler, R. S., & Robinson, M. (1982). THe development of numerical understandings. In H. Reese & L. P. Lipsitt (Eds.), *Advances in child development and behavior, Vol. 16*. New York: Academic Press.

Siegler, R. S. & Shrager, J. (1984). Strategy choices in addition and subtraction: How do children know what to do. In C. Sophian (Ed.), *Origins of cognitive skills* (pp. 229–293). Hillsdale, NJ: Lawrence Erlbaum Associates.

Siegler, R. S., & Taraban, R. (1986). Conditions of applicability of a strategy choice model. *Cognitive Development, 1*, 31–51.

Winkelman, J., & Schmidt, J. (1974). Associative confusions in mental arithmetic. *Journal of Experimental Psychology, 102*, 734–736.

# 7

# Guided Learning and Transfer: Implications for Approaches to Assessment

Joseph C. Campione
Ann L. Brown
*University of California at Berkeley*

## INTRODUCTION

In this chapter, we describe an approach to the assessment of academic status. The goals of the enterprise are to devise assessments that complement the information afforded by standard tests of ability and achievement, and to develop evaluations that can serve to inform instruction. The approach is an attempt to integrate several different lines of research having to do with: (a) dynamic assessment methods; (b) the centrality and interpretation of learning and transfer processes; and (c) the distinction between domain-specific and domain-general processing capabilities. In the remainder of this section, we outline the rationale underlying dynamic assessment approaches in general, enumerate the theoretical reasons for concentrating on learning and transfer processes as indicants of individual differences, and consider the implications of the domain-specific–domain-general controversy for assessment.

In the next two sections, we illustrate our methods and provide an overview of the results obtained to date. The studies reviewed in the first of the two sections were the earliest in the series and were designed to explore the psychometric properties of the learning and scores we generated. They were also concerned with relatively free-content, free-learning skills and their relation to academic ability. In contrast, in the next section, we describe research set in a particular academic domain, early mathematics, and emphasize more domain-specific procedures. In the final section, we outline further questions and directions for future research aimed at integrating assessment and instruction.

## Dynamic Assessment

The first influence involves the contrast between static and dynamic forms of assessment. The major impetus for dynamic assessment is a concern with several perceived limitations of standardized "static" tests. In such tests, students are asked for particular information or required to solve certain types of problems. They work alone responding to the items, and the tester is careful to avoid providing any information that might be helpful. The resulting score is based on the products of their prior history and represents an estimate of current, independent competence. The interpretation of such test results rests strongly on the assumption that all testees have had equivalent opportunities to acquire the knowledge or routines being evaluated. When this condition is not met, the general level of performance an individual attains may represent a dramatic underestimate of his or her potential skill level.

Although approaches to dynamic assessment have differed, a major common feature is the attempt to assess as directly as possible the functioning of psychological processes involved in task performance, rather than to infer their operation from the products of prior experience. In this way, it is argued, it should be possible to identify children who may not have had access to the information or skills being assessed, but who would be able to master them readily if given the opportunity. Our specific approach to assessment was influenced strongly by certain translations of Vygotsky's writings, notably *Mind in Society* (1978), and observations of Soviet clinicians' uses of his ideas (Brown & French, 1979). The "zone of proximal development" was defined by Vygotsky (1978) in terms of the difference between the levels of performance a student could achieve working independently or in collaboration with others. He argued that in evaluating this difference, we would be led to consider, not simply the products of past experience, but also the processes of acquisition themselves. That is, by observing learning in the zone of proximal development, we would glean information about the efficiency with which students could acquire new cognitive resources.

This product–process distinction has been made frequently in the literature on testing (Brown & Campione, 1986; Mann, 1979). In general, developers of dynamic assessment methods modify the testing environment so that it is possible to estimate how readily testees can improve on their unaided performance levels. This modification can take several forms, including altering the problem formats, providing feedback about performance, encouraging reflection, providing instruction in domain-relevant problem-solving strategies, or teaching more general control strategies. Attention is then directed to the ease with which these strategies can be learned, or the magnitude of improvement in task performance that comes about following help. Budoff (1974), for example, distinguished "gainers," those who improve from the initial test to a second test following instruction, and "non-gainers," those whose posttest performance is not much different from that achieved prior to the instruction.

His data support the view that gainer status is a good predictor of later academic accomplishments, providing information beyond that obtained from the original static test. Budoff also found that the sensitivity of the dynamic measures was most pronounced for minority students.

In this context, it is interesting to note that dynamic assessment approaches have been particularly salient to those working with disadvantaged populations. For both Vygotsky (1978) and Feuerstein (1980), a major motivation for their attempts to develop alternative assessment methods was the need to work with individuals who had been exposed to, to say the least, suboptimal learning environments. Vygotsky, in his role as the Director of the Institute of Defectology in Moscow, had the task of dealing with children raised in the aftermath of the Russian Revolution. Feuerstein worked with children who were refugees from displaced persons camps in the wake of the Second World War. In both cases, it was safe to say that those students' opportunities for learning had been severely restricted, and that performance on standard tests would provide virtually no valid information that could be used to guide either classification or instruction. In the case of Vygotsky and Feuerstein, their approach was to observe students as they were actually learning to deal with novel problems, and to use this performance as the basis for prediction.

## Learning and Transfer Processes

The emphasis on assessment of process has a number of potential advantages. The first, already discussed, is the capability of distinguishing poor performance due to impoverished cognitive capacities from poor performance reflecting inadequate opportunities for learning. In addition, the ability to pinpoint the processes distinguishing good from poor performers can provide information that can be used to guide instruction. It is in the latter area, the use of test results to inform instruction, that standardized tests have been most severely criticized (e.g., Brown & Campione, 1986).

Given the decision to pursue a dynamic approach to assessment, there are still a number of remaining issues. The most basic, of course, is exactly what should be assessed. For a number of theoretical and empirical reasons, we have chosen to emphasize global learning and transfer processes. These processes have long had a central place in theories of intelligence and academic ability (e.g., Campione, Brown, & Ferrara, 1982; Campione & Brown, 1984). They are ideal candidates for the kinds of general, relatively content free, processes likely to be involved in students' coming to deal with new academic areas. There are also good empirical reasons for this emphasis.

*Why Learning and Transfer?*    Presumably, the goal of assessment is to evaluate the operation of processes that are exploited differentially by successful and unsuccessful students. To do this requires a theory about the components of successful academic performance and some indication of which components within that theory distinguish students of varying ability. Many hypotheses have been put forth, including durability and capacity of short-term or long-term memory, the speed of executing basic cognitive operations, regulating one's own cognitive resources, and so forth (see Campione & Brown, 1978; Campione, Brown, & Ferrara, 1982, for reviews). To the extent that this theoretical exercise is effective, there are likely to be clear implications for assessment practices; the ability to point to specific areas distinguishing successful and unsuccessful students should provide a basis for suggestions about the contents of diagnostic tests.

Evidence showing that this form of theoretical analysis can result in effective assessment and instruction comes from the memory literature. We reasoned that if some component of performance on memory tasks was hypothesized to be a particular source of difficulty for, say, slow-learning children, then teaching them to execute that component should both improve their performance and reduce the performance differential between them and other, more capable students (see Belmont & Butterfield, 1977; Brown & Campione, 1978; Campione & Armbruster, 1984; Campione & Brown, 1977; Campione et al., 1982, for discussions of the strengths and weaknesses of this approach). For example, our theoretical analysis indicated that poor performance on a certain class of memory problems was due to failure to employ appropriate strategies. Given this, we would predict that instruction in the strategies should have beneficial effects. And this is indeed true (e.g., Butterfield, Wambold, & Belmont, 1973; Brown, Campione, Bray, & Wilcox, 1973); dramatic improvements in memorial accuracy could be achieved.

It should be noted that the design of these instructional studies depended on the development of a theory about memory performance that could be used to specify individuals' strengths and weaknesses. The success of the training programs stands in marked contrast, for example, to that attempted by William James (1890). Lacking a theory of the components of memory performance and of the potential sources of difficulty, he tried to bring about improvement in memory performance through intense practice in memorizing. Almost 40 days of continual practice resulted in no improvement in his ability to memorize (Brown & Campione, 1986).

One feature that emerged regularly from instructional studies was that instruction needed to be extremely explicit and detailed before clear benefits emerged. In these studies, the bottom line seemed to be that the weaker the student, the more the need for detailed and explicit instruction before maximal gains could be expected. A nicely programmatic line of research that corroborated that view was provided by Rohwer (1973), who studied the role of mediational processes in paired-associates learning in children differing widely in age and ability.

The implication of these findings for assessment is that response to instruction be included as a component of test performance. If it is the case that students of varying ability differ with respect to how readily they respond to instruction, this ability should be assessed directly. This conclusion was reinforced by another line of research. In a series of studies in our laboratory, a test–train–test procedure was used. Baseline levels of competence were evaluated, instruction afforded, and then postinstructional levels of performance measured. The main finding for our purposes was a "divergent effect"; groups differing in age or ability performed equivalently during baseline testing, but even though they received comparable instruction—in both content and duration—they differed on the posttest measure, with the older or more capable group outperforming the younger or less capable students (Brown & Barclay, 1976; Brown & Campione, 1977; Brown, Campione, & Barclay, 1979; Brown, Campione, & Murphy, 1974; Day, 1980, 1986; see also Snow & Yalow, 1982). Groups that appeared comparable on the basis of an initial assessment were differentiated following instruction, again the suggestion being that an estimate of response to instruction provides important information about groups of students, more information in fact than their initial level of performance.

If we consider the longer term effects of instruction, another consistent finding emerged. Even when weak students were taught strategies or procedures enabling them to deal with a variety of cognitive tasks, they were reluctant to transfer what they had been taught to novel, but related, situations. In fact, in many cases, students who were taught to execute a strategy correctly, and who performed well during the instructional sessions, would abandon use of the strategy on the exact same task when the experimenter ceased prompting its use. Although these failures of maintenance (Campione & Brown, 1977) could be overcome with extensive practice, it took more serious modifications of the teaching package before any transfer effects could be detected. Even with more explicit instruction designed to increase transfer, weak students appeared able to tolerate only minor changes in task structure before transfer failures recurred (Borkowski & Cavanaugh, 1979; Brown, 1978; Campione & Brown, 1977, 1978; Campione, Brown, & Ferrara, 1982).

The overall picture that emerged from these earlier studies was that the weaker the students, the more explicit the instruction needed to be before they could master what was being taught. Further, even then, they had particular difficulties transferring what they had learned to novel situations, with these difficulties increasing as the similarity between the training and transfer tasks decreased. The suggestion was that the rapidity with which students responded to instruction and the ease with which they transferred the fruits of that learning to related situations should be included directly in assessment packages.

***How Might We Evaluate Learning and Transfer?***    Although the results of these instructional studies did seem to indicate that learning and transfer efficiency may distinguish students of varying academic ability, the evidence remained weak for two reasons. First, most of it was culled from cross-experiment comparisons or from studies demonstrating, for example, what seemed to be extreme reluctance to transfer on the part of weak students. Given the evidence that college students also fail to transfer on many occasions (e.g., Gick & Holyoak, 1980, 1983; Reed, Ernst, & Banerji, 1974), it would be nice to have more direct comparative data bearing on the issues. Second, there was no clear metric of either amount of instruction required, nor of transfer flexibility, built into those studies. Despite these limitations, the data were consistent with the notion that learning and transfer scores, obtained in the course of teaching students rules and principles set within some domain would provide important diagnostic information.

This was instructive, as prior attempts to link either learning or transfer performance with academic ability had been generally unsuccessful. In the 1920s, it was assumed by many that intelligence tests measured the ability to learn—intelligence was identified with the ability to learn (e.g., Buckingham, 1921; Dearborn, 1921). However, in reviewing the studies done in the first half of the century, Woodrow (1946) concluded that there was essentially no relation between intelligence and either learning or transfer performance. The question, then, was how to reconcile our assumptions about the centrality and diagnostic value of learning and transfer processes with that pessimistic history, or, alternatively, how one might design an assessment vehicle that would produce positive results. Our first goal then was to see if we could develop estimates of learning and transfer efficiency that would be sensitive to variations in academic capabilities.

As we have argued elsewhere (Campione & Brown, 1984), the negative findings were obtained in studies where learning was seen as an asocial process dependent primarily on feedback regarding correctness of responses. Subjects worked alone and unaided on the learning tasks. Further, because the dominant theories of the day viewed learning as a very general process that could be observed in virtually any situation, learning was seen simply as improvement with practice, and that improvement could be evaluated on any task. Subjects were asked to learn arbitrary responses in randomly selected contexts, for example, sorting forms (circle, square, etc.) into different boxes. Finally, in part as a consequence of the emphasis on the learning of arbitrary responses, transfer tasks such as sorting colored pegs were chosen without regard to either theories of transfer or metrics of task similarity.

In contrast, we assumed that if we obtained learning and transfer measures that centered on the learning of *rules and principles* of some generality via *guided instruction* set *within a structured domain,* we would be approximating conditions of school learning and hence be more likely to generate metrics that provided diagnostic information about individual students.

It is this view of learning that mapped nicely onto the instructional work we and others had carried out. In that work, learning was socially mediated, and efficiency was seen as the ability to profit from incomplete instruction (see also Resnick & Glaser, 1976). Whereas capable students would adopt a variety of problem-solving or memory strategies when given general hints about their appropriateness, less capable students would require an in-depth exposition and demonstration of the strategy before they would come to use it effectively.

This approach is also consistent with Vygotsky's (1978) general views about learning and development. Vygotsky emphasized that much of learning was socially mediated. Children experience cognitive activities in social situations and come to internalize them gradually over time. At the outset, the child and an adult work together, with the adult doing most of the cognitive work while simultaneously serving as a model. As the child acquires some degree of skill, the adult cedes the child responsibility for part of the job and does correspondingly less of the work. Gradually, the child takes more of the initiative, and the adult serves primarily to provide support and help when the child experiences problems. Finally, the child becomes able to take over complete responsibility for the task and carries it out independently. Within this system, readiness can be regarded as the degree of adult help needed before the child can come to perform independently.

Toward this end, we conducted a series of experiments in which we evaluated how much instruction students needed to come to deal with problems they could not solve individually. The student was set to work on a problem, and the tester/teacher provided a series of hints until the student could solve the problem. The hints provided a form of scaffolding to enable the student to progress. The tester estimated the level of hint required by a student, providing more or less help as needed, just as in "natural" scaffolding. Early hints consisted of quite general indications about the problem, later hints were much more specific, with the tester eventually providing a blueprint for solving a particular problem if the learner failed to catch on. This phase of the process continued until the student could solve an array of target problems with no help from the teacher. The amount of help each student needed was taken as the estimate of learning efficiency within that domain and at that time. It is important to note that the selection of hints rests on a theoretical analysis of the domain being studied. Without such a theory, it is difficult, if not impossible, to determine what hints to give and how to sequence them.

Following this accomplishment, the student was given a series of transfer problems, varying in terms of their similarity to the ones learned originally—again an analysis of the domain is needed to generate appropriate transfer tasks. The idea was to evaluate the extent of lateral transfer (Gagne, 1970) that individuals could accomplish, based on a metric of "transfer distance." Transfer problems were classed as involving near, far, or very far transfer as a function of the number of transformations performed on the learning problems to generate the transfer probes. The amount of help needed to deal with each of the transfer problems was then used as an estimate of the student's "transfer propensity" (Campione & Brown, 1984). This transfer performance was taken as an index of the extent to which the students understood the procedures they had been taught;

that is, having learned the procedures, could they access and modify them in flexible ways.

*Unpacking learning and transfer.*    To this point we have talked as though learning and transfer were global, undifferentiated processes. And this is the view that dominated the early research reviewed by Woodrow (1946). In contrast, current theories regard learning as a highly complex constellation of many separate processes, any set of which might or might not be relatable to academic proficiency, either generally or within a specific domain. The next issue, then, is an analysis of the components of efficient learning and transfer. What does it mean for someone to be an effective learner or a flexible transferrer? Where and how do those who perform well differ from those who do less well? These more detailed analyses are necessary for several reasons. If we can isolate some of the processes that underlie individual differences, we could sharpen our assessment approaches by focusing more directly on them. Second, being able to identify those processes would indicate the form that remedial instructional programs should take. Knowing that a feature of weak students is a failure to monitor their learning activities and progress would make it clear that these monitoring activities should be addressed explicitly in instruction. Our own conclusion from the instruction work we and others have conducted is that learning and transfer differences reflect in good part the operation of a number of "metacognitive," self-regulatory skills, such as planning problem-solving approaches, seeking additional information, searching for and using analogies, monitoring progress, that are at the heart of the poor performance of academically weak students (Brown, 1974, 1978; Brown, Bransford, Ferrara, & Campione, 1983; Campione & Brown, 1978; Campione, Brown, & Ferrara, 1982).

There are several lines of evidence consistent with this emphasis on metacognitive skills. For one, much recent work with academically delayed students has converged on the finding that those students experience particular difficulties with the on-line regulation of their learning activities. Second, for instructional programs to be successful with those students, it is necessary that they include an emphasis on metacognitive activities as part of the training program. Instruction that focuses exclusively on the training of learning strategies that lack explicit instruction in their regulation results in, at best, limited gains (Brown & Campione, 1978; Brown et al., 1983; Campione, 1984; Campione & Armbruster, 1984). Finally, this view is consistent with information-processing approaches that highlight the importance of "general but weak" methods as students begin to deal with relatively new problem domains (e.g., Anderson, 1987; Campione et al., 1982; Newell, 1979).

Given that one assumes that learning rests in good part on the use of these methods, one might ask why our assessment procedures do not aim directly at those processes, that is, attempt to evaluate individuals' ability to plan, monitor, revise approaches, and so on. This is, for example, what Feuerstein (1979) aims to do with his Learning Potential Assessment Device. We have chosen, in contrast, to evaluate the operation of those skills in the context of learning and using domain-specific resources. There are two reasons for this choice.

One is that we believe that the most important role metacognitive skills play is as mediators of learning and transfer, and that they can best be assessed in the context of actually coming to use novel skills within some principled domain. In the final section of this study, we present some evidence consistent with this interpretation. In addition, as we outline in the next section, we believe that situating assessment in particular content areas makes it much more likely that the assessment can serve to inform instruction. Evaluating the operation of self-regulatory processes in the context of mathematics learning, for example, should provide information to those interested in students' mathematical capabilities. Also, such assessments allow the possibility that some students may be efficient regulators of their learning within some domains but not others. That is, rather than assume the domain-independence of these skills, that issue is left as an empirical question.

## Domain-General versus Domain-Specific Assessment

The final factor influencing our approach is a consideration of the domain-generality versus domain-specificity of the processes being assessed. As we have indicated, our preference is to situate assessment within the context of specific academic domains, that is, to evaluate the learning and transfer of, say, mathematics or physics principles. This is not to deny the existence of general processing skills; in fact, some of the results from our work are consistent with the existence of such skills. Rather, we simply want to argue that: (a) there are also important domain-specific skills and procedures that need to be evaluated; and (b) the operation of more general skills *can* vary across domains as a function of variations in the availability of those more specific capabilities. Thus, situating assessment within a specific area has several advantages. First, it should provide more accurate descriptions of individual learners. Second, if we can evaluate processing strengths and weaknesses within a domain, the "leap to instruction" (Brown & Campione, 1986) problem can be reduced. Knowing something about sources of difficulties associated with doing subtraction problems provides information that can be used to design instruction, whereas knowing that someone has an auditory sequencing problem does not.

There is a third, and equally important, advantage, one with strong social policy implications. Emphasizing the potential variability in use of learning and transfer skills across domains and across time within domains reduces the likelihood that diagnoses will be "fixed for all time." When a general intelligence test is given, and a student receives an IQ score of, say, 80, it is frequently assumed that the student is never likely to be capable of a higher level of functioning than that score implies. In contrast, concluding that a student is experiencing particular difficulties at this time with some operations does not imply that similar difficulties will continue to exist in the future.

The requirement for such assessment, of course, is that we have available a good analysis of the processing skills required in various domains, and a good analysis of the domain in question. It is in this area that recent developments in cognitive science fit in nicely. Over the last several years, there has been increasing interest in understanding the requirements and skills involved in a variety of areas, including elementary physics, reading comprehension, early mathematics, and electronics. We believe that the methods we have been developing, coupled with these advances, can result in dramatic changes in the extent to which assessment and instruction can be integrated.

## SUMMARY OF INITIAL FINDINGS

The first experiments were undertaken to see if the learning and transfer scores we obtained had reasonable psychometric properties. Did they distinguish between students of varying abilities? The specific questions concerned concurrent and predictive validity. Would groups of students of higher ability learn more rapidly and transfer more broadly, on the average, than those of lower ability? And, would an individual's learning and transfer scores provide important information about him or her that could not be obtained from standard, static tests? In turn, these "standard, static tests" could be ones tapping either general ability (e.g., intelligence) or domain-specific ability (entering competence in the domain being assessed). The studies addressing these issues involved inductive reasoning skills and are reviewed in the next two sections.

### Concurrent Validity Studies

Several studies were done comparing the performance of students of varying ability (Campione, Brown, Ferrara, Jones, & Steinberg, 1985; Campione & Ferrara, in preparation; Ferrara, Brown, & Campione, 1986), either retarded versus nonretarded or average versus above average students. By way of further introduction to the specific procedures we have used, we describe the task featured in the Ferrara et al. study. The subjects were third and fifth graders of average (mean IQ=101) and above average (mean IQ=122) ability.

The experimental problems, letter series completion tasks, are illustrated in Table 7.1. Each problem consisted of a series of eight letters followed by four blank spaces in which the subject was to complete the pattern. The specific pattern was determined by the combination of a certain periodicity and by certain alphabetic relations (*Next*, the appearance of letters in alphabetical sequence; *Identity*, the repetition of letters; and *Backward-next*, the appearance of letters in reverse alphabetical sequence). On the learning items, the children learned to

TABLE 7.1
Examples of Learning, Maintenance, and Transfer Items

| Problem Type and Pattern[a] | Sample Problem | Correct Answer |
|---|---|---|
| Original learning: | | |
| NN............................................... | N G O H P I Q J  _ _ _ _ | (R K S L) |
| NINI............................................ | P Z U F Q Z V F  _ _ _ _ | (R Z W F) |
| Maintenance (learned pattern types; new instantiations): | | |
| NN............................................... | H Q I R J S K T  _ _ _ _ | (L U M V) |
| NINI............................................ | T J F O U J G O  _ _ _ _ | (V J H O) |
| Near transfer (learned relations and periodicities, but in new combinations): | | |
| NI ............................................... | D V E V F V G V  _ _ _ _ | (H V I V) |
| NNNN ........................................ | V H D P W I E Q  _ _ _ _ | (X J F R) |
| Far transfer (new relation, backward-next; or new periodicity, three letters): | | |
| BN ............................................... | U C T D S E R F  _ _ _ _ | (Q G P H) |
| NBNI ........................................... | J P B X K O C X  _ _ _ _ | (L N D X) |
| NIN.............................................. | P A D Q A E R A  _ _ _ _ | (F S A G) |

Very far transfer ("secret code" items embodying backward-next as well as next relations and "periodicity" of two letters, but relations must be sought between strings of letters rather than within a string)

| Instructions |
|---|
| Pretend that you are a spy. You want to send the message on top in a secret code that only your friends will understand. Someone has begun coding the message for you on the second line. Try to figure out the secret code and finish coding the message by filling in the blanks with the letters that follow the code. |

        SIX SHIPS GONE
        THY RIHQR  _ _ _ _ _ (H N O D)

*Note:* Adapted from Brown and Ferrara, 1985, p. 287. Adapted by permission.
[a] The letters themselves in the pattern notations refer to the alphabetic relations (i.e., N = next, I = identity, B = backward-next). The number of letters in each pattern notation equals the periodicity.

deal with the Next and Identity relations, and with periodicities of two (the *NN* problems) and four (the *NINI* problems).

On each problem, the child and the experimenter worked together to solve the item. If the child could not come up with the correct answer, the experimenter gave a series of hints that provided progressively more information about the solution. These hint sequences differed for each problem type, and a sample, for the *NINI* problems, is given in Table 7.2. The hints are designed to emulate the

TABLE 7.2
Hint Sequence for the Following NINI Problem:
P Z U F Q Z V F _ _ _ _

---

1. "Is this problem like any other you've seen before?" If so: "How did you solve the other problem?"
2. "Read the letters in the problem out loud. . . . Did you hear a pattern in the letters?"
3. "Are any of the letters written more than once in the problem? . . . Which ones? . . . Does that give you any ideas about how to continue the pattern?"
4. "How many other letters are there between the two Z's? . . . And how many other letters are there between the two F's? . . . Does that give you any ideas about how to complete the pattern?"
5. "Are any of the letters in the problem next to each other in the alphabet? . . . Which ones? . . . Does that help you to solve the problem?"
6. "How many other letters are there between the P and the Q in the problem? . . . And how many other letters are there between the U and the V? . . . Does that give you any ideas about the answer?"
7. "Point to the P and the Q in the alphabet . . . and to the U and the V. . . . Does that help at all?"
8. Tester superimposes the "bee" transparency and says: "The bee is flying from the P, skipping three letters, landing on the Q, skipping three more letters, and landing on the *first* blank. If he were going to *continue* that pattern, what letter do you think he'd put in the blank?"
9. Use of the "rabbit" transparency and verbal accompaniment similar to that for the first transparency.
10. Use of the "butterfly" transparency and verbal accompaniment similar to that for the first transparency.
11. Use of the "bird" transparency and verbal accompaniment similar to that for the first transparency.
12. Tester fills in first blank with correct letter (R).
13. Tester fills in second blank with correct letter (Z).
14. Tester fills in third blank with correct letter (W).
15. Tester fills in fourth blank with correct letter (F).

---

processing an expert might go through in solving the problem. Note that they begin by being very general and proceed through more and more specific levels until they provide a formula for generating the correct answer to the stated problem. This joint activity continued until the child solved six problems in a row with no help from the experimenter. The total number of hints he or she required to reach this criterion served as the measure of learning efficiency.

After the children learned to solve these problem types, they were given the sets of maintenance and transfer problems (see Table 7.1). *Maintenance* items involve no transformations, but are simply novel exemplars of the originally learned problem types. *Near transfer* items involve the same principles (relations and periodicities) learned originally but in different combinations. *Far transfer* items involve the application of a novel periodicity (three) or relation (Backward-next). And *Very far transfer* items involve the use of novel principles in a novel context. Again, hint sequences were developed, and the child and experimenter worked together to solve the problems. In this phase, a predetermined number of problems of each type was presented, and the maintenance and various transfer scores consisted of the numbers of hints required for each child to solve the problems.

The results were uncomplicated. Younger students and those of average ability required more hints to solve the original sets of problems than their older and more capable counterparts. Grade and ability differences were also obtained on the transfer items, and the magnitude of the differences increased as transfer distance increased (see Fig. 7.1). There were no significant grade or ability differences on the maintenance or near transfer items—indeed virtually no help was needed on those problems—but differences on the far and very far transfer items were statistically reliable.

Campione and Ferrara (in preparation) repeated this experiment, this time incorporating a comparison of retarded and nonretarded children. Essentially the same results were obtained, with one notable exception. As in the previous study, the groups differed in terms of both their learning and transfer scores; and group differences on transfer increased as transfer distance increased. Also consistent with the previous study, the nonretarded sample required virtually no help to deal with the maintenance and near transfer problems. However, the retarded students did need help, even with these problems; and the differences on those problems were statistically significant.

The final study (Campione et al., 1985) also involved a comparison of retarded and nonretarded students. This study differed from the previous ones in two

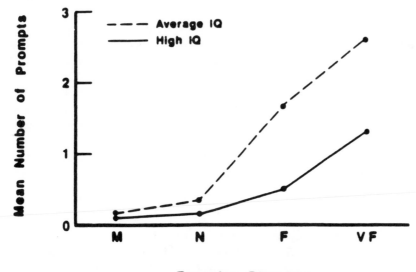

FIG 7.1.   Title TK

ways. First, the problems employed were variants of the Raven Progressive Matrices, rather than letter series completion tasks. Second, the "tutor" was a computer rather than a live experimenter. The PLATO system was used to provide a series of hints, including animation when appropriate, to guide the students to problem solution.

The change in problem types and the nature of the "social" interaction made little difference to the results. In this study the groups of retarded and nonretarded were equated on their ability to solve relevant Raven's problems at the outset. The groups then differed in terms of both chronological and mental age, as well as in IQ scores. Possibly due to this matching procedure, there were no significant group differences obtained during the original learning phase of the study (although the data did favor the nonretarded group). There were, however, large differences during transfer, with the nonretarded students requiring fewer hints than the retarded group. As in the previous study, the nonretarded students took virtually no help on maintenance problems. The retarded group, in contrast, did need help; and the group difference was significant. Transfer performance also differed, with the nonretarded group again requiring less assistance. As in each of the preceding studies, the magnitude of group differences increased as transfer distance increased.

In summary, the learning and transfer indices obtained in the context of guided instruction do possess concurrent validity. Both sets of scores distinguish students of varying academic ability, with the transfer scores doing a more consistent job. Further, the clarity with which the groups are differentiated increases as transfer distance increases. As the need for flexibility in applying what one has learned to the task of solving novel but related problems increases, more capable students show a progressively larger advantage.

In addition to looking at group differences, we can also ask how "far" along the transfer continuum subjects can go before they begin to need help. Viewed in this way, the data are also consistent. Retarded students do not go very far; even on maintenance items (the exact kinds of problems they have learned to solve to criterion earlier) they require some assistance. Nonretarded students, in contrast, needed no help on either maintenance or near transfer probes, but were able to tolerate those variations readily. It was only on far transfer, where new principles had to be discovered, that they needed further guidance. Thus, the retarded groups differ from the nonretarded ones in terms of when they begin to need help, as well as in how much help they need.

## Predictive Validity Studies

Having found that learning and transfer scores could distinguish groups of students differing in ability, we asked whether they could provide diagnostic information about *individual* students. Would the ease with which individuals learned new problem-solving skills, or transferred them to related problems, predict anything about their future performance? Would the dynamic scores provide information beyond that available from knowledge of the person's general ability and/or skill levels prior to any intervention?

Bryant (1982; Bryant, Brown, & Campione, 1983) undertook a series of studies investigating this issue. In an effort to look further at the generality of the effects, Bryant worked with considerably younger children, 4- and 5-year-olds. The problems were again inductive reasoning tasks. The design began with a pretest including both evaluations of general ability (subscales of the WPPSI used to generate an overall IQ estimate and the Raven Coloured Progressive Matrices) and a task-specific pretest. In the latter, baseline levels of performance on the *items to be included* in the learning and transfer sessions were obtained. This was followed by learning and transfer sessions and a final posttest. The posttest was a readministration of the pretest, and our major interest here was with the gain from pretest to posttest performance that resulted from the learning and transfer sessions. That is, in addition to looking at the relation between general ability and learning/transfer scores, we were concerned with the relation between the various static and dynamic scores, on the one hand, and improvement within the domain, on the other. Our expectation was that the best predictors of improvement from the pretest to the posttest would be the dynamic scores.

Two separate studies were conducted, one involving a simplified version of the series completion task and one a simplified version of the matrices task. The major results are shown in Tables 7.3 and 7.4, which show the results of a series of multiple regression analyses. The first thing to note is that there are significant correlations between the ability scores and the learning and transfer metrics, thus replicating the results of the previous studies. Children of higher ability tended to require fewer hints to reach criterion on the original learning problems and to deal with the transfer probes.

TABLE 7.3
Multiple Regression Summary Table for Series Completion Task

| Criterion Variable | Predictor Variable | Zero-Order Correlation | Multiple Correlation | Changes in $R^2$ |
|---|---|---|---|---|
| Training | Block Design | −.48* | .48 | .227* |
| | Vocabulary | −.43* | .68 | .153* |
| Transfer | Block Design | −.58* | .58 | .338* |
| | Animal House | −.48 | .64 | .073 |
| Residual gain | Estimated IQ | .52* | .52 | .272* |
| | Ravens | .35 | .58 | .062 |
| | Training | −.46* | .60 | .020 |
| | Transfer | −.69* | .75 | .221* |
| | Far Transfer | −.56* | .75 | .000 |

* $p<.05$

TABLE 7.4
Multiple Regression Summary Table for Matrices Task

| Criterion Variable | Predictor Variable | Zero-Order Correlation | Multiple Correlation | Changes in $R^2$ |
|---|---|---|---|---|
| Training | Information | −.44* | .44 | .193* |
| | Coding | −.04 | .59 | .152* |
| Transfer | Information | −.39 | .39 | .151* |
| Residual gain | Estimated IQ | .49* | .49 | .235* |
| | Ravens | .47* | .61 | .135* |
| | Training | −.61* | .77 | .224* |
| | Transfer | −.60* | .88 | .173* |
| | Far Transfer | −.70* | .88 | .014 |

*$p < .05$

We are more concerned with the analyses of the residual gain scores. In both cases, the effects of an estimated IQ score—based on the WPPSI subscales—and the Raven Coloured Progressive Matrices score were extracted first. As can be seen, they did account for significant portions of the variance in gain scores. Following this, the effects of the learning and transfer scores were extracted. In both cases, the dynamic scores did account for significant additional portions of the variance in gain scores, 24% in the case of the series completion task and 41% with the matrices. Also consistent across the experiments, the transfer scores did most of the predictive work. Finally, in both studies, if we consider the simple correlations involving residual gain, the dynamic scores were better predictors of gain than the static measures. These patterns are consistent with those obtained in the prior studies, where ability group differences were larger on transfer than during learning. If the goal is to distinguish groups of students differing in ability, or to predict the future trajectory of individual students, the best indicator is performance on the transfer problems.

## Cross-Task Consistency

We have also looked at the cross-task consistency of learning and transfer measures. Two samples of third- and fourth-grade children have been tested on both the letter series completion and modified Raven Progressive Matrices tasks. We reasoned that this comparison would provide a reasonable test of consistency. The tasks are similar at a very general level, both involving inductive reasoning, but also different in important ways, for example, in tapping figural versus verbal processes.

In the first sample, reported in Ferrara et al. (1986), 21 children were included. The learning scores correlated .66 across the two tasks, and the transfer scores .39. A second sample run later involved a total of 23 children, and the learning and transfer correlations were .58 and .55, respectively. All correlations were statistically reliable. Thus, scores obtained in one inductive reasoning task were somewhat predictive of performance in a second.

## Summary

These data indicate the usefulness of the dynamic measures in providing diagnostic information about individual students. Given the task of predicting how well an individual is likely to do in progressing within a domain, his initial response to instruction and particularly the flexibility with which he uses whatever he learns turn out to be more powerful indicants than static tests of either general ability or entering competence. If one wants to be sure that a student is "ready" to proceed further within a domain, the suggestion is that we need to evaluate not simply whether he has mastered sets of rules or procedures, but also the extent to which he can make use of or modify them in the service of solving related problems.

Another major issue for assessment practices is the extent to which the assessment procedure provides information that can be translated into suggestions for instruction. The data from these initial studies do not go far toward that goal, but they were not really intended to. We wished first to establish that the learning and transfer scores we generated from these procedures did possess reasonable psychometric properties, and in that endeavor we were successful. The only suggestion that follows from these data is that it is important to pay attention to transfer performance when designing instruction. Our data, in the context of both assessment and instruction, indicate that simply having students, particularly weak students, master skills or principles is not sufficient to guarantee that they can use them effectively. In the current studies, for example, even after all students learned sets of rules to a fixed criterion, the groups diverged sharply when required to make use of those rules. Although this "suggestion" may appear empty (or obvious) to some, we do not believe that such is the case, at least in the area of special education—and recall that much of our work has been with these populations. In this arena, there is a considerable history of emphasizing the acquisition of subskills involved in complex areas such as reading and mathematics. Individualized intervention programs emphasize drill and practice activities, the goal being to make sure that the "building blocks" of the domain are in place before proceeding to more complex processing. If nothing else, these data can serve to remind us that unless we maintain attention to flexible use of resources that are being acquired, the acquisitions may have less consequence than we would like.

It was partly to work toward the goal of integrating assessment with instruction and partly to evaluate in more detail the utility of dynamic versus static measures that we undertook the next step in the research effort. We wished to leave the domain of inductive reasoning and situate the work in an area that was both richer and of more direct educational interest. The reasons for these interests are elaborated in the next section.

## EXTENSION TO EARLY MATHEMATICS

Having established that guided learning and transfer measures have reasonable psychometric properties, we were interested in extending the method to academically more salient, and conceptually richer, domains. Our choice was early mathematics. This step was taken for both theoretical and practical reasons. Theoretically, there is a dominant view that individual or developmental differences can be explained largely in terms of variations in amount and quality of domain knowledge. In contrast, although not denying the role of knowledge factors, we emphasize the importance of processing skills underlying the acquisition and use of that knowledge. One central issue is, how did individuals come to have different amounts of knowledge in the first place (Brown, Bransford, Ferrara, & Campione, 1983)? The strong interpretation of the knowledge position is that students, equated for amount and quality of knowledge, are equally "ready" to proceed within a domain and should improve at comparable rates. Our contrasting, dynamic view is that students may have taken different routes acquiring that knowledge, and that predictions of future trajectories require an examination of individuals' learning/transfer efficiency as well. Although the results of our early studies were consistent with the dynamic view, they could not be said to provide a particularly strong comparative test. Inductive reasoning tasks are featured on standard ability tests in good part because they do not require much specific background knowledge. Students are thus equated for knowledge by their lack of it.

Mathematics is of course a rich domain, and that richness means there is a good chance that we can develop a sound test of knowledge or competence. The fact that there has been a considerable amount of research on the development of early number and arithmetic skills also means that there is an extensive literature to draw on to guide attempts to develop a comprehensive knowledge test. This endeavor is theoretically important in its own right. To the extent that current theories have identified some of the factors underlying mathematical skill, they should provide cues about the development of a diagnostic test of early counting and mathematics ability. Attempts to use those theories to produce a useful assessment thus provide an indirect evaluation of the theories.

In addition, we are concerned with integrating assessment and instruction. An assessment vehicle that is based on sound theoretical analyses of the skills and knowledge required for performance within a domain does have the potential to provide that kind of information (the child does not have rapid access to number facts, does not understand one-to-one correspondence, counts all rather than counts on, and so on). Thus, we believe that the best way of effecting an assessment–instruction link is to situate the assessment within a particular domain rather than to target presumably general components of cognitive competence (Brown & Campione, 1986).

## Knowledge Assessment

Although we cannot go into detail here, we can summarize some aspects of the knowledge test. Eleven subscores, listed in Table 7.5, are obtained. Three of the subscores reflect the child's knowledge of the conventional number–word sequence. Four are measures of the child's knowledge of basic principles of counting that have been described by Gelman and Gallistel (1978). The final four tap advanced counting skills.

The knowledge test has been administered to several samples of preschoolers with consistent results. Factor analysis indicates the existence of three factors that account for approximately 60% of the variance in test performance. Ferrara identified these factors as: (a) a Verbal factor, having to do with children's knowledge of the conventional number–word sequence and of what one says when counting; (b) a Contextual component, having to do with an appreciation of the contexts in which counting occurs; and (c) an Action component, referring to performance aspects of object counting. In addition, the relations among the three factors indicated the presence of a higher order or general factor involved in early counting ability. It is also of interest that performance on this theoretically based test correlates well with other standardized tests of mathematics ability. The measures were highly related to scores on the mathematics subtest (Part A) of the Stanford Early School Achievement Test administered by school personnel. Performance on that test correlated .71 with the general factor and .69, .69, and

TABLE 7.5
Subscores Involved in Mathematics Knowledge Test

*Knowledge of number–word sequence*
    Rote counting—length of child's count sequence
    Counting-on—ability to count on from a given number
    Backward counting

*Counting principles: Gelman & Gallistel, 1978*
    One–one principle
    Stable order principle
    Cardinal principle
    Order-irrelevance principle

*Advanced counting*
    Counting spatially separated arrays—subsets separated in space
    Counting random arrays—items haphazardly arranged in space
    Generating sets of given numerosity
    Numeral recognition

.26 with the Verbal, Contextual, and Action factors, respectively. Details of this instrument and the data are given in Ferrara (1987).

## Dynamic Assessment

The second phase of the research involved 5-year-old children learning to solve word arithmetic addition and subtraction problems. Ferrara obtained IQ scores, standardized math scores, the initial indices of each subject's ability to solve the targeted problems, along with the knowledge scores derived from the new instrument.

Examples of the learning and transfer problems are shown in Table 7.6. During the initial learning sessions, the student and tester worked collaboratively to solve problems that the student could not solve independently. The problems were simple two digit addition problems, for example, $3 + 2 = ?$, presented as word problems, such as:

> Cookie Monster starts out with 3 cookies in his cookie jar, and I'm putting 2 more in the jar. Now how many cookies are there in the cookie jar?

When the student encountered difficulties, the tester provided a sequence of hints or suggestions about how to proceed. These sequences, a sample of which is shown in Table 7.7, were standardized and proceeded from general to specific. The interaction continued until the student could solve a series of such problems without help, and Ferrara measured the amount of aid needed to achieve this

TABLE 7.6
Numerical Representations of Learning and Transfer Problems

*Original Learning* (Three sums later presented across several toy contexts until mastery is achieved)

| | | |
|---|---|---|
| $3 + 2 = ?$ | $4 + 3 = ?$ | $5 + 4 = ?$ |

*Maintenance* (Three original sums above set in a new toy context and presented in a follow-up session)

*Near Transfer* (New sums of mostly familiar quantities set in the new toy context)

| | | |
|---|---|---|
| $4 + 2 = ?$ | $5 + 3 = ?$ | $6 + 4 = ?$ |

*Far Transfer* (New sums of familiar quantities set in the new toy context, but involving two additions)

| | | |
|---|---|---|
| $4 + 2 + 3 = ?$ | $5 + 3 + 2 = ?$ | $6 + 4 + 1 = ?$ |

*Very Far Transfer* (New sums of familiar quantities set in the new toy context, but the addend is unknown and the sum is prespecified)

| | | |
|---|---|---|
| $4 + ? = 6$ | $5 + ? = 8$ | $6 + ? = 10$ |

*Note:* Items were always set within a supportive toy context and stated in a word-problem format.

## TABLE 7.7
### Hint Sequence Scheme and an Instantiation for the Following Problem

*This* **time Miss Piggy is starting out with** *4* **pennies in her purse (briefly display to the child and then turn away), and I'm putting** *3 more* **pennies into the purse. (Show them in the palm of your hand and then add them to the hidden display.)** *Now* **how many pennies are there** *altogether* **in the purse?**

| | |
|---|---|
| SIMPLE NEGATIVE FEEDBACK | Hint 1.) [If child's response is incorrect but there seems some chance for self-correction, say the following:] That's a good try, but it's not quite right. Do you want to try again? |
| WORKING MEMORY "REFRESHERS" Repeat starting quantity (x) | Hint 2.) [Repeat parts of the problem verbatim if the child requests it or if he clearly was not attending originally. Wherever possible, phrase hint as a question first, e.g., "How many pennies were in the purse to start with?"] Miss P had 4 pennies in her purse . . . |
| Repeat operation Repeat added quantity (y) | 2a.) . . . and I put in some more pennies . . . 2b.) . . . I put in 3 more pennies. So how many pennies does Miss P now have altogether in her purse? |
| NUMERALS AS MEMORY AIDS Represent x numerically | Hint 3.) [If child again forgets the "known" quantities, give the following two hints as necessary.] There were 4 pennies in the purse to start with this time. So why don't you put a number "4" right here [point] on the magnet board to remind yourself? |
| Represent y numerically | 3a.) And since I put 3 more pennies into the purse, why don't you put a number "3" right here [point] to remind yourself of that amount? [Assist, as necessary.] |
| "TRANSFER" HINT | Hint 4.) Why don't you try playing this game like we played the other games? [Not relevant on first problem.] |
| ENUMERATIVE STRATEGY HINTS Suggest general strategy Instruct to make a set of size x | Hint 5.) Why don't you try pretending that each of these wooden knobs is a *penny* and act it out (like you did the other times)? 5a.) Since Miss P had 4 pennies to start with this time, put 4 knobs here [point]. We'll pretend that those are the pennies she had to start with. |
| —Correct set size | 5b.) [Correct quantity placed on board if necessary.] |
| Instruct to make a set of size y —Correct set size | 5c.) And since I put 3 more *pennies* into the purse, put 3 more *knobs* over here [point]. 5d.) [Correct quantity added if necessary.] |

*(continued)*

TABLE 7.7 *(continued)*

| | |
|---|---|
| —Facilitate accurate set formation | 5e.) Count each knob as you put it out. [Demonstrate, if necessary.] |
| " | 5f.) If you leave a little space here between the old knobs and the new ones that you're adding, it's easier to keep track of how many new ones you're adding. [Demonstrate spacing.] |
| " | 5g.) If you place the knobs in a row, they're easier to count. [Assist.] |
| " | 5h.) If you spread the knobs out a little, they're easier to count. [Assist.] |
| Instruct to count-all (of superset) | 5i.) So how many pennies does Miss P have altogether in the purse? You can figure it out by counting all the *pretend-pennies* here [point] in your working space—all these knobs. |
| —Correct counting | 5j.) You counted wrong. [Describe error, if possible.] Try again more slowly and carefully. |
| Instruct on cardinality | 5k.) [If child simply gives the count sequence as the solution . . .] So *how* many pennies are there altogether in the purse? Seven was the last number you counted, so 7 is the number of pennies there are altogether. |
| COMPLETE DEMONSTRATION & RATIONALE | Hint 6.) [If child has needed all of the instructions for implementing the target strategy as well as some strategy corrections or "facilitating tips," give a complete demonstration of the enumerative procedure with rationale.] |
| "STRATEGIC-ORIENTATION" HINT | Hint 7.) [If child did not attempt some reasonable strategy until prodded, say the following:] It's easy to figure out the right answer when you use your magnet board, isn't it? . . . Next time, why don't you act it out with the magnets *right away while I'm showing you the pennies* so you don't forget the numbers? OK? . . . So clear the working space and get ready for the next game. Let's see if you can act out the next one *all by yourself.* |
| "ABANDON-INEFFECTIVE-STRATEGY" HINT | Hint 8.) [If child is using a different strategy that is not always effective, such as number fact retrieval, say the following:] Your way is very clever, but it doesn't always work for you. My way—with the knobs—always works if you do it carefully. So why don't you try it my way unless you're *absolutely positively* sure of the answer? OK? |

degree of competence, that is, how much help does the student need to master the specific procedures?

Following this, Ferrara presented a variety of transfer problems in the same interactive, assisted format. These problems (see Table 7.6) required the student to apply the procedures learned originally to a variety of problems that differed in systematic ways from those worked on initially. Some were quite similar (near transfer: addition problems involving new combinations of familiar quantities and different toy and character contexts); others more dissimilar (far transfer: 4 + 2 + 3 = ?); and some very different indeed (very far transfer: missing addend problems, 4 + ? = 6). What was scored was the amount of help students needed to come to solve these transfer problems on their own. The aim of the transfer sessions was to evaluate *understanding of the learned procedures*. That is, the goal was to both program transfer and use the flexible application of routines in novel contexts as the *measure of understanding*. Can students use only what they were taught originally, or can they go farther and apply their routines flexibly?

After these learning and transfer sessions were completed, a posttest was given to determine how much the student had learned during the course of the assessment/instruction, the gain from pretest to posttest. The question of interest concerns which variables or combination of variables best predict the gain scores. The major data are summarized in Table 7.8. The main features are that the dynamic scores are better predictors of gain (mean correlation $= -.57$) than are the static knowledge and ability scores (mean correlation $= .38$). Further, in a hierarchical regression analysis, although the static scores when extracted first did account for 22.2% of the variance in gain scores, addition of the dynamic scores accounted for an additional 33.7% of the variance, with transfer performance doing the majority of the work; it accounted for 32% of the variance.

There is one additional finding of interest. Note that the IQ variable did not correlate significantly with the gain score, nor did it contribute significantly in the regression analysis, a finding that is discrepant with the earlier patterns. In looking at the knowledge assessment results, Ferrara found considerable variability. She also found that during the learning sessions, approximately ⅓ of her subjects spontaneously developed alternative strategies for solving the problems

TABLE 7.8
Stepwise Multiple Regression on Mathematics
Residualized Gain Scores

| Step | Variable | Zero-Order Correlation | Multiple Correlation | Changes in $R^2$ |
|------|----------|------------------------|----------------------|------------------|
| 1 | Background Knowledge | .47* | .47 | .22* |
| 2 | IQ | .28 | .47 | .00 |
| 3 | Learning | −.41* | .49 | .02 |
| 4 | Transfer | −.73* | .75 | .32* |

* $p < .05$

(alternative in the sense that they differed from the one implicit in the sequence of prompts). These latter children outperformed the remainder of the sample in many ways. They got more items correct on the math pretest, obtained better scores on the knowledge assessment, took fewer hints during the learning and transfer sessions, and showed a larger pre-to-post residual gain score. Interestingly, they did not differ from the remainder of the sample in IQ.

A regression analysis was performed on the 21 remaining subjects, termed novices by Ferrara. The results of that analysis were consistent with that performed on the full sample—with one exception. Whereas in the overall sample, IQ did not correlate significantly with gain ($r = .28$), nor did it account for significant gain score variance, in the novice sample, the IQ–gain correlation ($r = .60$) was significant, and IQ accounted for an additional 17% of the gain variance beyond background knowledge. After knowledge and IQ effects were extracted, the learning (4%) and transfer (32%) scores accounted for an additional 36% of the variance in gain. These results suggest that individual differences in responsiveness to instruction involve a complex interplay of a number of factors, and that the role of these factors may vary with the development of expertise within a domain. Because novices have relatively little prior knowledge of a topic to draw on, they must rely not only on their meager stores of specific knowledge, but also on more general knowledge and skills that they possess (many of which are assessed on IQ tests). However, as they acquire more expertise within the particular domain, this specific knowledge can assume more power in driving further learning within that domain, and may compensate for relatively poorer general intellectual ability. The results, however, also indicate that even *across* stages of expertise, the processes underlying transfer abilities remain extremely important in determining how responsive a child will be to instruction—whether the transfer involves more general knowledge by the novice, or more domain-specific knowledge as the child acquires further expertise within the domain. Thus, responsiveness to instruction is determined not only by what children already *know* (as a number of current theories suggest), but also by their abilities to *apply* recently acquired knowledge to novel but related situations.

## Summary

The results are consistent with those from the earlier studies. Although measures of general ability and task-specific competence do predict the amount of gain individuals achieve, the dynamic measures—learning and transfer scores—are better individual predictors of gain; they account for significant additional variance in gain scores beyond ability and knowledge; and transfer scores are significantly more diagnostic than learning scores. If the interest is in predicting the learning trajectory of different students, the best indicant is not their IQ or how much they know originally, nor even how readily they acquire new procedures, but how well they understand and make flexible use of those procedures in the service of solving novel problems.

## CONCLUSIONS AND SUGGESTIONS

There are two sets of issues driving this research program. One is concerned with the extent to which we can identify those likely to experience academic difficulties in a particular field. Much of our early work on dynamic assessment addressed the first issue. The argument is that observing the products of prior experience may result in underestimating the capabilities of students who have not been exposed to a rich array of potential learning experiences, either specific to a domain or in general. More direct observation of the processes underlying change should supplement the product information and provide a better basis for prediction. The second thrust concerns methods of integrating assessment and instruction. Here we have done less research, but we believe that there are clear suggestions that follow from what has been done thus far. We summarize these issues here.

### Assessment and Prediction

We undertook this program of research on the assumption that measures of learning and transfer efficiency would provide important information about individuals' academic strengths and weaknesses. We chose to treat "learning efficiency" as an inverse function of the degree of explicitness an individual would need to be able to acquire new skills. Similarly, we regarded "transfer propensity" as the extent to which those skills could be applied in novel situations, again as far as possible with little direct input from an expert. We regarded transfer performance as an index of the extent to which students understood the rules, principles, and knowledge they had acquired in the early portions of the experiments. Finally, to look at transfer distance, or the extent of lateral transfer an individual could achieve, we designed test problems that differed in terms of the number of transformations distinguishing the original learning contexts from the various transfer situations. Having chosen this way to assess learning and transfer, we were able to establish clear relations between those processes and overall ability scores—a sharp contrast with the earlier literature.

In the next series of studies, we were also able to show that the dynamic scores were better individual predictors of an individual's likelihood to profit from instruction in an academically interesting domain, early math, than estimates of either general ability or entering domain-specific competence. Also, the dynamic measures accounted for significant proportions of variance in individuals' improvement scores within that domain even after the effects of general ability and domain competence were extracted. The most consistent finding was that the transfer scores were by far the most sensitive indices of individual differences. Even though all students learned the original sets of rules and procedures to the same criterion, the students differed considerably in terms of how flexibly they could apply those resources to related problems; and that capability was the best indicator of how well they would progress in learning that domain.

By way of summarizing the emphasis on "flexibility," there is a consistent picture that emerges from the overall series of experiments. After all students have learned to apply a set of rules to solve a number of problems, students with the lowest ability level or the least understanding of those rules begin to experience difficulties when required not only to execute those rules but also to *select* the appropriate one. This occurs during tests of *maintenance* when the different problem types are presented either in an unpredictable order or in the context of additional problem types. At the next level are situations where students are asked to apply the rules, not singly but in combination. These instances of *near transfer* add an additional bit of information about student capability. Finally, and most sensitive, are cases where students are asked to extend what they have been explicitly taught. On tests of *far transfer,* they must use what they have learned about the relation between problem statements and specific rules or principles, and apply that information to the task of inducing novel principles to solve related but unfamiliar problem types. This far transfer performance both generates the strongest contrast between groups of different ability and is the best predictor of an individual's subsequent performance within the domain. It is what one does with the resources available that is the most accurate index of current capacity. Students with a greater understanding of rules they have learned apply them to a broader range of situations and are able to build on what they know to generate additional rules enabling them to deal with previously unencountered problems.

Beyond the prediction issue, there was another theoretical issue with which we were concerned. We wanted to evaluate contrasting views of developmental and individual differences that emphasized the primacy of knowledge base or processing capabilities as determinants of readiness. To do that required having good estimates of individuals' knowledge in the targeted domain, along with measures of learning and transfer efficiency. Given that information, it would be possible to pit one against the other, knowledge versus process, to see which afforded a better prediction of later accomplishments. The results from the earlier, inductive reasoning studies were consistent with views emphasizing the centrality of processing skills. However, given a weak measure of knowledge and the fact that the domains were designed to eliminate or severely reduce knowledge factors, we could not speak directly to the issue of which was the better predictor. The move to early mathematics was motivated in part by a desire to work in an area where we could develop and use a more thorough and theoretically defensible knowledge assessment vehicle. When this was done, in Ferrara's dissertation, the results continued to support the view that learning and transfer efficiency are the most sensitive predictors of potential for growth within a domain. We do not wish to argue that knowledge factors are unimportant, only that they are not the only or best indicators. It is clear that a theoretically defensible measure of knowledge factors, together with information about process, can paint a clear and detailed picture of an individual's capabilities.

The data from all the experiments converge on the conclusion that if the goal is to distinguish students who are likely to do well within some area from those likely to experience difficulties, estimates of their initial response to instruction and of their ability to make use of newly acquired resources are powerful tools. They also indicate that the most diagnostic indicator is transfer performance. Insuring that new skills have been learned, even to some constant criterion across students, is no guarantee that those skills will be useful subsequently. If we want to monitor progress through a domain, it is essential that we constantly check to see if "acquired" skills can be used flexibly, or whether they remain "welded" or "inert," triggered only by a relatively complete instantiation of the context in which they were learned.

## Integrating Assessment and Instruction

In addition to helping predict how well individuals may do in some domain, it is highly desirable that the assessment process produce some payoff in terms of contributing directly to the instructional process. In one sense, the approach we have taken does this automatically—instruction is an integral part of assessment. While students are being evaluated, they are also being taught something about the domain in question. In the ideal case, the hints that are given are based on a detailed task analysis of the components of competence within the domain; as such, they provide a model of how one should proceed to solve the problems presented. If the hints are internalized to some degree, the subjects acquire relevant skills. That learning does take place is clear enough—in all the studies we have conducted, subjects have shown large gains from the pretest to the posttest.

From our perspective, an ideal way of integrating assessment and instruction would involve the interspersing of dynamic assessment sessions with regular instructional sessions. The assessment segments would provide current information on how quickly individuals were able to acquire *and use* new skills, as well as helping teach those skills. Although the sessions are time-consuming, the fact that the hints are preprogrammed makes it feasible to carry them out on a computer, and we have in fact done that successfully in our own work. As a result, the assessments could be done without taking up teacher time. The main point is that checking regularly for students' ability to use new resources would reduce the likelihood that they are acquiring progressive bits of knowledge that remain encapsulated and relatively inaccessible. If tests of "current competence" are solely in terms of the extent to which particular routines have been mastered and have become usable within familiar contexts, it is easily possible that some students would have acquired a repository of inert facts and procedures.

In addition to signalling that some student may be in particular difficulty, it is also desirable that the assessment process provide specific information about the kinds of help that individual may need to advance more quickly. One approach is to develop sequences of prompts that can be organized qualitatively. In that way, in addition to determining the number of hints individuals require, information about the specific kinds of hints they need would also be available. This information could then be used to devise more specific remedial instruction. For example, Ferrara's hints included simple negative feedback (giving an opportunity for subjects to correct their initial response), verbal memory aids (reminders of the quantities involved in the problem), concrete memory aids, scaffolding (supportive prompts designed to help the child structure the problem), strategy suggestions, and so on. Although we have not run enough subjects as yet to know if the additional information is helpful, this approach is one we are currently pursuing.

## On Learning, Transfer, and Instruction

Another comment concerns an interpretation of the learning/transfer differences, and the implications for instruction. As we described earlier we assume these differences reflect in good part the operation of a class of metacognitive, self-regulatory processes, such as planning problem-solving approaches, looking for analogies, monitoring progress, and so forth. To evaluate this claim requires an in-depth, qualitative analysis of the differences between more and less successful students. Toward this end, we have run a group of students on the PLATO matrices tasks and asked them to provide on-line "talk alouds" as they work on the problems. These data, together with the sequence of instructions they give the computer when trying to generate the correct answer (see Campione et al., 1985), provide a good picture of students' approaches to the task.

The results of these analyses accord well with our assumption. More efficient learners and more flexible transferrers spend more time planning, and analyzing and classifying, the problems before they attempt to offer an answer. They are more likely to take advantage of opportunities to check their reasoning during the course of working on a problem. They are better able to engage in a number of efficient fix-up strategies when they seem to be getting off track. Poorer performers, in contrast, begin generating solutions much more quickly. They try out alternative rules in a fairly random order, trying one to see if it works, and when informed that they are wrong, moving on to another one. When beginning to work on a new problem, they are less likely to refer back to prior problems. Overall, the global learning and transfer indices do appear to reflect the operation of an array of monitoring and self-regulatory skills, or weak but general methods.

The implication of this result for instruction is that programs for students experiencing academic difficulties should emphasize these components of performance. That is, "training for transfer" involves explicit instruction in the orchestration and monitoring of the resources being taught. This suggestion is, of course, quite consistent with many analyses of successful instructional programs.

## On Evaluating Transfer

Having emphasized the importance of transfer phenomena, we conclude by summarizing some of the methods we have used to evaluate transfer proficiency. The goal is to include a range of test items reflecting near and far transfer. This in turn requires some objective method of evaluating transfer distance. We have devised several methods of generating transfer sequences; they all involve making the problem *setting* or *statement* more complex than was the case during the original learning sessions. During those sessions, the students typically learned a set of rules or principles that could be used to solve a set of distinct problem types. The settings were simple in that only a few problem types were involved, and those problem types might be presented in separate blocks. Both factors conspire to make the task of identifying or classifying the problem types quite simple. The statements were also simple in that the problems included all and only the information needed to specify and solve the problems. Following this setup, a continuum of items tapping *maintenance, near transfer,* and *far transfer* was devised.

The maintenance items themselves form a continuum. The defining feature of these items is that they involve the identical problem types dealt with originally. At the simplest level, the same settings and problem statements might be used; that is, the test format is exactly the same as that of the learning sessions. At the next stage, more complicated settings are introduced. Here, the problem types can be presented in an unpredictable order or in the context of additional problem types (types introduced either before or after the specific types being tested). In addition, the problem statement can be modified. For example, in working with algebra word problems, we begin with problem statements that include all and only the numerical information needed to work the problems. On later maintenance tests, we include conditions where: (a) there is not enough information to solve the problem; (b) there is additional, extraneous information provided; and (c) there is enough information available to solve a number of problems, including the stated one.

In each case, the specific application of the rules taught originally is sufficient to solve the problems. Complexity is added by increasing the difficulty of identifying or classifying the problem type and by making it more difficult for the student to extract the relevant information from the problem statement. The next step along the transfer continuum is to near transfer, where the problems cannot be solved by the application of one of the rules. Rather, these problems require the students to invoke novel combinations of those rules. In the system we have used, the defining feature of far transfer probes is the need on the part of the student to discover additional principles that were not explicitly instructed during the original phase of the assessment. Note that this is made possible by the fact that the measure of transfer is a dynamic one. Students are not expected to solve these problems without help (although of course some do). They are given help to do so, and it is the amount of help they take that serves as the indicator of their readiness to proceed.

## ACKNOWLEDGMENTS

Preparation of this manuscript and the research reported therein were supported by Grants PO1-HD-05951 and RO1-HD-15808 from the National Institute of Child Health and Human Development

## REFERENCES

Anderson, J. R. (1987). Skill acquisition: Compilation of weak-method problem solution. *Psychological Review, 94*, 192–210.

Belmont, J. M., & Butterfield, E. C. (1977). The instructional approach to developmental cognitive research. In R. V. Kail, Jr. & J. W. Hagen (Eds.), *Perspectives on the development of memory and cognition* (pp. 437–481). Hillsdale, NJ: Lawrence Erlbaum Associates.

Borkowski, J. G., & Cavanaugh, J. C. (1979). Maintenance and generalization of skills and strategies by the retarded. In N. R. Ellis (Ed.), *Handbook of mental deficiency: Psychological theory and research* (pp. 569–617). Hillsdale, NJ: Lawrence Erlbaum Associates.

Brown, A. L. (1974). The role of strategic behavior in retardate memory. In N. R. Ellis (Ed.), *International review of research in mental retardation* (Vol. 7, pp. 55–111). New York: Academic Press.

Brown, A. L. (1978). Knowing when, where, and how to remember: A problem of metacognition. In R. Glaser (Ed.), *Advances in instructional psychology* (Vol. 1, pp. 77–165). Hillsdale, NJ: Lawrence Erlbaum Associates.

Brown, A. L., & Barclay, C. R. (1976). The effects of training specific mnemonics on the metamnemonic efficiency of retarded children. *Child Development, 47*, 71–80.

Brown, A. L., Bransford, J. D., Ferrara, R. A., & Campione, J. C. (1983). Learning, remembering, and understanding. In J. H. Flavell & E. M. Markman (Eds.), *Handbook of child psychology* (Vol. 3, pp. 77–166). New York: Wiley.

Brown, A. L., & Campione, J. C. (1977). Training strategic study time apportionment in educable retarded children. *Intelligence, 1*, 94–107.

Brown, A. L., & Campione, J. C. (1978). Permissible inferences from the outcome of training studies in cognitive development research. *Quarterly Newsletter of the Institute for Comparative Human Development, 2*, 46–53.

Brown, A. L., & Campione, J. C. (1986). Psychological theory and the study of learning disabilities. *American Psychologist, 41*, 1059–1068.

Brown, A. L., Campione, J. C., & Barclay, C. R. (1979). Training self-checking routines for estimating test readiness: Generalization from list learning to prose recall. *Child Development, 50*, 501–512.

Brown, A. L., Campione, J. C., Bray, N. W., & Wilcox, B. L. (1973). Keeping track of changing variables: Effects of rehearsal training and rehearsal prevention in normal and retarded adolescents. *Journal of Experimental Psychology, 101,* 123–131.

Brown, A. L., Campione, J. C., & Murphy, M. D. (1974). Keeping track of changing variables: Long-term retention of a trained rehearsal strategy by retarded adolescents. *American Journal of Mental Deficiency, 78,* 446–453.

Brown, A. L., & Ferrara, R. A. (1985). Diagnosing zones of proximal development: An alternative to standardized testing? In J. Wertsch (Ed.), *Culture, communication and cognition: Vygotskian perspectives* (pp. 273–305). New York: Cambridge University Press.

Brown, A. L., & French, L. A. (1979). The cognitive consequences of education: School experts or general problem solvers. Commentary on "Education and cognitive development: The evidence from experimental research" by Sharp, Cole, & Lave. *Monographs of the Society of Research in Child Development, 44,* (1–2, Serial No. 178).

Bryant, N. R. (1982). *Preschool children's learning and transfer of matrices problems: A study of proximal development.* Unpublished master's thesis, University of Illinois, Urbana, IL.

Bryant, N. R., Brown, A. L., & Campione, J. C. (1983, April). *Preschool children's learning and transfer of matrices problems: Potential for improvement.* Paper presented at the Society for Research in Child Development meetings, Detroit.

Buckingham, B. R. (1921). Intelligence and its measurement: A symposium. *Journal of Educational Psychology, 12,* 271–275.

Budoff, M. (1974). *Learning potential and educability among the educable mentally retarded.* Final Report Project No. 312312. Cambridge, MA: Research Institute for Educational Problems, Cambridge Mental Health Association.

Butterfield, E. C., Wambold, C., & Belmont, J. M. (1973). On the theory and practice of improving short-term memory. *American Journal of Mental Deficiency, 77,* 654–669.

Campione, J. C. (1984). Metacognitive components of instructional research with problem learners. In F. E. Weinert & R. H. Kluwe (Eds.), *Metacognition, motivation, and learning* (pp. 109–132). West Germany: Kuhlhammer.

Campione, J. C., & Armbruster, B. B. (1984). Acquiring information from texts: An analysis of four approaches. In S. Chipman, J. Segal, & R. Glaser (Eds.), *Thinking and learning skills: Relating instruction to basic research* (Vol. 1, pp. 317–359). Hillsdale, NJ: Lawrence Erlbaum Associates.

Campione, J. C., & Brown, A. L. (1977). Memory and metamemory development in educable retarded children. In R. V. Kail, Jr., & J. W. Hagen (Eds.), *Perspectives on the development of memory and cognition* (pp. 367–406). Hillsdale, NJ: Lawrence Erlbaum Associates.

Campione, J. C., & Brown, A. L. (1978). Toward a theory of intelligence: Contributions from research with retarded children. *Intelligence, 2,* 279–304.

Campione, J. C., & Brown, A. L. (1984). Learning ability and transfer propensity as sources of individual differences in intelligence. In P. H. Brooks, C. McCauley, & R. Sperber (Eds.), *Learning and cognition in the mentally retarded* (pp. 265–293). Baltimore: University Park Press.

Campione, J. C., Brown, A. L., & Ferrara, R. A. (1982). Mental retardation and intelligence. In R. J. Sternberg (Ed.), *Handbook of human intelligence* (pp. 392–490). New York: Cambridge University Press.

Campione, J. C., Brown, A. L., Ferrara, R. A., Jones, R. S., & Steinberg, E. (1985). Breakdowns in flexible use of information: Intelligence-related differences in transfer following equivalent learning performance. *Intelligence, 9,* 297–315.

Campione, J. C., & Ferrara, R. A. (in preparation). Ability-related differences in the learning and transfer of inductive reasoning principles.

Day, J. D. (1980). *Training summarization skills: A comparison of teaching methods.* Unpublished doctoral dissertation, University of Illinois, Urbana, IL.

Day, J. D. (1986). Teaching summarization skills: Influences of student ability level and strategy difficulty. *Cognition and Instruction, 3,*(3), 193–210.

Dearborn, W. F. (1921). Intelligence and its measurement: A symposium. *Journal of Educational Psychology, 12,* 210–212.

Ferrara, R. A. (1987). *Learning mathematics in the zone of proximal development: The importance of flexible use of knowledge.* Unpublished doctoral dissertation, University of Illinois, Urbana, IL.

Ferrara, R. A., Brown, A. L., & Campione, J. C. (1986). Children's learning and transfer of inductive reasoning rules: Studies in proximal development. *Child Development, 57*(5), 1087–1099.

Feuerstein, R. (1979). *The dynamic assessment of retarded performers: The learning potential assessment device, theory, instruments, and techniques.* Baltimore: University Park Press.

Feuerstein, R. (1980). *Instrumental enrichment: An intervention program for cognitive modifiability.* Baltimore: University Park Press.

Gagné, R. M. (1970). *The condition of learning* (2nd ed.). New York: Holt, Rinehart & Winston.

Gelman, R. & Gallistèl, C. R. (1978). *The child's understanding of number.* Cambridge, MA: Harvard University Press.

Gick, M. L., & Holyoak, K. J. (1980). Analogical problem solving. *Cognitive Psychology, 12,* 306–355.

Gick, M. L., & Holyoak, K. J. (1983). Schema induction and analogical transfer. *Cognitive Psychology, 15,* 1–38.

James, W. (1890). *Principles of psychology* (Vol. 1). New York: Holt.

Mann, L. (1979). *On the trail of process: A historical perspective on cognitive processes and their training.* New York: Grune & Stratton.

Newell, A. (1979). One final word. In D. T. Tuma & F. Reif (Eds.), *Problem solving and education: Issues in teaching and research* (pp. 175–189). Hillsdale, NJ: Lawrence Erlbaum Associates.

Reed, S. K., Ernst, G. W., & Banerji, R. (1974). The role of analogy in transfer between similar problem states. *Cognitive Psychology, 6,* 436–450.

Resnick, L. B., & Glaser, R. (1976). Problem solving and intelligence. In L. B. Resnick (Ed.), *The nature of intelligence* (pp. 205–230). Hillsdale, NJ: Lawrence Erlbaum Associates.

Rohwer, W. D., Jr. (1973). Elaboration and learning in childhood and adolescence. In H. W. Reese (Ed.), *Advances in child development and behavior* (Vol. 8, pp. 1–57). New York: Academic Press.

Snow, R. E., & Yalow, E. (1982). Education and intelligence. In R. J. Sternberg (Ed.), *Handbook of human intelligence* (pp. 493–585). Boston: Cambridge University Press.

Vygotsky, L. S. (1978). *Mind in society: The development of higher psychological processes.* (M. Cole, V. John-Steiner, S. Scribner, & E. Souberman, Eds. & Trans.). Cambridge, MA: Harvard University Press.

Woodrow, H. A. (1946). The ability to learn. *Psychological Review, 53,* 147–158.

# The Assisted Learning of Strategic Skills:
## Comments on Chapters 5, 6, and 7

Sherrie P. Gott
*Air Force Human Resources Laboratory*

There are two intersecting themes concerning cognitive diagnosis, instructional treatment, and learning that I wish to consider in this commentary. The themes illustrate the important guiding principles that are shared by what otherwise may be viewed as three highly dissimilar research endeavors. First, like other contributors to this volume, Campione and Brown, Gadd and Pople, and Siegler and Campbell focus their diagnosis *not* on the static products that result from cognitive performances but rather on the explicit *processes* that enable variable types and levels of achievement. More specifically, it is *strategic control processes* such as planning, knowledge deployment, and performance control and monitoring that are targeted.

A diagnostic focus on *strategic* knowledge turns out to have considerable utility. First of all, problem-solving strategies are generally regarded as filling a critical role in skilled performance (Anderson, Boyle, Farrell, & Reiser, 1984; Brown, 1978; Gott, 1989; Greeno, 1978; Kieras, 1987). A strategy establishes the general plan (or approach or goal structure) that guides the solver through the problem space. As a type of performance "blueprint, energizer, and regulator," it deploys the knowledge and skill components that are needed along the way, and it produces the glue that bonds all the detailed steps together. Secondly, strategic knowledge has repeatedly been found to differentiate novice from expert performers in various domains of study. Interestingly, these same strategic control skills are often ignored in traditional instructional programs (Brown, Bransford, Ferrara, & Campione, 1983; Gott, 1989; Soloway, 1986). The conclusion to be drawn from these circumstances is that if not directly taught, strategic knowledge can only be acquired through problem-solving experience. However, once acquired, the experienced performer's strategies and goal structures have a tendency to become highly compiled (to use the computer metaphor) and thus inaccessible to the performer to articulate to a novice learner. In short, strategic knowledge tends to be *tacit* knowledge (Gott, 1989; Greeno, 1978). As a consequence, strategic components seldom become direct targets of instruction because they are not made explicit for learning. Analytic and diagnostic methods that access and represent these vital underlying processes (that is, make them explicit and thus knowable) reduce the "leap to instruction" and strengthen its content with the very skill components that appear to be central to advanced levels of performance and thus to developmental growth and change.

The second theme that connects these three studies is the characterization of instructional experiences as "learning with help." As a pedagogical approach, assisted learning is consistent with the type of socially mediated learning that occurs in naturalistic settings. For purposes of cognitive diagnosis, the level of assistance needed for task performance can be used to gauge an individual's readiness to move toward higher levels of understanding and skill. This view of cognitive skill acquisition takes the following position: In most fields of human endeavor, we reach mature levels of practice through a process of successive approximations. Partial understandings build on each other toward completeness, and limited procedural skills mature and expand to accommodate more task components as well as task variants. During the early stages of acquisition (the initial approximations), the learner needs considerable external support to compensate for voids and weaknesses. In time, the support can be withdrawn as the performance becomes increasingly integrated and complete.

For Gadd and Pople, guided and assisted learning is evident in the Socratic dialogue and the collegial discourse of hospital teaching rounds. For Siegler and Campbell, children's overt, adaptive procedures (e.g., counting fingers) support their early cognitive functioning in arithmetic. And for Campione and Brown, *assisted learning* takes on even greater significance as they formalize the concept in the principles and methods of dynamic assessment. To illustrate the point, the key diagnostic indicator in dynamic assessment is the level of assistance needed by the learner to perform a task. These researchers view one's response to instruction (in terms of assistance required for learning) as the most informative piece of evidence regarding a student's readiness for change, that is, his/her learning potential.

Let me now briefly elaborate each of these themes as they are instantiated in the three studies. My primary foci include (a) the nature of the *strategic processes* that are *modeled* and (b) how the models in turn inform diagnosis and instruction. Of particular interest is how clearly instruction is projected—even blueprinted—by the resulting diagnostic findings.

# MODELING THE PROCESS OF PROBLEM SOLVING

## Medical Expertise

Gadd and Pople are motivated by the goal to improve the teaching of the *process* of medical diagnosis. More specifically, their interest is in intermediate clinical reasoning—the diagnostic stage at which hypotheses are formed and evaluated, and initial lines of reasoning are drawn. (Others have called such activity problem representation and/or strategic planning.) They pursue this goal by studying clinical reasoning as it actually unfolds during hospital teaching rounds, that is, under realistic conditions of use. The objective is to explicate human problem-solving discourse as a means of creating a *clinical* reasoning process model. This approach also enables their distal instructional goal, namely, a computer-based assessment and learning environment directed at creating human–machine interactions that approximate the human problem-solving discourse that is in the model. The instructional system is informed by the modeling of social interactions and the cognitive support processes of human discourse that lead to coherence and synthesis in diagnosis as well as by the tutoring processes displayed by the senior physician/teacher. These latter topics are discussed in a later section that addresses "learning with help."

By focusing on the processes of clinical reasoning situated in actual problem contexts, Gadd and Pople have come to "where the action is" in medical problem solving. Superior achievement in clinical diagnosis depends on the orchestrated contribution of many specialized, multifaceted sources of knowledge (Nii, 1986). Real-time diagnosis establishes the appropriate conditions to exercise and test orchestration (strategic) capabilities as well as the completeness and interconnectedness of the knowledge sources that are activated. The realism of the context also benefits cognitive diagnosis in another way. Problems are often ill-structured in complex domains such as medicine, meaning no well-defined algorithms exist for solution, goals are poorly defined, and/or criteria for evaluating solution acceptability are weak (Newell, 1969). Under such conditions the performer must construct the goals and sequences of actions that are most effective for moving through a problem space. Complicated strategic decision processes are involved. A cognitive model makes those processes explicit for measurement and instructional purposes.

Experts tend to have well-supported decisions that shape the solution paths that they construct. This finding illustrates Clancey's (1986) point that diagnosis is not the name of a disease, (i.e., it is not a static product), but rather it is a dynamic, self-improving *argument*. The evolving argument systematically relates symptom manifestations to responsible agents in cause-and-effect terms. A model of expertise that follows from this view is one of *dynamic opportunistic reasoning,* where optimal solutions are crafted in response to particular situations by applying just the right piece of knowledge at just the right time. Strategic processes are central to deft, opportunistic planning and execution, and yet, as previously noted, such processes are often ignored instructionally. Instead, the multiple declarative and procedural knowledge components of complex performances tend to be taught in isolation, and students are given little direct training in how to integrate and deploy knowledge in clinical contexts. It is precisely this void in medical education that interests Gadd and Pople.

The analytic approach used by the authors for modeling diagnostic reasoning succeeds in capturing the clinical context of building a diagnostic argument by representing the human discourse that occurs during hospital teaching rounds. Transcripts of consultation dialogues between an expert clinician and students and colleagues with varying levels of expertise provide the basic data. From multiple discourse transcriptions, Gadd and Pople have abstracted a process model that defines a general framework for diagnosis. Their data show that the expert diagnostician engages in multiple levels of diagnostic activity; adopts heuristics to focus, constrain, select, and evaluate disease alternatives; displays remarkable data manipulation processes to combine and synthesize partial findings; and perhaps most importantly, continuously feeds back new information to test working assumptions and improve hypotheses.

Though informative, this litany of expert clinical skills is a rather static description of the diagnostician's argumentation tendencies and tools. Of more interest to both cognitive diagnosis and instruction would be a dynamic representation that illustrates how the argument builds and how the tools are used in attacking a problem. The dynamic model that emerges (from the Gadd and Pople work as well as from other studies of expertise in medical problem solving) is one that reveals the building of an evolving diagnostic interpretation (argument) that in its final formal form is both elegant and complete in handling the data. The physician's goal is to create a coherent picture of the disease processes from the partial representations that are triggered by each additional finding. In the beginning, given limited information by way of symptoms, clinical tests, and so forth, the interpretation is very general; however, the early interpretations behave like schemata, establishing expectations for handling subsequent findings. As more data emerge, additional alternative interpretations are considered, but the expert carefully controls the cognitive load with what Gadd and Pople call a heuristic problem-focusing strategy. With this strategy the hypothesis set is kept to a manageable size. The expert uses pragmatic rules and operators to execute the strategy, for example, invoking Occam's razor, which in this case means choosing the simplest of competing hypotheses. At the same time, the expert uses new information to question his assumptions and reformulate his favored hypothesis when necessary.

There are also pedagogical advantages inherent in this *dynamic* process model. As illustrated by the metaphor of overlays used by Gadd and Pople, the "real time" building of the interpretation can be decomposed to reveal both the component structures of the expert's knowledge (including the rich set of associated relations and procedures) as well as the evolving interpretation of the disease processes, including disease subprocesses. The subprocesses in turn decompose into manifestations or clusters of manifestations and causal and/or nosological links between manifestations and diseases.

There is a companion process model of the physician as teacher/cognitive diagnostician that also emerges from the human discourse approach. It bears interesting similarities to the clinical-reasoning model detailed earlier. The physician as teacher works on an evolving interpretation (understanding) of student capability. The interpretation is built through the same synthetic processes of piecing together partial representations of student knowledge into a coherent diagnostic picture, establishing expectations regarding student competence based on previous interactions and new data from present teaching rounds, and consistently testing and modifying assumptions about the student's knowledge and reasoning ability.

In sum, in the Gadd and Pople work we see the following particular strategic processes being modeled: general-to-specific reasoning to construct a diagnostic argument that becomes increasingly complex and explicit and at the same time parsimonious with respect to the data; synthesizing partial findings and opportunistically deploying knowledge structures rich with relations; and carefully regulating performance to (a) avoid cognitive overload, (b) ensure the evolving argument is self-improving by feeding back new findings and continually questioning underlying assumptions, and (c) monitor progress toward solution. These strategic models have high face validity given their origin in *authentic* clinical contexts. However, there may still be a need (as we have found in our work with expert electronic troubleshooters) to *rehash* transcripts with experts to maximize the representation of strategic knowledge that shapes and unifies the sequence of diagnostic steps (Gott, 1989; Gott & Pokorny, 1987).

For example, we have found that experts have specific *reasons* that support the sequence of diagnostic stages—even the order of individual diagnostic steps—that they follow. An expert might elect to pursue $X$ as a probable cause of failure before $Y$, even though the available evidence implicates $X$ and $Y$ equally. The $X$-$Y$ sequence choice may be supported by various reasons, such as efficiency of time and equipment resources. Very often such reasons do not surface even in a more directive verbal protocol session, much less in a sampling of naturalistic human discourse as in the Gadd and Pople approach. Post hoc rehashes could in effect fully establish the rationale for the sequencing of the "overlays," that is, reveal the substance (supporting reasons) that is the glue of the discourse process.

Because the envisioned instructional system (human–machine discourse) described by Gadd and Pople is not yet available to examine, one can only speculate as to how and how well their strategic process models can inform cognitive diagnosis and instruction. The most appealing aspect of the models (for these

purposes) is their evolving character, which allows decomposition of the argu-
ment-building process. With the data taking this form, it is quite easy to imagine
the tutoring system using the decomposed structure of the diagnostic protocols
as the basis for a learning trajectory to map out successive approximations of
clinical expertise. Similarly, diagnostic assessment would also be aided by such
a well-defined course of skill development.

## Arithmetic/Comprehension Skills

In the second study addressed in this commentary, Siegler and Campbell focus
on the processes of performance by studying children's adaptiveness and use of
various decision rules in determining which solution procedure to deploy, given
the features of a particular arithmetic or vocabulary task. The author's *strategy
choice model* depicts a multiphase process where decisions affect procedural
accuracy and speed. The initial phases involve retrieval of the answer from
memory, the quality of which is affected by the length of the memory search the
child is willing to undertake and by the level of confidence the child has in the
retrieved answer. Subsequent phases entail *elaboration* of the problem representation, either through external procedures, such as using and eventually manipulating fingers to visually and kinesthetically model the addition or subtraction
operation, or through elaborated internal representations, such as mentally im-
aging the number of objects specified and eventually operating on that internal
representation to achieve addition or subtraction goals.

The authors report data that support their claim that the strategy choice model
accounts for the high correlations among percentage of overt strategies used on
a problem, percentage of errors on the problem, and problem solution time. In
other words, strategy choice is related to the quality and timeliness of the solution.
The studies reported by Siegler and Campbell also present the argument that
arithmetic knowledge is essentially rule-based in character, meaning that knowledge develops as rules and associations are strengthened through constructive
practice. In point of fact, it is the presence of peaked associations, that is,
strong associations between the arithmetic stimuli in the problems and the correct
responses stored in memory, that Siegler and Campbell interpret as the single
best indicator of level of achievement. In turn, they prescribe instructional remediation that is generally directed at improving or strengthening the associative links.

There are, however, other theoretical frameworks that have proved useful in
characterizing the nature of arithmetic knowledge. For example, a more propositional knowledge-based view of the domain would focus less on rulelike associations and more on the basic principles of counting (Gelman & Gallistel, 1978).
Such principles include the "one–one principle" that every item in an array must
be associated with one and only one unique tag and the *cardinal* principle that
the last tag in a count sequence represents the numerosity of an array. This
alternative theory is mentioned to illustrate the existence of other interpretations

that would posit different sources of difficulty in addition and subtraction operations besides weak associative links.

In the present case, however, the strategic processes that are modeled are postulated to be in the service of developing strong associations between external stimuli and memory stores. Moreover, the authors argue that the strategies reveal the sequence of understandings that children pass through en route to mastery. Both these points are perhaps best illustrated in the author's cluster analysis study to investigate patterns in children's use of strategies. Three distinct groups emerged from the analysis: "good students," "not-so-good students," and "perfectionists." The contrasting strategic patterns are quite interesting. When compared to the not-so-good group, the good students were more accurate, faster, and more adaptive in strategy use. More specifically, their accuracy levels were higher whether they used a retrieval strategy or an elaboration (nonretrieval) strategy. Also, they were *faster* in executing overt strategies as well as in retrieving addition and subtraction answers from memory. They also used retrieval on 10% more of the arithmetic trials than the not-so-good students.

Both accuracy and speed are viewed by Siegler and Campbell as by-products of a concentration of associative strength in a single answer. The stronger the association, the quicker the retrieval process and the higher the likelihood of the retrieved answer meeting imposed confidence criteria and thus being stated. In short, the "good students" used both internal and external strategies with better effect, made better choices in fitting the strategy to the problem, and made better decisions regarding confidence criteria to impose. In contrast, the "not-so-good" students were correct only 42% of the time and took twice as long on retrieval trials, though they used the retrieval strategy frequently (74% of trials). Moreover, and perhaps most importantly, their backup (external) strategies were slow and inaccurate.

These patterns begin to suggest a form of developmental trajectory (or sequencing of understandings, to use Siegler and Campbell's words). Correct *external strategies* appear to be important in the initial stages of learning so that strong associations are built up. Once the associations exist internally, the external support gradually disappears. Without the accurate external strategies, however, learning can be seriously impaired and advanced levels of functioning blocked.

The profile of the third group—the "perfectionists"—supports this developmental view, but it also adds other interesting strategic implications. As reported by Siegler and Campbell, the perfectionists broke the typical pattern of relationships among strategy use, errors, and solution times. They were the *most accurate* of the three groups but used *retrieval* (the fastest strategy and the one that signals internalized representations) *least often*. The opposite might be expected from the most skilled group, that is, a predominance of retrieval trials because of strong, internal associations. The authors interpret this somewhat unexpected outcome to mean that although perfectionists have highly peaked distributions (which account for the accuracy of their solutions), they also set extremely high confidence criteria for retrieval tasks. As a result they generally *reject* answers retrieved from memory, except those with the highest associative strengths, that is, those that can meet the stringent confidence criteria that the perfectionists impose. This group's profile lends further support to the argument of a developmental progression because they were the most accurate of the three groups in executing the external backup strategies.

In sum, although the strategic processes examined by Siegler and Campbell are quite simple compared to physicians' clinical reasoning processes, the general principles guiding this work are the same as for Gadd and Pople: Strategic decisions that activate and regulate knowledge and procedural skill can profoundly affect performance outcomes and therefore need to be studied in their own right and modeled explicitly for purposes of cognitive diagnosis and instruction. In the *strategy choice model,* the authors denote memory activation processes (retrieval) as well as counting procedures as strategies, but the actual strategic processes would appear to be the decision/selection rules that *deploy* the particular process or procedure—decisions that set the length of the memory search, for example, or impose the confidence criteria to be met by the retrieved answer. The developmental or learning trajectory that emerges from this work presents a theory of knowledge/skill acquisition for simple arithmetic tasks. The acquisition process appears to proceed from external to internal elaborations as associative links are established and strengthened. The trajectory as well as the identified strategic processes have important implications for instruction.

Siegler and Campbell propose particular forms of instructional remediation for each of the three groups based on the strategic models and the assumed learning trajectory. For example for the "not-so-good" students, improvement of their backup (external) strategies is proposed, and for perfectionists, encouragement to lower their confidence criteria is recommended. Alternatively, perfectionists could be given practice on problems that they are still solving by external elaborations so that associations are strengthened. It seems rather unlikely, however, that perfectionists would respond to simple encouragement to "lower their standards," and such a tactic may even be ill-advised. Instead, it seems useful to consider engineering the demand characteristics of certain tasks so that *speed* is valued over accuracy in order to prompt a change in strategy by the perfectionists. With no incentive to be speedy, they are probably being sensible by optimizing accuracy. Instruction that directly targets self-regulatory processes such as strategy adaptation is central to the third study, which is addressed next.

## Global Learning and Transfer Skills

Campione and Brown identify their targets of cognitive diagnosis as the psychological processes that are directly involved in cognitive *growth* and *change*—the processes that account for global learning and transfer. They have explicated these processes through empirical assessment and instructional studies. In order to capture *change* processes during "acts of learning," Brown, Campione, and colleagues have developed assessment methods with dynamic properties. The methods target the dynamics of change by assessing the learner's *response* to new instruction (as an index of learning potential) and by constantly updating the learner's diagnostic profile to reflect ongoing developmental progress (not unlike Gadd and Pople's expert physician/teacher). More specifically, the approach tests the boundaries and transfer potential of students' existing capabilities to determine how independently they can use what they already know to solve novel problems.

The results of such dynamic assessments provide informative diagnostic indicators of a student's *readiness* to advance to higher levels of functioning. Readiness in turn is postulated to depend on the availability of certain metacognitive strategic processes that enable the learner to transfer acquired concepts and procedures to the solution of new problems. Campione and Brown report findings from studies in arithmetic and reading comprehension that provide impressive evidence that learning and transfer "readiness" indicators are indeed better predictors of gain—or future learning trajectory—than traditional measures of general ability and task-specific competence.

The metacognitive learning and transfer processes that appear instrumental to learning are similar to those studied by both Gadd and Pople and by Siegler and Campbell, namely, planning, employing adaptive problem-solving strategies, seeking and using additional information, searching for and using analogies, and monitoring progress. Campione and Brown view these components as mediators of learning and transfer that perform on-line regulation of cognition to foster the flexible use of existing knowledge as well as to aid in the acquisition of new knowledge and skill. It is important to examine this mediation function closely in order to be as clear as possible about the strategic processes in question.

In the Campione et al. diagnostic/instructional approach, learning is mediated as the student gains access (via an instructor) to the strategic knowledge that is embodied in tutorial *hint structures*. The objective is to support learning and transfer with gradations of hints that provide feedback and direction for cognitive growth. For example, in Ferrara's (1987) work in arithmetic, the hint structure contains the following levels, or gradations: first, the learner is provided simple negative feedback at a very general level to offer him/her the opportunity to self-correct: "That's a good try, but it's not quite right. Do you want to try again?" The next level provides working memory aids in the form of verbal elaborations, followed by concrete memory aids in the form of visible elaborations such as writing down starting quantities. Next would come more localized assistance or scaffolding such as supportive prompts, and then suggestions (even demonstrations) of strategies to pursue, for instance, a prompt to use an analogy or a suggestion to abandon an inefficient strategy. The mediating strategic processes are designed to emulate the manner in which skilled learners generalize their knowledge and acquire new skill, that is, by using analogies, providing support to working memory, and monitoring progress to reduce inefficiencies.

Several aspects of this hint structure are familiar because the same strategic principles and processes were encountered in the two studies previously reviewed. The model of clinical reasoning derived by Gadd and Pople also follows a general-to-specific progression, and the expert physician employed heuristics to manage the cognitive load on working memory. The students of Siegler and Campbell similarly used elaborations as working memory and performance aids, with concrete, visible support, such as counting fingers, signaling early stages of skill development. A developmental progression from *external,* concrete supports (such as using fingers to assist in counting) to *internalized,* abstract representations characterizes both the skill acquisition process in the arithmetic studies of Siegler and Campbell and the hint structure in Ferrara's study. Finally, both the advanced arithmetic students (Siegler and Campbell) and the expert physician (Gadd and Pople) engaged in self-regulation by imposing stringent standards for acceptable solutions and by continuously evaluating their own progress toward solution by testing underlying assumptions and revising, on-line, the course of reasoning.

Campione and Brown report a body of empirical findings to further support the general role of strategic processes in skilled performance and the particular role of strategic knowledge in learning and transfer. They note that more efficient learners and more flexible transferers work first at a general level of analysis as they represent the problem and plan an approach. In contrast, novice performers begin generating local solutions much more quickly and proceed by trying alternative procedures in random fashion without benefit of a plan or goal structure. Further, the weaker the student, the greater the need for explicit and detailed external support (instruction) that is concrete in nature. They report that weak students can only tolerate minor changes in task structure before transfer failures occur. By comparison, strong students can apply learned routines more flexibly, presumably because they engage in the types of learning and self-regulatory processes modeled in the hints, such as searching for analogies in previously learned problems and monitoring progress to evaluate the adequacy of their current strategy and to generally "check their work." They also tend to have more efficient fix-up strategies to use as self-corrections if they do stray off course.

In sum, Campione and Brown emphasize the role of strategic processes in the *on-line regulation of learning,* much as other investigators (including Gadd and Pople) have identified strategic knowledge as a vital component of advanced forms of experience. Strategic processes are those that produce plans and goal structures, that reduce working memory load during the solution search, that use prior knowledge and procedures as analogical bridges to solutions in novel problems, and that continuously monitor progress so that self-correction and on-line adjustment are efficiently executed. By performing these functions, metacognitive processes are believed to *mediate* learning by enabling partial knowledge structures to grow qualitatively and by enabling brittle procedural skills to gain wider utility and flexibility. The authors support this claim with empirical data that lead to the following general conclusion: "If we want to monitor progress through a domain, it is essential that we constantly check to see if 'acquired' skills can be used flexibly, or whether they remain 'welded' or 'inert,' triggered only by a relatively complete instantiation of the context in which they were learned."

Toward that end, Campione and Brown advocate an integrated assessment–instruction approach, where dynamic assessment sessions are interspersed with regular instructional sessions in order to check the flexibility and generality of acquired knowledge. The assessment segments both diagnose how quickly individuals are acquiring and flexibly using new skills (and thereby progressing in a domain) as well as help to teach the targeted processes. The hint structures that are used in dynamic assessment do, in fact, have inherent instructional value, given the underlying principles of supported learning on which they are based. Also, the concept of supported learning is clearly integral to the acquisition of the strategic processes targeted by Campione and Brown. As a result, their integrated assessment–instruction approach provides a convincing instantiation of the second theme of this commentary—learning with help.

## Summary: Modeling the Strategic Control Processes of Problem Solving

The foregoing account of models of strategic knowledge attempts to make explicit the cluster of metacognitive control processes that are the *common* foci for three research endeavors. In each effort, cognitive diagnosis is targeted at the strategic and self-regulatory processes that enable both advanced levels of competence in a domain as well as learning and transfer, or knowledge acquisition, capabilities. Besides making strategic knowledge (which is typically tacit) *explicit* and thus knowable by learners, the modeling of these metacognitive processes has revealed important features of skill acquisition that help not only to highlight the role of metacognition in learning but perhaps more importantly to bring much needed attention to the construct of *learning trajectories* (or developmental skill progressions).

I refer in particular to the presence across research programs of a developmental transition from heavily (externally) supported performances to independent levels of competence, presumably made possible by internalized skill and knowledge representations. Findings relevant to the course of skill and knowledge acquisition have considerable utility in linking cognitive analysis and diagnosis to instruction. To elaborate the point, diagnosis that focuses on the processes that underlie various levels of achievement also, in effect, postulates a learning continuum comprised of developmental stages of competence (or successive approximations of expertise). Even if the continuum is no more explicit than to reflect movement from externally supported activities to internalized mental representations, as in Ferrara's study, an elaborated hint structure can be generated that moves students toward independent levels of performance in a principled way.

Ideally the three programs of research considered here would have instructional systems at comparable stages of development so that the interplay among cognitive diagnosis, skill acquisition trajectories, and instruction could be uniformly examined. However, such is not the case; nonetheless, it *is* possible to comment on skill acquisition and related pedagogical principles that are either implicitly or explicitly shared by the three programs. In the process, the second theme of this commentary is formally treated.

## ASSISTED, SOCIALLY MEDIATED LEARNING OR LEARNING WITH HELP

I begin with the Campione and Brown research, where instructional programs predicated on the concepts of integrated assessment–instruction and assisted learning are most mature, for example, Ferrara's (1987) work in arithmetic and Brown and Palinscar's (1984) work in comprehension monitoring. (See Brown & Palinscar, 1989, for a review of relevant studies in this area.) In a recent review article, Glaser and Bassok (1989) noted that the instructional principles proposed and followed by Brown, Campione, and colleagues are rooted in certain theoretical conceptions of developmental psychology. One conception has particular relevance to this commentary. It is the notion of the social genesis of learning. This view has been advanced by two leading developmental theorists, among others—Piaget (1926) and Vygotsky (1978). It is in fact possible to trace many of the pedagogical principles seen in the Campione and Brown work (as well as in other studies of naturalistic apprenticeship learning) to this postulate, namely, that much of human learning in naturalistic settings is *socially mediated* (Collins, Brown, & Newman, 1989; Papert, 1980). The social character of the out-of-school learning of adults has even been highlighted recently to call attention to the discontinuity between in-school and out-of-school learning experiences in terms of social context (Resnick, 1987). Consider the following brief illustrations of the point: Children initially experience cognitive activity, such as language development, in social situations, and adults frequently learn and perform in groups or teams, work under the direction of a mentor, with the informal support of colleagues, and so forth.

There are two key elements in such experiences that are critical to skill acquisition: First, an *observable model* of the targeted performance is constantly projected by one or more of the advanced, more skilled participants, and second, the *external support* needed to assist with the knowledge acquisition of the less skilled participants is available via the social context. With scaffolding and other forms of guidance, the learner gradually internalizes the modeled skill and conceptual understandings and acquires the capability to generate the cognitive activity independently, without external models or other forms of social mediation. This model of externally (socially) supported skill acquisition is clearly prominent in the studies considered in this commentary. It is important to note, however, that internalization as a mechanism of learning has yet to be fully explicated, either theoretically or empirically (Glaser & Bassock, in press).

## Campione and Brown

The hint structures of dynamic assessment techniques and the general instructional approach proposed by Campione and Brown emanate from a developmental framework that posits the centrality of social mediation in learning. The mediation occurs as modeling, coaching, scaffolding, and collective problem solving provide pedagogical activities that are rich in socially supportive interactions. The Brown et al. (1983) research group as well as others working in this area report successful instructional interventions where cooperative learning has been effectively used to enhance metacognitive, self-regulatory processes such as comprehension monitoring as well as domain-specific skill acquisition (Brown & Palincsar, 1984; Ferrara, 1987; Ferrara, Brown, & Campione, 1986; Scardamalia, Bereiter, & Steinbach, 1984; Schoenfeld, 1985).

A key feature of the Campione and Brown instructional approach (and related training studies) is the embodiment of *situated* learning. The pedagogy ensures that learning is situated in a structured subject matter domain, as opposed to separating the metacognitive learning skills from the cognitive resources to be regulated, namely, the domain knowledge and procedural skill of a subject matter. Further, learning and transfer skills are clearly (externally) modeled for the learner, and scaffolding is provided as assistance to foster internalization of the modeled skills. More specifically, the social setting enables a *joint* negotiation of understanding where the adult begins as model, critic, and interrogator and gradually relinquishes these functions as children assume responsibility for their own self-regulatory processes. As previously noted, the principle indicator of learning in this approach is the extent to which procedures are well enough understood to be extended, modified, and otherwise flexibly applied, given varying levels of assistance. In effect, the level of assistance one needs to learn and perform as instructed reveals vital (diagnostic) information regarding the internalized character, completeness, and flexibility of knowledge and skill. The instructor then uses the diagnostic results to "calibrate" (adapt) subsequent instructional events.

## Gadd and Pople

Socially mediated learning is likewise the context in which Gadd and Pople have chosen to model clinical diagnostic reasoning. It is, in fact, their pedagogical interest in the cognitive support processes and social interactions of human discourse that is responsible for the selected modeling and learning context, that is, hospital teaching rounds. As with Campione and Brown, their pedagogy embraces socially supported, situated learning; explicit, observable models of expert reasoning; joint negotiation of understanding; and adaptive (dynamic) tutoring calibrated to student developmental progress. These dimensions have emerged from a tutorial process model of the expert physician/teacher who directs the teaching rounds.

The general pedagogical approach of the modeled teacher–physician is a form of expanded Socratic dialogue where interrogation of student understanding by the master teacher is supplemented with group discourse. In the expanded group context, a cooperative exchange of viewpoints, understandings, and interpretations among participating physicians occurs. In effect, the Socratic dialogue, which is inherent in hospital teaching rounds, is viewed as "explicitly reflective," meaning that the reasoning processes, conceptions, and interpretations generated by the student (and the group in general) are examined and reflected upon as the group attempts to produce a coherent and elegant diagnostic argument. For example, the expert physician/teacher requires students to explain statements, defend conclusions, and evaluate the assumptions of favored hypotheses when new data suggest that previously suppressed alternatives should be examined. In the process, the teaching physician attempts to generate on-line a model of each student's present level of competence so that the tutoring dialogue can be adapted accordingly.

The student modeling/diagnosis engaged in by the teaching physician is specifically informed by the student's *response to instruction* from him and/or the group—for example, how the student defends against or assimilates a suggested alternative hypothesis to explain emergent findings. Similarities to the Campione and Brown dynamic assessment approach are obvious. Further, the second critical element of socially mediated learning is satisfied in the teaching rounds context as the teacher–physician *models* the synthetic nature of problem solving. Various interpretations of the data (and their underlying assumptions) are examined and evaluated as new findings are encountered, and the use of early findings to establish expectations (schemata) as a rational guide to subsequent inquiry is made visible to the student physicians.

This expanded, socially supported form of Socratic diaglogue maps quite well onto the Campione and Brown concept of an integrated assessment–instructional system. An integrated system of this form is in fact the distal instructional goal of Gadd and Pople's work. They envision their system as facilitating a natural consultation dialogue among physicians. In the enhanced Caduceus system, they foresee a computerized consultation environment where important features of human medical discourse are emulated so that "more collegial joint man–machine problem-solving experiences" can be afforded to medical students. The socially supported, machine learning environment is intended to mirror (as possible) the assisted learning context of hospital teaching rounds.

## Siegler and Campbell

In the Siegler and Campbell study, cognitive activity is clearly supported by external aids such as overt finger-counting strategies, but the concept of *socially* supported learning is not explored. As these investigations extend this line of research to the design and eventual empirical test of arithmetic and/or vocabulary comprehension training studies, they might consider pedagogical approaches where cooperative learning contexts are used. Existing models of effective, socially mediated instruction in these domains with similar age groups are available (Brown & Palinscar, 1984, 1989; Bransford, Sherwood, Vye, & Rieser, 1986).

To take the suggestion a bit further, consider the fact that in the diagnosis-oriented work reported here, children who are better performers not only have superior external counting strategies but they have learned *when* to deploy such backup strategies and when to rely on internalized representations (i.e., learned associations). One can imagine cooperative learning instructional scenarios where these advanced performers could provide models and scaffolding for less skilled children whose overt procedures are underdeveloped. Similarly, the superior performers could provide explicit models of the strategic processes to use in deciding when to use external versus internal counting procedures by verbalizing their own decision-making processes. Such reflection on their own decision processes may even turn out to be sufficient "self-scaffolding" for the perfectionists to increase the flexibility of their own strategic choice processes, such as recognizing conditions under which to optimize speed over accuracy.

## SUMMATION

On the surface, studies directed at physicians' clinical reasoning, children's arithmetic and vocabulary understandings, and the global learning and transfer processes of a range of learners across several subject matter domains would appear to share little common ground. On closer examination, however, one finds that these three endeavors work from similar principles regarding cognitive models, diagnosis and assessment, knowledge acquisition, learning trajectories, and instruction. Although the observable performances of the three sets of learners are quite different, a common core of underlying metacognitive processes appears to operate to structure, deploy, regulate, and indeed extend their domain-specific cognitive resources, whether they be medical concepts, arithmetic rules, or vocabulary knowledge. What makes this collection of studies important to diagnostic assessment and instruction is their focus on these influential control processes.

Although strategic knowledge has been clearly established as a distinguishing dimension of skilled performance, the processes that produce plans and goal structures, regulate cognition to maximize efficiency and effectiveness, and foster learning are seldom the *targets* of instruction. Instead, learners are generally taught the domain specific resources, for instance, declarative knowledge and procedural operations, in isolated, unnatural contexts, not under their natural conditions of use. It has been by preserving the natural conditions of knowledge use in cognitive task analysis studies that our understanding of how knowledge is deployed and generalized has grown. Similar conditions should be injected into instruction so that learning is situated in realistic contexts. Under such conditions, the cognitive resources specific to the domain must be activated, regulated, and adapted. Strategic knowledge responds by providing how-to-decide-what-to-do-and-when knowledge. These three studies call attention to the importance of modeling, diagnosing, and teaching this form of knowledge in its own right as an influential determinant of developmental growth.

Finally, this collection of studies enlightens us about skill and knowledge *acquisition*. The role of strategic-control processes in global learning and transfer is examined as the transfer skills of superior learners are modeled and the on-line student diagnosis/modeling that is executed by a superior teaching physician is made explicit. The results suggest that readiness to advance in a domain is signaled by a student's ability to adapt and extend existing knowledge to meet the demands of altered contexts or novel problems. In short, flexible use of knowledge in response to instruction signals learning potential. In turn, tutoring that provides varying levels of assistance to students in executing the needed metacognitive processes has been shown to be effective in promoting acquisition, that is, advancing learners to higher levels of functioning. This provides a striking realization of cognitive models that are primarily viewed as informing the *content* of instruction, also informing pedagogical *method*. The cognitive models of learners at various levels of achievement revealed developmental progressions from externally supported, socially mediated activity to independent performances, presumably enabled by internalized skill and knowledge representations. Used in this manner, diagnostic findings generate the tight coupling of assessment to instruction that many believe is a key contribution of cognitive theory to the field of psychological measurement.

## REFERENCES

Anderson, J. R., Boyle, C. F., Farrell, R. G., & Reiser, B. J. (1984). Cognitive principles in the design of computer tutors. *Proceedings of the Sixth Cognitive Science Society Conference*, Boulder, CO, pp. 2–8.

Bransford, J., Sherwood, R., Vye, N., & Rieser, J. (1986). Teaching thinking and problem solving: Research foundations. *American Psychologist, 41*(10), 1078–89.

Brown, A. L. (1978). Knowing when, where, and how to remember: A problem of metacognition. In R. Glaser (Ed.), *Advances in instructional psychology*. (Vol 1, pp. 77–165). Hillsdale, NJ: Lawrence Erlbaum Associates.

Brown, A. L., Bransford, J. D., Ferrara, R. A., & Campione, J. C. (1983). Learning, remembering, and understanding. In J. H. Flavell & E. M. Markman (Eds.), *Handbook of child psychology* (Vol 3, pp 77–166). New York: Wiley.

Brown, A. L., & Palincsar, A. S. (1984). Reciprocal teaching of comprehension-fostering and monitoring activities. *Cognition and Instruction, 1,* 175–77.

Brown, A. L., & Palincsar, A. (1989). Guided, cooperative learning and individual knowledge acquisition. In L. B. Resnick (Ed.), *Knowing, learning, and instruction: Essays in honor of Robert Glaser.* Hillsdale, NJ: Lawrence Erlbaum Associates.

Clancey, W. J. (August, 1989). From GUIDON to NEOMYCIN, and HERACLES in twenty short lessons: ONR final report 1979–1985. *AI Magazine, 7*(3), 40–60.

Collins, A., Brown, J. S., & Newman, S. E. (1989). Cognitive apprenticeship: Teaching the craft of reading, writing, and mathematics. In L. B. Resnick (Ed.), *Knowing, learning, and instruction: Essays in honor of Robert Glaser* (pp. 453–494). Hillsdale, NJ: Lawrence Erlbaum Associates.

Ferrara, R. A. (1987). *Learning mathematics in the zone of proximal development: The importance of flexible use of knowledge.* Unpublished doctoral dissertation, Department of Psychology, University of Illinois at Urbana-Champaign.

Ferrara, R. A., Brown, A. L., & Campione, J. C. (1986). Children's learning and transfer of inductive reasoning rules: Studies in proximal development. *Child Development, 57*(5), 1087–1099.

Gelman, R., & Gallistel, C. R. (1978). *The child's understanding of number.* Cambridge, MA: Harvard University Press.

Glaser, R., & Bassok, M. (1989). Learning theory and the study of instruction. In M. R. Rosenzweig & L. W. Porter (Eds.), *Annual review of psychology* (Vol. 40, pp. 631–666). Palo Alto, CA: Annual Reviews.

Gott, S. P. (1989). Apprenticeship instruction for real-world tasks: The coordination of procedures, mental models, and strategies. In E. Z. Rothkopf (Ed.), *Review of Research in Education.* Washington, DC: American Educational Research Association.

Gott, S. P. & Pokorny, R. (1987). The training of experts for high-tech work environments. *Proceedings of the Ninth Interservice/Industry Training Systems Conference.* Washington, DC, pp 184–190.

Greeno, J. G. (1978). A study of problem solving. In R. Glaser (Ed.), *Advances in instructional psychology* (Vol. 1, pp. 13–75). Hillsdale, NJ: Lawrence Erlbaum Associates.

Kieras, D. E. (1987). *What mental model should be taught: Choosing instructional content for complex engineered systems* (Tech. Rep. No. 24 TR-87/ONR-24). Ann Arbor, MI: University of Michigan.

Newell, A. (1969). Heuristic programming: Ill-structured problems. In J. Aronowsky (Ed.) *Progress in Operations Research, Vol III* (pp 360–414). New York: Wiley.

Nii, H. P. (1986). Blackboard systems part two: Blackboard application systems. *AI Magazine, 7*(3), 82–106.

Papert, S. (1980). *Mindstorms: Children, computers, and powerful ideas.* New York: Basic Books.

Piaget, J. (1926). *The language and thought of the child.* London: Routledge & Kegan Paul.

Resnick, L. B. (1987). Learning in school and out. *Educational Researcher, 16*(9), 13–20.

Scardamalia, M., Bereiter, C., & Steinbach, R. (1984). Teachability of reflective processes in written composition. *Cognitive Science, 8,* 173–190.

Schoenfeld, A. H. (1985). *Mathematical problem solving.* New York: Academic Press.

Soloway, E. M. (1986). Learning to program equal learning to construct mechanisms and explanations. *CACM, 29*(9), 850–858.

Vygotsky, L. S. (1978). *Mind in society: The development of higher psychological processes.* Cambridge, MA: Harvard University Press.

# Parsimonious Covering Theory In Cognitive Diagnosis and Adaptive Instruction

James A. Reggia
C. Lynne D'Autrechy
*University of Maryland*

> Find out the cause of this effect, or rather say, the cause of this defect, for this effect defective comes by cause.
>
> William Shakespeare

This chapter summarizes recent work on a formal model of diagnostic reasoning referred to as *parsimonious covering theory* and discusses its relevance to cognitive diagnosis. Parsimonious covering theory represents diagnostic knowledge as a network of causal associations. It models diagnostic reasoning as a hypothesize-and-test procedure whose goal is to account for observed symptoms with a plausible explanatory hypothesis. The term *parsimonious covering theory* reflects the fact that a plausible explanatory hypothesis is a simple or economical (parsimonious) set of disorders that accounts for (covers) the observed symptoms. This theory, which is still evolving, captures several important features of human diagnostic inference. It directly addresses the issues of diagnostic context and of multiple, simultaneous causative disorders, and it provides a conceptual framework within which to view recent work on diagnostic problem solving in general.

The viewpoint taken here is that parsimonious covering theory and related abstractions are of direct relevance to adaptive instruction in at least two ways: as the basis of overlay models and student simulations in instructional tasks where the student is learning to solve diagnostic problems in some application domain, and as a method for automating the cognitive diagnosis process in any type of intelligent/adaptive tutoring situation. With this in mind, the material in the remainder of this chapter is organized as follows. First, a brief summary of some recent studies of diagnostic problem solving and computer models of diagnostic reasoning is presented to motivate the approach taken in parsimonious covering theory. The basic ideas of parsimonious covering theory are then presented from an intuitive rather than a formal, derivational perspective. Finally, we address the relevance of parsimonious covering to cognitive diagnosis and adaptive tutoring systems.

## DIAGNOSTIC REASONING AND COMPUTATIONAL
## MODELS OF DIAGNOSTIC INFERENCE

Diagnostic reasoning has received a great deal of attention over the last few years by cognitive psychologists, artificial intelligence (AI) researchers, and educators (e.g., Barrows, 1972; Elstein, Shulman, & Sprafka, 1978; Kassirer & Gorry, 1978; Pauker, Gorry, Kassirer, & Schwartz, 1976; Rouse, 1979; Rubins, 1975; Wortman, 1966). This section first briefly reviews past empirical studies of the diagnostic reasoning process, and then discusses computational models of this process.

### Empirical Studies of Diagnostic Reasoning

Although a variety of experimental designs have been used in empirical studies of diagnostic reasoning, perhaps the most common has been the use of simulated diagnostic problems. Based on these studies, diagnostic reasoning is generally accepted to be a sequential hypothesize-and-test (hypothetico–deductive) process during which the diagnostician conceptually constructs a model of the underlying causative disorders. This model, or hypothesis, is based primarily on the manifestations that are known to be present (for instance, a patient's symptoms). It postulates the presence of one or more disorders that could explain the given manifestations. Each cycle of the inference process can be viewed as consisting of three phases: disorder evocation, hypothesis construction, and question generation (hypothesis testing). In reality, these three phases overlap extensively.

Disorder evocation is the retrieval from long-term memory of causative disorders as the diagnostician detects a new manifestation in the information available about a problem. Ideally, the diagnostician's knowledge base or long-term memory includes the set of al possible causative disorders for each manifestation, and the set of all possible manifestations for each disorder (Wortman, 1966). Usually a single manifestation (rather than combinations of manifestations) is responsible for evoking new disorders for incorporation into the evolving hypothesis (Kassirer & Gorry, 1978).

The second phase of the hypothesize-and-test cycle, hypothesis construction, involves the incorporation of possible causes of the new manifestation into the hypothesis. This may require attributing the manifestation to some disorder already assumed to be present, or adding new disorders evoked by the manifestation to the hypothesis. The diagnostician's hypothesis may at times be relatively complex. Not only may it contain a great deal of uncertainty about which of several diagnoses account for a certain manifestation, but it might also presume the simultaneous presence of multiple disorders. The empirical evidence suggests that the hypothesis can best be viewed as a resolution of two conflicting goals[1]:

---
[1] In statistical terms, coverage can be viewed as maximizing explained variance, and parsimony as using few degrees of freedom.

*Coverage goal.* The goal of explaining all of the manifestations that are present.
*Parsimony goal.* The goal of minimizing the complexity of the explanation.

The second goal is sometimes referred to as Occam's razor.

It is important to appreciate the iterative nature of diagnostic reasoning. As the diagnostician gradually learns information about a problem, his or her hypothesis changes to reflect this new information. For example, if a patient complains of sudden onset of chest pain, a physician's initial hypothesis might be something like:

*Hypothesis H1:*
Heart attack, *or* pulmonary embolus, *or.* . . .

As further details become available, some of the initially possible disorders might be eliminated. In the preceding example, if it was then learned that the patient also had a chronic cough, the hypothesis might change to

*Hypothesis H2:*
heart attack, *or* pulmonary embolus, *or* . . .
*and*
bronchitis, *or* asthma, *or* . . .

reflecting the physician's belief that at least two diseases must be present to account for this patient's symptoms. Note that at this point, the hypothesis contains both uncertainty (indicated by *or*) and the presumption that multiple simultaneous disorders are present (indicated by *and*).

Another aspect of hypothesis construction is the ranking of the likelihood of competing disorders. The term *competing disorders* refers to hypothesized alternatives that can account for the same or similar manifestations, such as heart attack and pulmonary embolus in Hypothesis H1. Perhaps surprisingly, human diagnosticians appear to use only a three-point weighting scheme to rank competing disorders: a particular finding may be "positive, noncontributory or negative with respect to a particular hypothesis" (Elstein, Shulman, & Sprafka, 1978). At the end of a problem-solving session, diagnosticians are thus able to rank competing disorders only in a very coarse fashion (for instance, disorder *d* is definitely present, *d* is very likely to be present, *d* may be present, *d* is possible but improbable).

The third phase of the hypothesize-and-test cycle is question generation, and it represents the test phase. The word *question* here is being used in a general sense to indicate not only verbal questions, but also any type of information-gathering activity (for instance, measuring a voltage in a malfunctioning circuit). Investigators studying human diagnostic problem-solving often divide such questions into two categories: protocol driven and hypothesis driven. Protocol-driven questions are those that a diagnostician generally asks as a routine during any diagnostic session, and these are not of further concern in this chapter. In contrast, hypothesis-driven questions seek information that is specifically needed to modify the evolving hypothesis.

Many aspects of the diagnostic-reasoning process are incompletely understood at the present time. For example, it is unclear how a diagnostician reasons about multiple simultaneous disorders. In such situations the manifestations must be attributed to appropriate disorders, and competing disorders must be ranked in the context of other disorders assumed to be present. It is also unclear exactly how diagnosticians decide to terminate the diagnostic process because a "solution" has been reached.

## Computational Models of Diagnostic Problem Solving

A great variety of approaches has been taken in representing and processing knowledge in computational models of diagnostic problem solving (Reggia & Tuhrim, 1985; Ramsey, Reggia, Nau, & Ferrentino, 1986). Regardless of the method used, it is convenient to view these systems as having two components: a *knowledge base* and an *inference mechanism*. The knowledge base is a collection of encoded knowledge that is needed to solve diagnostic problems in some specific application, for instance, electronics. The inference mechanism is a program that, given a problem description, uses the information in the knowledge base to generate a diagnosis.

Three prominent examples of such methods are statistical pattern classification, rule-based deduction, and association-based abduction. In systems using statistical pattern classification, the knowledge base typically consists of tables of probabilities, and the inference mechanism involves the calculation of posterior probabilities of disorders using formulas such as Bayes' theorem. Models of this type have clearly achieved expert-level performance, at times outperforming human diagnosticians (deDombal, 1975; Zagoria & Reggia, 1983), but are of limited value in situations where multiple, simultaneous disorders may occur, and are difficult to use for many real-world problems because the necessary probabilities are not available. It is important to what follows to note that models using statistical pattern classification have a strong theoretical foundation in probability theory.

Computational models of diagnostic problem solving using rule-based deduction typically have a knowledge base consisting of conditional rules and an inference mechanism based on making logical deductions (e.g., modus ponens or proof by refutation). As with statistical pattern-classification models, systems of this type have clearly been demonstrated to exhibit an expert level of performance in empirical testing (Kingsland et al., 1983; Reggia, Tabb, Price, Banko, & Hebel, 1984), but reformulating naturally occurring knowledge as rules has proven to be extremely difficult in general diagnostic domains. Rule-based, deductive systems also have a strong theoretical foundation, in this case in first-order predicate calculus.

A third approach to building diagnostic expert systems is association-based abduction. In contrast to deductive rule-based systems, whose inferences might in their simplest form be characterized by the syllogism:

given fact $A$ and rule $A \rightarrow B$, infer $B$,

systems of this type inherently involve *abductive inference* of the form:

given fact $B$ and association $A \rightarrow B$, infer *plausible A*.

Although the $\rightarrow$ in the deductive syllogism refers to logical implication, in the abductive syllogism as used in diagnostic problem solving it refers to a qualitative causal association between $A$ and $B$: "Disorder $A$ is capable of causing manifestation $B$, and manifestation $B$ is known to be present, so perhaps disorder $A$ is causing it."

The term *abduction* refers to any reasoning in which the goal is to derive the best explanation(s) for a given set of observed facts (Charniak & McDermott, 1985; Josephson, 1982; Peirce, 1955; Reggia, 1985; Thagard, 1978). Tasks that are abductive in nature typically involve probabilistic, context-sensitive disambiguation of problem features using associative knowledge. They involve the *construction* of a solution, as well as selection from alternative solutions. Diagnosis is just one example of an abductive task. Many aspects of natural language understanding and high-level scene interpretation can also be viewed as abductive (Charniak & McDermott, 1985; Reggia, 1985).

Abductive models of diagnostic problem solving not only aim for a high level of performance, but are also often explicit attempts to model the underlying reasoning of the diagnostician. Information in the knowledge base, typically causal associations, is generally represented in a descriptive or "object-oriented" fashion, and a sequential hypothesize-and-test inference process is used. The key point here for what follows is that association-based abductive models of diagnostic inference, in marked contrast to models using statistical pattern classification and rule-based deduction, do *not* have a readily identifiable, well-developed theoretical foundation. It is in large part due to this absence of a theoretical basis that AI research on abductive expert systems is sometimes dismissed as ad hoc (e.g., Ben-Bassat et al., 1980). The parsimonious covering theory described in this chapter represents an attempt to fill this gap.

## PARSIMONIOUS COVERING THEORY

Our approach to providing a theoretical model of human diagnostic reasoning, and of association-based abductive computational systems, has been to develop a formal abductive logic referred to as *parsimonious covering theory* (Reggia,

Nau, & Wang, 1983, 1985; Peng & Reggia, 1986, 1987a, 1987b). This nondeductive theoretical model has been used as the basis of a number of implemented diagnostic expert systems (Reggia et al., 1983), and has proven quite powerful. It supports a descriptive knowledge representation and answer justification[2] (Reggia, Perricone, et al., 1985), and it handles many of the difficulties that arise in the context of multiple, simultaneous disorders.

This section begins by describing the method used to represent diagnostic problem-solving knowledge in parsimonious covering theory and the formulation of diagnostic problems. Algorithmic models of the reasoning processes used during diagnostic problem solving are then presented for certain classes of diagnostic problems. Finally, several issues involved in extending the basic theory are discussed. The emphasis in the following is on explaining the intuitions behind parsimonious covering theory. Readers interested in the mathematical details are referred to the literature cited here.

## Knowledge Representation and Problem Formulation

In parsimonious covering theory, diagnostic knowledge is represented as an associative network of causal relationships. Disorders, indicated by nodes in set $D$, are causally related to intermediate pathological states, and ultimately to measurable manifestations (set $M$). For example, in medicine, *heart attack* would be a disorder, *shock* a pathological state, and *confused* a manifestation. A heart attack may cause shock, which in turn may cause someone to be confused. The state of being confused is considered to be a directly observable abnormality, making it a manifestation, whereas shock and heart attack are not considered to be directly observable (their presence must be inferred).

In many real-world domains, the associative knowledge used in diagnostic problem solving is very large, complex, and ill-structured (for instance, in medicine). One approach to formalizing the structure and use of this knowledge is to examine the most general case possible. Although this is obviously the ultimate goal, as a starting point in explaining parsimonious covering it introduces a large amount of complexity and detail that obscures the central ideas of the theory. Thus, we initially consider only the simplest meaningful version of parsimonious covering theory. Once this basic formulation is understood, the assumptions are reexamined to explain why more general formulations are useful.

In the simplest version of parsimonious covering theory, the underlying knowledge for a diagnostic problem is organized as pictured in Figure 9.1a. There are two discrete, finite sets that define the scope of diagnostic problems: $D$, representing all possible disorders $d_i$ that can occur, and $M$, representing all possible manifestations $m_j$ that may occur when one or more disorders are present. For

---

[2] Answer justification refers to the ability of an expert system to explain how or why it arrived at a specific solution to a problem.

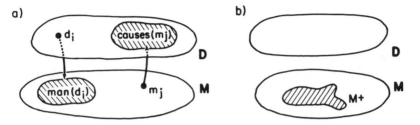

FIG. 9.1.   Causal network ($D$ = disorders, $M$ = manifestations) underlying diagnosis problems. Links or arcs in this network represent causal associations.

example, in medicine, $D$ might represent all known diseases (or some relevant subset of all diseases), and $M$ would then represent all possible symptoms, examination findings, and abnormal laboratory results that can be caused by diseases in $D$. We assume that $D$ and $M$ have no elements in common, and that the presence of any $d_i$ is not directly measurable.

To capture the intuitive notion of causation, we assume knowledge of a relation $C$ involving individual disorders and manifestations. Stating that $d_i$ can cause $m_j$ does not imply that $m_j$ always occurs when $d_i$ is present, but only that $m_j$ may occur. For example, a patient with a heart attack may have chest pain, numbness in the left arm, loss of consciousness, or any of several other symptoms, but none of these symptoms is necessarily present.

Given $D$, $M$, and $C$, the following sets can be defined:

$$\text{man}(d_i) = \{m_j \mid d_i \text{ causes } m_j\} \quad \text{for each disorder } d_i \text{ in } D, \text{ and}$$
$$\text{causes}(m_j) = \{d_i \mid d_i \text{ causes } m_j\} \quad \text{for each manifestation } m_j \text{ in M.}$$

These sets are depicted in Figure 9.1a, and represent all possible manifestations caused by $d_i$, and all possible disorders that cause $m_j$, respectively. These concepts are intuitively familiar to the human diagnostician. For example, medical textbooks frequently have descriptions of diseases that include, among other facts, the set man($d_i$) for each disease $d_i$. Physicians often refer to the *differential diagnosis* of a symptom, which corresponds to the set causes($m_j$). Clearly, if man($d_i$) is known for every disorder $d_i$, or if causes($m_j$) is known for every manifestation $m_j$, then the causal relation $C$ is completely determined. We will use

$$\text{man}(D_I) = \bigcup_{d_i \,\varepsilon\, D_I} \text{man}(d_i) \text{ and causes}(M_J) = \bigcup_{m_j \,\varepsilon\, M_J} \text{causes}(m_j)$$

to indicate all possible manifestations of a set of disorders $D_I$ and all possible causes of any manifestation in $M_J$, respectively.[3]

---

[3] If X and Y are sets, then X $\cup$ Y is the *union* of X and Y, or the set formed by combining their elements together. For example, if X = {A,B}, and Y = {B,C}, then X $\cup$ Y = {A,B,C}.

Finally, there is a distinguished subset $M^+$ of $M$ that represents those manifestations which are known to be present (see Figure 9.1b). Whereas $D$, $M$, and $C$ represent general knowledge about a class of diagnostic problems, $M^+$ represents the manifestations occurring in a specific case.

Using this terminology, a *diagnostic problem P* is defined by specifying $D$, $M$, $C$ and $M^+$. We assume in what follows that diagnostic problems are well formed in the sense that man($d_i$) and causes($m_j$) are always non-empty sets.

Having characterized a diagnostic problem in these terms, we now turn to defining the solution to a diagnostic problem by first introducing the concept of explanation.

An *explanation E* for $M^+$ is a set of disorders where

(i) $M^+$ is a subset of man(E), or E *covers* $M^+$; and

(ii) E is *parsimonious*.

An explanation represents a plausible diagnostic hypothesis. The definition of an explanation captures many features of what one intuitively means by "explaining a set of manifestations," and is central to parsimonious covering theory. Part (i) specifies the reasonable constraint that an explanation $E$ must be able to cause the manifestations known to be present in the case being diagnosed. In other words, an explanation $E$ must be a *cover*: a set of disorders that can account for or cover $M^+$. If one assumes that the manifestations in $M$ do not occur spontaneously, but only when caused by disorders, then one can prove that whenever $M^+$ occurs it must be the case that one of its covers is also present (Nau & Reggia, 1984).

Part (ii) of the definition specifies that $E$ must also be *parsimonious*, reflecting an intuitive principle often referred to as Occam's Razor: The simplest explanation is the preferable one. Thus, an impotant issue raised by the definition of an explanation is how one should go about formalizing the notion of parsimony or simplicity. Here are some examples of definitions of parsimony that have been proposed on intuitive grounds for various diagnostic applications in the past:

(ii-a) Single disorder assumption[4]: $|E| = 1$;

(ii-b) Minimal cardinality: $|E| \leq |D_1|$ for any cover $D_1$ of $M^+$;

(ii-c) Irredundancy[5]: no proper subset of E covers $M^+$; and

(ii-d) Relevancy: E is a subset of causes ($M^+$)

Each of these parsimony criteria can be viewed as a generalization of those listed before it.

Assuming that only a single disorder can occur at one time (ii-a) may be appropriate in some applications (Reggia et al., 1983; Shubin & Ulrich, 1982),

---

[4] For a set X, the notation $|X|$ means "the number of elements in X." For example, if X = {A,B,C}, then $|X| = 3$. The size of a set is often referred to as it cardinality.

[5] Irredundancy is sometimes called *minimality*, but the former term is used here to avoid any confusion with the term *minimal cardinality*.

but is obviously too restrictive for general diagnostic problem solving. Minimal cardinality (ii-b) says that only the smallest sets of disorders should be considered to be viable or plausible hypotheses. Minimal cardinality covers have been used in a number of computational models of real-world diagnostic reasoning (Reggia et al., 1983). However, minimal cardinality covers are currently viewed as too restrictive. For example, suppose that either a very rare disorder $d_1$ alone, or a combination of two very common disorders $d_2$ and $d_3$, could cover all present manifestations. If minimality is chosen as the parsimony criterion, then $\{d_1\}$ would be chosen as a viable hypothesis whereas $\{d_2,d_3\}$ would not, even though $\{d_2,d_3\}$ might be considered to be more plausible by a human diagnostician. Thus, in many diagnostic applications, such selection of plausible hypotheses based on minimal cardinality might miss the most probable hypothesis.

On the other hand, relevancy (ii-d) requires only that any disorder in an explanation be causally related to some manifestation in $M^+$. Intuition suggests that such a parsimony criterion would result in consideration of a large number of obviously implausible diagnostic hypotheses. Therefore, solely on an intuitive basis, a growing number of researchers in this area have adopted irredundancy as a parsimony criteria (Nau & Reggia, 1984; Reggia, Nau, & Wang, 1985; Peng & Reggia, 1986; Reiter, 1987; deKleer & Williams, 1987). Using this criterion, a set of disorders $D_I$ that can account for the given manifestations $M^+$ is to be considered as a plausible hypothesis if and only if no proper subset of $D_I$ can cover $M^+$. In the example in the preceding paragraph, using irredundancy as a parsimony criterion results in both sets $\{d_1\}$ and $\{d_2,d_3\}$ being considered to be explanations or plausible hypotheses.

In general diagnostic problem solving, there are typically several sets of disorders that satisfy the definition of explanation, and one often wishes to identify all of these plausible hypotheses. Thus, the solution to a diagnostic problem is defined to be the set of all explanations for $M^+$, or some most highly ranked subset of all explanations for $M^+$.

Example. To illustrate the above concepts, let $D = \{d_1, d_2, \ldots, d_9\}$, $M = \{m_1, \ldots, m_6\}$, and let man($d_i$) and causes($m_i$) be as specified in Table 9.1. Let the observable manifestations be $M^+ = \{m_1, m_4, m_5\}$. Note that no single disorder can cover (account for) all of $M^+$, but that some pairs of disorders do cover $M^+$. For instance, if $D_1 = \{d_1,d_7\}$ then $M^+$ is a subset of man($D_1$), so $D_1$ covers $M^+$. Because there are no covers for $M^+$ of smaller cardinality than $D_1$, it follows that $D_1$ is an explanation for $M^+$ if minimal cardinality is used as a parsimony criterion. Careful examination of Table 9.1 should convince the reader that, using minimal cardinality for parsimony, the solution to this diagnostic problem is

$$\left\{ \{d_1,d_7\}, \{d_1,d_8\}, \{d_1,d_9\}, \{d_2,d_7\}, \{d_2,d_8\}, \{d_2,d_9\}, \{d_3,d_8\}, \{d_4,d_8\} \right\},$$

the set of all explanations for $M^+$. Alternatively, using irredundant covers as explanations,

TABLE 9.1
Knowledge about a Class of Diagnostic Problems

| $d_i$ | $man(d_i)$ |
|---|---|
| $d_1$ | $m_1 m_4$ |
| $d_2$ | $m_1 m_3 m_4$ |
| $d_3$ | $m_1 m_3$ |
| $d_4$ | $m_1 m_6$ |
| $d_5$ | $m_2 m_3 m_4$ |
| $d_6$ | $m_2 m_3$ |
| $d_7$ | $m_2 m_5$ |
| $d_8$ | $m_4 m_5 m_6$ |
| $d_9$ | $m_2 m_5$ |

| $m_i$ | $causes(m_i)$ |
|---|---|
| $m_1$ | $d_1 d_2 d_3 d_4$ |
| $m_2$ | $d_5 d_6 d_7 d_9$ |
| $m_3$ | $d_2 d_5 d_6$ |
| $m_4$ | $d_1 d_2 d_5 d_8$ |
| $m_5$ | $d_7 d_8 d_9$ |
| $m_6$ | $d_4 d_8$ |

Note: The relation $C$ is implicitly defined by either the top or bottom half of this table.

$$\Big\{ \{d_1, d_7\}, \{d_1, d_8\}, \{d_1, d_9\}, \{d_2, d_7\}, \{d_2, d_8\}, \{d_2, d_9\}, \{d_3, d_8\}, \{d_4, d_8\},$$

$$\{d_3, d_5, d_7\}, \{d_3, d_5, d_9\}, \{d_4, d_5, d_7\}, \{d_4, d_5, d_9\} \Big\}$$

is the solution or set of all irredundant covers.

In summary, the basic formulation of parsimonious covering theory presented here represents diagnostic knowledge as an associative network where causal relations link disorders to manifestations. Specifying a diagnostic problem involves specifying this associative network and a set of manifestations $M^+$ that are present in a specific problem. The goal of problem solving is then to construct a set of explanations or plausible hypotheses for the given manifestations. Each explanation takes the form of a set of disorders that "parsimoniously cover" or account for $M^+$.[6]

---

[6] The reader interested in how this formulation of diagnostic problems relates to cognitive diagnosis may wish at this point to scan the section "As a Framework for Cognitive Diagnosis" later in this chapter.

## Procedural Models of Diagnostic Reasoning

Given a diagnostic problem formulated within the framework of parsimonious covering theory, the next issue is how to formally model the abductive, hypothesize-and-test reasoning process of the human diagnostician. A number of provably correct procedural models exist under a variety of assumptions (Peng & Reggia, 1986, 1987b; Reggia, Nau, & Wang, 1985). In the following, we presume that manifestations are discovered one at a time (rather than all being available initially) to illustrate the flavor of parsimonious covering procedures through an informal example.

The tentative hypothesis at any point during problem solving is defined to be the solution for those manifestations already known to be present, assuming, perhaps falsely, that no additional manifestations would be subsequently discovered. To construct and maintain a tentative hypothesis like this, three pieces of information prove useful:

MANIFS: the set of manifestations known to be present
SCOPE: causes(MANIFS), the set of all disorders $d_i$ for which at least one manifestation is already known to be present; and
HYPOTHESIS: the tentative solution for just those manifestations already in MANIFS; typically, HYPOTHESIS is represented as a collection of generators, and should be thought of as the current working hypothesis.

The term *generator* used here needs further definition. Rather than representing the solution to a diagnostic problem as an explicit list of all possible explanations for $M^+$ or MANIFS, it is advantageous to represent the disorders involved as a collection of explanation generators. An explanation generator is a collection of sets of competing disorders that implicitly represent a set of explanations in the solution and can be used to generate them. If $A$, $B$, and $C$ are sets of disorders, then $A \times B \times C$ (read as "one of $A$ and one of $B$ and one of $C$") is a generator that represents all explanations of the form $\{d_A, d_B, d_C\}$, that is, all explanations where one disorder comes from $A$, one from $B$, and one from $C$.[7] Hypotheses H1 and H2 given early in the summary of diagnostic reasoning are each generators. To illustrate further this idea, consider the example diagnostic problem presented earlier (Table 9.1). Assuming minimal cardinality covers are explanations, two generators are sufficient to represent the solution to that problem: $\{d_1, d_2\} \times \{d_7, d_8, d_9\}$ and $\{d_3, d_4\} \times \{d_8\}$. The second generator here implicitly represents the two explanations $\{d_3, d_8\}$ and $\{d_4, d_8\}$, whereas the first generator represents the other six explanations in the solution.

---

[7] A generator is thus analogous to a Cartesian set product, the difference being that the generator produces unordered sets rather than ordered tuples.

There are at least three advantages to representing the solution to a diagnostic problem as a set of generators. First, this is usually a more compact form of the explanations present in the solution. Second, generators are a very convenient representation for developing algorithms to process explanations sequentially. Finally, and perhaps most importantly, generators are closer to the way the human diagnostician organizes the possibilities during problem solving (e.g., the *differential diagnosis*).

Using the three data structures MANIFS, SCOPE, and HYPOTHESIS, a hypothesize-and-test algorithm based on parsimonious covering can perform diagnostic problem solving. The HYPOTHESIS represents the tentative or working hypothesis at any point during problem solving. The algorithm, described informally, is:

1. Get the next manifestation $m_j$ and add it to MANIFS.
2. Retrieve causes($m_j$) from the knowledge base.
3. Replace SCOPE with SCOPE $\cup$ causes($m_j$).
4. Adjust HYPOTHESIS to accommodate $m_j$.
5. Repeat this process until no further manifestations remain.

Thus, as each manifestation $m_j$ that is present is discovered, MANIFS is updated simply by adding $m_j$ to it. SCOPE is augmented to include any possible causes $d_i$ of $m_j$ that are not already contained in it (derived by taking the union of causes($m_j$) and SCOPE). Finally, HYPOTHESIS is adjusted to accommodate $m_j$ based on operations involving causes($m_j$) and the sets of disorders in the existing generators. These latter operations are done such that any explanation that can no longer account for the augmented MANIFS (which now includes $m_j$) are eliminated, and any possible new explanations are automatically constructed.

The key step in this process is Step 4, the adjustment of the HYPOTHESIS or working hypothesis. The exact form of the algebraic operations on the HYPOTHESIS depends on which parsimony criterion is being used, but in general these operations are referred to as generator *division* and *remainder* operations. Perhaps the best way to get a basic understanding of this step is to follow a simple example. Recall the abstract knowledge base illustrated in Table 9.1, and consider the same diagnostic problem $M^+ = \{m_1, m_4, m_5\}$ that was used earlier. Assume that irredundant covers are explanations. The order in which information about manifestations is discovered is determined by question-generation heuristics, as discussed later. Assuming all manifestations are found, this order does not affect the final solution. For now, suppose that the sequence of events occurring during problem solving are ordered as listed in Table 9.2.

Initially, MANIFS, SCOPE and HYPOTHESIS are all empty ($\varnothing$ is the empty set). When $m_1$ is discovered to be present, $m_1$ is added to MANIFS, and the new SCOPE is the union of the old SCOPE with causes($m_1$). Since previously there

TABLE 9.2
Sequential Problem Solving Using Parsimonious Covering Based
on Irredundant Covers

| Events in order of their discovery | MANIFS | SCOPE | HYPOTHESIS (generator form) |
|---|---|---|---|
| Initially | 0 | 0 | 0 |
| $m_1$ present | $\{m_1\}$ | $\{d_1 d_2 d_3 d_4\}$ | $\{d_1 d_2 d_3 d_4\}$ |
| $m_2$ absent | $\{m_1\}$ | $\{d_1 d_2 d_3 d_4\}$ | $\{d_1 d_2 d_3 d_4\}$ |
| $m_3$ absent | $\{m_1\}$ | $\{d_1 d_2 d_3 d_4\}$ | $\{d_1 d_2 d_3 d_4\}$ |
| $m_4$ present | | | $\{d_1 d_2\}$ |
| | | | and |
| | $\{m_1 m_4\}$ | $\{d_1 d_2 d_3 d_4 d_5 d_8\}$ | $\{d_3 d_4\} \times \{d_5 d_8\}$ |
| $m_5$ present | | | $\{d_1 d_2\} \times \{d_7 d_8 d_9\}$ |
| | | | and |
| | | | $\{d_8\} \times \{d_3 d_4\}$ |
| | | | and |
| | $\{m_1 m_4 m_5\}$ | $\{d_1 d_2 d_3 d_4 d_5 d_7 d_8 d_9\}$ | $\{d_5\} \times \{d_3 d_4\} \times \{d_7 d_9\}$ |
| $m_6$ absent | | | $\{d_1 d_2\} \times \{d_7 d_8 d_9\}$ |
| | | | and |
| | | | $\{d_8\} \times \{d_3 d_4\}$ |
| | | | and |
| | $\{m_1 m_4 m_5\}$ | $\{d_1 d_2 d_3 d_4 d_5 d_7 d_8 d_9\}$ | $\{d_5\} \times \{d_3 d_4\} \times \{d_7 d_9\}$ |

were no generators in the HYPOTHESIS, a new generator is created, in this case consisting of causes($m_1$). In the terms defined earlier, this generator represents a solution for $M^+ = \{m_1\}$. It tentatively postulates that there are four possible explanations for $M^+$, any one of which consists of a single disorder. The HYPOTHESIS thus asserts that "$d_1$ or $d_2$ or $d_3$ or $d_4$ is present."

The absence of $m_2$ and $m_3$ does not change this initial hypothesis. However, when $m_4$ is discovered to be present, MANIFS and SCOPE are augmented appropriately. A new HYPOTHESIS is developed by "dividing" the only preexisting generator set in HYPOTHESIS by causes($m_4$), which in this case corresponds to intersecting causes($m_4$) with the only set of disorders in the HYPOTHESIS. A new generator $\{d_1\ d_2\}$ is the result of this "division" or intersection, while the other new generator $\{d_3\ d_4\} \times \{d_5\ d_8\}$ is constructed as a "remainder" from the division process. In other words, the second new generator is built from $\{d_3\ d_4\}$, which is the part of HYPOTHESIS not kept in the division/intersection, and $\{d_5\ d_8\}$, which is the part of causes($m_4$) not kept in the division/intersection. Note that the two generators at this point represent all irredundant covers for the manifestations known to be present so far. These covers have either one or two disorders in them.

When $m_5$ is noted to be present, MANIFS and SCOPE are again adjusted appropriately. Similar "division" and "remainder" operations are used to create a new HYPOTHESIS representing 12 irredundant covers, each containing either two or three disorders. Because $m_6$ is found to be absent, the resulting three generators represent exactly the irredundant covers in the final solution; compare them with the explicit listing of all irredundant covers for $M^+ = \{m_1, m_4, m_5\}$ given in the earlier example.

## FURTHER ISSUES

The previous section has attempted to present the flavor of parsimonious covering theory in an informal fashion, using a simplified model of the associative knowledge involved. Clearly, as outlined earlier, more complex associative networks can be involved, and many additional issues need to be examined. This section outlines some of these issues. The first part addresses a number of extensions to the basic version of parsimonious covering theory described above. The second part examines another extension, integration with probability theory, in some detail. Finally, the third part mentions recent attempts to generalize the theory in a number of ways so that it addresses more complex diagnostic problems.

### Extensions to the Basic Formalism

Using the basic form of parsimonious covering theory described in the previous section as the basis of computational models requires that a number of issues be addressed and resolved. Two related issues are how questions should be generated during sequential problem solving to obtain additional information, and when problem solving should terminate. These are open research questions in AI today. Diagnostic expert systems based on parsimonious covering theory (Reggia et al., 1983) and related nonformal models (Miller, Pople, & Myers, 1982; Pople, 1982) have generally used a heuristic approach to question generation and termination. Questions are generated in a hypothesis-driven fashion based on which disorders are currently under active consideration. Recently, an entropy-minimizing metric has been proposed for abductive reasoning models (deKleer & Williams, 1987). All of these methods for question generation are limited in their utility and accuracy as a model of human problem solving.

Another issue is how $M^+$ should be extracted from information describing a problem. The formulation of parsimonious covering theory in the preceding section presumes that $M^+$ is readily available, but in some applications obtaining $M^+$ is nontrivial and must be inferred from a large amount of data about the system being diagnosed. For example, in the description

> The patient is a 31 year old diabetic female with a complaint of headaches. Her temperature is 101°F, BP is 115/75, the pulse is 72/min, the neck is supple and without bruits, and the neurological examination is unremarkable except for distal loss of proprioception in the lower extremities.

taken from a patient's chart it must somehow be appreciated that $M^+$ consists of three manifestations (headache, fever, proprioception loss).

In general, identifying $M^+$ involves examining the *differences* between normal behavior of a system and observed behavior. This differencing process is quite simple in some cases. For example, identifying fever as an element in $M^+$ in the above description just involves recognizing that the given temperature is outside of the normal range. In other situations, extracting $M^+$ from observed behavior is much more involved and requires a significant amount of inferencing itself. The problem of extracting $M^+$ has been examined in some detail in such applications as analysis of models of biological tree growth (Tagamets & Reggia, 1985), classification of errors in sequential processes (Ahuja & Reggia, 1986), and in diagnosis of faults in electronic systems (Reiter, 1987; DeKleer & Williams, 1987).

Another practical aspect of diagnostic problem solving is the possible availability of partial solutions. For example, in the above patient description the fact that the patient is diabetic represents an assertion that a disorder is present, not a manifestation. Applying parsimonious covering in the face of such volunteered information requires not only that diabetes be part of any overall diagnostic hypothesis, but that those elements of $M^+$ presumably caused by diabetes (proprioception loss) should be handled accordingly. Algorithms that perform parsimonious covering in the context of volunteered partial solutions have been developed for fairly general classes of diagnostic problems (Peng & Reggia, 1987b).

Finally, it should be appreciated that human diagnosticians can justify their diagnostic hypotheses, and that automated justification of problem solutions is an important feature for acceptability of diagnostic expert systems. For this eason, basic methods for automated justification of diagnostic hypotheses formulated as parsimonious covers have been studied (Reggia, Perricone, Nau, & Peng, 1985), but much work in this area remains to be done.

## Integration with Probability Theory

An alternative approach to determining the plausibility of a diagnostic hypothesis based on a *subjective* notion of parsimony is to *objectively* calculate its probability using formal probability theory. The difficulty with this approach in the past has been that general diagnostic problems are multimembership classification problems (Ben-Bassat et al., 1980): multiple disorders can be present simultaneously. A hypothesis $D_1 = \{d_1, d_2, \ldots, d_n\}$ represents the belief that disorders $d_1$ and $d_2$ and . . . and $d_n$ are present, and that all $d_i$ not listed in $D_I$ are absent. Such problems are very difficult to solve (Ben-Bassat et al., 1980; Charniak, 1983). Among other things, letting $N = |D|$ be the total number of possible disorders, the set of $2^N$ diagnostic hypotheses $D_I$ that must be ranked in some fashion is incredibly large in most real-world applications. For example, in medicine, even constrained diagnostic problems may have $50 \leq N \leq 100$, and thus $2^{50}$ to $2^{100}$

hypotheses to consider; see (Reggia et al., 1983). Furthermore, there has not been any generally accepted method to rank hypotheses $D_I$ relative to one another in multimembership problems.

Recently, we have been successful in integrating formal probability theory into the framework of parsimonious covering theory in a way that overcomes some of these past difficulties (Peng & Reggia, 1986, 1987a). This is achieved as follows. In the knowledge base, a prior probability $p_i$ is associated with each disorder $d_i$ in $D$ where $0 < p_i < 1$. A *causal strength* $0 < c_{ij} \leq 1$ is associated with each causal association in $C$, representing how frequently $d_i$ causes $m_j$. For any $d_i$ and $m_j$ not in $C$, $c_{ij}$ is assumed to be zero. A very important point here is that $c_{ij} \neq P(m_j|d_i)$.[8] The probability $c_{ij}$, defined as $c_{ij} = P(d_i$ causes $m_j|d_i)$, represents how frequently $d_i$ causes $m_j$ when $d_i$ is present; the probability $P(m_j|d_i)$, which is what has been used in previous statistical diagnostic models, represents how frequently $m_j$ occurs when $d_i$ is present. Because typically more than one disorder is capable of causing a given manifestation $m_j$, $P(m_j|d_i) \geq c_{ij}$. For example, if $d_i$ cannot cause $m_j$ at all, $c_{ij} = 0$, but $P(m_j|d_i) \geq 0$ because some other disorder present simultaneously with $d_i$ may cause $m_j$. More concretely, if $d_i$ = "nail in left front tire" and $m_j$ = "car will not start," then $c_{ij} = 0$ because a nail in a tire does not cause a car to fail to start. However, $P(m_j|d_i)$ is greater than zero because it is the case that from time to time a car with a nail in a tire will not start (e.g., coincidentally its battery is dead).

By introducing the notion of causal strengths, and by assuming that disorders are independent of each other, that causal strengths are invariant (whenever $d_i$ is present, it causes $m_j$ with the probability $c_{ij}$ regardless of other disorders that are present), and that no manifestation can occur without being caused by some disorder, a careful analysis derives a formula for $P(D_I|M^+)$, the probability of any diagnostic hypothesis $D_I$ given the presence of any $M^+$, from formal probability theory (Peng & Reggia, 1986, 1987a). Here $D_I$ denotes the event that all disorders in $D_I$ are present and all other disorders absent, while $M^+$ denotes the event that all manifestations in $M^+$ are present and all others absent. In particular, it can be shown that

$$P(D_I \mid M^+) = K(M^+) \cdot L(D_I, M^+)$$

where $K(M^+)$ is a constant for all $D_I$ given any $M^+$, and $L(D_I, M^+)$, called the relative likelihood of $D_I$ given $M^+$, involves only probabilistic information related to $d_i \, \varepsilon \, D_I$ and $m_j \, \varepsilon \, M^+$ instead of the entire associative network. For this reason, $L(D_I, M^+)$ is computationally very tractable.

These results make it possible to compare the relative likelihood of any two diagnostic hypotheses $D_I$ and $D_J$ using

---

[8] The notation $P(m_j|d_i)$ means the probability of $m_j$ given that $d_i$ is known to be present, and is referred to as the conditional probability of $m_j$ given $d_i$.

$$\frac{P(D_I \mid M^+)}{P(D_J \mid M^+)} = \frac{L(D_I, M^+)}{L(D_J, M^+)} .$$

In addition to providing a method for ranking a set of parsimonious covers identified as the solution to a diagnostic problem, there are some other immediate benefits to be derived from this result.

By applying this form of Bayesian classification extended to work in the framework of parsimonious covering theory, we have been able to examine various intuitive/subjective criteria for hypothesis plausibility in an *objective* fashion. Consistent with intuition and concepts in parsimonious covering theory, probability theory leads to the conclusion that a set of disorders must be a cover to be plausible hypothesis (noncovers have zero probability). Further, conditions can now be stated for when various criteria of simplicity or parsimony are reasonable heuristics for judging plausibility, based on whether or not they are guaranteed to identify the most probable hypothesis (Peng & Reggia, 1986). For example, minimal cardinality is only appropriate to consider when all disorders are very uncommon and of about equal probability, and causal strengths are fairly large. If some disorders are relatively much more common than others, or if some causal strengths are weak, using minimal cardinality as a heuristic to select plausible diagnostic hypotheses is inadequate. In this latter situation, typical of most real-world problems, the criterion of irredundancy may be appropriate.

Irredundancy is generally quite attractive as a plausibility criterion for diagnostic hypotheses, and the set of all irredundant covers of a set of given manifestations $M^+$ can be shown usually to include the most likely hypothesis. However, there are two difficulties with directly generating the set of all irredundant covers for consideration as diagnostic hypotheses. First, this set may itself be quite large in some applications, and may contain many hypotheses of very low probability. Second, and more serious, it may still miss identifying the most probable diagnostic hypothesis in some cases (Peng & Reggia, 1986). This latter difficulty is an insight concerning plausibility criteria that has not been previously recognized.

Fortunately, both difficulties are surmountable. A heuristic function based on a modification of $L(D_I, M^+)$ can be used to guide a heuristic search algorithm to first locate a few most likely irredundant covers for $M^+$. Then, a typically small amount of additional search of the "neighborhood" of each of these irredundant covers can be done to see if any relevant but redundant covers are more likely. An algorithm to do this and a proof that it is guaranteed to identify the most likely diagnostic hypothesis has been presented in detail elsewhere (Peng & Reggia, 1987a).

There are a number of generalizations that could be made to these results concerning probability theory, and we view these as important directions for further research. Our use of Bayesian classification with a causal model assumed that disorders occur independently of one another. Because in some diagnostic problems this is unrealistic, a logical extension of this work would be to generalize it to such problems. Some related work has already been done along these lines in setting bounds on the relative likelihood of disorders with Bayesian classification (Cooper, 1984). In addition, we have developed only one method of ranking hypotheses (Bayes' Theorem) to work in causal domains involving multiple simultaneous disorders. It may be that with suitable analysis other approaches to ranking hypotheses could also be adopted in a similar fashion, for example, Dempster-Shafer theory (Dempster, 1968; Shafer, 1976). Some initial work along these lines with fuzzy measures has already been done (Yager, 1985).

## Advanced Issues and Challenges

There are a number of other generalizations or extensions that have been or can be made to parsimonious covering theory, and we point some of these out here. Perhaps the most obvious is that more general associative networks can be used. This involves the use of associative or *causal chaining:* A causes B, and B causes C, so A indirectly causes C (the first two causal associations are "chained together" to form the third, reflecting the fact that causation is a transitive relationship). It has been possible to develop provably correct algorithms that peform parsimonious covering in fairly general situations involving causal chaining (Peng & Reggia, 1987b).

Other work in progress is investigating several related topics:

1. Incorporation of classification taxonomies into parsimonious covering theory.
2. Extension of the theory to work with causal associations involving quantified variables.
3. Modification of parsimonious covering theory so that it can be used for nondiagnostic abductive tasks such as natural language processing (Dasigi & Reggia, 1987).
4. Integration of the theory with underlying causal mechanism models.

Many of these topics are being examined in the context of developing a large, real-world diagnostic reasoning model (Reggia, Tuhrim, Ahuja, et al., 1986).

## ROLE IN COGNITIVE DIAGNOSIS
## AND ADAPTIVE INSTRUCTION

There is a great deal of interest today in developing automated systems for *adaptive instruction:* computer programs that dynamically adjust their instruction to fit the individual student's competence, learning rate, and abilities (Gable & Page, 1980; Sleeman & Brown, 1982). Such intelligent tutoring systems must be able to model the student and, to some extent, must assess his/her cognitive state, a task sometimes referred to as *cognitive diagnosis* (Ohlsson, 1986). In the following, we use this term in a somewhat more specific fashion consistent with the more widespread use of the word *diagnosis*. In particular, we define *cognitive diagnosis* to be the task of inferring the *differences* between a person's cognitive state and some desire or target state.

From this perspective, parsimonious covering theory can be seen to be directly relevant to adaptive instruction in a number of ways. As a method for performing diagnostic inference, it is generally applicable to any adaptive instructional task involving cognitive diagnosis. It may also be of general relevance to development of a subsequent teaching strategy. In the special case where the knowledge and skills being taught are in some diagnostic application area (e.g., tutoring involving the topic of medical or electronic diagnosis), parsimonious covering theory may also be important as the basis of a student model. In this latter role it can provide a framework for developing overlays or student simulations (Ohlsson, 1986). These issues are discussed below. Although we have applied parsimonious covering to a number of real-world tasks, we have not yet applied it to a cognitive diagnosis problem, so the following discussion should be viewed as proposed applications awaiting empirical study.

## As a Framework for Cognitive Diagnosis

Parsimonious covering theory can be used to perform cognitive diagnosis by applying it to infer the *differences* between a student's cognitive state and a desired or target state. For our purposes we define a student's cognitive state as having three components. These are the information currently in working memory, the information currently in long-term memory consisting of both procedural and nonprocedural knowledge, and an inference mechanism used to reason with the existing knowledge. Because an individual's cognitive state is not directly observable, we are restricted to observing a student's responses to ascertain it. For clarity, we simplify and are concerned only with inferring errors in procedural or nonprocedural, long-term memory in the following discussion.

To be specific, we now consider how a cognitive diagnosis problem can be mapped onto the framework of parsimonious covering theory. Formally, a diagnostic problem is specified by $D$, the set of all possible disorders; $M$, the set of all possible manifestations; $C$, the causal relationship that exists between $D$ and $M$; and $M^+$, the set of manifestations present in a specific problem. In cognitive diagnosis, $D$ represents the set of all possible disorders or *faults* in a student's cognitive state. Such faults could include missing knowledge about the existence of important concepts or associations between concepts, incorrect associations, or mistakes in procedural information (e.g., in a sequence, omission of a step, addition of an extraneous step, reversal of the order of two steps, substitution of one step for another, etc.; for discussion of generic errors in sequential processes, see Ahuja & Reggia, 1986 or Sankoff & Kruskal, 1983).

Similarly, $M$ represents the set of all possible observable errors (incorrect answers) that a student can make. An observable error, defined as any difference between a student's response and the target response, represents a manifestation. (A target response is any acceptable response that would be generated by the "target cognitive state," the correct knowledge that is to be conveyed to the student.) For example, for the arithmetic task "subtract 268 from 513," the target or correct response is 245. Given a student answer of 355, the set of student errors might be represented as the manifestations

$$M^+ = \{\text{"the first digit is 1 too large," "the second digit is 1 too large"}\}$$

reflecting the differences between the target and actual answers.

The relation $C$ represents causal associations between faults in the student's cognitive state (disorders) and possible observable errors in the student's response to questions (manifestations). For example, suppose a student's knowledge of how to do subtraction contains a Borrow-no-decrement[9] fault. In this case the knowledge base in a cognitive diagnosis system should contain a causal relation between this disorder and manifestations representing "non-rightmost digits in the answer are one greater than the correct value." Thus, a Borrow-no-decrement error in a student's cognitive state could account for or cover an answer of 355 in subtracting 268 from 513.

The set $M^+$ represents those errors observed in a specific student's response or answer during a tutoring session. The existence of an incorrect answer (observable error) implies that at least one disorder or fault exists somewhere in the student's cognitive state. Parsimonious covering would then seek to find an explanation for all detected manifestations, $M^+$, that are present, in terms of faults in a student's cognitive state. For example, if a student gives an answer of 355 in subtracting 268 from 513, and the causal associations described in the preceding paragraph exist, and no other information is available so that

$$M^+ = \{\text{"the first digit is 1 too large," "the second digit is 1 too large"}\}$$

contains two manifestations, then the resultant solution to this cognitive diagnosis task would include the parsimonious cover

$$D^+ = \{\text{Borrow-no-decrement}\}$$

containing a single disorder. Of course, other parsimonious covers might also be possible.

To apply parsimonious covering successfully to a cognitive diagnosis task, it seems clear that a great deal of thought needs to go into formulating the sets $D$,

---

[9] Student fails to decrement appropriate minuend digits when borrowing during subtraction.

$M$ and $C$ for specific tutoring applications. Further, the set of existing student errors, $M^+$, must be established dynamically during problem solving. This involves finding any differences between a student's responses and the target responses. Given $M$, $D$, $C$, and $M^+$, parsimonious covering can determine plausible sets of disorders or faults in a student's cognitive state that can serve as hypotheses for why the observed student errors occurred. Multiple disorders or faults in a cognitive state may be present, and a strength of parsimonious covering is that it still functions even when a single disorder does not account for all of the observed student errors. Once the disorders are found, the adaptive instructional system can focus its tutoring efforts accordingly.

In addition, it is possible that parsimonious covering could also be used for selection of a teaching strategy once a plausible cognitive diagnosis has been achieved. This application of parsimonious covering is of great theoretical interest because, although parsimonious covering has been used for diagnostic problem solving in the past, until recently it was not applied to the problem of treatment selection. Figure 9.2 depicts the causal relationship between manifestations and disorders, and a relation $R$ between disorders and teaching strategies that could be used to correct them. Cognitive diagnosis involves information in the lower portion of Fig. 9.2, whereas selection of a teaching strategy would involve information in the upper portion.

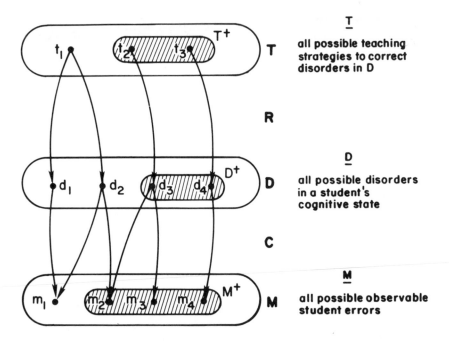

FIG. 9.2.   An associative network used in cognitive diagnosis and teaching strategy selection.

To select a teaching strategy, let $D^+$ be the set of disorders responsible for the observed errors in $M^+$, and let $R$ be the relationship between $D$ and $T$ as they are illustrated in Fig. 9.2. Given $D$, $T$, $R$, and $D^+$, we believe that parsimonious covering could be applied to select appropriate teaching strategies in $T$ to parsimoniously correct hypothesized disorders in $D^+$. For example, in Figure 9.2, teaching strategies $t_2$ and $t_3$ would be selected when disorders or faults $d_3$ and $d_4$ are found to exist in a student's cognitive state.

Recently, parsimonious covering was used as an inference mechanism in an expert system that proposed instructional programs for teachers who were responsible for educating disabled children (Haynes, Pilato, & Malouf, 1986). It was felt that this approach was closer to that used by experts than rule-based deduction, and that it was particularly advantageous for constructing multicomponent plans. However, the parsimony criterion utilized (minimal cardinality; criterion ii-b) proved to be too restrictive, and further assessment of parsimonious covering for selecting teaching strategies is clearly needed.

Some difficult issues are introduced in applying parsimonious covering to perform cognitive diagnosis or other aspects of adaptive tutoring, and a great deal of work remains to be done to produce a working model. As noted earlier, the extraction of the set $M^+$ of differences between observed and target responses can be difficult or computationally expensive. Defining the sets $D$ and $M$, and the causal relation $C$, may also prove to be difficult tasks. For example, in contrast to many diagnostic applications such as medicine, where the sets man($d_i$) and causes ($m_j$) are at least theoretically available in textbooks, in cognitive diagnosis these sets need to be constructed (see Ahuja & Reggia, 1986, for some discussion on this point). It is also not clear yet that this theory could currently be used in an interactive tutoring system due to performance constraints. A student expects a system to react promptly and could become impatient while waiting if the system proved to be too slow. Further application-oriented research should shed light on many of these issues.

## As a Target Student Model

We now turn to a second way in which parsimonious covering could be applied in adaptive instruction. Consider an application, such as medicine, where the goal of the tutoring system is to teach diagnostic problem solving itself. In this scenario, the tutoring system would have access to a medical expert system capable of doing diagnostic problem solving. This medical diagnostic expert system would serve as the desired or target cognitive state for the student, that is, the diagnostic expert system could serve as part of a target student model. To the extent that parsimonious covering models human diagnostic associative memory and inference mechanisms, it could thus serve as the basis for an overlay model or student simulation (Ohlsson, 1986) and be used in this fashion to assess a student's cognitive state.

In an overlay model, a student's knowledge is "laid over" an expert's knowledge to determine how much of the subject matter the student already knows (Carr & Goldstein, 1977; Ohlsson, 1986). Using a medical diagnostic problem-solving system, the tutorial subject matter would be represented by medical concepts in the sets $M$, $D$, and $C$. In our scenario, a student would be given a medical diagnosis problem to solve and the tutoring system would mark the information in the sets $M$, $D$, and $C$ that the student presumably used in solving the problem. At any time during a tutorial session, the marked items would represent the student's knowledge and the unmarked items represent the expert knowledge that the student has not yet been shown to have mastered.

A student simulation is a description of a student's cognitive state that generates the same behavior as the student when applied to a task in the same domain (Ohlsson, 1986). When teaching medical diagnosis, a diagnostic expert system could be used to simulate a student's diagnostic problem-solving behavior. The existing sets $M$, $D$, and $C$ can be masked, marked, or altered to reflect only the knowledge or faults a student has demonstrated. If the correct masking has been done, when parsimonious covering is applied to the sets $M$, $D$, and $C$ that represent the student's medical knowledge, the diagnostic system should mimic the behavior of the student. A simulation could be used to test a hypothesis regarding why a student reasons incorrectly.

It should be appreciated that although we have focused on medical diagnosis as a concrete example in this section, the comments made are generally applicable to any diagnostic application area to which parsimonious covering could be applied (e.g., electronics or mechanics).

## CONCLUSION

This chapter has introduced and summarized the ideas in parsimonious covering theory, and explored ways in which they relate to cognitive diagnosis and adaptive instruction. Although a number of significant results have been obtained in developing parsimonious covering theory, much work remains to be done to extend the formalism and increase its generality. A pressing need at present is to test further the concepts in parsimonious covering theory through their application in real-world computational systems.

We are currently developing a large, knowledge-based diagnostic expert system that uses parsimonious covering theory. The system, called NEUREX for *Neuro*logical *Expe*rtise, can be applied to perform neurological localization and diagnosis (Reggia, Tuhrim, Ahuja, et al., 1986). The purpose of the NEUREX system is to serve as a substantial real-world application to permit the critical evaluation of concepts used in parsimonious covering theory. Parsimonious covering would not only be used to perform the application-related, diagnostic problem solving, but it would also be used to support cognitive diagnosis during adaptive instruction in the ways outlined here. Ultimately, parsimonious covering would be tested as a method for selecting a teaching strategy.

The use of parsimonious covering theory in this fashion is a departure from diagnostic methods used in previous cognitive diagnosis systems. For example, DEBUGGY uses an exhaustive search of a fi> .1 set of hypotheses followed by some problem-reduction techniques (Burton, 1982), and the Diagnostic Pathfinder uses a selective search guided by psychological criteria (Ohlsson & Langley, 1985). Further, parsimonious covering uses a knowledge base represented as a causal associative network. In contrast, many previous tutoring systems, such as the LISP tutor (Anderson, Boyle, Corbett, & Lewis, 1986) and GUIDON (Clancey, 1982), model knowledge using production rules. The extent to which the differences in the approach taken in parsimonious covering could be useful in real-world cognitive diagnosis systems remains to be determined.

## ACKNOWLEDGMENTS

Preparation of this chapter was supported in part by NSF Award DCR-8451430 with matching industrial funds from Software A&E, AT&T Information Systems, and Allied, and in part by NIH Award NS-16332. Technical assistance by Gloria Handy in preparing this manuscript is gratefully acknowledged.

## REFERENCES

Ahuja, S., & Reggia, J. (1986). Using abductive inferencing to derive complex error simulations for discrete sequential processes. In D. Kembler (Ed.), *Proceedings of the Nineteenth Annual Simulation Symposium* (pp. 207–225). Washington, DC: IEEE Computer Society Press.

Anderson, J. R., Boyle, C. F., Corbett, A., & Lewis, M. (1986). *Cognitive modelling and intelligent tutoring* (Tech. Rep. No. ONR-86-1). Pittsburgh, PA: Carnegie-Mellon University, Psychology Department.

Barrows, H. (1972). The diagnostic (problem solving) skill of the neurologist. *Archives of Neurology, 26,* 273–277.

Ben-Bassat, M., Carlson, R., Puri, V., Davenport, J., Schriver, M., Latif, M., Smith, R., Portigal, L., Lipnick, E., & Weil, M. (1980). Pattern-based interactive diagnosis of multiple disorders: The medas system. *IEEE Transactions on Pattern Analysis and Machine Intelligence, 2,* 148–160.

Burton, R. R. (1982). Diagnosing bugs in a simple procedural skill. In D. Sleeman & J. S. Brown (Eds.), *Intelligent tutoring systems* (pp. 157–183). New York: Academic Press.

Carr, B., & Goldstein, I. (1977). *Overlays: A theory of modelling for CAI* (MIT AI Memo 406). Cambridge, MA: Massachusetts Institute of Technology.

Charniak, E. (1983). The Bayesian basis of common sense medical diagnosis. *Proceedings of the National Conference on Artificial Intelligence* (pp. 70–73). Los Altos, CA: Kaufmann.

Charniak, E., & McDermott, D. (1985). *Introduction to artificial intelligence* (Ch. 8 & 10). Reading, MA: Addison-Wesley.

Clancey, W. J. (1982). Tutoring rules for guiding a case method dialogue. In D. Sleeman & J. S. Brown (Eds.), *Intelligent tutoring systems* (pp. 201–225). New York: Academic Press.

Cooper, G. (1984). *NESTOR: A computer-based medical diagnostic aid that integrates causal and probabilistic knowledge* (Tech. Rep. No. STAN-CS-84-1031). Palo Alto, CA: Stanford University.

Dasigi, V., & Reggia, J. (1987). Abduction in discourse processing: A parsimonious covering model. In J. Boudreaux, B. Hamill, & R. Jernigan (Eds.), *The role of language in problem solving* (pp. 49–67). Amsterdam: North Holland.

deDombal, F. (1975). Computer assisted diagnosis of abdominal pain. In J. Rose & J. Mitchell (Eds.), *Advances in medical computing* (pp. 10–19). New York: Churchill-Livingston.

deKleer, J., & Williams, B. (1987). Diagnosing multiple faults. *Artificial Intelligence, 32*, 97–130.

Dempster, A. (1968). A generalization of Bayesian inference. *Journal of Royal Statistical Science, 30*, 205–247.

Elstein, A., Shulman, L., & Sprafka, S. (1978). *Medical problem solving: An analysis of clinical reasoning*. Cambridge, MA: Harvard University Press.

Gable, A., & Page, C. (1980). The use of artificial intelligence techniques in computer-assisted instruction: An overview. *International Journal of Man-Machine Studies, 12*, 259–282.

Haynes, J., Pilato, V., & Malouf, D. (1986). Expert systems for educational decision making. *Education Technology*.

Josephson, J. (1982). *Explanation and induction*. Unpublished doctoral dissertation, Ohio State University, Columbus, OH.

Kassirer, J., & Gorry, G. (1978). Clinical problem solving: A behavioral analysis. *Annals of Internal Medicine, 89*, 245–255.

Kingsland, L., Sharp, G., Capps, R., Benge, J., Kay, D., Reese, G., Hazelwood, S., & Lindberg, D. (1983). Testing of a criteria-based consultant system in rheumatology. In J. vanBemmel, M. Ball, & O. Wigertz (Eds.), *Proceedings of MEDINFO-83* (pp. 514–517). Amsterdam: North Holland.

Miller, R., Pople, H., & Myers, J. (1982). INTERNIST-1, An experimental computer-based diagnostic consultant for general internal medicine. *New England Journal of Medicine, 307*, 468–476.

Nau, D., & Reggia, J. (1984). Relationship between deductive and abductive inference in knowledge-based diagnostic problem solving. In L. Kerschberg (Ed.), *Proceedings of the First International Workshop on Expert Database Systems* (pp. 500–509). Melo Park, CA: Benjamin/Cummings.

Ohlsson, S. (1986). Some principles of intelligent tutoring. *Instructional Science, 14*, 293–326.

Ohlsson, S., & Langley, P. (1985). Psychological evaluation of cognitive diagnosis. In H. Mandl & A. Lesgold (Eds.), *Learning issues for intelligent tutoring systems*. New York: Springer-Verlag.

Pauker, S., Gorry, G., Kassirer, J., & Schwartz, W. (1976). Towards the simulation of clinical cognition. *American Journal of Medicine, 60*, 981–996.

Peirce, C. (1955). *Abduction and induction*. New York: Dover.

Peng, Y., & Reggia, J. (1986). Plausibility of diagnostic hypotheses: The nature of simplicity. *Proceedings of the National Conference on Artificial Intelligence* (pp. 140–145). Los Altos, CA: Kaufmann.

Peng, Y., & Reggia, J. (1987a). A probabilistic causal model for diagnostic problem-solving. *IEEE Transactions on Systems, Man and Cybernetics, 17*, 146–162 & 395–406.

Peng, Y., & Reggia, J. (1987b). Diagnostic problem-solving with causal chaining. *International Journal of Intelligent Systems, 2*, 265–302.

Pople, H. (1982). Heuristic methods for imposing structure on ill-structured problems: The structuring of medical diagnostics. In P. Szolovits (Ed.), *Artificial intelligence in medicine* (pp. 119–190). Boulder, CO: Westview.

Ramsey, C., Reggia, J., Nau, D., & Ferrentino, A. (1986). A comparative analysis of methods for expert systems. *International Journal of Man–Machine Studies, 24*, 475–499.

Reggia, J. (1985). Abductive inference. In K. Karna (Ed.), *Proceedings of Expert Systems in Government Symposium* (pp. 484–489). Washington, DC: IEEE Computer Society Press.

Reggia, J., Nau, D., & Wang, P. (1983). Diagnostic expert systems based on a set covering model. *International Journal of Man–Machine Studies, 19*, 437–460.

Reggia, J., Nau, D., & Wang, P. (1985). A formal model of diagnostic inference. *Information Sciences, 37,* 227–285.

Reggia, J., Perricone, B., Nau, D., & Peng, Y. (1985). Answer justification in diagnostic expert systems. *IEEE Transactions on Biomedical Engineering, 32,* 263–272.

Reggia, J., Tabb, D., Price, T., Banko, M., & Hebel, R. (1984). Computer-aided assessment of transient ischemic attacks: A clinical evaluation. *Archives of Neurology, 41,* 1248–1254.

Reggia, J., & Tuhrim, S. (1985). An overview of methods for computer-assisted medical decision making. In J. Reggia & S. Tuhrim (Eds.), *Computer-assisted medical decision making* (Vol. 1, pp. 3–45). New York: Springer-Verlag.

Reggia, J., Tuhrim, S., Ahuja, S., Pula, T., Chu, B., Dasigi, V., & Lubell, J. (1986). Plausible reasoning during neurological problem-solving. In *Proceedings of the Fifth World Congress on Medical Informatics* (pp. 17–21). Amsterdam: North Holland.

Reiter, R. (1987). A theory of diagnosis from first principles. *Artificial Intelligence, 32,* 57–95.

Rouse, W. (1979). Problem solving performance of maintenance trainees in a fault diagnosis task. *Human Factors, 21,* 195–203.

Rubins, A. (1975). The role of hypothesis in medical diagnosis. *Fourth International Joint Conference on Artificial Intelligence* (pp. 856–862). Los Altos, CA: Kaufmann.

Sankoff, D., & Kruskal, J. (1983). *Time warps, string edits, and macromolecules.* Reading, MA: Addison-Wesley.

Shafer, G. (1976). *A mathematical theory of evidence.* Princeton, NJ: Princeton University Press.

Shubin, H., & Ulrich, J. (1982). IDT: An intelligent diagnostic tool. *Proceedings of the National Conference on Artificial Intelligence* (pp. 290–295). Los Altos, CA: Kaufmann.

Sleeman, D., & Brown, J. (Eds.). (1982). *Intelligent tutoring systems.* New York: Academic Press.

Tagamets, M., & Reggia, J. (1985). *Abductive hypothesis formation and refinement during construction of natural system models* (Tech. Rep. No. 1463). College Park, MD: University of Maryland, Department of Computer Science.

Thagard, P. (1978). The best explanation: Criteria for theory choice. *Journal of Philosophy, 75,* 76–92.

Wortman, P. (1966). Representation and strategy in diagnostic problem solving. *Human Factors, 8,* 48–53.

Yager, R. (1985). Explanatory models in expert systems. *International Journal of Man–Machine Studies, 23,* 539–549.

Zagoria, R., & Reggia, J. (1983). Transferability of medical decision support systems based on Bayesian classification. *Medical Decision Making, 3,* 501–510.

# Rules and Principles
# in Cognitive Diagnosis

Pat Langley
James Wogulis
*University of California, Irvine*

Stellan Ohlsson
*Learning Research and Development Center*
*University of Pittsburgh*

## A FRAMEWORK FOR COGNITIVE DIAGNOSIS

One of psychology's central goals is the description of human behavior. However, it has become increasingly clear that psychology faces several complications in its pursuit of that goal. The most important of these complications is that individual differences appear to be an essential aspect of the human condition. Different people have different experiences and thus acquire different knowledge and skills. Moreover, the behavior of even a single human varies over time as he gains more experience and more expertise.

In this chapter, we present one response to the problems of how to deal with individual differences and change over time. Our approach builds on three related research methodologies. The first is cognitive simulation, a paradigm for constructing process models of human cognitive behavior. The second is heuristic search, one of the mainstays of artificial intelligence. The third component is machine learning, the subfield of artificial intelligence that focuses on computational methods for improving performance over time. Out goal is to *automate* the process of constructing cognitive simulations. This is the problem of *cognitive diagnosis* (Ohlsson & Langley, 1986), and we employ methods from heuristic search and machine learning to this end.

Within the field of computer-aided instruction (CAI) and intelligent tutoring systems, the problem of cognitive diagnosis goes by another name—*student modeling*. Unlike most CAI systems, human teachers employ some model of the student's knowledge state to determine their instructional actions. Intelligent teaching systems would also gain from such student models, but they must first have some means to infer the student's knowledge from his or her overt behavior.

Because this problem is equivalent to that confronting the cognitive psychologist attempting to construct a model of some subject, we use the more general term *cognitive diagnosis* in our discussion.

## Testing and Cognitive Simulation

Before delving into the problem of cognitive diagnosis and our proposed solution, we should review a major alternative to this approach. The testing tradition in psychology has a long and venerable history, dating back to Galton and Binet. The basic paradigm involves identifying dimensions of intellectual variation and designing tests to measure ability along these dimensions. Thus, test psychology has explicitly focused on the problem of individual differences, and has led to many practical results over the years. Tests are easy to apply and interpret, making them attractive in many settings. This approach has been particularly useful in predicting academic success, making it quite popular within educational psychology.

However, the testing paradigm makes a number of limiting assumptions. First, it does not attempt to generate a theoretical description of an individual's state of knowledge; it is content to summarize a person's behavior in terms of empirically derived test scores. Second, test psychology interprets these scores as stable properties of the individual, thus ignoring the changes that occur over time as the result of learning. Finally, the testing framework focuses on quantitative descriptions of behavior, and this representation severely limits its descriptive and explanatory power.

Now let us turn to the paradigm of cognitive simulation, a quite different approach with a much shorter history, first formulated by Newell, Shaw, and Simon (1960). Like the testing approach, this framework also focuses on individual analyses. However, it differs in that the goal is a detailed description of the subject's cognitive behavior. This description takes the form of a running computer program that simulates the subject's performance, hence the term *cognitive simulation*. These simulations specify the structures and processes leading to behavior, rather than providing numeric descriptions like those in test psychology. Finally, the approach also has potential for modeling learning, and thus accounting for changes in performance over time.

Despite these advantages, the methodology of cognitive simulation has gained relatively few adherents in the years since its inception. Undoubtedly, one reason is the difficulty of gathering and analyzing data such as verbal protocols, and another is the skill and patience involved in constructing a detailed cognitive simulation that explains these data. In contrast, tests are easy to administer and their results are simple to interpret. Our long-term goal is to automate the process of constructing simulation models, making the framework of cognitive diagnosis as manageable and attractive as the testing approach.

## Assumptions for Cognitive Diagnosis

Before we can automate the diagnostic process, we must establish the framework within which we can operate. There exists a variety of schemes for modeling cognitive processes in computational terms, and the more constrained our models, the better chance we have to automate their construction. Let us consider the assumptions underlying our cognitive models, along with the alternatives.

The most basic assumption is that knowledge is represented using *symbols*, and that these symbols are grouped into propositions. Newell (1980) has referred to this general approach as the *physical symbol system* hypothesis. For instance, we can represent the subtraction problem $43 - 21$ with propositions like (in 4 column-1 row-1), (in 3 column-2 row-1), and so forth. In such representations, the symbols themselves have meaning; thus, *4* represents the number *four* and row-1 stands for a particular position.[1] One could easily map our propositional scheme onto other symbolic paradigms, such as semantic networks. However, both frameworks contrast sharply with research in the connectionist paradigm that relies on the *subsymbolic* hypothesis—that meaning is represented by configurations of nodes in a network (Anderson & Hinton, 1981). We do not attempt to justify our alignment with the symbolic approach, except to note that this approach has proven very useful in modeling a wide range of cognitive behavior.

Of course, a cognitive simulation requires more than a representation of knowledge—it also requires some processes to manipulate that knowledge. These processes can be organized in various ways, and computer science has traditionally focused on *algorithmic* control schemes. However, this is not the only such organization, and artificial intelligence has emphasized the alternative organization of *heuristic search*. In this framework, one systematically searches a space of possible states, deciding at each point which is most likely to lead to a problem solution. Many AI tasks lend themselves to this approach, including problem solving and language understanding.

A central concept in the heuristic search framework is the *problem space*, which can be defined in terms of an initial problem state and a set of operators for generating new states. Newell and Simon (1972) have put forward the *problem space hypothesis*—that all human cognition involves search through some problem space. In this view, even algorithmic behavior can be viewed as search, though this search is so constrained that behavior is determined at each point. We rely heavily on the problem space hypothesis in the following pages. Again, we do not argue for this assumption, except to mention that it has been successfully applied to many aspects of intelligent behavior.

Although the problem space hypothesis significantly constrains one's models of cognition, it does not specify the representation of operators or the heuristics used to control search. One response is to represent operators as opaque

---

[1] These are examples of declarative knowledge, but as we see shortly, we also assume that procedural knowledge is represented symbolically.

procedures (e.g., LISP functions) that are applied to a given state. The alternative is to represent operators as transparent *production rules* in which the conditions and results are stated as abstract propositions. One can represent heuristic knowledge as some numeric evaluation function that ranks states according to predicted distance to the goal. This approach has a sizable following within artificial intelligence, partially because it is amenable to formal analysis (Pearl, 1984). However, one can also represent control knowledge as heuristic conditions on rules, and this scheme is a natural companion to the transparent operator representation.

Newell (1972, 1973), Anderson (1976), and others have proposed production rules as a general framework for modeling human cognition. A *production system* is a collection of production rules that operates in cycles. On each cycle, the conditions of each rule are matched against the contents of a dynamic working memory. From those rules with conditions that successfully match, some are selected for application and their actions are carried out. These actions alter the contents of working memory, causing new rules to match on the next cycle. This recognize/act cycle continues until no rules are matched or an explicit halt action is evoked. We assume that all procedural knowledge is represented as such condition–action rules. This *production system* hypothesis constitutes our third assumption. Taken together, our three assumptions significantly restrict the class of models that we must consider in constructing cognitive simulations.

## Three Stages of Cognitive Diagnosis

Newell and Simon (1972) identified three successive stages in the diagnostic process, each providing a more detailed model of behavior. First, one must identify the problem space in which a given subject is operating. This involves selecting some representation for states and operators, including the legal conditions on the latter. One must also specify some termination criteria; this is usually represented as one or more tests for detecting when a goal state has been reached. Identifying the subject's problem space is a very difficult task, and we have not attempted to automate this aspect of cognitive diagnosis.

Second, one must identify the path followed by the subject while working on each problem. This involves examining the subject's behavioral record and inferring a sequence of state selections and operator applications. Newell and Simon (1972) employed the method of protocol analysis to this end, but verbal protocols are difficult to analyze and not always available, especially in educational settings.[2] Another approach is to focus on *answer data,* such as a student's responses to test questions. Although such data have a lower temporal density than

---

[2] Waterman and Newell (1972) made some progress towards automating the analysis of verbal protocols, but more work must be done on this problem before it reaches the applications stage.

verbal protocols, they are much easier to collect and may limit the diagnostician to one or a few path hypotheses.

Finally, one must identify some production system model of the subject's behavior that accounts for his or her performance across a number of problems. This set of condition–action rules makes up a running cognitive simulation, and constitutes an hypothesis about the strategy the subject used to solve the problems. Of course, knowledge of the problem space and path traversal can be used to constrain this model. Unfortunately, one cannot always assume that a subject's behavior is consistent across different problems, and this makes the inference process more difficult. Also, we see later that for educational applications, such models may be less useful than the path hypotheses themselves. Thus, it is not clear that one always need generate a complete simulation of the subject's behavior.

## THE SUBTRACTION DOMAIN

Early work in cognitive diagnosis focused on puzzle-solving and reasoning tasks. However, one of the most carefully analyzed areas is that of multicolumn subtraction problems, and we have chosen this domain to test our approach to automated diagnosis. We consider the nature of these problems and the types of errors that arise when students attempt to solve them. After this, we review some previous approaches to diagnosing these errors.

### The Standard Subtraction Algorithm

At first glance, the task of multicolumn subtraction seems relatively straightforward: given two multidigit integers, one must simply find their difference. For instance, $345 - 211 = 134$, $642 - 13 = 629$, and $406 - 138 = 268$. However, the standard algorithm for such problems contains unexpected complexity, and this complexity causes difficulty for many students of arithmetic. Close examination of these three examples reveals some of the reasons.

The first example, $345 - 211$, is the simplest of the set. In this case, one merely finds the difference in the rightmost column (4) and writes down this result. One then moves to the second column, finds the difference there (3) and records the result. Finally, one moves to the leftmost column, finds the last difference (1), and writes the final result, giving the complete answer 134.

The second problem, $642 - 13$, is more difficult because it involves borrowing. One cannot directly subtract 3 from 2, because this would give a negative result. Instead one moves to the adjacent column, decrements the 4 by one to give 3, and then adds ten to the original column, transforming the existing 2 into 12. Now one can subtract 3 from 12, producing the result 9. Next one shifts to the second column and finds the difference between 3 (the decremented 4) and 1, records the result of 2 in this column, and moves to the leftmost column. Because no digit exists in the second row, the digit in the top row (6) is carried down into the result, giving the final answer 629.

Our third example, 406 − 138, is even more complicated, because it involves borrowing from zero. As before, one cannot subtract 8 from 6, so the only option is to borrow from the top digit in the adjacent column. However, one cannot borrow from zero, so one must move over yet another column. Borrowing from the 4 in the leftmost column transforms this digit into 3 and the 0 in the middle column into 10. Now one can borrow from the 10, replacing this number with 9 and the 6 (the original cause of the problem) with 16. These actions let one compute the results for each column in turn, giving the final result 268.

## Errorful Subtraction Algorithms

Brown and Burton (1978) and VanLehn (1982) have carried out detailed analyses of student's subtraction behavior, noting the different types of errors (*bugs*) that occur on various problems. They have identified over 100 basic bugs that students make in this domain. Table 10.1 lists the eleven most common subtraction bugs, along with their relative frequency and an example of each error type. Let us consider some of these procedural misconceptions.

Nearly all subtraction errors occur on borrowing problems. One of the most common borrowing bugs is the smaller-from-larger strategy. In this algorithm, the student subtracts the smaller digit from the larger in a given column, regardless of which is above the other. Thus, the answer generated for 81 − 38 would be 57 (rather than the correct answer 43). Note that this method bypasses the need for decrementing digits and adding ten, making it much simpler than the correct strategy.

TABLE 10.1
Common Subtraction Bugs

| Bug | Example | Frequency |
|---|---|---|
| Correct strategy | 81 − 38 = 43 | |
| Smaller from larger | 81 − 38 = 57 | 124 |
| Stops borrow at zero | 404 − 187 = 227 | 67 |
| Borrow across zero | 904 − 237 = 577 | 51 |
| 0 − N = N | 50 − 23 = 33 | 40 |
| Borrow no decrement | 62 − 44 = 28 | 22 |
| Borrow across zero over zero | 802 − 304 = 408 | 19 |
| 0 − N = N except after borrow | 906 − 484 = 582 | 17 |
| Borrow from zero | 306 − 187 = 219 | 15 |
| Borrow once then smaller from larger | 7127 − 2389 = 5278 | 14 |
| Borrow across zero over blank | 402 − 6 = 306 | 13 |
| 0 − N = 0 | 50 − 23 = 30 | 12 |

Some types of errors occur only when borrowing from zero is involved. For instance, in the borrow-across-zero bug, the student decrements the digit left of the zero twice to avoid borrowing from zero. Thus, this algorithm generates 577 for the problem $904 - 237$, rather than the correct answer 667. The borrow-across-zero-over-zero is a variation on this bug, in which the errorful behavior is only invoked when two zeros occur in the same column. This strategy generates 408 (instead of 498) as the answer for $802 - 304$, while producing the correct answer for $904 - 237$.

Young and O'Shea (1981) have used the label *pattern errors* to refer to another class of misconceptions. One of these is the $0 - N = N$ bug, in which the student avoids borrowing by using the digit in the second row as the answer for the current column. The $0 - N = 0$ bug has a very similar flavor. For the problem $50 - 23$, the first strategy generates the answer 33, whereas the second method produces 30 as the final result. Special cases of these algorithms also exist, such as $0 - N = N$ except after borrow.

These examples give only a flavor of the errors that can occur on multicolumn subtraction problems, but they should help the reader understand the complexity of the behaviors we hope to diagnose. Moreover, the various bugs may occur in combination, producing even more complex errors than is possible by each in isolation. Finally, students are not always consistent in their errorful behavior, sometimes using different algorithms at the beginning and the end of the same test; VanLehn (1982) has called these *bug migrations*.

## DEBUGGY and Bug Libraries

In addition to empirical studies of subtraction errors, a number of researchers have developed computational models of this behavior. The earliest and best known effort along these lines was Brown and Burton's (1978) DEBUGGY system. This system used a hierarchical procedural network to represent the correct algorithm for multicolumn subtraction. Associated with some nodes in this network were 'buggy' versions of that subroutine. If one of these buggy routines were used in place of the standard node, the algorithm would still run, but it would generate an incorrect answer.

Langley, Ohlsson, and Sage (1984) call this the *bug library* approach to cognitive diagnosis. One of its main advantages is that it decomposes behavior into a number of relatively independent components. These can be used in isolation or in combination to explain observed deviations from correct behavior. The key word here is 'deviations.' The bug library framework attempts to model errors as minor variations on the correct strategy. This approach has also been successfully applied to other domains; for instance, Sleeman and Smith (1981) have used bug libraries to model errors in algebra problem solving.

The main disadvantage of bug libraries is that they require extensive empirical analysis to identify bugs that actually occur in the domain. For example, VanLehn

(1982) has reported over 100 distinct procedural errors that occur in multicolumn subtraction, and DEBUGGY would represent each of these misconceptions as another alternative subroutine in its procedural network.[3] In addition, the farther a subject's behavior from the standard algorithm, the more difficult it is to develop a buggy model. Different bugs can interact with one another, making it difficult to diagnose algorithms involving multiple misconceptions.

However, DEBUGGY did much more than represent errorful subtraction algorithms; the system also *inferred* a student's strategy from his observed answers. The simplest approach would involve a generate-and-test scheme in which each bug is inserted into the procedural network and checked to see whether it explains the student's behavior. If none of the bugs is sufficient by itself, then all pairs of bugs would be considered, then triples, and so forth. Although this scheme is guaranteed to work if the subject's behavior is covered by the bug library, it is combinatorial in nature, and thus very expensive. In fact, DEBUGGY used a more sophisticated diagnostic method based on a discrimination network. Particular types of errors would suggest different bugs, and the system would then gather the evidence for each competing hypothesis.

## Production System Models of Subtraction

Young and O'Shea (1981) have taken a quite different approach to explaining subtraction errors. Rather than representing arithmetic algorithms as procedural networks, they employed a production system formalism. The researchers modeled the standard subtraction strategy as a set of condition–action rules, explaining errors in terms of slight variations on this model. In many cases, they were able to model errors simply by deleting one or two production rules. Using this approach, they explained many of the most common subtraction bugs described by Brown and Burton (1978).

Although Young and O'Shea did not implement an automated diagnostic system, the rule deletion approach provides a natural foundation for such a system. Given a set of production rules for the correct algorithm, one can easily check to see whether removing various rules will explain a subject's errors. This approach is possible because production rules are relatively independent of each other and, when a production system model is carefully formulated, it will continue to run (though incorrectly) when rules are removed. Although the nodes in a procedural network are independent, they do not have this latter feature.

Unfortunately, Young and O'Shea were forced to introduce additional production rules to model certain subtraction errors, and this complicates the diagnostic method we just outlined. These rules contained standard actions for the subtraction domain, but applied those actions under the incorrect conditions. One could

---

[3] Brown and VanLehn (1980) have tried to remedy this drawback with their repair theory, which attempts to explain the origin of subtraction bugs.

generate a set of such incorrect rules and employ them in diagnosis, but with this modification the approach begins to take on the flavor of a bug library.[4]

# A NEW APPROACH TO SUBTRACTION DIAGNOSIS

Although the Young and O'Shea framework has limitations, it points the way to a more flexible approach to diagnosis. If we assume that *all* errors are due to rules with the correct actions but the wrong conditions, then diagnosis consists of determining the subject's conditions for each rule in the domain. This is the approach we take to automating the diagnostic process in the subtraction domain. The 'correct actions' correspond to the operators in a problem space, whereas the 'subject's conditions' correspond to the heuristic conditions for applying those operators.

## Identifying a Problem Space

As we have seen, the first step in our approach requires one to identify the problem space in which the subject is operating. This is a very difficult problem and little work in AI and cognitive science has addressed the issue. Rather than automating this aspect of the diagnostic process, we use the standard subtraction space as defined by Ohlsson and Langley (1986).

The first step in defining a problem space involves specifying the *problem states* contained in that space. We represent states in the subtraction domain as lists of relations between objects; this decision is consistent with previous analyses of student problems (VanLehn, 1982). The objects consist of digits, columns, and rows in the problem display. Relations between these objects include predicates like *above, left-of, in,* and so forth. A given problem state is represented as a set of such relations between objects. For example, the initial state for the two column subtraction problem 93 − 25 would be represented by the list of relations shown in Table 10.2.

In addition to such relational information, a problem state can also contain control information. For example, the statement (*processing column-1*) in the table signifies that the subject is attempting to find a result for a column-1. Similarly, the focused-on predicate indicates which column is being considered for borrowing operations. Although not shown in the table, a state may also include information about the last operation performed. For example, after the Find-Difference operator has been applied, the problem description would contain the element (*just-did find-difference*).

---

[4] In fact, Sleeman and Smith (1981) used just such a rule-based approach in their LMS system for algebra diagnosis. Their program included both correct algebra productions and *mal-rules* that led to errors.

TABLE 10.2
Initial problem state for 93–25

| | |
|---|---|
| (in 9 column-2 row-1) | (above row-1 row-2) |
| (in 2 column-2 row-2) | (left-of column-2 column-1) |
| (in 3 column-1 row-1) | (processing column-1) |
| (in 5 column-1 row-2) | (focused-on column-1) |
| (result blank column-2) | |
| (result blank column-1) | |

TABLE 10.3
Operators for subtraction

**Add-Ten (number, row, column)** Takes the number in a row and column and replaces it with that number plus ten.

**Decrement (number, row, column)** Takes the number in a row and column and replaces it with that number minus one.

**Find-Difference (number1, number2, column)** Takes the two numbers in the same column and writes the difference of the two as the result for that column.

**Find-Top (column)** Takes a number from the top row of column and writes that number as the result for that column.

**Shift-Column (column)** Takes the column which is both focused-on and being processed and shifts both to the column on its left.

**Shift-Left (column)** Takes the column which is focused-on and shifts the focus of attention to the column on its left.

**Shift-Right (column)** Takes the column which is focused-on and shifts the focus of attention to the column on its right.

Table 10.3 presents one set of operators for multicolumn subtraction. These operators can be used to generate new problem states, and this lets one systematically search the problem space, starting from the initial state. The first two operators—Add-Ten and Decrement—are responsible for borrowing. The second pair—Find-Difference and Find-Top—write the result for a particular column. The final three operators—Shift-Column, Shift-Left, and Shift-Right—influence the control symbols processed and focused-on.

These operators assume a certain set of primitive actions, including the ability to add ten to a digit, subtract any two numbers between 0 and 19, shift attention between columns, and write a result for a column. Such primitive skills define a given level of abstraction, but note that other choices are possible. For instance, we could have also broken the Decrement operator into three simpler operators, one for crossing out a digit, another for subtracting 1 from that digit, and a third for writing the decremented number in its place. This level of description would let us describe subjects' behaviors in more detail, but only at the cost of a much larger problem space.

Similarly, we could have replaced the Decrement and Add-Ten operators with a single Borrow operator, giving a more abstract problem space. This would produce fewer problem states, but we would be unable to model many observed subtraction errors. We believe that the operators in Table 10.3 constitute an optimal level of abstraction for the subtraction domain, but this assumption is open to empirical tests.

The final component of a problem space is the termination condition that specifies when search should halt. In the subtraction domain, this occurs when one has written results for all of the columns, and when these results agree with the subject's answer to the problem. Again, remember that the goal is not to find the correct answer, but to explain how the subject arrived at the observed answer.

## Path Hypotheses

Given a problem space for subtraction and a subject's answer for a particular test problem, we must find some *path hypothesis* that explains the observed answer. Such a path hypothesis consists of the states traversed by the subject, along with the instantiated operators connecting those states.

For the problem–answer pair $93 - 25 = 68$, one explanatory path hypothesis that uses the operators from Table 10.3 would be:

> Shift-Left(column-1)
> Decrement (9, row-1, column-2)
> Shift-Right(column-2)
> Add-Ten(3, row-1, column-1)
> Find-Difference(13, 5, column-1)
> Shift-Column(column-1)
> Find-Difference(8, 2, column-1)

For any problem–answer pair, there could be several path hypotheses, each one providing an explanation of how the subject could have obtained the observed answer.[5]

We can also use path hypotheses to explain *incorrect* answers to subtraction problems. Ohlsson and Langley (1986) have shown how a number of different incorrect answers can be explained through paths in the standard subtraction space. For example, the smaller-from-larger bug (in which the subject always subtracts the smaller number from the larger one in a given column) would give the answer 72 to the problem $93 - 25$. Within our problem space, one path hypothesis that explains this answer would be:

---

[5] In general, there may be more than one 'correct' procedure or algorithm in that all produce the correct answer to all subtraction problems. For instance, the order in which one performs the Add-Ten and Decrement operators does not affect the final answer.

Find-Difference(5, 3, column-1)
Shift-Column(column-1)
Find-Difference(9, 2, column-2)

Note that this path is much shorter than the one needed to generate the correct answer. Empirically, buggy paths appear to be shorter than correct paths for the same problem. We return to this fact when we consider methods for inferring path hypotheses.


## Production System Models

Having generated plausible path hypotheses for a number of problem–answer pairs, we would like some production system model that would generate the inferred solution paths. The mapping from problem space onto production system is straightforward: The working memory on each cycle corresponds to a particular problem state, the action sides of productions represent the operators for generating new states, and the condition sides of productions correspond to the legal and heuristic conditions on these operators.

In a traditional production system, multiple productions can match on any given cycle, and some *conflict resolution* scheme determines which rule to apply. However, one of our goals is to construct diagnostic models that can be easily understood, and we believe that reliance on conflict resolution methods obscures the semantics of such models. Instead, we formulate production rules with mutually exclusive conditions; these guarantee that only one rule matches on each cycle, and this in turn should lead to clearer models.

Table 10.4 presents a production system model of the standard subtraction algorithm. This model includes all of the operators from Table 10.3, and each rule contains both legal conditions (necessary to instantiate the action side) and heuristic conditions (necessary to ensure correct behavior). Heuristic conditions have been enclosed in braces to distinguish them from the legal conditions. (The reader should ignore conditions in brackets; we return to these later.) This model generates the correct answers for all subtraction problems, including the borrowing problem 93 − 25 we saw earlier. In solving this problem, the model produces the first path hypotheses we examined.

Note that two rules in the model—Shift-Left-To-Borrow and Shift-Left-Across-Zero—employ the Shift-Left operator in their action side. Each of these productions covers a different situation in which it is appropriate to shift the focus of attention to the left. This is equivalent to placing *disjunctive* conditions on the Shift-Left operator. In general, a diagnostic system may need to infer that a student uses an operator in such disjunctive situations.

But we are more interested in modeling incorrect subtraction behavior than the correct algorithm. Table 10.5 presents a production system model of the smaller-from-larger bug described earlier. Some aspects of this incorrect strategy

TABLE 10.4
Rules for correct subtraction strategy

---

Add-Ten:
    If *number-a* is in *column-a* and *row-a*,
        {[and you are focused on *column-a*]},
        {[and *row-a* is above *row-b*]},
        {[and there is no result for *column-a*]},
        {[and *number-a* is less than ten]},
        {and you just did Shift-Right},
    then replace *number-a* with *number-a* plus ten.

Decrement:
    If *number-a* is in *column-a* and *row-a*,
        {[and you are focused on *column-a*]},
        {[and *number-a* is not zero]},
        {[and *row-a* is above *row-b*]},
        {[and you did not just Decrement]},
        {[and you are not processing *column-a*]},
        {[and *column-a* is to the left of *column-b*]},
        {[and there is no result for *column-a*]},
        {[and you have not added-ten to *column-b*]},
        {and you did not just Shift-Right},
    then replace *number-a* with *number-a* minus one.

Find-Difference:
    If *number-a* is in *column-a* and *row-a*,
        and *number-b* is in *column-a* and *row-b*,
        {[and you are processing *column-a*]},
        {[and you are focused on *column-a*]},
        {[and there is no result for *column-a*]},
        {and *row-a* is above *row-b*},
        {and *number-a* is greater than or equal to *number-b*},
    then write the difference between *number-a* and *number-b*
    as the result for *column-a*.

Find-Top:
    If *number-a* is in *column-a* and *row-a*,
        and *row-a* is above *row-b*,
        {[and you are processing *column-a*]},
        {[and there is no result for *column-a*]},
        {[and you are focused on *column-a*]},
        {[and there is no number in *column-a* and *row-b*]},
    then write *number-a* as the result for *column-a*.

Shift-Column:
    If you are processing *column-a*,
        and you are focused on *column-a*,
        and *column-b* is to the left of *column-a*,
        {[and there is a result for *column-a*]},
    then shift your focus from *column-a* to *column-b*,
        and process *column-b*.

---

*(continued)*

TABLE 10.4    *(continued)*

---

Shift-Left-to-Borrow:
  If you are focused on *column-a*,
    and *column-b* is to the left of *column-a*,
    [and there is no result for *column-a*],
    [and you did not just Decrement],
    [and you did not just Add-Ten],
    {[and *number-a* is in *column-a* and *row-a*]},
    {[and *number-b* is in *column-a* and *row-b*]},
    {[and *row-a* is above *row-b*]},
    {[and you did not just Shift-Right]},
    {and you are processing *column-a*},
    {and *number-b* is greater than *number-a*},
  then shift your focus from *column-a* to *column-b*.

Shift-Left-Across-Zero:
  If you are focused on *column-a*,
    and *column-b* is to the left of *column-a*,
    [and *number-a* is in *column-a* and *row-a*],
    [and you did not just Decrement],
    [and you did not just Add-Ten],
    [and there is no result for *column-a*],
    {[and *row-a* is above *row-b*]},
    {[and you did not just Shift-Right]},
    {and you are not processing *column-a*},
    {and *number-a* is zero},
  then shift your focus from *column-a* to *column-b*.

Shift-Right:
  If you are focused on *column-a*,
    and *column-a* is to the left of *column-b*,
    [and you did not just Shift-Left],
    [and you are not processing *column-a*],
    {and you just did Decrement},
  then shift your focus from *column-a* to *column-b*.

---

can be accounted for by missing operators; because borrowing never occurs, our model has no need for the Decrement, Add-Ten, Shift-Right, or either Shift-Left rules. The model includes Shift-Column and Find-Top in their correct forms because students with the smaller-from-larger bug still process all columns and behave correctly when no digit exists in the lower row.

However, the model's version of the Find-Difference rule lacks the *above* condition present in the correct model. This means it would subtract the smaller digit in a column from the larger, independent of their spatial relation. Given a nonborrowing problem like 54 − 31, this model gives the correct answer 23. But given a borrowing problem such as 93 − 25, the Find-Difference variant would subtract 3 from 5, giving the incorrect answer 72. In solving the problem in this manner, the system generates the second path hypothesis we saw above.

TABLE 10.5
Production rules for smaller-from-larger bug

---

Find-Difference:
  If *number-a* is in *column-a* and *row-a*,
    and *number-b* is in *column-a* and *row-b*,
    {[and you are processing *column-a*]},
    {[and you are focused on *column-a*]},
    {[and there is no result for *column-a*]},
    {and *number-a* is greater than or equal to *number-b*},
  then write the difference between *number-a* and *number-b*
    as the result for *column-a*.

Shift-Column:
  If you are processing *column-a*,
    and you are focused on *column-a*,
    and *column-b* is to the left of *column-a*,
    {[and there is a result for *column-a*]},
  then shift your focus from *column-a* to *column-b*,
    and process *column-b*.

Find-Top:
  If *number-a* is in *column-a* and *row-a*,
    and *row-a* is above *row-b*,
    {[and you are processing *column-a*]},
    {[and there is no result for *column-a*]},
    {[and you are focused on *column-a*]},
    {[and there is no number in *column-a* and *row-b*]},
  then write *number-a* as the result for *column-a*.

---

To review, our framework divides the task of cognitive diagnosis into three stages—identifying a problem space, generating a path hypothesis that explains the subject's behavior on each problem, and finding a production system model that explains these path hypotheses. We have chosen to focus on the domain of multicolumn subtraction problems, both because of the empirical work that has been done in this area and because of the earlier diagnostic work. Now that we have seen some examples of problem spaces, path hypotheses, and production system models for this domain, let us examine a method for generating these hypotheses and models.

## A SYSTEM FOR AUTOMATED COGNITIVE DIAGNOSIS

In order to test our approach to cognitive diagnosis, we have implemented ACM, an artificial intelligence system that constructs cognitive models of behavior. The user provides the system with an appropriate problem space and a set of problem–

answer pairs. The program outputs a path hypothesis for each problem, along with a production system model that generates the inferred paths.

ACM's basic method rests on the notion of *problem reduction* (Nilsson, 1980), in which one decomposes a difficult problem into a number of independent, simpler problems. Once each of these subtasks has been solved, the results are recombined to form an answer to the original problem. We can apply this approach to cognitive diagnosis by realizing that the ultimate goal—generating a complete production system model—can be divided into a number of independent tasks— one for each operator in the problem space. In each case, we must determine the heuristic conditions on that operator that lets us predict when it would be invoked by the subject. Once we determine these conditions (which may be disjunctive), we simply combine the resulting production rules into our final model. The resulting set of rules can be used to simulate the subject's observed behavior and to predict his behavior on future problems.

In determining the conditions on an operator, ACM employs a method for *learning from examples*. A variety of such methods have been described in the machine-learning literature (Mitchell, 1982; Michalski, 1983; Quinlan, 1983), but all rely on a division of the data into *positive* instances and *negative* instances. We see that one can use path hypotheses to generate such a division, and that these instances can in turn be used to find the conditions on each operator. Thus, we first consider ACM's approach to formulating path hypotheses and only then describe its condition-finding method. Finally, we consider how these two components interact to produce a complete diagnostic system

## From Behavior to Path Hypotheses

Given a subtraction problem and a subject's answer to that problem, ACM must generate some path hypothesis to explain the observed answer. A path hypothesis consists of a sequence of operator instantiations that takes one from the initial problem state to the observed final state. But given only the legal conditions, many operators will match against most states. This leads to a combinatorial explosion of possible paths, and we need some means for managing the alternatives. Fortunately, AI provides a variety of methods for finding paths through combinatorial problem spaces, all revolving around the notion of *search*.

The basic action in these search methods consists of expanding a problem state by applying all operator instantiations that match against that state. One begins by expanding the initial state, selecting one of its successor states for expansion, generating still more states, and continuing this process until the termination condition is met or until no operators match. Alternative search algorithms differ radically in their methods for deciding which state to expand, but all generate a *search tree* of the alternative paths explored to date. The leaves of this tree represent those states which have not yet been expanded.

Figure 10.1 presents a search tree generated by ACM when solving the

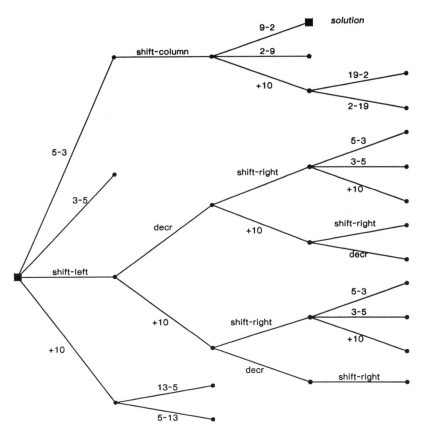

FIG 10.1.   Search tree for solution to 93 − 25 = 72.

subtraction problem 93 − 25 = 72. The search tree shows all paths with five or fewer steps. For this problem, there was one solution path that led to a final state consistent with the subject's answer of 72. One issue that ACM must handle is the possibility that multiple path hypotheses can explain the subject's answer. In such cases, the diagnostic system must determine which path(s) provides the most plausible explanation of the observed behavior.

Different search methods arise when one alters the method of selecting which state to expand. If one selects the least recently generated state, then *breadth-first* search results. This method examines all states at the first level, then all states at the second level, and so forth until the solution is reached. Breadth-first search is guaranteed to find the shortest solution path, but its memory requirements are very high, because one must remember all states at the previous level. If one selects the most recently generated state, then *depth-first* search results. This method pursues a single path until the solution is found or until some depth-limit is reached. In the latter case, the algorithm backtracks to the next most recent state, follows it downward, and so forth. This method has very low memory requirements, but it is not guaranteed to find the shortest solution path.

Both breadth-first and depth-first search are *exhaustive* algorithms in that they systematically consider all possibilities. They place an organization on the combinatorial explosion, but they do not eliminate it. In contrast, *heuristic search* methods use knowledge of the domain to reduce the combinatorics inherent in the problem space. In some methods, this knowledge takes the form of a numeric evaluation function that determines which state should be expanded.[6] Another approach encodes heuristic knowledge in the conditions placed on operators, giving fewer operator instantiations and causing fewer states to be generated.

We have chosen to use this latter method in ACM. As we have seen, each operator has an associated set of legal conditions that specifies the constraints under which that operator can be applied. For example, in multicolumn subtraction one cannot shift attention to the left when one is already in the left-most column. We can further constrain each operator by adding similar conditions that keep the operator from generating path hypotheses that seem psychologically implausible. For instance, one might not allow the decrement operator to be applied to the same position twice in succession. The production rules in Table 10.4 show these search-constraining conditions in brackets. These should not be confused with the acquired heuristic conditions, which are enclosed only by braces.

To see the need for a heuristic search solution of this sort, consider solving a four-column problem using the rules shown in Table 10.4 with only their legal conditions. Because we need one step to write the result for each column and one to shift columns, we cannot generate any solution (correct or otherwise) in fewer than seven steps. Given the generality of the conditions on each rule, we estimate an average of ten instantiations for each state in the problem space.

Carrying out an exhaustive search of this space to a depth of seven would require us to generate $10^8 - 1$ states. If we assume each node can be generated in 1/100th of a second, then this search would take over 11 days to perform. A five-column subtraction problem would require two additional steps, increasing the depth to a minimum of nine. This would multiply the number of states generated by 100, requiring over 3 years to search.

In contrast, the additional conditions we have placed on the operators lead to an average branching factor of three. This lets us consider only $3^8 - 1$ states during a depth seven search, which can be generated in slightly over one minute.[7]

---

[6] Ohlsson and Langley (1986) have described DPF, a diagnostic system that uses numeric evaluation functions to direct the search for path hypotheses. The heuristics of DPF incorporated knowledge of the human information processing system, such as limited short-term memory.

[7] There is a price to be paid for this reduction in search; one may be unable to model certain errors. For example, VanLehn (1982) reports one buggy strategy in which the student decrements a number in the bottom row, which ACM cannot model using the current set of initial conditions.

But regardless of the number of states involved, we must still organize the search in some fashion. To this end, ACM carries out a depth-first search to a depth one step longer than the length of the *correct* solution path. However, the details of this search differ from the standard depth-first algorithm in two respects.

First, the system rejects all states in which the partial answer diverges from the observed answer. This not only eliminates the current state; it also eliminates all of its successors, reducing the combinatorial explosion. Second, ACM does not halt upon finding a single path hypothesis. Instead, it continues until it has considered all solutions with the specified length or less. In this way, the program finds all path hypotheses that explain the subject's answer on the current problem while requiring very little in the way of memory.

Our depth limit requires some justification. We noted earlier that very few errorful subtraction strategies require more steps than the correct algorithm. One theory of bug origins suggests that errors result from memory limitations during the learning process, and such an explanation would also account for the simple nature of most bugs. But whatever the reason, the vast majority of buggy solution paths are shorter than the correct solution path, and this means we can use the latter's length as a heuristic cutoff in our search.

## From Path Hypotheses to Rules

Recall that our ultimate goal is a production system model of the student's behavior on a set of problems. We have already mentioned that ACM takes a problem-reduction approach to constructing such models, determining the conditions on each operator independently and combining the resulting rules into the final production system. In finding the conditions for an operator, the system employs a method for learning from examples that requires its input be divided into positive instances and negative instances.

The ACM system constructs these sets using a method that Sleeman, Langley, and Mitchell (1982) have called *learning from solution paths*. Given a solution path to some problem, one labels all instantiations of an operator that lie along the path as positive instance of that operator. Similarly, one labels all instantiations that lead one step off the path as negative instances of the operator.[8] We have already seen how ACM infers path hypotheses for each problem–answer pair, and the system uses these paths to classify each operator instantiation.

Given this information, the program looks for conditions on each operator that cover (match against) the positive instances, but that fail to cover the negative instances. The conditions on each operator let it propose steps that lie along the inferred path hypothesis, but avoid paths that lead off the path. Thus, the resulting

---

[8] One ignores states that lie two or more steps off the path, since the system would never have reached that point given the right conditions on its operators.

rules (when combined) let one replicate the subject's behavior—whether correct or errorful—without the need for search.

ACM uses a particular condition-finding method that is based on Michalski's (1983) $A^q$ algorithm.[9] We can summarize the basic method in three steps. Let *Pos* be the set of positive instances for an operator, *Neg* the set of negative instances, *D* the empty set, and *C* the initial conditions on the operator:

1. Randomly select an example *p* from *Pos*.

2. Determine a set of heuristic conditions *H* which (when added to *C*) covers the positive instance *p*, but which covers none of the instances in *Neg*. Let $C' = C \cup H$.

3. Remove all instances from *Pos* that are covered by *C'* and add the conditions *C'* to the set *D*. If *Pos* = $\varnothing$, then halt; otherwise go to step 1.

At the end of this process, *D* contains a set of condition sets that, taken as a disjunct, covers all of positive instances of the operator and none of the negative instances. ACM then proceeds to simplify each set in *D* by removing component conditions that do not significantly aid in distinguishing positive from negative instances. The resulting simplified rules may cover some negative instances or fail to cover some positive ones; these cases are interpreted as noisy data.

This outline has left many details unspecified, the most important being the method for generating a new set of conditions from a single positive instance. In order to explain the technique, we must first review ACM's representation of instances, its representation of conditions, and the relation between them. In the subtraction domain, each state is described as a set of relations between numbers, rows, and columns like those shown in Table 10.2. Thus, the working memory against which rules are matched would contain elements like (in 3 column-1 row-1), (in 5 column-1 row-2), and (above row-1 row-2).

Within the production system framework, the conditions of rules have forms analogous to elements in working memory, but in which some constant terms have been replaced by pattern matching variables. Thus, one set of conditions that would match the elements given above is:

$$((\text{in } \textit{number-a column row-a})$$
$$(\text{in } \textit{number-b column row-b})$$
$$(\text{above } \textit{row-a row-b}))$$

where pattern matching variables are shown in italics. This condition set should match a state description in which two numbers (*number-a* and *number-b*) occur

---

[9] An earlier version of ACM (Langley & Ohlsson, 1984) used a method for constructing decision trees similar to that described by Quinlan (1983).

in the same column, with *number-a* above *number-b*. Variables can match against any symbol, but they must bind consistently in different conditions.

The positive and negative instances each have two components. The first consists of the working memory elements present in memory when that operator was applied; this represents the overall state description. The second component consists of the variable bindings for the legal conditions that allowed the operator to match. Together with the legal conditions on the operator, this information lets ACM generate conditions for discriminating between positive and negative instances.

This generation process can be viewed in terms of heuristic search. The initial state in this search consists of the operator's legal conditions, whereas the final state consists of conditions that cover some of the positive instances but none of the negative instances. At each step in the search, ACM transforms all working memory elements in the instance into potential conditions. This involves replacing all constant symbols with the variables to which they were bound in the instantiation. For example, if *row-a* were bound to row-1 and *row-b* to row-2, the element (above row-1 row-2) would be transformed into the condition (above *row-a row-b*). Those constants not already bound to some variable are replaced with a new variable, except for predicates like above, left-of, and in.

The system also considers two types of conditions that are not based on elements present in the instantiation. User-defined predicates such as greater, equal, and zero lead to conditions relating all numeric variables. Thus, if *number-a* and *number-b* were already mentioned in the existing conditions, ACM would consider conditions such as (greater *number-a number-b*) and (zero *number-a*). The program also considers negated conditions that must *not* match for an operator to apply, basing them on elements that were present in negative instances of the operator.

The problem is that ACM can generate very many conditions in these ways, and somehow it must select among them. Because its goal is to find a set of conditions that discriminate between positive and negative instances of the operator, the system employs the $\chi^2$ statistic to measure the ability of each competitor in distinguishing between the two classes. Thus, conditions that match many of the positive instances and few of the negative instances are preferred to those that fail to discriminate.

At each point in its search, ACM selects that condition with the highest score on the $\chi^2$ metric, selecting one at random in case of ties. This condition is added to the set, and the element on which it was based is removed from the instantiation so it cannot be regenerated. As more conditions are added, fewer and fewer negative instances would be covered, until ultimately all have been eliminated. At this point, the conditions are combined with the operator to form a production rule that is added to the diagnostic model. In summary, ACM employs a form of hill climbing through the space of conditions, using the $\chi^2$ measure to direct its search.

The system employs the same statistic during the simplification process. After

ACM finds a set of conditions that covers some positive instances but none of the negatives, it considers the effect of dropping each condition in turn. If the elimination of a condition significantly reduces a production's $\chi^2$ value, then that condition is retained; otherwise it is dropped from condition side of the rule. In this way, the system eliminates extra conditions that were introduced accidentally during the search process.

## Combining the Methods

In an earlier version of ACM (Ohlsson & Langley, 1984), the path-finding component and the rule-finding component worked independently of each other. The system first generated path hypotheses for all of the problems and then used these paths to formulate a production system model that explained them. There were two serious flaws in this approach. First, the amount of search required for twenty subtraction problems of even moderate complexity was prohibitive. Second, the pathfinding often generated multiple path hypotheses for each problem, and ACM had no means for determining which explanations were consistent with each other.

The current version of the system takes a new approach that overcomes these limitations. The basic idea involves interleaving the generation of path hypotheses with the formulation of production system models. ACM begins by finding one or more solution paths that explain the subject's answer to the first problem. Based on each path, the system constructs a production system model that predicts that path. However, because these models are based on small amounts of data, they are likely to be nondeterministic. Thus, they would be able to reproduce the path hypotheses, but they would generate other paths as well.

However, the total amount of search is greatly reduced when ACM encounters the next problem–answer pair. This time it uses the partial rules generated during the first round, and each tentative model leads to a second set of path hypotheses. These determine new positive and negative instances, and these in turn let the system refine its models by adding discriminating conditions. The process is repeated on successive problems, gradually giving more detailed models of the student's strategy. The production rules slowly become more specific, and this reduces the amount of search required at each step. If the subject's behavior is sufficiently regular, the model eventually becomes algorithmic and search is eliminated.

One interesting complication can arise within this framework. In some cases, the rules generated from problems 1 through $n$ cannot generate the answer observed for problem $n + 1$. The natural interpretation of this situation is that the subject has exhibited a *bug migration* (VanLehn, 1982). That is, he has shifted from one errorful strategy to a different algorithm. The appropriate response is to retain the existing production rules as the model for behavior on the first $n$ problems, but to construct an entirely new model for the remaining problems.

This is the approach that ACM takes when its cannot find an adequate path hypothesis.

To illustrate how the combined method operates, let us work through an example diagnosis of a subject with the smaller-from-larger bug. We use the productions in Table 10.4 (with only the legal and bracketed conditions) as the initial rules, and we use the subtraction problems: $647 - 45 = 602$, $885 - 297 = 612$, and $83 - 44 = 41$. The correct answer to the first of these problems requires five steps; when ACM searches to a depth of six, it finds only one path hypothesis to explain the observed answer 602:

Find-Difference(7, 5, column1)
Shift-Column(column1, column2)
Find-Difference(4, 4, column2)
Shift-Column(column2, column3)
Find-Top(column3)

For the sake of simplicity, we focus on the Find-Difference operator. The inferred path has a single negative instance for this operator: Find-Difference(5, 7, column1); and three positive instances: Find-Difference(7, 5, column1) and Find-Difference(4, 4, column2); the last of these occurs twice, once for 4 in both positions.

Based on these instances, ACM finds a set of conditions that covers all the positive instances but not the negative example. However, the lack of data leads the system to reject all of these conditions during the simplification process, so search continues unrestrained on the second problem: $885 - 297 = 612$. Again the correct solution takes five steps, so the program searches to a depth of six. Only one solution path accounts for the answer, but this time it differs from the correct solution path:

Find-Difference(7, 5, column1)
Shift-Column(column1, column2)
Find-Difference(9, 8, column2)
Shift-Column(column2, column3)
Find-Difference(8, 2, column3)

Three positive examples are generated from this path hypothesis: Find-Difference(7, 5, column1), Find-Difference(9, 8, column2), and Find-Difference(8, 2, column3). In addition, three negative examples are produced: Find-Difference(5, 7, column1), Find-Difference(8, 9, column2) and Find-Difference(2, 8 column3).

ACM now has seven positive instances of Find-Difference, along with three negative instances. This is enough to allow the most discriminating condition to be retained during the simplification process. This condition is (*greater number1 number2*), which matches six of the seven positive instances and none of the negative instances. Another likely condition is (*above number1 number2*), but this only matches three of the seven positive instances and none of the negative instances, causing it to be dropped during simplification.

With its new Find-Difference rule, ACM attempts to solve the next problem: $83 - 44 = 41$. Because of the additional condition on the new rule, the system generates only two instantiations of Find-Difference, both of which lie on the final path hypothesis:

Find-Difference(4, 3, column1)
Shift-Column(column1, column2)
Find-Difference(8, 4, column2)

This solution path provides two additional positive examples: Find-Difference(4, 3, column1) and Find-Difference(8, 4, column2). Provided the subject is consistent on future subtraction problems, the program only considers instances of the operator that lie along the inferred solution path. In this case, ACM has arrived at a nearly complete model of the subject's behavior after the first two problems. Before generating the complete smaller-from-larger model shown in Table 10.5, it also requires some problems that use the Find-Top operator, but little search occurs on the intervening problems.

This example was simplified in that ACM never found more than one path hypothesis that accounted for the subject's answer on a problem. This, in turn, effectively eliminated search through the space of alternative production system models. In general, the system may discover multiple solution paths, and when this occurs it constructs a separate production system model based on each path (together with previous paths). ACM then examines each model's ability to explain the current path and all previous paths. This involves running the model on earlier problems to see how many positive and negative instances it generates for each operator. The $\chi^2$ measure is also used in this evaluation process, with the highest-scoring model being retained, along with the path hypothesis on which it was based.

## Advantages of the Approach

The approach we have taken to automating cognitive diagnosis has a number of benefits. For instance, the method's reliance on the $\chi^2$ measure lets it tolerate noise. The learned conditions on an operator need not cover all of its positive instances, nor must they mismatch all negative instances. As long as a condition accounts for significant regularities in the data it is retained in the resulting production system model.

The method can also formulate models in which an operator has disjunctive conditions. The $\chi^2$ statistic prefers condition sets that cover more of the positive instances, and thus prefers conjunctive rules when these cover the data. But when two or more sets of conditions are necessary, ACM has no difficulty in generating such disjuncts. These are represented as separate rules in the final production system.

In addition, the system detects bug migrations when the model produced from the first $n$ problems cannot solve the $n + 1$st problem. Earlier versions of ACM (Ohlsson & Langley, 1984) did not have this ability. Schlimmer and Granger (1986) have identified a closely related issue in learning from examples, which they term *concept drift*. This task involves distinguishing between noisy data and changing environments, and they argue that this is a very difficult problem. We do not claim to have a complete solution to such ambiguities, but we have made a start.

In fact, the above three problems remain basic research issues in the field of machine learning. Few AI learning systems can acquire disjunctive rules and even fewer can learn from noisy data. Very little work has examined the problem of concepts that change over time, which corresponds to our bug migration. Although our main goal is to automate the process of cognitive diagnosis, ACM can also be viewed as responding to the joint issues of disjuncts, noise, and concept change.

A final advantage of the approach is that it measures the quality of the final production system model. After all problems have been solved, ACM computes the $\chi^2$ score for the final model in terms of its ability to predict the positive and negative instances of each operator. The greater the number of steps along the inferred path hypotheses that are predicted by the model, the higher its descriptive power. Although Newell and Simon (1972) proposed methods for evaluating their hand-crafted models, their approach was not linked to standard statistical measures.

We have implemented ACM in Interlisp-D on the Xerox Lisp Machine and we have successfully applied it to some common subtraction bugs. Recall that Table 10.1 lists the eleven most frequent subtraction bugs reported by VanLehn (1982). For each bug, we provided the system with twenty test problems and the answers that would result from an idealized application of that strategy. Given these data, ACM generated plausible production system models to account for all eleven buggy strategies (including the correct strategy).

For example, one of the bugs listed in Table 10.1 is *borrow-from-zero* in which the subject needing to borrow from zero changes the zero to a nine instead of continuing left to borrow. The model ACM formed for the buggy procedure is identical to the model it formed for the correct procedure except for the Shift-Left and Add-Ten operators. In the correct procedure, there are two rules for shifting left: Shift-Left-To-Borrow and Shift-Left-Across-Zero. The model that ACM formed for the borrow-from-zero bug includes the version of the Shift-Left-To-Borrow rule it had formed for the correct procedure, but excludes the Shift-Left-Across-Zero rule entirely. This second rule is not needed to model the borrow-from-zero bug because when the subject is confronted with borrowing from zero, he simply changes the zero to a nine and has no need to continue shifting left. For the Add-Ten operator, ACM forms the version of the rule used for the correct procedure, as well as the following (paraphrased) rule: *If you are focused on a column in which the top number is zero, and you just shifted left, then change the zero to a ten.* Whenever this rule is used, the conditions for the Decrement rule are subsequently met, and the ten is then decremented to a nine and the processing continues as in the correct procedure. Together these rules form a production system that correctly models the buggy procedure *borrow-from-zero.*

We have also tested the system on idealized subtraction data containing bug migrations. For the same twenty problems, we provided ACM with the correct answers to the first ten problems, but with incorrect answers to the last ten problems that would be produced by the smaller-from-larger strategy. The system detected when the bug migration occurred and produced two separate production system models: one for the first ten correct answers, and another for the last ten buggy answers. We have not yet tested ACM on actual subject data in the subtraction domain. However, earlier work suggests that such data should contain both noise and migrations, and such tests are one of our highest research priorities.

## RULES AND PRINCIPLES IN COGNITIVE DIAGNOSIS

All existing work on automated cognitive diagnosis, including the approach we have described in the preceding pages, builds on some procedural analysis of the skill being diagnosed and results in some description of the subject's procedure or strategy. Before closing, we should consider an alternative framework for diagnosis that may be more relevant in the long run, at least for educational purposes.

### Bugs and Misconceptions

As the field of cognitive psychology has progressed, our understanding of errorful behavior has become more sophisticated. Researchers began with the simple distinction between correct and incorrect performance as measured by tests. This simplistic view has been superceded by the distinction between forgetting errors (due to memory limitations) and procedural errors (due to faulty strategies). Even more recently, researchers have started to distinguish different types of procedural errors. Brown and Burton's (1978) work on DEBUGGY was instrumental in clarifying the difference between systematic errors (bugs) and those caused by carelessness.

In this section, we would like to propose a further refinement within the set of systematic errors, namely between *bugs* and *misconceptions.* A bug is a syntactic entity, involving some fault in a procedure that can be corrected by a set of editing operations on the code of the procedure, such as adding or replacing conditions. In other words, a bug is inherently procedural in nature. A misconception, on the other hand, involves a person's beliefs about the world. These are more declarative in nature, though they must interact with problem-solving processes to impact behavior. Misconceptions imply faulty *understanding* rather than faulty *performance*.

Procedural bugs can be modeled by clearly defined programming languages, and thus lend themselves to formal analysis. Unfortunately, we have no formalisms analogous to programming languages that would make possible a formal treatment of misconceptions. In order to proceed, we follow the lead of several other researchers interested in understanding and assume that understanding resides in *principles*, that is, propositions of general validity within a task domain. This view of understanding has virtually no basis, except that principles are commonly used within well-understood domains such as mathematics and natural science.[10] However, we currently have no viable alternative. Given this model of understanding, it seems natural to model misunderstanding as involving the violation of some principle or, equivalently, the use of an incorrect principle.

In a task domain like arithmetic, one would expect some relationship between understanding and performance, between misconceptions and bugs, between principles and heuristics. Resnick (1982) has explicitly argued that subtraction bugs can be seen as corresponding to violations of specific subtraction principles. Indeed, it seems natural to hypothesize procedural bugs as being *caused* by misconceptions. In other words, the process of acquiring procedures results in buggy algorithms due to a lack of constraints (or due to wrong constraints), and these follow from a lack of understanding.[11]

From a pedagogical point of view, misconceptions are more central than bugs. Not only can faulty understanding cause bugs, but in a hierarchically organized subject matter like mathematics, faulty understanding at one level is likely to create difficulties at the next level of learning. Indeed, one could argue that the schools' main goal should be to communicate understanding, and that faulty understanding indicates failure even in the presence of correct performance. Even if one rejects this stance, it seems clear that remedial teaching should be directed toward misconceptions rather than bugs whenever possible. This in turn raises the problem of *diagnosing misconceptions:* Given a set of observed answers to problems in some domain, and given a set of principles that encode understanding of that domain, identify a set of misconceptions (violated principles) that explain the observed answers.

---

[10] See Rissland (1978) for a view of mathematical knowledge and understanding which adds considerable richness to the notion of a '*principle.*'

[11] Resnick and Omanson (in press) have reported experimental evidence against this hypothesis, but we do not feel their results are sufficient to justify abandoning the view at this point.

In considering this problem, we should naturally attempt to build on existing results from cognitive diagnosis. If possible, we should adapt earlier techniques to the new goal of finding misconceptions in place of buggy heuristics. We consider two approaches to diagnosing misconceptions, both of which build on the notion of path hypotheses and the problem space hypothesis. Thus, these methods share features with the ACM system described earlier, even though they make no attempt to construct process models to describe the inferred paths.

### Principles as Evaluation Functions

We assume a set $P$ of principles $P_1$, $P_2$, . . . , $P_n$ for a task domain $T$. We further assume a set of problems, $T_1$, $T_2$, . . . , $T_m$, to which some person has produced a set of answers $A_1$, $A_2$, . . . , $A_m$; the person can be viewed as a function $a$ that maps problems to answers, $A_i = a(T_i)$. As before, we incorporate the notion of a problem space and path hypotheses, so $A_i$ is (strictly speaking) a *path*. We assume that an answer is generated by some procedure, strategy, or collection of heuristics that traverses the states in some problem space, thus generating a path from the initial state in the space to the goal state.

The central idea is that principles are related to paths, rather than to answers or procedures. We argue that *solution paths are best viewed as obeying or violating the principles of the task domain* in which behavior occurs. As an example, consider the general arithmetic principle of *compensation* as proposed by Resnick (1982). This principles states that when a number is re-decomposed into additive components, its value remains constant only when a quantity that has been subtracted from one component is also added to another component. Suppose that we observe the solution of a subtraction problem in which there are decrements that are not paid back, or in which increments are not preceded by any borrowing operation. Any solution path in the standard subtraction space that has unequal numbers of applications of the Add-Ten and Decrement operations thus violates the principle of compensation.

This framework suggests that *all* principles of a domain can be viewed as *path constraints* (Carbonell, 1986), and this suggests our first method for diagnosing misconceptions. The basic ideas is *to use the number of constraint violations as the evaluation function for heuristic search through the problem space*. In other words, we start with some problem space (such as the standard subtraction space) and with a set of principles, and we formulate the principles in terms of constraints on paths through that space. We then carry out a best-first search through the space, always selecting for expansion that node with the lowest score. We measure this score by the number of principle violations occurring along the path to that node, rejecting paths that do not lead to the same digits in the same columns as the observed answer.[12] This procedure finds the path through the problem space that accounts for the observed answer using the assumption of minimal number of misconceptions.

This method for diagnosing misconceptions in terms of principle violations has a number of interesting features:

1. If we use the $A^*$ search algorithm, the method discovers the best possible diagnosis; this follows from properties of the $A^*$ algorithm.

2. The diagnosis contains not only the number of principle violations, but also a list of *which* misconceptions are implied by the path. From this we can hypothesize that the subject fails to understand these principles.

3. The method bypasses the need for a procedure to generate the correct path. Neither the correct path nor the correct procedure play any role in this technique.

4. The method diagnoses the misconceptions *without* diagnosing the buggy procedure. The method matches *paths* against principles, thus avoiding the need to infer the subject's strategy.

This diagnostic method is closely related to our earlier work on the Diagnostic Path-Finder (Ohlsson & Langley, 1986). In the DPF system, the best-first search was also guided by principles. However, DPF employed general psychological principles to evaluate the plausibility of any one path hypothesis. In effect, our new method applies the same computational machinery, but with a very different interpretation. The principles now represent the content of the domain, rather than general theoretical principles based on our knowledge of the human information processing system. The psychological theory embedded in DPF has been replaced with the single assumption that the path that violates the least number of domain principles is the most plausible one.[13]

Like all best-first search methods, the new method is only guaranteed to find the optimal path if each node in the state space is expanded completely. This means that all its (one-step) descendents must be explicitly generated (and evaluated). In spaces with large branching factors, this means that even a very selective search (in the sense that only a few nonprofitable paths are explored) would

---

[12] The $A^*$ algorithm for best-first search also requires some estimate of the cost of the remaining path. One simple cost estimate for the subtraction domain is the number of columns that still have no result. Because each column takes at least one operator application to generate a result, this measure is guaranteed to underestimate almost any cost function, as required by the $A^*$ algorithm to guarantee optimal results. Another issue is the monotonicity of the cost function. If we formulate the path constraints so that each violation is associated with a single step, then monotonicity is satisfied.

[13] Note that this scheme could also be used as a module in the current ACM system to find solution paths. This diagnostic method does not *forbid* production system models, it simply does not *rely* on them.

nevertheless generate a very large number of states. This follows from the fact that evaluation functions provide selectivity only *after* a node has been expanded and its successors generated.

In general, this problem can be overcome by introducing selectivity during the process of *generating* new nodes. In the current context, this means using domain principles to constrain the branches leading out from a search node. In other words, we would like to find a way to move the selective power of the principles from the node-selection stage to the step-generation stage. We outline an alternative method for diagnosing misconceptions that incorporates this idea.

## Principles as Condition Generators

The use of principles as path constraints arose from the idea that misconceptions can be diagnosed separately from the buggy procedure that generated them. However, this approach ignores the relation between principles and problem-solving rules. We see that one can also use principles to *generate* such rules, and that one can use these rules to propose steps through the problem space which violate some specific principle. Instead of first generating all logically possible states and then using the principles to evaluate them, we can use rules based on the principles to selectively generate steps that violate those principles. This method involves three successive stages: constructing rules for correct performance, generating rules that produce specific misconceptions, and using these rules to perform cognitive diagnosis.

First, let us consider the relation between principles and correct performance. The total set of principles for a domain like subtraction should dictate exactly which steps to take during problem solving. This suggests a technique for systematically generating rules for correct performance in a domain. For each operator in the problem space, create a rule that applies that operator. For each principle, add to the rule *those conditions that ensure that the application of the operator does not violate the principle*. If we do this for each principle, then the operator would only be applied when its action obeys all the principles. If we carry out this scheme for each operator, the resulting set of productions performs in accordance with the given principles, producing correct behavior.

The importance of such problem-solving rules is *not* that they constitute a plausible model of human performance. Humans do not acquire procedures using the method just described, and we doubt the resulting production system would be a good cognitive model. By the same reasoning, one should not attempt to teach such rules to students. The importance of such rules is that we can use them as a step generator with known properties. Recall that each condition in these rules is motivated by some particular domain principle. From this it follows that *removing a condition from a given rule produces a rule that violates the corresponding principle*. In other words, because we know which condition corresponds to which principle, we can generate variants on the correct rules that generate steps that violate specific principles.

For instance, imagine a correct rule that includes a condition that the first argument of the Find-Difference operator be *above* the second argument in the problem display. This condition is motivated by the principle that says the purpose of subtraction is to subtract the subtrahend from the minuend, rather than vice versa. Removing this condition leads to a rule that generates steps violating this principle; the surface symptom of this is the smaller-from-larger bug we described earlier.

In short, we start with the set of rules for correct performance. For each rule, we create one variant for each principle by deleting those conditions that ensure that the rule's actions obey the principle. The resulting set of rules is a step generator that does *not* explore every path in the problem space, but *only those paths that can be interpreted in terms of violations of the stated principles*. The functional- or operational-branching factor in this space is independent of the logical branching factor. Instead, it is dependent upon the number of principles and the different ways in which they can be violated.[14]

Because our goal is diagnosis, we must search the reduced problem space in order to find a path explaining the observed answer, using the new rules as step generators. What kind of search is appropriate? Again, best-first search seems the right paradigm, with the number of rule violations as the evaluation function. However, expansion of a node no longer involves the exhaustive generation of all logically possible descendents, but only those generated by one or more of the rules. Also, there is no need to actually compare principles with the paths because we know which rule violates which principle. Therefore, one can determine which principles have been violated by inspecting the path itself.

Moving the principles into the step generator allows us to consider only that portion of the total problem space that involves misconceptions. Other (uninterpretable) faulty paths are not visited during search. Moreover, the method contains a criterion of consistency with respect to misconception: We can analyze a path in order to see whether a principle that was violated in one state was violated in every possible state. The approach also tells us when a diagnosis is ambiguous with respect to misconceptions. If a problem-solving step was generated by two different rules, then either of two misunderstood principles could be responsible for the problem. Thus, we can determine all interpretations of a student's errors. If the search through the space terminates without finding a path that explains the observed answer, then we know that the answer cannot be explained in terms of the given principles.

---

[14] Recall that in order to reduce ACM's search for path hypotheses to a reasonable size, we were forced to add conditions to our basic set of rules. The above method suggests a more principled response to this problem.

## SUMMARY

Cognitive simulation provides a framework for describing the complexities of human cognition, but this methodology (Newell & Simon, 1972) requires major effort in both the data-collection stage and the model-building stage. Initial attempts to automate the process of cognitive diagnosis have proved quite successful in limited domains, such as subtraction (Brown & Burton, 1978) and algebra (Sleeman & Smith, 1981). However, these approaches relied on hand-crafted bug libraries, which in turn required extensive analysis of subjects' errors in the domain.

In this chapter, we described an alternative approach to automated cognitive diagnosis that avoids the need for bug libraries. The method borrows two assumptions from other work in cognitive simulation—the problem space hypothesis and the production system hypothesis. One inputs some problem space for the domain by specifying the state representation and the operators for generating new states. One also provides a set of test problems and a subject's answers to those problems. Given this information, the method automatically infers path hypotheses that explain each answer, and then induces a production system model that explains the inferred paths.

This paradigm requires significantly less domain analysis than the bug library approach, and the method should be applicable to many procedural domains. We have implemented the technique as a running AI system called ACM, and we have tested this system on idealized buggy behavior in the subtraction domain. In addition, the particular methods it uses to infer paths, to induce rules, and to formulate production system models promise to handle three major issues that arise in cognitive diagnosis—disjunctive rules, noisy behavior, and bug migration. Our preliminary tests of ACM along these dimensions have been encouraging.

However, we need more serious tests of the system's capabilities, and this is a major direction for future work. First we must determine whether the program can model the majority of the observed subtraction bugs given idealized data. The next step is to provide ACM with actual subtraction data; this further tests the system's ability to handle noise and migrations. Finally, we hope to use the same system to model behavior in two additional domains—arithmetic with fractions and simple algebra. This means providing ACM with new problem spaces, but we hope that few modifications of the system itself will be necessary.

An entirely different research path would explore the role of principles in cognitive diagnosis. Rather than explaining subject's errors in terms of an algorithmic production system model, one can summarize behavior in terms of misconceptions about the domain. In this framework, one still searches for path hypotheses that explain the subject's answers, but one prefers those paths that violate fewer principles of the domain. The resulting paths identify which principles the subject has misunderstood, and this has more direct implications for remedial instruction than the errorful rules induced by ACM. We plan to follow this approach in parallel with our extensions of the rule-based framework.

We have no illusions about the difficulty of fully automating the task of cognitive diagnosis. This would force us to replicate the entire range of scientific reasoning in cognitive psychology, and we have no such pretensions. However, we believe that major components of the diagnostic process—the formulation of path hypotheses and the generation of production system models—*can* be automated using existing techniques from artificial intelligence and machine learning. We envision the day when psychologists interact with such a partially automated system to construct detailed models of a subject's behavior, and when intelligent teaching systems invoke similar modules to construct accurate student models. We do not predict the date when diagnostic systems become robust enough for these purposes, but we hope our efforts with ACM speed its arrival.

## ACKNOWLEDGMENTS

This work was supported in part by contracts N00014-85-K-0373 and N00014-85-K-0337 from the Personnel and Training Research Group, Office of Naval Research.

## REFERENCES

Anderson, J. A., & Hinton, G. E. (1981). Models of information processing in the brain. In G. E. Hinton & J. A. Anderson (Eds.), *Parallel models of associative memory* (pp. 9–48). Hillsdale, NJ: Lawrence Erlbaum Associates.

Anderson, J. R. (1976). *Language, memory, and thought.* Hillsdale, NJ: Lawrence Erlbaum Associates.

Brown, J. S., & Burton, R. R. (1978). Diagnostic models for procedural bugs in basic mathematic skills. *Cognitive Science, 2,* 155–192.

Brown, J. S., & VanLehn, K. (1980). Repair theory: A generative theory of bugs in procedural skill. *Cognitive Science, 4,* 379–427.

Carbonell, J. G. (1986). Derivational analogy: A theory of reconstructive problem solving and expertise acquisition. In R. S. Michalski, J. G. Carbonell & T. M. Mitchell (Eds.), *Machine learning: An artificial intelligence approach* (Vol. 2, pp. 371–392). Los Altos, CA: Morgan Kaufmann.

Langley, P., & Ohlsson, S. (1984). Automated cognitive modeling. *Proceedings of the National Conference on Artifical Intelligence,* 193–197. Austin, TX: William Kaufmann.

Langley, P., Ohlsson, S., & Sage, S. (1984). *A machine learning approach to student modeling* (Tech. Rep. No. CMU-RI-TR-84-7). Pittsburgh, PA: Carnegie-Mellon University, Robotics Institute.

Michalski, R. S. (1983). A theory and methodology of inductive learning. In R. S. Michalski, J. G. Carbonell & T. M. Mitchell (Eds.), *Machine learning: An artificial intelligence approach* (pp. 83–134). Palo Alto, CA: Tioga Press.

Mitchell, T. M. (1982). Generalization as search. *Artificial Intelligence, 18,* 203–226.

Newell, A. (1972). A theoretical exploration of mechanisms for coding the stimulus. In A. W. Melton & E. Martin (Eds.), *Coding processes in human memory*. New York: Winston.

Newell, A. (1973). Production systems: Models of control structures. In W. G. Chase (Ed.), *Visual information processing*. New York: Academic Press.

Newell, A. (1980). Reasoning, problem solving, and decision processes: The problem space hypothesis. In R. Nickerson (Ed.), *Attention and performance VIII*. Hillsdale, NJ: Lawrence Erlbaum Associates.

Newell, A., & Simon, H. A. (1972). *Human problem solving*. Englewood Cliffs, NJ: Prentice-Hall.

Newell, A., Shaw, J., & Simon, H. A. (1960). Report on a general problem-solving program for a computer. *Proceedings of the International Conference on Information Processing*, UNESCO, Paris.

Nilsson, N. J. (1980). *Principles of artifical intelligence*. Palo Alto, CA: Tioga Press.

Ohlsson, S., & Langley, P. (1984). Towards automatic discovery of simulation models. *Proceedings of the European Conference on Artificial Intelligence*.

Ohlsson, S., & Langley, P. (1986). Psychological evaluation of path hypotheses in cognitive diagnosis. In H. Mandl & A. Lesgold (Eds.), *Learning issues for intelligent tutoring systems* (pp. 42–62). New York: Springer.

Pearl, J. (1984). *Heuristics*. Reading, MA: Addison-Wesley.

Quinlan, J. R. (1983). Learning efficient classification procedures and their application to chess end games. In R. S. Michalski, J. G. Carbonell & T. M. Mitchell (Eds.), *Machine learning: An artificial intelligence approach* (pp. 463–482). Palo Alto, CA: Tioga Press.

Resnick, L. B. (1982). Syntax and semantics in learning to subtract. In T. P. Carpenter, J. M. Moser & T. A. Romberg (Eds.), *Addition and subtraction: A cognitive perspective*. Hillsdale, NJ: Lawrence Erlbaum Associates.

Resnick, L. B., & Omanson, S. F. (In press). Learning to understand arithmetic. In R. Glaser (Ed.), *Advances in instructional psychology* (Vol. 3). Hillsdale, NJ: Lawrence Erlbaum Associates.

Rissland, E. L. (1978). Understanding understanding mathematics. *Cognitive Science, 2*(4), 361–383.

Schlimmer, J. C., & Granger, R. H. (1986). Incremental learning from noisy data. *Machine Learning, 1*, 317–354.

Sleeman, D. H., & Smith, M. J. (1981). Modeling students' problem solving. *Artificial Intelligence, 16*, 171–187.

Sleeman, D. H., Langley, P., & Mitchell, T. M. (1982, Spring). Learning from solution paths: An approach to the credit assignment problem. *AI Magazine*, pp. 48–52.

VanLehn, K. (1982). Bugs are not enough: Empirical studies of bugs, impasses, and repairs in procedural skills. *Journal of Mathematical Behavior, 3*, 3–72.

Waterman, D. A., & Newell, A. (1972). *Preliminary results with a system for automatic protocol analysis* (CIP Report No. 211). Pittsburgh, PA: Carnegie-Mellon University, Department of Psychology.

Young, R. M., & O'Shea, T. (1981). Errors in children's subtraction. *Cognitive Science, 5*, 153–177.

# Trace Analysis and Spatial Reasoning: An Example of Intensive Cognitive Diagnosis and Its Implications for Testing

Stellan Ohlsson
*Learning Research and Development Center*
*University of Pittsburgh*

## ON METHODOLOGY

Mental life is invisible, and its expression in action is under voluntary, intentional control. The psychological sciences have been slow in accepting the methodological challenge posed by these two facts. Several evasive tactics have been tried. The first tactic was to observe mental life directly, by looking inward. The second evasive tactic was to decree that action itself is the object of study in psychology. Both of these tactics deny the necessity of inferring mental events from observations of actions. In a third evasive move, psychology was declared a part of the humanities, with the implication that interpretation of human behavior is necessarily, irrevocably subjective. While admitting the need for inferences, this stance denies the possibility of imposing a discipline on those inferences, a discipline that makes rational discussion and intersubjective agreement possible. We now know that the evasive tactics of introspectionism, behaviorism, and humanistic psychology do not work; they were worth trying but they failed. We are left with the sole option of tackling the methodological challenge of mental life head on.

One might take the view that a scientist should attack significant substantive problems, propose interesting theories, and discover novel facts. If this is done, the methodological development of his or her science will take care of itself. Methodology per se is boring, unending fiddling with technicalities, an activity best left to the pedantic introvert who brings no creativity to his or her work. A real scientist worries about ideas and problems, not about methods.

There are several mistakes hiding in this proud attitude. First, careful observation of scientific research by a knowledgeable and sympathetic observer like Toulmin (1972) has revealed that the knowledge transmitted by one generation of scientists to the next does not consist mainly of particular explanations, but, instead, of the procedures by which explanations are constructed. There is, then, evidence that our methods are closer to the center of scientific knowledge than the traditional disdain for methodological work admits. Second, methodology has to be distinguished from the perfecting of measuring instruments. Methodology certainly deals with the accuracy of observations in general and the precision of measurements in particular. But the core topics of methodology are: the nature of evidence, forms of description, patterns of inference, boundary conditions on the validity of inferences, the design of explanatory procedures, and the standards by which particular explanations are judged. Third, scientific breakthroughs are brought about by new methodologies as well as by new ideas. One need only mention the electron microscope, the carbon-14 dating method, and the cyclotron. Fourth, in the application of science to practical concerns, methods are often useful even in the absence of theory. For instance, the method of ascertaining verticality by suspending a weight from a string is useful for building a house even in the absence of a theory of gravitation. Methodology is essential both for the creation and the application of scientific theories.

Methodological innovation has not been a conspicuous feature of psychological research. The evasive tactics mentioned above discouraged serious thinking about how to infer states of mind from observations of behavior. Methodological development was restricted to the design of new statistical procedures, and methodological knowledge became limited to knowledge about the proper application of such procedures. But the cognitive revolution (Gardner, 1985) puts methodological innovation on the psychologist's agenda. Cognitive psychologists are collecting new types of data in support of new types of theories. We need a new view of methodology, new concepts to replace the stale dichotomies that dominated methodological debate in the past (description versus hypothesis testing, experimental versus correlational, laboratory control versus ecological validity, objective versus subjective, research versus application, standardized versus clinical, and so forth).

In order to take a fresh look at the fundamental dimensions of psychological methods, consider the following formulation of the basic problem: *Given a behavioral record of person P (at time t), infer a description of P's mental state (at t).* This formulation implies that the three fundamental dimensions of psychological methods are (a) the type of *behavioral record* to which a method applies (i.e., the input); (b) the type of *description* of mental states that a method generates (i.e., the output); and (c) the rules of inference—or, in the terminology of Toulmin (1972)—the *explanatory procedures* that are used to construct the description, given the behavioral record (i.e., the transformation of the input into the output).

With respect to input, we can distinguish between extensive and intensive methods. *Extensive methods* rely on relatively shallow analysis of a large number of performances, whereas *intensive methods* rely on a deep analysis of a small number of performances (possibly just one; see Dukes, 1968). For instance, the methods used by experimental psychology and by psychometrics are extensive, whereas the methods used by psychoanalysts are intensive. Furthermore, behavioral records vary with respect to whether they preserve *sequential* information or not, and methods that do preserve sequential information vary with respect to the *temporal density* of that information.

With respect to output, we can distinguish between singleton and aggregate descriptions. *Singleton descriptions* summarize observations that derive from a single individual, whereas *aggregate descriptions* summarize observations that derive from a group of individuals. For instance, psychometric and psychoanalytic methods produce singleton descriptions, whereas the methods used in experimental psychology typically produce aggregate descriptions.

With respect to explanatory procedures, we can distinguish between open and closed methods. The purpose of *open methods* is to reveal the structure in the behavioral record. Open methods proceed in bottom-up fashion from the data toward the description. The purpose of *closed methods* is to ascertain how closely the behavioral record fits a predefined structure. For instance, the methods used in psychoanalysis are typically open methods, whereas the methods used in experimental psychology are closed methods. The psychometric tradition has a double-sided relation to this dimension. The *construction* of tests uses open methods like factor analysis and cluster analysis, but the *application* of a test battery, once constructed, is an instance of a closed method.

In summary, I suggest that psychological methods should be discussed in terms of the type of behavioral records they apply to, the type of description of mental states they generate, and the type of explanatory procedures they use to transform the record into the description. The rest of this chapter presupposes this schema for the analysis of methods.

A major new type of behavioral record introduced into cognitive psychology in recent years[1] is that of *protocols,* in particular think-aloud protocols (Newell, 1966; Newell & Simon, 1972; Ericsson & Simon, 1984; Williams & Hollan, 1981; Williams & Santos-Williams, 1980). A protocol is a verbatim transcript of spontaneous talk on the part of a subject about a task. There are two frequently used methods for the processing of protocols. The simplest is the *method of excerpts,* which has been practiced in the humanities for a long time. It consists of selecting a part of the corpus and printing it in full, thus letting the reader see for himself/herself, as it were. The excerpt is selected so as to exhibit a typical case, to prove the existence of some phenomenon, or to make a point of some

---

[1] The use of verbal protocols was not *invented* in recent years, but rather rediscovered. See the historical section in Ericsson and Simon (1984, pp. 48–61).

kind; frequently, two excerpts are shown side by side in order to illustrate a difference or a contrast.

The other popular method for processing verbal protocols is known in social psychology as *content analysis*[2] (Holsti, 1968). In content analysis one proceeds by defining a set of categories of textual events and counting the frequency with which each category occurs in a corpus of protocols. These frequencies can be used as dependent variables in experimental studies. Cognitive psychologists reinvented this method and have used it frequently in recent years, without, however, paying attention to the rather extensive experience of social psychologists with respect to its applicability, reliability, and validity (Holsti, 1968).

Newell (1966) and Newell and Simon (1972) have proposed a new method for the analysis of protocols. They did not name their method; for convenience, I refer to it as *trace analysis*. In the terms introduced above, trace analysis is an intensive, open method that aims for singleton descriptions. The type of behavioral record to which trace analysis applies is a think-aloud protocol. The type of description produced is a specification of an information-processing system that behaves like the observed person. The explanatory procedures that generate an information-processing system for a think-aloud protocol are rather complicated; they are presented below in the context of an example. Trace analysis breaks new ground in that it combines an interest in the meaning of protocol fragments (which is characteristic of the method of excerpts) with a concern for imposing a discipline on the process of analysis (which is characteristic of content analysis). Also, it makes use of the sequential information in a protocol, a type of information that is destroyed by methods that build on category frequency.

Trace analysis has been all but ignored. Today, eighteen years after its introduction, there exists, to the best of my knowledge, no published research report that uses it, other than the book in which it was originally introduced. One possible explanation for this fact is that the description of the method is somewhat obscure, and, moreover, buried in a single chapter of a large and rather difficult book (Newell & Simon, 1972, Chap. 6). Another possible explanation is that Newell and Simon introduced trace analysis in the context of a specific application, namely a study of so-called cryptarithmetic problems.[3] Because human performance on cryptarithmetic problems is not a hot *substantive* topic, researchers might bypass Newell and Simon's study as not relevant to their interests, thus missing the *methodological* contribution of that study. Also, researchers might fail to distinguish between different *types* of protocol analysis. Researchers who use either the method of excerpts or the method of content analysis may believe

---

[2] This is an unfortunate misnomer. For content analysis to yield intersubjectively valid results, the categories used must be defined on the basis of syntactic, lexical, or other criteria which ignore content.

[3] In cryptarithmetic problems words are treated as numbers, as in SEND + MORE = MONEY. The task is to replace the letters with digits in such a way that the arithmetic operation is correct.

that they *are* using the method proposed by Newell and Simon, and consequently feel no need to study the original description of trace analysis. Yet another possible explanation is that trace analysis breaks so radically with the methodological traditions of academic psychology that it has not been understood.

The purpose of this chapter is to develop the implications of trace analysis for standardized testing, and to facilitate and promote wider discussion and use of trace analysis in both research and practical contexts. The introduction to trace analysis presented here is, I believe, more accessible than the original presentation by the inventors of the method. Also, the task domain chosen for the application— verbally presented spatial reasoning problems—is different enough from cryptarithmetic to provide some evidence for the generality of the method.

The chapter is organized as follows. The next section puts forth the rationale of trace analysis. The section that follows is devoted to an application of trace analysis to spatial reasoning. The final section contains a speculative proposal for a nonpsychometric methodology of standardized testing that builds on trace analysis.

## THE ENACTION THEORY AND TRACE ANALYSIS

Newell and Simon have proposed that we think by mentally enacting alternative sequences of actions with respect to a problem (Newell, 1966, 1980, 1987; Newell, Shaw, & Simon, 1958; Newell & Simon, 1972). Although they did not name their theory, I have called it the *Enaction Theory* in other contexts (Ohlsson, 1983), and I will continue to do so here. The main methodological implications of the Enaction Theory are that cognitive diagnosis should be based on a sequentially ordered and temporally dense trace of the performance to be diagnosed, and that a diagnostic description should take the form of a specification of an information-processing mechanism that can reproduce the observed performance. Think-aloud protocols fulfill these methodological requirements better than other types of behavioral records. Trace analysis is primarily a method for the analysis of think-aloud protocols. Both the Enaction Theory and the method of trace analysis are described below.

### The Enaction Theory of Thinking

The Enaction Theory asserts that cognitive processing takes the form of *heuristic search through a problem space*. The process of heuristic search consists in using a *strategy*, that is, a collection of problem-solving heuristics, in order to decide which *operator*, that is, cognitive skill, should be applied to the current *knowledge state*, that is, mental representation of a problem. The application of an operator generates a new knowledge state. The successive application of operators continues until a knowledge state is reached in which the problem solver's *goal* is satisfied. These concepts may need some clarification.

Consider a person confronted with an intellectual task, such as the Tower of Hanoi puzzle, a chess problem, an algebra problem, Maier's Two-String Problem, or a geometric proof problem. In order to solve the task he/she must construct a mental representation of the given information, the problem-as-presented. The internal description of the problem is called the *initial knowledge state*. For instance, in the Tower of Hanoi puzzle[4] the problem-as-presented can be seen as a pyramid of discs; in a verbal reasoning task the givens might be conceptualized as a list of related facts. The problem solver must also build a mental representation of what is supposed to be done with the task, that is, of what counts as having solved it. This representation is his/her *goal*. The goal specifies when to terminate the problem-solving effort. For instance, in the Tower of Hanoi puzzle the goal might be conceptualized as *transport the pyramid of discs to another peg*. The initial knowledge state and the goal together constitute an understanding of the problem.

Once the task has been understood, the thinker must call up a repertory of mental actions, or cognitive skills, with which to process the problem. These actions, or skills, are called *operators,* because they operate on the current mental representation of the problem to generate a new representation (namely a representation of what the problem situation would be like if the physical action corresponding to the operator were to be carried out). The application of operators is a mental, rather than a behavioral, process. The theory asserts that the thinker is acting out *in his or her mind* what would happen if such and such an action were to be taken with respect to the problem. For instance, in solving a chess problem, the thinker is likely to imagine what would happen if he or she were to make such and such a move; in an algebraic proof problem, the thinker might anticipate what a particular formula would look like, if a certain transformation were applied to it. The theory claims that the problem solver at any one time considers only a small ensemble of operators that he or she has judged as relevant for the current problem. The problem solver may or may not be correct in his/her relevance judgments, so the operator ensemble may or may not include all operators necessary to solve the problem.[5]

The initial knowledge state and the repertory of relevant operators (or the operators the problem solver believes are relevant) implicitly specify a space of solution candidates to the problem, known as the *problem space.*[6] A solution

---

[4] Given three pegs and $N$ discs of different sizes stacked on one of the pegs in order of increasing size, move the discs to another peg by moving one disc at a time, without ever putting a larger disc on a smaller (Simon, 1975).

[5] This principle has been used to explain the phenomena of restructuring and insight in problem solving (Ohlsson, 1984c).

[6] The terminology chosen by Newell and Simon is unfortunate on this point. "Solution space" would have been more descriptive than "problem space." Grave misunderstanding of the theory results if a problem space is construed as *a space of problems* instead of as *a space of solution candidates for a particular problem.*

consists in the application of some operator to the initial state, then another (not necessarily distinct) operator to the resulting state, then yet another operator to its result, and so on, until the goal has been reached. A solution candidate consists in a sequence of operator applications, known as a *path* through the problem space. For instance, *pick up the hammer, tie the hammer to one of the ropes, set the rope swinging, walk over to the other rope, grab the first rope as it comes swinging, untie the hammer, and tie the ropes together* is a sequence of steps that constitutes a solution to Maier's Two-String Problem.[7] The initial state and the repertory of operators together generatively define the set of all possible solution candidates. The Enaction Theory asserts that thinking consists in the mental exploration of this set.

In routine action, the sequence of operators that lead to the goal is known beforehand. For instance, in solving a multicolumn addition task, any competent adult knows to begin with the column to the right, add within a column, carry to the next column to the left, and so on. Such a task is not properly called a *problem*. A task is a problem when the solution path is not known beforehand, but has to be found by trying out various operator sequences, judging how promising they are, and selecting one for execution. If the selected action sequence does not, in fact, lead toward the goal, the problem solver has to go back and try a different sequence, a process that naturally enough is called *backup*. The process of exploring alternative paths is called *search*. The search is anticipatory; we search in the head before we search in the flesh, as it were, a decision-making technique that has considerable survival value.

A problem space can be searched systematically, by exploring all possible paths. But simple combinatorial calculations show that the number of possible operator sequences is astronomical, even if the repertory of actions is small and the length of the solution path short. For instance, if there are 5 relevant operators and if the solution path is 10 steps long, then there are 5 to the 10th power, or approximately 10 million, different solution candidates. Systematic search is not feasible. Instead, the Enaction Theory claims, problem solvers search selectively, applying rules of thumb called *heuristics*. Such a rule contains information about which operator is most likely to lead toward the goal in some particular type of situation. For instance, a useful heuristic for geometry proof problems is: *if the task is to prove two geometric objects congruent, and if the given figure contains many straight lines, try to find congruent triangles*. A problem-solving strategy consists of a collection of such rules. The efficiency of problem solving is a function of how accurately the available heuristics sort out blind alleys and focus the search on a path that leads to the goal. The Enaction Theory explains expert performance in knowledge-rich domains (Newell & Simon, 1972, Chap. 11-13) as a product of a large number of very selective heuristics.

---

[7] Two ropes are suspended from the ceiling; the distance between them is too wide to allow a person to reach one rope while holding the other. A variety of everyday objects is provided. The task is to tie together the two ropes (Maier, 1970).

The Enaction Theory is a successful theory. The notion of heuristic search through a problem space has been articulated with respect to a wide range of human behaviors, from syllogistic reasoning (Newell, 1980) to the configuration of computers (Rosenbloom, Laird, McDermott, Newell, & Orciuch, 1985). The theory explains why some problems are more difficult than others (see Kotovsky, Hayes, & Simon, 1985). It explains individual differences in thinking (see Newell & Simon, 1972, Chaps. 7, 10, and 13). During recent years, the Enaction Theory has been the basis for several theories of learning (see the collections of articles edited by Anderson, 1981; by Bolc, 1987; and by Klahr, Langley, & Neches, 1987a). The Enaction Theory carries definite implications for education (Frederiksen, 1984; Ohlsson, 1983; in press); indeed, it is solid enough to support the design of the intelligent tutoring systems (Anderson, Boyle, & Reiser, 1985). There is at the current time no other theory of human thinking with comparable scope, precision, empirical grounding, and practical utility.

## The Method of Trace Analysis

If the Enaction Theory of thinking is correct, what kind of empirical method do we need in order to explain particular problem-solving performances? The theory implies that a psychological explanation consists of three parts: An hypothesis about the subject's problem space (his/her understanding of the problem, and the mental resources he/she has available for processing it), an hypothesis about his/her solution path (the sequence of mental states traversed on the way to the goal), and an hypothesis about his/her strategy (the collection of heuristics that generated the solution path). The empirical observations we collect and the procedures by which we analyze them must enable us to identify those three constructs.

Newell and Simon (1972) proposed that think-aloud protocols is an ideal type of behavioral record for the study of problem solving, and they invented *trace analysis*[8] as a method for the processing of such protocols. The main methodological works on trace analysis are Newell and Simon (1972, Chapter 6) and Ericsson and Simon (1984). Trace analysis proceeds in a bottom-up fashion through three main steps:

1. Construct the subject's problem space: (a) infer his/her *mental representation* of the task from the words used to describe the problem; (b) infer his/her *ensemble of operators* from recurring patterns of activity that give rise to new conclusions; and (c) infer his/her *goal* by noticing when, under

---

[8] The name *trace analysis* is preferred over *protocol analysis*, because I do not want to imply that the method invented by Newell and Simon is the *only* possible method for the analysis of protocols.

what conditions, the subject declares himself/herself finished with the task.

2. Identify the subject's solution path by making use of the sequential information in the protocol in order to map it onto the problem space identified in step 1. This amounts to choosing a path through the problem space that explains as many of the events in the protocol as possible.

3. Hypothesize the subject's strategy by inventing problem-solving heuristics that can reproduce the subject's solution path. The strategy hypothesis is complete if for each state-step pair along the solution path, there is some heuristic in the strategy that can generate that step when applied in that state.

The description of the *subject* achieved with this method consists of a problem space and a strategy for how to search that space. The description of his/her *performance* consists of a solution path.

The three steps described above build on each other: Identification of the problem space enables the description of the solution path, and a description of the solution path enables identification of the heuristics. Only the first two steps build directly on the information in the data. The step of identifying the problem space makes use of the content of the protocol utterances, whereas the step of laying out the solution path builds on the sequential information in the protocol. The third step, however, builds on the previous two steps. The problem-solving heuristics used by the subject are inferred from the solution path, not from the protocol. In summary, the problem space constitutes a special purpose formalism for describing the solution path; the solution path is a low-level mini-theory that explains the behavioral record; the strategy is a slightly-higher-level mini-theory that explains the solution path.[9]

The Enaction Theory implies two methodological requirements that are difficult to fulfill with any type of behavioral records other than think-aloud protocols. The first requirement is that the behavioral record must enable us to infer the subject's conceptualization of the problem. We therefore need to hear the subject talk about the problem. How does he/she parse the problem situation into distinct objects, what properties does he/she assign to them, and what relations does he/she see between them? What representational formats does he/she use to encode those properties and relations? For instance, in so-called cryptarithmetic problems, the concept of *parity*—whether a number is odd or even—is often crucial to successful problem solving (Newell & Simon, 1972). It is obviously difficult

---

[9] The hierarchy of explanations does not end with the strategy, of course. The strategy is explained by a learning theory that, in turn, is explained by the structure of the cognitive architecture; the latter is related to the structure of the brain; and so on.

to know whether a person is using the concept of parity or not, unless we hear him or her talk about the problem. As a second example, Johnson-Laird (1983) has argued that people solve verbal-reasoning problems with mental models, rather than with propositional representations. It is obviously difficult to know what representational format a person is using unless we can hear him/her verbalize it.

The second methodological requirement of the Enaction Theory is that the behavioral record must enable us to infer the *sequence* of mental events that took place when the subject solved the experimental problem. Unless we know the solution path, we cannot infer the strategy. Different paths might lead to the same end-state, so a recording of the end-state or the time it took the subject to arrive at the end-state does not enable us to identify his/her path. We need to observe the intermediate stages of the problem-solving effort, the sequence of partial results created along the path to solution. The trace of the partial results should preferably be *temporally dense,* that is, have many observations of the performance per unit of time, in order to accurately discriminate the subject's path from alternative paths through the problem space.

Think-aloud protocols fulfill both of the above requirements. They reveal how subjects conceptualize the experimental problem, and they provide a sequentially ordered and temporally dense trace. Other types of behavioral records are less satisfactory. Interviews destroy sequential information, because the order of the subject's utterances is partially controlled by the order of the interviewer's questions. In retrospective interviews the sequential information is further corrupted by memory failures. In general, interviews reveal the subject's representation, but does not enable us to infer his/her solution path. Video tapes of behavior or the recording of key strokes on computer terminals provide sequential information, but they do not give us any insights into the subject's mental representation. In general, behavioral recordings reveal the path, but not the representation. Eye movement recordings may reveal the representation (since they tell us what features of the problem situation the subject attends to, or can discriminate between), but because they do not reveal what the subject *does* with the problem information, they do not enable us to infer the solution path. In short, think-aloud protocols fulfill the methodological requirements of the Enaction Theory better than other types of behavioral records.

In summary, human beings are hypothesized to think by mentally exploring alternative paths through some search space. The methodological implications of this hypothesis are that cognitive diagnosis should be based on a sequentially ordered and temporally dense behavioral record that is analyzed with the goal of designing an information-processing mechanism that can reproduce the observed behavior. A concrete example of this kind of cognitive diagnosis is worked out in detail in the next section. The implications of this methodology for the construction of standardized tests are developed in the fourth and final section.

1.  The Bench Problem

Some boys are sitting on a bench.

Jonas is further right than Ingvar.
Olof is further left than Ingvar.
David is immediately to the left of Jonas.

Who is immediately to the right of Ingvar?


2.  The Block Problem

A child is putting blocks of different colors on top of each other.

A black block is between a red and a green block.
A yellow block is further up than the red one.
A green block is bottommost but one.
A blue block is immediately below the yellow one.
A white block is further down than the black one.

Which block is immediately below the blue one?


3.  The Ice-Cream Problem

Some boys are standing in line at an ice-cream stand.

Rolf is further towards the front than Erik.
Sven is further towards the front than Ove.
Nils is immediately behind Mats.
Hans is frontmost but one.
Mats is further back than Ove.
Erik is immediately behind Hans.
Leif is further back than Mats.

Who is immediately behind Erik?

FIG. 11.1.   Three examples of spatial arrangement problems.


## TRACE ANALYSIS APPLIED TO SPATIAL REASONING

Consider the spatial reasoning problems in Fig. 11.1. Each problem consists of a short text describing a static situation by asserting certain spatial relations between some discreet, stable objects. It ends with a question concerning a relation not explicitly mentioned in the text. I call problems of this sort *spatial arrangement problems*. The relational concepts used are commonsense spatial concepts.[10] They include unary predicates like *bottommost,* tertiary predicates like *between,* and ambiguous predicates like *adjacent.* If the number of objects in such a problem is larger than three, it usually takes an adult more than a minute to solve that problem; if the number of objects is, say, ten, and if the relational structure embedded in the premises is complex, the solution time can be as long as 20 minutes.

From a problem-solving point of view, spatial arrangement problems are unusual in that they are static. Many problems used to study problem solving require a sequence of transformations of the given situation. In a spatial arrangement problem, on the other hand, the task is not to transform the given situation, but to understand it well enough to answer a question. From a psychometric point of view, spatial arrangement problems would be expected to have high loads on spatial ability, reasoning ability, and verbal ability. A main difference between spatial arrangement problems and typical test items is that spatial arrangement problems take more time to solve.

Empirical studies of spatial arrangement problems, using both trace analysis and experimental methods, have revealed a number of phenomena:

1. A majority of adults solve spatial arrangement problems with the help of a mental model,[11] rather than by reasoning exclusively in a propositional mode (Hagert, 1980a, 1980b; Johnson-Laird, 1983; Ohlsson, 1980a, 1984b). A small minority of adults use a propositional reasoning method based on the idea of elimination of alternatives (Ohlsson, 1980a, 1984b). An even smaller minority try to apply other, less rational approaches to the problem, such as trying to infer the quantitative distances between the objects (Ohlsson, 1980a).

2. The particular problem spaces used to implement the mental model-building strategy vary from one individual to the next, as do the heuristics used to search them, with substantial differences in the solution paths traversed by different persons as a consequence (Ohlsson, 1980a, 1980b, 1982).

3. Some subjects shift back and forth between model-building and propositional strategies. Subjects can be induced to make such strategy shifts, even when they do not show any spontaneous tendency to do so (Ohlsson, 1984a).

---

[10] The problem texts are translated from Swedish. Phrases like *bottommost but one* and *frontmost* may not be good English, but their Swedish counterparts are quite idiomatic.

[11] The term "mental model" is here used in the sense of Johnson-Laird (1983), who defines a model as an object which satisfies a set of propositions. This is the sense in which the term is used in the study of formal logic. The term is commonly used within cognitive science to refer to any integrated knowledge unit with a large grain size, particularly if it encodes knowledge about a physical mechanism or process. For examples of this alternative use of the term, see the collection of articles by Gentner and Stevens (1983).

4. Strategies for spatial arrangement problems have a large attention-allocation component. The solution to a spatial arrangement problem depends crucially on which premises are read in which order. Consequently, differences in attentional heuristics is a major source of individual differences in this task domain (Ohlsson, 1984b).

5. The spatial competence needed to solve spatial arrangement problems is large. A list of the inferences needed to build mental models of linear orderings from propositional descriptions contains over 100 distinct inference patterns (Ohlsson, 1980a).

6. Backups are frequent events in problem-solving efforts in this domain. However, a large proportion of backups are not followed by the exploration of new search paths, but by the retraversal of the already explored search path (Hagert & Rollenhagen, 1981; Ohlsson, 1980a). Hence, they are not backups in the search theory sense. These backups occur, I believe, because working memory capacity limitations make it necessary to recreate intermediate results from time to time. I call backups that are followed by repetition of previously performed inferences *consolidation backups*.

The general conclusions summarized above are based on large numbers of applications of trace analysis. For example, Study II of Ohlsson (1980a) was based on 50 protocols, each of which was analyzed with the help of trace analysis. A detailed diagnosis of a single performance is presented below.

## The Subject and the Behavioral Record

The performance to be diagnosed here was selected from a larger study (Ohlsson, 1980a, Study I). Twelve subjects participated in the study. They solved a variety of spatial arrangement problems under different conditions. The protocol to be discussed here was produced by a subject labeled SI6 while solving the Block Problem (see Fig. 11.1). It was selected for analysis on the basis of completeness and interest.

Subject SI6 was a 30-year-old psychology student, who participated in the experiment as part of a course requirement. She was not paid. The Block Problem was the third problem in the experimental session. In a previous session she had solved three simpler spatial arrangement problems.

The problem text was typed as it appears in Fig. 11.1 on a white index card that was handed to the subject at the beginning of the solution attempt. She had the card available throughout the solution attempt. She was not allowed the use of paper and pencil or any other tool and was instructed to think aloud. The exact instruction given was "give words to your thoughts as you have them." Further, the instruction was to begin the solution attempt by reading through the problem text aloud. The verbalizations were tape recorded and transcribed verbatim.

The complete protocol is shown in Fig. 11.2[12] F-numbers in the following analysis refer to protocol fragments in those figures. The protocol is 3 minutes and 40 seconds long (220 seconds), including the initial reading of the problem text. It contains a total of 314 words, which means that the subject's speech rate was approximately 1.4 words per second. There are no task-irrelevant passages in the protocol, nor any interactions with the experimenter. The solution attempt ended when the subject gave her answer, which was correct.

## Diagnosing the Subject's Problem Space

The problem space used by the subject is discussed in four subsections, dealing with her representation, operations, goal, and memory resources, respectively.

*Representation.*    The protocol shows that, as one would expect, the subject is capable of reading and comprehending the sentences in the problem text, and of making use of the propositional information conveyed by them. However, there are several classes of propositional constructions that are *not* used by this subject in this protocol. First, there are no examples of *negated* sentences in the protocol. SI6 does not use expressions of the form "Object X is not . . . ," for example, "The black block cannot be above . . ." Second, there is no evidence for the use of *quantifiers*. SI6 does not use expressions of the form "All objects are . . ." or "At least one object is . . ." Third, she does not use any *sentential connectives* (even though she uses "and" to connect arguments within propositions). In particular, she does not use any *if-then* constructs, such as "consequently," "therefore," "it follows that," and so on. In summary, simple predicate-argument conditions are sufficient to capture the subject's representation of propositional information about the task.

There is evidence in this protocol (as well as in other protocols from this subject) that the propositional format is not the only one used by SI6. In three places (F40, F44, and F47) she verbalizes her knowledge of the problem situation through a list of object names, for instance:

F40. white red black green

I take this as evidence that the subject is building a mental model of the problem situation, trying to see in her mind's eye the six blocks standing on top of each other.

A mental model of a linear ordering can be represented as a list of object symbols. Two refinements are needed to accurately represent this subject, namely end-anchors and a distinction between "adjacent" and "followed-by." First, the subject reads out her mental model in different directions at different times during the solution attempt (from top to bottom in F15-F17, and from bottom to top in,

---

[12] The subject spoke Swedish, so the text in Figure 11.2 is a translation of the original protocol.

F1. a child puts blocks in different colors on top of each other
F2. a black block is between a red and a green block
F3. a yellow block is further up than the red one
F4. a green block is bottommost but one
F5. a blue block is immediately below the yellow one
F6. a white block is further down than the black one
F7. what block is immediately below the blue one
F8. the black block is between a red and a green
F9. block
F10. well that does not mean that it must be exactly between
F11. could be something else between also
F12. a yellow block is further up than the red one
F13. a green block is bottommost but one
F14. a blue block is immediately below the yellow one
F15. the yellow one is higher up than the red one
F16. and immediately below the yellow one comes the blue one
F17. then comes a red one
F18. I'd say
F19. well
F20. a
F21. a yellow block is higher up than the red one
F22. a green block is bottommost but one
F23. a blue block is immediately below the yellow one
F24. below the yellow one is a blue block
F25. and a yellow block is higher up than the red
F26. below the yellow is then also a red
F27. a blue and a red are below the yellow one
F28. and a
F29. a blue and a red are under the yellow block
F30. and a green block is bottommost but one
F31. a black block is between the red and the green
F32. a black block
F33. a black block is between the red and the green block
F34. a white block is further down than the black one
F35. then there is a white
F36. and then we have a
F37. oh how difficult
F38. a white block is further down than the black one
F39. and the black one is between the red and the green
F40. white red black green
F41. I'll say then
F42. but the green is bottommost but one
F43. then I'll say
F44. white green black red
F45. instead
F46. then the white one is bottommost
F47. white green black and red
F48. and then we had the
F49. blue one which is immediately below the yellow
F50. the yellow is higher up than the read
F51. then it is topmost so far
F52. the yellow one
F53. and the blue one is immediately below
F54. then it comes topmost but one
F55. which one is then immediately below the blue one
F56. immediately below the blue one is then the red one

---

FIG. 11.2.   The complete protocol of subject S16 on Block Problem

for example, F40). This implies that her representation contains some device that allows her to keep track of the direction of a model. I assume that she does this with the help of *end-anchors*, that is, symbols that label the top and the bottom of the ordering respectively. In the formal model these are represented by the arbitrary symbols TOP and BTM.

Second, the subject is able to infer from premise 2 ("A yellow block is further up than the red one") and premise 4 ("A blue block is immediately below the yellow one") that the red block is below the blue block (see fragments F15-F17). This conclusion does not follow unless a distinction is made between two different relations, namely *x is adjacent to y*, which implies that there is no object between *x* and *y*, and *x is followed by y*, which does not say anything about proximity. Hence, the subject's mental model must contain some device for distinguishing between these two relations. In the formal model *adjacent to* is symbolized by a hyphen, and *followed by* with a blank space. For instance, (TOP *x-y* BTM) means that *y* is below and adjacent to *x*, (TOP *x y-*BTM) means that *y* is somewhere below *x*, that there could be other objects between *x* and *y*, and that there are no objects below *y*.

It is necessary to assume that the various kinds of knowledge elements used to represent the problem have different *modes*. These modes are symbolized in the analysis with the help of indices or *tags*. I assume that the subject can tag knowledge elements in four different ways:

new    a new result (i.e., an output from an operator);

old    information that has already been used as basis for an inference;

unc    a result that is experienced by the subject as unclear;

imp    a result that is impossible because it contradicts the given information.

The evidence for the *new* and *old* tags is indirect. It consists in the global observations that SI6 always works on newly produced information, and that old information never confuses her or interferes with her processing. The evidence for the *unclear* status is more direct: In fragment F18 (see Fig. 11.2) the subject directly verbalizes uncertainty about an outcome. The evidence for the *imp* tag, finally, is also direct: In the course of solving the problem the subject discovers a contradiction that leads her to revise the model; the fragments F42-F45 show that she is aware of this contradiction.

There are some types of information that are *not* used by SI6 in the solution to the Block Problem. First, she does not think about the *absolute positions* of the objects, in contrast to the relative positions the objects acquire in a partially completed model. For example, she does not ask herself questions like "What object goes into the topmost position?" or "What position should be assigned to object so-and-so?" Her representation is relative and topological in character, rather than absolute and positional.

A second and related point is that SI6 makes no use of *numerical information*. There is no evidence that she thinks in terms of number of objects: How many objects there are all in all, how many objects she has left to place, how many objects there could be room for in such-and-such a part of the model, and so on. Indeed, there is no evidence that she ever counts the total number of objects mentioned in the problem. (This raises the question of how she knows that her mental model has been completed.)

Third, there are no verbalizations of *goals,* plans, or intentions. SI6 never says anything about what she is trying to do, or what she would like to be able to do, for instance: "Next, I should find out the position of object X," or "I now want to find the object that is adjacent to object X."[13]

The representational format used by this subject on this task is summarized in a generative grammar on BNF form[14] in Fig. 11.3.

*Operators.* The subject shows evidence of using four basic problem-solving operators (mental processes that produce new results): *reading* the problem text (READ), *translating* propositional information into a mental model (TRNS), extending an existing mental model by *integrating* further propositional information into it (INT), and *answering* a question by reading off the answer from a mental model (ANSW). They are defined in Fig. 11.4.

It is worth emphasizing that the READ process is included among the problem-solving operators. In this analysis, reading new information from the display counts as a step forward in the problem space. This implies that a model of the subject's strategy must include assumptions about when and how she attends to the problem text. Heuristics for how to access the problem text play an important part in understanding human performance in this task domain.

The subject's world knowledge, or spatial competence, enters into the processing mainly through the TRNS, INT, and ANSW operators. They generate new conclusions. In order to model the subject's performance we need to know which spatial inferences these operators are capable of, that is, what inferential competence we should stock them with, as it were, in order to accurately simulate human behavior. Task analysis indicates that there are approximately 100 distinct inferences about linear orderings that adults in our culture would consider valid (Ohlsson, 1980a). The analysis of the inferential competence of this subject is not pursued further here.

*The goal.* The goal of solving a spatial arrangement problem is to answer the question at the end of the problem text. It is trivial to answer questions about a linear ordering, if one has access to a complete model of that ordering, that is,

---

[13] Other subjects in this study used position and numerical information in solving spatial arrangement problems, and gave clear evidence of setting themselves goals.

[14] The rules of the BNF notation can be found in many standard textbooks in computer science, and also in Newell and Simon (1972, pp. 44–46).

```
<knowledge-state>  ::= <knowledge-element> /
                       <knowledge-element> <knowledge-state>

<knowledge-element>  ::= <tag> <knowledge-element>  /
                         <proposition> / <question>  / <model>

<proposition>  ::= (<predicate> <object-sequence>)

<question>  ::= (<predicate> ? <object>)

<predicate>  ::= ABOVE / IMMEDIATELY-ABOVE /
                 UNDER / IMMEDIATELY-UNDER /
                 TOPMOST / TOPMOST-BUT-ONE /
                 BOTTOMMOST / BOTTOMMOST-BUT-ONE /
                 ADJACENT / BETWEEN / ANSWER

<model>  ::= (<end-anchor>.1 <element-sequence> <end-anchor>.2)

<end-anchor>  ::= TOP / BTM

<element-sequence>  ::= <element> / <element> <element-sequence>

<element> ::= <object> / <relation>

<object-sequence>  ::= <object> / <object> <object-sequence>

<object>  ::= red / black / white / green / yellow / blue

<relation>  ::= <followed-by> / <adjacent-to>

<followed-by>  ::= "blank space"

<adjacent-to>  ::= "colon"

<tag>  ::= old / new / unc / imp

<probe> ::= FIRSTPREM / SECPREM / THIRDPREM /
            FOURTHPREM / FIFTHPREM / NEXTPREM / QUESTION

<operator> ::= READ / TRNS / INT / ANSW
```

FIG. 11.3.   Mental representation of subject S16 for the Block Problem.

a model that includes all the objects mentioned in the problem text. I assume that the operative goal of SI6 was to achieve a complete mental model. The evidence for this is that as long as the model is incomplete, she does not read the question she is supposed to answer. However, as soon as her model is complete in the sense of containing all the objects, she attends to the question and answers it.

How did the subject decide that her mental model was complete? Logically speaking, there are only two possibilities: to check that each object mentioned in the problem text is included in the model, or, alternatively, to count the objects in the model, count the objects mentioned in the text, and verify that the counts are the same. SI6 does not show evidence of carrying out either process. The

READ(<probe>)    *Read from the problem text that item which is specified by the probe.* This operator accesses the external display, and delivers a proposition into working memory. The proposition is tagged as *new*, even if it has been read before. The probe is a description of that which is to be read. In the formal model, the probe can take the values FIRSTPREM, SECPREM, ... , etc., NEXTPREM, and QUESTION. These symbols are arbitrary, but their intended interpretation should be obvious.

TRNS(<proposition>)

*Translate a proposition into a mental model.* This operator takes a proposition as input, and delivers into working memory a model which satisfies that proposition. The proposition is tagged as *old* (given that the operator is successful), and the model as *new*. For instance, if the sentence "The blue block is immediately below the yellow one" (Premise 2 in the Blocks Problem) corresponds to the proposition "(Adjacent-Below blue yellow)", then TRNS[(Adjacent-Below blue yellow)] will result in the creation of the working memory element "(TOP yellow-blue BTM)".

INT(<proposition>)    *Integrate a proposition into the current model.* This operator takes a proposition as input, and tries to integrate its information into the current mental model. If it succeeds, it produces a new, extended model which is tagged as *new* and placed in working memory. The proposition is tagged as *old*. The previous model is deleted from working memory. For instance, if the current model is "(TOP yellow-blue BTM)", then INT[(Further-Below red yellow)] results in the extended model "(TOP yellow-blue red BTM)".

ANSW(<question>)    *Answer question.* This operator compares the question and the current mental model, and reads off the answer, if possible. The answer is then said, and the solution attempt ended. For instance, if the current model is "(TOP yellow-blue red BTM)", then ANSW[(Adjacent-Below blue ?)], where "(Adjacent-Below blue ?)" corresponds to the question "Which object is immediately below the blue block?", will result in the answer "red".

FIG. 11.4.    Basic problem-solving operators of subject S16 on the Block Problem.

protocol contains no clue as to how she knows that her mental model is complete. Recognition of a complete model does not seem to be an explicit inferential step. I assume that S16 infers that the model is complete when she fails to find any missing objects, that is, any objects not yet included in the model.

***Memory resources.***    A model of S16's reasoning must make some assumptions about her working memory capacity and her use of long-term memory. First, what working memory capacity should be presupposed? It turns out that a good account of the protocol can be constructed if we assume that this subject can reliably hold three knowledge elements in her head at any one time. (What counts as a knowledge element is defined by Fig. 11.3).

Second, the present analysis is based on the following hypotheses about long-term memory:

1. The inferential knowledge needed to solve spatial arrangement problems is stored (procedurally) inside the TRNS, INT, and ANSW operators.
2. Partial results are stored in long-term memory. More precisely, the current knowledge state is stored after each application of the TRNS and INT operators. Stored knowledge states can be retrieved and re-instated as the current state.[15]
3. The long-term memory trace contains only the path from the initial state to the current state, that is, search paths over which backups are made are deleted from memory.
4. Long-term storage is used for various bookkeeping purposes. For example, the READ operator is able to get the next premise from the problem text, that is, the premise immediately below the last premise to be read. This presupposes some memory of which premise was last read. Similarly, the SCAN operator can continue a scanning pattern from the last point of scanning, which presupposes some memory of where the previous scan was broken off.

## Diagnosing the Subject's Solution Path

Figs. 11.3 and 11.4 define the subject's problem space. If the hypothesis they express is correct, they specify generatively the entire set of paths subject SI6 *could* have traversed while solving the Block Problem. The next step in the construction of an explanation of SI6's performance is to identify which path was *actually* traversed. This is done by interpreting the protocol fragments in terms of the problem space operators and their inputs and outputs. The following three interpretative principles were applied in the present analysis:[16]

1. Verbalizations from the subject are interpreted as outputs from operators, unless this would complicate the overall interpretation.
2. Backups are assigned the shortest scope consistent with the evidence.

---

[15] Hence, a complete list of the subject's capabilities must include an operator that prepares for backup by storing the current state in long-term memory, and a backup operator that can retrieve a stored knowledge state. These operators are defined in Fig. 11.6.

[16] The reader may want to compare the interpretative principles used here with the discussion of protocol interpretation in Ericsson and Simon (1984).

3. Verbalizations that are identical to sentences in the problem text are assumed to be the result of reading aloud from the problem card, unless this complicates the overall interpretation. In cases of doubt, the audio tape was consulted.

These rules are applied below in mapping the protocol in Fig. 11.2 onto the problem space defined by Figs. 11.3 and 11.4. The result is an hypothesis about the subject's solution path that can be displayed graphically in the form of a *Problem Behavior Graph* (PBG).[17] The PBG generated from the protocol in Fig. 11.2 is shown in Fig. 11.5. The first subsection here describes how the PBG is generated. The second subsection asks whether the path hypothesis reveals any unusual or special events, events that are in special need, as it were, of being explained.

*Mapping the protocol onto the problem space.*    In the beginning the subject is simply reading the problem text, as she was instructed to do (F1-F7). Presumably there is some change of goals between F7 and F8, from *read the text* to *solve the problem,* but there is no trace of it in the protocol. SI6 then begins her solution attempt by reading the first premise (F8). The next step cannot be interpreted within the problem space: She reflects on the meaning of the term *between* (F10-F11). This does not produce any new result in terms of the problem space. (This is the only step outside the problem space.) In F12 the subject is back in the attempt to solve the problem. She continues to read the premises in the order in which they are written, that is, every time she reads, she reads the next premise (F12-F14). Upon reading the fourth premise, SI6 notices the repeated occurrence of the yellow block, and begins to make inferences. The content as well as the phrasing of the fragments F16 and F17 implies knowledge of the internal relations between the yellow, blue, and red blocks. I interpret F16 as an application of the TRNS operator to premise 4 and F17 as an application of INT to premise 2. The question of F15 then remains. The tone of voice on the tape does not support the hypothesis that premise 2 is being re-read at this point. Working memory considerations show that premise 2 should still be available. Therefore, it has been interpreted as a rehearsal, that is, not as a generation of a new result. The output from the sequence F15-F17 is probably tagged as *unclear* (F18) because it is followed by a consolidation backup (F19-F20).

The process is then repeated. In F21-F23 SI6 reads again the premises in the order in which they are written on the problem card. There is one difference: After having translated premise 4 (F24), she re-reads premise 2 (F25) before it

---

[17] The rules of PBG construction are set down by Newell and Simon (1972, p. 173). Briefly, time goes from left to right and from top to bottom. A knowledge state is a node, and an operator is a link. A backup results in a new node below the node representing the state to which the problem solver backed up; the two nodes are connected with a vertical line.

is integrated. No such re-reading was needed in the previous episode. However, as described above, in that episode SI6 felt a need to rehearse premise 2 before translating premise 4. The subject probably has some problem with working memory at this point, even though the assumption of a short-term capacity of three chunks predicts that premise 2 should still be available. At the end of this passage (F27-F29) SI6 again has the result *yellow blue red*.

The subject now continues by reading the two premises that she has skipped, namely premise 3 (F30) and premise 1 (F31), and the premise she has not yet looked at, namely premise 5 (F34), in that order. In F32 she is trying to do something with the black block, but it is unclear what. She fails, backs up, and re-reads premise 1 instead (F33).

In F35 the subject tries to work on the white block, but fails and backs up (F37). On trying again, she succeeds, achieving the result *white red black green* (F40). It must have happened through the translation of premise 5, followed by an integration of premise 1. In F42 the subject discovers a contradiction between her partial result and premise 3. This leads to a backup and revision of her mental model to *white green black red* instead (F44). She then integrates premise 3 into this model. We know this because in F46 she says that the white block is bottommost, a conclusion that only follows from the fact that the green is bottommost but one, combined with the fact that the white is below the green.

The subject then reminds herself that the blue block is still missing from the model and reads premise 4 that says that the blue block is immediately below the yellow one (F48-F49). There is no evidence that SI6 does anything with this premise. (Because neither the blue nor the yellow block are as yet placed in the model, no extension of the model is possible at this point.) Instead, SI6 reads premise 2 (F50), and integrates it (F51-F52). After that, the yellow block is part of the model, and premise 4 can be integrated (F53-F54). Finally, having placed all the objects in the model SI6 reads the question (F55) and derives the answer (F56).

The above path hypothesis is summarized graphically in the Problem Behavior Graph (PBG) in Fig. 11.5. Because the PBG contains 40 nodes and the solution time was 220 seconds, the *residence time*, that is, the time the subject spent in each knowledge state before deciding which operator to apply, was 5.5 seconds, a result that is compatible with other analyses of think-aloud protocols (Newell & Simon, 1972).

*Special events.*    Given the above interpretation of the subject's performance, we might ask if the solution path exhibits any remarkable features. Are there any events that are in particular need of explanation, as it were? There are five such events, or groups of events.

First, as the attentive reader has noticed, there is no trace of the partial result *yellow blue red* (which is achieved in fragments F16-F17) in the latter half of the protocol. SI6 creates the ordering *white red black green* (F40) and then continues

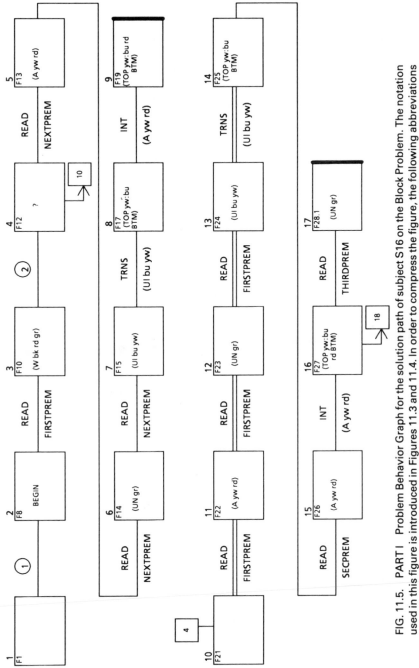

FIG. 11.5. PART I   Problem Behavior Graph for the solution path of subject S16 on the Block Problem. The notation used in this figure is introduced in Figures 11.3 and 11.4. In order to compress the figure, the following abbreviations are used for the predicate terms: A=Above, AI=Above, AM=Immediately-Above, AN=Topmost, AN=Topmost-But-One, U=Under, UI=Immediately-Under, UM=Bottommost, UN=Bottommost-But-One, I=Adjacent, and W=Between. The following abbreviations are used for the color terms: bl=black, bu=blue, gr=green, rd=red, yw=yellow, and wh=white.

273

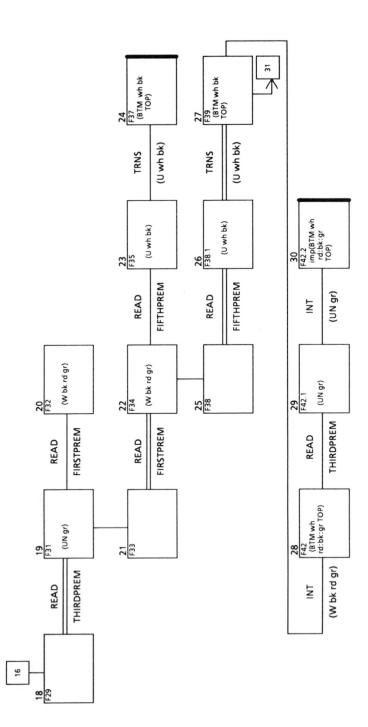

FIG 11.5. PART II

274

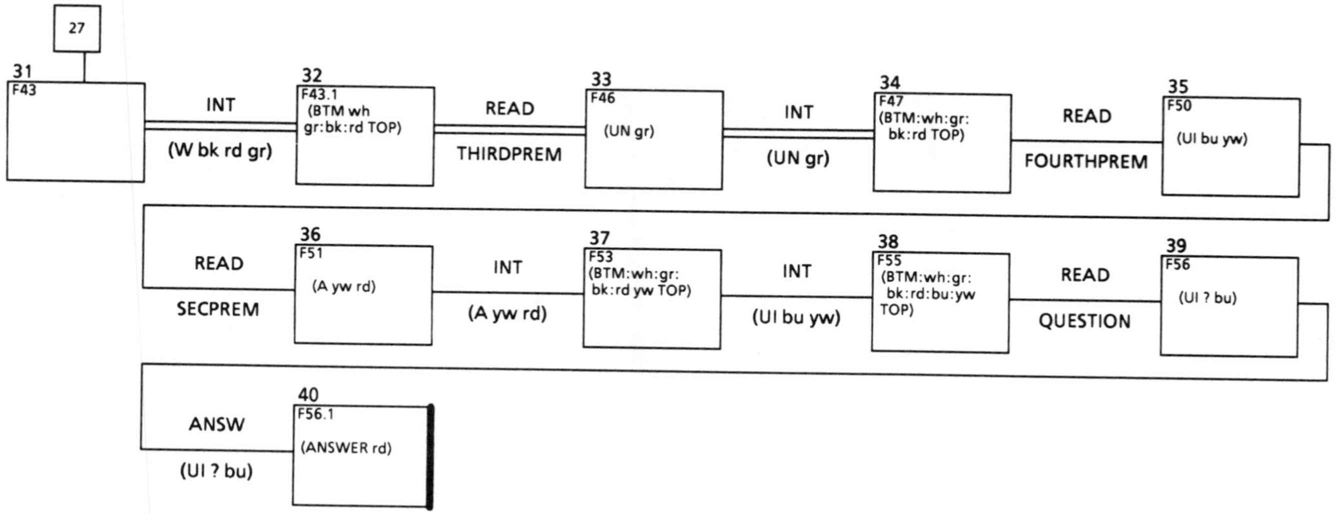


FIG. 11.5. PART III

to integrate the information about the yellow, blue, and red blocks into this ordering, as if she has no previous knowledge of their relative positions. Somewhere in the interval F29-F33 SI6 forgot the mental model that was being built. The problem is to explain why such a memory failure occurred at this point, but nowhere else in the solution attempt.

Second, the discovery of the contradiction between her mental model and premise 3 in F42 is crucial for the subject's solution. How did it come about? Premise 3 happens to be the only premise in the problem that could have shown her that the result achieved in F40 was wrong. What made her re-read this premise at such an appropriate time? Was it a chance event, or was she looking for such information? If she was looking for it, how did she know she needed it?

Third, in the beginning of the solution attempt, the subject *rehearses* premise 2 (F15); in the next pass over the premises, the subject *re-reads* premise 2 in the corresponding position (F25). In both cases, the assumption of a three-chunk working memory predicts that premise 2 should be available in working memory at that point. Thus, both the rehearsal and the re-reading are in need of explanation.

Fourth, in deriving the first partial result, *yellow blue red,* the subject worked with the model from the top and downwards (F16-F17). But later in the protocol, while constructing the sequence *white green black red,* she verbalizes the model from the bottom and upward instead (F40).

Fifth, there are four backups in the protocol that are not followed by the exploration of new paths in the problem space, but by repetitions of previously performed inferences (F19, F28.1, F32, and F37). I call them *consolidation backups.* There are two questions to be asked about each such event: "Why does it occur when it does?" and "What determines its scope?" (that is, how many previous steps are repeated?).

### Diagnosing the Subject's Strategy

The solution path (the PBG) is a low-level theory or explanation for the observed performance (the protocol). The next step in the diagnosis is to invent a higher level theory that explains the solution path. Such an explanation takes the form of a strategy for solving spatial arrangement problems that generates the hypothesized path when applied to the Blocks Problem.

It would be desirable to mechanize the process of inferring heuristics that explain a particular solution path. Several Artificial Intelligence systems have been proposed that invent a strategy hypothesis, given a protocol (Waterman & Newell, 1971), a problem space (Ohlsson & Langley, 1984, 1988), or a solution path (Langley, Ohlsson, & Sage, 1984). Langley, Wogulis, and Ohlsson (this volume) report some recent research with respect to this problem.[18] However,

---

[18] The reader is referred to Burton (1982) and to Lewis (1986) for examples of systems for the automatic generation of strategy hypotheses that are *not* based on the Enaction Theory.

such systems are not yet in practical use, so the practitioner of trace analysis has to be prepared to guess the subject's strategy, and then evaluate that guess by applying it to the path.

This section hypothesizes a strategy for SI6 and the next section evaluates that hypothesis. I first point out some global properties of SI6's style of problem solving, and then describe her problem-solving heuristics in detail.

***Global comments on SI6's strategy.***    There is a strong recency effect in SI6's protocol. The subject's inferences always deal with newly created information. Previous results never seem to confuse her, nor does she make use of them.

There is evidence that the inferential operators TRNS and INT are applied only when certain patterns of information are present. For instance, the subject reads four premises in the beginning of her problem-solving attempt before applying the TRNS operator, apparently waiting for some particular condition to be satisfied before starting to build the mental model. Similarly, the INT operator is not always applied as soon as there is a new proposition in working memory, but only under certain circumstances. Detailed hypotheses about the patterns she is looking for are stated later in this section.

The subject accesses the external display according to different heuristics during different phases of her problem solving. In the beginning, she is reading the premises in the order in which they are written. After the first application of the TRNS operator she looks around for information that has not yet been used. Finally, at the end, she is searching for information about particular objects.

The subject waits until the end to read the question. This confirms the data-driven character of the subject's processing; a goal-driven system would *begin* with the question.

***Formal description of SI6's strategy.***    In order to describe SI6's strategy as an information-processing system, four new operators, two attentional (FPP and FPM) and two perceptual (GMO and SCAN), are needed. They do not change the knowledge state as defined in Fig. 11.3 and 11.4 but they control attention, find arguments for the other operators, and access the external display. They are defined in Fig. 11.6 which also defines the two backup operators (BKUP and PREB).

The subject's strategy is here represented as a collection of heuristic rules. The rules are stated in a particular format known as a *production system*. In this format each rule has a *condition*, a conjunction of descriptive clauses, and an *action*, a list of problem-solving operators. The interpretation of the rule is that if a knowledge state satisfies the condition, then the operators described in the action should be carried out in that state. Production system models are common in the study of human cognition. The reader is referred to Davis and King (1976), Hunt and Poltrock (1974), Klahr, Langley, and Neches (1987b), and Waterman and Hayes-Roth (1978) for general overviews and discussions of production

| | |
|---|---|
| FPM(\<model\>) | *Find a proposition related to the current model.* FPM searches working memory for a proposition with one of its arguments already placed in the model. It returns that proposition, if any, or else it fails. |
| FPP(\<proposition\>) | *Find a proposition related to a given proposition.* This operator searches working memory for a proposition related in a particular way to the proposition given as argument. It returns that proposition, if any, or else fails. FPP is looking for a *chaining pattern*, i. e., a pair of binary relations such that the second argument of the first proposition is the same as the first argument of the second, e. g., (R x y)(P y z). |
| GMO(\<model\>) | *Generate missing objects.* This operator compares the current model and the text, and returns a list of objects which are not yet included in the model. If it cannot find any missing object, it fails. |
| SCAN(\<probe\>) | *Scan the text for the element described by the probe.* This operator takes a probe as input, and looks through the text for items that conform to the description in that probe. The probe can be an object, in which case SCAN finds the first premise that mentions that object. The probe can also be the constant UNUSED, in which case SCAN finds the first premise which has not yet participated in any inference. It returns a description of (the location of) the item it finds. |
| BKUP() | *Backup.* This operator retrieves the knowledge state that was current immediately before the last TRNS or INT inference, and reinstates it as the current knowledge-state. |
| PREB() | *Prepare for backup.* This operator stores the current knowledge state in long-term memory. It applies immediately before a TRNS or INT inference. |

FIG. 11.6.   Auxillary problem-solving operators for subject S16 on the Block Problem.

system languages. Although the production system formalism was introduced into psychology in connection with trace analysis (Newell, 1966; Newell & Simon, 1972), there is no inherent conceptual connection between trace analysis and production systems. Other formalisms for the representation of problem-solving strategies could be used to express the result of trace analysis.

The production system model of S16 on the Block Problem is shown in Fig. 11.7. The notation used is a variant of the standard BNF notation.[19] This notation is useful for discussing production systems, because it imposes some discipline on the statement of the production rules while at the same time allowing us to abstract from many of the technical details needed to make a running program.

---

[19] The rules for this notation can be found in Newell & Simon (1972, pp. 44–46).

```
A      <question> <model>    ===> ANSW(<question>)

C1     new(FAIL GMO)  ===>    READ(QUESTION)

I1a    <model> new<proposition> ===> FPM(<model>) (=> proposition);
                                     INT(proposition)

I2     new<model> <proposition>  ===> INT(<proposition>)

T1a    abs<model>  new<proposition>.1 <proposition>.2  ==>
                              FPP(<proposition>.1) (=> proposition);
                              TRNS(<proposition>.1)

B      imp<model>  ===> BKUP()

R3a    new<expression>  (REMAINS = NONE)  ===> GMO(<model>) (=> object);
                                               SCAN(object) (=> premise);
                                               READ(premise)

R2a    new<expression> (HASMODEL = YES)  ===>  SCAN(UNUSED) (=> premise);
                                               READ(premise)

R1     new<expression>  ===>  READ(NEXTPREM)

S1     BEGIN  ===>  READ(FIRSTPREM)
```

FIG. 11.7.   Production system model of subject S16 on the Block Problem.

Here I give a natural language paraphrase of, and sometimes a comment to, each production rule.[20]

A       *When the question has just been read, and a model is available, try to infer the answer.* The condition on this rule is very general, but SI6 does not read or attend to the question until already convinced that the model is complete. Hence, the fact that the question has been attended to is itself an indication that the model is completed, and that the ANSW operator should be applied.

C1      *When there are no more missing objects, read the question.* The fact that there are no more missing objects is a sign that the model is complete and that the problem-solving process can move into the question-answering stage.

I1a     *When both a new proposition and a model are available, check if the proposition has the right relation to the model, and, if so, try to*

---

[20] The reader need not worry about the somewhat elaborate labeling of the production rules. The labels are intended to facilitate comparison between this production system and other production systems for the same domain in other publications.

*integrate it.* The right relation is defined by the FPM operator: It returns a proposition that has at least one of its arguments placed in the model.

I2    *When a new model has been derived and there is at least one unused proposition in working memory, then try to integrate that proposition.*

T1a    *When there is no model in working memory, but at least one new and one old proposition, then check whether they have the right relation to each other, and, if so, try to translate the most recent of them into a model.* The right relation is in this case defined by the FPP operator: It is a chaining pattern like *(x R y)(y Q z)*. The three rules I1a, I2, and T1a regulate the effort to draw new inferences from newly created information.

B    *When the model contradicts the given information, then back up.*

R3a    *When all premises have been used at least once and there is nothing else to do, then find one or more missing objects, locate the premises that deal with those objects and read those premises (regardless of whether they have been read before or not).*

R2a    *When a new model has just been achieved and there are still unused premises, then read those premises.*

R1    *When a new model has just been achieved, read the next premise.* The productions R3a, R2a, and R1 represent three different heuristics for how to access the external display.

S1    *Start the problem-solving process by reading the first premise.*

In summary, the subject begins by reading the premises in the order in which they are stated in the problem text. When a chaining pattern appears, she starts building a mental model. Having begun building a mental model, she scans the problem text for unused information. Whenever extending the mental model, she tries to integrate any unused propositional information that is available in working memory. Having considered all premises without completing her model, SI6 identifies specific objects that are missing from the model, and reads any information—old or new—that is available about them. When the model is complete, she reads the question, and answers it by reading off the answer from the model.

## Evaluating the Strategy Hypothesis

The solution path in Fig. 11.5 is an hypothesis about the sequence of thoughts the subject had while solving the Block Problem. The list of production rules in Fig. 11.7 is an hypothesis about SI6's problem-solving strategy. We do not yet know whether the strategy explains the path or not. A strategy hypothesis must be evaluated by *applying* it to the relevant path. Its justification lies in its ability to generate or reproduce the solution path.

The basic method of applying a production system to a solution path is to ask for each state-operator pair along the path whether there is some production rule that has its condition satisfied in that state and has that operator as its action. If there is such a rule, that step is *covered* by the production system. If not, the system has made what is known as an *error of omission*. The method is complicated by the fact that several different rules might have their conditions satisfied in one and the same state, and by the fact that the path hypothesis is necessarily incomplete, that is, it cannot contain all the mental steps the subject actually went through. An explanatory procedure that takes these aspects into account is needed.

In the present analysis, the following procedure was used while applying the production rules in Fig. 11.7 to the solution path shown in Fig. 11.5. The reader might want to compare this procedure with the discussion in Newell and Simon (1972, pp. 197–199).

1. Suppose that the analysis has proceeded to the $n$th node in the PBG. The step to be explained next is the occurrence of the operator $Q$ leading out from that node. A list is made of all the productions that have such conditions that they could be evoked at that node. The production at the top of the list is assumed to have been evoked. Its action part is compared to the link in the PBG; if it can generate the operator $Q$, the step leading out from the $n$th node has been explained. The resulting change in the knowledge-state is computed, and the analysis proceeds from the next node.

2. If the action-part of the topmost production cannot generate the operator $Q$, the protocol is scanned for evidence that contradicts the assumption that the production was fired. If there is no such evidence, the production is assumed to have fired. A node is then interpolated between node $n$ and node $(n + 1)$.

3. The process now continues, until either of the following two events occur:

a. The production system finally generates an occurrence of the operator $Q$, without having contradicted any evidence in the protocol. If this happens, the whole sequence of production occurrences and the corresponding nodes is accepted as part of the solution path. The node that in the PBG appears as the $n$th node, is replaced by a sequence of nodes. The first node in the sequence is identical to the $n$th node, and the last link in the sequence is the occurrence of the operator $Q$. The occurrence of the operator has then been explained, the next node is computed, and the analysis proceeds from it.

b. The production system finally generates some production occurrences that cannot be reconciled with the protocol. Then the entire sequence of production occurrences interpolated after the $n$the node is discarded. The analysis is then resumed at the $n$th node. The topmost production is erased from the list of productions that could have fired at that node. The topmost among those remaining is then assumed to have fired, and the entire process is repeated.

4. If it happens that none of the productions that could have fired at the $n$th node is capable of giving rise to an explanation of the occurrence of the operator $Q$, the conclusion is that the production system cannot explain what happened at that node. A question mark is entered, the change caused by the operation $Q$ is computed, and the analysis resumes from the $(n+1)$th node.

In order to evaluate how well the production system explains the solution path, we have to consider a number of different dimensions, the most important of which are *coverage, simplicity,* and *realism.*

*Coverage.*    How many of the knowledge states in the complete solution path are covered by the production rules? There are 48 states, three of which lie outside the problem space. Of the remaining 45 nodes, 42 (93%) are covered. The corresponding figures for the Problem Behavior Graph are 37 and 31 (84%). (The figures differ because the procedure for applying the production system allows the interpolation of states between the nodes in the PBG.)

Another aspect of coverage is the number of special events in the solution path that the account explains. The production system explains the working memory failure in fragment F29-F33. It also explains the discovery of the contradiction in F42. However, the production system does not explain the rehearsal of premise 2 in F15, the re-reading of premise 2 in F25, the change in the order in which the mental model is verbalized, or the occurrence of the two consolidation backups in F28.1 and F32, nor does it explain the scope of any of the consolidation backups.

*Simplicity.*    Taken by itself, an analysis of coverage is not decisive. The problem of coverage can always be solved trivially by adding production rules until every step along the solution path is covered by some rule. In the limit, one could add a separate production rule for each step. Therefore, the drive toward completeness must be balanced by a concern for simplicity.

The number of different productions in Fig. 11.7 is 10. The average number of occurrences per production in the complete solution path is 4.8. There are three productions that are used only once: S1, A, and B. S1 and A begin and end a solution process; they fire of necessity only once each. B is the production that causes a backup upon the discovery of a contradiction; it fires only once because the subject discovered a contradiction only once. In short, each production rule adds general explanatory power to the strategy hypothesis, rather than just *ad hoc* coverage of some particular step.

***Realism.***    The production system formalism is a general format for the representation of procedures, but all production rules are not equal, psychologically speaking. In order to be psychologically plausible, rules must correspond to pieces of knowledge. The strength of a trace analysis is a function of to what extent it generates weird, complicated, or incomprehensible rules that have no other function than to reproduce the particular observed behavior, and to what extent it generates rules that correspond to useful pieces of heuristic knowledge.

The subjective way of deciding this is to inspect the production system and reflect on each rule, intuiting whether the rule makes sense and whether it is arbitrary. A more intersubjectively valid method is to translate the set of production rules into a running computer program, and then *run the program on other tasks than the one the subject solved*. If the program can solve other tasks, then the production rules are not arbitrary constructions specific to the observed path, but constitute a problem-solving strategy of some generality.

The production system in Fig. 11.7 was translated into a computer program. The language used was PSS, a production system language designed by the author (Ohlsson, 1979). It shares a family resemblence to such languages as PSG (Newell, 1973), OPS5 (Forgy, 1981), PRISM (Langley, 1983), and ACT (Anderson, 1983). The entire program is reproduced in the Appendix. The program solved the Blocks Problem correctly, generating a solution path that corresponds closely to the solution path followed by SI6, except for the lack of consolidation backups. In particular, the forgetting of the partial result *yellow blue red* is reproduced by the program, as well as the discovery of the contradiction with the given information in F42. The program was also run on fourteen other spatial arrangement problems of varying difficulty (Ohlsson, 1980a). It solved seven of them correctly. The computer runs showed that the program succeeds on some spatial arrangement problems of equal complexity to the Block Problem, but fails on others. The program also solved 5 out of 6 spatial arrangement problems of lesser complexity, but failed to solve any problems of higher complexity. The main weakness of the program is that it lacks heuristics for how to proceed when either the FPP or the FPM operator fails. This accounts for the failure on the simpler problems. For the more complex problems, the main source of failure was insufficient working memory capacity. The pattern of results is similar to what one would expect from a human subject.

In summary, the strategy hypothesis does rather well on each of the three basic evaluation dimensions. With respect to coverage, it handles almost all events in the think-aloud protocol. The events that are not explained—the rehearsal of premise 2 in F15, the re-reading of premise 2 in F25, the change in how the model is read out, the occurrence and scope of consolidation backups—are all related to working memory capacity. The first-approximation theory of working memory used in this analysis—a box with space for three chunks of information—is, not surprisingly, too coarse to capture the details of how working memory influenced the problem-solving effort. With respect to simplicity, the strategy hypothesis contains no more than ten rules, each of which covers, on the average, five nodes in the path. With respect to realism, computer implementation proved that the strategy can solve other spatial arrangement problems than the one it was designed to solve.

## A Do-It-Yourself Summary

The result of the trace analysis is a description of subject SI6 in terms of her problem space and her problem-solving strategy, and a description of her performance in terms of a solution path. The description claims that she successively integrates the propositional information given in the problem text into a mental model of the linear ordering, until the positions of all objects have been determined. The main difficulty in dealing with the task is that at each point of the process SI6 has to search the problem text for some premise that could enable her to infer the next extension of the model. While she is carrying out the search through the problem text, the mental model achieved up to that point is subject to working memory decay. The major determinant of the shape of SI6's solution effort is not her spatial knowledge, but her strategy for attention allocation.

In order to attempt this kind of cognitive diagnosis the reader should collect a think-aloud protocol from a task he or she is interested in, and then apply the following explanatory procedures:

1. Identify the subject's problem space:
   (a) Construct a representational language for the task by noticing the concepts and representation formats the subject is using in talking about the task.
   (b) Define a set of operators based on passages in the protocol that lead to new results or conclusions.
   (c) Hypothesize the goal of the subject.
   (d) Hypothesize a limit on the subject's working memory capacity.
2. Generate a solution path by mapping each fragment in the protocol onto some expression in the representational language. If the expression represents new knowledge about the task, then infer the application of an operator. The solution path is a description of the observed performance *in terms of* the problem space.
3. Invent problem-solving heuristics that capture the regularities in the solution path.
4. Evaluate the strategy hypothesis by investigating its coverage, simplicity, and realism.
5. Implement the strategy as a computer program and observe its performance on the experimental task, and on other tasks as well.

## IMPLICATIONS FOR STANDARDIZED TESTING

The process of generating an information-processing model with the help of trace analysis is a protracted process involving many decisions and much trial and error on the part of the analyst.[21] Standardized testing, on the other hand, requires that a description of cognitive functioning can be achieved with little enough effort and in short enough time to be useful in practical contexts. The purpose of this section is to discuss the nature of diagnostic tests that build on information-processing concepts, and the role of trace analysis in the construction of such tests.

The psychometric approach to standardized testing is based on the two ideas of measurement and standardization. I analyze these cornerstones of the testing movement in the first two subsections. The results of trace analysis are, I believe, incompatible with the idea of measurement, but quite compatible with the idea of standardization. I then propose a methodology for the construction of standardized tests based on information-processing concepts. This admittedly speculative proposal is called *theory referenced* test construction.

There are, of course, many different bridges to build between the psychometric and the information-processing traditions. The reader might want to compare the bridge built here with those constructed by, for example, Carroll (1976), Cooper (1982), Glaser (1986), Hunt (1986), Just and Carpenter (1985), and Snow (1980). A comparative analysis of different conceptualizations of the relation between psychometric and information-processing methods would be interesting, but falls outside the scope of the present chapter.

### Trace Analysis and Measurement

The psychometric tradition attempts to describe cognitive functioning with a measure, or, more accurately, a set of measures, defining a point in a multidimensional space (Nunnally, 1967; Sternberg, 1985). But analyses such as the one just presented here invalidate this type of description. A set of measures cannot accurately represent the nature of SI6's cognitive processes for two reasons.

First, the operation of a cognitive mechanism depends essentially on its *structure*. By *structure* I mean the breakdown of the mechanism into parts and the interactions between those parts. For instance, SI6's spatial reasoning depends critically on the interaction between her attention allocation and spatial inferences, as well as on the interaction between her problem-solving strategy and her short-term memory capacity. The abstraction involved in expressing

---

[21] The analysis presented in this chapter took approximately 6 weeks to carry out. The protocol was selected from a corpus of 50 protocols. The analysis of the entire corpus took more than 2 years.

SI6's spatial reasoning ability as a measure would inevitably hide those interactions.

Second, the operation of a cognitive mechanism depends essentially on the *content* of its knowledge. The crucial feature of a spatial reasoning is not *how many* inference rules a person knows, but exactly *which* rules he or she knows. The runs with the computer model of SI6 proved that a rule that is necessary for the solution of a one problem may or may not be necessary for the solution of some other problem at the same level of difficulty (as measured, say, by the number of inferences required to reach the solution). Measures of spatial reasoning ability inevitably abstract from the *content* of spatial knowledge.

In summary, cognitive mechanisms are not well described by measures. The major implication of information processing concepts with respect to testing is that tests should produce diagnostic descriptions that capture the structure and content of cognitive mechanisms. The complexity of the analysis of subject SI6 raises the question whether this implication is consistent with the notion of standardization.

## Trace Analysis and Standardization

The term *standardized* can be applied either to the behavioral record, to the output description, or to the explanatory procedures of a diagnostic method. It has a different meaning in each case.

The first meaning of standardization is that a test is a *fixed set of problems*. A test consists of problems with known properties that are used over and over again. The practitioner does not need to invent diagnostic problems, but can use existing ones. This is one way in which standardization contributes to practical usefulness. From the point of view of Enaction Theory, generating behavioral records with the help of a fixed set of problems is a great advantage, because of work of constructing a psychologically plausible problem space does not have to be done all over again for each new diagnosis.

The second meaning of standardization is that the purpose of diagnostic inquiry is *to select among predefined explanatory accounts*. More accurately, particular diagnoses are instances of well-known explanation patterns. For instance, the names of diseases refer to previously specified physiological states. A doctor who decides that a patient has, say, pneumonia is not discovering a new disease, or inventing a new theory of human physiology, or even constructing a novel account of a patient. The doctor is deciding that his or her patient is an instance of a known explanation schema. Similarly, a car mechanic who concludes that a car fails to start because of a broken wire is not constructing a theory, but applying a standard explanation type.[22]

---

[22] Clancey (1985) has developed the difference between *solution construction* and *solution selection* in an Artificial Intelligence context.

Research is our response to a phenomenon that we do not understand. It involves an element of discovery and creative thought precisely because the type of explanation that can account for the phenomenon is not known beforehand, but has to be invented as the explanatory effort proceeds. In a well-understood field of inquiry, on the other hand, we already know which types of explanation suffice to account for particular types of phenomena. Faced with an instance of a well-understood phenomenon, the task of the practitioner is to select which variant of the relevant explanation type to apply. This is, of course, a much simpler problem than inventing a new explanation type. For example, a medical doctor can diagnose many an infectious disease in a matter of minutes or at most hours, although the research that revealed the physiological mechanism of the disease might have taken many years. In short, the second meaning of *standardized* is that diagnosis does not aim to invent a new explanation, but to select among already known explanations. Diagnostic methods are, by definition, closed methods.

The implication of the above argument is that *standardized testing is only possible in a well-understood domain*. We cannot construct a standardized test for a psychological domain unless we have a theory for human performance in that domain, because the task of a diagnostic procedure is to select among the explanations provided by such a theory. Theory construction must precede test construction, a conclusion already reached by Frederiksen (1986) on the basis of other considerations.[23] This conclusion specifies the role of open methods like trace analysis in test construction: Open methods are needed for the construction of the relevant theory.

The third meaning of *standardization* is that there exists a *well-specified procedure* for mapping the set of test responses onto a diagnostic description. One of the great strengths of the psychometric approach is its repertory of well-specified procedures. Statistical theory provides the psychometrician with well-motivated, intersubjectively valid algorithms. But the explanatory procedures used in the psychometric approach are based on the idea of measurement, and so cannot be carried over into nonquantitative testing.

In the nonquantitative case diagnosis is a kind of classification (Clancey, 1985). The explanatory procedure classifies the pattern of observed responses as belonging to a particular explanation, or, equivalently, it discriminates between alternative explanations on the basis of the pattern of responses. Recent research in expert systems has shown that complex diagnostic procedures in a variety of domains, including medicine and electronic troubleshooting, can be specified with enough precision to be implemented on a computer (Clancey, 1985; Hayes-Roth, Waterman, & Lenat, 1983). There is, then, reason to believe that proce-

---

[23] This conclusion contradicts the idea of using tests as *research instruments*, that is, as instruments for data collection (rather than for diagnosis). If a theory is a prerequisite for test construction, then the data required to build that theory must have been collected before the relevant test existed.

dures for cognitive diagnosis based on information-processing concepts can be standardized in the form of computer programs, although there exists to-date only a handful of examples (Burton, 1982; Lewis, 1986; Ohlsson & Langley, 1988; Sleeman, 1984; Waterman & Newell, 1971).

In summary, the concept of standardization implies (a) that cognitive diagnosis is based on a fixed set of problems, (b) that the purpose of cognitive diagnosis is to select an explanation from a predefined set, and (c) that the selection of the explanation is based on a well-specified algorithm. The theories and methods of information-processing psychology are quite compatible with these requirements. It should therefore be possible to design a methodology for the construction of standardized psychological tests that build on information-processing, rather than psychometric, descriptions of mental states.

## Towards Theory Referenced Test Construction

The purpose of this section is to outline an admittedly speculative proposal for a methodology that I call *theory referenced test construction*. According to this methodology, the construction of a standardized psychological test proceeds through three phases: theory construction, item production, and algorithm design. Each phase is described in turn.

*Theory construction.*    The construction of a standardized test for diagnosing, say, spatial reasoning, should begin, I propose, with a descriptive investigation of spatial reasoning, using trace analysis and other open and intensive methods that aim for singleton descriptions. The question to be answered by the investigation is "What information-processing components (representations, operators, heuristics, goals, inference rules, and so forth) have to be postulated to explain a wide variety of human behavior in the relevant task domain?" The results of the investigation are summarized in an information-processing theory of human performance in that task domain. The function of that theory is to provide explanations of particular performances. Diagnosis is the process of mapping a particular performance onto the best-fitting explanation.

We can think of a theory of human performance as a space of information-processing models. Each model is a specification of an information-processing system that can generate (not necessarily correct or efficient) behavior with respect to the relevant task. Each model, that is, each point in the space, represents a standard (type of) explanation for behavior in the relevant task domain. To explain a particular problem-solving performance is to select that model in the space that most closely simulates that performance.

A model space for spatial arrangement problems has been constructed by Ohlsson (1980b, 1982), using trace analysis. A part of this space has been encoded in a *strategy grammar*, a formal device resembling a generative grammar (Ohlsson, 1980a). The model space is defined by a list of information-processing components and the rules for how to combine them into particular models. At the most global level of analysis there are several basic *approaches* to spatial arrangement problems. The two most important approaches are the *method of series formation*, which consists in constructing a complete mental model of the linear ordering, and the *method of elimination*, which consists in eliminating all possible answers but one. At the next level of analysis each approach is implemented in several different *problem spaces*. For instance, problem spaces for the method of series formation differ with respect to whether the mental model discriminates between adjacent and nonadjacent relations or not, with respect to whether there is an operator for posing hypotheses or not, and so on. (Subject SI6 uses the series-formation method, and her problem space—defined in Fig. 11.3 and 11.4—contains a symbolic device for discriminating between adjacent and nonadjacent relations, but it does not contain an operator for posing hypotheses.) Each problem space, in turn, can be searched with the help of different *strategies*, each strategy being represented by a set of *heuristics*. For instance, a strategy may or may not include the chaining heuristic. The approaches, problem spaces, and heuristics make up a modeling kit, as it were, out of which particular information-processing models can be assembled. To assemble a particular model, one selects an approach, then a problem space that implements that approach, and then a set of heuristics for searching that space. Ohlsson (1982) showed how different subjects can be modeled by different combinations of parts from this space.

The technique of representing a space of information-processing models by a modeling kit was first used by Young (1976, 1978) in a study of length seriation in children. Young presented a kit of production rules for seriation in which individuals at different levels of development are modeled by a different selection of rules. The same format was used by Young and O'Shea (1981) to describe a model space for multicolumn subtraction. Brown and Burton (1978) used a different but related approach to defining a space of models for subtraction. They encoded their space of subtraction models in a structure called a *procedure net*, a network of procedures with calling relations between them. A number of alternative versions of the correct procedure are stored at each node in the procedure net. For instance, there might be several incorrect versions of the borrowing procedure. By making a particular selection among the versions stored at each node in the network, a particular information-processing model is assembled, representing a standard explanation for incorrect subtraction answers (a so-called bug). Sleeman (1984) has produced a procedure space for algebra, based on the notion of selecting a set of rules, possibly including some incorrect rules, from a larger set.

Although examples of procedure spaces exist in the literature, they have not yet become common. *The proposal made here is that a procedure space should become a standard way of reporting the results of descriptive studies of human performance.* In particular, I am proposing that a procedure space is the first step in constructing a standardized psychological test. The individual procedures in the space correspond to particular, predefined explanations; the task of a diagnostic procedure is to map an individual onto one of those explanations on the basis of his or her performance on the test items.

*Item production.*    Given a space of information-processing models, the next task of test construction is to produce test items, problems, that discriminate between those models in the desired way. A problem discriminates between two information-processing models, A and B, if the performances on that problem predicted by model A differs in some observable way from the performance on that problem predicted by model B. The goal of the item-production phase is to find a set of problems that discriminates between all members of some given space of models, or that divides that space into equivalence classes.

Item production can be broken down into two processes, item generation and item selection. Both of these processes can be automated. A problem generator is a computer program that can generate possible test items. The art of programming problem generators is being explored in research on intelligent tutoring systems (Sleeman & Brown, 1982; Wenger, 1987). In brief, a problem generator needs an analysis of the relevant problem type into fixed and variable parts, and a list of the possible variations. For example, problems of the form $x + y = ?$ can be generated by replacing $x$ and $y$ with two random numbers. A problem generator for spatial arrangement problems would be more complicated to program, because it would have to check that the premises it generates make sense when taken together (that is, that the problem being generated has a solution). A problem generator for, say, electronic troubleshooting would be more complicated still. But problem generators for most tasks that are of interest to test constructors can be programmed with reasonable effort.

After item generation comes item selection. The fact that information-processing models are running computer programs can be exploited in order to automate the selection process as well. By running two or more simulation models on a particular problem, one can verify in an intersubjectively valid way whether that problem discriminates between those models or not. Models that generate identical solution paths for that problem are not discriminated, but models that generate different paths are. For instance, spatial arrangement problems that can be solved by integrating the premises in the order in which they are written in the problem text do not discriminate between different strategies for attention allocation, but other problems do. In short, I am proposing that test items should be validated by relating them to the theory of human performance that constitutes the basis for the test. It is this feature of the methodology proposed here that motivates the term *theory referenced test construction.*

Item production can be fully automated by interleaving item generation and item selection. A computer system for item production would generate an item, run the relevant models on it, and decide whether to keep the item on the basis of whether it discriminates between those models. The cycle of problem generation and model running would continue until the system has found a set of items that makes the desired discriminations between all the relevant models. That set of problems is then a test for whatever aspect of human cognition is described by that space of models.

*Algorithm design.*    The relationship between a pattern of responses on a test, on the one hand, and a space of information-processing models, on the other, can be very complex. If a test is to be useful in practical contexts, it must be possible to design an algorithm that quickly selects that model that best accounts for any particular pattern of responses. In principles, a pattern classifier consists of a discrimination tree that makes successive decisions depending upon the answers to each diagnostic item. The highly successful DEBUGGY system for classification of subtraction errors (Burton, 1982), and the construction of expert systems for medical diagnosis, electronic troubleshooting, and similar domains (Clancey, 1985) show that complex pattern classification algorithms can be designed and programmed.

Admittedly, the methodology for test construction outlined here cannot compete with the psychometric approach with respect to the processing of test responses. Given the psychometric idea of describing a mental state as a point in a multidimensional space, standard statistical techniques can be used to process the data from any test, regardless of the problems in the test, regardless of what the test measures, and even regardless of changes in the underlying theory, for example, changes in the assumptions about how many distinct abilities there are. In contrast, the methodology outlined here requires that a new classification algorithm is designed for each new test.

In summary, theory referenced test construction proceeds by (a) constructing a space of information-processing models, each model describing a possible state of mind, (b) producing a test, that is, a set of items that can discriminate between those models, and (c) designing a pattern classification algorithm that selects the best-fitting model for a particular set of responses to the test items.

This proposal is admittedly speculative. But the two last phases of the proposed methodology—item production and algorithm design—rely on standard programming techniques. No conceptual advances are needed to realize those two phases of the methodology. The speculative nature of the proposal comes to the fore in the first step. It is not obvious that we know how to construct model spaces that simulate people with enough accuracy to be used as bases for test construction, but the example provided by research on subtraction skills is encouraging (Brown & Burton, 1978; Burton, 1982). Furthermore, our ability to construct such model spaces is a function of the quality of our psychological theories. Presumably, continued psychological research will lead to better and more accurate theories of human cognition, and the better our theories, the more feasible the methodology of theory-referenced test construction.

## ACKNOWLEDGMENTS

The preparation of this manuscript was supported in part by ONR contract N00014-85-K-0337 and in part by a grant from the Swedish Council for Research in the Humanities and Social Sciences. The opinions expressed do not necessarily reflect the position of the sponsoring agencies, and no endorsement should be inferred. Goran Hagert was a constant and invaluable discussion partner during the early phase of the research, and Chris Wolfe played a similar role during the final phase. I thank Susanne Lajoie for helpful comments on an earlier version of the chapter, and editor Norman Frederiksen for his great patience with my extensive reworkings of the original draft.

## APPENDIX A. SIMULATION PROGRAM FOR S16

The following is a runnable simulation model of subject S16. It consists of the production rules in FIG. 11.7, written in a computer implemented production system language called PSS (Ohlsson, 1979).

```
(PO  (ANSWER X1)  ===>  SAY(X1);
                        STOPALL)

(P1  (NEW <QSTN>)  <MODEL>  ===>  UNMK((NEW <QSTN>));
                                  GOTO(ANSW))

(P2  (NEW (FAIL GMO))  ===>  UNMK((NEW (FAIL GMO)));
                             READ(QUESTION))

(P3A  (NTC: <PROP>)  <MODEL>  ===>  GOTO (INT))

(P3B  (NEW <PROP>)  <MODEL>  ===>  GOTO(FPM))

(P4  (NEW <MODEL>)  <PROP>  ===>  UNMK((NEW <MODEL>));
                                  NARK(<PROP> ; NTC:);
                                  GOTO(INT))

(P5A  (ABS <MODEL>)  (NTC: <PROP>.1)  <PROP>.2  ===>
                                  UNMK((NTC: <PROP>.1));
                                  RHRS(<PROP>.2);
                                  RHRS(<PROP>.1);
                                  GOTO(TRNS))
```

## Appendix A. Cont'd

```
(P5B (ABS <MODEL>) (NEW <PROP>.1) <PROP>.2 ===> GOTO(FPP)

(P6 (IMP <MODEL>) ===>  BKUP())

(P7A (NEW <EXPRESSION>)(MISSING: (X1)) ===>
                            UNMK((NEW <EXPRESSION>));
                            DEL((MISSING: (X1)));
                            SCAN((X1))(=> PREMISE);
                            READ(PREMISE))

(P7B (NEW <EXPRESSION>) (MISSING: (X1 <SEQ>)) ===>
                            UNMK((NEW <EXPRESSION>));
                            REPL((MISSING: X1 <SEQ>));
                                (MISSING: (<SEQ>)));
                            SCAN((X1))(=> PREMISE);
                            READ(PREMISE))

(P7C (NEW <EXPRESSION>) (REMAINS = NONE) ===>
                            UNMK((NEW <EXPRESSION>));
                            NTC(<MODEL>);
                            GMO(<MODEL>)(=> LIST);
                            MARK(<EXPRESSION> ; NEW);
                            INS((MISSING: LIST)))

(P8A   (NEW <EXPRESSION>)(UNUSED: (X1)) ===>
                            UNMK((NEW <EXPRESSION>));
                            DEL((UNUSED: (X1)));
                            READ(X1))

(P8B (NEW <EXPRESSION>) (UNUSED: (X1 <SEQ>)) ===>
                            UNMK((NEW<EXPRESSION>));
                            REPL((UNUSED: (X1 <SEQ>))
                                (UNUSED: (<SEQ.)));
                            READ(X1))

(P8C (NEW <EXPRESSION>) <MODEL> ===>
                            SCAN(UNUSED)(=> LIST);
                            INS((UNUSED: LIST)))

(P9 (NEW <EXPRESSION>) ===> UNMK((NEW <EXPRESSION>));
                        READ(NEXTPREM))

(P10 BEGIN ===> READ(FIRSTPREM)))
```

# REFERENCES

Anderson, J. R. (1981). *Cognitive skills and their acquisition.* San Francisco, CA: Freeman.

Anderson, J. R. (1983). *The architecture of cognition.* Cambridge, MA: Harvard University Press.

Anderson, J. R., Boyle, C. F., & Reiser, B. J. (1985). Intelligent tutoring systems. *Science, 228,* 456–462.

Bolc, L. (Ed.). (1987). *Computational models of learning.* Berlin: Springer-Verlag.

Brown, J. S., & Burton, R. R. (1978). Diagnostic models for procedural bugs in basic mathematical skills. *Cognitive Science, 2,* 155–192.

Burton, R. (1982). Diagnosing bugs in a simple procedural skill. In D. Sleeman & J. S. Brown (Eds.), *Intelligent tutoring systems* (pp. 157–183). London: Academic Press.

Carroll, J. B. (1976). Psychometric tests as cognitive tasks: A new "structure of intellect." In L. B. Resnick (Ed.), *The nature of intelligence,* (pp. 27–56). Hillsdale, NJ: Lawrence Erlbaum Associates.

Clancey, W. J. (1985, June). *Heuristic classification.* (Tech. Rep. No. STAN-CS-85-1066). Stanford, CA: Stanford University, Department of Computer Science.

Cooper, L. A. (1982). Strategies for visual comparison and representation: Individual differences. In R. J. Sternberg (Ed.), *Advances in the psychology of human intelligence* (Vol. 1, pp. 77–124). Hillsdale, NJ: Lawrence Erlbaum Associates.

Davis, R., & King, J. (1976). An overview of production systems. In E. W. Elcock & D. Michie (Eds.), *Machine Intelligence* (Vol. 1, pp. ). New York: Wiley.

Dukes, N. F. (1968). N = 1. *Psychological Bulletin, 64,* 74–79.

Ericsson, K. A., & Simon, H. A. (1984). *Protocol analysis. Verbal reports as data.* Cambridge, MA: The MIT Press.

Forgy, C. L. (1981). *OPS5 User's Manual.* (Tech. Rep. No. CMU-CS-81-135). Pittsburgh, PA: Carnegie-Mellon University, Department of Computer Science.

Frederiksen, N. (1984). Implications of cognitive theory for instruction in problem solving. *Review of Educational Research, 54*(3), 363–407.

Gardner, H. (1985). *The mind's new science. A history of the cognitive revolution.* New York: Basic Books.

Gentner, D., & Stevens, A. L. (Eds.). (1983). *Mental models.* Hillsdale, NJ: Lawrence Erlbaum Associates.

Glaser, R. (1986). The integration of instruction and testing. *Redesign of testing for the 21st century. Proceedings from the ETS Invitational Conference,* October 1985. Princeton, NJ: ETS.

Hagert, G. (1980a). *Cognitive processing in a spatial series task: A cognitive simulation study.* Working paper from the Cognitive Seminar (ISSN 0349–5124), University of Stockholm, No. 7.

Hagert, G. (1980b). Stability and change in strategies: Three simulations of one subject with one-year intervals. *Proceedings of the Fourth Conference on Artificial Intelligence and Simulation of Behavior,* Amsterdam.

Hagert, G., & Rollenhagen, C. (1981). *Learning in a spatial series task: A production system analysis.* Working paper from the Cognitive Seminar (ISSN 0349–5124), University of Stockholm, No. 14.

Hayes-Roth, F., Waterman, D. A., & Lenat, D. B. (1983). *Building expert systems.* Reading, MA: Addison-Wesley.

Holsti, O. R. (1968). Content analysis. In G. Lindzey, & E. Aronson (Eds.), *The handbook of social psychology: Vol. 2. Research methods* (2 ed.), (pp. 596–692). Reading, MA: Addison-Wesley.

Hunt, E. B. (1986). Cognitive research and future test design. *Redesign of testing for the 21st century. Proceedings of the ETS Invitational Conference,* (pp. 9–23), October 1985. Princeton, NJ: ETS.

Hunt, E. B., & Poltrock, S. E. (1974). The mechanics of thought. In B. H. Kantowitz (Ed.), *Human information processing: Tutorials in performance and cognition* (pp. ). New York: Wiley.

Johnson-Laird, P. N. (1983). *Mental models.* Cambridge, MA: Harvard University Press.

Just, M. A., & Carpenter, P. A. (1985). Cognitive coordinate systems: Accounts of mental rotation and individual differences in spatial ability. *Psychological Review, 92*(2), 37–171.

Klahr, D., Langley, P., & Neches, R. (Eds.). (1987a). *Production system models of learning and development.* Cambridge, MA: MIT Press.

Klahr, D., Langley, P., & Neches, R. (1987b). Learning, development, and production systems. In D. Klahr, P. Langley, & R. Neches (Eds.), *Production system models of learning and development* (pp. 1–53). Cambridge, MA: MIT Press.

Kotovsky, K., Hayes, J. R., & Simon, H. A. (1985). Why are some problems hard? Evidence from Tower of Hanoi. *Cognitive Psychology, 17,* 248–294.

Langley, P. (1983). Exploring the space of cognitive architectures. *Behavior Research Methods and Instrumentation, 15,* 289–299.

Langley, P., Ohlsson, S., & Sage, S. (1984). *A machine learning approach to student modeling.* (Tech. Rep. No. CMU-RI-TR-84-7). Pittsburgh, PA: Carnegie-Mellon University.

Lewis, C. M. (1986). *Intention-based diagnosis of novice programming errors.* Los Altos, CA: Kaufmann.

Maier, N. R. F. (1970). *Problem solving and creativity in individuals and groups.* Belmont, CA: Brooks/Cole.

Newell, A. (1966, June). *On the analysis of human problem solving protocols.* (Tech. Rep.). Pittsburgh, PA: Carnegie Institute of Technology.

Newell, A. (1973). Production systems: Models of central structures. In W. G. Chase (Ed.), *Visual information processing* (pp. 463–526). New York: Academic Press.

Newell, A. (1980). Reasoning, problem solving and decision processes: The problem space as a fundamental category. In R. Nickerson (Ed.), *Attention and performance.* (Vol. VIII, pp. 693–718). Hillsdale, NJ: Lawrence Erlbaum Associates.

Newell, A. (1987). Unitied theories of cognition. *The William James Lecture Series,* Harvard University.

Newell, A., Shaw, J. C., & Simon, H. A. (1958). Elements of a theory of human problem solving. *Psychological Review, 65*(3), 151–166.

Newell, A., & Simon, H. A. (1972). *Human problem solving.* Englewood Cliffs, NJ: Prentice-Hall.

Nunnally, J. (1967). *Psychometric theory.* New York: McGraw-Hill.

Ohlsson, S. (1979, September). *PSS3 reference manual.* (Working Papers from the Cognitive Seminar No. 4). Stockholm, Sweden: University of Stockholm, Department of Psychology.

Ohlsson, S. (1980a, January). *Competence and reasoning with common spatial concepts.* (Working Papers from the Cognitive Seminar No. 6). Stockholm, Sweden: University of Stockholm, Department of Psychology.

Ohlsson, S. (1980b, July). Strategy grammars. An approach to generality in computer simulation of human reasoning. *Proceedings of the AISB-80 Conference on Artificial Intelligence,* Amsterdam.

Ohlsson, S. (1982). *Problem-solving strategies in a reasoning task.* (Tech. Rep. No. 340). Uppsala, Sweden: University of Uppsala, Department of Psychology.

Ohlsson, S. (1983). The enaction theory of thinking and its educational implications. *Scandinavian Journal of Educational Research, 27,* 73–88.

Ohlsson, S. (1984a, June). Attentional heuristics in human thinking. *Proceedings of the Sixth Conference of the Cognitive Science Society.* Boulder, CO.

Ohlsson, S. (1984b). Induced strategy shifts in spatial reasoning. *Acta Psychologica, 57,* 47–67.

Ohlsson, S. (1984c). Restructuring revisited II. An information processing theory of restructuring and insight. *Scandinavian Journal of Psychology, 25,* 117–129.

Ohlsson, S. (1988). Computer simulation and its impact on educational research and practice. *International Journal of Educational Research, 12,* 5–34.

Ohlsson, S., & Langley, P. (1984). Towards automatic discovery of simulation models. *Proceedings from the Sixth European Conference of Artificial Intelligence,* Pisa, Italy.

Ohlsson, S., & Langley, P. (1988). Psychological evaluation of path hypotheses in cognitive diagnosis. In H. Mandl & A. Lesgold (Eds.), *Learning issues for intelligent tutoring systems.* New York: Springer-Verlag.

Rosenbloom, P. S., Laird, J. E., McDermott, J., Newell, A., & Orciuch, E. (1985). *R1 soar: An experiment in knowledge-intensive programming in a problem-solving architecture* (Tech. Rep. No. CMU-CS-85-110). Pittsburgh, PA: Carnegie-Mellon University, Department of Computer Science.

Simon, H. A. (1975). The functional equivalence of problem solving skills. *Cognitive Psychology, 7,* 268–288.

Sleeman, D. (1984). An attempt to understand students' understanding of basic algebra. *Cognitive Science, 8*(4), 387–412.

Sleeman, D., & Brown, J. S. (Eds.). (1982) *Intelligence tutoring systems.* London: Academic Press.

Snow, R. E. (1980). Aptitude processes. In R. E. Snow, P. A. Frederico, & W. E. Montague (Eds.), *Aptitude, learning and instruction: Vol. 1. Cognitive process analyses of aptitude* (pp. 27–63). Hillsdale, NJ: Lawrence Erlbaum Associates.

Sternburg, R. J. (1985). General intellectual ability. In R. J. Sternberg (Ed.), *Human abilities. An information processing approach* (pp. 5–30). New York: Freeman.

Toulmin, S. (1972). *Human understanding: Vol. 1. General introduction and Part 1. Oxford, U. K.:* Oxford University Press.

Waterman, D. A., & Hayes-Roth, F. (1978). An overview of pattern-directed inference systems. In D. A. Waterman & F. Hayes-Roth (Eds.), *Pattern-directed inference systems* (pp. 3–22). New York: Academic Press.

Waterman, D. A., & Newell, A. (1971). Protocol analysis as a task for artificial intelligence. *Artificial Intelligence, 2,* 285–318.

Wenger, E. (1987). *Artificial intelligence and tutoring systems.* Los Altos, CA: Kaufmann.

Williams, M. D., & Santos-Williams, S. (1980). Method for exploring retrieval processes using verbal protocols. In R. S. Nickerson (Ed.), *Attention and performance.* (Vol. VIII, pp. 671–689). Hillsdale, NJ: Lawrence Erlbaum Associates.

Williams, M. D., & Hollan, J. D. (1981). The process of retrieval from very long term memory. *Cognitive Science, 5,* 87–119.

Young, R. M. (1976). *Seriation in children. An artificial intelligence analysis.* Basel, Federal Republic of Germany: Birkhauser Verlag.

Young, R. M. (1978). Strategies and the structure of a cognitive skill. In G. Underwood (Ed.), *Strategies of information processing.* London: Academic Press.

Young, R. M., & O'Shea, T. (1981). Errors in children's subtraction. *Cognitive Science, 15,* 153–177.

---

## EDITOR'S NOTE

The editors regret that there is no commentary on the three preceding chapters. Delays in writing and editing one of the chapters delayed our sending it to the commentator, and subsequent illness and necessary travel made it impossible to meet the production schedule.

# 12

# Assessment Procedures for Predicting and Optimizing Skill Acquisition After Extensive Practice

J. Wesley Regian
Walter Schneider
*Learning Research and Development Center*
*University of Pittsburgh*

## INTRODUCTION

### Problem Statement

The problem considered in this paper is the design of selective and diagnostic testing procedures to optimize final performance in complex, procedural tasks. We are specifically concerned with high-performance tasks that require extended training to develop proficiency. Examples of applicable task domains are air traffic control, electronic troubleshooting, typing, and piloting; inapplicable task domains are practicing law, writing technical materials, and teaching history. For applicable task domains, we argue for a closer relationship between training, prediction, and diagnostic assessment. The principles discussed have limited utility for tasks that rely primarily on a declarative-knowledge base rather than performance components, and have greater utility in training environments where there is a strong investment in developing procedure-based skill.

Consider first the problem of predicting performance on a complex skill after a long training period. In many cases the level of prediction offered by assessment procedures is very modest. Prediction of performance after extended training is the goal of most college placement (4 years of training), military (1 to 4 years of training), and many corporate training programs. We briefly discuss one example of a failed assessment procedure.

### The Reagan Air Traffic Control Experiment

Early in his first term, President Reagan was confronted with a national strike of air traffic controllers. The president's decision to replace the striking ATC's resulted in an illustration of the limits on predicting performance after extended training. In order to identify a large pool of promising trainees, a group of 70,000 applicants was tested on an assessment battery. From this group of testees, the top 2% were selected for training. Such a stringent criterion was well warranted because the cost of ATC training was over $100,000 per person. In addition to their high standing on the assessment battery, these trainees were highly motivated to succeed. Success would mean a steady $35,000 per year job, and failure might mean unemployment. Nevertheless, about half failed and were dropped from the program during training. Why was the predictive utility of the assessment procedure so dismal?

## Two Pitfalls

We describe two pitfalls for the design of assessment procedures that seek to predict performance after practice. The first pitfall is a poor mapping between predictor measures and prediction criteria. In some cases, predictor measures are utilized that represent trivial components of the final task. In other cases, predictor measures are confounded in the sense that they themselves can be decomposed into more primitive components, only some of which are actually predictive of performance on the final task. In the Reagan experiment, in addition to verbal IQ tests, spatial tests were included because it was assumed that spatial skills were important for Air Traffic Controllers. Recent research has shown that spatial abilities can be decomposed into more primitive cognitive processes (Pellegrino, Alderton, & Regian, 1985). The psychometric literature on spatial ability has identified a diverse set of spatial 'abilities' or factors that vary independently across subjects (Lohman, 1979). More recently, individual differences on these spatial factors have been shown to be a function of individual differences in speed and accuracy of executing certain cognitive processes (Regian, Shute, & Pellegrino, 1985). Correlations among spatial tasks have been shown to depend on the degree of process overlap between tasks (Kosslyn, Brun, Cave, & Wallach, 1983). When seeking to predict performance on specific procedural tasks, it is critical to identify the trainees' potential ability to execute the cognitive processes invested in task solution in addition to identifying general ability factors related to task solution (e.g., verbal IQ).

The second pitfall is the variable plasticity of skills. Performance on many tasks changes drastically with practice, whereas other tasks show no appreciable practice effects at all. Moreover, for those tasks that do show practice effects, there is a great deal of variability across subjects as to the degree of the practice effects, and there is the possibility that subjects differ widely on the amount of prior exposure to the task. Most assessment procedures make the assumption that a stable ability is being measured, and so do not provide enough trials to observe performance changes. Ability measures before practice are often not well correlated with performance after practice (Ackerman, 1985). The problem of variable skill plasticity cannot be dealt with solely by developing better static ability measures, because task performance before practice is not even well correlated with performance on the identical task after practice (Kennedy, Jones, & Harbeson, 1958; Adams, 1953; Fleishman & Hempel, 1955). It is important to identify task components that are susceptible to practice effects, and to assess the trainees' ability to adapt to task demands.

The issues of selecting predictor measures and understanding practice effects have implications for both predicting and training performance. We discuss the implications of these pitfalls for assessment and training procedures, especially the utility of assessment procedures as diagnostic tools for training programs.

## FIRST PITFALL

### Selecting Predictor Measures

The first pitfall is due to the relationship between predictor measures and prediction criteria. Most assessment procedures use psychometric test scores, or factor scores based on psychometric tests, as predictor measures. This approach derives from factor-based theories of ability that assume that intellectual performance is appropriately characterized by describing ability factors. In this framework, predicting performance on a task reduces to a problem of identifying the intellectual factors required for task performance, and then assessing ability on those factors. However, as described above, the factors themselves can be further reduced to a description of the cognitive processes invested in task solution. We argue that both assessment and training of complex skills are facilitated by identifying important task components in addition to ability factors that are theoretically related to the skill.

### Psychometric Prediction

*Validity Studies.* A common use of psychometric assessment procedures is to select promising applicants to undergo long training programs. Examples are college entrance exams that seek to predict college success, military assessment procedures for predicting pilot success, law- and medical-school admission tests. In many cases, test-based selection procedures account for very modest proportions of variance in final task performance. For example, Humphreys (1968) reported a correlation of .21 between composite college entrance exams and final semester college grades. In this case, the predictors accounted for about 4% of the variance in final task success.

*Limits on Factor-Based Prediction.* In general, there have been only minor improvements in psychometric prediction during the last two decades. Moreover, recent advances in cognitive theory suggest methods of achieving enhanced predictive power in specific task domains. We are not arguing that factor-based prediction has no place in modern psychometrics. These methods are predictive when properly applied, and have the advantage of being economical. When the goal is to economically predict performance in a very general domain, such as performance in college, or to identify general aptitude strengths and weaknesses, then a factor-based aptitude battery is quite useful. When the goal is to predict performance in a specific training-intensive procedural task, then it may be cost-effective to develop very specific assessment procedures which look at task-specific cognitive processes. Psychometric ability factors say very little about the cognitive processes invested in task solution. The existence of a given factor is only a beginning toward understanding what processes are responsible for producing the factor. Vernon (1951) commented that "factors are indeed a kind of blurred average, for they derive from the common features displayed by a large group of people, they may stem from very diverse mental and physical processes in different people" (p. 9). The same point had already been made by Thurstone (1947): "The factorial methods were developed for the study of individual differences among people but these individual differences may be regarded as an avenue to the study of the processes which underlie these differences" (p. 55).

Relatively recently, a great deal of research has been done that sheds light on the processes that underlie factorially identified individual differences. We discuss the cognitive-components approach in order to illustrate: (a) the feasibility of modeling complex cognitive tasks; (b) the complex nature of ability factors; and (c) the utility of closely tying predictor measures to prediction criteria.

## An Information-Processing Approach

The hierarchical organization of intelligence theories is a function of the generality or specificity of the abilities at each order of nodes. If we conceive of $g$, or general ability, at the highest order, then less general ability factors break out at lower nodes. One can conceivably move far enough down such a hierarchy to discover the component processes involved in a specific task. Componential approaches to intellectual ability are an attempt to discover these processes.

Three points are of interest in considering componential approaches to intellectual ability. First, it is possible to generate valid process models of relatively complex tasks that result in substantial predictive ($r > .8$) and explanatory utility. Second, psychometric ability factors are a function of underlying cognitive processes. Third, the best predictor of ability on a specific task is some variant of the task itself, rather than a dissimilar task that is thought to overlap in the cognitive processes required.

*Cognitive Components.* The cognitive-components approach has been undertaken by Sternberg (1977, 1979, 1984), Pellegrino and Glaser (1980), Whitely (1980), and Snow (1980). This approach uses laboratory-adapted versions of marker tests from the psychometric tradition to identify cognitive processes invested in task solution. In one such study, Mumaw and Pellegrino (1984) developed a laboratory version of the Minnesota Paper Form Board (MPFB; Likert & Quasha, 1970) that systematically varied sources of item difficulty and allowed the experimenters to monitor solution latency for each item. The MPFB is a spatial ability test that assesses spatial visualization ability, a commonly identified spatial factor (Lohman, 1979). The authors identified four sources of item difficulty and postulated a cognitive-process model of task solution that proved to have extremely high internal validity ($R^2$ in the .90s). More importantly, processing parameters (latency and accuracy) from the task were significant predictors of the MPFB, accounting for 63% of test-score variance. Thus, by identifying specific cognitive processes invested in a spatial-visualization task, the authors were able to account for a good deal of the variance in the task.

## Summary—Specificity of Predictor Measures

In the cognitive-components approach to ability assessment, tests are chosen for performance modeling because they are consistently associated with a construct of interest (such as visualization ability in the case of the MPFB). The cognitive-components approach can also be applied directly to complex, real-world tasks. Such modeling is desirable because it allows for direct assessment and/or training of component processes. This requires a much greater investment in specific task analysis and task modeling than has been traditional in psychometric testing.

## SECOND PITFALL

### Plasticity of Skills

The second pitfall in assessment procedures is a result of the plasticity of skills. Performance on many skills is not stable over practice. The law of practice is ubiquitous in cognitive performance domains (Newell & Rosenbloom, 1981). For example, spatial abilities that were once thought to manifest stable performance characteristics have been shown to be highly susceptible to practice effects (Pellegrino, 1983).

*Unstable Skills.*    Human performance in almost any cognitive or motor skill shows profound changes with practice. Consider the changes that occur while learning to fly an aircraft, type, play a musical instrument, read, or play tennis. At first, effort and attention must be devoted to every movement or minor decision. At this stage, performance is slow and error prone. Eventually long series of movements or cognitive acts can be carried out with little attention, and performance is quite rapid and accurate. For example, in aircraft control, the novice may have difficulty just keeping the aircraft on the proper heading. However, the expert can fly complex aircraft formation maneuvers while performing a simultaneous digit-cancelling task (Colle & Demaio, 1978). It was once a commonly held belief that digit span was stable at around nine digits (Hunt, Frost, & Lunneborg, 1973). Chase and Ericsson (1981) demonstrated that with a year of training time this could be increased dramatically, in some cases up to 80 digits. An assessment of initial digit span would probably have been a poor predictor of digit span after 250 hours of training.

The fact that performance on many tasks is not stable has important implications for assessment procedures. For example, Spearman (1904) used tests employing pictorial stimuli to assess intelligence in a manner unconfounded by culture and education (see also U.S. Army Beta, 1917). To use spatial tests in this manner requires the implicit assumption that a stable ability is being measured. In the case of spatial ability, that assumption remained unchallenged for 70 years and has now been shown to be erroneous (Pellegrino, 1983; Pellegrino & Mumaw, 1980). Spatial abilities can be greatly enhanced by relevant experience. Pellegrino (1983) showed that test scores on a spatial relations test (Primary Mental Abilities—Spatial Relations) can be increased by 1.75 standard deviations with only 8 hours of training on mental rotation. This shift took subjects from below the 39th percentile on the test to above the 91st percentile, and the performance improvement was stable when subjects were retested 15 weeks after training. Other studies have shown that there are physiological determinants of spatial ability (McGee, 1979; Shute, 1984). Therefore, any spatial-ability assessment procedure that is of short duration must inevitably be confounding the interacting effects of ability and experience.

*Stable Skills.*    There are other examples of skills for which performance does not increase with practice. For example, measures of short-term memory capacity, such as memory-scanning rate for comparing random symbols (Kristofferson, 1972; Schneider & Shiffrin, 1977) or working-memory capacity (Chase & Ericsson, 1981), are insensitive to practice.

Diagnostic assessment can be viewed as having two aspects. First, one should assess those component skills that are stable and necessary for final performance. Second, one should try to assess the learning potential for components that change with practice in an attempt to predict practiced performance on these component skills. The differential effects of practice must be accounted for in any assessment or training procedure. The automatic/controlled processing framework provides a tool for distinguishing between trainable and untrainable skills.

## Automatic and Controlled Processing

The automatic/controlled processing framework provides an interpretation for practice effects and the differential trainability of skills. The framework posits two qualitatively different forms of processing that underly human performance

(Schneider, 1985; Schneider, Dumais, & Shiffrin, 1984; Schneider & Fisk, 1984; Shiffrin & Schneider, 1977). Automatic processing is fast, parallel, fairly effortless, not limited by STM capacity, not under direct subject control, and is used in performing well-developed skilled behaviors. This mode of processing develops when subjects deal with the experimental stimulus in a consistent manner over many trials. Controlled processing is slow, effortful, capacity limited, subject controlled, and is used to deal with novel, inconsistent, or poorly learned information. This mode of processing is expected at the beginning of practice on any novel task, and throughout practice when a subject's response to a stimulus varies from trial to trial. In this framework, trainable skills are trainable because they involve components that can be automatized.

Automatic and controlled processing serve different information-processing roles. Controlled processing is assumed to be instrumental in the development of new automatic processes. It is used to deal with novel tasks and tasks that cannot be carried out by automatic processing, to maintain the activity of nodes in memory, to activate nodes that enable automatic processes, and to block or modify automatic processes. Automatic processing is assumed to perform consistent component processing, to interrupt ongoing controlled processing in order to reallocate attention, and to bias and prime memory. Automatic processing develops over practice with a consistent task or task component. The two types of processes generally share the same memory structure and continuously interact.

In designing assessment or training procedures, two important findings from the automatic/controlled framework should be considered. The first centers on the distinction between consistent practice and varied (or inconsistent) practice. Consistent practice produces substantial improvements in performance as automatic processing develops (for example, 98% reduction in visual-search comparison rates, Fisk & Schneider, 1983). Varied practice utilizes only controlled processing and produces little improvement in performance (for instance, no change in letter-search performance over 4 months of training, Shiffrin & Schneider, 1977). The second finding centers on the amount of effort required to perform automatic-processing tasks. Consistent practice greatly reduces the amount of effort required to perform a task, allowing controlled processing to be allocated to another task. When subjects have already developed automatic processes to perform one task, they can learn to time-share another task with little or no deficit. After 20 hours of consistent practice in two search tasks, subjects were able to perform both tasks simultaneously nearly as well as they could perform each separately (Fisk & Schneider, 1983; Schneider & Fisk, 1982a, 1982b, 1984).

The acquisition of skill with practice is assumed to result from the development of automatic processes that are used to perform consistent task components. Any applied skill of reasonable complexity is likely to involve both consistent and inconsistent components. An empirically verified componential breakdown of a complex skill is useful for both assessment and training. Performance on consistent components is likely to change significantly over extensive practice, whereas performance on inconsistent components is likely to reach asymptote relatively quickly. Automatization of consistent components has the benefit of freeing up processing capacity that may then be applied to inconsistent components. Breaking the task up into its performance components allows performance on the two types of components to be independently assessed. Furthermore, automatization of consistent components may be facilitated during training by allowing trainees to attend fully to the isolated components.

An additional claim of the two-process theory is that for many tasks different processes may be involved in performance at different levels of experience. The concept of emergent abilities (Ferguson, 1956; Guilford, 1967, Horn, 1965) is especially relevant to understanding practice effects. Initial performance in a task is likely to be dependent on general abilities such as those involved in understanding instructions, selecting strategies, reasoning skills, and STM limitations. After task practice, these general abilities may give way to more specific determinants such as perceptual/motor coordination or speed and accuracy of executing specific cognitive processes (Fleishman & Hempel, 1955).

## Ability and Skill Acquisition

Improving the predictive capability of assessment procedures that are applied in training environments requires an understanding of the relationship between intellectual ability and skill acquisition. Cattell (1971) suggested a formal distinction between ability and experience. Cattell argued for two associated aspects of intelligence that he referred to as fluid intelligence ($Gf$) and crystallized intelligence ($Gc$). This distinction is very important for the specific assessment procedures we are currently concerned with. Process-oriented approaches to assessment are ideally suited to refining the distinction in task-specific contexts.

*Cognitive Components.*   If it is possible to train component processes that are invested in solution of test items, a prediction would be that scores on that test should reflect the training. Pellegrino has demonstrated this effect in several types of tasks. In one such experiment, briefly mentioned above, Pellegrino (1983) pretested subjects on psychometric tests of spatial ability, then trained subjects in mental rotation, and finally readministered the spatial battery. Many subjects who had tested in the 39th percentile on spatial relations before training moved to the 91st percentile after training. Further, the performance improvement was stable in that it remained in a subsequent posttest administered 15 weeks after training.

Static ability measures fail to discriminate adequately between ability on a task and performance differences due to differential experience on the task. Many of the subjects in Pellegrino's studies moved from low-ability groups before training to high ability after training. However, some subjects showed negligible effects of training. These results indicate that subjects may differ in the relevant experience they bring to a task as well as in their ability to acquire expertise in the task. Individual differences in learning ability have also been shown in studies of the development of automatic processing.

*Automatic and Controlled Processing.*   We have found that performance improvements for consistent tasks are variable across subjects, suggesting that skill-acquisition ability can and should be assessed. Individual differences in automatic/controlled processing appear in the rate of controlled processing, how quickly subjects develop automatic processing, and the range of tasks in which subjects develop automatic processing. In a consistent-search task, some subjects developed an automatic-search set in an hour, others showed no development after 6 hours. In another experiment, subjects were required to perform a category word search and digit task either separately or as a combined dual task. Although all subjects had roughly equivalent single-task performance, some subjects could not effectively perform the dual task. These subjects had difficulty inhibiting the allocation of control-processing resources to the automatic process. In an experiment examining context effects, about half the subjects did not appear to develop context-specific automatic processes (Schneider & Fisk, 1980). These findings suggest that for consistent tasks, initial performance is qualitatively different from trained performance, and it should be expected that assessment of initial performance should not be a strong predictor of final performance. Ackerman (1986) demonstrated that for consistent tasks, the predictive power of static ability measures goes down in proportion to the amount of training on the task. The explanation for this finding is straightforward. As training time increases, individual differences in skill-acquisition ability are more apparent (and initial differences in experience are less apparent). The effect is only found for consistent tasks, however. Ackerman (1986) showed that practice-related reductions in correlations between ability and performance are a function of the consistency of the task. Appropriate ability measures are good predictors of task performance for novel tasks. With extensive practice, however, only inconsistent tasks continue to be predicted by static ability measures. Static ability measures are only predictive of tasks with inconsistent mental processing demands.

## Summary—Ability and Experience

It is important to make a distinction between physiologically based limits on task performance and individual differences in task performance that are due to task or component familiarity, transfer of training advantages, and availability of relevant LTM information. These issues are all relevant to assessment, diagnosis, and training of complex skills.

   One of the implications of skill plasticity is that relevant experience plays an important role in an individual's skill performance at any point in time. Any heterogeneity of experience across individuals means that we are assessing the combined effects of experience and ability. For skills that can be shown to be trainable, if we assess current performance levels for a group of individuals we may be falsely assuming homogeneity of relevant experience.

The assumption of population homogeneity is probably reasonably safe in some situations and fallacious in others. In many research environments, the subject population is homogeneous with regard to many sorts of experience. Most research in cognitive psychology uses college students for subjects, and the majority of studies come from highly selective universities. By comparison, many training environments (e.g., military training environments) start with very heterogeneous groups. Avoiding this pitfall involves first making a distinction between trainable skills and stable skills. For trainable skills in heterogeneous groups it is critical to unconfound the effects of experience and ability.

An additional implication of dual-task studies is that speed and accuracy of performance may be insufficient measures. The automatic/controlled processing framework suggests that processing effort is a critical resource. Although the data are limited in this area, it cannot be assumed that all subjects are equally able to automatize performance. Consider the problem of trying to do calculus without first automatizing basic math and algebra skills. If the algebraic skills are not automatic, they would be unreliable when performed concurrently while allocating controlled processing to performance of the calculus task. The student would be more likely to be error prone, slow, and unable to perform complex problems. For many tasks it is important to automatize key components of the task. In assessment procedures, it may be relevant to assess speed, accuracy, and the ability to automatize performance. In designing training procedures, it may be important to empirically determine how much component training is required to automatize performance.


## ASSESSMENT FOR CANDIDATE TRAINEES

### Orientation

*Assumptions.*   We assume, according to the above discussion: a) that determinants of performance change drastically with practice; and b) that assessment procedures should assess both cognitive processes that determine task performance and abilities that are correlated with task performance.

*Assessment Categories.*   For purposes of selective assessment, there is a need to assess: a) stable component skills; b) the ability to automate performance on consistent components; c) motivation/perseverance to do the necessary practice to build automatic components; d) ability to perform important metacomponents of planning, monitoring, and decision making.

*Task Analysis.*   A detailed task analysis is required to identify: a) component skills that are stable; b) components skills that can be automatized, and the learning rate for those skills; and c) metacomponents. Our approach to this task analysis is to be guided initially by instructor recommendations on the appropriate task breakdown, along with our bias of seeking to reduce the task to consistent components where possible.

*Cost-Effectiveness.*   A cost-effectiveness balance must be achieved between assessment time and training time. For expensive, long-term training environments it may be cost-effective to train the subjects sufficiently to develop a reliable predictor of final task performance. One of the utilities of an assessment procedure is to save the time and cost of training individuals who would eventually wash out. Therefore, it is important to identify the break-even point by comparing the reduction in washout rate to the price (in time and money) of assessment.

## Hierarchical (Hurdle) Testing

*Limitations to Short-Term Assessment.*   There are serious limitations to short-term assessment due to instability of measures over experience, heterogeneous prior exposure, and insensitivity to motivation effects. The predictive limitations on short-term assessment procedures are greatest for the complex, procedural, training intensive skills that are the object of our approach. In many cases, hurdle testing may be useful for minimizing costs while maximizing prediction. We define hurdle testing as a series of increasingly discriminative assessment procedures with the goal of successively eliminating candidates at each assessment level. For example, the procedure should first assess any known minimal levels of acceptable knowledge or stable performance. These minimal levels should be assessed early in the procedure in order to wash out doomed applicants quickly. This first step would involve standard paper-and-pencil psychometric tests, and could therefore be completed at low cost. For the next hurdle, it might be appropriate to evaluate more fully the range of prerequisite declarative knowledge and performance on inconsistent (stable) components (e.g., working-memory capacity), selecting applicants who fall in the high range. The remaining group could then be evaluated on the learning of consistent (unstable) components. This final step would be relatively expensive, involving large numbers of trials on computer-controlled testing procedures. Our definition of hurdle testing is analogous to medical testing where short, general-purpose tests precede long-duration specialized diagnostic tests.

*Motivation.*   The issue of motivation consists of two related aspects. These are: a) motivational characteristics of the assessment procedure; and b) motivational characteristics of the testee. An argument can be made that it is important to design assessment procedures that are inherently motivating. The argument would claim that performance on the assessment procedure only reflects the ability of the testee to the degree that the testee is motivated to perform at full potential. This ignores the question of whether the testee/trainee is sufficiently motivated to complete a long and rigorous training procedure. Motivational characteristics of the testee are difficult to assess. Some possibilities are to use longer testing procedures, hurdle testing, include nearly impossible tasks, or (contrary to the above argument) to make the assessment procedure inherently unmotivating. It may also prove useful to look at the testees' life history and previous training performance to assess the motivation to practice. The military extensively tests the motivation of its officers in selecting people for promotion. For example, Ranger training in the U.S. Army is a 6-week, survival-oriented course. Trainees experience continuous tests of physical exertion and deprivation. The average weight loss during training is 25 pounds, and participants get only 4 hours of sleep per day while performing combat duties in mountains, deserts, and swamps. The trainee who survives this test is unlikely to fail further programs due to a lack of motivation. We consider motivation to be an important and currently underrepresented aspect of assessment.

*Time Compression.*    One of the benefits that falls out of a componential approach to assessment is the capability of providing a large number of trials for any given component in a relatively short period of time. For example, in the Air Traffic Control (ATC) training regime for radar operators it is important to be able to visually estimate the angular heading of a radar blip within 5 degrees accuracy. This level of accuracy takes an average of 2,000 training trials to achieve. Under normal training conditions, this number of trials would require about 5.5 weeks of training time. In a time-compressed, angle-judgment module, students perform a video-flash-card version of the task. In this form, students experience 2,000 trials of the critical task in 3 hours. The capability of observing performance on time-compressed training components makes it much more feasible to assess skill acquisition.

## DIAGNOSTIC ASSESSMENT DURING TRAINING

### Orientation

*Component Training.*    Many procedural training programs informally break down the training into parts that are trained individually and then in aggregate. For example, flight instructors often teach students a procedure to scan instruments during flight. This instrument drill is practiced in isolation until the student is comfortable with the procedure. Practice is provided on flight simulators, and students are sometimes encouraged to practice on aircraft in the hangar. By the time the student is actually flying an airplane, the instrument drill is supposed to be second nature. Under our perspective, the instrument drill is a task component that should be trained to automaticity so that control processing is freed up during flight for aircraft control. We believe it is desirable to formalize component training to enable instructors to objectively determine the student's level of component expertise, and when to add new components.

***How Much Component Training?***    How can we use diagnostic assessment to determine when to move on from component training to higher level skills? There is an optimal level of component training. Too little component practice can lead to overload when moving on to higher level components and to inefficient learning. In this case, the component skill may be poorly learned, resulting in unreliable component performance under the additional resource load of added task components, and learning of the added task components is impeded by the fact that control processing is still required for subcomponent performance. The other situation to avoid is too much component practice, which can lead to low marginal utility of practice and a waste of training resources. Once a component skill has been developed optimally,[1] training resources should be devoted to embedding the component in the higher level task components. We believe that the question of whether part-task training is better than whole-task training is a poorly phrased question. It is more useful to ask: what is the optimal task breakdown for training purposes and how much training is appropriate at each component level?

## Practice, Performance, and Promotion Guidelines

***Performance Measures.***    The problem of determining when a student has reached a desired performance level for a given component implies a set of performance measures that can be compared to empirically verified criteria. We believe that in addition to the commonly used measures of speed and accuracy, it is also important to measure the resource load of components during training. One of the observations that has been made by ATC instructors is that even among students who are very fast and accurate at performing simple intercept operations, excellent controllers are characterized especially as having the ability to do several things at once. The instructors are describing informally what we refer to as the problem of workload, or resource load. In our approach to diagnostic assessment, the student's component performance picture is only complete when we have knowledge of the student's speed, accuracy, and resource load for a

---

[1] The optimal level for development of a component skill is situationally determined. Generally, this is the point at which the component is sufficiently automatized so that controlled processing capacity is available to reliably execute the additional components.

given component. The performance picture is incomplete without any one of these three measures. For many complex skills, component speed is absolutely essential. The information provided by an ATC to a pilot is constantly changing, so that at any given point in time the ATC must quickly assess the current radar picture and extract the relevant information. Accuracy is also an important and commonly used performance measure, but accuracy asymptotes rapidly in many tasks, leading to a tendency to promote the student prematurely to higher level components. Although measures of speed change more continuously than accuracy, there is still the problem of identifying the appropriate criterion point. Even taken together, speed and accuracy may not predict when to add new tasks. Whereas it may be possible to predict resource load from speed and accuracy, there is no evidence to suggest a simple relationship between speed, accuracy, and resource load. To the contrary, findings suggest that there are large individual differences in the ability to automatize performance, and it is quite possible that this ability is not directly related to speed and accuracy. Assessment of component resource load requires extended training in addition to new assessment procedures. In designing an ATC diagnostic assessment battery, we are implementing a dual-task condition that allows assessment of component speed and accuracy under high workload in addition to isolated component speed and accuracy. Taken together, measures of speed, accuracy, and resource load may allow for the objective identification of component training promotion points.

## GUIDELINES AND EXAMPLE PROGRAM

In this section we provide a general description and specific example of how we are applying the principles discussed above. We are developing a selective and diagnostic assessment procedure for Naval Air Intercept Control (AIC) trainees. The goal is to select individuals who are likely to succeed after training in becoming proficient AIC's, and to provide guidelines during training to facilitate their success. This goal is pursued in seven steps. The first step is to obtain a description of the final task that serves as the goal of training, and of how proficient individuals perform the task. The second step is to break the task into components that reflect expert performance on the task and may serve as manageable instructional units. The third step is to evaluate learning rates, resource load, and the development of automaticity on task components, using novice subjects. The fourth step is to engineer the optimal distribution of training time and the optimal component-skill-sequencing procedure. The fifth step is to validate the training procedure by comparing trained subjects with existing experts on final task performance. The sixth step is to design the selective assessment battery based on task components that have been validated in step five. The seventh step is to validate the selection battery by administering the battery, training subjects, and observing final task performance.

## Task Description

The first step in designing selective and diagnostic assessment procedures is to specify explicitly what the final task is that is to be trained. Our approach is not to predict general job performance, but, rather, specific task performance. Predicting job performance is likely to involve a wide range of factors, including personality factors, interactions with supervisors, divergent skill areas, and others, and is beyond the scope of our approach.

Our specific goal is to develop an assessment procedure and diagnostically based training program for co-speed nearest collision intercepts (NCI). In this task, the controller is expected to guide a single fighter to rendezvous with a single bogey (i.e., the to-be-intercepted aircraft) at the earliest possible time after beginning the operation.[2] In order to perform the task with a single command, the controller must determine the nearest point where the fighter can intercept the bogey and instruct the fighter to turn left or right to the roll-out heading that would place the fighter on a collision course with the bogey. After the fighter is on a collision flight path with the bogey, the two aircraft constitute the end points of the two sides of an imaginary isosceles triangle that have equal length. Expert controllers are capable of imagining the nearest intercept triangle that can be achieved by the fighter, and accurately estimating the heading that the fighter should turn to in order to achieve the intercept triangle. The task as performed by experts is primarily a spatial task. At a purely descriptive level, the controller observes the locations and headings of the two aircraft on the radar screen and issues a command to the fighter. The command includes an identifying code for the fighter, a turn direction (either left or right), and a roll-out heading.

## Componential Task Analysis

The second step is to break the final task into components that reflect expert performance on the task and that may serve as manageable instructional units. By *manageable,* we mean that each important component of the task should be isolated from other important components so that they can be trained and assessed separately. In agreement with Sternberg, we believe that the definition of what constitutes a "primitive" component is a function of the desired level of analysis. In our approach, a complex task is broken down into consistent components where possible, leaving a minimum of inconsistent components. If a component is consistent, then performance on the component can be automatized and there is no need to break the component into finer grained components, even though this might be possible. Automatization of consistent task components allows controlled processing to be allocated to inconsistent components and metacompo-

---

[2] Co-speed refers to the fighter and bogey traveling at the same speed. NCI is an intercept where the fighter hits nose to nose with the bogey.

nents during final task performance. Moreover, assessment of inconsistent and consistent components differs, because performance on inconsistent components asymptotes quickly, whereas performance on consistent components does not.

In designing our training program, we discriminate between *totally consistent, context consistent,* and *inconsistent task components*. To illustrate the distinction, consider the problem of teaching an individual to drive a car. The skills of steering and tracking in an automobile may be considered totally consistent. In all cases, rotating the wheel clockwise causes the automobile to turn right, and the degree of the turn varies proportionally to the amount of steering wheel rotation. Contextually consistent components are those components that are consistent in a well-defined context. Manipulation of an automobile transmission is contextually consistent. The transmission may be automatic or standard, may be located on the steering column or on the floor, may involve three, four, or five gears, and so on. If we are interested in training an individual to drive a specific automobile, then manipulating the transmission is consistent in that context. Furthermore, it may be desirable to initially train on a consistent transmission so that this component can be automatized, and then later train for various transmissions after other components have been learned. As a general principle, it is sometimes expedient to hold constant and context of a contextually consistent component during early training, so that the trainee can devote more effort to learning other important components. Inconsistent components are those for which no consistent relation holds from trial to trial. For example, defensive driving courses teach that it is important to maintain an awareness of the locations of other automobiles while driving.[3] This allows the driver to make split-second decisions about alternative paths in the event of an imminent collision, and requires working memory to be maintained and updated constantly (therefore dis-allowing automatization).

Nearest collision intercept training can be broken down into four component skills. The component breakdown is based on the final task description, which may be worded as follows:

> The controller is assigned a fighter and a bogey. The identifying numbers of these aircraft are written on the radar screen. The mapping between these numbers and the radar blips, as well as the altitudes of these and any stranger aircraft,[4] must be maintained in working memory (component 1). Observing the locations of the two aircraft on the screen, the controller visually estimates the nearest intercept triangle that includes the intercept point (component 4). This estimation involves knowledge of the minimum turning radius of the fighter and the ability to project the flight path of the fighter after the turn to the point where it crosses the bogey flight path

---

[3] Such awareness includes information that is not always perceptually available, including an awareness of whether other vehicles currently occupy the drivers blind spot.

[4] The equipment that is at the disposal of the controller is capable of providing the altitude of any airplane that is represented on the screen. This is accomplished by placing a cursor over the blip and depressing a key. The altitude information is not continuously available.

(component 3). The final step is estimate the heading angle of the projected flight path (component 2) and instruct the fighter (component 1) to turn to the appropriate heading.

The numbering of the components is based on their hierarchical relationship. Component 4 involves components 3, 2, and 1; component 3 involves components 2 and 1; and component 2 involves component 1. Therefore, the components are ordered for purposes of assessment and training in an appropriate sequence. The general sequence is to proceed from simpler, lower level components to more complex, higher level components until one builds up to the final task. The componential task analysis is completed by describing each component in sufficient detail to enable training and assessment of consistent components, and assessment of inconsistent components.

**1. Working Memory.** The controller must maintain in working memory knowledge of which identifying number refers to which radar blip, and the altitudes of the various planes. This is an inconsistent component, and working memory capacity for this component is assumed to be fixed.

**2. Heading Judgment.** The controller must be able to visualize and identify compass headings of a radar track. Heading judgment is a consistent component. Regardless of the speed of the aircraft or the location on the screen of a r_. 'ar blip, the heading angle of an aircraft on a straight path is constant. Figure 12.1 shows the simulated radar screen for a single trial of the heading judgment training/assessment module. The trainee observes the flight path of the aircraft and inputs an estimate of the heading angle. The trainee is immediately shown the correct heading angle in the feedback window.

**3. Roll-Out Heading Identification.** The third component skill is roll-out heading identification. The controller must be able to specify when to roll out of a turn such that the aircraft would intercept a given point. This requires visualizing the turn radius of the aircraft and projecting the angular flight path to the point. Roll-out heading identification is a contextually consistent component. The turn radius of the aircraft is affected by the speed of the aircraft and also differs for various aircraft. Under the assumption of a specific aircraft at a standard speed, the turn radius is constant. Figure 12.2 shows the simulated radar screen for the roll-out point identification training/assessment module. The flight blip is in motion at real time and the other radar blip is stationary. The trainee inputs an estimate of the roll-out heading that would allow the fighter to cross the stationary point. The fighter then turns to the roll-out heading and continues in compressed time to allow the trainee to observe the accuracy of his estimate. The trainee is shown the correct roll-out heading in the feedback window.

**4. Visualization of Intercept Point.** The fourth component is visualization of the intercept point. The visualization requires imagining an isosceles triangle

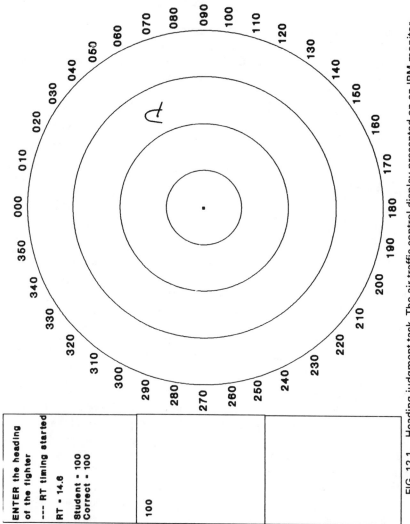

FIG. 12.1. Heading judgment task. The air traffic control display presented on an IBM monitor. The circle portrays the radar screen with rings every 5 miles and the compass headings in degrees. The half-circle object with a line coming out of it on the radar screen represents the fighter. The direction of the line from the center of the fighter indicates the heading of the aircraft. The box in the upper left hand corner indicates instructions to the controller. The middle box indicates the student input. This illustrates the heading judgment task. The student must estimate the angle of the fighter and enter that heading in degrees. On this trial the answer would be 50°. The student's input is shown in reverse video if it was in error and the correct answer below it.

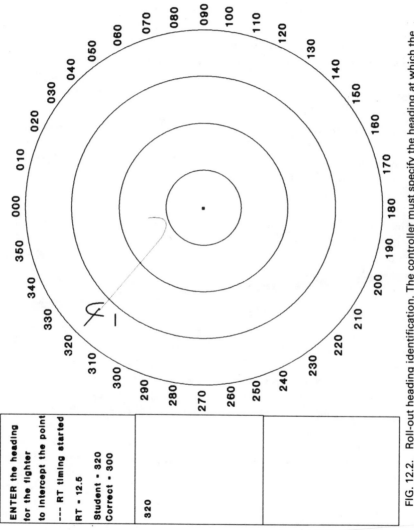

FIG. 12.2.  Roll-out heading identification. The controller must specify the heading at which the fighter rolls out of the turn to intercept the stationary point (rectangular box) on the radar screen.

with one edge on the bogey track and the other corner of the triangle near the fighter's current position. Visualization of the intercept point is a contextually consistent component. For co-speed intercepts, the intercept triangle is always an isosceles triangle. However, the location of the nearest intercept triangle is determined by the turn radius of the fighter. Figure 12.3 shows the simulated radar screen for the intercept point visualization training/assessment module. The fighter and the bogey are both in motion at real time. The trainee moves the + cursor (by manipulating a tracball) to the estimated nearest intercept point, and depresses a function key indicating completion of the estimation. The trainee is then shown the correct nearest intercept point and the fighter performs the best intercept in compressed time.

   **5. Final Task–Intercept Angle.** The final task is the fighter offset correction. In tactical intercepts, the controller must first visualize the intercept point by imagining the nearest collision triangle, and then turn at the appropriate point to hit the intercept point. When this is correctly executed, the AIC can set up the intercept with a single radio command. Figure 12.4 shows the simulated radar screen for the final task. The fighter and the bogey are both in motion at real time. The trainee inputs the identifying tag for the fighter, the turn direction (L or R), and the estimated roll-out heading. The fighter then performs the intercept (as input by the trainee) in compressed time, and the trainee is shown the correct command sequence in the feedback window.

## Learning Rates, Resource Load, and Automaticity

The next step is to evaluate learning rates and practice effects on component tasks. The practice performance curves for each of the component skills should be mapped out with experimental data relating the response time, accuracy, and resource load of each component and the final aggregate task. The resource load may be mapped out using a secondary task paradigm (for example, having subjects perform a concurrent auditory detection task while performing the component skill, see Schneider & Fisk 1982a). Performance on each consistent component improves with practice (reduced latency and increased accuracy). As the component becomes automatic subjects should be able to concurrently perform a secondary task. Promotion guidelines for component tasks are based on data derived during this step. The criterion performance for any given component is defined as the point when component speed, accuracy, and resource load has stabilized at a predetermined level. We do not add component tasks together until there is sufficient processing capacity to execute the additional components. Promotion decisions are based on promotion guidelines and on the perspective of the training environment. In some environments, it may be determined that trainees who cannot reach criterion after a certain amount of training are washed out of the training program. Alternatively, training may be individualized such that each trainee continues training on a component until criterion is reached.

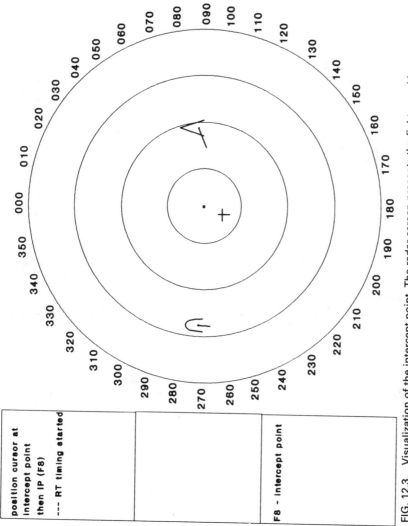

position cursor at
intercept point
then IP (F8)

--- RT timing started

F8 - intercept point

FIG. 12.3. Visualization of the intercept point. The radar screen presents the fighter and bogey object (the bogey is the triangle-shaped aircraft). A controller must move a cursor (the plus on the screen) along the bogey's track to indicate where the fighter would intercept the bogey. The feedback display places a rectangular box at the correct intercept location. The student also receives feedback as to the distance error in nautical miles.

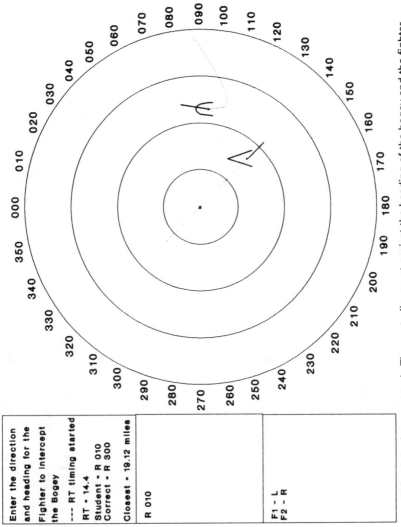

FIG. 12.4. Intercept task. The controller must project the heading of the bogey and the fighter aircraft. Controller must specify the turn that the fighter must execute in order to intercept the fighter aircraft. An accurate interception is one in which the fighter and bogey are within a mile distance. The student response time heading (RT = 8.7 seconds), (R 280), correct heading (R 260), and error (5.27 nautical miles) error feedback are presented.

318

In order to evaluate learning rates and practice effects for AIC components (and also for training and assessment), we have developed a microcomputer simulation of the AIC console. The simulation allows for time-compressed training (or assessment) of each component skill in isolation and the final task. The simulation also stores data for each trial so that learning rates and practice effects on performance measures can be derived. For each component, subjects are exposed to a great many trials over multiple sessions. In some sessions, subjects perform a secondary task so that component resource load can be evaluated. In secondary task sessions, subjects concurrently perform an auditory sound effects recognition task. In this task, the subject is presented with a short target series of sounds (1 to 3 sounds), followed by a longer test series. The subject is to respond if he or she detects the target series in the test series.

## Optimal Practice Trials and Task Sequencing

The next step is to empirically determine the optimal distribution of training time and the optimal component-skill-sequencing procedure. With regard to training time, various practice distribution schedules may be evaluated. Formulas for optimizing total performance (e.g., linear programming of component training time to maximize final score) may be developed. With regard to component skill sequencing, several possibilities should be evaluated. First, it should be determined whether training on each component independently contributes to final task performance. Next, it should be determined whether final task performance is optimized by training each component skill sequentially to criterion, or by training the component skills and final task concurrently.[5]

## Validation of the Training Procedure

The next step is to empirically validate the training procedure by comparing individuals trained with the procedure to individuals trained with conventional methods and to experts at the task.

AICs with a variety of skill levels (e.g., beginning student, student at middle and end of AIC course, operational AICs, and instructors) are being tested on the component training system. The system can provide detailed quantitative data on different performance levels (e.g., response time and closest point intercept data). This data allows comparison between students trained via the component training system and conventionally trained students.

---

[5] We find that the latter works better.

## The Selective Assessment Battery

The next step is the development of a selection test for task trainees. We have suggested that the most economical method is to use hurdle testing procedures.

The first hurdle in selective assessment for AIC training would include a psychometric assessment battery to derive measures of spatial visualization ability and working memory capacity. From scores on this hurdle, high ability subjects may be selected for further assessment.

The second hurdle would assess consistent component acquisition by observing component performance over large numbers of trials. For example, the time-compressed training of the intercept triangle visualization skill can compress the equivalent of 3 weeks of conventional intercept geometry perceptual training into 1 hour of training. The learning rate demonstrated during several hours of training is likely to be a good predictor of who succeeds in a 6-week course (see Ackerman & Schneider, 1985). Given the malleability of spatial skills, learning rate is likely to be a far better predictor of final performance than a short-term assessment procedure.

## Validation of Selection Battery

The final step is the empirical validation of the selection battery. This is accomplished by administering the selection battery to large groups of individuals and then observing the performance of these individuals in training and in the final task. During the validation phase, the selection battery is administered but all subjects are exposed to the training. After training, multiple regression techniques may be applied to predicting final task performance. Selective battery components that are not predictive of final performance would then be dropped from the assessment battery, and predictive components would be weighted according to their predictive contribution to final task performance.

## SUMMARY

Currently available assessment procedures for predicting skill acquisition in complex procedural tasks are often poor predictors of performance. Contemporary theoretical and empirical research suggests that optimizing traditional psychometric methods would result in little improvement beyond the current levels. We have argued that predicting performance after practice requires assessment of skill acquisition potential, motivation, and basic skills. The major drawback to the proposed assessment procedure is that it is difficult and time consuming. We suggest the use of hurdle testing procedures in order to keep costs reasonable. In addition to selective testing, diagnostic testing can be used during training programs to optimize skill acquisition. Our approach hinges on a closer relationship between training, prediction, and diagnostic testing. The utility of componentially describing a final task is in identifying and assessing actual task components, rather than abilities that are thought to correlate with task components. This serves to enhance prediction and diagnostic capabilities of the assessment procedure, and is useful in task training. The utility in task training derives from the approach of training task components to automaticity where possible, and in developing planning and time-sharing skills. Further, component training is enhanced by isolating each component during training.

## ACKNOWLEDGMENTS

This work was supported in part by the Office of Naval Research, Personnel and Training Contract N00014-84-K-008 (NR 154-527).

## REFERENCES

Ackerman, P. (1985). *Individual differences in skill learning: An integration of psychometric and information processing perspectives.* Unpublished manuscript.

Ackerman, P. (1986, April). *Attention, automaticity and individual differences in performance during task practice.* Paper presented at the meeting of the American Educational Research Association, San Francisco.

Ackerman, P., & Schneider, W. (1985). Individual differences in automatic and controlled information processing. In R. F. Dillon (Ed.), *Individual differences in cognition* (Vol. 2, pp. 35–64), New York: Academic Press.

Adams, J. A. (1953). *The prediction of performance at advanced stages of training on a complex psychomotor task* (Research Bulletin 53-49). Lackland AFB, TX: Air Research and Development Command, Human Resources Research Center.

Cattell, R. B. (1971). *Abilities: Their structure, growth and action.* New York: Houghton Mifflin.

Chase, W. G., & Ericsson, K. G. (1981). Skilled memory. In J. R. Anderson (Ed.), *Cognitive skills and their acquisition* (pp. 141–189). Hillsdale, NJ: Lawrence Erlbaum Associates.

Colle, H. A., & Demaio, J. (1978). *Measurement of attentional capacity load using dual-task performance of operating curves* (Interim Rep. AFHRL-TR-78-5). Brooks AFB, TX: Air Force Systems Command.

Ferguson, G. A. (1956). On transfer and the abilities of man. *Canadian Journal of Psychology, 10,* 121–131.

Fisk, A. D., & Schneider, W. (1983). Category and word search; Generalizing search principles to complex processing. *Journal of Experimental Psychology: Learning, Memory, and Cognition, 9,* 177–195.

Fleishman, E. A., & Hempel, W. E., Jr. (1955). The relation between abilities and improvement with practice in a visual discrimination reaction task. *Journal of Experimental Psychology, 49,* 301–316.

Guilford, J. P. (1967). *The nature of human intelligence.* New York: McGraw-Hill.

Horn, J. L. (1965). *Fluid and crystallized intelligence: A factor analytic study of the structure among primary mental abilities.* Unpublished doctoral dissertation, University of Illinois, Urbana.

Humphreys, L. G. (1968). The fleeting nature of the prediction of college academic success. *Journal of Educational Psychology, 59,* 375–380.

Hunt, E., Frost, N., & Lunneborg, C. (1973). Individual differences in cognition: A new approach to intelligence. In G. Bower (Ed.), *The psychology of learning and motivation* (Vol. 7, pp. 87–122). New York: Academic Press.

Kennedy, R. S., Jones, M. B., & Harbeson, M. M. (1958). Assessing productivity and well-being in Navy workplaces. In *Proceedings of the 13th Annual Meeting of the Human Factors Association of Canada*, (pp. 8–13). Ottawa: Human Factors Association of Canada.

Kosslyn, S. M., Brun, J. L., Cave, C. R., & Wallach, R. W. (1983). *Components of mental imagery representation* (Tech. Rep. No. 1). Waltham, MA: Brandeis University.

Kristofferson, M. W. (1972). Effects of practice on character classification performance. *Canadian Journal of Psychology, 26*, 54–60.

Likert, R., & Quasha, W. H. (1970). *Manual for the revised Minnesota Paper Form Board Test.* New York: The Psychological Corporation.

Lohman, D. F. (1979). *Spatial ability: A review and reanalysis of the correlational literature* (Tech. Rep. No. 8). Stanford, CA: Aptitude Research Project, School of Education, Stanford University.

McGee, M. G. (1979). Human spatial abilities: Psychometric studies and environmental, genetic, hormonal, and neurological influences. *Psychological Bulletin, 86*, 889–918.

Mumaw, R. J., & Pellegrino, J. W. (1984). Individual differences in complex spatial processing. *Journal of Educational Psychology, 76*, 920–939.

Newell, A., & Rosenbloom, P. S. (1981). Mechanisms of skill acquisition and the law of practice. In J. R. Anderson (Ed.), *Cognitive skills and their acquisition* (pp. 1–55). Hillsdale, NJ: Lawrence Erlbaum Associates.

Pellegrino, J. W. (1983, April). *Individual differences in spatial ability: The effects of practice on components of processing and reference test scores.* Paper presented at the meeting of the American Educational Research Association, Montreal, Canada.

Pellegrino, J. W., Alderton, D. L., & Regian, J. W. (1984, December). *Components of spatial ability.* Paper presented at NATO Advanced Study Institute in Cognition and Motivation, Athens, Greece.

Pellegrino, J. W., & Glaser, R. (1980). Components of inductive reasoning. In R. E. Snow, P-A Federico, & W. E. Montague (Eds.), *Aptitude, Learning, and Instruction (Vol. 1): Cognitive Process Analysis of Aptitude* (pp. 177–212). Hillsdale, NJ: Lawrence Erlbaum Associates.

Pellegrino, J. W., & Mumaw, R. J. (1980). *Multicomponent models of spatial ability.* Unpublished manuscript, University of California, Santa Barbara, CA.

Regian, J. W., Shute, V. J., & Pellegrino, J. W. (1985, June). *The malleability of spatial relations skills.* Paper presented at the meeting of Psychonomics, Boston.

Schneider, W. (1985). Toward a model of attention and the development of automaticity. In M. I. Posner & O. S. Marin (Eds.), *Attention and performance XI* (pp. 475–492). Hillsdale, NJ: Lawrence Erlbaum Associates.

Schneider, W., Dumais, S., & Shiffrin, R. M. (1984). Automatic and control processing and attention. In R. Parasuraman & D. R. Davies (Eds.), *Varieties of attention* (pp. 1–27). Orlando, FL: Academic Press.

Schneider, W., & Fisk, A. D. (1982a). Concurrent automatic and controlled visual search: Can processing occur without resource cost? *Journal of Experimental Psychology: Learning, Memory, and Cognition, 8*, 261–278.

Schneider, W., & Fisk, A. D. (1982b). Degree of consistent training: Improvements in search performance and automatic process development. *Perception & Psychophysics, 31*, 160–168.

Schneider, W. & Fisk, A. D. (1984). Automatic category search and its transfer. *Journal of Experimental Psychology: Learning, Memory, and Cognition, 10*, 1–15.

Schneider, W., & Shiffrin, R. M. (1977). Controlled and automatic human information processing: I. Detection, search, and attention. *Psychological Review, 84*, 1–66.

Shiffrin, R. M., & Schneider, W. (1977). Controlled and automatic human information processing: II. Perceptual learning, automatic attending, and a general theory. *Psychological Review, 84*, 127–190.

Shute, V. (1984). *Characteristics of cognitive cartography*. Unpublished PhD Thesis, University of California, Santa Barbara.

Snow, R. E. (1980). Aptitude processes. In R. E. Snow, P-A Federico, & W. E. Montague (Eds.), *Aptitude, Learning, and Instruction (Vol. 1): Cognitive Process Analysis of Aptitude* (pp. 27–60). Hillsdale, NJ: Lawrence Erlbaum Associates.

Spearman, C. (1904). General intelligence objectively determined and measured. *American Journal of Psychology, 15,* 201–293.

Sternberg, R. J. (1977). *Intelligence, information processing, and analogical reasoning: The componential analysis of human abilities*. Hillsdale, NJ: Lawrence Erlbaum Associates.

Sternberg, R. J. (1979). The nature of mental abilities. *American Psychologist, 34,* 214–230.

Sternberg, R. J. (1984). Toward a triarchic theory of human intelligence. *The Behavioral and Brain Sciences, 7,* 269–315.

Thurstone, L. L. (1947). *Multiple factor analysis*. Chicago: University of Chicago Press.

Vernon, P. E. (1951). *The structure of human abilities*. London: Methuen.

Whitely, S. E. (1980). Modeling aptitude test validity from cognitive components. *Journal of Educational Psychology, 72,* 750–769.

# 13

# Applying Cognitive Task Analysis and Research Methods to Assessment

Alan Lesgold
Susanne Lajoie
Debra Logan
Gary Eggan
*Learning Research and Development Center*
*University of Pittsburgh*

## INTRODUCTION

Tests have many different purposes. They can be used (a) to develop a description of a person's capabilities; (b) to search for an explanation for a person's level of performance; (c) to facilitate the adaptation of training to a particular person's capabilities; (d) as a screening device to warn about a student's lack of progress in learning a skill; or (e) to choose which of a set of people should be given a specific task. For some of these purposes, a global quantitative characterization is appropriate; for example, if we want only to be warned of any students who lag behind their peers in school, we can give a global achievement test and look for outlier scores. For other purposes, qualitative details are needed if a test is to be useful; for example, if a student has incomplete or incorrect knowledge that has led to systematic misconceptions, it is much more useful to know about the nature and basis of those misconceptions than simply to know that the student is not performing well on problems we wish he or she could solve.

Current psychometric methods, for the most part, use quantitative approaches to derive scales of measurement for predictor variables that have statistical relationships with more direct indicators of competence. Cognitive psychology provides an important basis for qualitative approaches to characterizing performance, and cognitive research has established a variety of methods for developing and verifying qualitative accounts of a person's knowledge. Perhaps some of the methods of cognitive psychology can be used to generate scales of performance measurement that are more directly related to underlying competence. Ideally, we would prefer to understand why particular performances or performance scores predict broader aspects of competence, just as physicians prefer to go beyond mere statistical indications to also consider causal models of healthy function and particular patients' departures from healthy function.

Such models may be more attainable now than in the past. The question considered in this book is whether new cognitive methods can contribute to building test instruments that have greater validity, in terms of their ability to inform training and selection decisions and to facilitate understanding and explanation of those decisions. In the sections that follow, we consider the possibilities for using cognitive psychological approaches to improve different forms of testing. Then, we discuss our own preliminary efforts to use cognitive approaches in ways that exemplify an emerging cognitive psychometrics. We discuss some of our measurement work in the area of electronics troubleshooting, specifically the isolation and repair of faults in aircraft navigation equipment. We also discuss forthcoming efforts to compare the effects of alternative training regimens for tutoring this technical skill and then reflect on cost/benefit analyses of training and transfer.

## Tests for Description

There are many reasons for wanting a description of a person's cognitive capabilities. For example, if a training course is to be revised, it would be useful to assess the capabilities of people who have taken that course. Detection of specific functional weaknesses would be useful in revising the training methods. Traditional psychometrics can handle this in part, because the personnel selection world has developed a variety of empirical methodologies for job sampling and performance assessment (cf. Hakel, 1986). However, because these techniques are either statistical or based only on modest laboratory research, the goal of being completely reliable and free of bias has yet to be attained.

The next step, to describe specifically what knowledge is missing, may require methodologies developed in cognitive research laboratories. It would be useful to be able to specify just what it is that inadequate performers *don't* know; this would be the obvious starting point for improved instruction. Equally important would be a specification of relevant knowledge that poor performers *do* know; this would avoid wasting time on improving training that is already successful. Trainees may also "know" some things that are not true, and this may have implications for training, because trainees will interpret new information in the context of what is already "known." All told, we see a major advantage in moving beyond a specification of the tasks the recipients of training can and cannot perform to include also specifications of the knowledge they need to perform the target skills and the aspects of that knowledge that are missing or incorrect.

## Tests for Explanation of Failures

In a sense, knowing what a trainee knows enables an explanation of the trainee's performance, which is another goal of testing. Many existing tests attempt to explain performance through the use of small subsets of items that appear to tap particular capabilities. For example, some of the achievement tests used in schools produce a variety of subscales that show strength or weakness in general curricular areas and even in components of those areas. A reading achievement test, for example, may include subscales for word recognition, literal comprehension of sentences, drawing inferences from text, and other subskills. If a student has trouble in reading, looking at such a profile of scores may permit a partial explanation of the sources of the trouble.

The problem with this approach is that it is mapped onto outcome categories rather than onto the underlying components of knowledge that permit the outcomes. The outcomes of successful word recognition performance, success in determining what a sentence means, and success on an inferential comprehension test depend on a number of specific reading skill components. A sound theory is required to specify just what these knowledge components are. If, on the basis of such a theory, we knew the specific knowledge components a student lacked, we would be more successful in designing instruction for that student. If the theory behind such a specification is weak, then an empirical approach based on clearly differentiated performance categories may be better. For reading, it is unclear whether our theories are yet adequate. For a number of areas of cognitive skill and knowledge where cognitive task analyses have yielded relatively specific accounts of the procedural knowledge that constitutes expertise (e.g., Lesgold, Lajoie et al., 1986), we believe that theory-based specifications of a student's knowledge and knowledge gaps would be more useful than the current empirically based specifications.

## Tests for the Adaptation of Instruction to a Student's Competences

Adaptation is the test of explanation. A critical purpose for tests is to provide the information needed by teachers to tailor the educational experience of a student. This tailoring can occur at many levels. A standard form of tailoring is to select different educational tasks for students as a function of their test performance. Computer-based testing and practice systems do this. The practice opportunities available to students are grouped into categories, and the system keeps track of student performance on tasks of each category. If a student performs extremely well on tasks of a particular category, it is assumed that the student already knows what those tasks are meant to teach and can be moved on to other categories. If the student performs extremely poorly, showing little improvement over successive instances of a category, it is assumed that the student is not yet "ready" for that category. Such methods require a representation of the prerequisite relations among the task categories, and students are generally given problems in categories whose prerequisites have been mastered. Significant trouble on a category might be handled by reverting to tasks from whichever of the prerequisite categories looks least strong.

In task domains where the tasks are more complex, the categories may be abstractions that are somewhat removed from the tasks at hand. For example, Wescourt, Beard, and Gould (1977) built BIP, a practice system for computer programming training. They assumed that each programming task their system could assign involved a number of skill components. These included the ability to use various BASIC commands, but they could easily have been abstracted further into categories such as the various forms of iteration procedures and input/output procedures. Success in solving a programming problem, then, was taken as evidence that the student knew all of the skill components designated for that problem. Failure was handled by trying to infer from the overall pattern of problem successes and failures which underlying skill components might be weak. For example, did the student have trouble whenever a problem involved iteration? Whenever a problem required use of the GOSUB command?

We can think of the BIP approach as being a cognitive testing approach to the extent that the underlying skill categories thought to be important in a problem are based on a cognitive analysis of the performance. As it happens, BIP was based instead on programming constructs in BASIC, not on fundamental cognitive procedures of program design. Most cognitive analyses of programming (e.g., Spohrer, Soloway, & Pope, 1985; Bonar, 1985) suggest that the relevant cognitive components are *plans* for accomplishing particular computational ends, not individual programming commands. BIP dealt instead with specific commands, such as FOR, GOSUB, and LET. Nonetheless, BIP's designers paved the way for a promising form of cognitive testing for adaptation.

A different approach to tailoring presents the same problems to all trainees but tailors the coaching and support it provides to individual diagnoses (student models). This is the approach of Sherlock, our electronics troubleshooting tutor. If, at a given point in trying to solve the problem, our measures suggest that the student should be able to handle the next step in the solution process, the support provided by the tutor is minimal. If it is known that the next step is beyond the student, then a hint may be provided that "gives away" what the student should do. In between, the character of hinting is based on a partial theory of instruction that specifies what sorts of coaching will be most useful for establishing the target knowledge.

It is only a difference in the cognitive specificity of its categories, and not some aspect of the general method, that keeps the BIP scheme from being a cognitive approach to tailoring. If we agreed with the task analysis, we would call the approach cognitive. This point is important because it may not be necessary for an entirely new measurement methodology to be developed. Rather, it may be possible to re-partition the knowledge categories used in some existing approaches. The new measurement instruments would infer the presence or absence of categories of knowledge from performances on tasks that require that knowledge. Psychometric approaches try to do this, too, but they differ in assuming that statistical techniques are sufficient to disentangle measures of abstract categories or scales from the specifics of test items. The statistical approach has not been sufficient so far; some amount of inference about the specific cognitive activities involved in performing test tasks seems to be needed to determine which procedural skill components a student has mastered.

## Tests for Warning

An alternative to the active approaches to adaptation just described is to provide a standard form of training to all students but to rely on tests to provide a warning about any trainee who is not making adequate progress and might need some form of remediation. Special training can then be made available to these students. This type of approach can be efficient if the cohort of trainees is sufficiently uniform in entering skills and aptitudes. Although the approach is far from ideal when long-term learning is the goal, many small-scale training requirements can be met quite well with relatively uniform instruction, so long as there is adequate means for detecting training failures. For example, in our own laboratories, we provide uniform training in the use of local word processing tools, but people who have difficulty can then seek help later. In a larger organization, one might want to test for such difficulties and plan for the remedial activity. The cognitive requirements for "warning" tests would be more or less identical to those for adaptation tests, except that the output of such tests would tend to be a broader category of cognitive skill that needs remediation.

## Tests for Selection

A final form of testing is for selection. Here, the importance of substantial cognitive modeling may depend on the specific situation. Selection tests are sometimes used to determine which of a group of people can profit from instruction or training and sometimes to decide who is best equipped to do a particular job. Depending on the relationship between the supply of talent and the number of trainees or workers needed, a cognitive approach may or may not provide an advantage. The existing psychometric techniques could probably do the best job of selecting the few people who are most likely to succeed from a large pool, simply because this is what the psychometric approach to predictive validity is optimized to do.

On the other hand, when the surplus of available candidates is not large, correlational methodologies are not well suited to deciding which people know everything needed to do a job or successfully complete a course. If we need to identify every available candidate who is likely to succeed, and the issue is deciding who has the prerequisite thinking and learning skills, the domain-specific cognitive procedures, and the understanding to do a job or be trained to do a job, then it might be worthwhile to base testing on detailed cognitive task analyses of the target job and the available training regimen.

We can compare the selection testing situation, and indeed all testing situations, to the practice of medicine. The various screening tests done by physicians often are based on statistical indicators (though usually physicians have a pretty good understanding of why the indicators work). So, for example, if the probability of a person having tuberculosis is relatively low (i.e., there are few TB victims to be selected from a large population), a skin test may be performed even if it has a moderate false-positive rate. On the other hand, if it is necessary to know with high probability whether a *particular* person has TB, then various examinations are conducted in order to gain a sufficient representation of that person's body state to know whether or not TB is present.

## DIAGNOSIS DURING THE COURSE OF LEARNING

Much current diagnostic testing is not triggered by signs of a problem. Rather, it is used for screening, like a tuberculin test; various subscores are used to produce statements about problems a student might have. For example, it might be sensible to warn a teacher that a student's math achievement score is, say, two grade levels below the reading score or that the student's vocabulary score on multisyllable words is well below the monosyllable score. However, such advice may be ludicrous if the scores are extreme. For example, scoring 4 years ahead of grade level on one subscale and 2 years ahead on another should not produce the message that a child needs extra work on the material for which he or she is only 2 years ahead (especially when the reliability of extreme scores is taken into account).

In the medical world, screening based on a sign that is very specifically associated with a given disease (e.g., antibodies to the AIDS virus) is often useful, whereas general screening (e.g., annual chest x-ray pictures) that is not associated strongly with a specific disease is usually ill-advised. We suspect that the same is true for education. General screening has a high false-positive rate, is likely to lead to substitution of unneeded special treatment for needed basic instruction, and tends to relieve instructors of their responsibility for optimizing individual students' learning. On the other hand, specific screening, such as checking of visual acuity, verifying the ability to pronounce all phonemes of our language correctly, finding specific bugs in arithmetic procedures, and so on, may be quite productive.

In addition to screening, education needs a technology of diagnosis in response to manifested problems, the sort of technology required for medical diagnosis. Given the discussions just mentioned, we would expect two approaches to be useful: (a) specific tests that can settle specific diagnostic questions, and (b) the basic differential sequential diagnosis strategy in which data are sought specifically to aid in the selection of one of several plausible alternatives. Both specific tests and sequential testing strategies are, of course, found in education. For example, the learning disabilities literature contains many specific tests, and there is a whole technology of sequential testing behind computerized adaptive tests such as those now used in military recruiting. However, these education and training applications really differ from the approaches taken in medicine, and we think we can learn a bit from the physician's experience.

The special education literature contains all sorts of tests for specific learning disabilities. What is often missing is a scientific underpinning for the "diseases" that are being diagnosed. Lacking such a framework, it is difficult to be sure what the test is saying or what to do about a particular diagnosis. This does not imply that such "soft" diagnosis is wrong; the problem is only that it depends excessively on the intuitive skills of the practitioner.

Sequential testing is a step in a positive direction, but it also turns out to suffer from the weakness of the tests from which it starts. Rather than being a means of ruling out alternative diagnoses, most sequential testing is simply a more optimal means of assigning a score on a scale, where the scale's diagnostic meaning, in terms of implications for actions, is weak. Knowledge of position in a scale does not reveal the contents or weak points of complex performances. To diagnose better, we need to have a clearer sense of the educational states we wish to differentiate and then to choose tests to maximize the chances of identifying the student's state. Because diagnosis and treatment are intimately linked, we need to be able to specify treatments precisely in order to build the science and technology of diagnosis.

This last point is critical. A diagnosis, when examined closely, derives from understanding of both a problem people have and a cure for the problem. The science on which any diagnosis rests must include the ability to specify the specific features of the "disease" that are present in a given case, the specific treatment components that are present in a specific therapeutic regimen, and what changes as a result of therapy. In medicine, individual diagnoses are, whenever possible, "patient-specific models" (Patil, Szolovits, & Schwartz, 1984). Statistical inferences are made when diagnostic procedures are evaluated, but the procedures themselves are grounded in inferences about mechanisms whenever possible.

Indeed, the basic behavior of medical diagnosticians (cf. Feltovich, 1981; Lesgold, 1984) is to quickly recognize the likely category of disease and then build and verify a specific model of the way in which the specific patient manifests a particular form of the disease. This is much different from a process that ends in a small number of numerical scores with minimal causal explanation of those scores. The goal of cognitive testing methodologies must be to know what is going on in the mind, just as medical diagnosis seeks to know what is going on in the body.

## AN EXAMPLE: AVIONICS TROUBLESHOOTING

The issues addressed here were brought into focus by a continuing effort to develop better techniques for analyzing the complex technical performances that are required in modern society. The Learning Research and Development Center was asked to take on a primary role in developing and testing a methodology for a large Air Force effort to improve the quality of training and performance measurement for a number of their more technical occupational specialties. Specifically, we were asked to explore the feasibility of using cognitive psychological approaches to task analysis. As that work proceeded and cognitive task analysis approaches were developed, we were also asked to demonstrate the efficacy of our analytic approaches by showing that the skills we identified as critical and not uniformly acquired would, if taught, make a difference in airmen's job performance. This latter effort is now underway. It involves development and field testing of an intelligent tutoring system. The specific domain for our work has been a specialty area in which nonautomated test equipment is used to diagnose and repair faults in navigational equipment for a particular airplane, the F-15.

### The Problem

To carry out this project, we had to develop specific measurement techniques that we believe are of broad general interest. In particular, we have developed a form of protocol analysis-based testing that we believe has broad applicability. Several other approaches have been developed (cf. Lesgold, Lajoie et al., 1986) that also seem likely to be useful. We have found it beneficial to compare subjects at multiple levels of competence so that we can describe competence as the presence or absence of certain key features during realistic (job-like) problem-solving performances. The features, in turn, signal specific procedural knowledge that seems to be differentially acquired by those who learn well on the job. Our current task is to try to provide, via intelligent, coached practice in a simulated job environment, this procedural knowledge and related conceptual (declarative) knowledge to airmen who lack it.

### Structured Interviews During Problem Solving:
### The Concept of Effective Problem Space[1]

In our first attack on this problem, Gitomer[2] developed a troubleshooting task that involved detection of complex faults in the test station used by our subjects. As a first formative approach, he simply videotaped subjects attempting to solve

---

[1] Portions of the material in this and the next section were also presented in a lecture to the Australian Society for Computers in Learning, Sydney, December, 1987, and published in the conference proceedings (Barrett & Hedberg, 1987).

[2] At the time a graduate student at LRDC, Gitomer is now at Educational Testing Service.

such fault-detection problems. He then examined the protocols (transcriptions of the tapes) and attempted to tabulate the activities that seemed relevant to either metacognitive or more tactical aspects of problem solving in this domain. Although the results (Gitomer, 1984) were of great interest, we wanted to move toward a testing approach that was less dependent on skilled cognitive psychological analysis. The Gitomer results told us a lot about what psychologists could see that was different in the cognitive processes of more- versus less-able problem solvers as they tackled hard troubleshooting problems. But we wanted to end up with a technology that directly reflected experts' views of what cognitive activities were critical to troubleshooting. Also, we wanted to make our approach reliably usable by domain experts—not just a laboratory demonstration. That, after all, is one aspect of what test development is largely about—rendering explicit the procedures that insightful researchers first apply in their laboratories to study learning and thinking. Also, because job skills are very much grounded in the specifics of the job (cf. Scribner, 1984), we expected a method heavily driven by domain expertise to be more productive than a "weak method."

An important contribution to our developing approach came from an electronics expert[3] who had extensive experience watching novice troubleshooting performances. He pointed out that it was quite possible to specify the entire *effective problem space,*[4] even for very complex troubleshooting problems. The effective problem space is a simplification of the complete problem space. Instead of considering activity at the microlevel of individual tests of the system that might be performed, it abstracts to the level of replaceable units, such as printed circuit boards. Because one printed circuit board might potentially have hundreds of tests performed on it, this is a major simplification. In addition, the effective problem space takes account only of the steps that an expert would take plus the steps that novices are likely to take in solving a troubleshooting problem. These steps could be specified because much of novice troubleshooting activity is observed and assisted by expert supervisors. In our first attempt to use the effective problem space approach, the task was to find the source of a failure in a test station that contained perhaps 40 cubic feet of printed circuit boards, cables, and connectors, but various aspects of the job situation constrained the task sufficiently so that the effective problem space could be mapped out.

One important key to success is to be sure that the effective problem space is complete with respect to the *key mental models* that guide expert problem

---

[3] Co-author Eggan was the domain expert in this work. He also had some background in cognitive psychology.

[4] This term is still evolving. Perhaps *abstracted problem space* is better, because there is both an abstraction of the level of activity and a pruning away of problem states that are not likely to ever occur.

solving. In the case of the manual F-15 avionics test station, the key model is the one that represents the state of the test station at the time failure is detected. If the effective problem space is relatively complete in having alternative planning structures for the small problem space region based on this model,[5] then it should contain the information needed both to diagnose trainee performance in troubleshooting the test station and to coach that performance; it can then provide hints toward problem solution that introduce or reinforce aspects of the key model. The key mental model for troubleshooting the test station references only a small part of the station, the part that is involved in the aircraft test that was anomalous. This model therefore heavily constrains the effective problem space. Our expert's specification of ideal troubleshooting and knowledge of novice behavior patterns specify the lower bound on the size of the effective problem space, and the model of the critical test specifies the upper bound, the set of plans for searching the space specified by the model.

Because the effective problem space could be specified, we could specify in advance a set of probe questions that would get us the information we wanted about subjects' planning and other metacognitive activity in the troubleshooting task. For what is probably the most complex troubleshooting task we have ever seen, there are perhaps 55 to 60 different nodes in the problem space; we had specific probe questions about strategy, tactics, or mental problem representation for about 45 of them.[6] Figure 13.1 provides an example of a small piece of the problem space and the questions we developed for it.

An examination of the questions in Fig. 13.1 reveals that some questions are aimed at very specific knowledge (e.g., *How would you do this?*), whereas others help to elaborate the subject's plan for troubleshooting (consider *Why would you do this?* or *What do you plan to do next?*). Combined with information about the order in which the subject worked in different parts of the problem space, this probe information permitted reconstruction of the subject's plan for finding the fault in the circuit and even provided some information about the points along the way at which different aspects of the planning occurred. In fact, we went a step further and asked a number of specific questions about how critical components work and what their purpose is. Finally, if a subject was headed well away

---

[5] There is terminological complexity here that cannot be avoided. The test station does tests. These tests enable a diagnosis of where in a piece of aircraft electronics a failure has occurred. Virtually all trainees can use the test station for this purpose. However, sometimes the test station itself fails. When this happens, a test performed by the test station on a piece of the aircraft produces an anomalous result. Finding out what is wrong with the test station is hard, and it is this skill that we were trying to diagnose in the airmen who use the station.

[6] Logan and Eastman have been refining this technology in our laboratories (Logan & Eastman, 1986), and we expect a more detailed account to be published by them at a later date.

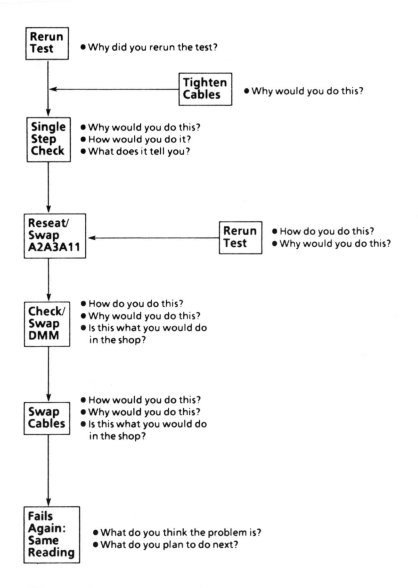

FIG. 13.1.  Structured interview diagram excerpt.

TABLE 13.1
Examples of Items Counted in each Subscale

---

I. Plans
   A. Extend and test a card.
   B. Trace through the schematic of an individual card.

II. Hypotheses
   A. There is a short caused by a broken wire or a bad connection.
   B. The ground is missing from the relay.

III. Device and system understanding
   A. Understanding and use of the external control panel.
   B. Understanding of grounds and voltage levels in the test station.

IV. Errors
   A. Misinterpreting/misreading the program code for a test that the test station carries out under computer control.
   B. Getting pin numbers for a test wrong.

V. Methods and skills
   A. Schematic understanding: Ability to interpret diagrams of relays, contacts, coils.
   B. Ability to run confidence check programs.

VI. Systematicity
   A. The subject returns to a point where he knew what was going on when a dead end was encountered.
   B. The path from the power source is checked.

---

from a reasonable solution path, we would, at predetermined points, redirect efforts back to more fertile ground.[7]

After reviewing the protocol, we developed 6 scales on which we scored each airman. Each of these scales could be further subdivided into subscales to permit more detailed and task-specific issues to be addressed. The 6 scales were titled *plans, hypotheses, device and system understanding, errors, methods and skills,* and *systematicity.* For each scale, Table 13.1 gives two examples of the items for which points could be earned (in the error scale, more points means more errors and thus is a lower score).

*Plans* was a count of the number of plans mentioned by the subject during the problem-solving efforts. Any time that the subject entered a new part of the problem space, we prompted the subject for a plan; however, the lower skill

---

[7] This was very controversial when we used our tests to validate our tutor. Our clients felt that redirecting the trainee back to the expert path biased our results; we felt that it allowed us to get additional information about the trainee's knowledge even after he had gone in a hopeless direction. Because our clients were using their own experts to provide a holistic evaluation of the trainee's problem-solving performance, our technique might well have made trainees look too good to those experts. By our reckoning, of course, the redirection occurred only after the trainee was thought to have little chance of cracking the problem.

subjects, especially, often did not have one. That is, they acted more or less randomly until a plan or hypothesis came to mind. A count was kept of the number of hypotheses offered by subjects at various points in their work. Again, subjects were prompted for hypotheses at the predetermined boundary points between regions of the problem space. The high-skill group entertained more hypotheses, which is what we would expect given that they are at intermediate skill levels. True experts could be expected to have a more constrained set of probable hypotheses (cf. Benbassett & Bachar-Bassan, 1984; Lesgold et al., 1988).

The *device and system understanding* scale was based on specific questions that were put to the subjects after they had performed the troubleshooting tasks. We asked a fixed set of questions about each of the components of the test station that played a role in the problems we had posed. These questions probed for knowledge about how the component worked, what role it played in the test station, what its general purpose in electronic systems was, and what it looked like.

The *errors* scale was simply a count of the number of incorrect steps taken by the airman in trying to troubleshoot the system. The *methods and skills* measure tallied which of the procedures needed to carry out the troubleshooting of the test station were successfully demonstrated by the subject. Finally, the *systematicity* measure consisted of a set of relatively broad criteria gauging the extent to which troubleshooting proceeded in a systematic manner rather than haphazardly or without a sense of goal structure.

This, then, provided a first and relatively global view of the skills that separated high- and low-skill airmen. We learned much from these analyses. High-skill airmen differed on most of the measures, except for *Plans*. Looking a bit more closely, the higher skill airmen seemed no more inclined to engage in metacognitive activity; rather, their planning, although still very domain-specific, was more general, less conditioned to the specific point in a specific problem solution at which they found themselves. On the one hand, a course in general "higher order thinking skills" does not seem called for, because both more- and less-skilled airmen engaged in such activity spontaneously. On the other hand, the less-skilled airmen seemed to operate at levels too microscopic and superficial in their representation of the problem and planning of a solution. The overall pattern of differences suggested to us that the missing knowledge to be taught to less-promising airmen was domain-specific planning, plus some specific skill components, such as tracing schematics and using meters for active-circuit measurement.

Again, though, the knowledge coming from the 6 scales, or even from slightly more specific tallies, was insufficient to drive the design or operation of an instructional system. To do that, we needed to be able to look at additional qualitative aspects of job-domain performance. An impressive example of how to do this was provided by Eggan, our domain expert, working with Roth of HumRRO. They took our methods and applied them to a slight variant of the domain we studied. However, instead of using general scales, they focused more specifically on comparing the specific problem space paths of experts and novices. The next few figures illustrate the yield of this work.

Diagnosis problems were developed that were characteristic of real problems faced in the work environment and likely to be solved correctly by the best technicians but not by many of the less-skilled, first-term airmen. People with experience in handling the tasks on which many airmen have difficulty tend to have a good sense of the kinds of problems that are in this class (representative of the domain, solvable by the better technicians, and not solvable by a substantial number of workers), and Eggan's analysis has now proven itself empirically. Figure 13.2 illustrates the effective problem space that was constructed for a troubleshooting problem in one of the job domains Eggan studied.[8]

Roth and Eggan then proceeded to run subjects on this problem. It was posed verbally to airmen who had access to the full set of Technical Orders (documentation for the devices involved). Technicians were encouraged to offer their hypotheses, state their plans, and announce specific steps they would take in attacking the problem. Whenever an overt step was stated by a subject, the subject was immediately informed of the outcome of that step. As predicted, almost all problem-solving activity fell within this space, for both experts and less-skilled workers.

Figure 13.3 shows the basic results that were obtained. The experts, whose actions are enclosed by a solid line, used a subset of the effective problem space, avoiding some of the steps that were less likely to be productive. The novices, whose composite empirical problem space is outlined with thick hash lines, failed to make some of the expert moves and did make some moves that experts would not make, such as swapping a disc pack (see bottom left of Fig. 13.3). Further, their empirical problem space was discontinuous, a set of four islands, whereas the more able technicians knew enough to make it completely through the problem without impasse.

To better understand what knowledge separated the experts from the novices, Roth and Eggan then tried to determine the specific knowledge that experts used at critical points in the problem space. Figure 13.4 shows the experts' empirical problem space with annotations of the knowledge that appeared to drive the moves experts made. Knowledge involved in making a move that experts make and novices generally do not make is a clear candidate for a general training. At the individual trainee level, a wrong choice at a decision point in the effective problem space becomes a mandate for specific instruction on the knowledge that could have led to correct performance.

A final issue that was addressed was the discontinuities in novice problem

---

[8] The problem involves deciding why efforts to download a piece of software from a mainframe computer to a workstation have failed. The symptoms lead to hypotheses concerning the disk drive to which the software is to be sent.

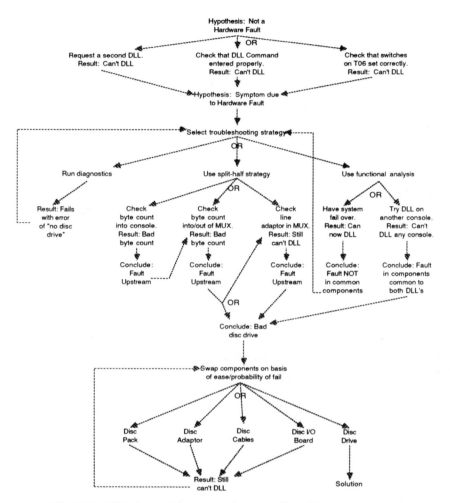

FIG. 13.2. Effective problem space for a small problem.

spaces. In essence, the gaps represent impasse points where the novice does not know what to do. Figure 13.5 shows, in boldface type, the extra steps taken by a novice outside the expert problem space. They involve relatively random behavior, driven by the snippets of knowledge the novice has. Initially, there is a period of board swapping that is not directed specifically at the problem. Then, there is an effort to think about the path involved in a download. The multiplexor (MUX) somehow becomes the focus of attention, and thought about the MUX continues until the novice is redirected toward the disc drive, whereupon the right possibilities are addressed, but without concern about the relative costs and benefits of the five alternatives.

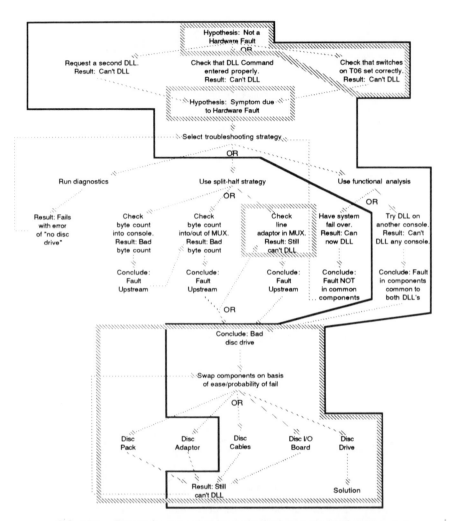

FIG. 13.3.  Expert (surrounded by solid line) and novice (surrounded by thick hashed lines) portions of effective problem space.

**Summary.**  Several things are clear from this work. First, there is a lot of variability from one subject to the next; statistical treatment of any coding of this sort of problem-solving performance is not easy when samples are small. Second, the summary measures of planning, systematicity, and so on, do not provide the detail on which instructional design and specific coaching must be based. Third, the validity of any conclusion about what a subject is doing must rest on a pattern of relationships among the observed details of performance, the expert knowledge of the domain, and the cognitive psychology of expertise. An electronics wizard

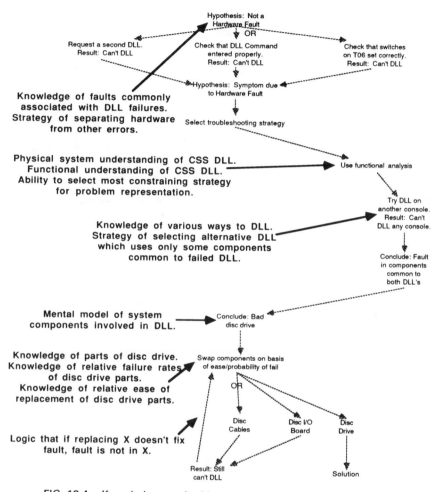

FIG. 13.4.   Knowledge required by nodes on expert problem solution path.

working with a cognitive psychologist can use cognitive extensions of rational task analysis to specify and elaborate the knowledge a novice has or does not have. This is a form of diagnosis more like what a physician does in an individual case than like what a testing expert does.

## From Testing to Tutor Development

The scientist can reasonably ask what empirical support there is for this approach. It must be demonstrated that differentiating people according to the kinds of rational diagnostic analyses just described is more than just some sort of psycho-

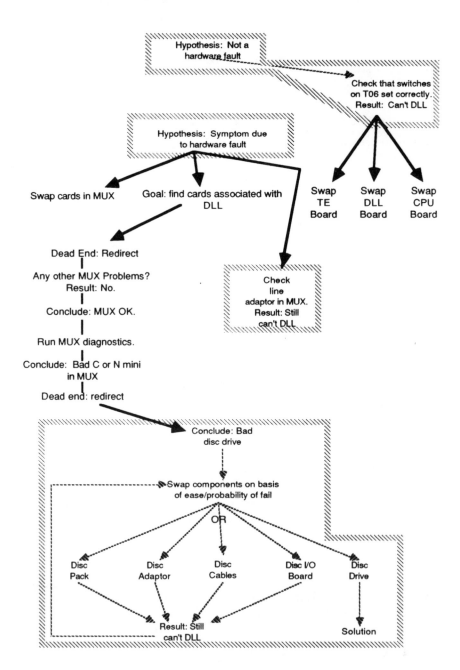

FIG. 13.5. Responses of one novice, including those outside the effective problem space.

logical version of astrology. The validation approach we have pursued is to show that diagnoses based on this approach can lead to effective instruction that is both individually tailored and generally effective.

At the group level, what is being tested is the effective problem space analysis. The question to be asked is whether people improve on the job after receiving instruction designed to teach them the mental procedures that would allow them to efficiently and coherently traverse the problem space. At the individual level, the empirical question is whether instruction tailored to one's current problem-solving performance, as interpreted with respect to these effective problem space analyses, is more productive than instruction that does not take account of such individual differences.[9] To help elaborate this validation approach, two important issues are addressed: (a) the nature of an instructional treatment model that might test such approaches, and (b) the nature of the student model with respect to which such a treatment might be individualized.

*The Treatment Model.*   The treatment model, in the terms we have been using, is simply the goal structure for instruction, a set of goals and subgoals that the instruction is intended to achieve. In our tutor, a computer programming object is associated with each subgoal. Each object is a semi-independent unit of code containing data relevant to the subgoal and methods for carrying out the work of the tutor with respect to that subgoal, as illustrated in Table 13.2. There must, of course, be information about how the nodes of the subgoal hierarchy interact. In addition, there must be information about just what knowledge the subgoal refers to and what parts of that knowledge the student has already acquired. In essence, curricular subgoals can, for some purposes, be thought of as checklists that show which parts of the curriculum the student has already mastered. Finally, there are certain procedural methods that must be available for each subgoal. *Instructional methods* generate the instructional treatments relevant to the subgoal. These include direct didactic instruction, coaching in an ongoing problem-solving session, selection of future problems, and other more indirect approaches.

*The Student Model.*   Each subgoal must also have diagnostic methods to decide whether a given student has or has not mastered the knowledge subsumed by the subgoal. These methods must infer mastery information from the trace of recent student learning and performance activities. The student model or curriculum for our avionics equipment troubleshooting tutor currently has the tentative structure shown in Fig. 13.6. This result is the product of considerable work of several kinds. First, we attempted to specify the missing knowledge that would have allowed novices or less-skilled airmen to behave more like experts on the problem-

---

[9] At the time this stage of our work was finished, the tutor field tests had just been completed. Although broad general indicators showed that the tutor was successful, the detailed analyses that could tie success to specific actions taken by the tutor were just being started.

TABLE 13.2
Contents of each curriculum subgoal node

---

Declarative Knowledge

Variables that identify how a given object's goals relate to the goals of others (i.e., which goals are prerequisite to the current one, and for which goals the current one is a prerequisite).

Variables that identify how the knowledge an object is trying to teach relates to the knowledge other objects are trying to teach (pointers to the knowledge layer).

Variables that represent the student's knowledge of the object's goal knowledge and functions that update those variables.

Procedural Knowledge

Functions (methods) that generate instructional interventions based upon the student model held by the given object, including both manipulations of the microworld and various forms of coaching or advising.

Functions that decide if the given object is to blame for problems that arise while objects for which it is prerequisite are in control (that is, if a student has trouble later on, the prerequisite objects can be asked if they see a reason for reviewing their lesson contents with the student).

---

solving tasks we had them do, as described above. Then we supplemented this with advice and observations from two electronics experts with considerable experience in training technicians.[10] Finally, we also considered some of the goals being developed by another research team at Bolt Beranek and Newman, Inc., for a related project focused more on conceptual than on procedural knowledge.[11]

It is important to note that the instructional methods tied to each curricular subgoal are independent in principle from the content goals of the instruction. That is, different researchers and designers might share a curriculum goal structure in terms of the subgoal hierarchy and the methods used to assess student knowledge, but they might still differ in the instructional methods they used to teach the knowledge. In fact, that is the current situation, for the most part, in the efforts of the Bolt Beranek and Newman group and our group. We want to know which methods of instruction do a better job of accomplishing which subgoals at what cost.

With this goal in mind, it becomes apparent that certain instructional goals

---

[10] The technicians were co-author Eggan and Richard Wolf, whom we thank for his participation in this work.

[11] This group consists of Allan Collins, John Frederiksen, and Barbara White, and it is working on tutors with more general skill goals. The two projects have been highly coordinated, because they have the same sponsor, the Air Force Human Resources Laboratory. Author Lesgold especially acknowledges the many insights gained from a discussion with Allan Collins during a train trip from Stuttgart to Heidelberg.

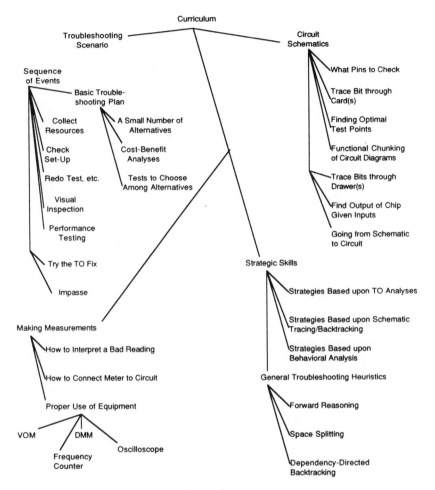

FIG. 13.6.   Curriculum for Sherlock.

may not be captured by the kinds of structures thus far described. Most notable is transfer. It is not immediately apparent that two different instructional efforts based on the kind of curriculum outline shown in Fig. 13.6 would necessarily produce the same transferability of learning. To decide issues of student transfer of knowledge, the student model (or curriculum goal structure) probably needs one of two types of changes. Perhaps it needs to be made into a more extended network, one in which each subgoal is not only part of a broader goal but also is to be achieved by the student for some part of the universe of situations in which the skill might be exercised. The other possibility, probably much better in the long run but not necessarily achievable today, is to understand the skills that produce transfer and explicitly include them in the curricular goals.[12] We believe that it is critical that the goals of instruction directly reflect concerns for transfer, by one means or the other.

***The Instructional Treatment.***   Given a clear goal structure of knowledge we want the student to acquire (both conceptual and procedural knowledge, presumably), the next issue is to specify the instructional treatments. Rather than discuss the treatments for our tutor specifically, we want to consider how treatments should be designed so that we can make determinations of their efficacy. Again, our goal is to be able to say useful things about which treatments produce which capabilities across which domains at what cost.

At one extreme, an instructional treatment is a very specific thing. We can think of it as being like a book or a particular piece of instructional software. If we consider a treatment in this sense, we can determine only whether it works better than some other specific treatment. Traditional educational psychology is full of these horserace demonstrations, and they do not give much guidance to instructional designers. However, at the other extreme, we can think of instructional principles driving intelligent instructional systems, where the instruction is assembled from the current situation and the student model according to a set of rules. These rules could be assessed by comparing them to other rules applied to the same range of teaching contexts, student capabilities, types of student models (curricular goals), and so on. If this were done, then tests of these instructional principles would have generality and would inform instructional designers.

Do we need the machine-based instruction to do this? In principle, we do not. We could ask different instructional designers to follow particular principles in their work and then test the work of a set of designers who followed one principle against those of another group who followed a different principle. In practice, this has not worked very well. Humans unintentionally color methods with their own interpretations, unconsciously want their students to do well, and thus sometimes use the methods they think would work best. What the intelligent tutoring system does in the testing arena is to add a bit of rigor to the experimental design, to more clearly separate treatments under more complex controls.

Of course, we cannot completely separate instructional principles from the specific domains in which they might apply. There is no reason to believe that instructional design knowledge is exempt from the general principle that all expertise has a substantial domain-specific component. But we can certainly use design approaches that make it easy to move from one domain to another that overlaps it. For example, whenever possible, the architectures of our tutors should be based on object-oriented programming styles (cf. Stefik & Bobrow, 1986), in

---

[12] Just because we are taking a new (cognitive) approach does not mean that we believe that new approaches to testing won't also be burdened by the incompleteness of psychological knowledge and analyses, just as were the older approaches. The progress made so far is incremental, and much is left to be done.

which the methods whereby procedures are carried out are only as particularized as is necessary. By relying heavily on inheritance hierarchies to specialize the instructional treatment methods from curricular subgoal objects, we can maximize our own transfer and develop robust methods.

## TOWARD ANALYSES OF INSTRUCTIONAL COSTS AND BENEFITS

If all of this can be done, then a variety of useful instructional experiments can be performed, and the needed tools to do these experiments can be the basis for part of a cognitive science of measurement. Here is a still partly imaginary scenario for what might transpire. The things we describe next have not yet been done, but we anticipate a first approximation to them within the next year or two.

We can develop problem samples from the various skill domains for which we want information, using domain experts to suggest problems that are informative, that is, of importance and likely to be solved well only by the better technicians. Then, we can use techniques such as the effective problem space analyses described earlier to understand better what skills are required for successful solution of such problems. Given such analyses, we can develop the curriculum goal structures for the family of domains being studied. Then, we can develop a basic tutor architecture for providing advice in the context of practice in solving realistic diagnosis problems. Finally, we can do experiments whose raw yield is a probability distribution over the student model structure, giving the probability of meeting each subgoal criterion after a specific period of time on an instantiation of the tutor with specific instructional principles driving it. Transfer can be tested by using problem samples drawn from a particular subset of the set of relevant domains.

### The Logical Character of Cognitive Measurements

This leaves a number of measurement issues, but the most critical are not statistical. For example, how should we infer general transfer from performance on a specific set of problems? More broadly, how do we summarize transfer evidence? That is, how do we represent in simplified form a probability distribution over a tree structure whose elements have interesting, and not necessarily simple, relationships with each other? Whatever we decide on as a summarization strategy is testable; further work samples can verify that assumptions about transfer implications are valid. That is, we can do experiments in which we test whether correctly carrying out a particular part of a problem solution implies the ability to handle similar parts of problems in other related domains. We can also test our ideas logically by trying to develop partial simulations of the problem-solving skills we are trying to teach.

## Instruction is Not Free: The Costs and Benefits
## of Instructional Principles and Actions

An exciting part of this scenario is that it offers a chance to begin developing a cost/benefit analysis methodology for instruction. Given a particular method of instruction, as represented by a particular set of principles or rules that drive instructional decisions in a tutor, we can test the efficacy of those rules. For each instructional subgoal at each relevant transfer criterion, we can determine the function that relates improvement in that subgoal to number of hours of tutor time with the rules that are being tested.

This may seem like a surplus of information at too fine a level of detail. Two replies can be made to that concern. First, it is a big improvement over the vague generality that Method A is better than Method B. Consider the recent controversies about whether the programming language LOGO is good for young children. Different schools and teachers take this product, make it available in different ways, and give very global tests of student capability after a single, fixed period of instruction. Only the language artifact LOGO is common to the instructional treatments, and it by itself seems to have no effect. Wouldn't we be in better shape if we could say that using LOGO in a particular kind of replicable instructional environment produced certain changes in a specific subset of the microcomponents of problem-solving skill in school arithmetic or algebra? In that way, we would know of effects that otherwise are hidden. For example, if most problems require three steps for solution, and LOGO only improves performance on the first, this is useful knowledge—more useful than just knowing that it is not general panacea.

A second reply to the above criticism is that we can now go on to develop ways of summarizing over the microstructure of instructional decisions and transfer subsets. A clear path has been posed that is substantive in nature. What does it mean to have learned a particular collection of subskills but to be missing others? Are there specific syndromes of partial learning that are worth watching for? Can we understand what causes there might be for particular syndromes in which only some skills that are directly addressed by instruction are learned and others are not? Can we, by recognizing such a syndrome, determine an instructional plan that is likely to be optimal?

## Diagnoses are Decisions: The Facade
## of Probabilistic Statements in Diagnosis

In a sense, the achievement tests of today, by not being tied very directly to the specifics of cognitive performance and by being reliable only as general statistical indicators, serve education as indicator categories as "grippe" once served medicine. What is needed to make further advances, at least in our ability to tailor instruction to individual student needs, is to be able to make causally integrated diagnoses. Just as a doctor is most satisfied when he can explain the mechanism that led to the manifestations in a patient, so we in instruction must be trying to develop explanatory diagnostic capability in which the relations between microindicators, or items, are a primary part of the diagnosis, or scoring. When all we can say is that certain scores indicate a certain probability of success in a broad, untunable curriculum, we should feel dissatisfied and be looking for more complete understanding.

## COGNITIVE APPROACHES TO TESTING ARE AT AN INTERMEDIATE LEVEL OF DEVELOPMENT

One final thought. When studying expertise in radiological diagnosis (Lesgold, 1984; Lesgold et al., 1988), we were impressed with the nonmonotonicity of performance over the course of acquiring diagnostic skill. First-year residents could make speedy judgments that were often accurate, but they weren't quite good enough. To get better, they had to learn a large body of medical diagnostic knowledge and integrate that knowledge with the perceptual learning that came from practice in recognizing signs in x-ray pictures. Experts with years of experience, although very fast, sometimes took most of their diagnosis time to build a mental model of the patient, one in which the diagnosis *made sense,* that is, was logically consistent with the many observed signs and symptoms. In between the superficial, but only moderately accurate, probabilistic thinking of the novice and the highly reliable logic-driven diagnosis of the expert, residents were often less accurate in complex cases than rank beginners were. The task they had undertaken was not yet sufficiently automated. Too many details had to be thought about. Too few syndrome models, or schemata, were sufficiently elaborated and quickly usable. Trying to learn to do diagnosis properly and at superhigh levels of accuracy, they forgot details as their minds became overloaded.

We believe that instructional testing is entering this middle phase in its development. The task of doing it right seems incredibly onerous compared to the quick, cheap methods of paper-and-pencil testing. But the easy way isn't good enough. The benefits of testing must be considered as well as the costs. Too many students fail to achieve what they could. Like doctors who are unwilling to let 15% of their patients go uncured just to make life simple, we must go on through a period of stumbling, of apparent inefficiency, to build efficient techniques of diagnosis— techniques driven by the criteria of coherence and completeness of explanation.

Pushing the metaphor one bit further, we must also remember that even very good doctors quite reasonably react to many minor crises by doing a bit of listening, almost no testing, and then providing a diffuse treatment ("take two aspirin and call me in the morning"). Our ultimate goal is not more detail and more complexity—that is just a stage through which we probably have to pass to get where we're going. The goal, which requires understanding of the course of acquisition for complex cognitive skills and of means for measuring that acquisition, is not simply to be more detailed and complete, but rather to understand when and how qualitative details of cognitive activity can lead to improved instructional design and better adaptation to individual student needs.

## ACKNOWLEDGMENTS

The work reported in this chapter was supported by contracts with the Air Force Human Resources Laboratory (through subcontracts with HumRRO and Universal Energy Systems) and with the Office of Naval Research. We are grateful for their support. None of these organizations necessarily endorse or agree with the views expressed herein.

## REFERENCES

Barrett, J., & Hedberg, J. (1987). *Using computers intelligently in tertiary education.* Kensington, Australia: University of New South Wales.

Benbassett, J., & Bachar-Bassan, E. (1984). A comparison of initial diagnostic hypotheses of medical students and internists. *Journal of Medical Education, 59,* 951–956.

Bonar, J. G. (1985). *Understanding the bugs of novice programmers.* Doctoral dissertation. Amherst, MA: University of Massachusetts.

Feltovich, P. J. (September, 1981). *Knowledge-based components of expertise in medical diagnosis* (Tech. Rep. No. PDS-2). University of Pittsburgh, Learning Research and Development Center.

Gitomer, D. H. (1984). *A cognitive analysis of a complex troubleshooting task.* Unpublished doctoral dissertation, University of Pittsburgh, Pittsburgh, PA.

Hakel, M. D. (1986). Personnel selection and placement. In M. R. Rosenzweig & L. W. Porter (Eds.), *Annual Review of Psychology,* 351–380.

Lesgold, A. M. (1984). Acquiring expertise. In J. R. Anderson & S. M. Kosslyn (Eds.), *Tutorials in learning and memory: Essays in honor of Gordon Bower* (pp. 31–60). San Francisco: W. H. Freeman.

Lesgold, A. M., Rubinson, H., Feltovich, P., Glaser, R., Klopfer, D., & Wang, Y. (1988). Expertise in a complex skill: Diagnosing x-ray pictures. In M. T. H. Chi, R. Glaser, & M. J. Farr (Eds.), *The nature of expertise* (311–342). Hillsdale, NJ: Lawrence Erlbaum Associates.

Lesgold, A. M., Lajoie, S. P., Eastman, R., Eggan, G., Gitomer, D., Glaser, R., Greenberg, L., Logan, D., Magone, M., Weiner, A., Wolf, R., & Yengo, L. (1986). *Cognitive task analysis to enhance technical skills training and assessment* (Tech. Rep.) University of Pittsburgh, the Learning Research and Development Center.

Logan, D. & Eastman, R. (1986). Unpublished raw data.

Patil, R. S., Szolovits, P., & Schwartz, W. B. (1984). Causal understanding of patient illness in medical diagnosis. In W. J. Clancey & E. H. Shortliffe (Eds.), *Readings in medical artificial intelligence* (pp. 339–360). Reading, MA: Addison-Wesley.

Scribner, S. (1984). Studying working intelligence. In B. Rogoff & J. Lave (Eds.), *Everyday cognition: Its development in social context* (pp. 9–40), Cambridge, MA: Harvard University Press.

Spohrer, J., Soloway, E. M., & Pope, E. (1985). A goal/plan analysis of buggy Pascal programs. *Human–Computer Interaction, 1,* 163–207.

Stefik, M. & Bobrow, D. G. (1986). Object oriented programming: Themes and variations. *AI Magazine, 6,* 40–62.

Wescourt, K. T., Beard, M., & Gould, L. (1977). Knowledge-based adaptive curriculum sequencing for CAI: Application of a network representation. *Proceedings of the Annual ACM Conference* (pp. 234–240). Seattle, WA.

# 14

## Monitoring Cognitive Processing in Semantically Complex Domains

Carl H. Frederiksen
Alain Breuleux
*McGill University*

The monitoring of a student's progress in acquiring knowledge and skill in knowledge-rich domains such as composition, biology, geography, or history is typically accomplished by such procedures as weekly quizzes, laboratory exercises, written papers, and midterm examinations. Such activities normally employ written materials and require that a student solve problems and compose written text. They usually are prepared by a teacher and are used to motivate students' learning by providing them with situations requiring that they acquire particular knowledge and skill. Standardized tests are generally administered at the end of the year when it is too late to make much use of them for teaching; they are used to provide a basis for evaluation of student learning and of the effectiveness of instruction (e.g., at the class, school, district, state or provincial level). Such tests generally employ the multiple-choice format for reasons of economy and objectivity, even though they are strongly biased toward the assessment of factual knowledge at the expense of comprehension, and toward the ability to recognize a correct solution to a problem rather than to actually generate a solution. There usually is no way for a teacher to discover to what extent a student has acquired a deep understanding of the concepts, principles and methods within a domain from scores on multiple-choice tests. Furthermore, there is an obvious mismatch between the types of tasks used to build competencies and monitor performance during learning, and the multiple-choice tests used to evaluate learning.

One common alternative to the multiple-choice examination is the essay examination, which is relatively easy to construct but is difficult and expensive to grade. In the case of English essays, a method called holistic scoring has been developed for large-scale testing in which judges are asked (after discussion about standards and practice scoring) to read each essay quickly and score it impressionistically. The pooled judgments of two or more judges may be reliable in the psychometric sense, but there is no way to know precisely what the score means in terms of knowledge, skill, ability, or comprehension.

In other domains, one can pose questions or problems to do with particular topics such as photosynthesis or the respiratory system, but if answers were graded impressionistically we still would not know how to interpret a score or discover what misconceptions were held by a student. Of course it would be possible to develop a set of *ad hoc* rules for scoring a particular essay topic by specifying what knowledge, principles, and conclusions a good written essay or response should contain. An essay could be scored in terms of the number and kinds of such elements it contained, but this would provide incomplete information at best. Furthermore, *ad hoc* rules would have to be developed for each domain; comparisons of performance across domains would be difficult due to the lack of comparable measures.

A student's conception of a problem, state of knowledge, or solution process could be described better by specifying the particular elements (e.g., concepts, rules) and relationships among elements that the student included or manipulated (and how), as well as those elements or manipulations that, although normally included by persons expert in the domain, were omitted by the student. Such a detailed description would be useful to the student for feedback, to the teacher for its diagnostic value, and to curriculum builders for evaluation and revision of teaching materials and methods. However, compared with the speed and accuracy of scoring multiple-choice tests, such scoring of essays or written responses to questions would not only be onerous and time consuming but also would require judgments by people highly trained in the analysis of natural-language discourse and problem-solving protocols. But with the development of precise models of conceptual knowledge based on the semantics of natural language and of computer methods for extracting such knowledge from natural language, computer-assisted scoring is now possible, and the possibility of totally computerized scoring is on the horizon.

This chapter examines the possibility of applying models and methods of semantic analysis to the monitoring of students' knowledge and performance in natural environments of comprehension, verbal production, and problem-solving such as occur in the knowledge domains mentioned previously. After reviewing current advances in modeling semantic representation, an approach to evaluating knowledge and processing is outlined and illustrated by means of examples in the domains of chemistry and written composition. The research that is described involved computer-aided analysis of verbal protocols and of expert-generated protocols to define models of expert knowledge in a domain. It should eventually be possible to write computer procedures to automate such analyses.

## SEMANTICALLY COMPLEX TASK DOMAINS

This chapter examines current models of semantic representation and processing from the point of view of their applicability for evaluating students' knowledge in subject matter domains and for monitoring their cognitive processing in *semantically complex task domains*. By *semantically complex domains* we mean task domains for which: (a) complex meaningful language and other symbolic expression, patterns, actions, and task structures occur; (b) successful performance requires complex conceptual and relational domain knowledge relevant to the task; and (c) successful performance depends on semantic representations and semantic processing operations. Semantic representation and processing are required to comprehend and produce linguistic messages and other symbolic expressions, patterns, actions, and task structures; to acquire, retrieve, and use conceptual knowledge; and to represent, plan, and control complex procedures and actions for the attainment of task-relevant goals.

Semantic representations and procedures for generating, retrieving, or operating on them are active areas of research within cognitive psychology, artificial intelligence, and computational linguistics. Well-defined models of semantic representation have been developed and applied in computational models and experimental studies of performance in semantically complex domains. By examining these models and their experimental applications, we hope to illustrate potentially fruitful approaches to monitoring and diagnosing knowledge and performance that may be implemented in computer-based learning and diagnostic systems.

All human cognitive processing involves knowledge—one's store of facts about the world, about actions, and about concepts symbolized in language— and the use of knowledge to represent meaning in language, symbols and patterns, and as a basis for representing and controlling actions to achieve situationally dependent goals. Consequently the acquisition, representation, and manipulation of conceptual knowledge has been a central concern of cognitive scientists. Research has been concerned with such diverse problems as the semantics of natural language, the comprehension and production of natural language texts, the structure of conceptual representations in memory, knowledge-based reasoning, the semantics of procedures and problems, and the formal representation of semantic structures in computer systems (for natural language processing and in knowledge-based systems). This work has converged in the development of formal theories of semantic representation that are relatively general (rather than specific to particular content domains). These employ the formalism of *semantic networks* (or equivalently, *conceptual graphs*), an innovation that may be traced to the work of Peirce in the late 19th century (cf. Roberts, 1973).

One branch of cognitive science has been concerned with *declarative* knowledge structure and representation. This concern with the form and content of conceptual knowledge (i.e., with "knowing that") is most prevalent in research on such problems as natural language processing, comprehension of connected discourse, text generation, learning (i.e., the acquisition and integration of knowledge), semantic memory, and reasoning in semantically rich domains. However, the conceptual representations associated with such *declarative* structures also have been found to be applicable to such meaningful information structures as procedures, experienced events, visual scenes or patterns, and even complex situations or task structures. For example, it has been recognized that procedural knowledge (i.e., "knowing how") may be represented declaratively, and that such declarative representations of procedures may be used as instructions to control actions, much as expressions within a computer programming language are interpreted by a compiler as instructions to be executed (Anderson, 1982; Frederiksen & Renaud, 1989). The advantage of having a declarative semantic system represent procedures is that complex networks of descriptive and control information may be expressed within a single conceptual structure. Therefore, research on conceptual representation is concerned with a broad range of semantic structures including both declarative and procedural knowledge.

A second branch of cognitive science has made the development of a theory of goal-directed human action the central concern. Cognition is described in terms of (a) procedural knowledge that represents and controls human action, and (b) the plans and heuristic strategies that govern the use of this knowledge to solve problems. Viewing human knowledge and action as problem-solving, Newell and Simon (1972) recognized that it was possible to develop and test models of human information processing in well-structured domains that are semantically restricted, that is, that have a restricted number of states that must be represented and thus allow for the possibility of identifying a delimited problem space within which one or more solution paths could be defined. The production-system formalism was developed to represent the procedural knowledge required to solve a problem.

Production systems are programs composed of condition-action rules that are applied to move from one state to another in the problem space until the solution state is reached. Although the conditions associated with production rules involve states whose descriptions are symbolically represented by a formal descriptive language[1], the emphasis has been placed on the development of rules rather than on the language used to describe problem states. Clearly, a general semantic representation "language" could serve the role of a state description language within the production system theory. Consequently, the theory is not limited to semantically restricted problem states. The theory could be extended to semantically complex domains if precise and general formalisms were available to represent the conceptual information involved in semantically complex problem states.

---

[1] Newell and Simon (1972) proposed the BNF grammar formalism to define a state description language.

Knowledge and the abilities associated with comprehension, reasoning, and problem-solving have long figured importantly in ability and achievement testing. However, such tests generally have not been based on formal theories of the processes that underlie performance, nor, due to a reliance on item-based, multiple-choice testing formats, have they employed task conditions that are representative of the natural environments of knowledge-based cognition (N. Frederiksen, 1984). Within cognitive psychology, the most serious attention given to individual differences was the effort made to model or simulate the problem-solving processes of individual subjects as reflected in their on-line think-aloud and performance protocols (Ericsson & Simon, 1984; Newell & Simon, 1972). Recent research on natural language processing has been modeling and studying on-line processing (e.g., Renaud & Frederiksen, 1988), and individual differences have received attention in the "expert-novice" literature (Glaser, 1985). However, this research has not yet led to the development and testing of general procedures for modeling the knowledge and processing of individual subjects.

Modeling individual subjects' on-line processing in complex tasks has been one objective of researchers involved in developing and evaluating intelligent tutoring systems to teach problem-solving in well-structured domains (Clancey, 1986a). In these systems, an individual's performance is continuously monitored to identify his or her state of knowledge and thereby to build a model of the student. In one approach, a student model is defined in terms of an expert system in which a learner is described in terms of his or her knowledge of production rules in the system. The student model is determined by inferring the rules the learner has applied on the basis of his or her responses (e.g., Clancey, 1986a). In another approach, the tutoring system incorporates a "qualitative model" of knowledge in a domain (such as electronic circuits) and a learner's knowledge is described in relation to this model. Clancey (1986b) has argued that this shift of orientation in intelligent tutoring systems from instruction based on models of experts' processing in a domain to instruction based on qualitative models of knowledge in a domain makes the study of network representations important as a "foundation for a science and engineering of qualitative models."

As domain knowledge models become semantically more complex, and as attempts are made to develop intelligent tutoring systems for instruction in a broader range of domains and with a wider range of teaching strategies, powerful and general semantic network models assume a greater importance in the development of learning and diagnostic systems. If tutoring or diagnostic systems ultimately are to be successful, they have to be capable of evaluating a student's knowledge and use of knowledge in a manner comparable to that of an expert teacher in a content area. Typically, this evaluation involves discourse communication between the teacher and the student. Evaluation, correction, and explanation are based on inferences concerning the student's knowledge and strategies as reflected in his or her actions and discourse, including planning and explanations of the reasons for his or her actions. Such teaching expertise requires the evaluation of semantic/conceptual representations acquired by a student in performing a task, of conceptual (including procedural) knowledge exhibited or used by a student, and of planning, reasoning, or other processes applied by the student in using knowledge as a basis for action.

Models of semantic representation and methods for analyzing the processes involved in generating and manipulating semantic structures ought to provide a basis for cognitive monitoring or diagnosis of learners' knowledge and performance in semantically complex tasks. Cognitive diagnosis in semantically complex domains involves the evaluation of: (a) an individual's state of knowledge in a domain, (b) the semantic representations an individual generates in the performance of a task, and (c) the processes that are employed in retrieving, generating, applying, modifying, or in other ways manipulating knowledge representations. However, before we can consider the application of semantic representation models and methods to cognitive diagnosis, we must first define more precisely what we mean by a semantic representation or semantic processing operation. This is the theme of the next section.

## MODELS OF SEMANTIC REPRESENTATION
## AND PROCESSING

### Defining Semantic Representations

Semantic representations are constructs proposed by cognitive scientists to model the internal symbolic structures that are used to represent conceptual meanings associated with language, perception, and thought. Although theories of conceptual representation derive from many sources (cf., Anderson & Bower, 1973; Sowa, 1984), the goal is to develop a unified model that can account for facts about natural language understanding and production, perception, memory, and reasoning. In psychology and computer science, an effort was made to use natural language semantics as a basis for identifying the nature and structure of conceptual relational structures in memory (Anderson & Bower, 1973; C. H. Frederiksen, 1975; Kintsch, 1974; Rumelhart & Norman, 1975; Schank, 1975). Since then, conceptual network models have become more precisely defined and linked to computational procedures for generating semantic representations, called *propositions*, from natural language. In addition, models of conceptual representations, called *conceptual frames*, have been proposed to represent particular types of connected knowledge structures represented in natural-language discourse and long-term memory. Conceptual frame theory provides a "bridge" from the semantic representation of natural language in terms of propositions to the structure of meaning in memory in terms of linked conceptual frame structures.

This section concentrates on the formal definition of propositions, of conceptual frames, and of procedures for generating them from natural language discourse. Although the examples given are based on the models and procedures developed in our laboratory, the descriptions and generalizations offered apply in varying degrees to the work done by other groups. The following section discusses the use of conceptual representations in evaluating knowledge and processing in semantically complex domains.

***Canonical Frames and Semantic Grammars.***   Formally, a semantic network (or "conceptual graph") is a type of data structure composed of two kinds of entities: nodes and links (or arcs). The basic structural unit is a relational triple composed of two nodes that are connected by a link into a relational structure. Networks are data structures composed of sets of relational triples. Nodes are either simple or complex. Simple nodes, **S-nodes,** refer to: (a) lexical concepts, (b) primitive concepts defined by a particular semantic model, or (c) proposition identifiers. Complex nodes, **C-nodes,** are nodes that are explicitly decomposed in a network into other nodes. **Links** are identified by names referring to the type of relation represented by the link.

To illustrate these ideas, consider the example in Fig. 14.1, which contains a semantic network generated for the following sentence taken from a procedural text in chemical engineering:

Collect the samples in an air-tight bottle.

In the Fig. 14.1, nodes in the network are enclosed in rectangles and relational links are enclosed in ellipses. Examples of S-nodes are "samples," "DEF," and "7.2," and an example of a C-node is "OBJECT." Notice that an OBJECT node is decomposed into a S-node and another complex node (DETERMINER). Arrows in Fig. 14.1 either connect nodes to links or they connect C-nodes to other nodes that decompose them. In the theory of conceptual graphs, S-nodes contain "identifiers," entities that label semantic information. This information may be (a) a *primitive concept* (for example, "TOK," token, a primitive determiner defined within the model); (b) a *lexicalized concept* represented by a word in the lexicon; or (c) a *proposition identifier,* a numeric label for a proposition or word referring to one or more propositions.

A proposition is a particular type of network structure, specified by a model, that is composed of nodes and relations, has a truth value, and is an independent unit of semantic information that may be expressed in natural language. In Fig. 14.1 there are three propositions: one event (proposition 7.1) and two states (propositions 7.2 and 7.3). When an arrow points from a relation to a proposition number (e.g., from RESULT.REL to "7.2"), the proposition labeled by the identifier is embedded in the node linked to the relation, that is, within another proposition. In the example, propositions 7.2 and 7.3 are embedded within 7.1 (i.e., in the "result node"). In the figure, positive truth-value is implicit and not marked explicitly.

Frequently, a "predicate-argument" notation is employed to represent propositions. In this equivalent notation, each proposition consists of a proposition number, followed by a predicate, followed by a series of labelled slots. To illustrate the conversion from conceptual graph to predicate-argument notation, the propositions represented in Fig. 14.1 may be written as follows:

| Prop. # | Predicate (head) | Argument slots |
|---------|------------------|----------------|
| 7.1 | (EVENT | (ACT(collect)) |
|  |  | (OBJECT.REL(OBJECT:samples(DETERMINER('DEF)(NUMBER('PLUR))))) |
|  |  | (RESULT.REL(7.2)(7.3)) |
|  |  | ('POS)) |
| 7.2 | (STATE | (STATE.OBJECT(OBJECT:samples(DETERMINER('DEF)(NUMBER('PLUR))))) |
|  |  | (LOCATIVE.RELATION.STATE(OBJECT:bottle(DETERMINER('TOK) |
|  |  | (NUMBER('SING))))) |
|  |  | ('POS)) |
| 7.3 | (STATE | (STATE.OBJECT(OBJECT:bottle(DETERMINER('TOK)(NUMBER('SING))))) |
|  |  | (ATTRIBUTE.RELATION.STATE(air-tight)) |
|  |  | ('POS)) |

Here each numbered proposition consists of a head followed by a series of labelled slots (slot labels are in upper case). For example, the head of proposition 7.1 is "EVENT" and the argument slots are ACT, OBJECT.REL (affected object relation), RESULT.REL (result relation), and POS (positive truth value). The ACT slot contains a lexical identifier *(collect)*; the OBJECT.REL slot contains the complex concept OBJECT that is decomposed into a lexical identifier *(samples)* and a DETERMINER having the values ('DEF) and (NUMBER ('PLUR); the RESULT.REL slot contains the proposition identifiers 7.2 and 7.3; and the truth value is POS. The reader familiar with list structures can recognize that the predicate-argument representations given above are list structure representations of the network in Fig. 14.1. The only modification was the movement of the proposition number out of the first slot to improve readability.

To define a semantic network model requires: (a) specification of the content of all nodes; (b) definition of all relational links and primitive concepts; and (c) specification of all patterns of relational structures and node decompositions that are permitted. Any model of semantic representation may be examined in terms of how it accomplishes these specifications. Two approaches have been taken in the literature on semantic representation to defining a semantic representation model: definition by means of **canonical frames** (e.g., Schank, 1975, Sowa, 1984), or definition by means of **semantic grammars** (Frederiksen, 1986).

A *canonical representation* (or *frame*) is a particular network structure or pattern that contains *variables*. Variables are symbols in a pattern that can be

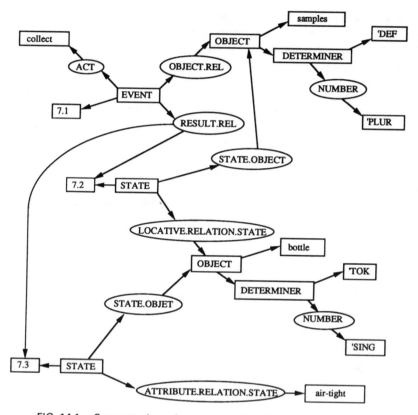

FIG. 14.1.   Conceptual graph representation of "Collect the samples in an air-tight bottle."

replaced by specific values. For example, in proposition 7.1, all S-nodes might be replaced by variables:

7.1 (EVENT (ACT(X))
(OBJECT.REL(OBJECT:Y(DETERMINER(P)(NUMBER(Q)))))
RESULT.REL(Z) ('POS))

that could be bound to (i.e., "assigned") the values given in proposition 7.1. Such a canonical frame could include *constraints* on values of variables; for example, X might be constrained to be a class of actions that includes *collect,* Y might be any object, and Z might be constrained to be a stative proposition or propositions specifying a location. A canonical frame defined in this way thus is capable of representing a large number of structures or "instantiations." The canonical frame approach to defining a propositional representation consists of defining an exhaustive set of such patterns, each of which represents a particular type of structural possibility. In computational semantic systems adopting this approach to propositional analysis, the set of such frames is stored in a dictionary. In linguistic terminology, this is an example of a *slot grammar*. The power of a slot grammar depends on the number and kinds of canonical frames included in the dictionary.

A *semantic grammar* adopts a generative approach to definition, specifying a model by means of rules that generate all acceptable patterns within the grammar. It is well known within the theory of generative grammar that a relatively small set of recursive rules can be much more powerful than a large set of canonical frames. To illustrate, in Fig. 14.2 we give the subset of rules from the semantic BNF grammar for propositions developed by Frederiksen (1986; Frederiksen, Décary & Hoover, 1988) that are required to generate the conceptual graph in Fig. 14.1. Rules are applied in order. Each rule specifies how a structure corresponding to the rule name may be formed by applying other rules (that are "called"). Eventually, the sequence of rules leads to lexical or proposition identifiers, or primitive concepts. The rules of this grammar are written so that rules whose names do not begin with the symbol # write their names into a parsing tree when they are applied. By this means, the application of rules directly generates a conceptual graph representation for each proposition.

*Generating Propositions: Frame Instantiation and Parsing.* These two approaches to defining a semantic representation have been associated with different computational approaches to generating propositions from natural language sentences (Ritchie, 1983). In the first approach, *frame instantiation*, propositions are generated by finding a canonical frame that can be matched to an input sentence. Frame matching normally involves matching semantic structures to syntactic patterns that instantiate them, and assigning variables values derived from sentence information (e.g., lexical values). Canonical frames are often specific to particular entries in the lexicon (e.g., verbs), so that much of the "work" that is done in building such a computational system involves building canonical frames into the lexicon.

In the second approach, *semantic parsing*, rules in a semantic grammar have associated with them tests that are applied to lexical, morphological, and/or syntactic representations of the sentence being analyzed and to information (e.g., semantic markers) in the lexicon. If the conditions associated with a test are satisfied, the rule is applied to generate a node in a parsing tree and transfer control to other rules (that are "called" by the rule). Most semantic parsing systems purport to carry out direct semantic parsing, that is, parsing in which there is no prior syntactic analysis of a sentence input to the system. However, Ritchie (1983) has observed that such systems inevitably incorporate *syntactic* categories into their semantic rules. Psycholinguistic evidence (Ferreira & Clifton, 1986; Morrow, 1986) and considerations involved in text generation systems

```
#PROPOSITION ::= EVENT I SYSTEM I STATE I PROPOSITIONAL.RELATION I
        IDENTITY.RELATION ALGEBRAIC.RELATION I FUNCTION I BINARY.DEPENDENCY I
        CONJOINT.DEPENDENCY
EVENT ::= #PROP.NUMBER ACT {#RESULTIVE.FRAME {#ACT.IDENTIFYING.RELATION}*
        {#TENSE} {R.ASPECT}* {R.ITERATIVE} {#MODALITY}* #TRUTH.VALUE*
ACT ::= #ACT.IDENTIFIER I 'EMPTY I 'WH-QUES
#RESULTIVE.FRAME ::= {AGENT.REL} {OBJECT.REL} {ACT.REL} {PROCESS.REL}
        {INSTRUMENT.REL} {RECIPIENT.REL} {SOURCE.REL} {RESULT.REL} {GOAL.REL}
OBJECT.REL ::= #AFFECTED.OBJ* I 'EMPTY I 'WH-QUES
#AFFECTED.OBJ ::= OBJECT I #PROPOSITION.LABEL*
RESULT.REL ::= #RESULT* I 'EMPTY I 'WH-QUES
#RESULT ::= OBJECT I #PROPOSITION.LABEL*
STATE ::= #PROP.NUMBER STATE.OBJECT #STATE.IDENTIFYING.RELATION* {#TENSE}
        {R.ASPECT}* {R.ITERATIVE} {#MODALITY}* #TRUTH.VALUE*
STATE.OBJECT ::= OBJECT* I 'EMPTY I 'WH-QUES
OBJECT ::= #DETERMINED.OBJECT I #PRONOUN.IDENTIFIER I #PROPER.NOUN.IDENTIFIER
#DETERMINED.OBJECT ::= #OBJECT.IDENTIFIER DETERMINER I #PROPOSITION.LABEL
        DETERMINER
DETERMINER ::= #NON.GENERIC I #GENERIC I 'EMPTY
#NON.GENERIC ::= #NG.DETERMINER #NG.QUANTIFIER {DETERMINER}
#NG.DETERMINER ::= 'DEF I 'TOK
#NG.QUANTIFIER ::= NUMBER I DEGREE
#STATE.IDENTIFYING.RELATION ::= CATEGORY.RELATION.STATE I IS.A.RELATION.STATE I
        PART.RELATION.STATE I IS.PART.RELATION.STATE I ATTRIBUTE.RELATION.STATE
        I LOCATIVE.RELATION.STATE I TEMPORAL.RELATION.STATE I
        DURATIVE.RELATION.STATE I THEME.RELATION.STATE
ATTRIBUTE.RELATION.STATE ::= #ATTRIBUTE.IDENTIFIER {DEGREE}*
        {ATTRIBUTE.RELATION}* I 'EMPTY I'WH-QUES
LOCATIVE.RELATION.STATE ::= #LOCATION* I 'EMPTY I 'WH-QUES
#LOCATION ::= #LOCATION.IDENTIFIER {DEGREE}* I OBJECT I #ACT.IDENTIFIER I
        #COORDINATES
NUMBER ::= #INTEGER I #NUMBER.IDENTIFIER {DEGREE}* I 'SING I 'PLUR I INTEGER.PAIR I
        'EMPTY I 'WH-QUES
#TRUTH.VALUE ::= 'POS I 'NEG I 'INT
```

BNF Notation:  Uppercase identifier = a rule name
        Quoted uppercase identifier = a primitive concept
        a # at the beginning of a rule name = a "hidden" rule
        ::= following a rulename = a rewrite rule
        I = or (choice among rule sequences separated by this symbol)
        { } enclose rules that are optional
        * following a rulename indicates that the rule is repeatable
        rules are applied in sequence given in the grammar

FIG. 14.2. Subset of rules from propositional grammar required to generate the example in Figure 14.1.

(in which sentences are generated from semantic representations, McKeown, 1985) dictate a "mixed" approach to semantic parsing.

In our computational system (Frederiksen, Décary, & Hoover, 1988), propositions are generated according to a mixed approach. Sentences are first analyzed syntactically by a deterministic parser that applies rules based on the current Government and Binding Theory of generative syntax (Chomsky, 1981). In the semantic component of our system, rules in the propositional grammar have associated with them sequences of "dynamic rules" that apply tests to the syntactic trees output by the syntactic parser (as well as to semantic markers in the lexicon). If a test is successful, the rule writes a trace of itself into the current proposition tree, and passes control to the next rule. Currently the system can analyze a relatively small subset of English expressing events and states as well as tense, aspect, modality and truth-value.

## Semantic Representation in Natural Language Processing

Research in the fields of natural language understanding and text comprehension have led to a stratified theory of natural language processing that we may describe as both multilevel and modular. The theory is multilevel in the sense that multiple representations are assumed to be generated for a natural language input. In its strongest form, these levels of representation are strictly ordered in the sense that each representation is assumed to be generated from representations generated at the level immediately preceding it. The theory is modular in the sense that distinct processes are associated with the generation of representations at each level, and these processes are assumed not to interact with one another (Fodor, 1983). In a modular system, component processes influence one another only by means of the data they output for consideration by another component process. Data obtained from eye movement, on-line reading times, and on-line text interpretation (Just, Carpenter & Woolley, 1982; Kieras, 1981; Raynor, Carlson & Frazier, 1983; Renaud & Frederiksen, 1988) provide evidence that the comprehension process is modular and parallel.

Levels of representation that have been identified in text comprehension are summarized in Fig. 14.3. These involve the following three categories of representations: *language units* (word/morpheme sequences, syntactic trees, syntactic dependency graphs), *propositions* (text base, augmented proposition sequences, derived propositions), and *conceptual graph structures* (descriptive semantic networks, linked semantic networks, and conceptual frames). Similar levels of representation have been identified in stratified models of speech understanding (Ermann, 1977), and the multilevel representation model also has its parallel in stratificational and dependency syntax approaches in linguistics (e.g., Mel'cuk, 1979).

*Representation of Linguistic Structures.*    We may identify three levels of representation of linguistic structure that are involved in providing input to the propositional analysis component: *word and morpheme sequences* (which form the input to the syntactic parsing component), *syntactic parse trees* (which summarize syntactic information available to the semantic analysis component), and *syntactic dependency relations* linking information in syntactic trees, for example, relations linking anaphoric elements such as pronouns to their referents (Halliday & Hasan, 1976), and thematically related elements across sentences (Grimes, 1975). Con-

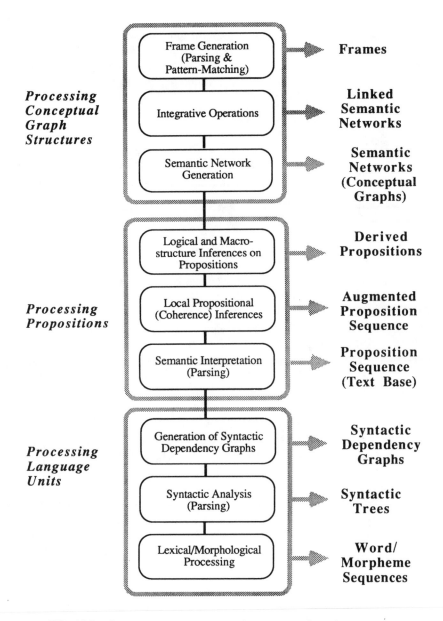

FIG. 14.3.   Component processes and representations in text processing.

vincing arguments for modular processing in sentence interpretation have been given based on experimental evidence (e.g., Ferreira & Clifton, 1986; Seidenberg & Tanenhaus, 1986). Properties of these various linguistic representations are known to exert independent effects on comprehension (Graesser, Hoffman & Clark, 1980) and to represent expressive alternatives in systems for text generation (McKeown, 1985).

*Propositional Representation.*    In current theories, a proposition is regarded as an intermediate semantic representation that is specialized both for the representation of chunks of conceptual information in natural language and for logical reasoning. As a semantic base for natural language, propositions represent all semantic distinctions that are reflected in natural language sentences. As a basis for reasoning, propositions serve as truth-valued and quantified predicates for logical reasoning operations (Sowa, 1984), probably according to a fuzzy logic (Zadeh, 1974). Once propositions are "extracted" from natural language, the only information that remains that is specific to language is the set of lexical identifiers that identify concepts in propositions. Propositional representations include propositions that are encoded directly in natural language, and in addition, propositions that are derived from local coherence inferences that bridge gaps or represent relations among a sequence of related propositions in discourse (e.g., Townsend, 1983; Tyler, 1983), and propositions that are derived to summarize or extend the literal discourse meaning through the application of "macrostructure" and logical operators (VanDijk & Kintsch, 1983).

Current propositional models are defined very specifically and represent a large proportion of the semantic distinctions found in linguistic research to be marked in natural language. In addition, the development of the theory of theta-roles in syntactic theory provides a formal mechanism for linking semantic structures to syntactic theories. Characteristics of propositional models are illustrated using the model of Frederiksen (1975; 1986; Frederiksen, Décary, & Hoover, 1988). Propositional models are capable of representing explicitly a great variety of semantic relations and structures found in natural language, mathematical expressions, chemical equations, or other symbolic languages. These include the following types of propositions (see Rule 1 in Fig. 14.2):

1. *Events,* causal systems involving a cause or *agent,* an *action,* and a change in a situation from a *source* (for example, a state) to a *result* (for example, a different state). Components of an event include: a *resultive frame* that specifies *case relations* representing the internal structure of events; and *act. identifying relations* that specify properties of actions such as attributes, location, time, duration, and so on. Like all types of propositions, events also include tense, aspect, iterative, modality, and truth value specifications.

2. *Systems*, structures representing a *process*, together with a *processive frame* that specifies the object characterized by the process (the patient), and any related objects, actions, states, processes or other information involved in the system. Systems also may include *process identifying relations* that specify properties of a process.

3. *States*, relations identifying properties of objects as well as their determination and quantification.

4. *Propositional relations*, properties of abstract concepts representing propositions;

5. *Identities*, relations linking concepts or propositions into identity sets;

6. *Algebraic relations*, transitive and intransitive *order* and *equivalence* relations applied to variables that may represent values identified in other propositions;

7. *Functions*, operations defined on *operands* that return *values*;

8. *Binary dependency relations*, relations that make one proposition depend on another such as *causative relations*, *conditional relations* and *logical* (material conditional and material biconditional) *implication*;

9. *Conjoint dependency relations: and, alternating or,* and *exclusive or* relations.

Such propositional representations, defined by semantic grammars, are sufficiently powerful that they may be applied to the analysis of a great variety of natural language discourse, including scientific and technical text, written discourse and think-aloud protocols obtained from experts or students performing in semantically complex tasks, mathematical expressions, chemical equations, and other formal languages. Although as yet only some propositions may be generated automatically from text by computer, we have developed software that guides a user in applying the rules of a grammar to generate tree structures as output. This program can be used with the propositional grammar or any other grammar expressed using BNF notation.

In the stratified theory of comprehension, the generation of propositions provides the semantic base information from which the construction of conceptual frame representations takes place.

*Conceptual Frame Representations.*    Conceptual frame representations are connected network structures that are assumed to provide the means by which knowledge is represented in long-term memory. Unlike propositions, conceptual frames are not cut up into isolated chunks of information, but rather they are vast networks of interconnected conceptual units. Research in the field of knowledge integration (Hayes-Roth & Thorndyke, 1979) has shown that when relational links between concepts are expressed close together in a text (i.e., within propositions or neighboring propositions) subjects are likely to learn the relationships, but when they are expressed in widely separated parts of a text subjects are less likely to remember the relationships. Such experiments suggest that there are distinct processes associated with linking conceptual information into a network that are required when information is not directly linked within propositions. This process is referred to as semantic network generation in Fig. 14.3. Figure 14.1 illustrates a result of this process, since the network representations for three propositions have been linked into a single network.

In addition to integrative operations within a text, research has repeatedly demonstrated that there are distinct processes associated with integrating text-derived information into existing conceptual information in long-term memory. Integrative processes include a variety of retrieval, inferential, and reasoning processes that operate in using prior knowledge to understand or interpret new text-derived conceptual information.

In addition to such descriptive conceptual networks constructed from a propositional base and prior knowledge, research on the comprehension of particular types of texts, such as stories, procedures, narratives, dialogue, and problems, has demonstrated that text understanding involves in addition high-level knowledge about these structures (C. H. Frederiksen, 1989). Both canonical frame and semantic frame grammar approaches have been applied to characterize this knowledge of high-level conceptual frame structures and the processes associated with using such knowledge. Evidence suggests that both frame instantiation and semantic parsing (i.e., application of rules in a semantic grammar) processes occur in comprehension. Frame instantiation processes are appropriate when relevant frames exist in prior knowledge that can be fit to the input information; rule-based frame generation occurs when a text is on an unfamiliar topic or is used as a basis for learning, that is, the acquisition of new conceptual information.

Conceptual frame representations may be illustrated using the example of Fig. 14.1. This sentence was taken from a chemical (pulp and paper industry) text that describes a procedure for measuring the amount of solids in the liquor produced in the production of wood pulp. The text was analyzed by applying a *procedure frame grammar* that consists of rules specifying the components and structure of a complex procedure (Frederiksen & Renaud, 1989). These rules are illustrated in the following listing that gives procedural information supplied in the example sentence:

**(PROCEDURE.NODE (R.NODE.ID N7)**
(R.PROCEDURE(CANONICAL.PROC(R.PROC.ID Collect liquor samples)
(R.VAR.BINDINGS EMPTY)
(R.VAR.CONSTRAINTS EMPTY)))

(R.IS.PART N5.1 sample liquor)

(R.PART N9 fill bottles)
(R.PART N10 stopper bottles)

**(PROCEDURE.COMP (R.PROC.ID Collect liquor samples)**
*(R.PROC.GOAL* (PROC.GOAL 7.2, 7.3 samples in air-tight bottles
(R.PROC.GOAL.ID NG7))

*(R.SITUATION* (SITUATION.DESC 7.3 air tight bottles; *source locations of
liquor in production: blow pits, diffuser, washers, evaporators, furnace*)

*(R.PROC.RULE*
*(TEST (R.CONDITION (CONDITION liquor present in a source location in
production POS)) (R.EXECUTE n7)*)
*(TEST(R.CONDITION(CONDITION liquor present in a source location in
production NEG)) (R.ENABLE obtain source of liquor)*)

*(R.PROC.DESC* (PROC.EVENT
(R.PROC.ACT collect)
(R.PROC.SOURCE *liquor in source location*)
(R.PROC.RESULT (PROC.RESULT 7.2 samples in bottles
(R.PROC.RES.ID NR7))
(R.PROC.AGENT *user*)
(R.PROC.INSTRUMENT*graduated pipette*)

*(R.GOAL.RULE* (GOAL.TEST
(GOAL.MATCH NG7 NR7 EXIT)
(R.ELSE debug collect samples)))

(Note—*'s indicate implicit information not given explicitly in the text.)


The grammar defines a *procedure node,* one node in a network representation of a procedure, together with relations linking it to other nodes. A complex procedure is represented by a *procedure frame* consisting of a set of linked procedure nodes. Corresponding to each node, there is a procedure component that specifies all information necessary to define a procedure. A procedure component consists of the following: (a) a goal (PROC.GOAL) that includes propositions defining the goal state of this procedure, (b) a situation description (SITUATION.DESC) that includes propositions specifying any states necessary to carrying out the procedure, (c) a procedure production rule (R.PROC.RULE) consisting of a set of tests of conditions necessary for the enactment of the procedure, (d) a description of the event (action or operation) associated with the procedure, and (e) a goal test that verifies that the goal was attained.

Procedural component nodes linked by a set of procedure relations (that is, part, category, temporal order, temporal equivalence, and conditional relations) define a procedural frame and represent a control structure for the application of component procedures (see Fig. 14.4). Altogether, a procedural frame may be

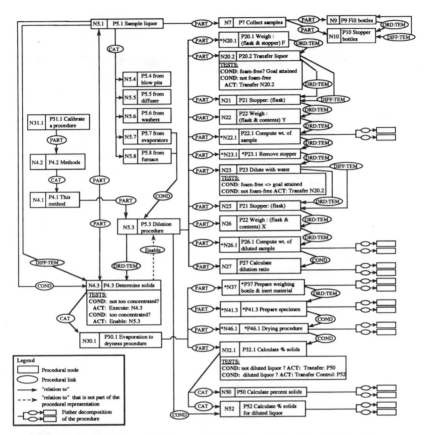

FIG. 14.4.    Procedural frame graph for the procedural text *Determination of Total Solids in Black Liquor: Method A: TAPPI Standard Method.*

thought of as a declarative representation of a program for controlling action in solving problems.

In the example, the following relations link this procedure node to other procedure nodes: procedure node N7 is linked to procedure nodes N9 and N10 by *part relations,* and to procedure node N5.1 by an *is part relation.*

Such models are tested in experiments investigating the ability of the model to represent the semantic content of expert protocols, and to predict expert and novice subjects' comprehension of procedural text, acquisition of procedural knowledge, and application of procedural knowledge in solving problems. To illustrate, in a study of acquisition of procedural knowledge from this text (Frederiksen & Renaud, 1989), it was found that expert knowledge (as reflected in expert-produced natural language protocols) may be represented in terms of declarative representations generated using the procedure frame model. Second, novice subjects' acquisition strategies were guided by the structure of the frame representation. Third, acquisition protocols, processing time measures, recall, and knowledge application all were predicted from properties of the frame model in novices and experts.

The semantics of procedures is but one problem involving the specification of a particular type of conceptual frame that has received attention. Other types of conceptual frames that have been studied in addition to descriptive networks and procedures include: (a) narrative frames (Frederiksen, Donin-Frederiksen & Bracewell, 1986; Trabasso & Nicholas, 1980), (b) dialogue frames (Frederiksen, Donin-Frederiksen, & Bracewell, 1986; Grosz, 1980; Sanford & Roach, 1987), and (c) problem frames (a principal component of a "story grammar," Newman & Bruce, 1986; Frederiksen, 1989; Gick & Holyoak, 1983; Stein & Policastro, 1984). There is extensive evidence in the experimental literature to support the contention that frame-based processing is important to the comprehension of texts expressing information interpretable in terms of one or more types of conceptual frames, and that frame-level processing may be either knowledge-based (i.e., involving the instantiation of frames previously stored in memory) or rule-based (i.e., generated by means of the application of rules in a frame grammar).

The existence of frame-level knowledge representations and processes associated with them implies that the description of an individual's performance in a semantically complex task is likely to involve frame knowledge and processes associated with generating or manipulating frames. Task-relevant knowledge and the states and procedures involved in solving a problem, therefore, should be represented conceptually as frame representations. Therefore, models of conceptual frame representation ought to be extremely useful in evaluating an individual's knowledge or processing.


## EVALUATING KNOWLEDGE AND PROCESSING
## IN SEMANTICALLY COMPLEX DOMAINS

In the first section of this chapter we identified characteristics of semantically complex domains and gave examples of semantically complex tasks. Central to all such tasks are conceptual representations that must be generated to represent task information and the problem structure of the task. Task information frequently consists of natural language text, but it also may include graphic information or expressions in formal languages; and the problem structure of a task includes problem states, goals, relevant solution procedures, and so forth, information that may be communicated explicitly or left implicit to be inferred by the student. Conceptual representations also constitute the form in which prior knowledge necessary to perform successfully on a task is represented. Prior conceptual knowledge includes knowledge of any methods or procedures relevant to successful performance on a task as well as knowledge of relevant facts and concepts. Successful performance in semantically complex tasks involves the generation and use of conceptual information of these kinds.

If a task is routine, task goals may be attained simply by executing procedures that already are a part of an individual's knowledge (e.g., solving quadratic equations by the quadratic formula). The evaluation of cognitive processing in routine tasks therefore should emphasize the domain knowledge an individual possesses and the operations required to apply that knowledge during performance on the tasks. Non-routine tasks, however, are tasks for which existing knowledge of procedures (methods and operations) is not sufficient to attain the goals required by the task. Evaluation of cognitive processing in non-routine tasks, therefore, requires not only evaluation of prior knowledge and operations in its application; required as well are methods for analyzing plans (i.e., procedures) that are generated by a student during performance on the task, and problem-solving strategies that the individual uses to develop successful plans.

The models of semantic representation described in the previous section provide a powerful formalism for modeling the conceptual information involved in semantically complex domains. Furthermore, the theory (and computational models) of text comprehension provide methods for the semantic analysis of natural language discourse that can be applied to develop conceptual frame representations for a task domain. These models and the methods for analysis of natural language based on them may be applied to the analysis of tasks and task supplied information, of discourse describing relevant background knowledge, and of protocols of experts performing on a task. On the basis of such analysis, conceptual frame models can be constructed for a given task. The resulting "*expert models*" can be used as a basis for evaluating knowledge and processing in semantically complex domains.

In this section, we describe a general approach to cognitive evaluation based on the construction and use of expert models. We then use an example to illustrate procedures for cognitive evaluation based on matching to an expert model. Finally, we use a second example to illustrate the application of semantic analysis methods to the analysis of student protocols, an approach that appears to be necessary on non-routine tasks for which successful performance depends on the student's ability to apply problem-solving strategies to generate plans for solving a problem.

## General Approach to Cognitive Evaluation

The components of a model of a student's knowledge and processing and the operations required to construct such a model are summarized in Fig. 14.5. We consider, first, the construction of an expert model, second, the components of a differential model of a student, and, third, procedures for developing a differential student model.

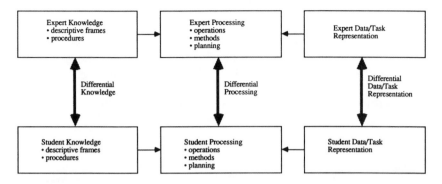

FIG. 14.5. Components of a differential model of a student's knowledge and processing.

***Expert Models.***    Modeling the expert involves modeling what the expert knows, how the expert understands a task, and how the expert uses his or her prior knowledge and task-derived information to successfully attain the task's goals. Working with detailed protocols obtained from experts, the following "expert models" are constructed by applying propositional and frame analysis methods:

1. *Model of expert knowledge:* model of task-relevant domain knowledge. The expert knowledge model normally would include particular sub-models corresponding to different conceptual representations or knowledge of procedures pertinent to the task.

2. *Model of expert data/task representation:* model of the task problem structure as understood by an expert, and semantic models of any task-supplied information, such as texts (if a source of information was natural language text), or other information sources, such as expressions in a formal language, experienced events (e.g., in a laboratory), graphic information, numeric data, and so on.

3. *Model of expert processing:* rules applied to specific task information and/ or domain knowledge to achieve task goals, and methods that experts apply to organize or control their application of rules. If the methods are routine applications of procedures, they are represented as a component of expert knowledge.

***Components of a Cognitive Model of the Student.***    If an expert is described in terms of these models (i.e., of relevant prior knowledge, of task information, and of applications of rules to these representations under the control of methods or plans), then a student may be described in relation to these models. Thus a student's knowledge and processing can be viewed (in comparison to the expert) in terms of:

1. Differential knowledge;
2. Differential representation of task structure and task-supplied information;
3. Differential processing; problem-solving operations, that is, rules used, specific prior knowledge or task-supplied information to which they are applied, and methods used to control operations including application of expert methods in routine tasks and/or strategies for planning in the generation of methods for non-routine tasks.

*Procedures for Developing a Differential Student Model.*   If we accept these as appropriate goals in developing a differential model of the student, we require a procedure for developing a differential model. In our experience with semantically complex task domains, differential models can be developed through a procedure of matching student responses to information in the appropriate expert model (with the exception of identifying students' planning strategies). We may organize this process as follows:

1. Evaluate the student's knowledge: identify units of information in the *domain knowledge model* used by the student in performing on the task (prior knowledge may be assessed independently before performance on the task using probe questions).
2. Evaluate the student's representation of the task: identify units of information in the *task model* used by the student in performing on the task (independent information concerning the student's comprehension of the task may be obtained through probe questions).
3. Evaluate the student's comprehension of task-supplied information: identify units of information in the *text model(s)* (and/or models based on other information sources) used by the student in performing the task (again, independent assessments can be obtained using recall or probed recall techniques).
4. Evaluate the student's processing operations: identify the specific *rules* the student used during performance of the task and the units of information in the *task model* and *domain knowledge model* to which the student applied the rules.

The evaluation of a student's use of control strategies and plans involves identifying sequences or subsets of operations on conceptual information; selective use of operations, knowledge, or task information; and methods or goals that are explicitly identified in student protocols that match methods or plans used by experts. When students employ methods that are not included in an expert model, or when they engage in planning strategies to generate a method, the use of matching methods to develop a differential model are not sufficient, and protocol analysis is necessary in addition to these matching techniques.

***On-Line Monitoring of Cognitive Processing.*** If differential student modeling is to be a part of a computer-based tutoring or learning system, then these evaluations have to be carried out on-line. This would require real-time matching of semantic information, operations, and methods used by subjects in order to make inferences concerning the student's use of information from the domain knowledge base, task information and structure, expert operations, and methods. Such an on-line system can vary in its "intelligence": in an "intelligent" system, the computer would actually simulate the student's processing by applying rules to the data structures operated on by a student and match its responses to that of the student (an approach advocated by exponents of intelligent tutoring systems); in a less "intelligent" system, the computer would rely on an exhaustive data-base consisting of conceptual models and listings of expert operations (i.e., rules correctly applied by experts to data structures during successful performance on the task) to which student responses are matched. This latter approach may be more realistic, and could be accomplished using general "shell" programs that operate using a structured data-base having defined properties. We would advocate basing the construction of such a data-base on conceptual networks found in experimental research to be adequate to represent knowledge and procedures of experts and students in the range of semantically complex tasks to which the tutoring system is to be applied.

The analysis of student-generated plans and problem-solving strategies requires real-time analysis of response protocols to determine methods the student has generated, and strategies used to generate them. Breuleux (1987, 1988) has experimented with computer-based semantic analysis of on-line protocols, and the techniques he has demonstrated could be applied in real-time learning environments.

## Cognitive Evaluation by Matching to an Expert Model

The use of matching procedures based on an expert model may be illustrated using data collected by Kubes (1988) in a study of expert-novice differences in the use of prior knowledge in knowledge integration tasks, that is, tasks requiring the incorporation of new knowledge into existing knowledge structure through the generation of inferred links between otherwise disconnected knowledge representations in memory (Hayes-Roth, 1977; Walker & Meyer, 1980). Kubes studied subjects' knowledge of a topic in chemistry (photosynthesis) and its use in integrative tasks requiring the interpretation of results obtained from an experimental demonstration of photosynthesis. That study is used to illustrate: (a) the development of a model of domain knowledge from expert-produced texts and its use in evaluating students' prior knowledge; (b) the development of a text model and its use in evaluating students' text comprehension; and (c) the identification of operations applied to domain knowledge and text-derived information in performing the explanation task (i.e., in generating links between domain knowledge concerning specific processes and experimental results).

***Prior Knowledge.***   To study integrative processes in science, Kubes asked experts in the field of chemistry to produce a text summarizing fundamental basic science knowledge concerning the process of photosynthesis. The text created from these expert texts included the following paragraph:

> *The basic reaction of photosynthesis indicates the formation of a simple carbohydrate, glucose, as the intermediate product of photosynthesis:*

$$6CO_2 + 6\,H_2O \rightarrow C_6H_{12}O_6 + 6O_2$$

> *There is, however, little free glucose produced in plants: instead glucose units are linked together to form starch, or are joined with fructose, another sugar, to form sucrose as described by the next general reaction:*

$$nCO_2 + nH_2O)) \rightarrow (CH_2O) + nO_2$$

> *As well as carbohydrates, amino acids, proteins, lipids (or fats), pigments, and other organic components of green tissues are also synthesized during photosynthesis. Starch is the primary product of photosynthesis. It is accumulated in the storage organs of plants, thus providing a reserve food supply.*

This expert-produced text was first analyzed to specify its propositional content, and descriptive frame graphs were generated from the propositions (Fig. 14.6). These constituted (in part) the expert domain knowledge model.

The graph in Fig. 14.6 represents the major compounds formed during the process of photosynthesis and contains graphs representing two of the major chemical reactions.

To evaluate subjects' (college students and graduate students in chemistry) prior knowledge of photosynthesis, Kubes obtained subjects' answers to probe questions derived from the expert text. Subjects' answers were matched to the expert frame graphs, and any nodes and links not present in the expert frame were added. This procedure yields a precise model of the prior knowledge each subject was able to access in responding to these probe questions. However, here the expert frame is used to illustrate cognitive diagnosis with reference to the knowledge integration tasks.

***Comprehension of Task Information.***   The knowledge integration task required subjects to interpret the results of experimental demonstrations of photosynthesis in terms of the relevant knowledge of the chemistry of photosynthesis. The last two paragraphs of the text of Experiment 1 (which describe the results and their interpretation) were as follows:

Experiment 1
*Testing for the Presence of Starch in Green Plants*

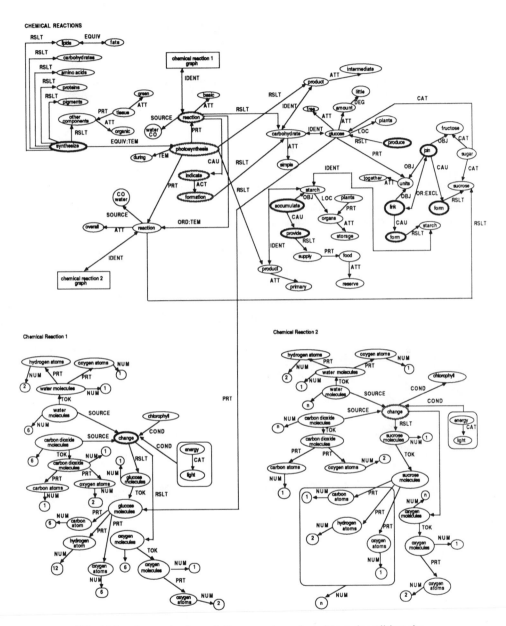

FIG. 14.6.   Conceptual graph for expert-produced text describing the major compounds formed during the process of photosynthesis.

*Results: During the process of boiling the leaves in water and alcohol, their green color gradually disappeared. After the leaves had been stained with iodine solution, they turned blue-black, except for the originally colorless spots.*

*Interpretation: The results of this experiment suggest that only the green parts of the leaves contain chlorophyll and can produce starch. When chlorophyll is removed from the leaves by boiling and extraction, the presence of starch can be detected with iodine reagent. The originally colorless spots of the leaves do not produce any starch.*

The frame representation for these paragraphs was constructed from a prior propositional analysis and is given in Fig. 14.7.

***Monitoring Processing Operations.***    These two frames (the "expert frame" and the "experiment frame") were used to evaluate subjects' use of prior knowledge in interpreting the experimental results. The knowledge integration problem just outlined required that a subject: (a) comprehend the experiment (that is, generate a representation for the experiment, including its results); (b) retrieve the relevant information from the prior knowledge frame for photosynthesis; and (c) generate the links needed to connect the two representations. In Kubes' study, a subject's representation (i.e., comprehension) of the experiment was evaluated using recall techniques (matching propositions in recall to experiment frame information).

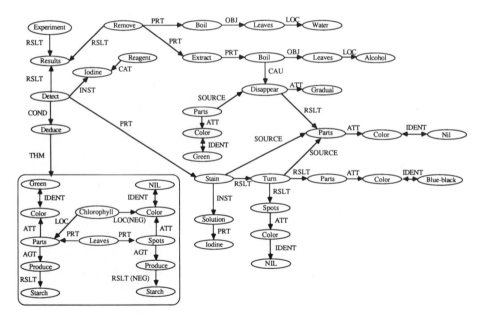

FIG. 14.7.   Conceptual graph for results of experimental demonstration of photosynthesis.

Subjects' prior knowledge was evaluated by analyzing nodes and links from the expert frame that subjects generated in response to prior knowledge questions. By matching subjects' responses to the knowledge integration questions (presented after the experimental text) against, first, the expert frame and, second, the experiment frame, both (a) their retrieval of prior knowledge, and (b) their procedures for generating links to the experimental results can be examined.

The responses of two graduate student subjects to one integrative question (question 2 for Experiment 1) were as follows:

*Integrative Question:*
*How does the demonstration of the production of starch in green plants contribute to our understanding of photosynthesis?*

*Responses of Graduate Student Subject #12:*
*The demonstration of starch production in green plants allows us to understand the fate of the glucose produced during the process of photosynthesis. That is, glucose is converted to its storage form—starch.*

*Response of Graduate Student Subject #13:*
*Starch is formed from one of the immediate products of photosynthesis, carbohydrate (glucose). Therefore, if starch is present, this is an indication that photosynthesis is taking place.*

The evaluation of Subject #12's retrieval of relevant prior knowledge is given in Fig. 14.8 in which nodes and links produced by the subject are overlayed on the expert frame of Fig. 14.6. Note that this subject has linked *starch* and *photosynthesis* through two stages of production (first, production of glucose, and then conversion of glucose to starch as specified in the expert frame). The only information from the expert frame that was represented in the Experiment 1 text was the production of starch. Thus, all other information was retrieved from prior knowledge in response to the integrative task. The subject recalled form the experiment that the production of starch in green plants had been demonstrated (Fig. 14.9). The subject then linked the description of the expert frame information (production of glucose and its conversion to starch) to the result of the experiment (production of starch in green plants) through an IF (i.e., material conditional) relation: the production of starch in green plants is an antecedent condition from which the subject inferred that there is production of glucose and its conversion to starch. This is an example of a forward reasoning operation, that is, reasoning from an experimental result (a given state) to a theoretical interpretation in terms of a chemical process (the goal state).

Subject #13's protocol exhibits retrieval of similar information from the expert frame, but a more complex linking of experiment frame information to prior knowledge. As may be seen in Fig. 14.10, this subject also linked photosynthesis to starch production through the mechanism of producing glucose as an intermedi-

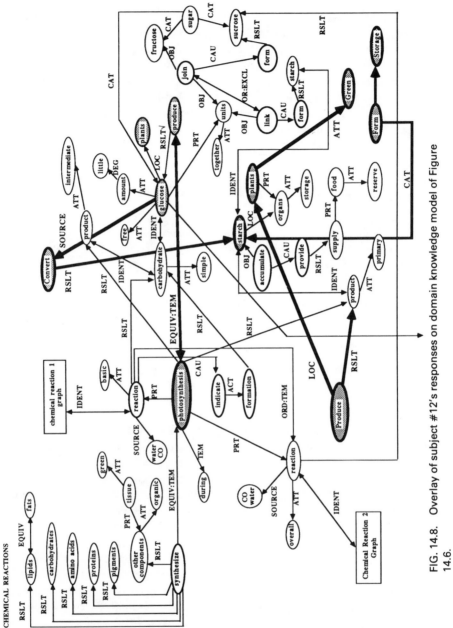

FIG. 14.8. Overlay of subject #12's responses on domain knowledge model of Figure 14.6.

378

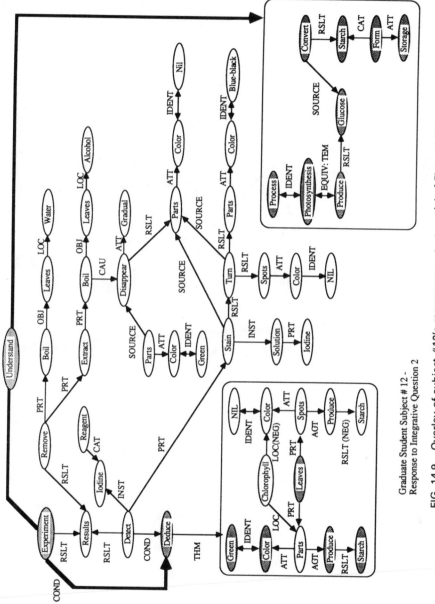

Graduate Student Subject # 12 -
Response to Integrative Question 2

FIG. 14.9. Overlay of subject #12's responses on text model of Figure 14.7.

379

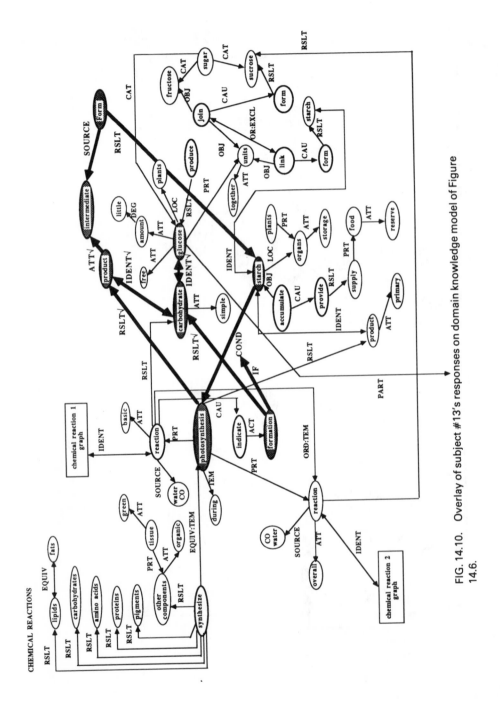

FIG. 14.10. Overlay of subject #13's responses on domain knowledge model of Figure 14.6.

380

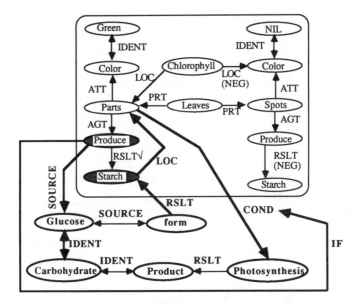

Graduate student subject #13
Response to Integrative Question 2

FIG. 14.11.   Overlay of subject #13's responses on text model of Figure
14.7.

ate product and forming starch from glucose. This subject recalled only that there
was starch production in the Experiment (Fig. 14.11). However, this subject
linked starch production in the experiment to the information from the expert
frame in a more complex way.

How this was done can be seen from Table 14.1, which summarizes the
dependency links (i.e., COND, CAU, and IF) generated in response to the
integrative question. Rule 1 states that if photosynthesis occurs, glucose is formed
(a CAU relation). Rule 2 states that there is a process in which if glucose is

TABLE 14.1
Rules Generated by Subject #13

| Rule # | Dependency Relation | Antecedent | Consequent |
|--------|---------------------|------------|------------|
| Rule 1 | CAU (RSLT) | photosynthesis | glucose is formed |
| Rule 2 | CAU (form) | SOURCE: glucose | RSLT: starch |
| Rule 3 | COND | starch present | photosynthesis |
| Rule 4 | IF | Rules #1,#2 | Rule #3 |

present, it is converted into starch. Both of these rules reflect prior knowledge. Rule 3 states that if starch is present (the given experimental data), this is a COND for photosynthesis to occur (the theoretical interpretation). Rule 3 is an example of *forward reasoning* (from data to theory). But Rule 4 states that given Rules 1 and 2 (retrieved information relevant to the goal), Rule 3 (which is based on the given data) may be inferred. This is an example of *backward reasoning* (from theory to data). Thus, the links established by this subject in response to the integrative question were more complex, involving *mixed forward and backward reasoning operations*.

These protocols illustrate that it is possible to achieve precise evaluations of students' prior knowledge and its use in text comprehension and knowledge integration domains. Although the evaluation procedures based on the domain-knowledge models are sufficient to differentiate subjects' procedures for retrieving relevant prior knowledge and generating links to experimental data, a real time evaluation of the operations students apply in on-line performance of these tasks would be necessary in computer-based learning environments.

## Evaluation of Problem-solving Strategies by Analysis of Protocols

The evaluation of problem-solving strategies is based on the analysis of on-line problem-solving data, usually in the form of think-aloud and performance protocols (Ericsson & Simon, 1984; Newell & Simon, 1972). The rationale for analysis may be described as follows.

In problem-solving situations, subjects are attempting to develop methods for attaining goals. They do this by searching for and evaluating a series of alternative actions (operations) appropriate to particular problem states in order to bring about a particular desired goal state. Their think aloud verbalizations reflect their organization of methods for implementing goals (Bobrow, 1975). Thus, transcripts of think aloud data contain verbalizations of the states and operators in the subject's problem-space, and of subjects' strategies for applying operators to states, strategies that usually involve goals and evaluations.

Analyzing think-aloud protocols involves encoding surface expressions in order to extract the problem-space and control knowledge used by the subject (Ericsson & Simon, 1984). In the well-defined tasks that are usually studied in problem-solving research, statements from a protocol are encoded as instances of one of the categories established by a prior analysis of the characteristics of the task (Newell, 1980; Newell & Simon, 1972). In cryptarithmetic, for example, this encoding can be carried out directly, without an explicit and formal set of rules (see Ericsson & Simon 1984 on *direct encoding*). Details of the processes and assumptions involved in this matching procedure are often left unexplained, mainly because they are obvious or simple. Because the knowledge required for handling the task is limited, it is possible, for example, to identify strategies like planning by reference to the "legality" of the operators involved: a plan is a set of statements involving moves that are illegal at the time stated and thus have to be decomposed into legal moves. The main advantage of this approach is that it reduces the need to rely on detailed natural language analysis of protocols.

However, in the case of complex and knowledge-rich tasks analyzing think-aloud protocols is somewhat problematic. The main reason for this is that a task analysis does not provide a workable set of elementary processes that could then be easily identified in the protocols. The analysis of ill-defined and unconstrained tasks also does not identify clear constraints that subjects follow and that would guide the analysis of their thinking-aloud. For example, no notion of legal moves can serve in defining control strategies; very few objects and operators can be given as part of a problem description; and it is not possible to anticipate reliably what knowledge would be used by subjects. In such situations, only general encoding categories, like operators and goal statements, are postulated, and a careful examination of the protocol itself is necessary to extract specific encoding categories that would further define the problem-space (see e.g., Kuipers & Kassirer, 1984; Patel & Groen, 1986). Thus, investigating behavior in ill-defined problems requires more systematic analysis of the verbal data, and techniques of semantic analysis of discourse are suitable for this purpose, especially those based on propositional analysis and procedural frame models. This situation contrasts with the analysis of protocols in well-defined tasks, usually carried out "informally," without specifying the formation rules of the particular semantic representation used.

In the remainder of this section, we examine planning as a strategy subjects adopt to solve problems in tasks such as writing that have complex states or imprecisely defined goals.

*Planning.*    Planning is the process of organizing goals and sub-goals hierarchically and sequentially to define a course of action, that is, a control structure or procedure (Miller, Galanter, & Pribram, 1960; Newell & Simon, 1972; Volpert, 1982). We emphasize here four aspects of planning and of plans.

First, planning is a problem-solving strategy consisting mainly in the *abstraction* of components of a problem to create a reduced and manageable representation of the space to be searched, which may produce a blueprint for the solution in the original problem space (Newell & Simon, 1972). The abstraction operates on the objects and operators of a problem and permits the exploration of possible solutions. The result of planning is the outline of a solution that can then be translated and tried in the original problem space. Newell and Simon (1972) have illustrated this aspect of planning. The usefulness of the strategy lies in the cognitive bargain resulting from a search over a small and abstract problem space, as opposed to working out a solution in the original, detailed problem space.

Two other important aspects of planning pertain to the cognitive structures that result from planning, and their execution. A plan coordinates the selection of operators, and its execution involves making behavior conditional on the state of the problem and a hierarchy of goals and sub-goals (Simon, 1975). Sacerdoti (1977) has convincingly argued that plans are complex cognitive structures that can be represented as networks in which the nodes are goals, mainly *actions*, and the links are *relations between actions*, that is, a kind of procedural frame. The actions represented in a plan are related one to another by hierarchical relations (specifying levels of detail and decomposition), logical relations (conjunction and disjunction), and temporal relations (specifying an order between actions). Consistent artificial planning has been demonstrated in computer systems capable of deriving plans at different levels of abstraction, gradually formulating more detailed plans until executable procedures are organized in a coherent sequence. The execution of plans relies heavily on the ability to *evaluate* desired and actual states of a problem and to compare them.

Finally, since goals represent desired situations or actions that take place in the future with a certain probability, elements of a plan are characterized by *eventuality* and *temporal antecedence* over action (Rips & Marcus, 1977; Simon, 1975).

These characteristics of planning can be used in defining an encoding scheme for the think aloud protocols of experts and novices in a complex problem-solving task.

*Planning in Semantically Rich Domains: The Case of Writing.*    Writing is a knowledge-rich domain, and writers need to explore and organize the complex pool of representations and processes relevant to a specific task. Planning provides an efficient strategy that is useful in writing mainly because it enables writers to explore at an abstract level the rich network of possible solutions to a writing assignment. This exploration is extremely valuable because of its reduced cognitive cost compared to the undertaking of a solution in the actual problem environment. Stepping into the problem without planning would require producing unnecessary text that must simultaneously satisfy a complex set of rules and constraints. By planning, a writer can delay many of these lower level decisions.

*Extracting Students' Plans and Methods in a Writing Task.*    Planning can be identified in think-aloud protocols of writers by specifying the semantic characteristics that instantiate the properties of planning found in their verbalizations. This can be thought of as applying a semantic grammar for plans. Table 14.2 presents an excerpt from a think aloud protocol produced by an experienced journalist who is writing background copy for a major feature.

Given that planning consists of the coordination of goals, the identification of a plan in a protocol requires, first, the identification of goal statements, and, second, the identification of relationships among goal statements. It is possible to specify the criteria for goal statements and the relationships between goal

TABLE 14.2
Section of Think Aloud Protocol from Subject GM1

| Segment no | Segment | Comment |
|---|---|---|
| 13— | first what I want to get down here is the in terms of a general introduction is what the prospects are | |
| 14— | and then explain why they are that way | |
| 15— | looking at the problem of summits generally first | |
| 16— | and then focusing on the American side and then Soviet side or vice versa | |
| 17— | so I should say some introductory introductory remarks now about my views of of what will happen next week | |
| 18— | *from all reports pessimism would appear to be the* the | Subject starts writing |
| 19— | what word am I looking for? | |
| 20— | the *predominant sentiment* | |
| 21— | one could say | |
| 22— | *going into the meetings* | |

*Note.* Segments in italic indicate information written by the subject, while talking.

statements that constitute a hierarchical or sequential organization. In the propositional representation used here, goals are mainly statements involving an action or a future state or a state with a modality marking; hierarchical relations consist of location, part-whole, theme, and equivalence relations; sequential organization is represented by the temporal order relation. Table 14.3 shows the propositional analysis for segment 13 of the protocol section presented in Table 14.2, and also segment 1 that illustrates how the temporal marking of the event in the propositional representation designates the segment as a goal statement. This marking corresponds to the future tense (TENSE:FUT) associated with the act identifier *write* in proposition 1.1. Segment 13 is an example of a verbalized volition, which is represented at the lexical level by the act identifier *want*.

In segments 13 and 14 (see Table 14.2), the subject is ordering two goals, the second being "decomposed." The ordering is identified by the *then* that is represented by the ORD:TEM: relation. The decomposition is identified by the inferred relation between *explain* and *looking at* (segment 15) and *focusing* (segment 16). In segments 15 and 16, the subject is putting an order between the goal of "looking at the problem of summits generally" and the two goals of "focusing on the American side" and "focusing on the Soviet side"; what is noticeable here is that the exact ordering of the *focusing* goals is explicitly not decided upon. A schematic of the plan to this point is presented in Fig. 14.12.

On the basis of such a definition of plans as goal structures in which nodes and links are explicitly specified, planning episodes from protocols can be identified

TABLE 14.3
Propositional Analyses for Segments 1 and 13 of Subject GM1

| Proposition Number | Head | Arguments |
|---|---|---|
| **Segment 1.** *I'll be writing an article on the prospects for success or failure at next week's summit meeting between Gorbachev and Reagan.* | | |
| 1.1 | "write" | agt:"I", thm: "article"(TOK,NUM:SUM)|TENSE:FUT, aspct:CONT,POS, |
| 1.2 | "article" | thm:1.3,1.4 |
| 1.3 | "meet" | pat:Gorbachev,Reagan,cat:"summit", att: "success" tem:"next week"|MOD:QUAL:*prospects* |
| 1.4 | "meet" | pat:Gorbachev,Reagan,cat:"summit", att: "failure" tem:"next week"|MOD:QUAL:*prospects* |
| 1.6 | ORALT: | [1.3],[1.4]; |
| **Segment 13.** *First what I want to get down here is, in terms of a general introduction, what the prospects are* | | |
| 13.1 | "want" | AGT:"I", THM:13.2,TEM:"first"|TENSE:PRES,POS, |
| 13.2 | "get down" | THM:13.3 |
| 13.3 | "what" | TENSE:PRES,MOD:QUAL*prospects*; |
| 13.4 | "introduction" | ATT:general, |
| 13.5 | EQUIV: | [13.3],[13.4]; |

reliably. We now illustrate this procedure with one simple example from the protocol of a student journalist writing an editorial for a student newspaper on the Challenger tragedy a few days after the accident.

Fig. 14.13 shows the overall pattern of planning and execution of plans for subject SH2. Plans are identified by a "head" (the thick oval nodes); the square nodes linked under a plan head represent the content of the plan, a

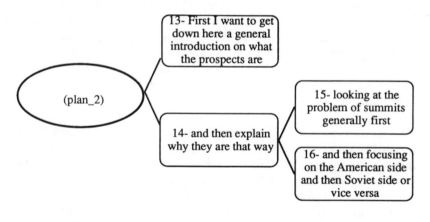

FIG. 14.12.  Graphic representation of plan in GM1's protocol (see Table 14.2).

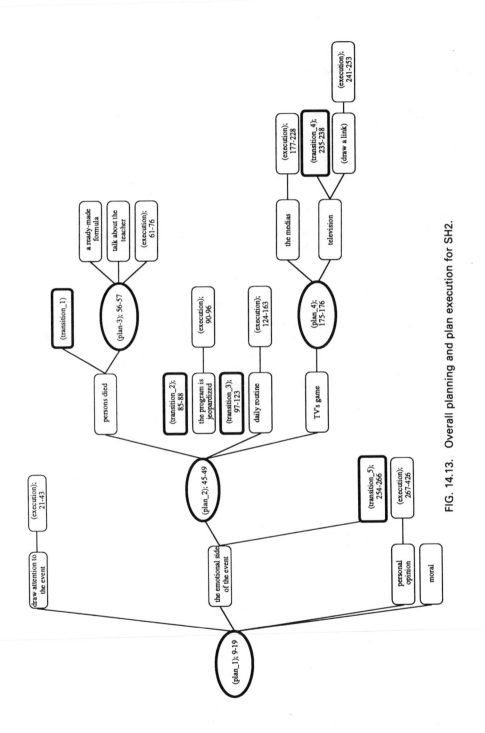

FIG. 14.13. Overall planning and plan execution for SH2.

387

structured set of goals. Numbers in plan heads correspond to segment numbers in the protocol, and can serve to indicate the order in which the planning episodes occurred. In the protocol in Fig. 14.13, planning episodes alternate with execution phases. The initial plan is gradually refined, each goal being expanded, usually through further planning, into a piece of discourse. The protocol represents a neat top-down treatment, but the subject does not expand his plan breadth-first by elaborating subgoals for all the goals in his initial plan. Another characteristic of the protocol is the occurrence of transition episodes (in thick square boxes). These episodes occur when the subject is evaluating aspects of the text produced as well as the high-level goals the text has to accomplish, in order to decide whether to plan further or to produce discourse. Plans are kept simple until the point of expansion, and the expansion process leads either to expression, elaboration of a sub-plan, or modification of a previous plan. The expansion process can be linked with transition episodes, during which subjects decide on the type of expansion by evaluating text and high-level goals. The plans in this protocol are remarkably simple and shallow: Very little hierarchical decomposition appears in the absence of actions. This suggests that the subject would rather not commit to particular objectives or that the subject cannot anticipate precisely the outcome of further processing (namely the expression process). Such plans are either decomposed locally or reorganized according to local properties of the problem-state (see Breuleux (1988) for a more detailed discussion).

These data illustrate how the tactic described for analyzing think-aloud protocols can serve to identify individual differences, as well as similarities, between subjects in a complex non-routine problem-solving task.

## CONCLUSION

We have shown in this paper how it is possible to develop, test, and use precise models of conceptual representation and processing by experts and learners performing semantically complex tasks that involve the integration of knowledge and the generation of problem-solving strategies. The basis for these models are generative rule-based systems defining conceptual representations, such as propositions, procedures, and plans, that can be generated from task information, discourse describing background knowledge, and protocols of subjects performing a task. These systems enable the differential modeling of individual subjects' knowledge, comprehension, and processing. Formal models constructed from data on experts make possible theory-based psychometric assessments and tutoring systems in which the performance of students in tasks involving comprehension, reasoning and problem-solving can be assessed and monitored, and diagnostic information obtained.

# REFERENCES

Anderson, J. R. (1982). Acquisition of cognitive skills. *Psychological Review, 89*, 364–406.

Anderson, J. R., & Bower, G. H. (1973). *Human associative memory*. Washington, DC: Winston.

Bobrow, D. G. (1975). Dimensions of representation. In D. G. Bobrow & A. Collins (Eds.), *Representation and understanding*. New York: Academic Press.

Breuleux, A. (1987). Discourse and the investigation of cognitive skills in complex tasks. In D. McCutcheon (Chair), *Cognitive Science and the Curriculum: Cognitive Models in the Educational Domain*, Symposium conducted at the annual meeting of the Cognitive Science Society, Seattle, WA.

Breuleux, A. (1988). *L'élaboration et l'exécution de plans dans une tâche de rédaction*. [The elaboration and execution of plans in a writing task.] Unpublished doctoral thesis. University of Montreal, Montréal, Québec.

Chomsky, N. (1981). *Lectures on government and binding*. Dordrecht, Holland: Foris Publications.

Clancey, W. (1986a). Qualitative student models. *Annual Review of Computer Science, 1*, 381–450.

Clancey, W. (1986b). *Intelligent tutoring systems: A tutorial survey* (Technical Report STAN-CS-87-1174). Stanford, CA: Stanford University, Department of Computer Science.

Ericsson, A., & Simon, H. A. (1984). *Protocol analysis: Verbal reports as data*. Cambridge, MA: MIT Press.

Ermann, L. D. (1977). A functional description of the Hearsay II speech understanding system. *Proceedings of IEEE-ICASSP*. Hartford, CT.

Ferreira, F., & Clifton, C. (1986). The independence of syntactic processing. *Memory and Language, 25*, 348–368.

Fodor, J. (1983). *The modularity of mind*. Cambridge, MA: Bradford Books-MIT Press.

Frederiksen, C. H. (1975). Representing logical and semantic structure of knowledge acquired from discourse. *Cognitive Psychology, 7*, 371–458.

Frederiksen, C. H. (1986). Cognitive models and discourse analysis. In C. R. Cooper & S. Greenbaum (Eds.), *Written communication annual: An international survey of research and theory, Vol. 1: Studying writing: Linguistic approaches*. Beverly Hills, CA: Sage.

Frederiksen, C. H. (1989). Text comprehension in functional task domains. In D. Bloom (Ed.), *Learning to use literacy in educational settings*. Norwood, NJ: Ablex.

Frederiksen, C. H., & Renaud, A. (1989). *Representation, acquisition and use of procedural knowledge in chemical engineering*. Paper presented at the annual meeting of the American Educational Research Association, San Francisco, CA.

Frederiksen, C. H., Décary, M., & Hoover, M. L. (1988). The semantic representation and processing of natural language discourse: Development of a computational model. *Proceedings of the International Colloquium on "Informatique et langue naturelle"*. Nantes, France.

Frederiksen, C. H., Donin-Frederiksen, J., & Bracewell, R. J. (1986). Discourse analysis of children's text production. In A. Matsuhashi (Ed.), *Writing in real time*. Norwood, NJ: Ablex.

Frederiksen, N. (1984). The real test bias: Influences of testing on teaching and learning. *American Psychologist, 39*, 193–202.

Gick, M. L., & Holyoak, K. J. (1983). Schema induction and analogical transfer. *Cognitive Psychology, 15*, 1–38.

Glaser, R. (1985). *Thoughts on expertise* (Tech. Rep. No. 8). Pittsburgh, PA: Learning Research and Development Center.

Graesser, A. C., Hoffman, N. L., & Clark, L. F. (1980). Structural components of reading time. *Journal of Verbal Learning and Verbal Behavior, 19*, 135–151.

Grimes, J. (1975). *The thread of discourse*. The Hague: Mouton.

Grosz, B. J. (1980). Utterance and objective: Issues in natural language communication. *AI Magazine, 1*, 11–20.

Halliday, M. A. K., & Hasan, R. (1976). *Cohesion in English*. London: Longman.

Hayes-Roth, B. (1977). Evolution of cognitive structures and processes. *Psychological Review, 84,* 260–278.

Hayes-Roth, B., & Thorndyke, B. W. (1979). Integration of knowledge from text. *Journal of Verbal Learning and Verbal Behavior, 18,* 91–108.

Just, M. A., Carpenter, P. A., & Woolley, J. D. (1982). Paradigms and processes in reading comprehension. *Journal of Experimental Psychology: General, 11,* 228–238.

Kieras, D. E. (1981). Component processes in the comprehension of simple prose. *Journal of Verbal Learning and Verbal Behavior, 20,* 1–23.

Kintsch, W. (1974). *The representation of meaning in memory.* Hillsdale, NJ: Lawrence Erlbaum Associates.

Kubes, M. (1988). *The use of prior knowledge in integration.* Unpublished doctoral thesis, McGill University, Montreal.

Kuipers, B. J., & Kassirer, J. P. (1984). Causal reasoning in medicine: analysis of a protocol. *Cognitive Science, 8,* 363–385.

McKeown, K. R. (1985). *Text generation.* Cambridge: Cambridge University Press.

Mel'cuk, I. A. (1979). *Studies in dependency syntax.* Ann Arbor, MI: Karoma Publishers.

Miller, G. A., Galanter, E., & Pribram, K. H. (1960). *Plans and the structure of behavior.* New York: Holt.

Morrow, D. G. (1986). Grammatical morphemes and conceptual structure in discourse processing. *Cognitive Science, 10,* 423–455.

Newell, A. (1980). Reasoning, problem-solving and decision processes: the problem space as a fundamental category. In R. Nickerson (Ed.) *Attention and Performance, Vol VIII.* Hillsdale, NJ: Lawrence Erlbaum Associates.

Newell, A., & Simon, H. A. (1972). *Human problem solving.* Englewood Cliffs, NJ: Prentice-Hall.

Newman, D., & Bruce, B. C. (1986). Interpretation and manipulation of human plans. *Discourse Processes, 9,* 167–195.

Patel, V. L., & Groen, G. J. (1986). Knowledge-based solution strategies in medical reasoning. *Cognitive Science, 10,* 91–116.

Raynor, K., Carlson, M., & Frazier, L. (1983). The interaction of syntax and semantics during sentence processing: Eye movements in the analysis of semantically biased sentences. *Journal of Verbal Learning and Verbal Behavior, 22,* 358–374.

Renaud, A., & Frederiksen, C. H. (1988). On-line processing of a procedural text. *Proceedings of the Cognitive Science Society.* Montreal, Quebec, Canada.

Rips, L. J., & Marcus, S. L. (1977). Suppositions and the analysis of conditional statements. In M. A. Just & P. A. Carpenter (Eds.), *Cognitive processes in comprehension.* Hillsdale, NJ: Lawrence Erlbaum Associates.

Ritchie, G. (1983). Semantics in parsing. In M. King (Ed.), *Parsing natural language.* New York: Academic Press.

Roberts, D. D. (1973). *The existential graphs of Charles S. Peirce.* The Hague: Mouton.

Rumelhart, D. E., & Norman, C. A. (1975). The active structural network. In D. A. Norman, D. E. Rumelhart, & The LNR Research Group (Eds.), *Explorations in cognition.* San Francisco, CA: W. H. Freeman.

Sacerdoti, E. D. (1977). *A structure for plans and behavior.* New York: American Elsevier.

Sanford, D. L., & Roach, J. W. (1987). Parsing and generating the pragmatics of natural language utterances using metacommunication. *Proceedings of the ninth annual conference of the Cognitive Science Society,* Seattle, WA.

Schank, R. C. (1975). *Conceptual information processing.* New York: American Elsevier.

Seidenberg, M. S., & Tanenhaus, M. (1986). Modularity and lexical access. In I. Gopnik (Ed.), *McGill studies in cognitive science.* Norwood, NJ: Ablex.

Simon, H. A. (1975). The functional equivalence of problem-solving skills. *Cognitive Psychology, 7,* 268–288.

Sowa, J. F. (1984). *Conceptual structures: information processes in mind and machine.* Reading, MA: Addison-Wesley.

Stein, N., & Policastro, M. (1984). The concept of a story: a comparison between children's and teachers' viewpoints. In H. Mandl, N. L. Stein, & T. Trabasso (Eds.), *Learning and comprehension of text.* Hillsdale, NJ: Lawrence Erlbaum Associates.

Townsend, D. J. (1983). Thematic processing in sentences and texts. *Cognition, 13,* 223–261.

Tyler, L. K. (1983). The development of discourse mapping processes: the on-line interpretation of anaphoric expressions. *Cognition, 13,* 309–341.

Trabasso, T., & Nicholas, D. W. (1980). Memory and inferences in the comprehension of narratives. In F. Wilkening, J. Becker, & T. Trabasso (Eds.), *Information integration by children.* Hillsdale, NJ: Lawrence Erlbaum Associates.

Van Dijk, T., & Kintsch, W. (1983). *Strategies of discourse comprehension.* New York: Academic Press.

Volpert, W. (1982). The model of the hierarchical-sequential organization of action. In W. Hacker, W. Volpert, & M. von Cranach (Eds.), *Cognitive and motivational aspects of action.* New York: North-Holland.

Walker, C. H., & Meyer, B. J. F. (1980). Integrating information from text: An evaluation of current theories. *Review of Educational Research, 50,* 421–437.

Zadeh, L. A. (1974). Fuzzy logic and its application to approximate reasoning. *Information Processing, 74,* 591–594.

# 15

# Diagnostic Approaches to Learning: Measuring What, How, and How Much
## Comments on Chapters 12, 13, and 14

Judith M. Orasanu
*U. S. Army Research Institute*

The purpose of the conference on Cognitive Issues in Measurement was to explore cognitive diagnosis, or new methods for determining what a learner knows, understands, and can do in order to further learning and performance. That cognitive diagnosis means something different to each participant became obvious with each presentation. The three chapters discussed here (by Regian & Schneider, by Lesgold, Lajoie, Logan & Eggan, and by C. Frederiksen & Breuleux) clearly illustrate those differences. They also share important commonalities that distinguish them as a group from traditional psychometric approaches to ability or achievement testing.

The most striking similarity among these three approaches is their goal of understanding what a learner needs to learn in order to master a skill, and to develop assessment within that context. Each offers the possibility of moving beyond the current right–wrong, or go–no go approach used in most education and training situations that provides little guidance for instruction. They all link testing with training; their aim is to yield pedagogically useful information. In addition, these three chapters describe efforts to develop methods for representing and assessing knowledge taken from real training problems, in contrast to artificial laboratory tasks. They deal with complex cognitive skills needed to interact with the new technologies appearing in schools, industry, and the military.

Despite their similarities in intent, the three approaches differ in significant ways, reflecting mainly differences in the kinds of knowledge or skill they address. Regian and Schneider focus on complex psychomotor tasks that require little declarative knowledge or understanding. In contrast, Lesgold and colleagues specifically address the declarative, procedural, and strategic knowledge required to reason about complex systems, such as in troubleshooting. Frederiksen and

Breuleux address the more basic linguistic–symbolic processes that are involved in knowing and reasoning with concepts rather than with procedures and systems.

Because of differences in the types of knowledge they seek to diagnose, the three approaches involve very different representations of the underlying knowledge and skill and ways of characterizing variation, both within and between individuals. These points are expanded in the following discussion of the major contributions and issues raised by each chapter.

## REGIAN AND SCHNEIDER

Regian and Schneider are concerned with predicting performance on complex tasks that require extensive practice in order to achieve expertise, such as air traffic controller performance. These involve clearly specifiable task components, some of which become automatized with practice. Most of these are perceptual–motor tasks, such as driving or radar control, that involve spatial judgment, motor control, and clear procedures. Specifically excluded is performance on tasks that are very heterogeneous and knowledge-dependent, such as leadership and teaching, which depend mainly on declarative knowledge and strategies.

Regain and Schneider offer a novel theory-based approach to diagnosis and prediction of performance on this class of tasks. It is characterized by the following advantages:

1. Their testing approach seeks greater predictive validity by replacing static aptitude tests with (a) tests that are actual subsets of the ultimate complex task to be predicted, and (b) testing based on rate of learning of a component skill. Job-sample testing has a long history, with variable success. What distinguishes Regian and Schneider's approach is that the subtasks are specified by a theory-driven analysis of the task into components that have various relations to ultimate task performance. By using rate of learning on task components, they seek to obtain more accurate measures of ability, unconfounded by prior experience with the task. Performance on static ability tests is always a joint product of ability and experience, with no way of teasing the two apart. Regian and Schneider recommend using knowledge about the malleability of certain aptitudes to determine a person's true ability, using combined testing and training. This allows one to distinguish between candidates with high ability but low prior experience and those with low ability but plenty of experience.

2. Regian and Schneider's approach can be used both for selection and for training purposes. When used for selection, a hierarchical, or hurdle-testing, strategy is recommended. This consists of a series of increasingly discriminant assessments predicated on emergent abilities and a componential analysis of the skills involved in a task. Emergent abilities are those that become dominant in performance of a skill at high levels, but are not evident during initial learning.

Initial learning more often depends on general learning strategies, short-term memory, or understanding of instructions, whereas later in skill acquisition, more task-specific perceptual or motor abilities may dominate. In Regian and Schneider's hierarchical scheme, initial pencil-and-paper testing screens out those falling below specified general ability or knowledge levels. Second-stage testing eliminates those lacking specific prerequisite skills, whereas third-stage testing involves extensive training on certain subtasks to determine aptitude through rate of learning.

3. Regian and Schneider's diagnostic testing approach relies on the distinction between stable and unstable task components. To briefly summarize this distinction, stable components are those that do not improve much with extensive practice. This results from a lack of consistency in stimulus–response pairings. For example, Shiffrin and Schneider (1977) found no change in letter-search performance over 4 months. In contrast, unstable components show continued improvement with practice. They are characterized by a consistent mapping of stimulus and response features, such as a car always turning left when the steering wheel is turned left.

After a substantial amount of practice, unstable components may become automatized, meaning that they can be performed quickly and efficiently with little conscious effort; other tasks may be performed concurrently. Stable task components continue to require cognitive effort, or control processing, and never become automatized. This distinction serves as the foundation for Regian and Schneider's diagnostic testing.

Such a framework is useful as it allows component skills to be characterized at various points in acquisition. Early in learning, all components are controlled; with practice, unstable components improve in accuracy and skill, and may become automatic. Stable components plateau early on both accuracy and speed, with little improvement. In second-stage hurdle testing, one measures performance on stable components and initial ability on unstable components. Following substantial training on unstable components, rate of improvement is measured in terms of accuracy, speed, and resource capacity.

An important aspect of Regian and Schneider's approach is its use of alternate performance measures. Accuracy may be achieved quite early in training, whereas speed continues to increase. Automaticity cannot be predicted by either accuracy or speed, but must be assessed through adding a secondary task. If a skill is not automatic, a greater performance decrement is observed than if it is well automated. From a practical point of view, this technique itself could yield more accurate assessment of an individual's readiness to perform a complex task, such as one needed in the military. For example, it is not sufficient to know whether a soldier knows how to track a target through a sight under ideal training conditions; the soldier's commander would want to know whether the soldier can do it under hostile conditions that demand attention to many sources of information or performance of multiple tasks. Testing for automaticity may provide just that information.

4. Analyzing skills into stable and unstable components provides a basis for designing tests that serve both diagnostic and selection purposes. There appear to be individual differences in the development of automaticity, as well as on stable components such as working memory. People with high ability may be selected based on learning rate and achievement of automaticity. But this information can also be used to prescribe a training regimen, especially one that involves integrating various components into complex tasks.

5. The final phase of hurdle testing takes into account motivation to undergo a lengthy training regime, a factor not tapped adequately by single-sitting tests, but critical to ultimate mastery of the predicted skill. Although standard ability tests can identify individuals with ability to learn, without sustained effort, those individuals do not learn. Researchers at the Army Research Institute have found effort and motivation, combined, to be one of five significant predictors of success across a broad range of jobs in the Army (Wise, Campbell, McHenry, & Hanser, 1986). In addition to treating motivation as a person variable, Regian and Schneider approach it as a task variable that can be manipulated to determine a candidate's commitment to a lengthy and sometimes boring training regimen.

## Issues

1. Regian and Schneider have described their theory of stable and unstable components in the context of a target-tracking task. One test of the adequacy of their theory is its application to other complex skills. How does one actually analyze stable and unstable components of real-world tasks in an efficient, cost-effective way? Regian and Schneider specify looking for consistency between stimulus and response requirements. Whether this is possible in practice remains to be seen.

For example, it would be useful to know how the recommended approach applies to basic Army soldiering skills categorized by Shields, Goldberg, and Dressel (1979) according to their training requirements. Some tasks require frequent (every month) refresher training to maintain a specified level of proficiency; others require little (once a year) or no refresher training. Examples of those requiring frequent refresher training include target identification and guided missile gunnery, both of which require speed and precision. Some tasks in this category have high memory components. Tasks requiring little refresher training include rifle marksmanship, typing, and tank driving. Presumably, skills in the latter category have become highly automated and should demonstrate the consistent stimulus–response relationship identified by Regian and Schneider.

2. A major concern in both civilian and military training is transfer from the classroom to practical contexts. The Regian–Schneider perspective provides a new framework for thinking about transfer. Do stable and unstable components transfer differently? Does transfer depend more on proficiency levels of the

whole task or of components? Traditional wisdom concerning training to enhance transfer recommends variation in context, which suggests that stable components should transfer better than unstable ones. Once skills have become automatic, are they readily transportable, or do they transfer only if the transfer conditions are identical to training conditions? Complex skills that have more stable components may be more flexible and transfer better than highly unstable ones.

3. Related to the issue of transfer is the development and use of strategies in the performance of a task. Strategies would seem to be more important for performing stable than unstable tasks because stable tasks do not offer the opportunity for improvement via practice with consistent mapping. A question not addressed by Regian and Schneider is whether strategies are relevant in acquiring unstable skills. Any improvements at all in performance on stable tasks may derive primarily from application of useful strategies. Consider, for example, improvements that occur with practice on rote verbal free recall tasks. Over time learners typically develop rehearsal or other mnemonic strategies that result in improved performance, even though the task offers no consistent stimulus–response mapping.

4. A final issue concerns the relation between componential analysis of skills and training. Specifically, how should the components be sequenced in training for optimal ultimate performance? Is it better to train each component to criterion and then put them together, or to train components in the context of the complete skill? Although sequential component training might seem to be a natural consequence of a componential testing approach, this conclusion does not necessarily follow. The situation might be called the Humpty-Dumpty problem: Training components to the level of automaticity in isolation may impede their reintegration with others needed for complete task performance due to powerful context effects operating on the components.

Some recent research on teaching reading, problem solving, and perceptual motor tasks such as those studied by Regian and Schneider indicates that it is more effective to teach component skills in the context of the complete task after some initial familiarization with components (see Au, Crowell, Jordan, Sloat, Speidel, Klein, & Tharp, 1986; Collins, 1988; Fabiani, Buckley, Gratton, Coles, Donchin, & Logie, 1988). Regian and Schneider themselves hint that teaching the context of the complete task is preferable. This suggests that it is important for the learner to have a clear understanding of how the components fit together in the complete task while they acquire the components. What is not known is how much of what kind of practice on what types of components is optimal for acquiring various complex skills.

Overall, the Regian–Schneider approach provides a rich framework for addressing the issues raised above in the context of complex perceptual motor skills.

## LESGOLD, LAJOIE, LOGAN, AND EGGAN

Lesgold and collaborators bring a very different approach to a different class of complex human skills. They aim to identify critical knowledge and skills that characterize expert troubleshooting of navigational equipment for F-15 fighter planes, and then to use that knowledge as a basis for examining novice performance in order to determine misconceptions or missing knowledge, which in turn serves as the basis for instruction.

What is unique about their approach is that they do not begin by developing a general theory of skill acquisition and diagnosis, but rather ground their approach in the specific knowledge of the system and troubleshooting strategies demonstrated by experts. Their effort reflects recent observations that problem-solving expertise is rooted in rich specific content knowledge and is not a general skill or ability. This has led them to examine both specific knowledge components, such as device or system understanding and troubleshooting methods, and meta-cognitive knowledge components such as plans and hypotheses and the way they are applied.

Especially notable aspects of the Lesgold et al. approach are the following:

1. Their purpose in developing diagnostic tests is to establish a basis for instruction. This goal contrasts with the psychometric approach of devising tests that maximally discriminate among people. Although a diagnostic test could certainly be used for comparing individuals, its primary use is to provide instructional guidance. Lesgold et al. have adopted a medical metaphor for their approach. In medicine, diagnostic tests are administered so that the doctor can prescribe a treatment. The most useful tests are those that discriminate most clearly between possible causes for the presenting symptoms.

Note that the information gained from good medical diagnostic tests enables the doctor to generate a causal explanation for the symptoms and to prescribe treatment that is directed at the cause of the ailment. Contrast such tests with those used for broad screening to identify people who have a particular feature, like an antibody, or are above a critical level on, say, blood pressure. These latter tests are more like general intelligence or ability tests that differentiate among people, but do not provide a basis for specific instruction. Knowing that a student has an IQ of 110 or 125 does not tell you how to teach her arithmetic.

2. The significance of Lesgold et al.'s goal of *complete* description of expert knowledge and strategies should not be minimized. Their aim is to determine all the relevant knowledge needed to perform a task, which includes detailed knowledge about the system, what its components do, how they can fail, the likelihood of various failures, appropriate troubleshooting strategies, and what information specific tests should yield. In other words, they are seeking a model of the expert's troubleshooting model, which includes a causal model of the system.

This approach stands in stark contrast to the usual approach to achievement testing found in both educational and military contexts that focuses on superficial elements of the task. These are frequently broken down into abstract theoretical or factual information and a set of fixed procedures applicable to specific situations. Unfortunately, traditional training and testing may never require that the two come together in any meaningful way. No understanding of the system, reasons for applying procedures, or conditions under which they are appropriate may be learned by the student.

In fact, considerable progress has been made in developing tests to measure knowledge in well-described domains. But the real problem in training people to solve problems is understanding the expert's rationale for generating a particular hypothesis, what his or her plan of attack is, and his or her understanding of how the system works. Strategies are specific to the device or system, so the two must be assessed together, not as independent components.

Student diagnosis is accomplished in a problem-solving context, with particular attention to critical impasse points to determine what is particularly difficult for novices to learn. By examining both specific device/system knowledge and metacognitive/strategic knowledge, the researchers generate a model of the learner's knowledge that led to the particular failure, and then design instruction to address specific knowledge gaps. Expert approaches at those impasse points guide the instructional design. The complete model of task knowledge and performance can thus serve both as a guide to instruction and as a basis for evaluating the effectiveness of that instruction.

3. A final benefit of the Lesgold et al. cognitive task analysis approach is that it would provide a basis for cost/benefit analysis of instruction. Lesgold et al. acknowledge that the cognitive diagnosis approach they propose would be very expensive to conduct routinely for all learners. However, much current instruction is wasteful because it does not address learner needs, being either too far beyond the learner's understanding, redundant with what she or he already knows, or completely missing a student's misconception. Cognitive task analysis should lead to understanding of patterns of subskills or syndromes of partial learning that would lead to optimal, and eventually economical, instructional plans.

## Issues

1. One issue that must be addressed is how to validate the cognitive task analysis that serves as the foundation for diagnosis. One obvious way is concurrence among a number of experts. The other is by determining whether instruction aimed at deficiencies identified by the task analysis leads to improved performance. However, a problem that must be considered is how to interpret the findings if performance does not improve following such instruction. Failure to

improve may indicate that the task analysis was inadequate, but it could also mean that the instruction was inadequate.

At this point the Lesgold et al. analogy to medical diagnosis breaks down. In medicine, once a diagnosis is correct, the treatment options are generally known. Treatment is largely specified by the diagnosis, with the caveat that its application may need to be modulated by patient factors, such as age, history, and other conditions. Lesgold et al. acknowledge that diagnostic information does not prescribe instructional remedies. The nondeterministic nature of the relation between diagnosis and instruction suggests that other means of validating the cognitive task analysis should be sought. They point out that the troubleshooting problem used in their initial work was well defined. They and their subject-matter expert were confident that their problem-space mapping was exhaustive. Procedures for doing so with less well-defined subject domains remain a serious methodological problem, but their approach opens the door to dealing with complex domains.

2. For cognitive diagnosis to be possible, in addition to having a valid task analysis, a second essential component is a theory of skill acquisition. It is not enough to describe the target state of knowledge and skill as evident in the expert. It is also necessary to know the sequence, logical prerequisites, and interdependencies among different aspects of knowledge as one moves from being a novice to an expert. For example, one would want to know how much knowledge about system components is needed before simple troubleshooting strategies can be acquired. Can strategic planning be learned at the outset, or must other specific knowledge be mastered first? We have no reason to assume that uniformity exists across experts in any domain, or that all learners follow the same path of acquisition.

This difficulty is exacerbated by the fact that we do not have a good causal model of the relation between instruction and learning. The teacher teaches a lesson; the student learns something; and we conclude a causal relation. But the dynamics are poorly understood. We do not fully know how a teacher's questions, explanations, or assignments lead to new understanding or knowledge on the student's part. A theory of cognitive diagnosis in the absence of a thorough understanding of learning and teaching process is bound to be incomplete.

3. Finally, Lesgold et al. are searching for a pattern of logical relations among details of performance to create a model of student knowledge. This reflects confidence that a coherent model can be constructed. Such a model may exist more in the eyes of the beholder than the learner. Initial observations of students' troubleshooting performance suggested that their knowledge was fragmentary as they resorted to trial-and-error strategies when reaching an impasse. That is not to say that students do not develop misconceptions that lead to consistent errors; it does suggest that investigators may need to set some limits on their search for consistency that may not exist.

## FREDERIKSEN AND BREULEUX

Frederiksen and Breuleux are tackling the very difficult problem of assessing conceptual understanding of knowledge in a rich domain. Unlike the other two approaches discussed here, their emphasis is on declarative knowledge rather than procedures, strategies, or skills. Their focus is most closely related to traditional achievement tests in content areas, such as chemistry, social sciences, or history, where essay type assessments are common, although multiple-choice questions frequently prevail.

In general, their goal is to provide a theoretical foundation for assessing knowledge acquisition, integration and use after reading (or, presumably, hearing) extended text. Much like a teacher who uses a student's answers to questions as a basis for inferring the student's understanding of a text, Frederiksen and Breuleux want to model the student's (a) concept of the task (question), (b) prior knowledge, (c) current knowledge, and (d) response-production processes.

Although their progress to date is limited to a small domain, they have developed a theoretical framework for representing expert knowledge to use as the source for differential modeling. This includes analysis of discourse produced as answers to questions in syntactic, propositional, and conceptual terms. The effort builds on Frederiksen's earlier work on discourse analysis that developed a method for characterizing text base.

Frederiksen and Breuleux's approach offers four major advantages compared to the more limited multiple-choice or short-answer approaches:

1. For the first time, it would be possible to use freely produced discourse as a response in an automated system, instead of multiple-choice or short-answer types of questions. This allows the student to explain answers, yielding a richer source of information about that student's understanding. In the past this has not been possible because no valid and economical means of analyzing the semantic content of that discourse has been available. The effort hinges on a workable and thorough representation of the expert knowledge—the text base—for comparison with the student's discourse.

2. The differential modeling approach permits a broader assessment of the student's knowledge because it allows richer specification of ways in which the student's knowledge differs from the expert's. With an automatic system for creating a conceptual network of the student's knowledge, it should be possible to identify missing or incorrect concepts or relations. If a student gives an incorrect or incomplete answer to a question, the differential model guides the selection of follow-up questions that pin down misconceptions by identifying gaps. Such flexibility is impossible with a test using a fixed-item pool.

3. Frederiksen and Breuleux's semantic representation would also make it possible to evaluate inferences drawn from the presented text or resulting from

incorporation of new information into the student's existing knowledge. The propositional base provides a foundation for analyzing derived propositions on a flexible basis. However, a theory of inferencing is needed in order to determine the nature of the inferences and how they relate to explicit information.

4. Finally, use of propositional rules and conceptual frames for differential modeling makes it possible to assess student knowledge on the basis of underlying concepts, rather than on superficial aspects of discourse. A consequence is that different surface representations should yield the same underlying structure when the knowledge is truly equivalent. Such an approach should reduce negative judgments of student comprehension that are based on poor linguistic production instead of incomplete knowledge. One difficulty in the classroom when teachers evaluate students' understanding from either oral or written replies is the possibility of a halo-effect based on a student's fluency and style, which often distort underlying knowledge or camouflage ignorance. A propositional analysis goes beyond surface features to represent the concepts and their relations.

## Issues

Although Frederiksen and Breuleux's approach is powerful and could revolutionize evaluation of comprehension, there are potential pitfalls along the way to full implementation.

1. The most critical strength of the system—its reliance on a propositional base for its differential modeling—is also its potential Achilles' heel. Linguistic performance is used as the basis for assessing underlying competence. A critical question is whether the method is in fact able to generate an unconfounded representation of underlying conceptual understanding from the language used to express it. Would the system be able to generate identical conceptual frames from different but equivalent linguistic expressions? Its ability to do so depends primarily on the adequacy of the transformational theory. This is essentially a validity question.

2. A reliability question centers on a theory of question answering. If a student is twice asked the same question about a just-read text, does the student give the same answer both times? One may guess that the answers may vary slightly, both as a function of performance factors—it is difficult to remember exactly what you said even a minute ago—and also as a function of retrieving the information for the first answer. Presumably Frederiksen and Breuleux would not be bothered by this. They would want to extract all relevant knowledge from the student, along with appropriate inferences. Probe questions are proposed to achieve just this purpose.

An associated problem is that different students may interpret the same question differently, as a function of differences in relevant conceptual or linguistic knowledge. Although the authors specifically propose to assess the student's understanding of the question, they do not indicate how they plan to determine and represent this understanding. Responses would then need to be conditionalized on the student's representation of the task. If the student understands a question differently than an expert, which is quite likely, differences in their answers may be misleading because they are in effect answering different questions. However, the striking advantage of Frederiksen and Breuleux's approach is that it would explicitly identify such differences, which would be systematically analyzed—a possibility not offered by other approaches.

3. In addition to assessing the understanding that results from reading a text, the authors propose to assess process, but little attention is devoted to this facet. By *process* they mean the operations involved in answering a comprehension question about the just-read text, that is, accessing and using relevant information acquired from the text. Accomplishing this requires a theory of question answering, but none is provided (see, for example, Graesser & Murachver, 1987). Given that they would use an expert model for comparison, they would be faced with the dilemma of separating out differences in process (weak versus strong methods) from differences in knowledge, as in other expert–novice comparisons, an issue they would need to address.

A different approach is illustrated in their chapter for characterizing discourse production when no expert model is available. An example is provided of a journalist writing an article to accomplish a specific purpose. They analyze the writing in light of the journalist's stated goal and subgoals, which takes the place of the expert model. A conceptual frame is developed for the evolving article, coordinated with the strategy protocol, obtained from interviewing the journalist. Although this approach yields descriptive data, its utility for diagnostic purposes is not apparent, mainly because of the nondeterministic nature of language. Frederiksen and Breuleux must tell us what it is they want to characterize and measure. Interesting related work is currently being done by researchers studying case-based and analogical reasoning (see Holyoak & Thagard, in press; Kolodner, 1988). They are wrestling with the problem of how information relevant to a current problem is accessed and retrieved from memory, a task not unlike that needed for answering questions in Frederiksen and Brueleux's formulation.

4. Frederiksen and Breuleux distinguish between frame-based and rule-based processing, the former used when the task is routine and sufficient relevant knowledge is available for a frame to have been created already. Rule-based processing occurs when the task and information are new to the student. The authors do not indicate how they can infer from a student's response whether the processing is rule or frame based, or the significance of these two types of processing. They do plan to assess prior relevant knowledge through probe questions that presumably would shed light on the type of processing. Also, the nature of inferences generated should indicate whether a frame is operating. Clearly, frame-based processing is the default, when available.

# SUMMARY

The chapters discussed here describe different diagnostic approaches that deal with different kinds of skills. Regian and Schneider are concerned with developing a general theory that accounts for skills involving some degree of automaticity in performance. Their effort focuses on understanding *degrees* of learning of various skill components.

Lesgold et al. are primarily concerned with analyzing the components of knowledge and skill. The focus on *what* and *how,* not on how much. The kinds of abilities they address are complex cognitive skills characterized by detailed knowledge, understanding, and strategies.

Frederiksen and Breuleux are concerned with assessing the contents and structure of knowledge in rich conceptual domains. They too are interested in measuring the *what.*

Expertise according to Regian and Schneider consists of automaticity of unstable components of a skill. According to Lesgold et al. it consists of highly organized models of how devices and systems work and metacognitive plans and strategies. For Frederiksen and Breuleux, expertise is defined by the completeness and richness of the conceptual network.

Regian and Schneider have proposed a general theory that cuts across many psychomotor tasks and does not depend on the specific content of the skill. Lesgold et al. are focusing on a very specific kind of skill, with the hope of building a more general theory once the specific case is understood. Frederiksen and Breuleux are developing a method for representing complex knowledge at various levels.

A critical issue for all three approaches is the type of metric they require for measuring an individual's progress in acquiring knowledge or skill, or for comparing learners with each other. Regian and Schneider's approach directly yields numerical performance measures that can be used for both purposes. Note that their measures involve determining *how much*—measured by speed, accuracy, or automaticity. Lesgold et al. and Frederiksen and Breuleux have not yet gotten to the point of determining a unit of knowledge. Questions must be asked about the relative importance of each bit of information. Are all bits equal? Does the same scale hold for system, strategy, and test probe knowledge? In Frederiksen and Breuleux's conceptual framework, are some nodes more essential than others? How is progress to be measured?

We might also ask whether alternative methods such as Regian and Schneider propose (accuracy, speed, workload) should also be applied to the other two schemes. Would it be useful to know how well some bit of declarative or strategic knowledge has been learned, in addition to whether it can be retrieved at all? One might want to test the information's accessibility in various contexts. An advantage of the Lesgold et al. approach is that it is testing knowledge in use, rather than being retrieved just to pass a test. Frederiksen and Breuleux are likewise concerned with the use of information in answering questions.

Clearly these three approaches are complementary and are equally valid, but they yield different information. It may well be that students cannot learn or perform certain aspects of troubleshooting until some component skills are automated. A complete approach to diagnosis would require analysis of both what a student knows and how well he or she knows it, which in turn requires a theory of the task and its acquisition. All three efforts discussed here are making substantial progress toward achieving this goal. These three approaches currently are in the proof-of-concept stage. In their next stage they must yield principles that others can apply to new domains to test their usefulness and adequacy.

## REFERENCES

Au, K. H., Crowell, D. C., Jordan, C., Sloat, K. C. M., Speidel, G. E., Klein, T. W., & Tharp, R. G. (1986). Development and implementation of the KEEP reading program. In J. Orasanu (Ed.), *Reading comprehension: From research to practice* (pp. 235–252). Hillsdale, NJ: Lawrence Erlbaum Associates.

Collins, A. (1988). *Cognitive apprenticeship and instruction technology*. (Tech. Rep. No. 6899). Cambridge, MA: BBN.

Fabiani, M., Buckley, J., Gratton, G., Coles, M. G. H., Donchin, E., & Logie, R. (1988). *The training of complex task performance*. (Tech. Rep. No. CPL 88-1). Champaign, IL: University of Illinois.

Graesser, A. C., & Murachver, T. (1985). Symbolic procedures of question answering. In A. C. Graesser & J. B. Black (Eds.), *The psychology of questions*. Hillsdale, NJ: Lawrence Erlbaum Associates.

Holyoak, K., & Thagard, P. (in press). A constraint-satisfaction approach to analogue retrieval and mapping. In K. Gilhooly, M. Keane, R. Logie, & G. Erdos (Eds.), *Lines of thought*. Chichester, U.K.: Wiley.

Kolodner, J. (1988). Retrieving events from a case memory: A parallel implementation. In *Proceedings of the DARPA Workshop on Case-Based Reasoning*, pp. 233–249. San Mateo, CA: Morgan-Kaufmann.

Shields, J. L., Goldberg, S. L., & Dressel, J. D. (1979). *Retention of Basic Soldiering Skills*. (Research Report 1225). Alexandria, VA: US Army Research Institute for the Behavioral and Social Sciences.

Shiffrin, R. M., & Schneider, W. (1977). Controlled and automatic human information processing: II. Perceptual learning, automatic attending, and a general theory. *Psychological Review, 84*, 127–190.

Wise, L. L., Campbell, J. P., McHenry, J. J., & Hanser, L. M. (1986). A latent structure model of job performance factors. In *Improving the selection, classification, and utilization of Army enlisted personnel: Annual Report, 1986 Fiscal Year—Supplement to ARI Technical Report 813101*. (Research Note 813704), pp. 413–446. Alexandria, VA: US Army Research Institute for the Behavioral and Social Sciences.

# 16

## Diagnostic Testing by Measuring Learning Processes: Psychometric Considerations for Dynamic Testing

Susan Embretson[1]
*University of Kansas*

The current impetus for diagnostic testing stems from a longstanding effort to link testing to instruction. Glaser (1985) points out that the substantive foundations for diagnostic testing are emerging through the connection of both instruction and aptitude theory to cognitive theory. However, Glaser suggests, the psychometric foundations for diagnostic testing have not yet emerged.

This chapter examines the observation of learning processes that occur while one is taking a test as a method for diagnostic testing. More specifically, learning processes are measured by examining the consequences of instruction or using structured cues on the examinee's performance level. This method of testing is currently known as dynamic testing.

The measurement of learning processes has a controversial status in psychology. Therefore, prior to the new developments, the theoretical views and results that support the measurement of learning processes are contrasted with the psychometric concerns about test-related learning. Fortunately, a reconceptualization of the issues is now possible. Both theoretical and technological developments in the last decade are radically changing psychological measurement. The various psychometric issues are reconsidered in light of these developments, which include the cognitive-component analysis of aptitude, latent trait models, and computerized adaptive testing.

Next, a series of new developments are presented as a psychometric basis for measuring learning processes. The first subsection presents two examples that show how dynamic tests can be designed to measure specified learning constructs. Experimental cognitive methods can be applied to control the test content so that

---

[1]Susan Embretson has also published as Susan E. Whitely.

performance changes are linked to specified theoretical constructs. The second subsection examines some scaling problems in measuring change. Cronbach and Furby's (1970) classic article reviewed many problems in measuring change and suggested that change scores should be abandoned. This chapter shows that change scores from tests that are based on classical test theory do lead to differences in scores that are purely scaling artifacts. However, these problems are solved by computerized adaptive testing that is based on item response theory (i.e., latent trait models). The third subsection presents a multidimensional latent trait model for measuring change. In this model, the experimental design of the dynamic testing procedure controls the abilities that are measured in the latent trait model.

It should be clearly noted that this chapter presents new developments rather than a discussion of currently implemented psychometric methods. Although linking the concerns of diagnostic testing to current psychometric theory seems desirable on the surface, it proves to be a nearly insurmountable task. In fact, papers on diagnostic testing often emphasize the inappropriateness of traditional psychometric techniques (e.g., Glaser, 1985). Two major problems are that (a) the psychometric concept of static latent traits does not interface well with a concern for diagnosing multifaceted differences in performance that can be prescriptive for guiding subsequent learning, and (b) the psychometric techniques for item analysis begin only after the items are constructed, whereas diagnostic testing is concerned with item content.

## MEASURING LEARNING PROCESSES: A CONTROVERSIAL TOPIC

### Supporting Views

Measuring individual differences in intelligence by measuring the actual progress of learning has a long history of interest in psychology. At the first major conference on the measurement of intelligence, many participants stressed capacity for learning as a major aspect of intelligence. But one participant (Dearborn, 1921, p. 130) noted, ". . . most tests in common use are not tests of the capacity to learn, but are tests of what has been learned."

Interest in directly measuring learning clearly continues in contemporary psychology. Resnick and Neches (1984, p. 276) point out that viewing static tests as measures of learning processes is based on the (probably faulty) assumption that ". . . the processes required for performance on the tests are also directly involved in learning." Another indicator of continuing interest among American psychologists (e.g., Campione, Brown, Ferrara, Jones & Steinberg, 1985) is the increasing popularity of Vygotsky's (1978) thesis about measuring the zone of proximal development. Vygotsky hypothesized that the sensitivity of an examinee's performance to external aids and cues is theoretically revealing of his or her learning potential.

The recent interest in diagnostic testing has also rendered measuring the progress of learning an important concern. The goal for diagnostic testing is to facilitate the adaptation of instruction to the individual by diagnosing the cognitive basis of performance (Glaser, 1985). That is, assessment should be concerned not only with an individual's performance level, but also with the cognitive processing components, strategies, and knowledge structures that underlie his or her performance. Thus, diagnostic testing is grounded in the use of cognitive theory to monitor skill and knowledge acquisition processes so that instruction may be adaptively selected.

Some recent developments in testing (cf. Lidz, 1987), seemingly hold promise as a foundation for measuring learning processes. These developments concern *dynamic testing*, in which the changes in an examinee's performance are observed following instruction or structured cues. Recently, several studies have reported positive results both for increasing predictive validity (Babad & Budoff, 1974; Carlson & Weidl, 1979; Hamilton & Budoff, 1974) and for diagnosing specific cognitive deficits that may be remedied by instruction (Feuerstein, 1979, 1980; Campione et al., 1985).

## Psychometric Concerns

Despite the continuing interest in measuring learning directly on a test, the psychometric view is currently quite negative for several reasons. First, practice effects during testing are a threat to the appropriateness of the popular latent trait models, such as the one-, two-, or three-parameter logistic latent trait models. The popular latent trait models are unidimensional and must assume that no learning occurs on the test. Only one ability is measured, one that reflects a person's response potential throughout the test. Furthermore, the models assume that an item's difficulty is constant, regardless of whether the item occurs early or late in the test. Thus the models have no way to represent improvements in performance that occur by learning during the taking of a test.

Second, performance gains that accompany test-related instruction are also viewed as a threat to the psychometric properties of the test. Test-related instruction is regarded as coaching, which is viewed as a potential threat to test validity. Major effort has been expended to examine the impact of coaching on scores for major tests (e.g., Messick & Jungeblut, 1981).

Third, many psychometricians do not believe that learning ability is a viable construct. The early studies on learning ability provided seemingly negative evidence about the validity of measuring ability by changes in performance. Woodrow's (1938) findings that learning was task specific and unrelated to school achievement are often cited as evidence against the learning ability construct.

Fourth, the measurement of change is beset with so many problems that some psychometricians have suggested abandoning change measures altogether (e.g.,

Cronbach & Furby, 1970). Later in this chapter I show that, in fact, the problems in measuring change by any score that is based on classical test theory are even worse than envisioned by Cronbach and Furby (1970).

Fifth, the currently available dynamic testing procedures also have major faults: The procedures are individually administered, and they often involve unstandardized procedures. The properties required for psychometrically adequate dynamic tests include: (a) presentation of the test in a format appropriate for mass testing, (b) standardized instructional sets or cue structures, (c) well-specific contingencies for the administration of the instruction or the cues, and (d) appropriate normative or item calibration data.

## A Reconceptualization

Despite the currently negative psychometric view, I believe that dynamic testing should become a major approach to testing in the future. A dynamic testing procedure may influence validity in at least three different ways (see Embretson, 1987b, for details): It may (a) improve incremental validity by adding a direct measure of learning ability from the modifiability of cognitive performance to initial ability status; (b) improve construct validity by providing better measures of intended aptitude constructs (by reducing the influence of task dependent or construct irrelevant sources of individual differences in performance; and (c) improve diagnostic validity by measuring the modifiability of specific cognitive deficits (from supplying cues or instructional sets that influence known cognitive components, strategies, or knowledge structures).

Several major developments in the last decade that include the cognitive component analysis of aptitude, computerized adaptive testing, and latent trait models permit the psychometric issues to be reconceptualized. First, latent trait models that are appropriate for measuring learning can be developed by including parameters that model performance increases during the testing. One such model, a multidimensional normal ogive model for measuring change is presented in this chapter.

Second, dynamic testing procedures may lessen the impact of coaching on test scores. Currently, coaching introduces a new and undesirable source of individual differences in test scores, because it is unstandardized and unequally utilized by examinees. By standardizing instruction about the test and including it as part of the testing procedures, the impact of coaching can be minimized. An added advantage of "standardized coaching," is that the resulting individual differences in score modifiability can be measured, and such scores may provide incremental validity when added to initial status (e.g., Carlson & Weidl, 1979; Embretson, 1987a).

Third, the status of learning ability as a theoretical construct may begin to be resolved. Since the Woodrow studies, it has become clear that the early negative findings are due at least partially to methodological flaws (see Stake, 1961) in measuring learning, such as failing to clearly differentiate the various parameters of a learning curve (i.e., intercept, slope, asymptote). Another significant factor is the nature of the learning tasks that were studied. The early studies used relatively simple perceptual or conceptual tasks that depend little on higher order executive processing strategies or the acquisition and utilization of knowledge structures. In fact, the negative results on measuring learning should not have been surprising, because even the very earliest studies showed that simple tasks have had little validity to predict criterion performance in settings such as education or training (e.g., Wissler, 1901).

The recent studies on dynamic testing differ substantially from Woodrow's early studies. The performance gains are not only measured on more complex tasks, but gain is more closely related to specific cognitive processes that are targeted by the dynamic testing procedure.

Fourth, although the measurement of change is clearly problematic for tests that are based on classical test theory, a solution to the scaling problems exists. Computerized adaptive testing, in which individuals are measured by items that are selected to equate information about their ability, solves the scaling problems that arise from scores that are based on the number of items passed. This issue is considered in detail later.

Fifth, computerized adaptive testing entails other technological changes that can allow dynamic testing procedures to become sufficiently objective and standardized for large-scale testing programs. Most importantly, computerized presentation of items can replace many functions of an individual examiner in dynamic testing. Dynamic testing requires (a) the precise display of each item (or cue), (b) interactive item selection according to specified response contingencies, and (c) the recording of auxiliary indices of cognitive processing, such as response time. Computerized administration of items, fortunately, can meet all these requirements. In fact, computerized item presentation makes the technology of testing similar to cognitive experiments. Cognitive research now routinely uses microcomputers to precisely vary task presentation conditions according to an experimental design. Thus, computerized presentation of items gives the testing situation the same stimulus control capabilities as cognitive experiments.

Another advantage of computerized adaptive testing is that it decreases testing time. Precise measurement is obtained from fewer items than the traditional fixed content tasks (Weiss, 1982). Thus, additional time is available for dynamic testing procedures.

## A PSYCHOMETRIC BASIS FOR MEASURING LEARNING PROCESSES

Measuring learning processes through dynamic testing requires three classes of developments: (a) experimental designs are needed to manipulate and assess the construct representation of performance, including the cognitive components, strategies, and knowledge structures that are involved in performance under various conditions (i.e., instruction versus control, cues versus no cues, etc.); (b) test development procedures must assure that dynamic testing is sufficiently objective for use in large scale testing (i.e., the individualized testing needs to be replaced by a more objective testing format); and (c) an adequate psychometric model for measuring score changes under the various conditions is necessary because measuring gain reliably presumes that stringent scale properties have been achieved.

In the next several sections, experimental designs and psychometric models for measuring learning processes are considered.

## CONSTRUCT REPRESENTATION
## AND DIAGNOSTIC TESTING

In this section, experimental designs for the measurement of learning processes are presented. First, the relationship between experimental design and construct representation is considered. Then examples of possible experimental designs are given for two item types: mathematical reasoning and spatial aptitude. These two aptitudes were selected because they involve different dynamic testing procedures: The mathematical reasoning example employs structured cues to increase performance level, whereas the spatial aptitude example uses instructional sets.

### Construct Representation and Experimental Designs
### for Dynamic Testing

Construct validation can be viewed as two separate research stages (see Embretson, 1983). Construct representation concerns the cognitive components, strategies, and knowledge structures that are involved in solving the test item. It is assessed by decomposing the task into more elementary components, using a variety of methods that are current in cognitive psychology. The theoretical nature of the construct that is measured by the test is assessed by construct representation research. Nomothetic span, on the other hand, concerns the utility of a test as a measure of individual differences. Nomothetic span is assessed by the pattern, magnitude, and span of relationships of test scores with other measures of individual differences.

The linkage of aptitude to cognitive theory, such as is provided by cognitive component analysis (Sternberg, 1982), means that the construct representation of a test is becoming increasingly explicit. Cognitive component analysis makes it possible for the designing of a psychological test to become a science rather than an art. That is, the test can be designed just like a cognitive experiment in which a task is systematically varied so that specified constructs are measured (Embretson, 1985). Dynamic testing can be viewed as another aspect of test design in which the nature of the supplied item cues or instruction also manipulate cognitive processing. Dynamic testing, in conjunction with cognitive component analysis, makes it possible to design precisely the dynamic testing procedure to measure specified constructs.

For diagnostic testing, the primary objective is to associate individual performance levels with various conditions so as to diagnose specific aspects of cognitive processing that could have implication for instruction. Three well-established methods for linking performance changes to cognitive processing can be readily employed in dynamic testing: (a) an instructional method that changes an examinee's cognitive processing in taking an ability task (cf. Butterfield, 1985, for summary), (b) an additive factor method in which the cognitive components that are required for solution are varied by the task structure (Pachella, 1973), and (c) a subtractive factor method that utilizes subtasks to manipulate processes. The latter two methods can be considered as structured cue methods because they involve changes in the task content. With all three methods, it is important to provide empirical data, such as mathematical modeling of response time and accuracy, and protocol analysis to support the attribution of gain to the targeted cognitive processes.

*Example 1: Mathematical Reasoning.*    Mathematical reasoning, as assessed by word problems such as those shown in Table 16.1, is easily tested by dynamic procedures because promising theoretical foundations have been developed. The cognitive processing of word problems has been studied from contrasting theoretical views (Kintsch & Greeno, 1985; Mayer, Larkin, & Kadane, 1984). These studies provide a good foundation for targeting manipulations of the stimulus content of word problems through structured cues to vary the dependence on specified aspects of processing.

A recent study in my laboratory (Wheeler & Embretson, 1986) examined 25 published mathematical reasoning items from the Scholastic Aptitude Test (SAT). Mayer, Larkin, & Kadane's (1984) taxonomy was applied to separate sources of errors in solving these word problems. Table 16.2 shows that this taxonomy postulates four types of error in solving a word problem—errors in translation,

TABLE 16.1
Examples of Word Problems from the SAT

*Example 1*
If 45 cards can be copied in 30 minutes, how many *hours* will it take to copy 540 such cards at the same rate?
(A) 3          (B) 6          (C) 12          (D) 18          (E) 24

*Example 2*
A woman made 5 payments on a loan, with each payment being twice the amount of the preceding one. If the total of all 5 payments was $465, how much was the first payment?
(A) $5          (B) $15          (C) $31          (D) $93          (E) $155

TABLE 16.2
Four Types of Knowledge Required in Solving
An Algebra Story Problem

| Phase | Type of Knowledge | Example from Algebra Problem |
|---|---|---|
| 1. Translate | linguistic and factual knowledge | Variables are (TOTAL OXYGEN), OXYGEN PER ASTRONAUT PER DAY), (NO. OF DAYS), (NO. OF ASTRONAUTS). |
| 2. Understand | schematic knowledge | "Time-Rate" problem schema is TOTAL = RATE × TIME. |
| 3. Plan | strategic knowledge | First figure out TIME, (TIME = NO. OF DAYS) × (NO. OF ASTRONAUTS). Then figure out TOTAL, (OXYGEN) = (OXYGEN PER ASTRONAUT PER DAY) × (TIME). |
| 4. Execute | algorithmic knowledge | Carry out procedure for 3 × 5, such as adding 5 + 5 + 5. |

Reprinted with permission from Mayer, R.E., Larkin, J.H., & Kadane, J.B. (1984). A cognitive analysis of mathematical problem-solving ability. In Sternberg, R.J. (ed.), *Advances in the Psychology of Human Intelligence, Vol. 2.* Hillsdale, NJ: Lawrence Erlbaum Associates.

understanding, planning, and executing. These errors imply deficiencies in factual/linguistic knowledge, schematic knowledge, strategic knowledge, and algorithmic knowledge, respectively.

A goal for diagnostic testing could be to pinpoint the specific sources of error that are prominent in an individual's performance. Instruction could then be geared to remediating this source.

To design a dynamic testing procedure, it is desirable to determine which knowledge structures are associated with relatively high error rates. An initial study on mathematical reasoning (Wheeler & Embretson, 1986) has shown substantial error rates on some components of constructing the problem algorithm. In this study, college freshmen were first given the SAT problems in their standard format. After completing the test, they were required to write protocols that described how they solved each problem. The written protocols were scored by two raters according to whether they contained an error in each of Mayer's four knowledge types. High reliability was achieved for factual/linguistic, schematic, and strategic knowledge. Errors in algorithmic knowledge were rarely detected, and hence were eliminated from subsequent analysis.

Figure 16.1 shows accuracy on the standard word problem (labeled Full Task) that examinees had taken before writing out their problem-solving methods, and the three types of knowledge that were scored from the written protocols. It can be seen on Fig. 16.1 that factual/linguistic knowledge was associated with the

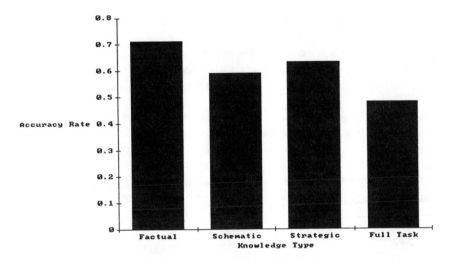

FIG. 16.1.   Accuracy rate on four types of mathematical knowledge.

highest accuracy levels, whereas schematic and strategic knowledge had lower accuracy. These results suggest that factual, schematic, and strategic knowledge could all be assessed by dynamic testing. For those problems that are missed, one approach could be to supply the necessary prerequisite knowledge with the item. For a rate problem, for example, the general rate formula shown on Table 16.2 could be supplied with the item and subsequently performance accuracy could then be observed. Similarly, the translation of the problem or solution strategy could be supplied to examine performance changes.

Wheeler and Embretson (1986) also provided evidence that structured cues could increase performance levels. The study supplied cues with each problem that, if applied appropriately, would lead to solution. Only one complete set of cues was supplied, so that the various types of knowledge were not separated in this study. Accuracy levels increased significantly ($t = 3.58; p < .001$), showing the feasibility of dynamic testing for mathematical reasoning ability.

*Example 2: Spatial Aptitude.*   The second example employs an instructional method to manipulate cognitive processing in the spatial reasoning area. In this study, a pretest was followed by an intervention that was intended to increase performance levels. Then a posttest was administered. Two scores were obtained from the design. The initial ability score was obtained by a Rasch latent-trait model scaling of the pretest. A modifiability score was obtained as residualized gain score (as recommended by Cronbach and Furby, 1970). The modifiability score reflects the impact of the dynamic testing procedure. It should be noted that the posttest scores were also scaled by the Rasch model prior to obtaining the residentialized gain scores.

As stated above, the instructional method requires that a good theory of the task be available so that performance changes can be attributed to specific components, strategies, or knowledge structures. Ideally, instruction should be precisely targeted, and empirical data should be collected to support further which aspect of processing is influenced. The current example partially meets these goals.

A good theoretical foundation is available for the spatial folding task, two items of which are presented in Fig. 16.2. Several investigations have supported similar processing models for the spatial folding tasks (Carpenter & Just, 1982; Just & Carpenter, 1985; Pellegrino, Mumaw, & Shute, 1985; Regian & Pellegrino, 1985; Shepard & Metzler, 1971). Although differences between subjects in spatial processing are sometimes observed (e.g., Just & Carpenter, 1985), and while it is possible that subjects switch strategies during testing, a general processing model often provides reasonably good fit to the task response data. Thus, the various theories support at least three general processing stages that include: (a) anchoring part of the unfolded figure to the folded alternative, (b) rotating the sides to fold the figure, and (c) confirming that the mentally folded side of the unfolded figure appears as shown on the alternative.

In the dynamic testing of spatial aptitude (Embretson, 1987a), the intervention was targeted to facilitate spatial processing by providing concrete training on the physical analogue of the task. That is, large cutouts of the unfolded figure were presented, with prefolded edges, so that the subject could physically compare the folded shape to the various alternatives. The series of studies (Embretson, 1987a) showed that performance was significantly increased by the intervention and that

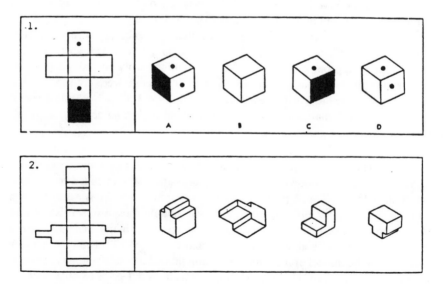

FIG. 16.2.  Two spatial folding items.

anchoring and confirming were less-important sources of item difficulty on the posttest. Specifically, mathematical models of item responses revealed that a stimulus factor that influences the anchoring and confirming processes was significant on the pretest, but not the posttest, in modeling item difficulty. The stimulus factors that influence rotation did not differ in explaining item difficulty on the pretest and posttest. A last study in the series on spatial aptitude obtained positive support for validity in predicting vocational training in text editing (previous studies, such as Egan and Gomez, 1985, had found spatial reasoning to be a major predictor of text editing performance).

So, in summary, the Embretson (1987a) studies showed that: (a) ability scores are significantly increased by dynamic testing, as the posttest ability mean was about .66 standard score units higher than the pretest ability mean); (b) the dynamic testing procedure significantly changed cognitive processing, as indicated by the differences in the mathematical models of item difficulty between the pretest and the posttest; and (c) most importantly, incremental validity for predicting success in vocational training was found as the modifiability score significantly, and substantially, increased prediction beyond the initial ability score alone.

## PSYCHOMETRIC MODELS

The relationship of psychometric models to the measurement of change is considered in this section. The classical test theory model, unidimensional latent trait models, and multidimensional latent train models were examined for appropriateness in measuring change. Finally, a new multidimensional latent trait model is introduced that links experimental designs for measuring learning to ability measurement.

### Classical Test Theory: Who Gains the Most?

In classical test theory, the test score is typically a linear transformation of the number of items passed. Thus, the scale properties of the raw score persist in the derived standard score. The basic problem is that the level and dispersion of item difficulties within tests influences the metric of the scores. Comparing gains between individuals requires that: (a) the scores employ the same metric for two tests, (b) interval measurement be achieved within each test, and (c) equal precision of measurement be achieved for all abilities. This section shows that these properties cannot be achieved under the assumptions of classical test theory.

The basic problem is that the regression of item-solving success on ability is nonlinear, as has long been known. If the item-solving probability is calculated for groups that are homogeneous for raw score levels, the normal ogive shown on Fig. 16.3 typically provides a good approximation of the data. The threshold of the item is given by the ability score at which the probability of passing is .50. Small changes in ability around the item's threshold lead to large changes in response probabilities. At the extremes, however, large changes in ability lead to small changes in response probability.

Raw scores, as linear combinations of responses, do not take into account the level and dispersion of items within the test. The effect is devastating for the measurement of change.

The following concrete examples show more clearly how the measurement of change is influenced by an underlying nonlinear item response model. Figure 16.3 shows an item characteristics curve that is typically obtained from items in cognitive tests. The ordinate axis is the probability that the item is solved, and the abscissa is ability. The logistic latent trait models often show quite adequate fit to cognitive test data that generate item characteristic curves, such as presented on Fig. 16.3.

For the purpose of demonstration, it is assumed for the examples that the underlying model is the one-parameter logistic latent trait model, in which the probability of solving an item, $P_{(X_{ij}=1)}$, is given from the log linear difference of ability, $\Theta_j$ and item difficulty, $b_i$, as follows:

$$P_{(X_{ij}=1)} = \frac{e^{(\theta_j - b_i)}}{1 + e^{(\theta_j - b_i)}}$$

Where
$b_i$ = difficulty for item $i$
$\theta_j$ = ability for person $j$

Consider four individuals—Oscar, Mario, Maxwell, and Olaf—who are measured in a test–intervention–test design. These individuals vary widely in initial abilities of $-2.00$, $-.50$, $1.00$ and $2.50$, respectively, which makes them evenly spaced on the ability continuum with an interval of $1.50$. Suppose that the pretest and posttest are perfectly parallel forms with symmetrically distributed item difficulties that are appropriate for a general population. That is, the item-solving probabilities range from about .40 to .60, with a mean of 0.50. Suppose further that only three item difficulty levels are used, and the symmetrically distributed $b_i$ equal $-.50$, $0.00$ and $.50$. Assuming that the population mean is .00, inserting these item difficulties into Equation 1 with $\Theta_j$ equal to .00 yields item probabilities of .62, .50 and .38, respectively. That is, for $b_i$ equal to .50,

$$P_{(X_{ij}=1)} = \frac{e^{(.00 - .50)}}{1 + e^{(.00 - .50)}}$$

$$= .38.$$

Table 16.3 shows the probability of solving each item for each of the four individuals. If a test consists of 30 items, 10 for each difficulty level, the expected raw scores on the pretest is given by multiplying the probabilities by 10 and

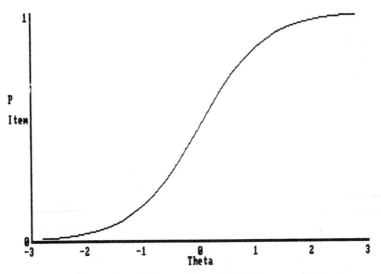

FIG. 16.3.   Regression of item-solving probability on ability.

summing across items. Table 16.3 presents the expected pretest raw scores. It can be seen that although the individuals are evenly spaced along the ability continuum, their raw scores are not.

Suppose that these four individuals profit equally from the interventions, so that ability increases by 1.00 for everyone. Thus, their relative separations on posttest ability are the same as on the pretest (i.e., an interval of 1.50). The probabilities for each posttest item are given on Table 16.3 and the expected raw

TABLE 16.3
Item Solving Probabilities for Four Persons on a Symmetric Test

|  | Item Probability (P_{ij}) | | | Expected Raw Scores | |
|  | $b_i = -0.5$ | $b_i = 0.0$ | $b_i = 0.5$ | Initial | Gain |
|---|---|---|---|---|---|
| *Pretest Ability* | | | | | |
| Oscar ($\Theta_j = -2.0$) | .18 | .12 | .08 | 3.80 | — |
| Mario ($\Theta_j = -0.5$) | .50 | .38 | .27 | 11.50 | — |
| Max ($\Theta_j = 1.0$) | .82 | .73 | .62 | 21.70 | — |
| Olaf ($\Theta_j = 2.5$) | .95 | .92 | .88 | 27.50 | — |
| *Posttest Ability* | | | | | |
| Oscar ($\Theta_j = -1.0$) | .38 | .27 | .18 | 8.30 | 4.50 |
| Mario ($\Theta_j = 0.5$) | .73 | .62 | .50 | 18.50 | 7.00 |
| Max ($\Theta_j = 2.0$) | .92 | .88 | .82 | 26.20 | 4.50 |
| Olaf ($\Theta_j = 3.5$) | .98 | .97 | .95 | 29.00 | 1.50 |

[a] Expected Raw Score = 10 ($P_{ij}$)

scores for a 30-item test. Note that the spacing between individuals is unequal, but different, than on the pretest.

But do the raw scores appropriately reflect the true gain? The answer is clearly no. It can be seen on Table 16.3 and on Fig. 16.4 that Mario shows a very large expected raw gain whereas Olaf shows a very small gain. In fact, Mario's expected raw gain is 5.7 items more than Olaf's expected raw gain. Thus, individuals with equal true gains show unequal raw gains. Furthermore, these raw gains would not be appropriately corrected by using a residualized gain score (see Cronbach & Furby, 1970) or by regressing the posttest on the pretest. Figure 16.4, under the label *Symmetric Test,* shows that although the higher initial score has the lowest gain (Olaf), the lowest score (Oscar) did not have the highest gain. Thus, gain is clearly not negatively related to initial ability. In fact, Fig. 16.4 shows that the relationship of initial ability and gain is not even monotonic.

A second example shows that the magnitude of raw score gain also depends on item dispersion. Item-solving probabilities and expected raw scores on pretest and posttest were calculated for the same four individuals, but for another set of parallel tests. In this case, although the mean item difficulty is .00 (so that the average item probability is .50), the item difficulties are asymmetrically distributed. That is, the difficulties are $-1.00$, $-1.00$ and $2.00$. It can be seen on Table 16.4 that, as on the symmetrical tests, the raw scores are not evenly spaced on either the pretest or posttest. More crucial, however, is the fact that the raw gain scores are again unequal, although the separations between the individuals is not the same as for the first set of parallel tests. Figure 16.4 also presents the raw gains for the asymmetrical test, under the label *Asymmetric Test.*

These examples show that individual differences in gain may reflect only the

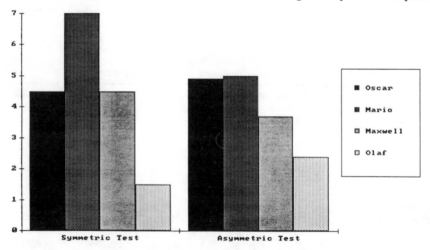

FIG. 16.4. Raw score gains for four persons on both a symmetric and asymmetric test.

TABLE 16.4
Item Solving Probabilities for Four Persons on a Asymmetric Test

| | Item Probability $(P_{ij})$ | | | Expected Raw Scores | |
| | $b_i = -.01$ | $b_i = -1.0$ | $b_i = 2.0$ | Initial | Gain |
|---|---|---|---|---|---|
| *Pretest Ability* | | | | | |
| Oscar ($\Theta_j = -2.0$) | .27 | .27 | .02 | 5.60 | — |
| Mario ($\Theta_j = -0.5$) | .62 | .62 | .08 | 13.20 | — |
| Max ($\Theta_j = 1.0$) | .88 | .88 | .27 | 20.30 | — |
| Olaf ($\Theta_j = 2.5$) | .97 | .97 | .62 | 25.60 | — |
| *Posttest Ability* | | | | | |
| Oscar ($\Theta_j = -1.0$) | .50 | .50 | .05 | 10.50 | 4.90 |
| Mario ($\Theta_j = 0.5$) | .82 | .82 | .18 | 18.20 | 5.00 |
| Max ($\Theta_j = 2.0$) | .95 | .95 | .50 | 24.00 | 3.70 |
| Olaf ($\Theta_j = 3.5$) | .99 | .99 | .82 | 28.00 | 2.40 |

[a] Expected Raw Score = 10 $(P_{ij})$

scale properties of the tests that are used. In both examples, individuals with true gains that are equal have different raw score gains.

The four individuals who were considered varied widely in initial ability levels, but gained equally. Examples could also be constructed to show that individuals who have the same initial ability level, but different true gains, are not appropriately separated by differences between their raw gain scores.

To anticipate more generally the relationship between test characteristics and raw gain, Fig. 16.5 pinpoints items that would show the greatest change in

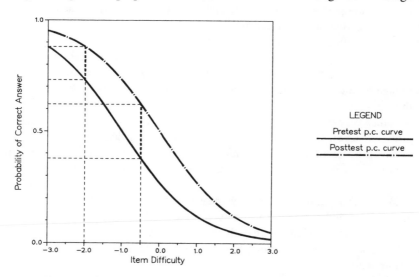

FIG. 16.5. Person characteristic curves for a single person at pretest and posttest.

response probabilities between a pretest and posttest. It presents two characteristic curves that show the probability that a person would solve items at various difficulties (shown on the horizontal axis). The two curves represent the same person, at pretest, where ability equals $-1.00$, and at posttest, where ability equals $0.00$. Items with the greatest vertical separation between the curves show the greatest difference in pretest and posttest response probabilities.

Figure 16.5 shows dashed lines that indicate response probability differences between pretest and posttest for an item difficulty of $-.50$ and an item difficulty of $-2.00$. It can be seen that the response probability difference is much greater for this person when item difficulties are at $-.50$. In this case, the pretest probability of .38 can be subtracted from the posttest probability of .62, yielding a probability difference of .24. When the item difficulties are at $-2.00$, subtracting the pretest probability of .73 from the posttest probability of .88 yields a probability difference of only .15. Thus, the person shown on Fig. 16.5 would have a larger response probability difference between pretest and posttest if he or she received items with a difficulty of $-.50$ than if he or she received items with a difficulty of $-2.00$.

To summarize, Fig. 16.5 shows that items between the threshold levels of the pretests and posttest abilities show the greatest changes in response probabilities. Because a raw score can be regarded as the sum of the person's item probabilities, it can be deduced readily that the largest raw score difference between pretest and posttest occurs for items with difficulties that show the greatest separation between the pretest and posttest person characteristics curve. Thus, the level of raw gain that is observed for a person depends not only on the person's true gain, but also on the person's initial ability and its relationship to the characteristics of the test items that he or she received.

The main conclusion to be drawn from this presentation is that individual differences in true gain cannot be adequately diagnosed from individual differences in raw scores. The item characteristics of the test are crucial in determining the magnitude of raw score differences. Thus, scaling artifacts are confounded with true gain.

Another very crucial point is the reliability of the gain scores. Item response theory has shown that the item characteristics of tests determine the precision with which different ability levels are measured. If an individual receives items at his or her threshold, then the highest reliability is achieved. However, items that are out of range, either much too easy or much too hard, provide little information about ability. Hence, the measurement error is high. Therefore, item difficulty level and dispersion also influence the reliability with which ability gain is measured. An individual with high ability who gains a great deal would not be reliably measured on the posttest unless a sufficient number of very difficult items are administered.

Computerized adaptive testing, which uses latent trait models to scale ability, makes the measurement of gain feasible for two major reasons. First, interval measurement can be achieved because the ability estimates take into account the characteristics of the items that are administered. The models estimate the ability that gives the person's response pattern the highest likelihood, given the specific items that were administered, and the response probabilities are determined by latent trait models that directly account for the nonlinear threshold effects of the items. Second, and equally important, equal precisions of measurement for varying ability levels can be achieved by selecting those items that provide the most information. Given an adequate item bank, items can be adaptively selected to yield equal reliabilities for both the pretest and the posttest. Such a procedure assures that each individual is administered items that are equally near that individual's threshold level.

## LATENT TRAIT MODELS FOR MEASURING LEARNING PROCESSES

The preceding section elaborates the advantages of latent trait models over classical test theory for measuring learning processes. However, the latent trait model that generated the examples above is adequate for measuring learning only when a single dimension characterizes all measurements that are obtained during the dynamic testing process. Thus, change is not explicitly modeled, nor is ability linked explicitly to the experimental designs of the dynamic testing procedure. This section presents multidimensional latent trait models that are appropriate for measuring change.

Two general types of multidimensional models have been postulated. They differ with regard to whether the multiple dimensions are compensatory or noncompensatory in the probability of solving an item. A noncompensatory model that is appropriate for processing components is the multicomponent latent trait model (Embretson, 1984; Whitely, 1980). This model contains both person and item parameters for each component. In this case, *noncompensatory* implies that each component is necessary for item solving, so that the model is multiplicative. Thus, a low ability in one component implies a low probability of item solving regardless of the ability levels on the other components. Given the appropriate method to identify the model parameters learning processes can be assessed on several dimensions; for example, in the mathematical reasoning items subtasks could be constructed to separate translation processes from planning processes.

A compensatory latent trait model is the multidimensional normal ogive model (Lawley, 1943; Lord, 1952). In this model, a person's response potential for a given item depends on the item's threshold and a weighted combination of several abilities. The weights vary between items. An effective algorithm for estimating the parameters has recently been implemented by Bock, Gibbons, and Muraki (1985). However, the model is not quite appropriate for measuring learning processes because the dimensions are defined by common factors that are empirically extracted from the data rather than by the design of the dynamic testing procedures.

I believe that the key to developing psychometric models that are appropriate for measuring the processes involved in learning is to represent the experimental design structure for observing these processes directly in the model. Prior to presenting these psychometric models, some sample design structures are reviewed. Then the multicomponent latent trait model is presented, and it is shown that it implicitly incorporates one design structure. Last, a multidimensional latent trait model for measuring learning processes is developed. It is based on the multidimensional generalization of the two-parameter normal ogive model but contains special constraints that can be specified by the design structure of the dynamic testing procedure.

## Mathematical Model for Experimental Design Structures

The two examples of dynamic testing that were elaborated in the section on construct representation led to rather different experimental designs. In this section, some sample design structures are presented.

Recent studies have shown that under certain assumptions the item discrimination parameters in latent trait models are like factor loadings (Mislevy, 1986; Thissen & Steinberg, 1984). When the assumptions are met, it also seems feasible to extend to latent trait models some specified designs for the orientation of the ability dimensions, analogous to confirmatory factor analysis (Joreskog, 1974). Thus, it is postulated here that specifying a design structure to identify the targeted abilities is identical to specifying matrices for confirmatory factor analysis. These design structures need to be formally checked for their potential to identify the targeted dimensions in the same way as for factor analysis models.

Consider first the mathematical reasoning example. In this case, Mayer, Larkin, & Kadane's model of four knowledge structures (factual/linguistic, schematic, strategic, and algorithmic) was postulated to describe cognitive processing on mathematical word problems. For this example, the most obvious for dynamic testing is to diagnose which knowledge structure(s) lead to errors in performance for an examinee.

The four sources of errors in solving mathematical reasoning problems may be identified by supplying cues with the items according to a specified design structure. A major feature of Mayer, Larkin, & Kadane's (1984) model is that the four knowledge structures are sequentially dependent during problem solution. For example, successfully inducing a schema requires that the examinee have the requisite factual/linguistic knowledge to read the problem. Similarly, applying a strategy to solve the problem requires that the appropriate problem schema be induced.

Table 16.5 presents a design structure for cues to be supplied with the problem. This design is like an additive factors design in which the task content is varied systematically to manipulate the knowledge structures involved in solving the problem. The entries on Table 16.5 show the knowledge structures that are involved in performance for each item set, where *X* means that the structure must be supplied by the subject, whereas *O* means that the structure need not be supplied by the subject because a sufficient cue has been supplied. For the first set of items, no cues are supplied, so that all knowledge structures must be supplied by the subject. Then, the following sets supply successively more cues. Thus, solving Set 2 items requires the subject to supply one less knowledge structure than solving Set 1 items. In the last set, all knowledge structures except the arithmetic algorithm are supplied. In each set, the requisite knowledge for some elements are supplied so that any remaining performance errors depend only on sequentially dependent knowledge in the later processing stages.

Table 16.6 presents a different design structure for the mathematical word problems. In this design, as for the preceding design, the total item requires that the subject supply all the knowledge structures. However, the other item sets require only one knowledge structure for solution. For example, subtasks can be constructed from the total item to reflect only one knowledge structure. Subtask 2 asks the examinee to produce the appropriate schema to solve the problem, and the other knowledge structures are eliminated; that is, the requisite factual knowledge is supplied and the examinee is not asked to plan or execute a solution to the problem.

The spatial reasoning example that was presented earlier leads to yet another conceptualization of the appropriate design structure. In an instructional design, the interventions can be targeted to influence specified aspects of processing. To illustrate an appropriate design structure more completely, assume that two different instructional units are administered so that the full design is test–intervention–test–intervention–test.

In this example, the most appropriate goal for dynamic testing is to measure an examinee's modifiabilities following the instructional units. Table 16.7 presents a design structure of two sequentially administered interventions that separates two

TABLE 16.5
A Design Structure for Mathematical Reasoning Items Using
Additive Factors

| | Knowledge Structure | | | |
|---|---|---|---|---|
| Items | Factual | Schematic | Strategic | Algorithmic |
| Set I | X | X | X | X |
| Set II | O | X | X | X |
| Set III | O | O | X | X |
| Set IV | O | O | O | X |

X = Structure Present
O = Structure Absent

TABLE 16.6
A Design Structure for Mathematical Reasoning
Using Subtask Responses

| | Knowledge Structure | | | |
|---|---|---|---|---|
| | Factual | Schematic | Strategic | Algorithmic |
| Set I—Total | X | X | X | X |
| Subtask I | X | O | O | O |
| Subtask 2 | O | X | O | O |
| Subtask 3 | O | O | X | O |
| Subtask 4 | O | O | O | X |

X = Structure Present
O = Structure Absent

TABLE 16.7
A Design Structure for Spatial Aptitude Items

| | Abilities | | |
|---|---|---|---|
| Items | Initial | Gain 1 | Gain 2 |
| Set 1 | X | O | O |
| Set 2 | X | X | O |
| Set 3 | X | X | X |

X = Ability Present
O = Ability Absent

types of gain from initial status. Following the first intervention, performance is characterized as a weighted combination of initial status and a gain factor. The gain factor is a different factor than initial status. Following the second intervention, performance is characterized as a weighted combination of initial status and two gain factors.

## Multicomponent Latent Trait Models

The multicomponent latent trait model (MLTM) estimates abilities and item difficulties on each underlying component in the model. For the mathematical reasoning example, then, abilities for each person and difficulties for each item on factual knowledge, schematic knowledge, strategic knowledge, and algorithmic knowledge would be given.

MLTM requires two types of data to estimate the parameters and test fit of the model: (a) responses to the standard item, and (b) responses to subtasks that are constructed from the item to represent the components. Thus, for example, the mathematical word problem in its standard form would first be administered.

Then, subtasks asking about each type of knowledge would be introduced successively, with the requisite knowledge from the preceding being supplied.

MLTM expresses the probability of solving the standard item as the product of the probabilities of solving the individual components, as follows:

$$P_{(X_{ijT} = 1)} = \prod_k P_{(X_{ijk} = 1)} \tag{2}$$

Where

$P_{(X_{ijT} = 1)}$ = probability that person $j$ solves total item $i$

$P_{(X_{ijk} = 1)}$ = probability that person $j$ solves component $k$ on item $i$

In turn, the probabilities for the components are given by the one parameter logistic latent trait model, similar to Equation 1, as follows:

$$P_{(X_{ijk} = 1)} = \frac{\exp(\theta_{jk} - b_{ik})}{1 + \exp(\theta_{jk} - b_{ik})} \tag{3}$$

Where

$\theta_{jk}$ = ability of person $j$ on component $k$

$b_{ik}$ = difficulty of item $i$ on component $k$

The design structure presented on Table 16.6 reflects the assessment of abilities and item difficulties by MLTM. Because each component is identified by items that load uniquely on the component, correlated abilities can be estimated. The item threshold or difficulty parameters that are obtained also correspond uniquely to the components. Thus, MLTM allows for the assessment of the cognitive demands of individual items. As shown elsewhere, this assessment of items should be very useful for selecting items to measure specified aspects of processing (Embretson, 1985).

## Multidimensional Latent Trait Model for Change

The multidimensional latent trait models require only responses to whole items; abilities are combined additively and the weightings of the various abilities can vary between items. However, abilities have compensatory relationships, so that a weakness in one ability can be compensated by a strength in another ability. In this section, a multidimensional latent trait model is presented that is appropriate for measuring performance changes. This is accomplished by using the design matrices for the dynamic testing procedure to place constraints on the model. Thus, the ability dimensions that are represented by the model are defined by the design structure, analogous to confirmatory factor analysis (Joreskog, 1969).

The multidimensional generalization of the two-parameter normal ogive model postulates that item responses are determined by response potential, so that if the item's threshold (i.e., difficulty), $b_i$, is equaled or exceeded, then the person passes the item, as follows:

$$X_{ij} = \begin{bmatrix} 1, & \text{if } Y_{ij} > b_i \\ 0, & \text{if } Y_{ij} < b_i \end{bmatrix}$$

Response potential is determined by a weighted combination of the person's abilities, $\Theta_j$, and a residual, $v_j$, as follows:

$$Y_{ij} = \lambda_{i1}\theta_j + \ldots \ldots \lambda_{ik}\theta_j + v_i$$

It is assumed that the residuals are independent over items and examinees and that they are distributed $N (0, O_j)$.

The multivariate extension of the two-parameter normal model for latent traits is given as follows:

$$P_{(X_{ij} = 1)} = \frac{1}{\sqrt{2\pi}\,\sigma_i} \int_{b_i}^{\infty} \exp -\frac{1}{2}\left(v - \sum_k \lambda_{ik}\theta_j\right)^2 dv \qquad (4)$$

$$= F\left(\frac{b_i - \sum \lambda_{ik}\theta_j}{\sigma_i}\right)$$

Essentially, Equation 4 indicates that the probability of solving an item is a cumulative normal density function of the difference between the item's difficulty threshold and the weighted sum of the person's abilities, where the weights depend on the item's discrimination on the various abilities.

One attractive feature of the multidimensional normal ogive model is that it is directly related to factor analysis. Thus, estimation of the item parameters of the multidimensional latent trait models can be obtained from a factor analysis that is appropriate for binary items.

Thus, a factor analysis model of item correlations for the multidimensional normal ogive model can be given as follows:

$$\Sigma_{i \times i} = \Lambda_{i \times k}\Psi_{k \times k}\Lambda'_{k \times i} + \Phi_{i \times i} \qquad (5)$$

Where

$\Lambda_{i \times k}$ = factor loadings (i.e., discriminations for item $i$ on ability $k$)

$\Psi_{k \times k}$ = ability correlations

$\Phi_{i \times i}$ = unique covariances

Current implementations of this model assume that abilities are uncorrelated and that the unique variances are given as follows:

$$\Phi_{i \times i} = I - \text{diag}(\Lambda_{i \times k} \Psi_{k \times k} \Lambda'_{k \times i}) \qquad (6)$$

Further, it is assumed that no constraints are placed on the item discrimination matrix.

To measure learning processes, it is postulated that certain values must be constrained to zero in the item discrimination or factor loading matrix to reflect the design structure of the dynamic testing procedure. That is, estimation of the parameters can be accomplished in the context of confirmatory factor analysis.

Table 16.5 presents a design structure that constrains certain values to be zero, depending on whether the knowledge structure is supplied by a cue or not. Thus, the appropriate item discrimination matrix for the multidimensional latent trait model is the following:

$$\Lambda_{i \times k} = \begin{bmatrix} x & x & x & x \\ 0 & x & x & x \\ 0 & 0 & x & x \\ 0 & 0 & 0 & x \end{bmatrix}$$

If the ability correlation matrix of identity is also specified in confirmatory factor analysis, the model would be formally identified.

Similarly, the design structure presented on Table 16.7 can also be readily accommodated by the multidimensional latent trait model. In this case, the design structure for the factor loading or item discrimination matrix is as follows:

$$\Lambda_{i \times k} = \begin{bmatrix} x & 0 & 0 \\ x & x & 0 \\ x & x & x \end{bmatrix}$$

Again, the $\Psi_{k \times k}$ matrix of ability correlations must be set equal to an identity matrix to formally identify the model.

Actually, this particular design achieves some important desiderata for measuring gain. Because raw gain is typically correlated (negatively) with initial status, the most satisfactory derived score should measure gain that is independent of initial status. Cronbach and Furby (1973) recommend residualized gain scores. The posttest score is regressed on the pretest score, and the unpredicted or residual posttest score is a measure of gain that is uncorrelated with initial status that is indexed by the pretest. In the design structure in Table 16.7, because the correlation of initial status with the gain factors is set to zero, both gain factors are residualized for initial status.

The design structures presented above are merely a few examples. Many other design structures could be devised for dynamic testing sequences. For any design, however, it is necessary to check its adequacy to identify the targeted abilities prior to use in a psychometric model.

## SUMMARY

This chapter presents a new approach to diagnostic testing—the measurement of learning processes by dynamic testing. The history of measuring learning processes has been controversial. Although substantive interest in directly measuring learning on tests remains high, it has been shown that classical test theory was inappropriate for measuring learning. A reconceptualization of the psychometric issues is presented that shows that substantive and psychometric developments during the last decade can lead to psychometrically satisfactory measurements of learning.

The psychometric reconceptualization for measuring learning as presented in this chapter involves both experimental designs to manipulate designed cognitive processes and psychometric models that directly incorporate the experimental design structure. Not only are design structures for change impossible under classical test theory, but failure to consider the item characteristics in estimating abilities leads to scaling artifacts that preclude reliable change measurement. Latent trait models provide a solution to these scaling artifacts, but still do not incorporate the experimental design for change into the model.

Two multidimensional latent trait models for measuring change have been presented. In both models, the design structure for measuring change can be represented so that the abilities measured directly reflect the intended learning processes. The multicomponent latent trait model (Whitely, 1980) was originally developed for measuring component processes, and it can be adapted to measuring learning in experiments involving various designs.

The multidimensional latent trait model for measuring change is a new development that is first presented here. It is appropriate for designs that involve repeated measurements of performance in which the conditions of the task presentation vary systematically. That is, the task can be varied according to the additive factor, subtractive factor, or instructional design to measure an individual's performance modifiability in response to specified cues that are presented under standardized conditions. These modifiabilities have potential to diagnose the specific sources of an initially low or moderate level of performance. Further, the assessment of performance modifiability also may have potential to provide a measure that is diagnostic of success in specific educational interventions. The various measurement designs discussed here are, in a sense, a sample of material that could be supplied in a more extended intervention. The individual's responsiveness to the specific types of cues or instruction could indicate sensitivity to the more extended intervention.

## REFERENCES

Babad, E. Y., & Budoff, M. (1974). Sensitivity and validity of training—potential measurement in three levels of ability. *Journal of Educational Psychology, 66,* 439–447.

Bock, D. R., Gibbons, R. D., & Muraki, E. (1985). Full information factor analysis. (MRC Report No. 85-1). Chicago: National Opinion Research Center.

Butterfield, E. (1985). Instructional methods in studying the entogery of human intelligence. In D. K. Detterman (Ed.), *Current topics in human intelligence: Volume 4* (pp. 202–222). Norwood, NJ: Ablex.

Campione, J. C., Brown, A. L., Ferrara, R. A., Jones, R. S., & Steinberg, E. (1985). Breakdowns in flexible use of information: Intelligence-related differences in transfer following equivalent learning performance. *Intelligence, 9,* 297–315.

Carlson, J. S., & Weidl, K. H. (1979). Toward a differential testing approach: Testing-the-limits employing the Paven's matrices. *Intelligence, 3,* 323–344.

Carpenter, P., & Just, M. (1982). Spatial ability: An information-processing approach to psychometrics. In R. Steinberg (Ed.), *Advances in the psychology of human intelligence.* Hillsdale, NJ: Lawrence Erlbaum Associates.

Cronbach, L. J., & Furby, L. (1970). How we should measure change—or should we? *Psychological Bulletin, 74,* 68–80.

Dearborn, D. F. (1921). Intelligence and its measurement: A symposium. *Journal of Educational Psychology, 12,* 123–147 & 195–216.

Egan, D., & Gomez, L. M. (1985). Assaying, isolating and accommodating individual differences in learning a complex skill. In R. F. Dillon (Ed.), *Individual differences in cognition* (Vol. 2, pp. 110–141). New York: Academic Press.

Embretson, S. (1983). Construct validity: Construct representation versus nomothetic span. *Psychological Bulletin, 93,* 179–197.

Embretson, S. E. (1984). A general latent trait model for response processes. *Psychometrika, 49,* 175–186.

Embretson, S. E. (1985). *Test design: Developments in psychology and psychometrics.* New York: Academic Press.

Embretson, S. E. (1987a). Improving the measurement of spatial ability by a dynamic testing procedure. *Intelligence, 11,* 333–358.

Embretson, S. (1987b). The psychometrics of dynamic testing. In C. Lidz (Ed.), *Dynamic testing* (pp. 209–230). Beverly Hills, CA: Guilford Press.

Feuerstein, R. (1979). *The dynamic assessment of retarded performers: The learning potential assessment device, theory, instruments and techniques.* Baltimore: University Park Press.

Feuerstein, R. (1980). *Instrumental enrichment: An intervention program for cognitive modifiability.* Baltimore: University Park Press.

Glaser, R. (1985, October). *The integration of instruction and testing.* Paper presented at the ETS Invitational Conference on the Redesign of Testing for the 21st Century. New York.

Hamilton, J. L., & Budoff, M. (1974). Learning potential among the moderately and severely mentally retarded. *Mental Retardation, 12,* 33–36.

Joreskog, K. G. (1969). Analyzing psychological data by structural analysis of covariance matrices. In D. H. Krantz, R. C. Atkinson, R. D. Luce, & P. Suppes (Eds.), *Contemporary developments in mathematical psychology.* San Francisco: Freeman.

Just, M., & Carpenter, P. (1985). *Cognitive coordinate systems: Accounts of mental rotation and individual differences in spatial ability.* Psychological Review, 92, 137–172.

Kintsch, W., & Greeno, J. (1985). Understanding and solving word problems. *Psychological Review, 92,* 109–129.

Lawley, D. N. (1943). On problems connected with item selection and test construction. *Proceedings of the Royal Society of Edinburgh, 61-A,* 273–287.

Lidz, C. (1987). *Dynamic testing.* Beverly Hills, CA: Guilford Press.

Lord, F. M. (1952). A theory of test scores. *Psychometric Monographs* (Whole No. 7).

Mayer, R., Larkin, J., & Kadane, P. (1984). A cognitive analysis of mathematical problem solving ability. In R. J. Sternberg (Ed.), *Advances in the psychology of human intelligence* (Vol. 2, pp. 231–273). Hillsdale, NJ: Lawrence Erlbaum Associates.

Messick, S., & Jungeblut, A. (1981). Time and method in coaching for the SAT, *Psychological Bulletin, 89,* 191–216.

Mislevy, R. (1986). Recent developments in the factor analysis of categorical variables. *Journal of Educational Statistics, 11,* 3–31.

Pachella, R. G. (1973). *The interpretation of reaction time in information processing research.* (Tech. Rep. No. 45), Human Performance Center. Ann Arbor, The University of Michigan.

Pellegrino, J. W., Mumaw, R. J., & Shute, V. (1985). Analyses of spatial aptitude and expertise. In S. Embretson (Ed.), *Test design: Development in psychology and psychometrics* (pp. 45–76). New York: Academic Press.

Regian, J. W., & Pellegrino, J. W. (1985, November). *The modifiability of spatial processing skills.* Paper presented at the 26th annual meeting of the Psychonomic Society, Boston.

Resnick, L. B., & Neches, R. (1984). Factors affecting individual differences in learning. In R. J. Sternberg (Ed.), *Advances in the psychology of human intelligence* (Vol. 2). Hillsdale, NJ: Lawrence Erlbaum Associates.

Shepard, R. N., & Metzler, J. (1971). Mental rotation of three-dimensional objects. *Science, 171,* 701–703.

Stake, R. (1961). Learning parameters, aptitudes and achievements. *Psychometric Monographs,* No. 9.

Sternberg, R. J. (1982). *Beyond IQ: A theory of human intelligence.* Cambridge, MA: Cambridge University Press.

Thissen, D., & Steinberg, L. (1984). A response model for multiple close items. *Psychometrika, 44,* 501–519.

Weiss, D. J. (1982). Improving measurement quality and efficiency with adaptive testing. *Applied Psychological Measurement, 6,* 379–396.

Wheeler, A., & Embretson, S. (1986). *The effects of test anxiety on the cognitive components of mathematical reasoning.* Unpublished manuscript.

Whitely, S. E. (1980). Multicomponent latent trait models for ability tests. *Psychometrika, 45,* 479–494.

Wissler, C. (1901). The correlation of mental and physical tests. *Psychological Review Monograph Supplement 3* (No. 16).

Woodrow, H. (1938). The relationship between abilities and improvement with practice. *Journal of Educational Psychology, 29,* 215–230.

Woodrow, H. (1946). The ability to learn. *Psychological Review, 53,* 147–158.

Vygotsky, L. S. (1978). *Mind in society: The development of higher psychological processes.* Cambridge, MA: Harvard University Press.

# 17

# Generating Good Items
# for Diagnostic Tests

Sandra P. Marshall
*San Diego State University*

Recent advances in our understanding of human information processing have led to a new class of psychological models of knowledge acquisition. These models contain a specificity of detail never before attempted, details of both the structure of knowledge and the mechanisms by which it is encoded, stored, and retrieved. The models invite us to consider monitoring the way in which an individual learns a particular cognitive skill. To do so requires considerable cooperation between cognitive psychologists and psychometricians to adapt existing statistical procedures of testing to the new form of information to be evaluated.

For the past several years, I have been concerned with the problems involved in diagnosing individuals' cognitive skills. I have investigated procedures for selecting optimal or near-optimal diagnostic items (Marshall, 1980, 1981), and I have studied the nature of the information that can be derived from different types of items (Marshall, 1986). It has become increasingly clear to me that there are four questions that are important to both cognitive psychologists and test theorists who are concerned with monitoring the acquisition of knowledge.

The first question is: What constitutes an item? Just as models of knowledge acquisition have changed, so, too, has our conception of items that test that knowledge.

The second question looks at the objective of diagnosis. What distinguishes diagnostic testing from other testing situations?

A third question focuses on individual differences. How can diagnosis take them into account? If individuals have different knowledge structures, then it stands to reason that successful diagnosis requires highly specific test items that are responsive to the individual and to the situation.

The fourth and final question concerns the criteria under which diagnostic items are selected. What are the important constraints? If diagnosis is to be informative, we must select items carefully. This chapter discusses each of these questions in turn, raises some issues related to them, and offers some possible answers.

## WHAT IS AN ITEM?

Items vary widely. They may be as diverse as a traditional test problem, an ill-structured problem used in protocol analysis, a physical model such as a circuit in electricity, or a collection of disease symptoms observed in a patient. Most researchers in cognitive science present items to individuals (or to computer simulation models) as a means of gathering information about problem-solving strategies or knowledge representation. At the conference on which this volume is based, for example, items included a computer program to find N! (Anderson), multicolumn subtraction problems (Langley), a set of blocks (Ohlsson), a demonstration of photosymthesis (Carl Frederiksen), and a description of air traffic control (Schneider).

Fundamentally, an item is any situation we define in which we ask an individual to respond. We have great latitude in defining what this response may be and how it may be interpreted. The response format may be fixed (as in multiple-choice items) or open (as in protocol responses). There may be unique, identifiable correct responses to the situation or there may be no single one.

In traditional testing situations, we define an item to be a problem or question to which students respond. Typical items on an arithmetic test, for example, include computational problems (e.g., $25 \times 9 = ?$), story problems (e.g., Joe has 10 marbles. Bill gives him 6 more. How many does Joe have now?), identification problems (e.g., What is the numerator of the fraction 4/7?) and so on. A student usually responds by selecting one of several alternative answers, although open-ended questions are occasionally used.

In many psychological tasks, items are less clearly defined. Frequently, the objective is to determine how an individual thinks about a particular concept, and the individual is presented with an ill-structured problem and asked to "think aloud." A record of his/her verbalization is kept (e.g., a protocol), and the researcher studies the particular strategies and subgoals used as the individual works with the problem. A detailed example is provided by Ohlsson's chapter in this volume. In such situations, the question is broad; the individual is asked to find a solution to a problem and to verbalize the accompanying thoughts as this is done. The solution is less important than the process by which it was achieved.

In other situations, an individual may be given a model or a diagram to decipher and explain. For example, students learning basic electricity work with diagrams or circuits. They are expected to know the components of a circuit as well as how it works. The problem may be a representation of a working or a flawed circuit, depending on the situation. The question posed may be to explain how the correct circuit works or to find out what's wrong in the flawed circuit. The process and the correct solution are both important in this case.

Still another notion of *item* comes from a collection of features about an unknown concept. The most frequent example of this situation is a medical evaluation of a patient's symptoms (as illustrated in Reggia's and Pople's chapters). The issue here is to decide which questions to ask the patient and which laboratory tests to perform in order to reach a decision about the cause of the symptoms.

Many of these conceptions of an item differ significantly from the traditional view of a test item. Not only is the structure of the response different (e.g., open-ended versus fixed format) but the nature of the question asked is different as well. In all cases, however, the item elicits information from the individual being evaluated.

It is now important to ask how we may gather relevant information that tells us what we want to know about the individual's thinking processes. What specific question do we ask? What is a *diagnostic* item? The answers to these questions depend on our view of diagnosis.

## WHAT IS THE OBJECTIVE OF DIAGNOSIS?

According to my dictionary, diagnosis has three meanings: (a) "the act or process of deciding the nature of a diseased condition by examination"; (b) "a careful investigation of the facts to determine the nature of a thing"; and (c) "the decision or opinion resulting from such examination or investigation."[1] The meaning we choose influences the way in which we build diagnostic items.

Consider the first meaning. By definition, such diagnosis requires examination. Consequently, we must devise a testing procedure that leads to a decision about the condition of an individual. In this case, the emphasis is upon how the decision is made, because the term *diagnosis* is defined as "the process of deciding." Several assumptions underlie this view of diagnosis. First, the nature of the condition is covert rather than overt. We cannot simply observe and record it. Second, this hidden nature means that we cannot make in general a definitive statement about the nature. Therefore, we are in a probabilistic mode of operation. Third, this kind of diagnosis is a process; it is not a static, unchanging operator that can be applied to a situation. Process implies change.

Now consider the second meaning: "a careful investigation of the facts to determine the nature of the thing." The most obvious difference between this and the previous definition is that we are no longer asked to focus on the process of making a decision. Rather, we can look directly at a record of observations and

---

[1] From Webster's *New World Dictionary, College Edition*.

make a determination. Implicit here is the notion of a deterministic rather than a probabilistic investigation. If we just look long enough and hard enough, we can come to the correct diagnosis.

Finally, we have diagnosis as the conclusion of the examination or investigation. This is the product, as opposed to the process, or diagnosis. The product may be the diagnostic outcome or, as Clancey (1985) suggests in the NEOMYCIN system, the history or *trace* of the process used to obtain the diagnosis. Hence. it becomes necessary to seek an explicit representation of the means by which the diagnostic outcome was achieved.

It seems to me that much of the confusion over diagnostic evaluation comes from our lack of agreement about the fundamental character of diagnosis. Most psychometricians have been concerned with the first definition: What is the nature of the decision process? What probabilistic measures are appropriate? How sure can I be of my hypotheses? Obviously, a good statistical model would be valuable. In contrast, most cognitive psychologists and artificial intelligence researchers have gravitated to the second meaning: the in-depth investigation of the phenomenon. For them, there is a lesser need for the statistical evaluation because they are able to probe deeper and deeper until they understand the topic being studied. By making detailed models, they aim to mimic or simulate the actual performance of individuals.

As researchers in both fields work together, we approach the third meaning: the conclusions that we draw from our researchers. There is room for both probabilistic approximation and detailed modeling of performance. Neither alone is entirely satisfactory. We run the risk of remaining too general when we use the statistical or psychometric approach by itself. On the other hand, it is virtually impossible to model by computer simulation the real-world understanding of many tasks simultaneously.

## WHAT IS A GOOD DIAGNOSTIC ITEM?

Not every question generates diagnostic information about cognitive skills. Knowing that an individual got the right or wrong answer does not tell us anything about how that individual processed the information in the problem. A diagnostic item must provide such information. The concern is with processing, not with particular content. Knowledge items requiring recall or recognition of facts are not diagnostic items about ability. They simply indicate the extent of an individual's factual store.

A good diagnostic item elicits the most information possible in a restricted amount of testing time. Thus, tied up in the notion of "good" are the psychometric or statistical qualities of sufficiency and efficiency. At any given point in most diagnoses, there are many possible questions that might be presented to an individual. Not all are equally good items. Some may provide redundant information. Some may be excellent items but not applicable for the particular individual being evaluated.

We must have a means of building items based on the knowledge possessed by a particular individual. One of the drawbacks of many tests is that the cognitive processes used by an individual do not influence item generation or selection. It seems reasonable to demand that good diagnostic items take into account both the capacity of the item to elicit a wide range of information and the ability of the student to make a response.

Students of psychometric principles should immediately recognize the potential application of item response theory in this setting. In its simplest form, item response theory (IRT) determines the probability of a correct response by an individual as a function of item characteristics (usually item difficulty) and of person characteristics (usually an ability measure of some sort). In more complex form, IRT considers several parameters for both item and person characteristics. An excellent discussion of IRT applications may be found in Lord (1980). Other chapters in this volume also address the topic (e.g., Embretson).

For the purposes of cognitive diagnosis, traditional measures of item difficulty and person ability are not directly useful. We are interested in identifying which of the individual's skills are strong, missing, or misguided rather than in classifying a person as a good, bad, or mediocre problem solver. Therefore, the first objective here must be to suggest alternative measures of item and person characteristics.

## Item Characteristics

There have been several recent attempts to incorporate cognitive characteristics of items into IRT estimates, notably by European psychologists. Fischer and Formann (1982) summarized this research and pointed out application of a special class of linearly restricted logistic models in domain such as calculus, intelligence testing, and syllogistic reasoning.[2] As one would expect, some of the efforts have been more successful than others. In one successful experiment, Fischer (1973) employed what he termed a linear logistic test model to analyze the psychological complexity of calculus problems. Item parameters were based on the cognitive structure of the items, defined according to the cognitive operations required for solution. His model incorporated both item difficulty estimates (in the usual Rasch model sense) and operation parameters, derived from the cognitive structure of the possible solution strategies.

Fischer's method of parameterization of the cognitive structures involves classifying problems according to presence or absence of a set of defined characteristics. Thus, he worked with a matrix of order $n \times p$, where $n$ is the number of items and $p$ is the number of psychological characteristics. Each item is defined

---

[2] Most of these studies are available only in German journals of psychology (see Fischer & Formann, 1982, for references).

by a vector of 0's and 1's, indicating absence or presence of the psychological factors.

This procedure should be generalizable to other domains of study. For example, in research on the architecture of arithmetic story problems, there appears to be a small number of basic schemas that represent underlying semantic relations (Riley, Greeno, & Heller, 1983; Marshall, 1985). Both simple and complex problems could be coded by vectors of 1's and 0's, representing presence and absence of the semantic relations. It should then be possible to derive estimates of item difficulty based on the cognitive structure of the items using Fischer's procedure.

## Person Characteristics

In many systems of item response theory, person characteristics are estimates of an individual's ability over a specified domain. Frequently, this is a measure of achievement indicating the proportion of items on a test that the person can answer correctly.

It seems reasonable to assume that measures of cognitive abilities would be useful in IRT estimates of person characteristics, just as they are in determining item parameters. Many possibilities come to mind. For example, one might include reaction time measures of short-term memory span or of processing time in retrieving information from long-term memory. One could use estimates of image processing or spatial organization. Whatever the measures, the focus is on incorporating as much specific information about the individual's cognitive processing as possible into the generation of appropriate diagnostic items.

## HOW ARE DIAGNOSTIC ITEMS SELECTED?

We turn now to the methods by which items are chosen. This is the heart of the diagnostic problem: Under what restrictions, conditions, or rules is an item selected? In most real world situations, there are many questions that could be asked. All may appear to be equally good and to provide satisfactory (if different) information about the individual being examined.

The organization of the knowledge to be tested guides the selection process as well as the model of student learning. I consider two cases here: hierarchically structured knowledge and a tangled network (quasi-hierarchical).

### Hierarchical Structure

Suppose the material to be evaluated consists of a set of two cognitive skills, $C_1$ and $C_2$, and their combination, $C_{12}$. Under the usual restriction of hierarchical relationships, success on any combination implies success on all components forming the combination. Thus, a correct response to $C_{12}$ means that an individual has mastered all the skills of the set.

As I have discussed elsewhere (Marshall, 1981), for such a simple case it is possible to determine the optimal policy of item selection through principles of dynamic programming. The system is a Markov process. For any item type ($C1$, $C2$, or $C12$), there are three possible outcomes: It is mastered, it is not mastered, it has not yet been presented. The number of states in the Markov model can be determined by $3^k$, where 3 is the number of outcomes, and $k$ is the number of distinct items that may be tested. The goal is to estimate the probability that an individual has learned any particular skill or combination.

The difficulty with finding an optimal policy of selection by this technique is that the number of states of the Markov process becomes excessive with only a moderate number of distinct skills. The backward enumeration process of dynamic programming involves a large number of intermediate states that make the calculation excessively slow. Consequently, we generally use heuristic approximations of an optimal policy.

Two heuristics have been developed (Marshall, 1981).[3] Both heuristics take a Bayesian approach, with the probability of a correct response on any item depending on the individual's previous responses. Both heuristics keep track of an individual's ability to answer correctly the possible items (including all logical combinations) by computing a matrix of skills by ability. For the very simple case just described, the matrix has the form given in Table 17.1.

In Table 17.1, the value $1$ indicates mastery of the skill and $0$ denotes nonmastery. At every point in the diagnostic process, there is some probability that an individual may be characterized by one of the ability vectors. Thus, we have a probability distribution, $S$, over the vectors. Some of the elements of $S$ may be zero because it is possible to have zero probability for some vectors. For example, if the individual has not mastered $C_1$, he or she has a zero probability of ability vector 1, complete mastery of all skills.

In the absence of better information, one typically begins the diagnostic process by assuming equal probabilities for all ability characterizations. As each item is presented and answered, a new probability distribution, $S$, is computed. The diagnostic objective is to identify one ability vector with sufficiently high probability.

The first heuristic seeks to maximize the number of zero elements in the probability distribution, $S$. A next-item function computes the new value of $S$ for each possible item from the set of skills and selects the item that minimizes the number of nonzero entries for the updated $S$. Thus, each step in the testing procedure reduces the number of possible states by which the individual may be classified.

---

[3] In an earlier publication, I gave details of two approximations (Marshall, 1981). The reader is referred to that article for complete mathematical details.

TABLE 17.1
Matrix of Skills by Ability Vectors

| Ability Vectors | Skills | | |
|---|---|---|---|
| | $C_1$ | $C_2$ | $C_{12}$ |
| 1 | 1 | 1 | 1 |
| 2 | 1 | 1 | 0 |
| 3 | 0 | 1 | 0 |
| 4 | 1 | 0 | 0 |
| 5 | 0 | 0 | 0 |

The second heuristic uses the statistic of information from information theory (Attneave, 1959). Under this theory, the more probable a correct response, the less information it provides. The heuristic seeks to maximize information, where information is defined as usual as

$$I(x_i) = -\log_2 \text{prob}(x_i) \tag{1}$$

where $x_i$ is the individual's response to item $i$. The expected value of $I$ is

$$E(I) = -\text{prob}(x_i) \log_2 \text{prob}(x_i) \tag{2}$$

Each item contains only two messages: either an individual answers correctly or answers incorrectly. It is relatively simple to show that given only two outcomes, $E(I)$ is maximized when the probability of a correct response is .50. Therefore, the second heuristic seeks the item having a probability value closest to .50, given the current probabilities $S$. I have shown elsewhere that both of these heuristics approximate well the optimal policy given a uniform prior distribution over ability vectors (Marshall, 1981).

*Applications.* In what circumstances would these heuristics be useful? One application is in mathematical procedures. For example, in solving subtraction problems, there are distinct skills that are required, such as finding the difference between two single-digit numbers, learning to compute from right to left in a multi-digit problem, and carrying out the borrowing or regrouping procedure. These have a hierarchical relationship: Students who have not mastered the simple skills such as finding the difference between two single-digit numbers are unable to compute successfully the difference between two multi-digit numbers.

A second application is basic electricity. As several recent research studies have pointed out, students have difficulty understanding circuits (e.g., Larkin, Reif, Carbonell, & Gugliotta, 1985; Reif, 1986). The knowledge needed is hierarchical. Unless an individual understands the function of a resistor, the nature of Ohm's law, and what is meant by parallel resistors, he or she is unable to describe correctly the function of circuits consisting of several elements.

There are obviously many other areas in which these heuristics could be applied. The requirements are that the individual skills be specified, that they have a hierarchical composition, and that the ways in which they form higher order or more complex combinations be defined.

## The Tangled Network

Much of the current research in cognitive psychology is focused on knowledge representation in complex domains (e.g., Anderson, 1983; Anderson, Boyle, Corbett, & Lewis, 1986; Larkin et al., 1985). The particular knowledge structure under investigation is the schema. A schema is a generic representation of an experience, a situation, or a concept. Although psychologists are not in complete agreement about the precise nature of a schema, they generally agree that the form of this knowledge structure is a network in which one finds descriptive terms, preconditions, and various goal-setting rules.

Generally, a schema is represented by a network rather than a directed hierarchy. One can imagine a very simple network in which every element is related only to other elements within the network. Such is the case for Fig. 17.1 (A). On the other hand, one can also envision what may be called *tangled networks* (following Anderson's, 1983, description of tangled hierarchies) in which some elements of one network are also shared by a second, as seen in Fig. 17.1 (B).

In general, any specific instance of a schema activates only a sample of the elements that characterize the full schema. There are at least three distinct sets

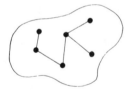

(A) SIMPLE NETWORK:  ALL NODES BELONG
TO A SINGLE SCHEMA

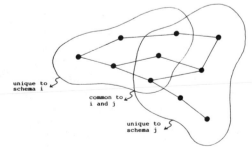

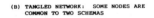

(B) TANGLED NETWORK:  SOME NODES ARE
COMMON TO TWO SCHEMAS

FIG. 17.1.  Two Networks

of elements: declarative facts, preconditions, and subsequent procedures or rules. Any test item for a schema would call for subsets of these three sets. The diagnostic problem is to test various subsets and thereby to estimate efficiently the completeness of an individual's knowledge of the schema.

There are three general questions to be asked about an individual's understanding and use of schemas: (a) How competent is the individual in mapping from an item to a schema? (b) Are all critical elements of a schema part of the individual's knowledge store? and (c) Are the critical elements linked together correctly? The first question addresses the problem of transferring and matching information from short-term (or working) memory to information stored in long-term memory. The latter two questions focus on the way in which information is stored in long-term memory. These are discussed separately below.

*Competency.*    To determine whether the individual correctly understands the stated form of the test problem, we must determine the individual's ability to recognize specific parts of the problem. To some extent, this is a more general issue than the understanding of any particular schema at all. At stake here is whether the individual is using schema knowledge. The individual may have the schema knowledge needed for an item and still fail to apply it. Therefore, testing of this competency serves two functions. It confirms that the individual is attempting to access a schema, and it assesses the competency of the individual in mapping the item to the schema.

We make a key supposition about an individual's mapping ability by assuming that this is a general skill and not one tied to a single schema. For example, suppose that we have four schemas that can be used to solve problems. If the individual can correctly relate one specific problem to a schema, we assume that the individual has the general mapping skills required for the remaining schemas. It is important to note that this is not the evaluation of whether the individual actually has the required elements of the schema in long-term memory (LTM). We are focusing instead on the mechanisms of pattern matching, through which elements in working (or short-term) memory are matched with elements in LTM. The contents and associated processes of LTM (i.e., the schemas) should be assessed separately.

We lack good assessment procedures for determining an individual's competency in this general area. Several experimental psychological paradigms are currently used. A common one involves a sorting task in which the individual is asked to arrange test items into several subgroups having similar characteristics. The elements of the test items are carefully developed to maximize certain common aspects of a schema structure. A second related situation presents the individual with a group of test items and requires him/her to explain what these items have in common. Additional methods of evaluation need to be developed.

***Schemas Stored in Long-Term Memory: The Critical Elements.***    Assuming the individual to have the necessary pattern-matching skills, we now turn our attention to the way in which information is stored in LTM. Again, there are many options for diagnostic questioning. One may want to determine whether a specific piece of information is present or absent (declarative knowledge). One may want to examine interactions among a set of condition–action rules (procedural knowledge). Or, one may want to study the schemas that govern the use of declarative and procedural knowledge. The first two options can be addressed by using known methods of psychometrics (see the discussion in Marshall, 1986). The third option is the topic of this section.

Schema information is viewed as being stored as a network of linked nodes. To assess the size and relationships of the network, consider the network from the perspective of graph theory. The network is a graph in which the components are nodes. If two nodes are related, they are connected by an arc. For the moment, we require the graph to be undirected and simple; that is, arcs have no directionality, there are no arcs that start and end at the same node, and there is at most one arc between any two nodes.

Suppose we have an individual to be evaluated. It is reasonable to begin diagnosis with an estimate of how fully developed the individual's schema knowledge structure is. We have two options; both use statistical inferences from graph theory (Frank, 1971).[4] First, we can estimate the size of the graph by considering the number of nodes, and, second, we can estimate the degree of relationship within the graph by considering the number of arcs.

We begin with a model of a fully developed schema network (such as Figure 18.1A) with two known sets—the number of nodes and the number of arcs. This model corresponds to the target of an established instructional sequence. We also have a second graph or network whose size is initially unspecified. This is the model of the student. Our objective is to determine how similar (or dissimilar) the student model is to the instructional model. We need, therefore, to estimate the size of the student graph and to compare the estimate with the target of the full network. We make the estimates by employing the technique of sampling subgraphs.

There are many ways to sample nodes and arcs from a graph. For example, one can employ Bernoulli sampling, random sampling, or stratified sampling. The simplest case is to select randomly a group of nodes, then generate test items calling for use of those and only those nodes.

***Estimating the Number of Nodes.***   The estimate of the number of nodes present in the student's schema graph depends on four things: the sampling scheme used to derive the sample, the number of nodes sampled from the graph, the number of items needed to test the sampled nodes, and the sampling probabilities of the

---

[4] Much of the statistical theory described in this section comes from Frank, *Statistical inferences in graphs*. Proofs and details of the unbiased estimators are given in Chapters 4 through 6 of Frank's book. It must be stressed, however, that some of the ideas presented here are general extensions of Frank's estimators, and the statistical properties remain to be developed.

nodes. I consider the simplest case first and then suggest several modifications for more complicated diagnosis.

Let $G$ be the instructional model graph containing $N$ nodes. We assume that each node is equally likely to be learned by the student and is not conditional upon other nodes. Take a random sample from $G$. The sample contains $S$ nodes, where $S < N$. Sampling is done without replacement. Thus, the probability of sampling any node on the first selection is $1/N$, the probability of sampling any node once a single node has already been selected is $1/(N-1)$, the probability of sampling a node once two nodes have been selected is $1/(N-2)$, and so on.

Construct a set of items, $I$, to test the sampled nodes of $S$. In the extreme case, one might sample all $N$ nodes, and one might evaluate each node by one test item, so that $N = S = I$. For the moment, assume that $N > S = I$. That is, we sample a subset of nodes $S$ and construct one item to test each node. Present the items to the individual, and score the response as 1 or 0 according to the individual's success or failure in responding. Denote the responses as $X^i$, with $i = 1,\ldots,S$. The overall success of the individual can be expressed by

$$p = 1/S \, X^i \qquad (3)$$

which, of course, is simply the proportion of nodes corresponding to correct responses.

The estimate of the total number of nodes known by the individual is computed from the values of $p$, the measure of the individual's success with the sample, and the total number of nodes in $G$:

$$T(\text{node}) = pN. \qquad (4)$$

*An Example.*    A simple numerical example may be useful here. Let $G$ be the graph of Fig. 17.2, with $N = 10$. Let $G^*$ be the true state of the student that is initially unknown and is to be estimated. $N^*$ is the corresponding number of nodes in $G^*$. For this example, $N^* = 6$. In practice, $N^*$ is unknown and we estimate it by $T(\text{node})$.

Arbitrarily, set the sample size of nodes to be tested at 5, so that $S = 5$, and make a random sample, such as:

$$S = \{1,3,4,7,8\}. \qquad (5)$$

Assuming no measurement error, it is clear that the individual would respond correctly to items assessing nodes 1, 7, and 8 and would respond incorrectly to items testing nodes 3 and 4 (because these are not present in the student's network). Thus, a summary of the student's performance is:

$$X_1 = 1$$
$$X_2 = 0$$
$$X_3 = 0$$
$$X_4 = 1$$
$$X_5 = 1$$

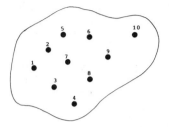

(A) THE INSTRUCTIONAL TARGET GRAPH G

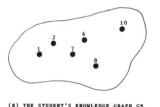

FIG. 17.2.    The Nodes    (B) THE STUDENT'S KNOWLEDGE GRAPH G*

Summing over the $X^i$s and dividing by 5, the sample size, we have

$$p = \frac{3}{5} = .6. \tag{6}$$

The total number of nodes estimated to be in the student's graph is

$$T(\text{node}) = pN = (.6)10 = 6. \tag{7}$$

*Some unresolved issues.*    There are two important issues to be addressed at this point. First, how large a sample is required to achieve a satisfactory estimate of $T(\text{node})$? And, second, how many items do we need to construct to measure the node sample?

Obviously, the sample of nodes can range from 1 to $N$, the number of nodes in the instructional graph. When $N$ is small, one might consider the deterministic process of evaluating each possible node. When $N$ is large, however, a probabilistic estimate is necessary. This corresponds to setting an acceptance confidence interval and computing the values of $N$ that satisfy the bounds of the interval.

Return to the example above. Suppose the sample size is 2. Table 17.2 contains ten samples drawn at random and the $p$ values associated with each. Clearly a sample of size 2 is too small. The estimated values of $T$ have too large a variance to be acceptable.

Table 17.2 also contains estimated values based on samples of size 3, 4, and 5. As sample size increases, the range of estimates of $T$ decreases. Good estimates of $T$ require large samples. However, at some point there would be a trade-off

TABLE 17.2
Expected Node Totals Under Differing Sample

| S = 2 | | | S = 3 | | | S = 4 | | | S = 5 | | |
|---|---|---|---|---|---|---|---|---|---|---|---|
| nodes | p | T | nodes | p | T | nodes | p | T | nodes | p | T |
| 18 | 1.00 | 10 | 123 | .67 | 7 | 1345 | .25 | 3 | 23458 | .40 | 4 |
| 46 | .50 | 5 | 693 | .33 | 3 | 2489 | .50 | 5 | 34578 | .40 | 4 |
| 23 | .50 | 5 | 867 | 1.00 | 10 | 1248 | .75 | 8 | 23469 | .40 | 4 |
| 34 | .00 | 0 | 845 | .33 | 3 | 1259 | .50 | 5 | 23457 | .40 | 4 |
| 27 | 1.00 | 10 | 326 | .67 | 7 | 2678 | 1.00 | 10 | 12689 | .80 | 8 |
| 85 | .50 | 5 | 437 | .33 | 3 | 2457 | .50 | 5 | 12679 | .80 | 8 |
| 13 | .50 | 5 | 736 | .67 | 7 | 1247 | .75 | 8 | 26789 | .80 | 8 |
| 79 | .50 | 5 | 147 | .67 | 7 | 1678 | 1.00 | 10 | 13467 | .60 | 6 |
| 24 | .50 | 5 | 315 | .33 | 7 | 4568 | .50 | 5 | 34569 | .20 | 2 |
| 49 | .00 | 0 | 149 | .33 | 3 | 5689 | .50 | 5 | 12359 | .40 | 4 |

between the number of items that can be presented efficiently (in terms of time and cost) and the acceptable confidence bounds for $T$.

The problem of sample size is influenced by the second issue of interest here—the number of nodes to test per item. Whereas the first issue of sample size is essentially a statistical problem, the issue of how many nodes can be constituents of a single item is a psychological problem. One must examine the logical structure of multi-node items and determine whether such items can be constructed easily. One suspects that, in practice, most items that address schema knowledge are multi-node. If this is the case, we should take advantage of the item structure as a means of expediting the testing process.

One searches for an efficient testing process in which the number of items is less than the number of nodes in the sample, which is itself less than the total number of nodes in the instructional graph, so that

$$I < S < N. \tag{8}$$

This requires item construction in which more than a single node can be assessed. The number of nodes that can be accurately evaluated by a single item is not known and probably depends upon the domain being tested. In theory, one might use a single item (such as a very broad item to which the individual responds by thinking aloud). In practice, it is more reasonable to expect that any item calls on between two and five distinct nodes.

The use of multi-node items would improve estimates of $T$(node), the total number of nodes in the network. The primary constraint of the example presented above is the number of *items* used in diagnostic testing, not the number of *nodes* to be tested. With multi-node items, we can increase the size of the sample of nodes without increasing the number of items. For example, if each test item evaluates two nodes, one could assess the presence or absence of eight nodes with only four items. Such items can only be constructed if the domain is well understood and the schema knowledge is clearly defined and represented as a network.

As our understanding of schema structure develops, we can expect to move to sampling schemes that are more sophisticated than the one just illustrated. For example, if there are several distinct types of knowledge that may be embedded in a schema, we probably want to stratify the sample to cover each one. The acquisition of nodes is almost certainly not uniformly probable. There may be dependency among nodes or some may be almost impossible to assess. As the relationships among nodes is better understood, the statistical procedures can be refined to produce better estimates.

***Estimating the Number of Arcs.***   In addition to estimating the number of nodes in a schema, we want to know whether these elements are interconnected. It is important to estimate the number of nodes first, because there can be no connections unless the nodes are present. However, the degree of connectivity is the key element in the study of schema acquisition.

Again, we use a sample from the instructional target graph to construct test items. This graph now contains both the nodes and the relationships among them that the student is expected to have formed. For efficient testing, we restrict the total node set to those nodes already identified as being present in the student's schema graph. In other words, we are now investigating the degree of connectivity in the student's existing knowledge store.

To look at the relations among nodes, we must use multi-node items in the testing procedure because we need to determine whether the individual perceives connections between specified nodes. These relations are best assessed by presenting the individual with a test item and allowing him or her to think aloud about the solution. One expects that the student would reveal associations between nodes as he or she talks about the features of the item. Scoring such items is particularly difficult. Techniques of protocol analysis (e.g., Ericsson & Simon, 1984, or Ohlsson, Chap. 11 in this volume) are generally used to help interpret and guide inferences about knowledge representation and relationships among the nodes present in the item (i.e., in the sample).

The sampling procedure changes from that described for sampling nodes. For any set of nodes $N$, construct the set $M$ of possible node pairs, under the restriction that no node may appear more than once within a given element (e.g., there are no arcs linking a node with itself). The order of the nodes within a pair is unimportant ($jk = kj$), so the set of pairs has $N(N-1)/2$ members. We draw our sample from this set.

Again, let $S$ represent a random sample, with each member of $S$ corresponding to a particular pair of nodes. Each pair is tested by presenting an item containing both nodes to the individual. An individual's response is scored 1 or 0, depending on whether it indicates an association between the nodes. Thus, in testing the node pair $j$ and $k$:

$$X_i = \begin{cases} 1 & \text{if the connection exists between nodes } j \text{ and } k \\ 0 & \text{otherwise.} \end{cases}$$

One can proceed as described above for estimating nodes. First, compute $p$ as the average over the $X$ values in the sample. The total number of arcs can now be estimated by

$$T(\text{arc}) = pM. \tag{9}$$

***An Example.*** Suppose that the schema consists of the graph $G$ in Figure 17.3. It is determined through previous testing that the student knowledge base contains the nodes (1, 2, 6, 7, 8, 10). The true state of the student's knowledge of associations is based upon this set, as shown in $G^*$ of Figure 17.3. As before, the true state is unobservable and must be estimated.

We begin by enumerating the members of $M$, the eligible pairs of nodes. For the 6 nodes, $M$ contains $(6)(5)/2 = 15$ pairs. Let $S$ contain a random sample of 4 pairs (this number is chosen arbitrarily):

$$S = \{(2,6)(7,8)(1,10)(1,2)\}. \tag{10}$$

Construct items containing these pairs of nodes and present them to the student whose knowledge structure is reflected in Figure 17.3. The responses to the items would be (0, 0, 0, 1), indicating that the only arc present of the sampled pairs is

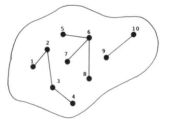

(A) THE INSTRUCTIONAL TARGET GRAPH G

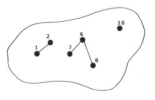

FIG. 17.3.    The Arcs

(B) THE STUDENT'S KNOWLEDGE GRAPH G*

between nodes 1 and 2. The value $p$ is therefore 1/4 or .25, and the total number of arcs estimated to be in $G^*$ is

$$T(\text{arc}) = pM = (.25)(15) = 3.75 \simeq 4. \tag{11}$$

***Unresolved Issues.***   As before, the sample size is an important variable in the problem of estimating the total number of arcs. The points made earlier regarding nodes are equally pertinent here.

There are several potential problems associated with determining the number of items to present to the individual. As before, time may be a limiting factor in the diagnostic process. This may be especially true in diagnosing whether an association exists between two nodes, because the response time in talk-aloud situations is usually greater than the response time for fixed-format items. Scoring of these items is also more difficult.

A second problem arises when we consider the combination of more than two nodes in a single item. Consider the graphs in Fig. 17.4. Graph (A) is fully connected, the arcs connecting every pair of nodes. Graph (B) illustrates the situation in which there exists a path connecting all nodes but not every pair is joined. Graphs (C) and (D) each contain two arcs but represent different understanding. And, finally, Graph (E) is completely unconnected. If we construct an item containing nodes 1, 2, and 3, we may have difficulty determining whether graph (A) is most appropriate or whether graphs (B) and (C) are more characteristic of the student's knowledge. The problem is that we cannot easily distinguish between the fully connected set of nodes and the set in which a path exists to connect them.

***Related Questions.***   The estimates of size and connectivity have been presented here as if they are to be assessed separately. In practice, one may not wish to test the same material twice to derive the two estimates. To do so would defeat our objective of efficient diagnosis. The decision of whether to estimate these two values simultaneously or sequentially depends on the domain being studied.

One can envision several extensions of statistical inference in graph theory as

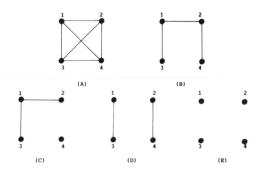

FIG. 17.4.   Several Graphs with Four Nodes

we investigate cognitive skills. I have not touched on the techniques of sampling partial graphs or estimating the number of linked components of graphs. It is reasonable to assume that as schema knowledge grows, first the individual develops several isolated but internally linked subsets of nodes. Estimation of the number and identities of these would be valuable.

It is also of interest to estimate the number of isolated nodes in schema knowledge. Some nodes may be harder to incorporate into a network than others. Can we estimate how many and can we identify them? Frank (1971) outlines the general case for estimating isolates but how the theory applies to schema networks remains unspecified.

A by-product of the method described here is the identification of specific nodes and arcs already known to the individual. Although a central question may be to make estimates of the size of the node set and arc set, a second and perhaps equally important question is the specification of which particular nodes are present and absent. This question is especially important in diagnostic testing. If there are key nodes or arcs that one knows a priori to be important in a knowledge domain, one may wish to test these independently. Conversely, if an individual appears to have only a few nodes or arcs, it is imperative to identify them so that future instruction can build on them.

## SUMMARY

I have attempted to define some of the issues that need to be addressed jointly by cognitive psychologists and psychometricians. These have been framed within the four questions of (a) how to define a test item, (b) what the objective of diagnosis is, (c) what makes an item diagnostic, and (d) how to determine the selection procedures that drive the testing process. In particular, I have focused on the form of knowledge representation and the statistical procedures that might be applied to it. A central theme is the nature of the information to be diagnosed.

In addition to describing the theoretical concerns involved in selecting and constructing good diagnostic test items, I have pointed out several unresolved issues. In particular, there is a need for better items that have fixed-format responses, such as those used on standardized assessment tests. We need to explore the use of free-response items in diagnostic tests. We need to expand the use of item–response theory and broaden the parameters to include cognitive characteristics of items and persons. We need to create new methods for studying an individual's abilities to map and pattern-match information from an item to information stored in long-term memory. I hope that these are issues to be addressed by researchers in the near future.

In psychological research, we strive to advance our understanding of knowledge representation. One way to do so is to advance our psychometric and statistical measurement of the representation. New methodology is needed to monitor cognitive development. As described here, techniques of item–response theory and statistical graph theory seem particularly pertinent to current psychological models. Through them, we should be able to refine our models of knowledge acquisition. At the same time, our psychological models should also be beneficial to statisticians. So far we have general statistical procedures. As we develop more detailed models of memory and learning, we increase our knowledge of the underlying mechanisms. This knowledge can then be used to devise more specialized and efficient statistical methodology.

## ACKNOWLEDGMENTS

Some of the research reported in this chapter was supported by the Office of Naval Research under Contract No. N00014-85-K-0661.

## REFERENCES

Anderson, J. R. (1983). *The architecture of cognition.* Cambridge, MA: Harvard University Press.
Anderson, J. R., Boyle, C. F., Corbett, A., & Lewis, M. (1986). *Cognitive modelling and intelligent tutoring* (Tech. Rep. No. ONR-86-1). Advanced Computer Tutoring Project, Carnegie-Mellon University, Pittsburgh, PA.
Attneave, F. (1959). *Applications of information theory to psychology.* New York: Holt.
Clancey, W. J. (1985). *Acquiring, representing, and evaluating a competence model of diagnostic strategy* (Tech. Rep. No. 13, Contract No. N00014-85-K-0305). Washington, D.C., Office of Naval Research.
Ericsson, K. A., & Simon, H. A. (1984). *Protocol analysis: Verbal reports as data.* Cambridge, MA: The MIT Press.
Fischer, G. (1973). The linear logistic test model as an instrument of educational research. *Acta Psychologica, 37,* 359–374.
Fischer, G., & Formann, A. K. (1982). Some applications of logistic latent trait models with linear constraints on the parameters. *Applied Psychological Measurement, 6,* 397–416.
Frank, O. (1971). *Statistical inference in graphs.* Stockholm: FOA Repro Forsvarets Forskningsanstalt.
Larkin, J., Reif, F., Carbonell, J., & Gugliotta, A. (1985). *FERMI: A flexible expert reasoner with multi-domain inferencing* (Tech. Rep. ONR No. N-00014-82-C-0767). Carnegie-Mellon University, Pittsburgh, PA.
Lord, F. (1980). *Applications of item response theory to practical testing problems.* Hillsdale, NJ: Lawrence Erlbaum Associates.
Marshall, S. P. (1980). Procedural networks and production systems in adaptive diagnosis. *Instructional Science, 9,* 129–143.
Marshall, S. P. (1981). Sequential item selection: Optimal and heuristic policies. *Journal of Mathematical Psychology, 23,* 134–152.
Marshall, S. P. (1985, December). *Using schema knowledge to solve story problems.* Paper presented at Office of Naval Research Contractors' Meeting, San Diego, CA.
Marshall, S. P. (1986, February). *Assessing knowledge structures in mathematics: A cognitive science perspective.* Paper presented at the Conference on New Directions in Educational Measurement, Orlando, FL.

Reif, F. (1986). *Interpretation of scientific or mathematical concepts: Cognitive issues and instructional implications* (Tech. Rep. No. CES-1). Department of Physics and School of Education, University of California, Berkeley, CA.

Riley, M., Greeno, J., & Heller, J. (1983). Development of children's problem solving ability in arithmetic. In H. Ginsburg, (Ed.), *The development of mathematical thinking* (pp. 153–196). New York: Academic Press.

# 18

# Toward an Integration of Item-Response Theory and Cognitive Error Diagnosis

Kikumi K. Tatsuoka
*Educational Testing Service*

## INTRODUCTION

Finding the sources of misconceptions possessed by students is a difficult task because it is impossible to see what is happening in their heads. The only directly observable outcomes are the students' responses to the test items. Studying their think-aloud protocols is one method for discovering how students solve or think through problems. Several computer programs that are capable of diagnosing students' misconceptions have been developed in the past decade (Brown & Burton, 1978; Marshall, 1980; Ohlsson & Langley, 1985; Sleeman, 1984; Tatsuoka, Baillie, & Yamamoto, 1982; VanLehn, 1983). The common ground for these cognitive diagnostic systems is that they infer the unobservable cognitive processes from logical interrelationships among cognitive tasks, subtasks, and goals involved in problems representing the domain of interest. It is important that we be able to retrieve invisible things from the "black box" and put them into a useful form so that valuable information can be obtained for improving educational quality.

Efforts to incorporate the findings of cognitive or educational theories into the construction of test items is not new. Bloom and associates (1956), for example, created a taxonomy of educational objectives for the cognitive domain, and it has become very popular among educational practitioners in the past decades. However, some people have had considerable difficulty in classifying test items according to Bloom's taxonomy. Statistical properties of the taxonomy have been investigated (Madaus, Woods, & Nuttall, 1973; Miller, Snowman, & O'Hara, 1979; Roid & Haladyna, 1982), and the results suggested only two cognitive factors—fluid and crystallized intelligence (Cattell, 1971).

More recent advances in cognitive theory provide new insights into human thinking and learning processes. As a result, it has become apparent that the need for a new kind of test has arisen—tests that may be used as an integral part of instruction. In order to be of greater use, the new assessments should promote learning and the improvement of instruction.

Linn (1985) pointed out that "there are a number of barriers that will need to be overcome if the envisioned improvements in testing are to be even partially realized" (p. 69). He described three barriers: a lack of technical or methodological theories that are appropriate to handle dynamic aspects of modern learning theory, an economic barrier, and an ideological barrier. The ideological barrier has to do with the researchers and practitioners who in dealing with current theories of educational and psychological statistics perceive "noise" or "response errors" as incidental factors and fail to seek reasons for the errors. Aberrant responses may be seen as errors even though they coincide with the responses resulting from the perfect application of wrong rules (Birenbaum & Tatsuoka, 1982). Linn (1985) said, "It is important to understand the obstacles to change, whatever their nature, in order to overcome them" (p. 70).

In this chapter, a new methodology that is capable of diagnosing cognitive errors and analyzing different methods for solving problems is introduced and illustrated with fraction subtraction problems. This new approach, called *Rule Space*, integrates Item-Response Theory (IRT) and the algebraic theory of databases (Lee, 1983). The rule space model is general enough to apply to any domain where classification and selection of students and diagnoses of misconceptions are done by Bayes' decision rules for minimum errors (Fukunaga, 1972), or where any other equivalent decision rules are applied to a set of systematic errors determined prior to the analyses. The first section of the chapter discusses important objectives and criteria for the construction of cognitive diagnostic tests. Then the rule space model is introduced and related to a distribution theory, to the construction of a "bug" library and a rule space, and finally to an operational classification scheme.

## ON THE CONSTRUCTION OF ITEMS
## FOR COGNITIVE DIAGNOSTIC TESTING

Special care has been taken in selection of the items for cognitive diagnostic testing. For example, one of the popular misconceptions in fraction subtraction problems is held by about 3% of seventh- or eighth-graders. When it is necessary to increase the numerator of the first fraction of a subtraction problem, a student with this misconception reduces the whole number part by 1 and adds 10 to the numerator of the fraction (Shaw, 1984), presumably by analogy with borrowing in whole number subtraction. But if the denominator of the first fraction happens to be 10, the procedure produces the correct answer

$$\left(2\tfrac{5}{10} - \tfrac{6}{10} = 1\tfrac{15}{10} - \tfrac{6}{10} = 1\tfrac{9}{10}; \quad 2\tfrac{1}{5} - \tfrac{2}{5} = 1\tfrac{11}{5} - \tfrac{2}{5} = 1\tfrac{9}{5}\right)$$

Therefore, in order to detect the misconception, at least one item must have a denominator not equal to 10 in the first fraction, while another item must have the denominator of 10. Then the response pattern (1 for the correct answer and 0 for wrong answers) yielded by the right rule is (1,1), but the rule adding 10 to the numerator produces the response pattern of either (1,0) or (0,1).

Traditionally, item construction was based on the concept of content validity, that is, "how well the content of the test item covers the class of situations or subject matter about which conclusions are to be drawn" (APA, AERA, & NCME, 1954 (p. 13)). However, Angoff (1986), Messick (1980), and Cronbach (1975) came to the same conclusion offered by Loevinger in 1957: "Content validity is essentially *ad hoc* and does not have scientific value" (p. 636). Recently, content validity has generally been replaced by construct validity.

To establish construct validity it is necessary, according to Messick (1984), to examine the psychological trait, or construct, presumed to be measured by the test and investigate relationships between the data from the test and the theory underlying the construct. Further, Angoff (1986) stated that "Construct validation is a process, not a procedure; and it requires many lines of evidence, not all of them quantitative" (p. 26). According to this view, a validation study may include logical task analyses such as those done by Klein, Birenbaum, Standiford, and Tatsuoka (1981) for predicting bugs or erroneous rules of operation, and the construction of test items by which all the predicted bugs would be covered. Protocol studies have also become an important component of the validation process.

Glaser (1985) suggested a new direction for educational measurement in achievement tests. He wrote, "Test items can be comprised of two elements—information that needs to be known and information about the conditions under which use of this knowledge is appropriate" (p. 47). There are obviously various stages of competence in students' knowledge, including cognitive skills. And as Glaser implied, it is important to discover what knowledge structures the students have. Greeno (1980) pointed out that the acquisition of declarative and procedural knowledge is usually an object of instruction, but strategic knowledge that enables one to set goals and subgoals and to form plans for attaining goals is not explicitly taught. It is often left to individuals to acquire it by induction. Some item types require the students to decide which solution path should be taken, beginning with what should be done first to reach the final answer. Many erroneous rules discovered in the studies of signed-number and fraction addition and subtraction problems indicate that the students do not even recognize that different item types require different solution paths and different sequences of subtasks. They did not have the slightest idea of why the strategic skills described by Greeno were necessary.

The new test design must be capable of detecting the different knowledge structures possessed by individuals. Each different structure requires its own unique strategic skills. For example, there are two contrasting methods for solving mixed-number fraction subtraction problems. One is to separate whole number parts from fraction parts (Method B), and the other is to convert mixed numbers to improper fractions first and then subtract the two numbers (Method A). If a student using Method A has excellent computational skills in the arithmetic of whole numbers, then he/she does not have to learn how to borrow one from the whole number part. So Method A always gives the correct answers for subtraction of mixed numbers. The student using Method A can get high scores without really understanding numbers and the number system.

Modern cognitive theory concludes that one of the important stages in learning processes is "theory change" (Glaser, 1985). When learning takes place, students evaluate their hypotheses and then modify as necessary their current theories on the basis of the new information. New methods of educational measurement must take into account such volatile theory changes by an individual and be able to capture the traces of performance changes in detail.

The goals to be attained in modern measurement theory are not easy. As Linn (1985) stated, the technical barrier is high and the traditional theories of educational measurement and testing have only limited power, or are simply inapplicable to the new goals. IRT is not an exception if we conceptualize IRT at the level of individual items.

Thus the usual definition of construct validity has to be expanded, and traditional test theory needs to be reconceptualized in order to explain the dynamic aspects of learning and to express knowledge structures in terms of relational databases. None of the traditional test theories can handle theory changes or assess knowledge structures.

Glaser (1985) categorized the main objectives of assessing new achievement measures into four parts: The first is to diagnose the *principles of performance;* the second is to assess *theory changes;* the third is to evaluate the *structure or representation of problems;* and the fourth is to assess the *automaticity of performing skills.* The automaticity is important to reduce demands on attention. Carrying out single-component processes may be easy, but it may not be easy to work on several components together unless one or more have become automatic. The importance of such orchestration of several component tasks seems often to be neglected by textbooks and in classroom teaching.

The four objectives just listed simply need new achievement measures that are descriptive and qualitative. Psychometrics, on the other hand, is concerned mainly with *quantitative* theories of educational and psychological measurement. Test theory has supported the development of standardized testing throughout a long history of contributions to American education, and the development of IRT has led to many improvements in such areas as item analysis, test design, test equating, and procedures for detecting item bias. Test theory should also be useful in supporting the development of the new achievement measures.

The basic concept underlying IRT is latent traits. As stated by Lord and Novick (1968, p. 358), "A theory of latent traits supposes that an individual's behavior level can be accounted for, to a substantial degree, by defining certain human characteristics called traits, quantitatively estimating the individual's standing on each of these traits, and then using the numerical values obtained to predict or explain performance in relevant situations." Messick (1984) projected a view of new achievement assessment as a combination of trait theory and the descriptive theory used in differential psychology. However, there is no guarantee that traits exist in any physical or physiological sense. "It is sufficient that a person behaves as if those amounts substantially determined his behavior," according to Lord and Novick (1968, p. 358). Convincing intepretation of trait variables have never been given in the past.

Returning to the definition of construct validity given by Angoff (1986), let us examine the psychological traits or constructs as viewed by traditional psychology. Cattell (1971) described ability as organized complexes of transferable concepts and skills. Guilford (1967) described it as information-processing skills. Sternberg (1977) treated abilities as constellations of information-processing components. Snow and Lohman (1984) conceived abilities as structures of assembly and control processes, as well as of performance processes.

On the other hand, psychometricians have developed probabilistic models to measure invisible constructs. Two general classes of the models have been proposed: continuum and state models. Two conflicting views are at the root of the models: For continuum models, trait acquisition is assumed to be continuous in nature, whereas state models take the position of all-or-none, discrete processes. Continuum models would appear to be more relevent to supporting the learning tests of the future.

As for the continuous models, several pioneers have developed various types of item response theory models (Birnbaum, 1968; Lord, 1953; Lord & Novick, 1968; Rasch, 1960). Since then, several extentions or modifications of the original IRT models have been developed (Bock, 1972; Embretsen, 1984; Fischer, 1973; Mislevy, 1983; Mokken & Lewis, 1982; Reckase, 1985; Samejima, 1969). The IRT models express a trait by the variable $\theta$ and express item characteristics by continuous probability functions. That is, item scores $x_j$ ($j = 1, 2 \ldots n$) are related to a trait $\theta$ by a function that gives the probability of each possible score on an item for a randomly selected examinee of given ability. These functions are response curves (formerly called item characteristic curves by Lord & Novick, 1968). Although the models fit the datasets of various standardized tests, the clear meaning of $\theta$ remains undetermined through data analysis. Spada and McGaw (1985) investigated cases for which the one-parameter logistic model and Fischer's linear logistic test model (LLTM) are applicable. They concluded that "the simple Rasch model is applicable only if global learning of item-specific learning occurs, with constant gains for all persons. Person-specific learning falsifies the model. The same is true for application of LLTM that decompose item-specific learning into changes in the difficulties of elementary cognitive operations" (p. 189).

A discrete learning model pioneered by Lazarsfeld and Henry (1968) also has branched out to many modified, extended models (Alvord & Macready, 1985; Macready, 1982; Muthén, 1984; Paulson, 1985; Yamamoto, 1987). Paulson, in particular, extended the latent structure model to apply to the detection of rules of operation in signed-number addition problems. Each rule was treated as a discrete state in his model. Some basic assumptions in the state models are too restrictive and unrealistic to incorporate into the modern learning theory. They assume a priori how many latent classes or states the model has. Then, every subject must belong to exactly one of the finite sets of classes that are mutually exclusive and together exhaustive. Thus the explanation of theory changes by state models is conceptually very difficult. The restriction in the number of states to be included in modeling before the parameters are estimated critically limits the flexibility of this approach. Although recent advances in methods of estimating parameters (Bock & Aitken, 1981; Bock & Mislevy, 1982) are significant, it is still an expensive task with respect to computer time, and it requires a dataset of astronomical size in order to obtain accurate estimates of many parameters.

Tatsuoka and associates (Tatsuoka, 1983, 1985, 1986; Tatsuoka & Tatsuoka, 1983, 1987a) have developed a new probabilistic model that takes advantage of both the continuous and discrete models. They named it the *Rule Space* model.

## THE RULE SPACE MODEL

### Philosophy Behind the Rule Space Model

Whatever the invisible traits or constructs stand for, the statistical meaning of the estimated latent variable is virtually equivalent to the proficiency levels of the performances on the test items because the total score or weighted total score is a sufficient statistic for estimating the true $\theta$ by the maximum likelihood method in the one- and two-parameter logistic models (two of the basic IRT models) and nearly so in the three-parameter logistic and other related IRT models.

Suppose item j is scored 1 or 0; then $x_j$ is a random variable related to $\theta$ by a probability function as follows:

$$P_j(\theta) = \text{Prob}(x_j = 1|\theta) = 1 - Q_j(\theta) = 1 - \text{Prob}(x_j = 0|\theta). \qquad (1)$$

The one-parameter logistic function defines a basic type of model called the Rasch Model. Equation (2) gives the two-parameter logistic function, where $a_j$ is item discrimination power and $b_j$ is item difficulty:

$$P_j(\theta_i) = \frac{1}{1 + \exp\left[-1.7a_j(\theta_i - b_j)\right]}. \tag{2}$$

If $a_j$ is set equal to 1, then it becomes the Rasch model.

Tatsuoka and Linn (1983) discussed the relationship between item response function $P_j(\theta_i)$ and person response function $P_i(b_j)$. The person response function (or curve) is defined by the same equation (2), but $P_j(\theta_i)$ is a function of a continuous variable $\theta$ for fixed $b_j, a_j$ (and other parameters such as $c$, if present), whereas $P_i(b_j)$ is a function of variable $b$ (assuming there are infinitely many items) for a fixed level of $\theta_i$ and fixed $a$. In particular, the one-parameter logistic function is a symmetric function with respect to $\theta$ and $b$.

The person-response function is the probability function of person $i$ with $\theta_i = \theta$ getting the correct answer for an item with difficulty $b_j$. Since Mosier explored person response curves in 1941, several researchers have found them very useful for explaining the relation between ability $\theta$ and item difficulty $b$ (Carroll, 1987; Trabin & Weiss, 1979). By using the one-parameter logistic model, Carroll (1987) explored the relation between both the curves with several ability tests in order to obtain an answer to the question, "What is an 'ability'?" (p. 1). The assumption is, "The existence of an ability can be demonstrated when it can be shown that for any individual there is a systematic, monotonic, and close relation between the individual's probability of correct or satisfactory performance and the difficulties of a series of tasks, and when there are variations over individuals in the parameters of this relation" (p. 22). Carroll's conclusion is that the ability is defined in terms of the attribute(s) of the tasks that cause differences in task difficulty. This conclusion is applicable to the situation such that the space of the difficulties resulting from various combinations of attributes involved in the tasks is unidimensional. Then this conclusion is mathematically sound because of the symmetric relation of the Rasch model.

As long as we interpret $\theta$ as the latent ability or construct that influences the performances on the tests, we may face the philosophical dilemmas of IRT models, such as the dimensionality of $\theta$ or $b$, or the impossibility of explaining gain scores or Glaser's theory changes. Because a composite of several factors (or abilities) influences the performance of an item, and each item in the test is likely to require a different composite or possibly a different set of abilities, the psychological meaning of $\theta$ is very complicated and difficult to interpret (Stout, 1987).

IRT models are formulated by utilizing a response pattern or binary vector with $n$ elements. There are two distinct independent pieces of information in a response pattern. One is quantitative, telling us how many items are correctly answered (total score), and the other is qualitative, telling us which items are correctly answered and which are missed. Because IRT assumes local independence (Lord & Novick, 1968), the likelihood function is expressed in terms of both pieces of information. The item and person parameters can be estimated from the likelihood function by applying the maximum likelihood procedure.

However, Tatsuoka (1987) investigated what really determines the item response curves, a task somewhat similar to Carroll's quest regarding "what is an ability." Starting from a painstaking logical task analysis, Tatsuoka constructed sets of items such that each item involves a unique combination of cognitive subtasks. The study showed that the underlying cognitive processes for solving an item determine the slope and location parameters of an IRT curve. If this is true for any domain, then it is important to expand our view from a localized, narrow interest in IRT curves to a broader global concept. After IRT models were introduced, refinement and improvement in psychometric techniques have generally been limited to dealing with individual items separately.

A new model has to be able to achieve the measurement objectives of modern learning theory. In order to achieve this demanding goal, it is helpful to see item-response curves as a whole, as a set, and to investigate algebraic and topological properties of this function space. Many IRT models have been proposed recently, and their probability functions provide a finer or more accurate measure of $\theta$ than simple basic IRT models. They can also be used to formulate the rule space model; thus, it is not necessary to be restricted only to one- and two-parameter logistic models. Such an expansion of the perspectives of test theories to functional analysis leads to some important and useful conclusions. For example, Tatsuoka (1975) reformulated classical test theory in Hilbert space, and proved the existence of the true score.

The theory of functional analysis treats a function as a "point" and utilizes the methods of algebra and topology in a set of functions. Ramsay (1982) outlined the concept of functional analysis as an extension of classical statistical techniques and explained least squares, principal components, and canonical correlation analyses in the context of functional analysis: "The data must be viewed as an element in a space of possible functions taking a domain space into a range space" (p. 352). Ramsay concluded with the remark that "functional analysis already has revolutionized numerical analysis so that any issue of a major journal [in that discipline] now has a number of papers using this technology. I claim that this is about to happen to statistics" (p. 394). The rule space model is an application of functional analysis using a projection operator.

The third objective listed by Glaser was to assess the structure of knowledge possessed by an individual. This dimension requires a leap to a new world for the field of educational measurement, because it is apparent that the algebraic theory of relational databases is needed to achieve this objective. If a set of items is carefully constructed, then various relationships among the items should reflect the relationships among cognitive subtasks underlying each item. By examining bugs and sources of misconceptions, one can see which subtasks caused scores of ones or zeros on the items. For example, Tatsuoka (1984c) represented 27 erroneous rules of operation found in signed-number addition problems as ordered pairs of (a) the number of cognitive steps taken correctly, and (b) the value of the Norm Conformity Index, one of several indices that measure appropriateness of response patterns (Tatsuoka & Tatsuoka, 1982). The latter assesses the degree of conformity of the sequence of cognitive steps followed by each bug to the expert's procedural steps. That is, the second value measures how early or how late an erroneous rule causes departure from the correct steps in the procedural network. The result of the study indicated that an early derailment has more serious consequences than one at a later stage. Cluster analysis separated bugs caused by early and frequent derailments from those due to later and less-frequent derailments. The former were named "seriously ill-composed rules." Later studies (Birenbaum & Tatsuoka, 1987; Shaw, 1986) indicated that wrong rules that are not seriously ill-composed can be remediated by giving correct answers, or even by the feedback of OK or NO to each response to the item.

The Norm Conformity index (Tatsuoka & Tatsuoka, 1982) characterizes the quality of information of a response pattern and expresses its characteristics quantitatively. The rule space uses a similar index (called IRT-based caution index) defined in the context of the IRT curves (Tatsuoka, 1984b). However, in order to explain what the rule space model is, we have to clarify the terms *bug* and *erroneous rules of operation,* which have been used without specific definitions so far.

## What are Rules?

A systematic error over the test items can result from a combination of one or more bugs or erroneous rules. If a student applies an erroneous rule with perfect consistency to the items in the test, then his/her responses to the test would be perfectly matched with the responses generated by a computer program. We call systematic errors *erroneous rules.*

*Correct rules* would, by definition, produce the right answer to all the items, but sometimes wrong rules may produce the right answer to some subset of the test items. Moreover, some rules are combinations of the right rule and wrong rules, and others are combinations of two or more different wrong rules. We consider them as new rules as long as they are consistently applied to all the items (Tatsuoka & Tatsuoka, 1988). If we construct the test items carefully so that the important, predicted common errors can be expressed by unique item-response patterns of ones and zeros, or component-response patterns specified in a task analysis, then the rules can be distinguished by response patterns. In other words, we can assume that rules are expressed by binary response vectors.

The rule space model was developed to solve a specific classification problem in which the entities to be classified are the rules in some well-defined domain such as arithmetic, algebra, or science. As was mentioned earlier, two kinds of information are included in a response pattern. They are the quantitative information of the total number of 1s and the qualitative information of *which* items had 1s. The former is represented by $\theta$, the latter, by $\zeta$, an index expressing atypicality (or inappropriateness) of the response patterns for a given group (Tatsuoka,

1984b). Any rule can be expressed by an ordered pair of $\theta$ and $\zeta$ or, equivalently, $\theta$ and the numerator of $\zeta$, denoted by f(**x**) (Tatsuoka, 1985). We assume that, at least at the very beginning, the rules are determined a priori through a logical task analysis. A later section explains this in detail.

## Bug Distribution

The distribution of observations plays an important role in statistical theories. When we deal with students, random errors or slips due to careless errors or uncertainty always affect the outcomes of performance on a test. A slip on item $j$ occurs when a student does not use his/her rule exactly on item $j$, and as a result, the response to item $j$ does not match the response yielded by the rule. The response that deviated from the rule-based response may, of course, be the correct response. Even if a student possesses some systematic error, it is very rare to have the response pattern perfectly matched with the patterns theoretically generated by its algorithm (Tatsuoka, 1984a; VanLehn, 1983). Some systematic errors may produce more slips, whereas others have a small number of slips. Also, some items may be prone to produce more slips than other items. It is very important that we be able to predict the probability of having slips on each item for each systematic error (or rule). Knowing the theoretical distribution of observed slips of a rule enables us to see and predict statistical properties of observed responses yielded by the rule.

Tatsuoka and Tatsuoka (1987a) derived the theoretical distribution of observed slips and named it the *Bug Distribution*. First, the probability of having a "slip" on item $j$ ($j = 1, 2, \ldots, n$), is denoted by $p_j$ for item $j$, ($j = 1, 2, \ldots, n$) and it is assumed that slips occur independently across items. The bug distribution of a rule R follows a compound binomial distribution with different slip probabilities for the items.

$$\text{Prob (having up to } s \text{ slips/R)} = \sum_{m=0}^{s}\left[\sum_{\Sigma u_j = m}\prod_{j=1}^{n}p_j{}^{u_j}(1-p_j)^{1-u_j}\right] \tag{3}$$

where $u_j$ is a random variable such that $u_j = 1$ if a slip occurs on item $j$ and $u_j = 0$ if not. The expectation and variance of the bug distribution of Rule R whose corresponding binary vector is $\mathbf{x_R}$—in which we assume, without loss of generality, that the first $r$ elements are ones and the rest are zeros (i.e., $x_{R_j} = 1$ for $j = 1, \ldots, r$ and $x_{R_j} = 0$ for $j = r + 1, \ldots, n$)—are given by

$$\mu_R = \sum_{j=1}^{r}p_j + \sum_{j=r+1}^{n}q_j \tag{4}$$

$$\sigma_R^2 = \sum_{j=1}^{n} p_j q_j \tag{5}$$

where $q_j = 1 - p_j$.

The bug distribution of rule R is a function defined on the slip random variable $u_j$, and it relates algebraically to the conditional probability that a subject in the state of possessing rule R would respond correctly to item $j$ (Tatsuoka & Tatsuoka, 1987b).

## A Mapping Function of Response Patterns x.

The rule space model begins by mapping all possible binary response patterns, $\mathbf{x}$'s, into a set of ordered pairs $\{[\theta, f(\mathbf{x})]\}$. The mapping function $f(\mathbf{x})$ is the inner product of two residual vectors, $\mathbf{P}(\theta) - \mathbf{x}$ and $\mathbf{P}(\theta) - \mathbf{T}(\theta)$, where $P_j(\theta)$ $j = 1, \ldots n$ are the logistic functions and $\mathbf{P}(\theta) = [P_1(\theta), \ldots P_n(\theta)]$ and $\mathbf{T}(\theta) = [T(\theta), \ldots T(\theta)]$, $T(\theta)$ being the average of $P_j(\theta)$, $j = 1 \ldots, n$. Because $f(\mathbf{x})$ is a linear function, the bug distribution of Rule R mapped into the rule space will have the centroid $[\theta_R, f(\mathbf{x}_R)]$, where $f(\mathbf{x}_R)$ is given by Equation (6), and the variance–covariance matrix of Equation (7) (Tatsuoka, 1985).

$$f(\mathbf{x}_R) = -\sum_{j=1}^{r} Q_j(\theta_R)[P_j(\theta_R) - T(\theta_R)] \tag{6}$$

$$+ \sum_{j=r+1}^{n} P_j(\theta_R)[P_j(\theta_R) - T(\theta_R)]$$

$$\sum_R = \begin{bmatrix} \dfrac{1}{I(\theta_R)} & 0 \\ 0 & \displaystyle\sum_{j=1}^{n} P_j(\theta_R)Q_j(\theta_R)[P_j(\theta_R) - T(\theta_R)] \end{bmatrix} \tag{7}$$

where $\theta_R$ is the $\theta$-value for Rule R, $Q_j(\theta_R)$ is $1 - P_j(\theta_R)$ and $I(\theta_R)$ is the information function of the test at $\theta_R$.

On the other hand, the slip variable $u_j$ is related to the item-score variable $x_j$ on item j as follows:

$$\begin{cases} u_j = 1 \text{ if a slip occurs and hence } x_j \neq x_{R_j} \\ u_j = 0 \text{ if a slip does not occur and hence } x_j = x_{R_j}, \end{cases} \tag{8}$$

or, equivalently $u_j = |x_{R_j} - x_j|$ by Tatsuoka and Tatsuoka (1987b). The conditional probability of having a slip on item $j$ for a given rule R is as follows:

$$\text{Prob } (u_j = 1 \,|R) = \text{Prob } (x_j \neq x_{R_j}|R). \tag{9}$$

Tatsuoka (1985) showed that the function f(**x**) maps binary response patterns {**x**} into a set of ordered pairs {[$\theta$, f(**x**)]} one-to-one in the one-parameter logistic model, and also empirically confirmed with several sets of Monte Carlo data that this relation would be true for the two-parameter logistic model as well, provided the number of items is large and the $a_j$ are spread out. Therefore, the relationship in (9) can be rewritten, within the context of IRT models, in Equation (10).

$$\text{Prob } (x_j \neq x_{R_j} \,|\, R) = \text{Prob } [x_j \neq x_{R_j} \,|\, \theta_R, \text{f}(\mathbf{x_R})]. \tag{10}$$

The relation (10) is true for any IRT model as long as the mapping of response patterns {**x**} into ordered pairs of ability level $\theta$ and the image of **x** is one-to-one. The mapping function that is used to formulate the rule space can be other person fit statistics such as those of Drasgow, Levine, and McLaughlin (1987), of Wright and Stone (1979) or of Molenaar (1987). If the value of f(**x**) is close to the $\theta$-axis in the rule space, the response pattern **x** is typical and conforms well to the response patterns produced by a majority of subjects in a population. In other words, rule R is a popular rule that is used by many students. Because the expectation of f(**x**) is zero (Tatsuoka, 1984b, 1985c), and the purpose of this study is to investigate further properties of IRT functions, extremely unusual rules of operation (or latent classes) are not considered here. Under this condition, Equation (10) becomes (11):

$$\text{Prob } [x_j \neq x_{R_j} \,|\, \theta_R, \text{f}(\mathbf{x_R})] = \text{Prob } (x_j \neq x_{R_j} \,|\, \theta_R) \tag{11}$$

$$= \begin{cases} \text{Prob } (x_j = 1 \,|\, \theta_R) = P_j(\theta_R) \text{ if } x_{R_j} = 0 \\ \text{Prob } (x_j = 0 \,|\, \theta_R) = Q_j(\theta_R) \text{ if } x_{R_j} = 1 \end{cases}$$

By expressing Equation (11) as a weighted average of IRT functions, Equation (12) of slip probability on item j is given as follows:

$$S_j(\theta) = (1 - x_{R_j}) \, P_j(\theta_R) + x_{R_j} Q_j(\theta_R). \tag{12}$$

Indeed, the variance of a bug distribution of R given in (5) will be mapped into $\sum_{j=1}^{n} p_j q_j [P_j(\theta) - T(\theta)]^2$ (Tatsuoka & Tatsuoka, 1987a). If $\mathbf{x_R}$ is a typical rule for the majority of students in the population where the IRT parameters are estimated, then $p_j q_j$ will be $P_j(\theta) Q_j(\theta)$, and thus the image of the bug distribution of R in the rule space is the variance–covariance matrix given by Equation (7).

By standardizing f(**x**), IRT-based caution index $\zeta$ (Tatsuoka, 1985) becomes

$$\zeta = \frac{f(\mathbf{x})}{\sum_{j=1}^{n} P_j(\theta_R)Q_j(\theta_R) \left[P_j(\theta_R) - T(\theta_R)\right]^2}$$    (13)

The mechanism of how the index $\zeta$ distinguishes atypical response patterns from typical ones is described in Tatsuoka and Tatsuoka (1988); so a more detailed explanation than that given on pp. 474–477 is not given in this paper. But the statistical properties of the bug distributions are discussed later in the context of the theory changes mentioned earlier.

The next section introduces an elementary relational structure of the items that are used for preparing a list of erroneous rules in the bug library.

## Differential Ordering of Items by Underlying Cognitive Processes

If a content domain for constructing a cognitive diagnostic test is determined, then logical task analysis can nominate cognitive attributes. The attributes may refer to production rules, procedural operations, item types, or, more generally, any cognitive subtasks. A set of $n$ items can be characterized by $K$ nominated attributes and expressed by $K$-element vectors. Let us call this matrix an *attribute × item* matrix, or **Q**-matrix (Embretsen, 1984). The initial task analyses could be carried out by several experts or master teachers. If two or more experts use different methods to solve a given set of problems, then they may get entirely different attribute × item matrices.

In this study, all the nodes of a directed process network will be called "attributes" and denoted by $A_1$, $A_2$, . . . $A_K$. Items will be characterized by placing one in the $(k, j)$ cell of the **Q**-matrix if item $j$ involves attribute $A_k$, and placing a zero when item $j$ does not involve attribute $A_k$,

$$q_{kj} = \begin{cases} 1 & \text{if item } j \text{ involves attribute } A_k, \\ 0 & \text{otherwise} \end{cases}$$    (14)

For example, in Figure 18.1b Method B is an attribute × item matrix for fraction subtraction problems solved by Method B (separate whole number and fraction parts).

The purpose of introducing an attribute × item matrix is, first, to make it easier to construct a set of items relevant to diagnosing misconceptions that result from a lack of knowledge or misunderstanding of an attribute or combination of several attributes. The second aim is to extract a set of binary patterns of $n$ items from the matrix, each pattern being produced by a systematic application of an

**Method A** (Always convert mixed numbers to improper fractions.)

| ATTRIBUTES | ITEMS 1 | 2 | 3 | 4 | 5 | 6 | 7 | 8 | 9 | 10 | 11 | 12 | 13 | 14 | 15 | 16 | 17 | 18 | 19 | 20 |
|---|---|---|---|---|---|---|---|---|---|---|---|---|---|---|---|---|---|---|---|---|
| 1. Convert a whole number to a fraction | 0 | 0 | 0 | 0 | 0 | 0 | 1 | 0 | 1 | 0 | 0 | 0 | 0 | 0 | 1 | 0 | 0 | 0 | 1 | 0 |
| 2. Convert 1st mixed number to fraction | 0 | 0 | 0 | 1 | 1 | 0 | 1 | 0 | 1 | 1 | 1 | 0 | 1 | 1 | 0 | 1 | 1 | 1 | 1 | 1 |
| 3. Convert 2nd mixed number to fraction | 0 | 0 | 0 | 1 | 1 | 0 | 0 | 0 | 0 | 1 | 1 | 0 | 1 | 1 | 0 | 1 | 0 | 1 | 0 | 1 |
| 4. Simplify before subtracting | 1 | 0 | 0 | 1 | 1 | 0 | 0 | 0 | 0 | 1 | 1 | 1 | 0 | 0 | 0 | 0 | 0 | 1 | 1 | 1 |
| 5. Find a common denominator | 1 | 1 | 1 | 0 | 1 | 0 | 0 | 0 | 0 | 0 | 0 | 0 | 1 | 0 | 0 | 0 | 0 | 0 | 0 | 0 |
| 6. Column borrow to subtract numerator | 1 | 0 | 0 | 0 | 1 | 0 | 0 | 0 | 1 | 0 | 0 | 0 | 1 | 0 | 0 | 0 | 0 | 1 | 1 | 1 |
| 7. Reduce answer to simplest form | 0 | 0 | 0 | 0 | 1 | 0 | 0 | 0 | 1 | 1 | 1 | 1 | 0 | 0 | 1 | 1 | 1 | 1 | 1 | 1 |

**Method B** (Separate mixed numbers into whole and fraction parts.)

| ATTRIBUTES | ITEMS 1 | 2 | 3 | 4 | 5 | 6 | 7 | 8 | 9 | 10 | 11 | 12 | 13 | 14 | 15 | 16 | 17 | 18 | 19 | 20 |
|---|---|---|---|---|---|---|---|---|---|---|---|---|---|---|---|---|---|---|---|---|
| 1. Convert a whole number to fraction or mixed number | 0 | 0 | 0 | 0 | 0 | 0 | 1 | 0 | 1 | 0 | 0 | 0 | 0 | 0 | 1 | 0 | 0 | 0 | 1 | 0 |
| 2. Separate whole number from fraction | 0 | 0 | 0 | 1 | 1 | 0 | 1 | 0 | 1 | 1 | 1 | 0 | 1 | 1 | 1 | 1 | 1 | 1 | 1 | 1 |
| 3. Simplify before getting final number | 0 | 0 | 0 | 1 | 1 | 0 | 1 | 0 | 0 | 1 | 1 | 1 | 0 | 0 | 1 | 0 | 0 | 1 | 1 | 1 |
| 4. Find the common denominator | 1 | 1 | 1 | 0 | 1 | 0 | 0 | 0 | 0 | 0 | 0 | 0 | 1 | 0 | 0 | 0 | 0 | 0 | 0 | 0 |
| 5. Borrow 1 from whole number part, change numerator and whole | 0 | 0 | 0 | 1 | 0 | 0 | 0 | 0 | 0 | 1 | 1 | 0 | 1 | 0 | 0 | 0 | 1 | 1 | 1 | 1 |
| 6. Column borrow to subtract 2nd numerator from 1st | 1 | 0 | 0 | 0 | 0 | 0 | 0 | 0 | 0 | 1 | 0 | 0 | 0 | 0 | 0 | 0 | 0 | 1 | 0 | 0 |
| 7. Reduce answer to simplest form | 0 | 0 | 0 | 0 | 1 | 0 | 0 | 0 | 0 | 1 | 0 | 1 | 0 | 0 | 0 | 0 | 0 | 0 | 0 | 0 |

FIG.18.1. *Attribute x item* matrices of fraction subtraction problems by using Methods A and B.

erroneous rule resulting from a misconception, incomplete knowledge of a targeted attribute, or a combination of several attributes.

Starting from such an attribute × item matrix, many researchers in a variety of disciplines such as biology, differential psychology, engineering, and sociology have investigated clustering techniques. Although the author has applied such techniques to the attribute × item matrix, the results were disappointing. By using a dataset, results of the analysis may be more objective, but interpretability of analysis results may be reduced to a great extent. The frequent lack of interpretability of factors obtained by factor analysis of the estimated trait variables is well known. Thus there is a problem of trade-off between establishing objectivity and interpretability. At this stage of making a diagnostic test, we take the value of interpretability of data into account. However, it is not our intention to neglect objectivity. This issue is discussed again in the summary and discussion.

Each item, represented by a column vector $\mathbf{Q}_j$ of the attribute × item matrix, is now characterized by a specific combination of attributes. Similarly, each attribute, a row vector $\mathbf{Q}_k$, contains the information as to which items involve attribute k. Let $R$ be a relation on a set of the column vector $\mathbf{q}_j$, $j = 1, \ldots, n$, where $n$ is the number of items.

The definition of $R$ is as follows:

$$\mathbf{q}_i \leq \mathbf{q}_j \text{ if } q_{ik} \leq q_{jk} \text{ for } k = 1, \ldots, K. \tag{15}$$

Or equivalently, if item $j$ includes the attributes involved in item $i$, then item $j$ requires no fewer tasks than item $i$. This relation satisfies the reflexive and transitive laws:

1) $\mathbf{q}_i \leq \mathbf{q}_i$, (reflexive law);
2) if $\mathbf{q}_i \leq \mathbf{q}_j$ and $\mathbf{q}_j \leq \mathbf{q}_l$, the $\mathbf{q}_i \leq \mathbf{q}_l$ (transitive law).

With this relation, a set $\{\mathbf{q}_1, \ldots, \mathbf{q}_n\}$ has a partial ordering. If the symmetric law is satisfied by $\mathbf{q}_i$ and $\mathbf{q}_j$, then $\mathbf{q}_i$ and $\mathbf{q}_j$ are equivalent, and it is written as $\mathbf{q}_i \sim \mathbf{q}_j$. Let $\{\mathbf{q}_j\}$ be a set of items expressed by vectors of $K$ attribute elements where $\mathbf{q}_j$, $j = 1, \ldots n$. From the attribute × item matrix a set of totally ordered items is extracted. When relation $R$ exists for any two elements in a set S, then S is said to be totally ordered.

In Fig. 18.1b, Method B, Items 6, 8, 12, and 10 are totally ordered but 6, 2, and 12 are not. Denote a set of totally ordered items by $S_i$. Then a list of the totally ordered sets of the items extracted from Fig. 18.1, Method B, is presented in Table 18.1.

In Fig. 18.2b, Method B, a tree of the items is constructed from the list of totally ordered sets in Table 18.1. If two items are connected by a directed arc, then the items are totally ordered.

The number (or numbers) in a box represent the item(s) involving the attributes listed next to the box. An advantage to using such an item tree is that a structural interrelationship among the items can be portrayed schematically. With the pro-

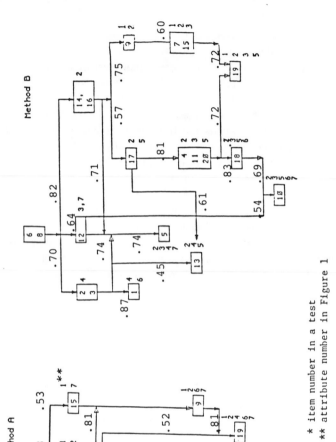

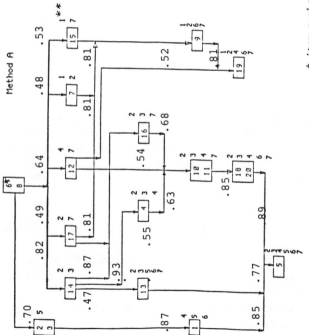

* item number in a test
** attribute number in Figure 1

FIG.18.2. Two item trees constructed from the *attribute x item matrices* for Methods A and B.

TABLE 18.1
A List of Totally Ordered Sets of the Items Extracted
from Figure 18.1, Method B

| | |
|---|---|
| 1. | 6(8)*,2(3)*,1 |
| 2. | 6(8) ,2(3) ,13 |
| 3. | 6(8) ,12  ,5 |
| 4. | 6(8) ,12  ,10 |
| 5. | 6(8) ,14(16)*,17,13 |
| 6. | 6(8) ,14(16) ,17,4(11,20)**,18,10 |
| 7. | 6(8) ,14(16) ,17,4(11,20)  ,19 |
| 8. | 6(8) ,14(16) , 9,7,19 |

*Items 6 and 8, 2 and 3, 14 and 16 are equivalent.
**Items 4, 11, and 20 are equivalent.

cess network it is difficult to see all the different solution paths taken by 20 items in a single graph, and it is also difficult to pinpoint why and where a student's response pattern deviates from the perfect responses. For example, Tatsuoka (1984a) described Rule 8 as "The student subtracts the smaller from the larger in corresponding parts when the two numbers are different" (p. 4). With Rule 8, items 12 and 14 ($1\frac{1}{8} - \frac{1}{8}$, $3\frac{4}{5} - 3\frac{2}{5}$) have correct answers, whereas 2 and 17 ($\frac{3}{4} - \frac{3}{8}$, $7\frac{3}{5} - \frac{4}{5}$) do not. By marking each box in the item tree of Method B with * for the correct answers and × for the wrong ones, the sources of misconceptions producing Rule 8 (referred to as G14) are represented clearly, as can be seen in Fig. 18.3; they are borrowing, getting a common denominator, and converting a whole number to a fraction.

## Preparation of the Bug Information Bank or Bug Library

The rule space model has been developed by emphasizing the importance of interpretability of statistics estimated from the data. Most psychological models have been less concerned with interpretability. Fischer and his associates (Embretson, 1985; Fischer, 1973), for example, expressed item difficulties in the Rasch model by a linear combination of component subtasks, and also by unobservable frequencies with which each component influences the solution of each item. Because the models contain several parameters in the logistic functions, the estimation of the item parameters has become a major task in the past 10 years (Fischer & Formann, 1972). Scheiblechner (1972) estimated item difficulties from the Rasch model first, and then regressed the estimated item difficulties onto the hypothetical frequencies contained in the task matrix **Q**. Estimated $\beta$-weights approximate fairly well the estimates of component subtasks obtained by a conditional maximum likelihood procedure. However, Spada and McGaw (1985) stated, "Despite the value of the LLTM's analysis of task performance in terms of performance on elementary operations, there are some difficulties in interpreting the parameters of the model. The decomposition of the item difficulties is,

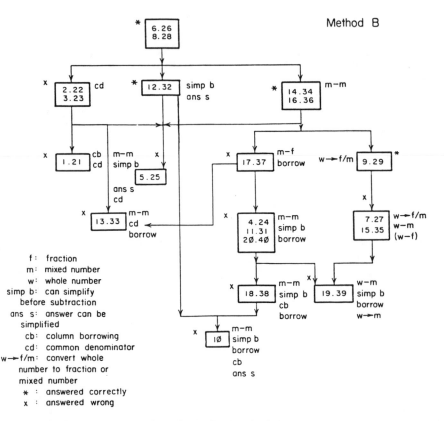

FIG.18.3. Representation of rule G14 by the item tree.

of course, quite precisely defined but its psychological interpretation is not equally clear" (p. 180). Such difficulties in interpreting the estimates of the psychological models are very common in psychometrics. It is difficult to maintain the interpretability of estimated parameters in terms of underlying cognitive tasks in the current psychological modeling approaches. New approaches must be flexible enough so that individual differences unaccounted for during the process of formulating a model not only improve the interpretability of the estimates but are also able to determine the existence of subjects who do not fit the model. Because the item trees are constructed from the inclusion relationships among attributes, interpretability is clearly retained.

***Use of Multiple Regression.*** A multiple regression of analysis of the attributes on the item difficulties of 40 items was carried out, as was done by Scheiblechner (1972). The analysis showed that the four attributes—converting a whole number to a fraction or mixed number, getting the common denominator, borrowing in whole-number subtraction, and borrowing one from the whole-number part to make the numerator larger—have significant $\beta$-weights to predict the item difficulties (Chevalaz, 1983). Also, the number of attributes involved in each item correlates with the item difficulty, ($r = .57$). Therefore, it is true that the greater the number of attributes involved in the items, the more difficult the items are.

Suppose that a student who uses Method A cannot get the lowest common multiple of two denominators but can do the remaining attributes. Then the response pattern of the performance on the 40 items would be 0 for the items involving the attribute $cd$ in the Method A item tree and 1 for those not involving the attribute $cd$. Because getting the common denominator has a substantial $\beta$-weight, this error can be a good indicator for determining a list of rules in a bug library.

*Use of the Item Tree.*    There are $2^7$ possible response patterns obtainable from the attribute $\times$ item matrix in each method. However, the item trees in Figure 18.2 enable us to select a smaller number of rules and bugs that are substantially important in designing and evaluating lessons.

The numbers shown near the directed arcs of Fig. 18.2 are conditional probabilities, Prob $(X_i = 1 \mid X_{i-1} = X_{i-2} = \ldots X_1 = 1)$ where i − 1, i − 2, ..., 1 are antecedent items of $i$, and $X_i$ is the score of item $i$.

Because $\mathbf{q}_i \geq \mathbf{q}_{i-1}$ (i.e., item $i$ includes all the attributes involving item $i − 1$) a drastic decrease in the value of the conditional probability implies that a newly added attribute (or attributes) causes the change. For instance, for Method B, the new attribute added to item 17 is indeed a difficult subtask—borrowing. If a student cannot do this new attribute but can do the other attributes perfectly well, then subsequent items not including the borrowing attribute can be answered correctly. Thus, a binary response pattern corresponding to the student's performance would be 0s for the items that involve borrowing and 1s for nonborrowing items. This conjecture with respect to borrowing may be confirmed by examining the arc between items 12 and 10.

Next, the conditional probability value between items 9 and 7 is .60, which is low enough to merit attention. The new attribute in the second box is "w to f or m"—converting whole numbers to fractions or mixed numbers. Therefore, the second response pattern resulting from this case is 0s for the items with whole numbers such as 3 − ½, and 1s for the items not including whole numbers in their first position. By proceeding in this manner we would obtain a set of response patterns that are logically interpretable. Thus, representing the structural relationships among the items with respect to their underlying cognitive attributes facilitates error analysis. We have developed a computer program to make an item tree from an attribute $\times$ item matrix and extract a set of totally ordered items. Then, applying the method just mentioned, a list of 39 rule classes is prepared. They are coded as G1 through G39. For instance, G2 is the binary pattern of 1s for items 6, 8, 26, and 28, and G13 is binary pattern of ones for easy nonborrowing items. The interpretation of G2 is that a student can subtract two numbers if no attribute in Figure 18.1 is involved. Then their centroids and variance–covariance matrices are stored in the bug library for later use.

## Stochastic Behavior of the Rules: Inferences From the Bug Distribution

***Which Rules are More Consistently Applied?***    The bug distribution of Rule R defined on the neighboring response patterns of R was introduced in the previous section. It was expressed by a compound binomial distribution with the slip probabilities $S_j(\theta_R)$, $j = 1, \ldots, n$. Let $S(\theta_R)$ be the mean of $S_j(\theta_R)$, $j = 1, \ldots$ $n$. Because any rule can be used as R, $\theta$ instead of $\theta_R$ will be used hereunder. Walsh (1954) expanded the compound binomial in powers of $S_j(\theta) - S(\theta)$ where $S(\theta)$ is the average of $S_j(\theta)$. Suppose $U$ is a random variable of slip and $s$ is the number of slips, then the probability of having $s$ slips is given by (16),

$$\text{Prob }(U = s) = P_n(s) + \tfrac{1}{2}nV_2C_2(s) + \tfrac{1}{3}nV_3C_3(s) + (\tfrac{1}{4}nV_4 - \tfrac{1}{8}n^2V_2^2) \quad (16)$$

$$C_4(s) + (\tfrac{1}{5}nV_2 - \tfrac{1}{6}n^2V_2V_3)C_5(s) + \ldots, s = 0, 1, 2, \ldots, n,$$

$$\text{where } P_n(s) = \binom{n}{5}S(\theta)^s[1 - S(\theta)]^{n-s} \text{ for } s = 0, 1, 2, \ldots n,$$

$$C_r(s) = \sum_{v=0}^{r}(-1)^{v+1}\binom{r}{v}P_{n-r}(s - v),$$

$$V_r = \frac{1}{n}\left\{\sum_{g=1}^{r}\left(S_j(\theta) - S(\theta)\right)\right\}^r, r = 2, 3, \ldots, n.$$

Let us use G2 and G13 for illustrating the relationship between the rule the probability of having s-slips away from the rules.

As can be seen in Table 18.2, the probability of having a slip at item 6 is .610 for Rule G2 and .240 for G13. Because the scores for item 6 of both G2 and G13 are 1, the probability of having a slip, 1 to 0, at item 6 is higher for G2 than for G13. That is, Prob $(X_6 \neq X_{G2_6} \mid G2) = .610$ and Prob $(X_6 \neq X_{G13_6} \mid G13) = .240$. Item 6 produces more slips for G2 than for G13. Table 18.3 shows the theoretical frequency distributions of Rules G13 and G2. The probability of having 5 slips for G2 is .225 and for G13 is .150. The frequency distribution of G13 reaches the mode at $s = 6$ whereas that of G2 reaches the peak at $s = 5$. A close examination of the bug distributions indicates that as $\theta$ comes closer to the sample mean, the rule associated with such $\theta$ produces more slips. As $\theta$ becomes larger

TABLE 18.2
Slippage Probabilities of the First 20 Items for Rules $G_2$ and $G_{13}$

| Item | $G_2$ Slippage Probability | $X_{R_j}$ | $G_{13}$ Slippage Probability | $X_{R_j}$ |
|------|---------------------------|-----------|------------------------------|-----------|
| 1 | .043 | 0 | .175 | 0 |
| 2 | .025 | 0 | .164 | 0 |
| 3 | .025 | 0 | .128 | 0 |
| 4 | .154 | 0 | .308 | 0 |
| 5 | .285 | 0 | .435 | 0 |
| 6 | .610 | 1 | .240 | 1 |
| 7 | .006 | 0 | .037 | 0 |
| 8 | .495 | 1 | .331 | 1 |
| 9 | .430 | 0 | .448 | 1 |
| 10 | .002 | 0 | .020 | 0 |
| 11 | .012 | 0 | .076 | 0 |
| 12 | .269 | 0 | .592 | 0 |
| 13 | .001 | 0 | .005 | 0 |
| 14 | .192 | 0 | .444 | 1 |
| 15 | .006 | 0 | .048 | 0 |
| 16 | .208 | 0 | .490 | 1 |
| 17 | .003 | 0 | .029 | 0 |
| 18 | .021 | 0 | .099 | 0 |
| 19 | .000 | 0 | .001 | 0 |
| 20 | .001 | 0 | .014 | 0 |

TABLE 18.3
Bug Distributions of Rules $G_{13}$ and $G_2$ (N = 1000)

| No. of Slips | Frequencies of $G_{13}$ | Frequencies of $G_2$ |
|--------------|-------------------------|----------------------|
| 0 | 1 | 1 |
| 1 | 5 | 11 |
| 2 | 18 | 48 |
| 3 | 49 | 122 |
| 4 | 98 | 198 |
| 5 | 150 | 225 |
| 6 | 181 | 188 |
| 7 | 176 | 119 |
| 8 | 141 | 58 |
| 9 | 93 | 22 |
| 10 | 51 | 6 |
| 11 | 23 | 1 |
| 12 | 9 | |
| 13 | 9 | |

473

or smaller, such rules produce fewer slips. This implies that the students with near-average $\theta$ values test their hypotheses more actively than those with $\theta$-values close to the two extremes. Thus, theory changes are observed most often among the students who have not quite mastered a topic yet. This conjecture, derived from theoretical bug distributions conforms well with the results of error analysis performed on fraction addition problems as well as on signed-number subtraction problems (Tatsuoka, Birenbaum, & Arnold, in press).

**Which Rules are Atypical?.**    The IRT models assume the local independence of reponses to the items. Therefore, the likelihood of each rule can be computed by Equation (17). For each rule $R_i$,

$$L_{\mathbf{R}_i} = \prod_{j=1}^{n} P_j(\theta)^{R_{ij}} [1 - P_j(\theta)]^{1 - R_{ij}}. \tag{17}$$

It is known that the likelihood correlates very highly with $\zeta$ (Birenbaum, 1985, 1986; Harnisch & Tatsuoka, 1983). The numerator of $\zeta$ is the function f($\mathbf{x}$), which is linear in $\mathbf{x}$, as follows,

$$f(\mathbf{x}) = \mathbf{P}(\theta) [\mathbf{P}(\theta) - \mathbf{T}(\theta)] - x [\mathbf{P}(\theta) - \mathbf{T}(\theta)] \tag{18}$$

Because IRT curves are sensitive to the underlying cognitive processes as mentioned earlier (Tatsuoka, 1987), the deviation of $P(\theta)$—denoted by $P(\theta) - T(\theta)$— also reflects those cognitive processes. But the shapes of the function $P_j(\theta) - T(\theta)$ are different from those of the original logistic function. Figure 18.4 shows three curves where the difficulty of item 27 is smaller than the average function $T(\theta)$, and that of item 28 is greater than $T(\theta)$. Let us take $T(\theta)$ as the horizontal axis and the value of $P_j(\theta)$ as the vertical axis and draw the deviations of item response curves. Then graphs of deviations $P_j(\theta)$ would be as in Fig. 18.5.

Easier items are located in the upper half of the space, whereas more difficult items are in the lower half. If a student with ability $\theta$ takes the score of 1 for easier items and 0 for harder items, then the value f($\mathbf{x}$) would be smaller. If the student scores 0 for easier items and 1 for harder items, then the values of f($\mathbf{x}$) tend to become larger. The same relation holds for Equation (17), the likelihood function.

For example, if a student has a wrong rule for the borrowing operation in fraction subtraction, then that student's response pattern consists of 1s for the items that do not require borrowing and 0s for those requiring borrowing. Figures 18.6 and 18.7 show two sets of strikingly different curves of the deviation of $P_j(\theta)$. The first set of items, in Fig. 18.6, contains items 4, 10, 11, 13, 17, 18, 19, and 20, which require borrowing before subtraction of the numerators is carried out. The second set of items, Fig. 18.7, includes nonborrowing items 1, 2, 3, 5, 6, 8, 9, 12, 14, and 16; items 7 and 15 are excluded. Items 7 and 15

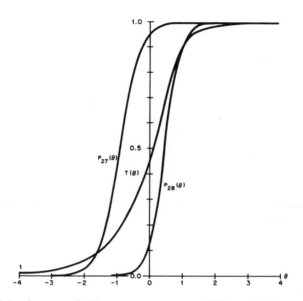

FIG.18.4. Average of 40 item response curves, T(Θ), and IRT curves of Items 27 and 28.

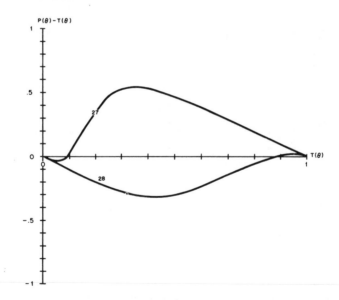

FIG.18.5. The curves of $P_{27}(\Theta)$—T(Θ) and $P_{28}(\Theta)$ - T(Θ) over T(Θ).

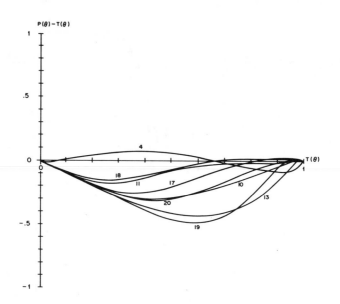

FIG.18.6.   The curves of eight items requiring borrowing.

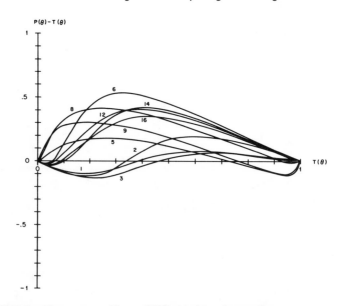

FIG.18.7.   The curves of items NOT requiring borrowing.

476

need conversion of a whole number to an improper fraction or mixed number. All the items in Fig. 18.6 (except item 4) have the functions $P_j(\theta) - T(\theta)$ below the x-axis that scales the average function $T(\theta)$. The functions in Fig. 18.7 all have curves above the horizontal axis.

The response pattern associated with the borrowing error has the following binary vector:

$$G19 = (111011011001110100001110110110011010000)$$

and the maximum likelihood estimate of the latent variable $\theta$ is .09. The value of $T(\theta)$ for G19 is obtained by substituting $\theta = .09$ into the item response functions and yields $T(.09) = .48$. Next, let us examine the values of the functions $P_j(\theta) - T(\theta)$ at $T(.09) = .48$. As can be seen in Fig. 19.6 and 19.7, the functions $P_j(\theta) - T(\theta)$ at $T(\theta) = .48$ have clearly different values for borrowing than for nonborrowing items. Because the value of Equation (18) at a given $\theta$ depends on the item score of 1 or 0, the $\zeta$ value of G19 is a negative number. By dividing the value of f(G19) by the standard deviation at $\theta$, the value of Equation (13) is obtained. Thus, G19 corresponds to (.09, $-2.26$) in the rule space.

The rule space model starts by mapping all possible binary response patterns into a set of ordered pairs $\{(\theta,\zeta)\}$ and representing it by a Cartesian product space. A list of rule-class response patterns $\{Gr, r = 1, \ldots 39\}$ produced from the item tree program (Baillie & K. Tatsuoka, 1985) would be expressed by a set of ordered pairs $(\theta_r, \zeta_r)$. Table 18.4 lists the 39 points.

Figure 18.8 shows the 39 centroids of 39 bugs in the rule space; their values are given in Table 18.4. In Fig. 18.8, the cluster represented by circled + signs are the rule classes or bugs derived from the item tree by Method A, and the squares are those by Method B. It is interesting to see that the two sets of bugs derived from the two entirely different structures of the item trees partition the rule space, and yet spread evenly over the $\theta$-axis. Because the points below the $\theta$-axis conform better to the order of item difficulties, they are more typical performances on the test items. If a rule is very unusual, then the location of the rule is in the upper part of the space. Thus, the location within the space tells whether or not the rule is atypical with high scores or low scores. The same is true for typical rules with high or low $\theta$s. Figure 18.9 contains a selected set of ellipses whose major and minor axes are $1/I(\theta)$ and 1, respectively (Tatsuoka, 1985).

## OPERATIONAL CLASSIFICATION SCHEME

If all rules prepared in the bug library are mapped into a set of ordered pairs, $\{(\theta_R,\zeta_R)\}$ along with their neighboring response patterns with several slips away from each rule, then the topography would be like that in Fig. 18.9.

The population of points would exhibit modal densities at the rule points, and

TABLE 18.4
The 39 Centroids Representing 39 Different Error Types
in Fraction Subtraction Tests ($N = 535$, $n = 40$)

| Groups | $\Theta$ | $\zeta$ | No. of Items | $I(\Theta)^{-1}$ | Rule Classes | $\Theta$ | $\zeta$ | No. of Items | $I(\Theta)^{-1}$ |
|---|---|---|---|---|---|---|---|---|---|
| 1 | −2.69 | −.80 | 1 | .85 | 21 | .24 | −.89 | 22 | .01 |
| 2 | −1.22 | −.69 | 4 | .08 | 22 | −.22 | −1.23 | 14 | .02 |
| 3 | −.75 | −.68 | 8 | .05 | 23 | .62 | −1.55 | 32 | .01 |
| 4 | −.46 | .75 | 10 | .03 | 24 | 1.04 | −.61 | 38 | .03 |
| 5 | .11 | .91 | 18 | .02 | 25 | .75 | −.05 | 34 | .01 |
| 6 | .64 | 1.74 | 30 | .01 | 26 | −.51 | −1.62 | 10 | .04 |
| 7 | −.17 | 1.48 | 13 | .02 | 27 | −.87 | −.56 | 6 | .05 |
| 8 | .40 | −.16 | 25 | .01 | 28 | −1.99 | 1.01 | 2 | .29 |
| 9 | .60 | −.43 | 31 | .01 | 29 | −.19 | 1.53 | 12 | .02 |
| 10 | .57 | −.24 | 29 | .01 | 30 | −.24 | 2.74 | 10 | .03 |
| 11 | .99 | .72 | 37 | .03 | 31 | −1.18 | 1.46 | 4 | .07 |
| 12 | 1.19 | .86 | 39 | .05 | 32 | −1.45 | .58 | 4 | .11 |
| 13 | −.60 | −1.58 | 10 | .04 | 33 | .57 | −.66 | 31 | .01 |
| 14 | −.44 | −2.31 | 12 | .03 | 34 | .59 | −1.39 | 30 | .01 |
| 15 | −.18 | .67 | 14 | .02 | 35 | −1.66 | −1.96 | 4 | .16 |
| 16 | −.08 | −1.81 | 16 | .02 | 36 | −.52 | −.94 | 10 | .04 |
| 17 | .16 | −.86 | 20 | .02 | 37 | −.32 | −1.26 | 14 | .03 |
| 18 | −.01 | −2.12 | 18 | .02 | 38 | −.41 | −2.57 | 13 | .03 |
| 19 | .09 | −2.26 | 20 | .02 | 39 | .17 | −2.34 | 22 | .01 |
| 20 | .29 | −1.51 | 24 | .01 | | | | | |

each rule forms the center of an enveloping ellipse with the density of points getting rarer as we depart farther from the center in any direction. Furthermore, the major and minor axes of these ellipses are parallel to the vertical and horizontal reference axes, respectively. The set of ellipses with Mahalanobis distance as the metric gives a complete characterization of the rule space. If the ellipses represent misconceptions possessed by a majority of students, then any response-pattern point can be classified as most likely being a random slip from some rule. For a student's response-pattern point we search the two nearest ellipses by computing the Mahalanobis distances of the student's point to the centroids of the ellipses. Then, Bayes' decision rule for minimum error is applied to classify the point and to determine error probabilities.

However, computation of error probabilities (the probability of misclassifications) is not an easy task. If the two ellipses nearest the student's point have equal variance–covariance matrices and if the mapped distributions of the response patterns around the rules $R_1$ and $R_2$ into the rule space follow multivariate normal distributions, then the logarithm of the likelihood-ratio function becomes linear. Therefore, computation of the error probabilities is reduced to the integration of the posterior conditional density functions (Tatsuoka & Tatsuoka, 1987a). More detail of the general procedure can be found in Fukunaga (1971). The assumption

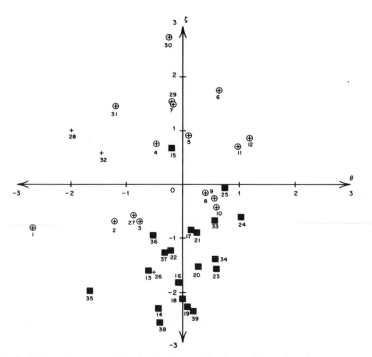

FIG.18.8.   The centroids of 39 Big Distributions. Note: Black squares
are the bugs predicted from Method B. White circles are from Method
A.

of equal variance–covariance matrices of $R_1$ and $R_2$ must, needless to say, be
thoroughly examined.

## The Results of Classification

The 535 students' responses on the 40-item fraction subtraction problems are
mapped into the rule space, and almost 90% of the students are classified into
39 sources of misconceptions. Table 18.5 summarizes the number of students
classified into the ellipses derived from the item trees of Method A and B in Fig.
18.2.

The distribution of Method A users and Method B users over the $\theta$-axis, is
fairly even and not much different in terms of the level of $\theta$s. In an earlier study
by Tatsuoka (1984a), 275 out of 535 students, most of them seventh graders in
a local junior high school, had never been taught Method B. The remaining 260
students were from a different school, and most of them were in the eighth grade.
Moreover, quite a few students used both methods. If they do not need borrowing,
then they use Method B; otherwise they switch their method from B to A (Shaw,

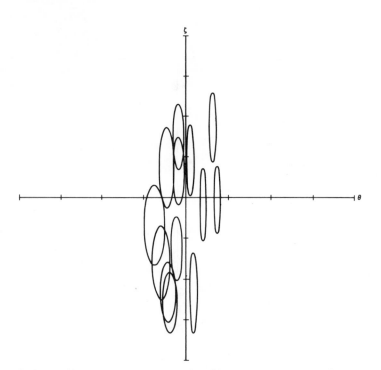

FIG.18.9.   Fifteen ellipses representing fifteen error types randomly chosen from the 39 sets of ellipses.

1984, p. 43). Method A does not require the borrowing skill. These students are left undiagnosed in this study because the item trees utilized in producing a list of bugs are of either Method A or B and the combination tree of Methods A and B is not constructed. One of the advantages of using the rule space model is that uncertain errors on the test can be left classified without forcing them into one of the ellipses. They can subsequently be further investigated for their underlying cognitive processes. Therefore, the model can be exploratory and sensitive to any changes that affect students' performance.

Regarding the psychological meaning of $\theta$, the content of Table 18.5 is investigated in detail. The frequency distributions of both groups over the $\theta$-axis are shown in Fig. 18.10.

The $\theta$ values in the two groups are not significantly different, but the $\zeta$ values are different. The two histograms for $\theta$ overlap and cannot be distinguished from each other. However, the Method B users had a deeper understanding of the number system, and many of them were later advanced to an algebra class. If $\theta$ is really an ability influencing the scores of the 40-item fraction subtraction test, it is only natural to assume that the Method B users should have higher ability levels than those of the Method A users. As Resnick (1983) stated, Method A

TABLE 18.5
Frequencies of Students Who Used Either Method A or B

| Range of $\Theta$ | Method | Frequencies | Method B | Frequencies |
|---|---|---|---|---|
| $\Theta \leq -3$ | | | | |
| $-3 < \Theta \leq -2.5$ | 1 | 29 | | |
| $-2.5 < \Theta \leq -2$ | | | | |
| $-2 < \Theta \leq -1.5$ | | | 36 | 12 |
| $-1.5 < \Theta \leq -1$ | 2,31 | 25 | | |
| $-1 < \Theta \leq -0.5$ | 3,27 | 27 | 13,37 | 12 |
| $-0.5 < \Theta \leq 0$ | 4,7,29,30 | 42 | 14,15,16,18,22,38 | 39 |
| $0 < \Theta \leq 0.5$ | 5,8 | 46 | 17,19,20,21,39 | 31 |
| $0.5 < \Theta \leq 1$ | 6,9,10,11 | 78 | 23,25,34,35 | 73 |
| $1 < \Theta$ | 12 | 50 | 24 | 26 |
| Total | 16 rule classes | N = 306 | 18 rule classes | N = 193 |

requires a better short-term memory with accurate computational skills, whereas Method B requires sophisticated manipulation of the numbers.

Tatsuoka, Linn, Tatsuoka, and Yamamoto (1988) analyzed the dataset more carefully and found that Method B users had higher mean scores for most subtasks except for borrowing, which clearly demonstrated that borrowing skills caused differential item performances. This study indicates that the rule space model is useful for studying item bias and for investigating the causes of item bias.

## SUMMARY AND DISCUSSION

This chapter discussed some important issues for theories in educational measurement and testing. Recent findings in modern learning theory have raised tough challenges to psychometricians. Glaser categorized these challenges into four main objectives that new achievement measurement should take into account. These objectives are to develop assessment methods that are descriptive, dynamic, structure oriented, and that through automation make it possible to orchestrate several component tasks.

The pros and cons of two representative approaches of probabilistic modeling commonly used in psychometrics were discussed. Their common, basic principle is that an individual's proficiency level is explained, to a substantial degree, by defining certain human characteristics called traits. These traits are invisible; the only observable evidence of their existence is based on students' responses to the test items.

Modern physics and advances in the theory and practice of electricity and electronics share this problem with us. We have to infer the outcomes of invisible traits (if they exist), the unobservable cognitive processes, knowledge structures, and theory changes from observable responses to test items. Modern physicists

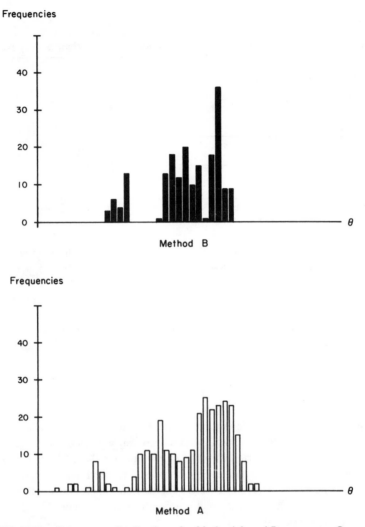

FIG.18.10.   Frequency distributions for Method A and B users over Θ.

have discovered neutrons, electrons, and other elementary particles by modeling observable physical phenomena as logical relationships.

It would seem that a new addition to the current theory and techniques of psychometrics is needed to respond to the new challenges raised by modern learning theory. This addition must overcome an ideological barrier as well as a technological one (Linn, 1985). At the same time, the new addition requires an expansion of our commonsense to more abstract levels and a re-examination of the basic principles of test theories. The time is ripe for such developments, and, finally, research that manifests this new trend has begun to appear in several journals. This includes, for example, renewed concepts of construct validity proposed by Messick (1980, 1984), Angoff (1986), and Cronbach (1975), and a new technology, called rule space, introduced by Tatsuoka (1983) and associates.

This chapter introduced a part of the rule space model. The model consists of four major components: (a) item construction and preparation of the bug library, which consists of response patterns resulting from various sources of misconceptions, sources of incomplete knowledge, and erroneous rules of operation; (b) estimation of parameters, including item parameters of IRT models and bug distributions; (c) execution of decision rules; and (d) evaluation of the information in the bug library and update of the contents.

The first component was discussed mainly by introducing a method for constructing an item tree. Making a tree is an application of deterministic relational databases. Each item tree reflects a unique process structure underlying the problem-solving activities. The values of conditional probabilities computed on a specific directed path help to identify the attribute that causes difficulties in doing the test.

After locating sources of error types, or combinations of misconceptions that require special attention in teaching, remediation, or designing instructions, the item tree program converts them into a list of response patterns. Because the attributes can be production rules, the item tree can be a descriptive representation of a production system.

One of the main differences between the traditional modeling approach and the rule space approach lies in the ways they utilize the information obtained from a detailed task analysis. The former approach defines a set of new variables and formulates them as parameters in a probability function, or as probabilistic relationships among probability functions. The rule space approach utilizes algebraic relationships among item-response functions for expressing the information obtained from the task analysis. Each rule corresponds to its unique bug distribution over slips, and it is represented as true points in the rule space, which is a Cartesian product of two quantities, $\theta$ and $\zeta$. Each rule is the center of an enveloping ellipse, with the density of points decreasing as we depart farther from the center in any direction. Further, the major and minor axis of these ellipses are asymptotically orthogonal (Tatsuoka, 1985). An observed response, on the other hand, would be classified into one of the ellipses if possible. Statistical pattern recognition techniques are applied to classify the observed point. By examining the probability of errors, the student's performance on the test may be diagnosed in terms of a hypothetical knowledge structure and an interpretable prescription.

Because $\theta$ is taken as denoting the levels of proficiencies (and not as latent traits or constructs that determine the levels of test performance), the change scores resulting from hypothesis-testing activities of testees are explained (through a bug distribution of the random slip variable around rule R) without any philosophical difficulties. The rule space model has treated $\theta$ as a quantitative variable and attributed an important role to the contents of the bug library.

## ACKNOWLEDGMENTS

This research was sponsored by the Personnel and Training Research Programs, Psychological Sciences Division, Office of Naval Research, under Contract No. N00014-82-K-0604, Contract Authority Identification Number NR 150–495.

The author wishes to acknowledge Robert Baillie for computer programing, Betty Dowd and Kentaro Yamamoto for collecting data and miscellaneous assistance, Jocelyn Smith and Rose Nygaard for typing this manuscript and drawing the charts, and Maurice Tatsuoka for his critical review and editorial help.

The author is especially grateful to Bob Linn, Robert Mislevy, Bill Stout, and Maurice Tatsuoka for valuable discussions and comments.

The data used in this report was obtained from a study supported by the National Institute of Education.

Some of the analyses presented in this report were performed on PLATO[R] system. The PLATO[R] system is a development of the University of Illinois, and PLATO[R] is a service mark of Control Data Corporation.

The NovaNET[SM] system is a development of the University of Illinois and NovaNET[SM] is a service mark of University of Communications, Inc.

## REFERENCES

Alvord, G., & Macready, G. B. (1985). Comparing fit of nonsubsuming probability models. *Applied Psychological Measurement, 9*(3), 233–240.

American Psychological Association, AERA, & NCME. (1954). *Standards for educational and psychological tests*. Washington, DC: American Psychological Association.

Angoff, W. H. (1986). Validity: An evolving concept. In H. Wainer & H. I. Braun (Eds.), *Test Validity* (pp. 19–32). Hillsdale, NJ: Lawrence Erlbaum Associates.

Baillie, R. K., & Tatsuoka, K. K. (1985). *Item-Tree*. A computer program. Urbana, IL: University of Illinois.

Birenbaum, M. (1985). Comparing the effectiveness of several IRT based appropriateness measures in detecting unusual response patterns, *Educational and Psychological Measurement, 45*, 523–534.

Birenbaum, M. (1986). Effect of dissimulation motivation and anxiety on response pattern appropriateness measure. *Applied Psychological Measurement, 10*(2), 167–174.

Birenbaum, M., & Tatsuoka, K. K. (1982). On the dimensionality of achievement test data. *Journal of Educational Measurement, 19*(4), 259–266.

Birenbaum, M., & Tatsuoka, K. K. (1987). Effects of "on-line" test feedback on the seriousness of subsequent errors. *Journal of Educational Measurement, 24*(2), 145–155.

Birenbaum, A. (1968). Some latent trait models and their use in inferring an examinee's ability. In F. M. Lord & M. R. Novick (Eds.), *Statistical theories of mental test scores* (pp. 397–472). Reading, MA: Addison-Wesley.

Bloom, B. S., Engelhart, M. D., Furst, E. J., Hill, W. H., & Krathwohl, D. R. (1956). *Taxonomy of educational objectives: The Cognitive Domain*. New York: Longmans, Green.

Bock, R. D. (1972). Estimating item parameters and latent ability when the responses are scored in two or more nominal categories. *Psychometrika, 37*, 29–51.

Bock, R. D., & Aitken, M. (1981). Marginal maximum likelihood estimation of item parameters: Application of an EM algorithm. *Psychometrika, 46*, 493–459.

Bock, R. D., & Mislevy, R. J. (1982). Adaptive EAP estimation of ability in a microcomputer environment. *Applied Psychological Measurement, 6*, 431–444.

Brown, J. S., & Burton, R. R. (1978). Diagnostic models for procedural bugs in basic mathematical skills. *Cognitive Science, 2*, 155–192.

Carroll, J. B. (1987). New prespectives in the analysis of abilities. *Proceedings of the Buros-Nebraska Symposium on measurement and testing, the influence of cognitive psychology on testing and measurement*. Lincoln, NE: University of Nebraska.

Cattell, R. B. (1971). *Abilities: Their structure, growth, and action*. New York: Houghton Mifflin.

Chevalaz, G. M. (1983). *A comparative analysis of two order analytic techniques: Assessing item hierarchies in real and simulated data*. Unpublished master's thesis, University of Illinois: Urbana, IL.

Cronbach, L. J. (1975). Beyond the two disciplines of scientific psychology revisited. *American Psychologist, 30*, 116–127.

Drasgow, F., Levine, M. V., & McLaughlin, M. E. (1987). Detecting inappropriate test scores with optimal practical appropriateness indices. *Applied Psychological Measurement, 11*, 59–79.

Embretson, S. E. (1984). A general latent trait model for response processes. *Psychometrika, 49*, 175–186.

Fischer, G. H. (1973). The linear logistic test model as an instrument in education research. *Acta Psychologica, 37*, 359–374.

Fischer, G. H., & Formann, A. K. (1972). *An algorithm and a FORTRAN program for estimating the item parameters of the linear logistic model* (Research Bulletin No. 11). Vienna: Institute for Psychology, University of Vienna.

Fukunaga, K. (1972). *Introduction to statistical pattern recognition*. New York: Academic Press.

Glaser, R. (1985). *The integration of instruction and testing*. Paper presented at the ETS Invitational Conference on the Redesign of Testing for the 21st Century, New York City.

Greeno, J. G. (1980). *Instruction for skill and understanding in mathematical problem solving*. Paper presented at the 22nd International Congress of Psychology, Leipzig.

Guilford, J. P. (1967). *The nature of human intelligence*. New York: McGraw-Hill.

Harnisch, D., & Tatsuoka, K. K. (1983). A comparison of appropriateness indices based on item response theory. In Hambleton (Ed.), *Applications of Item Response Theory*. Vancouver: British Columbia.

Klein, M., Birenbaum, M., Staniford, S., & Tatsuoka, K. K. (1981). *Logical error analysis and construction of tests to diagnose student "bugs" with addition and subtraction of fractions* (Tech. Rep. No. 81-6). Urbana, IL: University of Illinois, Computer-based Education Research Laboratory.

Lazarsfeld, P. F., & Henry, N. W. (1968). *Latent structure analysis*. Boston: Houghton Mifflin.

Lee, T. T. (1983). An algebraic theory of relational databases. *The Bell System Technical Journal, 62*(10), 3159–3206.

Linn, R. L. (1985). Barriers to new test designs. In E. E. Freeman (Ed.), *Proceedings of the 1985 ETS Invitational Conference* (pp. 69–79). The Redesign of Testing for the 21st Century: Princeton, NJ: Educational Testing Service.

Loevinger, J. (1957). Objective tests as instruments of psychological theory. *Psychological Reports, 3*, 635–694. (Monograph Supplement 9).

Lord, F. M. (1953). An application of confidence intervals and of maximum likelihood to the estimation of an examinee's ability. *Psychometrika, 18*, 57–77.

Lord, F. M. & Novick, M. R. (1968). *Statistical theories of mental test scores.* Reading, MA: Addison-Wesley.

Macready, G. B. (1982). The use of latent class models for assessing prerequisite relations and transference among traits. *Psychometrika, 47,* 477–488.

Madaus, G. F., Woods, F., & Nutall, R. L. (1973). A causal model analysis of Bloom's taxonomy. *American Educational Research Journal, 10,* 253–262.

Marshall, S. P. (1980). Procedural networks and production systems in adaptive diagnosis. *Instructional Science, 9,* 129–143.

Messick, S. (1980). Test validity and the ethics of assessment. *American Psychologist, 35,* 1012–1027.

Messick, S. (1984). The psychology of educational measurement. *Journal of Educational Measurement, 21,* 3, 215–238.

Miller, W. G., Snowman, J., & O'Hara, J. (1979). Application of alternative statistical techniques to examine the hierarchical ordering in Bloom's taxonomy. *American Educational Research Journal, 16,* 241–248.

Mislevy, R. J. (1983). Item response models for grouped data. *Journal of Educational Statistics, 8,* 271–288.

Mokken, R. J., & Lewis, C. (1982). A nonparametric approach to the analysis of dichotomous item responses. *Applied Psychological Measurement, 82,* 4, 417–430.

Molenaar, I. (1987). The many null distributions of person fit indices (personal communication).

Mosier, C. I. (1941). Psychophysics and mental test theory, II. The constant process. *Psychological Review, 48,* 235–249.

Muthén, B. (1984). A general structural equation model with dichotomous ordered categories, and continuous latent variable indicators. *Psychometrika, 49,* 115–132.

Ohlsson, S., & Langley, P. (1985). Psychological evaluation of path hypotheses in cognitive diagnosis. In H. Mandl & A. Lesgold (Eds.), *Learning issues for intelligent tutoring systems.* New York: Springer.

Paulson, J. A. (1985). *Latent class representation of systematic patterns in test responses* (ONR Research Report). Portland, OR: Portland State University.

Ramsay, J. O. (1982). When the data are functions. *Psychometrika, 47,* 379–396.

Rasch, G. (1960). Probabilistic models for some intelligence and attainment tests. (*Studies in mathematical psychology I.*) Copenhagen: Neilsen and Lydiche (for Danmarks Paedogagiske Institut).

Reckase, M. D. (1985). The difficulty of test items that measure more than one ability. *Applied Psychological Measurement, 9,* 401–412.

Resnick, L. B. (1983). A development theory of number understanding. In H. P. Ginsburg (Ed.), *The development of mathematical thinking* (pp. ). Orlando, FL: Academic Press.

Roid, G. H., & Haladyna, T. M. (1982). *A technology for test-item writing.* New York: Academic Press.

Samejima, F. (1969). Estimation of latent ability using a response pattern of graded scores. *Psychometrika, Monograph Supplement, 34*(4), Part 2.

Samejima, F. (1983). *A latent trait model for differential strategies in cognitive processes.* (Tech. Rep. ONR/RR-83-1). Office of Naval Research. Knoxville, TN: University of Tennessee.

Scheiblechner, H. (1972). Das Lernen und Lösen komplexer Denkaufgaben [Learning and solving of complex thought problems]. *Zeitschrift für Experimentelle und Angewandte Psychologie, 19,* 476–506.

Shaw, D. (1984). Fraction subtraction errors: Case studies. In K. Tatsuoka (Ed.), *Analysis of errors in fraction addition and subtraction problems,* (NIE Final Report, pp. 40–51). Urbana, IL: University of Illinois, Computer-based Education Research Laboratory.

Shaw, D. J. (1986). *The effects of using adaptive diagnostic test results as a basis for two types of computerized remediation.* Unpublished doctoral dissertation. University of Illinois, Urbana, IL.

Sleeman, D. (1984). *Basic algebra revisited: A study with 14-year-olds.* (HPP-83-9, ED 258 846). Stanford University, Department of computer science.

Snow, R. E., & Lohman, D. F. (1984). Toward theory of cognitive aptitude for learning from instruction. *Journal of Educational Psychology, 76,* 347–376.

Spada, H., & McGaw, B. (1985). The assessment of learning effects with linear test models. In S. E. Embretson (Ed.), *Test design: Developments in psychology and psychometrics* (pp. 169–191). Orlando, FL: Academic Press.

Stout, W. (1987). A nonparametric approach for assessing latent trait unidimensionality. *Psychometrika, 52*(4), 589–617.

Sternberg, R. J. (1977). *Intelligence, information processing, and analogical reasoning: The componential analysis of human abilities.* Hillsdale, NJ: Lawrence Erlbaum Associates.

Tatsuoka, K. K. (1975). *Vector-geometric and Hilbert space reformulation of classical test theory.* Unpublished doctoral dissertation, University of Illinois, Urbana, IL.

Tatsuoka, K. K. (1983). Rule space: An approach for dealing with misconceptions based on item response theory. *Journal of Educational Measurement, 20*(4), 345–354.

Tatsuoka, K. K. (1984a). *Analysis of errors in fraction addition and subtraction problems.* (NIE Final Report). Urbana, IL: University of Illinois, Computer-based Education Research.

Tatsuoka, K. K. (1984b). Caution indices based on item response theory. *Psychometrika, 49,* 95–110.

Tatsuoka, K. K. (1984c). Changes in error types over learning stages. *Journal of Educational Psychology, 76*(1), 120–129.

Tatsuoka, K. K. (1985). A probabilistic model for diagnosing misconceptions in the pattern classification approach. *Journal of Educational Statistics, 12*(1), 55–73.

Tatsuoka, K. K. (1986). Diagnosing cognitive errors: Statistical pattern classification and recognition approach. *Behaviormetrika, 19,* 73–86.

Tatsuoka, K. K. (1987). Validation of cognitive sensitivity for item response curves. *Journal of Educational Measurement, 24,* 233–245.

Tatsuoka, K. K., Baillie, R., & Yamamoto, Y. (1982). *SIGNBUG2: An error diagnostic computer program for signed-number arithmetic on the PLATO$^R$ system* (Computer program). Urbana, IL: University of Illinois, Computer-based Education Research Laboratory.

Tatsuoka, K. K., Birenbaum, M., & Arnold, J. (in press). On the stability of students' rules of operation for solving arithmetic problems. *Journal of Educational Measurement.*

Tatsuoka, K. K., & Linn, R. L. (1983). Indices for detecting unusual patterns: Links between two general approaches and potential applications. *Applied Psychological Measurement, 7*(1), 81–96.

Tatsuoka, K. K., Linn, R. L., Tatsuoka, M. M., & Yamamoto, K. (1988). An application of the Mantel-Haenszel procedure to detect item bias resulting from the use of different instructional strategies. *Journal of Educational Measurement, 25*(4), 301–319.

Tatsuoka, K. K., & Tatsuoka, M. M. (1982). Detection of aberrant response patterns. *Journal of Educational Statistics, 8*(3), 215–231.

Tatsuoka, K. K., & Tatsuoka, M. M. (1983). Spotting erroneous rules of operation by the individual consistency index. *Journal of Educational Measurement, 20*(3), 221–230.

Tatsuoka, K. K., & Tatsuoka, M. M. (1987a). Bug distribution and pattern classification. *Psychometrika, 52*(2), 193–206.

Tatsuoka, K. K., & Tatsuoka, M. M. (1987b). *Item response theory, latent classes and rule space.* (Tech. Rep. No. 87-2-ONR). Urbana, IL: University of Illinois, CERL.

Tatsuoka, M. M., & Tatsuoka, K. K. (1988). Rule space. In S. Kotz & N. L. Johnson (Eds.), *Encyclopedia of Statistical Sciences, 8,* (pp. 217–220). New York: Wiley.

Trabin, T. E., & Weiss, D. J. (1979). *The person response curve: Fit of individuals to item characteristic curve models.* (Research Rep. 79-7-ONR). Minneapolis, MN: University of Minnesota, Department of Psychology.

VanLehn, K. (1983). *Felicity conditions for human skill acquisition: Validity an AI-based theory*

(Research Rep. No. CIS-21-ONR). Palo Alto, CA: Cognitive & Instructional Sciences Group, XEROX Research Center.

Walsh, J. E. (1954). Approximate probability values for observed number of "successes" from statistically independent binomial events with unequal probabilities. *Sankhya, 15,* 281–290.

Wright, B. D., & Stone, M. H. (1979). *Best test design.* Chicago: MESA Press.

Yamamoto, Kentaro (1987). *A model that combines IRT and latent class models.* Unpublished doctoral dissertation. University of Illinois at Urbana-Champaign.

# Diagnostic Testing
## *Comments on Chapters 16, 17, and 18*

Robert L. Linn
*University of Colorado at Boulder*

There are a variety of published educational tests that include the label *diagnostic* in their titles or that purport to provide instructionally useful diagnostic information. Most of them, however, differ considerably from the type of diagnostic testing that was described in the three preceding chapters by Embretson, Marshall, and Tatsuoka. For example, published diagnostic tests are often used to classify students rather than to prescribe specific instructional activities. They generally lack a clearly articulated analysis of the tasks or a representation of the cognitive skills that the items are intended to measure. Finally, if they are based on psychometric theory at all, they rely on models that were developed for other purposes.

In contrast, the common goal of the diagnostic tests described by Embretson, Marshall, and Tatsuoka is to identify a student's specific instructional needs. To do this an explicit model of the instructional target is needed. Using Marshall's terminology, the relevant, fully developed schema network with all its nodes and arcs needs to be specified. This might include, for example, the time-rate problem schema for the algebra story problem in Embretson's Table 16.2, or the process of getting the common denominator in the case of Tatsuoka's subtraction of fractions problems. The nodes or arcs that are sampled by an item need to be specified, and the student's model needs to be inferred. The choice of a psychometric model is dictated by the goal and the target and student representations. The emphasis on the instructional content, task requirements of the items, and student cognitive processes is much greater in the work of the three authors than is typical of that underlying published diagnostic tests.

## LINKING PSYCHOMETRICS AND
## COGNITIVE SCIENCE

Measurement specialists have been challenged a number of times by such leaders in the field as Anastasi (1967), Glaser (1981), and Guttman (1970) to pay more attention to content, task requirements, and developments in other areas of psychology. It has also been suggested on several occasions that the psychometric methods that have served well the goals of selection and prediction are apt to be inadequate for the design of instructionally linked diagnostic tests (e.g., Bejar, 1984; Linn, 1986). Although relatively few have taken up these challenges, Embretson, Marshall, and Tatsuoka are among the small handful of researchers who are doing serious work that attempts to link psychometrics to developments in instructional research and cognitive science.

Embretson, Marshall, and Tatsuoka are clearly pioneers in an important new area of work. I find much to applaud in all three chapters and in the previous work of these three researchers. The line of work that they are engaged in is critical if we are to develop a new kind of testing, one that effectively serves instructional purposes rather than the more traditional purposes of sorting students that underlies our uses of tests for selection, placement, classification, and certification.

There are some significant differences between the conceptual approaches used in the work of Embretson, Marshall, and Tatsuoka that deserve consideration. However, there are also some important commonalities that differ from a traditional psychometric approach. Psychometrics has traditionally focused on the responses of test takers. The dominant modern psychometric theory even makes this focus explicit in its name: item-response theory. This is not to say that the content of the items is completely ignored. Item content plays a role in interpreting the results of factor analyses and in the creation of test specifications. It may also be important in deciding which items should be included when an item-response theory model is applied. However, the major emphasis is on the interrelationships of responses to items and on the relationships of test scores with other variables.

Responses are obviously important in the work of Embretson, Marshall, and Tatsuoka, but the role is not completely dominant as it often seems to be in psychometrics. Analyses of the stimulus and of the cognitive processes of the test takers are equal partners. These added dimensions of the work represent fundamental departures from much of psychometric theory and are essential to the development of sound diagnostic tests.

As was clearly articulated by Marshall, the emphasis on cognitive process leads to a different notion of what makes a good item. Merely knowing that an item discriminates high- and low-performing students in a given content area is not sufficient for inferring how a student processed the information. The student who gives the wrong answer to Embretson's algebra story problem may lack linguistic and factual knowledge, schematic knowledge, strategic knowledge, algorithmic knowledge, or some combination of these components. Similarly, the student who gives the wrong answer to one of Tatsuoka's fraction-subtraction problems may lack the skill of borrowing, finding the common denominator, or any of the other skills involved in the problem. Diagnostically useful testing needs to be able to make distinctions among possibilities such as these. The goal of making such distinctions is common to the work of Embretson, Marshall, and Tatsuoka, but the approaches to achieving this goal are different.

## ITEM-RESPONSE THEORY

All three researchers see a role for item-response theory, though none of them is satisfied with the traditional unidimensional models. Marshall suggests that additional item parameters are needed to represent the separate psychological characteristics required by an item. Furthermore, Marshall suggests a parallel expansion of person parameters to represent different skills, but the latter expansion is less well specified. The elaboration of the item parameters is closely related to Embretson's multicomponent latent-trait model, whereas the idea of expanding the person parameters may be more in keeping with the new multidimensional normal ogive model described by Embretson.

In previous work with signed-number arithmetic, Tatsuoka (1983) used a component-scoring procedure (sign-taking and number-taking) to estimate two parameters per person, which were then used to compute the probability of various erroneous rules. This IRT-based caution index used in conjunction with the standard person-parameter estimate is more flexible and may have broader applicability. It is less dependent on the peculiarities of the particular content, such as the existence of two distinct parts to a right answer (e.g., the sign and the numerical value in signed-number arithmetic). Although the rule-space approach with the IRT-based caution index might be useful in a variety of content areas, its use so far has been primarily in well-structured problem areas. Whether it would provide equally useful information for less well-structured problem domains remains to be seen.

The different approaches might be viewed as competitors, and to some extent they probably are. However, I prefer to think of them as alternatives that deal with slightly different problems. The choice of an approach should depend on the particular goals of the situation. Tatsuoka's rule space approach has been shown to provide very effective discrimination between the two methods of solving fraction subtraction problems. It also leads to good classification of students according to their use of particular erroneous rules. If the goal is the identification of specific misconceptions in a well-structured area such as arithmetic, then Tatsuoka's approach is very effective. Its utility for poorly structured problems deserves consideration, but, as was previously indicated, is not as well supported at this stage.

Although the two methods of teaching fraction subtraction were clearly distinguished in Tatsuoka's analysis of student responses, it is worth emphasizing
that the two groups had very similar distributions on the traditional IRT-based
performance dimension. The separation of the two groups of students was accomplished almost entirely by the IRT-based caution index. It would be of interest
to know the extent to which separate IRT analyses for the two groups of students
would have led to the definition of different performance dimensions. It may be,
for example, that the item-parameter estimates for some items would be quite
different when they are based on students using method A than when based on
those using method B. A traditional item-bias analysis (e.g., Lord, 1980) where
groups are defined by method of instruction might be considerably more revealing
than most item-bias studies. This is so because the definition of group membership
in terms of instructional experiences is apt to be much more relevant than race
or gender, the variables that have most often been studied.

In the multicomponent model, Embretson seeks to measure each separate
component as well as the overall item performance. In the story-problem example
this was done by having students write out their algorithms for solving each
problem after completing the test and scoring the algorithms in terms of the four
components. In some of Embretson's earlier work with verbal analogies (e.g.,
Embretson, Schneider, & Roth, 1986), separate tasks were devised for each
component. The goal of obtaining separate component scores is, of course, to
identify the specific source of error so that instruction can be targeted to that
source.

Embretson is well-known for innovations in item-response theory that attempt
to bring cognitive theory to bear on the model. Work on multicomponent latent
trait models (e.g., Embretson, 1984) provides a means of translating conceptions
of cognitive components into testable psychometric models. In a similar vein,
the multidimensional normal ogive model that was presented for the first time in
this book, attempts to provide a psychometric foundation that is appropriate for
the demands of dynamic assessment. The need for such a model was clearly
illustrated by the limitations of simple linear functions of number-right scores for
measuring change. Although I might question the assumption that the latent-trait
scale is itself equal interval, this is a minor issue and does not take away from
Embretson's major point.

The practical utility of Embretson's new multidimensional normal ogive model
for diagnostic testing remains to be demonstrated. It is not the first attempt to
specify a multidimensional model, and the previous attempts are yet to find much
in the way of practical application. However, Embretson's model differs in an
important way from previous attempts to specify multidimensional item-response
models. The constraints on the item-discrimination parameters and on the correlations among the latent traits are potentially important new features. The appeal
of the constraints is similar to that of Embretson's multicomponent model.
Namely, they are motivated by substantive considerations.

As noted by Embretson, the suggested multidimensional normal ogive model is compensatory. That is, the probability of a correct response depends on a weighted combination of several abilities. This is an important characteristic of the model that needs to be kept in mind in considering possible applications of the model. For some tasks it is likely that a weakness on one dimension can be compensated for by a strength on another dimension. Such compensation is not reasonable for all tasks, however.

## TEST ITEMS

Marshall's analysis of the goals of diagnosis makes some useful distinctions that help explain some of the differences between the approaches that are typically taken by cognitive scientists and test theorists. Possibly correlated with the distinction made between a probabilistic decision orientation of psychometricians and the deterministic, in-depth interpretations of cognitive scientists are concerns about efficiency and scale. Marshall alludes to these issues when suggesting that "an important objective facing diagnostic testing today is the development of fixed-response items to monitor development and maintenance of cognitive skills." The pervasive use of multiple-choice items in standardized tests, despite the frequent criticisms (see, e.g., Frederiksen, 1984), can be attributed to their efficiency and cost effectiveness. Multiple-choice items are effective at ordering people on a single dimension when testing and scoring times are limited. It is less clear, however, that they can serve the more demanding needs of identifying knowledge structures or the missing or misguided nodes and connections in the structure.

Marshall's sampling plans provide an efficient means for estimating the number of nodes or arcs. For many purposes, however, it is likely that it is more important to know which nodes or arcs are missing than to know how many are present. This suggests that systematic sampling may be needed to investigate the presence or absence of particular nodes and arcs.

Short-term changes and careless mistakes, or slips, on items pose a problem for diagnostic testing of the type considered by Marshall and Tatsuoka. The heavy demands for a large number of items in diagnostic testing would be greatly increased if several items are required to have sufficient confidence that a given node of connection is present or absent. The potential problem is apt to be exacerbated by the use of fixed-choice items where the test taker may sometimes select at random an answer that suggests that a given node or connection is present.

The estimates of the number of nodes and connections that would be derived from Marshall's sampling plans are apt to be degraded substantially when students can get the right answer by a chance selection of one of the fixed alternatives. A recent comparison of multiple-choice and open-ended fraction addition problems by Birenbaum and Tatsuoka (1987) found, for example, that the difference in item format made little practical difference when judged in terms of traditional reliability indices or mean estimated performance level. However, successful diagnosis of student misconceptions was considerably higher with the open-ended items than with the multiple-choice items, despite the fact that the multiple-choice items were carefully constructed so that distractors represented errors that were commonly found in the open-ended format.

## PRACTICAL CONSIDERATIONS
## FOR LARGE-SCALE APPLICATIONS

I consider the distinction between open-ended and fixed-choice formats to be potentially important, at least in the short run, if there are to be widespread applications of the type of diagnostic testing envisioned by Marshall and Tatsuoka. This type of testing is already very labor intensive. The development of the target cognitive structure or, as is illustrated by the two distinct methods for the simple case of fraction subtraction, alternative targets requires a substantial investment of time and energy. Designing tests that provide the level of detail about the student's knowledge and cognitive processes involves a good deal more research and effort. These are developmental costs, however, and may be justified if the end-product can be shown to improve student learning because the costs can be spread over a large number of potential users.

High costs for each test administration, whether measured in terms of teacher and student time or dollars, on the other hand, would be harder to justify. Even with efficient test designs, the amount of testing required for a system such as Tatsuoka's is an order of magnitude greater than that required for standardized achievement tests currently in widespread use. This can be illustrated by considering the number of fraction subtraction items that are included in the mathematics computation subtest of one of the widely used achievement test batteries.

The Comprehensive Tests of Basic Skills (CTB/McGraw-Hill, 1982) include a total of 40 computation items on each of the levels of the tests used in grades 4 through 12. Fraction subtraction items make up only a small fraction of this selection of the CTBS, however. There is one such item on the level of the test used at grade 4, three on the test for grades 5 and 6, four on the test for grades 7 and 8, and two on the test for grades 9 through 12. Furthermore, the whole set of 10 fraction subtraction items across the four levels of the test used at grades 4 through 12 fails to tap all the attributes listed for either method A or B in Tatsuoka's Table 18.2.

The attribute-by-item matrix based on method B is shown in Table 18.1 for the 10 CTBS fraction-subtraction items. Also shown are the test level and the item difficulty based on the national normative sample at selected grade levels. Note that none of the items taps attributes 3 or 6. Note also that there is only a single item, which appears on the form used at grades 9 through 12, that requires borrowing from the whole number part, an attribute that Tatsuoka's analysis found to cause considerable difficulty. This source of difficulty is borne out by the fact that only 58% of the national norming sample were able to select the right answer to that fraction subtraction problem at the end of the 12th grade. Presumably, that number would have been even smaller if the item had been presented in an open-ended response format. Item 4, the only item at grade 6 that involves finding a common denominator, is considerably more difficult than the other two items on that format of the test (items 2 and 3 in Table 19.1).

The CTBS is, of course, designed for quite different purposes than Tatsuoka's fraction subtraction tests, and it is hardly surprising that it gives so little coverage to this one particular computation skill. The point of the comparison is not to say that diagnostic testing has to get by with so few items. That would clearly be impossible. However, the comparison does provide a context in which to consider the need for efficiency. Fraction subtraction items represent only roughly 5% of the computation problem on the CTBS, and the entire mathematics computation subtest represents only about 15% of the total battery. Tatsuoka's diagnostic fraction subtraction test is 10 to 20 times as long as that part of the CTBS. Clearly,

TABLE 19.1
Tatsuoka's Item Attributes (Method B) for the Fraction Subtraction
Items on the CTBS and Item Difficulties at Selected Grade Levels

| Attribute* | Item | | | | | | | | | |
|---|---|---|---|---|---|---|---|---|---|---|
| | 1 | 2 | 3 | 4 | 5 | 6 | 7 | 8 | 9 | 10 |
| 1 | 0 | 0 | 0 | 0 | 0 | 0 | 0 | 1 | 0 | 1 |
| 2 | 1 | 1 | 1 | 1 | 1 | 1 | 0 | 1 | 1 | 1 |
| 3 | 0 | 0 | 0 | 0 | 0 | 0 | 0 | 0 | 0 | 0 |
| 4 | 0 | 0 | 0 | 1 | 0 | 1 | 1 | 0 | 1 | 0 |
| 5 | 0 | 0 | 0 | 0 | 0 | 0 | 0 | 0 | 1 | 0 |
| 6 | 0 | 0 | 0 | 0 | 0 | 0 | 0 | 0 | 0 | 0 |
| 7 | 0 | 0 | 0 | 0 | 1 | 0 | 0 | 0 | 0 | 0 |
| 8 | 0 | 0 | 0 | 0 | 0 | 0 | 0 | 1 | 0 | 1 |
| Level | F | G | G | G | H | H | H | H | J | J |
| Grade | 4.7 | 6.7 | 6.7 | 6.7 | 8.7 | 8.7 | 8.7 | 8.7 | 12.7 | 12.7 |
| p | .46 | .81 | .74 | .46 | .73 | .72 | .66 | .65 | .58 | .66 |

* 1. Converting a whole number to a fraction or mixed number.
  2. Separating whole number from fraction.
  3. Simplifying before the final answer is obtained.
  4. Getting the common denominator.
  5. Borrowing 1 from whole number part.
  6. Column borrowing for subtracting 2nd from 1st numerator.
  7. Simplifying the answer.
  8. Is a whole number in the problem?

a similar expansion in all of the content areas would represent a huge increase in testing. Furthermore, it is unclear that the degree of efficiency in diagnosis that Tatsuoka has been able to demonstrate in this content area can be realized in other, less well-structured, content areas. Hence, it is worthwhile to give serious consideration to the need for efficiency in diagnostic testing.

Even with the most efficient test designs, it is reasonable to expect that diagnostic testing would require much more student time than is currently devoted to standardized testing, which many people consider to be excessive already. Thus, it is even more important to consider how such testing can be justified. In this regard, I think that there are two essential considerations, both of which are related to the reasons that people object to the amount of time required by current tests. First, time devoted to standardized testing is often viewed as time lost to instruction. Second, the information provided by standardized tests is not considered to be very useful by teachers.

If the potential of diagnostic testing is to be realized, both of these perceived limitations of current testing must be overcome. The tests need to be seen as an integral part of instruction. In fact, the amount of time devoted to standardized testing represents only a small fraction of the total testing time. Considerably more time is devoted to the administration of teacher-made tests and little, if any, concern is expressed about that lost instructional time. This is so because the teacher-made tests are seen as a necessary and useful part of instruction. To realize the potential of the type of tests envisioned by Embretson, Marshall, and Tatsuoka, diagnostic tests need to be seen as serving instruction at least as well, and, it is hoped, considerably better, than current teacher-made tests.

This would require not only evidence that the information provided by diagnostic tests can enhance student learning but careful attention to the instructional programs themselves. It is also likely to require changes in the organization of schools and the ways in which instruction is delivered. As Glaser suggested several years ago, more flexible environments need to be created in schools that "would permit differential instructional practices that could be coordinated with useful diagnostic assessment so that testing and teaching become integral events" (Glaser, 1981, p. 925).

The conference on which this book is based took a small step toward the better integration of the results of cognitive science, instructional research, and testing. But the links between these different perspectives remain relatively weak. Instructional prescriptions that might accompany diagnosis, for example, have received relatively little attention and remain more implicit than explicit. Although some important progress has been made, the road to a fully integrated system of testing and instruction is likely to prove to be long and arduous. The potential benefits, however, are surely worth the effort.

# REFERENCES

Anastasi, A. (1967). Psychology, psychologists, and psychological testing. *American Psychologist, 22*, 297–306.

Bejar, I. I. (1984). Educational diagnostic assessment. *Journal of Educational Measurement, 21*, 175–189.

Birenbaum, M., & Tatsuoka, K. K. (1987). Open-ended versus multiple-choice response formats— It does make a difference for diagnostic purposes. *Applied Psychological Measurement, 11*, 385–395.

CTB/McGraw-Hill. (1982). *Comprehensive Tests of Basic Skills, Forms U and V*. Monterey, CA: CTB/McGraw-Hill.

Embretson, S. (1984). A general latent trait model for response processes. *Psychometrika, 49*, 175–186.

Embretson, S., Schneider, L. M., & Roth, D. L. (1986). Multiple processing strategies and the construct validity of verbal reasoning tests. *Journal of Educational Measurement, 23*, 13–32.

Frederiksen, N. (1984). The real test bias: Influences of testing on teaching and learning. *American Psychologist, 39*, 193–202.

Glaser, R. (1981). The future of testing: A research agenda for cognitive psychology and psychometrics. *American Psychologist, 36*, 923–936.

Guttman, L. (1970). Integration of test design and analysis. In *Proceedings of the 1969 Invitational Conference on Testing Problems* (pp. 53–65). Princeton, NJ: Educational Testing Service.

Linn, R. L. (1986). Barriers to new test design. *The redesign of testing for the 21st century: Proceedings of the 1985 ETS Invitational Conference*. Princeton, NJ: Educational Testing Service.

Lord, F. M. (1980). *Applications of item response theory to practical testing problems*. Hillsdale, NJ: Lawrence Erlbaum Associates.

Tatsuoka, K. K. (1983). Rule space: An approach for dealing with misconceptions based on item response theory. *Journal of Educational Measurement, 20*, 345–359.

# Author Index

**A**

Aaron, I.E., 128, *138*
Ackerman, P., 298, 305, 320, *321*
Adams, J.A., 299, *321*
Ahuja, S., 205, 208, 210, 212, 213, *214, 216*
Aitken, M., 458, *485*
Alderton, D.L., 298, *322*
Allen, J., 95, *111*
Alvord, G., 458, *484*
American Educational Research Assoc., 454, *484*
American Psychological Association, 454, *484*
Anastasi, A., 490, *497*
Anderson, J.A., 219, *249*
Anderson, J.R., 3, 5, *24*, 27, 28, 29, 35, *50*, 53, 71, *73*, 81, *86*, 148, *170*, 173, *188*, 214, *214*, 220, *249*, 258, 283, *294*, 354, 356, *389*, 441, *451*
Angoff, W.H., 454, 456, 483, *484*
Armbruster, B.B., 144, 148, *171*
Arnold, J., 474, *484*
Artley, A.S., 128, *138*
Ashcraft, M.H., 114, 124, *138*
Attneave, F., 440, *451*
Au, K.H., 397, *405*

**B**

Babad, E.Y., 409, *431*
Bachar-Bassan, E., 337, *350*

Baillie, R.K., 453, 477, *484, 487*
Banerji, R., 146, *172*
Banko, M., 194, *216*
Barclay, C.R., 145, *170*
Bardige, A., 82, *87*
Barrett, J., 332, *350*
Barrows, H., 192, *214*
Bassok, M., xi, *xiv*, 184, 185, *189*
Beard, M., 328, *350*
Bejar, I.I., 490, *497*
Belmont, J.M., 144, *170, 171*
Ben-Bassat, M., 195, 205, *214*
Benbassett, J., 337, *350*
Benge, J., 194, *215*
Bereiter, C., 185, *189*
Birenbaum, A., 457, *484*
Birenbaum, M., 454, 461, 474, *484, 485*, 494, *497*
Bloom, B.S., 27, *50*, 453, *485*
BMDP Statistical Software Manual, 130, *138*
Bobrow, D. G., 346, *350*, 382, *389*
Bock, D.R., 423, *431*
Bock, R.D., 457, 458, *485*
Bolc, L., 258, *294*
Bonar, J.G., 328, *350*
Borkowski, J.G., 145, *170*
Bovair, S., 53, 55, 58, 59, *73*
Bower, G.H., 356, *389*
Bowman, C.M., viii, *xiv*
Boyle, C.F., 3, 5, *24*, 81, *86*, 173, *188*, 214, *214*, 258, *294*, 441, *451*

Bracewell, R.J., 369, *389*
Bransford, J.D., 148, 158, *170*, 173, 185, 187, *188*
Bray, N.W., 144, *170*
Breuleux, A., 373, 388, *389*
Brown, A.L., 15, 20, *24*, 76, 82, *87*, 142, 143, 144, 145, 146, 147, 148, 149, 150, 151, 153, 155, 156, 158, 159, 168, *170, 171, 172*, 173, 184, 185, 187, *188, 189*, 408, 409, *431*
Brown, J.S., 3, 5, *24*, 27, *50*, 76, 77, 78, 81, 84, *86*, 184, *189*, 208, *216*, 222, 223, 224, 242, 248, *249*, 289, 290, 291, *296*, 453, *485*
Bruce, B.C., 369, *390*
Brun, J., 298, *322*
Bryant, N.R., 155, *171*
Buckingham, B.R., 146, *171*
Buckley, J., 397, *405*
Budoff, M., 142, *171*, 409, *431*
Burton, R.R., 76, 84, *86*, 214, *214*, 222, 223, 224, 242, 248, *249*, 276, 288, 289, 291, *294*, 453, *485*
Butterfield, E.C., 144, *170, 171*, 413, *431*

**C**

Campbell, J.P., 396, *406*
Campione, J.C., 15, 20, *24*, 142, 143, 144, 145, 146, 147, 148, 149, 150, 153, 155, 156, 158, 159, 168, *170, 171, 172*, 173, 185, *188, 189*, 408, 409, *431*
Capps, R., 194, *215*
Carbonell, J.G., 244, *249*, 440, 441, *451*
Carlson, J.S., 409, 410, *431*
Carlson, M., 362, *390*
Carlson, R., 195, 205, *214*
Carlson, S., x, *xv*, 2, *25*
Carpenter, P.A., 285, *295*, 362, *390*, 416, *431, 432*
Carr, B., 213, *214*
Carroll, J.B., 285, *294*, 459, *485*
Cattell, R.B., 304, *321*, 453, 456, *485*
Cavanaugh, J.C., 145, *170*
Cave, C.R., 298, *322*
Chall, J.S., 136, *138*
Chambers, D.L., ix, *xiv*
Charniak, E., 195, 205, *214*
Chase, W.G., 302, *321*
Chevalaz, G.M., 471, *485*
Choate, J., 82, *87*

Chomsky, N., 361, *389*
Chu, B., 208, 213, *216*
Clancey, W.J., 2, *24*, 175, *189*, 214, *214*, 286, 287, 291, *294*, 355, *389*, 436, *451*
Clanton, C.H., 91, *111*
Clark, L.F., 364, *389*
Clifton, C., 360, 364, *389*
Cohen, R., 19, *24*
Coles, M.G.H., 397, *405*
Colle, H.A., 302, *321*
Collins, A., 3, 5, *24*, 76, 77, 78, 81, 82, *86*, 184, *189*, 397, *405*
Cooper, G., 208, *215*
Cooper, L.A., 285, *294*
Corbett, A., 214, *214*, 441, *451*
Cronbach, L.J., 5, *24*, 408, 410, 415, 420, 429, *431*, 454, 483, *485*
Crowell, D.C., 397, *405*
CTB/McGraw-Hill, 494, *497*
Cuban, L., 76, *86*

**D**

Dasigi, V., 208, *215, 216*
Dauphine, W.D., xii, *xiv*
Davenport, J., 195, 205, *214*
Davis, R., 277, *294*
Day, J.D., 145, *171*
Dearborn, D.F., 408, *431*
Dearborn, W.F., 146, *171*
Decary, M., 360, 361, 364, *389*
deDombal, F., 194, *215*
deKleer, J., 84, *86*, 199, 204, 205, *215*
De Maio, J., 302, *321*
Dempster, A., 208, *215*
Donchin, E., 397, *405*
Donin-Frederiksen, J., 369, *389*
Dossey, J.A., ix, *xiv*
Dragow, F., 464, *485*
Dressel, J.D., 396, *405*
Dugdale, S., 84, *86*
Dukes, N.F., 253, *294*
Dumais, S., 303, *322*
Duran, A.S., 94, *111*
Dweck, C.S., 77, *86*

**E**

Eastman, R., 327, 332, 334, *350*
Eddy, D.M., 91, *111*

Egan, D., 417, *431*
Eggan, G., 327, 332, *350*
Eicholz, R.E., 128, *139*
Elstein, A.S., 93, 106, *111*, 192, 193, *215*
Embretson, S., 410, 412, 413, 414, 415, 416, 417, 423, 427, *431, 432*, 457, 465, 469, *485*, 492, *497*
Engel, G.L., 91, *111*
Engelhart, M.D., 453, *485*
Ericsson, A., 355, 382, *389*
Ericsson, K.A., 253, 258, 270, *294*, 447, *451*
Ericsson, K.G., 302, *321*
Ermann, L.D., 362, *389*
Ernst, G.W., 146, *172*
Eylon, B., 19, *24*


F

Fabiani, M., 397, *405*
Farrell, R., 3, *24*, 28, *50*, 173, *188*
Fehling, M.R., 4, *25*
Feltovich, P.J., 94, 96, *111*, 331, 337, 349, *350*
Ferguson, G.A., 304, *321*
Ferrara, R.A., 143, 144, 145, 148, 150, 151, 153, 156, 158, 160, 168, *170, 171, 172*, 173, 181, 184, 185, *188, 189*, 408, 409, *431*
Ferreira, F., 360, 364, *389*
Ferrentino, A., 194, *215*
Feuerstein, R., 143, 148, *172*, 409, *431*
Feurzeig, W., 15, 18, *24*
Fischer, G., 437, *451*, 457, 469, *485*
Fisher, C.W., x, *xiv*
Fisher, G.W., 113, *139*
Fisk, A.D., 303, 305, 316, *322*
Fleenor, C.R., 128, *139*
Fleishman, E.A., 299, 304, *321*
Fodor, J., 362, *389*
Ford, W.W., 114, *139*
Forgy, C.L., 283, *294*
Formann, A.K., 437, *451*, 469, *485*
Frank, O., 443, 450, *451*
Frase, L.T., 82, *87*
Frazier, L., 362, *390*
Frederiksen, C.H., 354, 355, 356, 358, 360, 361, 362, 364, 366, 368, 369, *389, 390*
Frederiksen, J., 3, 6, 8, 18, 19, *25*
Frederiksen, N., viii, x, *xiv, xv*, 2, *24, 25*, 78, 79, *86*, 258, 287, *294*, 355, *389*, 493, *497*
French, L.A., 20, *24*, 142, *171*
Frost, N., 302, *321*

Fukunaga, K., 457, 478, *485*
Furby, L., 408, 410, 415, 420, 429, *431*
Furst, E.J., 453, *485*


G

Gable, A., 208, *215*
Gagné, R.M., 147, *172*
Galanter, E., 383, *390*
Gallistél, C.R., 159, *172*, 178, *189*
Ganiel, U., 19, *24*
Gardner, H., 252, *294*
Gelman, R., 159, *172*, 178, *189*
Gentner, D., 82, *86*, 262, *294*
Gibbons, R.D., 423, *431*
Gick, M.L., 146, *172*, 369, *389*
Gilmartin, K., 96, *112*
Gingrich, P.S., 82, *87*
Gitomer, D.H., 327, 332, 333, *350*
Glaser, R., xi, *xiv*, 1, *24*, 76, *86*, 94, 96, *111*, 146, *172*, 184, 185, *189*, 285, *294*, 300, *322*, 327, 332, 337, 349, *350*, 355, *389*, 407, 408, 409, *431*, 454, 455, 456, *485*, 490, 496, *497*
Goldberg, S.L., 396, *405*
Goldstein, I., 213, *214*
Goldstein, I.P., 7, *24*
Gomez, L.M., 417, *431*
Gorry, G., 192, *215*
Gott, S.P., 173, 174, 177, *189*
Gould, L., 328, *350*
Graesser, A.C., 364, *389*, 403, *405*
Granger, R.H., 241, *250*
Gratton, G., 397, *405*
Greenburg, L., 327, 332, *350*
Greeno, J.G., 95, *111*, 173, 174, *189*, 413, *432*, 438, *452*, 455, *485*
Grice, H.P., 95, 108, *111*
Grimes, J., 362, *389*
Groen, G.J., 114, *139*, 383, *390*
Grosz, B.J., 369, *389*
Gugliotta, A., 440, 441, *451*
Guilford, J.P., x, *xiv*, 304, *321*, 456, *485*
Guttman, L., 490, *497*


H

Hagert, G., 262, 263, *294*
Hakel, M.D., 326, *350*
Haladyna, T.M., 453, *486*

Halliday, M.A.K., 362, *389*
Hamilton, J.L., 409, *431*
Hanify, G., 82, *87*
Hanser, L.M., 396, *406*
Harbeson, M.M., 299, *322*
Harnisch, D., 474, *485*
Hasan, R., 362, *389*
Hassesbrock, F., 94, *111*
Hayes, J.R., 258, *295*
Hayes-Roth, B., 365, 373, *389, 390*
Hayes-Roth, F., 277, 287, *295, 296*
Haynes, J., 212, *215*
Hazelwood, S., 194, *215*
Hebel, R., 194, *216*
Hedberg, J., 332, *350*
Heller, J., 438, *452*
Hempel, W.E., Jr., 299, 304, *321*
Henry, N.W., 458, *485*
Hill, W.H., 453, *485*
Hinton, G.E., 219, *249*
Hoffman, N.L., 364, *389*
Hollan, J.D., 253, *296*
Holsti, O.R., 254, *295*
Holyoak, K.J., 146, *172*, 369, *389*, 403, *405*
Hoover, M.L., 360, 361, 364, *389*
Horn, J.L., 304, *321*
Horwitz, P., 23n, *25*
Humphreys, L.G., 299, *321*
Hunt, E.B., 277, 285, *295*, 302, *321*

J

Jacobson, L., 78, *87*
James, W., 144, *172*
Jeffries, R., 35, *50*
Jenkins, L.B., ix, *xiv*
Jenkins, W.A., 128, *138*
Johnson, P.E., 94, *111*
Johnson-Laird, P.N., 260, 262, *295*
Jones, M.B., 299, *322*
Jones, R.S., 150, 153, 168, *171*, 408, 409, *431*
Jordan, C., 397, *405*
Joreskog, K.G., 424, 427, *431*
Josephson, J., 195, *215*
Jungeblut, A., 409, *432*
Just, M.A., 285, *295*, 362, *390*, 416, *431, 432*

K

Kadane, P., 413, 414, 424, *432*
Kahan, L.D., 113, *139*

Kassirer, J.P., 90, *111*, 192, *215*, 383, *390*
Kay, D., 194, *215*
Kaye, D.B., 114, *139*
Keating, D., 124, *139*
Keenan, S.A., 82, *87*
Kelman, P., 82, *87*
Kennedy, R.S., 299, *322*
Kibbee, D., 84, *86*
Kieras, D.E., 52, 53, 54, 55, 58, 59, 61, 66, 71, 72, *73*, 173, *189*, 362, *390*
King, J., 277, *294*
Kingsland, L., 194, *215*
Kintsch, W., 356, 364, *390, 391*, 413, *432*
Klahr, D., 258, 277, *295*
Klein, M., 454, *485*
Klein, T.W., 397, *405*
Klopfer, D., 337, 349, *350*
Kolodner, J., 403, *405*
Kosslyn, S.M., 298, *322*
Kotovsky, K., 258, *295*
Krathwohl, D.R., 453, *485*
Kristofferson, M.W., 302, *322*
Kruskal, J., 210, *216*
Kubes, M., 373, *390*
Kuipers, B.J., 383, *390*

L

Laird, J.E., 258, *296*
Lajoie, S.P., 327, 332, *350*
Langley, P., 214, *215*, 217, 223, 225, 227, 234, 235, 236, 238, 241, 245, *249, 250*, 258, 276, 277, 283, 288, *295, 296*, 453, *486*
Larkin, J., 96, *111*, 413, 414, 424, *432*, 440, 441, *451*
Latif, M., 195, 205, *214*
Lawley, D.N., 423, *432*
Lazarsfeld, P.F., 458, *485*
Lee, T.T., 457, *485*
Lenat, D.B., 287, *295*
Lesgold, A.M., 94, 96, *111*, 327, 331, 332, 337, 349, *350*
Levine, A.G., viii, *xiv*
Levine, M.V., 464, *485*
Lewis, C.M., 276, 288, *295*, 457, *486*
Lewis, M., 214, *214*, 441, *451*
Lidz, C., 409, *432*
Likert, R., 301, *322*
Lindberg, D., 194, *215*
Lindquist, M.M., ix, *xiv*

Linn, R.L., 78, *87*, 454, 455, 459, 481, 482, *485, 487,* 490, *497*
Lipkin, M., 91, *111*
Lipnick, E., 195, 205, *214*
Loevinger, J., 454, *485*
Logan, D., 327, 332, 334, *350*
Logie, R., 397, *405*
Lohman, D.F., 298, 301, *322,* 456, *487*
Lord, F.M., 423, *432,* 437, *451,* 456, 457, 459, *486,* 492, *497*
Lubell, J., 208, 213, *216*
Lunneborg, C., 302, *321*

Moller, J., 94, *111*
Monroe, M., 128, *138*
Morrow, D.G., 360, *390*
Mosier, C.I., 459, *486*
Mullis, I.V.S., ix, *xiv*
Mumaw, R.J., 301, 302, *322,* 416, *432*
Munro, A., 4, *25*
Murachver, T., 403, *405*
Muraki, E., 423, *431*
Murphy, M.D., 145, *171*
Muthén, B., 458, *486*
Myers, J.D., 90, *111,* 204, *215*

## M

MacDonald, N.H., 82, *87*
Macready, G.B., 458, *484, 486*
Madaus, G.F., 453, *486*
Magone, M., 327, 332, *350*
Maier, N.R.F., 257, *295*
Malouf, D., 212, *215*
Mann, L., 142, *172*
Manning, J.C., 128, *138*
Marcus, S.L., 384, *390*
Marshall, S.P., 433, 438, 439, 440, 443, *451,* 453, *486*
Matz, M., 76, *87*
Mayer, R., 413, 414, 424, *432*
McDermott, D., 195, *215*
McDermott, J., 96, *111,* 258, *296*
McGaw, B., 457, 469, *487*
McGee, M.G., 302, *322*
McGilly, K., 116, *139*
McGuire, C.H., viii, *xiv*
McHenry, J.J., 396, *406*
McKeown, K.R., 361, 364, *390*
McLaughlin, M.E., 464, *485*
Mel'cuk, I.A., 362, *390*
Messick, S., 409, *432,* 454, 456, 483, *486*
Metzler, J., 416, *432*
Meyer, B.J.F., 373, *391*
Michalski, R.S., 232, 236, *249*
Miller, D., 124, *139*
Miller, G.A., 383, *390*
Miller, R.A., 90, *111,* 204, *215*
Miller, W.G., 453, *486*
Minsky, M., 97, *111*
Mislevy, R., 424, *432,* 457, 458, *485, 486*
Mitchell, T.M., 232, 235, *249*
Mokken, R.J., 457, *486*
Molenaar, I., 464, *486*

## N

National Assessment of Education Progress, ix, *xiv*
Nattress, L.W., viii, *xiv*
Nau, D., 194, 196, 198, 199, 201, 205, 206, *215, 216*
NCME, 454, *484*
Neches, R., 258, 277, *295,* 408, *432*
Newell, A., 148, *172,* 175, *189,* 218, 219, 220, 241, 248, *250,* 253, 254, 255, 257, 258, 259, 267, 271, 272, 276, 278, 281, 283, 288, *295, 296,* 301, *322,* 354, 355, 382, 383, *390*
Newman, D., 369, *390*
Newman, S.E., 3, *24,* 76, 77, 78, *86,* 184, *189*
Nicholas, D.W., 369, *391*
Nii, H.P., 175, *189*
Nilsson, N.J., 232, *250*
Norman, C.A., 356, *390*
Novick, M.R., 456, 457, 459, *486*
Nunnally, J., 285, *295*
Nutall, R.L., 453, *486*

## O

O'Daffer, P.G., 128, *139*
O'Hara, J., 453, *486*
Ohlsson, S., 113, *139,* 209, 212, 213, 214, *215,* 217, 223, 225, 227, 234, 236, 238, 241, 245, *249, 250,* 255, 256, 258, 262, 263, 267, 276, 283, 288, 289, *295, 296,* 453, *486*
Omanson, S.F., 243, *250*
Orciuch, E., 258, *296*
O'Shea, T., 223, 224, *250,* 289, *296*

**P**

Pachella, R.G., 413, *432*
Page, C., 208, *215*
Palincsar, A.S., 76, 82, 87, 184, 185, 187, *189*
Papert, S., 184, *189*
Parkman, J.M., 114, *139*
Patel, V., xii, *xiv*, 383, *390*
Patil, R.S., 331, *350*
Pauker, S., 192, *215*
Paulson, J.A., 458, *486*
Pearl, J., 220, *250*
Pellegrino, J.W., 298, 300, 301, 302, 304, *322*, 416, *432*
Peng, S.S., viii, *xiv*
Peng, Y., 196, 199, 201, 205, 206, 207, 208, *215, 216*
Perlmutter, M., 124, *139*
Perricone, B., 196, 205, *216*
Piaget, J., 114, *139*, 184, *189*
Pierce, C., 195, *215*
Pilato, V., 212, *215*
Pokorny, R., 177, *189*
Policastro, M., 369, *391*
Polson, P.G., 54, 55, *73*
Poltrock, S.E., 277, *295*
Pope, E., 328, *350*
Popham, W.H., viii, *xiv*
Pople, H.E., 90, 93, 109, *111, 112*, 204, 215
Portigal, L., 195, 205, *214*
Pratt, C.C., 113, *139*
Pribram, K.H., 383, *390*
Price, T., 194, *216*
Prietula, M., 94, *111*
Pula, T., 208, 213, *216*
Puri, V., 195, 205, *214*
Pyle, W.J., 128, *138*


**Q**

Quasha, W.H., 301, *322*
Quinlan, J.R., 232, 236, *250*


**R**

Ramsey, C., 194, *215*
Ramsay, J.O., 460, *486*
Rasch, G., 457, *486*
Raynor, K., 362, *390*
Reckase, M.D., 457, *486*

Reed, S.K., 146, *172*
Reese, G., 194, *215*
Reggia, J., 194, 195, 196, 198, 199, 201, 205, 206, 207, 208, 210, 212, 213, *214, 215, 216*
Regian, J.W., 298, *322*, 416, *432*
Reif, F., 440, 441, *451, 452*
Reiser, B.J., 3, 5, *24*, 28, 29, *50*, 81, *86*, 173, *188*, 258, *294*
Reiter, R., 199, 205, *216*
Renaud, A., 354, 355, 362, 366, 368, *389, 390*
Resnick, L.B., 114, *139*, 146, *172*, 184, *189*, 243, 244, *250*, 408, *432*, 480, *486*
Richards, D.D., 113, *139*
Richards, J., 82, *87*
Rieser, J., 187, *188*
Riley, M., 438, *452*
Rips, L.J., 384, *390*
Rissland, E.L., 243, *250*
Ritchie, G., 360, *390*
Ritter, F., 15, 18, *24*
Roach, J.W., 369, *390*
Roberts, D.D., 353, *390*
Roberts, N., 82, *87*
Robinson, H.M., 128, *138*
Robinson, M., 115, *139*
Rohwer, W.D., Jr., 144, *172*
Roid, G.H., 453, *486*
Rollenhagen, C., 263, *294*
Rosenbloom, P.S., 258, *296*, 301, *322*
Rosenthal, R., 78, *87*
Roth, D.L., 492, *497*
Rouse, W., 192, *216*
Rubins, A., 192, *216*
Rubinson, H., 337, 349, *350*
Rulf, S., 113, *139*
Rumelhart, D.E., 356, *390*


**S**

Sacerdoti, E.D., 384, *390*
Sage, S., 223, 249, 276, *295*
Samejima, F., 457, *486*
Sanford, D.L., 369, *390*
Sankoff, D., 210, *216*
Santos-Williams, S., 253, *296*
Sauers, R., 28, *50*
Scardamalia, M., 185, *189*
Schank, R.C., 356, 358, *390*
Scheiblechner, H., 469, 470, *486*
Schiller, A., 128, *138*

Schlimmer, J.C., 241, *250*
Schmidt, H.G., xii, *xiv*
Schmidt, J., 124, *139*
Schneider, L.M., 492, *497*
Schneider, W., 302, 303, 305, 316, 320, *321,*
    *322,* 395, *406*
Schoenfeld, A.H., 76, 77, *87,* 185, *189*
Schriver, M., 195, 205, *214*
Schwartz, W., 192, *215,* 331, *350*
Scribner, S., 333, *350*
Seidenberg, M.S., 364, *390*
Shafer, G., 208, *216*
Sharp, G., 194, *215*
Shaw, D., 457, 461, 479, *486, 487*
Shaw, J., 218, *250,* 255, *295*
Shepard, R.N., 416, *432*
Sherwood, R., 187, *188*
Shields, J.L., 396, *405*
Shiffrin, R.M., 302, 303, *322,* 395, *406*
Shrager, J., 116, 123, 124, *139*
Shubin, H., 198, *216*
Shulman, L.S., 93, 106, *111,* 192, 193, *215*
Shultz, T.R., 113, *139*
Shute, V., 298, 302, *322,* 416, *432*
Siegler, R.S., 113, 114, 115, 116, 122, 123,
    124, 127, 129, *139*
Simon, D.P., 96, *111*
Simon, H.A., 95, 96, *111, 112,* 218, 219, 220,
    241, 248, *250,* 253, 254, 255, 256, 257,
    258, 259, 267, 270, 271, 272, 278, 281,
    *294, 295, 296,* 354, 355, 382, 383, 384,
    *389, 390,* 447, *451*
Sleeman, D., 27, *50,* 76, *87,* 208, *216,* 223,
    235, 248, *250,* 288, 289, 290, *296,* 453,
    *487*
Sloat, K.C.M., 397, *405*
Smith, M.B., 128, *138*
Smith, M.J., 223, 248, *250*
Smith, R., 195, 205, *214*
Snow, R.E., 5, *24,* 145, *172,* 285, *296,* 300,
    *323,* 456, *487*
Snowman, J., 453, *486*
Soloway, E.M., 173, *189,* 328, *350*
Sowa, J.F., 356, 358, 364, *390*
Spada, H., 457, 469, *487*
Spearman, C., 302, *323*
Speidel, G.E., 397, *405*
Spohrer, J., 328, *350*
Sprafka, S.A., 93, 106, *111,* 192, 193, *215*
Stake, R., 410, *432*
Staniford, S., 454, *485*
Stefik, M., 346, *350*

Stein, N., 369, *391*
Steinbach, R., 185, *189*
Steinberg, E., 150, 153, 168, *171,* 408, 409, *431*
Steinberg, L., 424, *432*
Steinberg, R.J., 412, *432*
Sternburg, R.J., 285, *296,* 300, *323,* 456, *487*
Stevens, A.L., 262, *294*
Stone, M.H., 464, *488*
Stout, W., 459, *487*
Sullivan, L.M., 128, *138*
Swanson, D.B., 94, *111*
Szolovits, P., 331, *350*

**T**

Tabb, D., 194, *216*
Tagamets, M., 205, *216*
Tanenhaus, M., 364, *390*
Taraban, R., 116, *139*
Tatsuoka, K.K., 453, 454, 458, 459, 460, 461,
    462, 463, 464, 465, 469, 474, 477, 478,
    479, 481, 483, *484, 485, 487,* 491, 494,
    *497*
Tatsuoka, M.M., 458, 461, 462, 463, 464, 465,
    478, 481, *487*
Thagard, P., 195, *216,* 403, *405*
Tharp, R.G., 397, *405*
Thissen, D., 424, *432*
Thorndike, E.L., 3, *25*
Thorndyke, B.W., 365, *390*
Thurstone, L.L., 300, *323*
Tomrose, M.K., 82, *87*
Toulmin, S., 252, *296*
Towne, D.M., 4, *25*
Townsend, D.J., 364, *391*
Trabasso, T., 369, *391*
Trabin, T.E., 459, *487*
Traub, R.E., x, *xiv*
Tuhrim, S.,194, 208, 213, *216*
Tyler, L.K., 364, *391*
Tyler, R.W., 83, *87*

**U**

Ulrich, J., 198, *216*

**V**

Van Dijk, T., 364, *391*
VanLehn, K., 76, *86,* 222, 223, 224, 225, 234,
    238, 241, *249, 250,* 453, 462, *487*

Vernon, P.E., x, *xiv*, 300, *323*
Volpert, W., 383, *391*
Vye, N., 187, *188*
Vygotsky, L.S., 142, 143, 147, *172*, 184, *189*, 408, *432*

## W

Walker, C.H., 373, *391*
Wallach, R.W., 298, *322*
Walsh, J.E., 472, *488*
Walters, J., 82, *87*
Wambold, C., 144, *171*
Wang, P., 196, 199, 201, 206, *215, 216*
Wang, Y., 94, 96, *111*, 337, 349, *350*
Ward, W.C., xii, *xvi, xvii*, 2, *25*
Waterman, D.A., 220, *250*, 276, 277, 287, 288, *295, 296*
Weidl, K.H., 409, 410, *431*
Weil, M., 195, 205, *214*
Weiner, A., 327, 332, *350*
Weintraub, S., 128, *138*
Weiss, D.J., 411, *432*, 459, *487*
Wenger, E., 290, *296*
Wepman, J.M., 128, *138*
Wescourt, K.T., 328, *350*
Wheeler, A., 413, 414, 415, *432*
White, B., 3, 6, 8, 18, 19, 23n, *25*
White, S.H., 83, *87*

Whitely, S.E., 300, *323*, 423, 430, *432*
Wilcox, B.L., 144, *170*
Williams, B., 199, 204, 205, *215*
Williams, M.D., 253, *296*
Winkelman, J., 124, *139*
Wise, L.L., 396, *406*
Wissler, 411, *432*
Wolf, R., 327, 332, *350*
Womer, F.B., viii, *xv*
Woodrow, H.A., 146, 148, *172*, 409, *432*
Woods, F., 453, *486*
Woolley, J.D., 362, *390*
Wortman, P., 192, *216*
Wright, B.D., 464, *488*

## Y

Yager, R., 208, *216*
Yalow, E., 145, *172*
Yamamoto, K., 458, 481, *487, 488*
Yamamoto, Y., 453, *487*
Yengo, L., 327, 332, *350*
Young, R.M., 223, 224, *250*, 289, *296*

## Z

Zadeh, L.A., 364, *391*
Zagoria, R., 194, *216*

# Subject Index

## A

ACT* theory, 28
Air traffic control experiment, 297–299
  assessment for trainees, 306–308
Assessment, *see also* Tests and testing
  diagnostic, *see* Diagnostic testing
  dynamic, 142–143, 160–164, 181–183
  for predicting skill acquisition after long-term
    training, 297–299
  for trainees, 306–308
  hierarchical, 307
  integration of with instruction, xii–xiii, 83–
    85, 167–168
  limitations of for short-term assessment,
    307
  of domain-general and domain-specific pro-
    cesses, 149–150
  of learning and transfer, 143–149
  of learning processes, 408, 411–412
  of learning strategies, 23
  of understanding, 403
  pitfalls of for design, 298–299
  plasticity of skills, 301–302
  reliability of, 402
  selecting predictor measures, 299–301
Assisted learning, 184–187
Automatic and controlled processing, 302–305,
    395, *see also* Cognitive diagnosis, auto-
    mated system for
Automaticity and learning rates, 316–319

## B

Bug distribution, 462–463
  inferences from, 472–477
Bug library, 223–224, 469–472
  use of for classification, 477–481
Bugs and misconceptions, 242–244

## C

Children's problem-solving strategies, 113–115
  adaptive value of diversity, 115–116
  development of, 122–126
  educational implications for cognitive diag-
    noses, 136–138
  individual differences in, 126–136
  model for strategic choice, 116–122
Cognitive approaches to testing, 349
Cognitive components, 300–301, 304–305
Cognitive diagnosis, 217–221
  and adaptive instruction, 208–213
  assumptions for, 219–220
  automated system for, 231–240, *see also* Au-
    tomatic and controlled processing
  advantages of, 240–242
  from path hypotheses to rules, 235–238
  methodology, 251–255
  role of parsimonious covering theory, 208–
    213
  rules and principles for, 242–247

**507**

stages of, 220–221
Cognitive processing, monitoring of, 351–352
Cognitive simulation, 51–55, 218
  acquisition of procedures, 55–58
  applications of, 55–70
  cost effectiveness of, 72, 399
  goals of, 52
  portability of representations, 72–73
Cognitive task analysis, 399
Componential analysis, 397
Computational models of diagnostic problem
  solving, 194–195
Computer-based testing for medical diagnoses,
  89–92, 93–95, 106–109
  a proposed representation of, 96–98
  influence of teaching rounds on, 93–95
  multiple roles of teaching rounds, 106–109
Construct representation and diagnostic testing,
  412–417
Construct validity, 454, 456
Conventional measurement theory, mapping to,
  16–17
Conventional tests, x–xi, 77–78
  effects of, vii–viii, 2, 77–78

**D**

Desiderata for new kinds of tests, 78–79
Diagnostic assessment during training, 308–310
Diagnostic knowledge and problem formulation,
  196–204
Diagnostic problem solving
Diagnostic reasoning, 192–195
  procedural models of, 201–204
Diagnostic test items, 436–438, 493–494
  good characteristics of, 436–438
  selection of, 438–450
Diagnostic testing, 15–16, 308–310, 395–396,
  412–417, 489
  constructing items for, 457–458
  items for, 436–438, 457–458, 493–494
  objectives of, 435–436
Discourse as a model for human-machine interaction, 92–93
Dynamic testing, 412–417, *see also* Assessment,
  dynamic

**E**

Enaction theory, 255–258
Evaluating knowledge in semantically complex
  domains, 369–388

cognitive evaluation, 370–373
  by analysis of protocols, 382–388
  by matching to an expert model, 373–382

**I**

Information processing, 300–301
Instructional costs and benefits, 347–349
Intelligent tutoring system, 80–83
  architecture of, 7
  cognitive modeling of, 6–7
  features of, 3–9
  mapping to conventional measurement theory,
    16–18
  model progressions for, 12
  problem-solving expert for, 9
  relation to cognitive theory, 27–29
  simulator for, 7–12
  use for assessment, 14–16
  validity of, 18–20
Item-response theory, 455, 458, 491–493
Items for diagnostic tests, 433–434
  applications, 440–441
  characteristics of good items, 436–438
  definition of an item, 434–435
  selection of, 438–440

**K**

Knowledge structures, 441–450

**L**

Latent-trait models for measuring learning, 423–
  426
  multicomponent latent-trait models, 426–430
Learning and transfer processes, 143–145, 180–
  183
  cross-task consistency, 156–157
  domain specificity of, 149–150
  evaluation of, 169–170
Learning environment, 2
Learning processes, measurement of, 408–412
Learning strategy, measuring the effectiveness
  of, 20–24
Learning theory to support assessment, xi–xiii
Learning with assistance, 174, *see* Assisted
  learning
  evaluation of, 145–148, 169–170

for mathematics, 158–164
validity of scores, 150–156, 165–167
LISP tutor, 29–34
    correlations between lessons, 44–48
    data analysis, 36–44
    theoretical premises of, 34–36


**M**

Mathematical learning and comprehension, 158–164, 178–180
Mathematical models for experimental design, 424–426
Medical expertise, 175–178, *see also* Parsimonious covering theory
Mental models, 13, 58–70, 332–340
Metacognitive learning and transfer, 181–183
Metacognitive skills, 148–149
Models of diagnostic problem solving, 95–96
Models of diagnostic reasoning, 201–204
Models of human-machine interaction, 92–93
Models of learning strategies, 23–24, 183–184
Models of strategic control processes, 183–184
Models of student knowledge, 400
    validity of, 18–20


**O**

Ordering of items by cognitive processes, 465–469


**P**

Parsimonious covering theory, 191
    as a framework for cognitive diagnosis, 209–212
    extensions to, 204–205
    integration with probability theory, 205–208
    procedural models of, 201–204
    role in cognitive diagnosis and instruction, 208–212
    use in knowledge representation and problem formulation, 196–200
Path hypotheses, 227–228
Performance measures, 309–310
Plasticity of skills, 301–302
Problem solving, *see also* Diagnostic problem solving
    human-machine interaction, 92–93, 95–98

modeling of, 175–178, 183–184
strategies for, 122–136, 179–184
    children's, 113–115, 179–180
    choices of, 122–127, 178–180
    diversity of, 113–116
    individual differences in, 126–136
    model for choices, 116–122, 183–184
Problem space, 225–227, 332–334
    instruction for, 346–347
    of experts, 337–338
    scales for assessment of, 333–341
    student model, 343–346
    treatment model, 343
Procedural models, 201–204
Production system, models of, 224, 228
Protocol analysis, 382–388
Psychometric foundations for diagnostic testing, 407, 409–411
Psychometric methods, uses of, 325–330
Psychometric models of learning, 417–423, *see also* Latent trait models
Psychometric prediction, 299–300
Psychometrics and cognitive science, 490–491


**Q**

QUEST, 6


**R**

Rule space model, 458–461
    mapping function of, 463–465


**S**

Schema or schemata, *see* Knowledge structures
Semantic representations
    definitions of, 356–362
    in natural language processing, 362–369
Semantically complex task domains, 353–356
Skills, 178–180
    acquisition of, 304–306
    plasticity of, 301–302
    stable and unstable components, 301–302, 396
Strategic control processes, 173
Subtraction problems
    algorithms for, 221–224
    path hypotheses for, 227–228

production system models for, 224–225, 228–231

T

Task analysis, componential, 311, 316, 394
Task sequencing, 319
Teaching rounds, 93–95
  an example of, 98–106
  implications of, 106–109
Test format, influence of, viii–x, 493–494
  practical considerations, 494–496
Test item, definition of, 434–435
Tests and testing, 218, 395–399, 412–413, 489
  adaptive, 327
  conventional, vii–xi, 77–78
  for description of cognitive skills, 326
  for explanation of failure, 326–327
  for selection, 329–330
  integration with teaching, 83–85

item construction for, 457–458
nonconventional, 78–79
purposes of, 326–330
Tests, diagnostic, see Diagnostic testing
Testing and cognitive simulation, 218
Trace analysis, 258–261
  applications to
    evaluation of strategy hypothesis, 280–284
    diagnosis of solution path, 270–276
    diagnosis of spatial reasoning, 261–263
    diagnosis of strategy, 276–280
    standardized testing, 285–291
Transfer of training, 396–397, see Learning and transfer processes
Trouble shooting, avionics, 332

V

Validation of an assessment and training procedure, 319–320, 394